How to access the supplemental web study guide

We are pleased to provide access to a web study guide that supplements your textbook, *Contemporary Sport Management, Fifth Edition.* This resource includes dynamic and interactive activities that will help you master the subject matter of the text. Learning in action and web search activities help you apply and discover new knowledge. Job opportunities help you learn about the myriad jobs in sport management. Portfolio activities allow you to apply ethical decision making and critical thinking skills. Day in the life activities let you see how current professionals do their jobs.

Accessing the web study guide is easy!
Follow these steps if you purchased a new book:

1. Visit **www.HumanKinetics.com/ContemporarySportManagement.**

2. Click the fifth edition link next to the corresponding fifth edition book cover.

3. Click the Sign In link on the left or top of the page. If you do not have an account with Human Kinetics, you will be prompted to create one.

4. If the online product you purchased does not appear in the Ancillary Items box on the left of the page, click the Enter Key Code option in that box. Enter the key code that is printed at the right, including all hyphens. Click the Submit button to unlock your online product.

5. After you have entered your key code the first time, you will never have to enter it again to access this product. Once unlocked, a link to your product will permanently appear in the menu on the left. For future visits, all you need to do is sign in to the textbook's website and follow the link that appears in the left menu!

→ Click the Need Help? button on the textbook's website if you need assistance along the way.

How to access the web study guide if you purchased a used book:

You may purchase access to the web study guide by visiting the text's website, **www.HumanKinetics.com/ContemporarySportManagement**, or by calling the following:

800-747-4457 . . . . U.S. customers
800-465-7301 . . . . Canadian customers
+44 (0) 113 255 5665 . . . . European customers
08 8372 0999 . . . . Australian customers
0800 222 062 . . . . .New Zealand customers
217-351-5076 . . . . .International customers

For technical support, send an e-mail to:
support@hkusa.com . . . . U.S. and international customers
info@hkcanada.com . . . . Canadian customers
academic@hkeurope.com . . . . European customers
keycodesupport@hkaustralia.com . . . . . Australian and New Zealand customers

 HUMAN KINETICS
The Information Leader in Physical Activity & Health

06-2014

Product: Contemporary Sport Management, Fifth Edition, web study guide

Key code: PEDERSEN-NPF6ZG-OSG

This unique code allows you access to the web study guide.

Access is provided if you have purchased a new book. Once submitted, the code may not be entered for any other user.

CONTEMPORARY SPORT MANAGEMENT

Fifth Edition

Paul M. Pedersen, PhD

Indiana University

Lucie Thibault, PhD

Brock University

Editors

HUMAN KINETICS

Library of Congress Cataloging-in-Publication Data

Contemporary sport management / Paul M. Pedersen, Ph.D., Indiana University, Lucie Thibault, Ph.D., Brock University, editors. -- Fifth edition.
    pages cm
 Includes bibliographical references and index.
1. Sports administration. 2. Physical education and training--Administration. I. Pedersen, Paul Mark, editor of compilation. II. Thibault, Lucie, 1962- editor of compilation.
 GV713.C66 2014
 796.06'9--dc23

                    2013045771

ISBN-13: 978-1-4504-6965-4 (print)

Acquisitions Editor: Myles Schrag
Developmental Editor: Amanda S. Ewing
Associate Managing Editor: Anne E. Mrozek
Copyeditor: Joy W. Hoppenot
Proofreader: Red Inc.
Indexer: Dan Connolly
Permissions Manager: Dalene Reeder
Senior Graphic Designer: Keri Evans
Cover Designer: Keith Blomberg
Photograph (cover): JB Autissier/FEP/Panoramic/Icon SMI
Photo Asset Manager: Laura Fitch
Photo Production Manager: Jason Allen
Art Manager: Kelly Hendren
Associate Art Manager: Alan L. Wilborn
Illustrations: © Human Kinetics, unless otherwise noted
Printer: Courier Companies, Inc.

Printed in the United States of America   10 9 8 7 6 5 4 3 2 1

The paper in this book was manufactured using responsible forestry methods.

Human Kinetics
Website: www.HumanKinetics.com

United States: Human Kinetics
P.O. Box 5076
Champaign, IL 61825-5076
800-747-4457
e-mail: humank@hkusa.com

Canada: Human Kinetics
475 Devonshire Road Unit 100
Windsor, ON N8Y 2L5
800-465-7301 (in Canada only)
e-mail: info@hkcanada.com

Europe: Human Kinetics
107 Bradford Road
Stanningley
Leeds LS28 6AT, United Kingdom
+44 (0) 113 255 5665
e-mail: hk@hkeurope.com

Australia: Human Kinetics
57A Price Avenue
Lower Mitcham, South Australia 5062
08 8372 0999
e-mail: info@hkaustralia.com

New Zealand: Human Kinetics
P.O. Box 80
Torrens Park, South Australia 5062
0800 222 062
e-mail: info@hknewzealand.com

E6280

Paul and Lucie once again wish to enthusiastically dedicate the new edition of *Contemporary Sport Management* to Janet B. Parks. As we noted in the fourth edition, we dedicate this book to Dr. Parks because she is one of the most influential pioneers, professors, researchers, and leaders in our field of sport management. Besides having a leading role in founding the North American Society for Sport Management (NASSM) and the *Journal of Sport Management*, she had the foresight and dedication to develop and publish, along with coeditor Beverly R.K. Zanger, the first edition of this textbook more than two decades ago. Over the years, she has led several revisions of *Contemporary Sport Management* with coeditors. In addition to all her accomplishments in sport management, she is our friend! Dr. Parks, once again, no one is more deserving of this dedication!

CONTENTS

5 Managing and Leading in Sport Organizations 110

Shannon Kerwin, PhD • Jerome Quarterman, PhD • Ming Li, EdD

PART II   SELECTED SPORT MANAGEMENT SITES 137

6 Community and Youth Sport 140

Marlene A. Dixon, PhD • Jennifer E. Bruening, PhD

7 Interscholastic Athletics 162

Warren A. Whisenant, PhD • Eric W. Forsyth, PhD • Tywan G. Martin, PhD

8 Intercollegiate Athletics 190

Ellen J. Staurowsky, EdD • Robertha Abney, PhD

9 Professional Sport 216

James ("Jay") M. Gladden, PhD • William A. Sutton, EdD

10 Sport Management and Marketing Agencies 240

Catherine Lahey, MBA, MSBM • Jezali Ratliff, MBA, MSBM • William A. Sutton, EdD

11 Sport Tourism 264

Heather Gibson, PhD • Sheranne Fairley, PhD

PART III SELECTED SPORT MANAGEMENT FUNCTIONS 289

12 Sport Marketing 292

Ketra L. Armstrong, PhD

13 Sport Consumer Behavior 318

Andrea N. Eagleman, PhD • Cara Wright, PhD • B. Christine Green, PhD

14 Communication in the Sport Industry   338

G. Clayton Stoldt, EdD • Stephen W. Dittmore, PhD • Paul M. Pedersen, PhD

15 Finance and Economics in the Sport Industry   360

Timothy D. DeSchriver, EdD • Daniel F. Mahony, PhD • Marion E. Hambrick, PhD

16 Sport Facility and Event Management   384

David K. Stotlar, EdD • Coyte G. Cooper, PhD

PART IV CURRENT CHALLENGES IN SPORT MANAGEMENT 403

17 Legal Considerations in Sport Management   406

Anita M. Moorman, JD • R. Christopher Reynolds, PhD, JD • Samuel Olson, JD

18 Sociological Aspects of Sport   426

Nicole M. LaVoi, PhD • Mary Jo Kane, PhD

19 A North American Perspective on International Sport   450

Ted G. Fay, PhD • Luisa Velez, PhD • Lucie Thibault, PhD

20 Sport Management Research   476

Jess C. Dixon, PhD • Wendy Frisby, PhD

ACKNOWLEDGMENTS

Paul M. Pedersen and Lucie Thibault would like to express deep gratitude to numerous individuals, groups, and organizations whose collective contributions made this edition of *Contemporary Sport Management* a reality.

This project could not have been accomplished without the input and expertise of the 41 contributing authors—numerous national and international leaders and rising stars in various areas of study—who wrote most of the chapters in this fifth edition. The quality of this book is a direct result of the contributors' outstanding efforts. Please refer to the back of the textbook for more information about the activities and accomplishments of the contributors.

We express our sincere gratitude to Andrea Eagleman (Massey University) who served as the textbook's international sidebar liaison. She solicited, coordinated, and edited an outstanding group of international vignettes and learning activities for this fifth edition. We sincerely thank those who contributed the vignettes and learning activities that are integrated throughout the chapters: Hassan Assadi (Iran), Alina Bernstein (Israel), Veerle De Bosscher (Belgium), Donna de Haan (England), Karen Danylchuk (Canada), Lesley Ferkins (New Zealand), Yair Galily (Israel), Shane Gibson (New Zealand), Morris Glimcher (Canada), John Harris (Scotland), Ma Hongjun (China), Isaac Mwangi Kamande (Kenya), Adam Karg (Australia), Elsa Kristiansen (Norway), Reinhard Kunz (Germany), Sanghak Lee (South Korea), Melinda Maika (Canada), Dimitra Papadimitriou (Greece), John Paton (Canada), Pamm Phillips (Australia), Brent W. Ritchie (England), Florian Schnellinger (Germany), Richard Shipway (England), Ricardo João Sonoda-Nunes (Brazil), Babs Surujlal (South Africa), Ilan Tamir (Israel), Victor Timchenko (Russia), Jasper Truyens (Belgium), Yosuke Tsuji (Japan), and János Váczi (Hungary). In addition to the contributions of the international sidebar authors, we are truly grateful to Corinne Daprano, University of Dayton, for revising and updating the instructor guide, test package, and web study guide. Furthermore, we are appreciative of the time, effort, and input of the sport industry professionals who are featured throughout the textbook. Students will enjoy—and benefit from—reading all of the sport management profiles included in this fifth edition.

Special notes of appreciation go to our educational institutions and publisher for their outstanding support. We are grateful to Indiana University and Brock University for providing the resources that facilitated the completion of this book. We are privileged to be university professors and fortunate to work in environments that support our efforts. As always, we extend gratitude to the thousands of students whom we have had the privilege of teaching across the years. Furthermore, we sincerely appreciate Human Kinetics and the publisher's remarkable editors and professionals associated with this project. Although numerous individuals from Human Kinetics have assisted and facilitated this fifth edition, we would like to acknowledge two editors in particular. Myles Schrag, our acquisitions editor, again provided valuable advice and assistance as we conceptualized this fifth edition. The quality of the final product is due, in large measure, to Myles' expertise, imagination, energy, and enthusiasm. We are also grateful for the diligent, committed, and talented help provided by Amanda Ewing, the developmental editor for this book. Myles and Amanda made our jobs much easier by always being there with valuable information, assistance, and advice.

We are indebted to the anonymous reviewers and the instructors and students who have provided us with thoughtful suggestions, ideas, and critiques of previous editions of the textbook. Their contributions, which are evident throughout these chapters, have improved the book.

Lastly, we would like to acknowledge our various family members who have provided tremendous support of our work on *Contemporary Sport Management*. In particular, we are grateful for the patience and understanding of Brock, Carlie, Hallie, Jennifer, and Zack.

A LETTER TO STUDENTS AND INSTRUCTORS

Welcome to the fifth edition of *Contemporary Sport Management*. Whether you are a student or an instructor, this letter will provide you with information that explains the goals, updates, and features of this new edition. Many new updates and features make this fifth edition an exciting and valuable resource, one that we are sure will broaden your understanding of sport management.

Goals of This Book

As with the previous editions, the goal of this fifth edition of *Contemporary Sport Management* is to introduce students to sport management, both as an academic major and as a professional endeavor. Toward that end, the book provides a broad overview of sport management rather than detailed instructions about how to manage sport enterprises. This distinction is important because the book must meet the needs of two types of students: those who have already decided to major in sport management and those who are still thinking about their choice of a major. If you are currently majoring in sport management, you probably anticipate learning more about the field, particularly about the variety of professional opportunities that await you. Those of you who are currently considering a major in sport management probably want to gain general knowledge about the field before making a final decision. After studying the information in this book, some of you will be even more intrigued with the idea of seeking a career in sport management, and you will pursue the remainder of your curriculum with enhanced understanding, insight, and maturity of purpose. Others among you may discover that sport management is not really what you had envisioned or a field in which you want to work, and you will choose a different major. In either case, the book will have served a valuable purpose.

Contemporary Sport Management contains 20 chapters written by the two of us in concert with 41 other contributors, 11 of whom are new arrivals for this fifth edition: Kathy Babiak (University of Michigan), Coyte G. Cooper (University of North Carolina at Chapel Hill), Andrea N. Eagleman (Massey University), Marion E. Hambrick (Syracuse University), Shannon Kerwin (Brock University), Catherine Lahey (Wasserman Media Group), Tywan G. Martin (University of Miami), Brian P. McCullough (Bowling Green State University), Samuel Olson (Eastern Michigan University), Jezali Ratliff (Wasserman Media Group), and Cara Wright (Pacers Sports and Entertainment). The authors, both new and returning, are experts in their fields and are committed to sharing their knowledge with you, the next generation of sport managers. The photographs and brief biographies of the editorial team and the 41 contributors are included at the back of the book. We are hopeful that seeing their faces and reading about their accomplishments will personalize the material in the chapters and make the book more meaningful for you. We know that you will be impressed with each contributor's experience and depth of knowledge.

Scope and Organization of the Book

The Commission on Sport Management Accreditation (COSMA) is the accrediting body for sport management curricula. This fifth edition of *Contemporary Sport Management* addresses each of the common professional component (CPC) topical areas that COSMA considers essential to the professional preparation of sport managers. These content areas—according to the COSMA's guide, *Accreditation Principles and Self Study Preparation*—include social, psychological, and international foundations of sport management; sport management principles, leadership operations, event and venue management, and governance; ethics in sport management; sport marketing and sport communication; finance, accounting, and economics; legal aspects of sport; and integrative experiences (e.g., strategic management, internship, thesis, project, comprehensive examination). The book provides basic information in all these content areas. In addition to the coverage of the sport management topical areas in specific chapters (e.g., the content areas of sport marketing and sport communication are covered in chapter 12, "Sport Marketing," and chapter 14, "Communication in the Sport Industry"), every chapter includes a specific section or vignette on international aspects of the field and ethics in sport management, two requirements of the COSMA standards for accreditation. As you progress through the professional preparation curriculum at your college or university, you will study each content area covered in this textbook (and required by programs to meet COSMA standards) in much greater depth.

The 20 chapters of the book are organized within the following separate parts: "Introduction to Sport Management," "Selected Sport Management Sites," "Selected Sport Management Functions," and "Current Challenges in Sport Management." Each of these parts begins with a brief description of its purpose, an explanation of the types of information that you will find in the chapters in that part, and a section titled "For More Information" that identifies additional resources related to the chapter topics. After studying all the chapters, completing the international learning activities within the chapters and the additional learning activities in the web study guide (WSG), and taking advantage of the "For More Information" sections in the part openers, you should be able to (1) define sport management, (2) discuss the significance of sport as an international social institution, (3) exhibit desirable professional skills and attitudes, (4) describe the nature and scope of professional opportunities in the sport industry, (5) explain a variety of functions that sport managers typically perform, (6) demonstrate an understanding of theories associated with management, leadership, and organizational behavior and of how these theories are applied in sport enterprises, (7) demonstrate critical thinking skills to evaluate major challenges confronting various segments of the industry, (8) explain the relevance of legal, historical, sociological, and psychological concepts to the management of sport, (9) engage in socially responsible activities and make principled decisions through a thorough knowledge of the ethical decision-making process, (10) demonstrate an appreciation of diversity through the use of unbiased language and an inclusive approach to human relations, (11) identify research questions in sport management and demonstrate the ability to analyze and interpret published research, and (12) become a member of the profession who will have a positive influence on the way that sport is managed in the future.

Updates to the Fifth Edition

This is the fifth edition of *Contemporary Sport Management*. We are gratified that many students over the years have found the first four editions useful, and we hope that the new, improved version will serve your needs even better. The changes in this edition range from new material (e.g., each chapter now contains a bio and question-and-answer section on a sport industry professional) to revised and updated sections. We believe that you will appreciate and benefit from the significant modifications and updates. For instance, the inclusion of a social media sidebar in each of the 20 chapters is needed (future sport managers should possess expertise across a variety of social media platforms), relevant (the sport industry has been particularly affected by the social media phenomenon over the past decade), and interesting (the topics covered often involve some of the unique challenges and opportunities encountered in social media engagement).

The textbook once again has an updated web study guide (WSG). This study guide (which can be accessed under the Student Resources heading at www.HumanKinetics.com/ContemporarySportManagement) provides multiple interactive learning experiences that will help you more fully understand and apply the concepts covered in each chapter. Icons throughout each chapter point you to the various activities:

 Job announcements. These fabricated, but realistic, position announcements related to employment opportunities within particular sport settings will help you understand the skills that prospective employers are seeking. You can select the traits and characteristics you think are most applicable to each position. Sport management practitioners will then identify the traits and characteristics they think are most applicable to each position.

 Comprehension activities. These learning in action activities, including matching exercises and multiple choice, will challenge you to complete a specific task that helps drive home the information covered in the chapter.

Web searches. Web activities give you the opportunity to explore a specific website related to a chapter's content and complete an assignment that connects the website's content to the chapter content.

Day in the life. These activities, which are tied to the professional profile sidebars, ask you to evaluate how professionals spend their time.

Portfolio. The critical thinking and ethics sections in selected chapters provide background information that you will use to answer specific questions in the WSG. After completing these questions, you will have built a portfolio that highlights your thoughtful considerations of myriad issues related to sport management.

eBook available at your campus bookstore or HumanKinetics.com

As noted previously, the fifth edition has four distinct parts, each of which contains at least four relevant chapters. In the first part, five unique chapters introduce you to sport management. These opening chapters provide an overview of the field, information on becoming an effective and professional sport manager, historical elements of sport management, and managerial and leadership concepts associated with this dynamic field. In the second part, six chapters detail the major settings that contain many sport management positions. These chapters examine professional and amateur sport management sites in addition to areas involving positions in sport management agencies and sport tourism. The third part of this new edition has five chapters that convey key functional areas of sport management. These areas involve sport marketing, sport consumer behavior, sport communication, finance and economics in sport, and sport facility and event management. In the fourth part, four chapters examine issues that sport managers currently encounter and that you will face as you enter the sport industry. These challenges (and opportunities) include sport management issues related to law, sociology, globalization, and research in this field. We believe the organization of the chapters into these four unique parts will assist you in understanding the field of sport management.

Each chapter has been updated and some have been significantly revised. The historical moments that accompany each chapter have also been expanded. We hope that the history chapter and historical moments throughout the chapters will capture your attention as they visually communicate historical developments and connections among key events over time. Instructors can incorporate the historical information and the attendant learning activities into their lectures, assignments, and tests.

Although the chapters deal with various competencies that you should acquire as a future sport manager, two key ones examined in select chapters are the ability to make principled ethical decisions and to think critically. First, sport managers need an understanding of ethical principles and moral psychology so they can act in a socially responsible manner and deal effectively with the numerous ethical issues they will confront. Second, because of the myriad issues that will confront you throughout your career as a sport manager, you need critical thinking skills to guide you in making sound decisions. Therefore, because of the importance of ethical decision making in the field of sport management, we once again dedicate separate sections in chapters to ethics and critical thinking, in which the authors have analyzed issues on this theme related to their respective topics.

Also, because of the increased attention paid to sport as an international pursuit and the overall activities leading to the globalization of sport, current and future sport managers need an understanding and appreciation of international issues and cultures. Besides offering a specific chapter on international sport and providing steps to help you prepare for effective involvement in the global community, this edition (as with the previous edition) also provides a new international vignette in each chapter. Andrea Eagleman from Massey University (New Zealand) served as the international liaison. An examination of the variety of individuals, countries, and topics represented will reveal her outstanding contribution to this edition. Each international sidebar, written by someone from outside the United States, addresses the chapter topic from the perspective of that culture and country. Because we respect the linguistic customs of all countries, we have retained the voices of the sidebar authors. Consequently, some of them contain words, expressions, and spellings that might be new to you. We encourage you to take advantage of the opportunities that these new vocabularies provide to learn more about cultures outside the United States. We are hopeful that you will find these essays informative and that they will whet your appetite for learning more about sport and its management in other countries.

› Some key features of this fifth edition of *Contemporary Sport Management* are carried over from previous editions. For instance, the chapters in this edition once again reflect the inclusion of diverse populations (e.g., people of different ages, genders, abilities, social classes, sexual orientations, races, ethnicities, cultures). The inclusive nature of the text fosters a better understanding and appreciation of the variety of stakeholders that exist in the sport industry. Another feature of this edition is its use of gender-inclusive language, which is a conscious attempt to reflect and embrace the diversity that is celebrated in many other ways throughout the book.

› Although each chapter of the book addresses a particular aspect of sport management, many of the chapters have important similarities. For example, most of the chapters that cover careers in sport management include lists of publications, governing bodies, and professional associations (lists of such organizations and publications are also included in each part opener). Several chapters address ethical, legal, economic, and communication concerns. By including these topics in several chapters, we hope to reinforce important concepts that you will find useful as you progress in your professional preparation program. Furthermore, some chapters contain real-life scenarios, case studies, or news stories that illustrate a point. We believe that these features make the book more user-friendly.

› Each chapter has at least one feature of a sport industry professional. The features include a photograph of the professional, an introduction to the featured professional, a question-and-answer section, and a WSG activity. The profiles include Alex Alston (Tulsa Sports Commission), Jill Bodensteiner (University of Notre Dame), John Brunner (University of North Carolina at Chapel Hill), Becky Burleigh (University of Florida), Kellie A. Cavalier (USA Rugby), Derek Eiler (Fermata Partners), Claude Grubair (Ransom Everglades School), Christy Hammond (Detroit Red Wings), Samantha Hicks (Indiana Fever and Pacers Sports

and Entertainment), Jeff Ianello (Phoenix Suns and Phoenix Mercury), Kalen Irsay (Indianapolis Colts), Mike Kern (Missouri Valley Conference), Carley Knox (Minnesota Lynx), Hunter Lochmann (University of Michigan), Donna Lopiano (Sports Management Resources), AJ Maestas (Navigate Research), Sydney Millar (Canadian Association for the Advancement of Women and Sport and Physical Activity), Tiffany Patterson (TownLake YMCA), Aprile Pritchet (D.C. United), Gene Smith (The Ohio State University), Bruce Whitehead (National Interscholastic Athletic Administrators Association), and Tim Whitten (Kentucky Derby Festival). Those featured in this edition include professionals in sport ownership, law, marketing and branding, management, facility and event operations, professional and amateur sports, intercollegiate and interscholastic athletics, sport tourism, for-profit and nonprofit organizations, sport finance, community sport, sport entrepreneurship, and other areas and segments of the sport industry.

Features of the Book

This text provides many learning aids to help you understand and retain the information:

› Each of the chapters begins with learning objectives. These objectives serve as an outline for reading and studying the chapter.

› A "Historical Moments" section in each chapter presents key moments in the development of the study and practice of sport management. These key moments include dates that mark the establishment of a sport organization, the commencement of a sport journal, the arrival of a sport leader, and so on.

› A running glossary provides in-margin definitions of key terms and phrases.

› References to the WSG link the text with opportunities to practice with the material. We included a wide variety of exercises throughout the book and WSG to accommodate different learning styles and preferences.

› The review questions at the end of each chapter are linked to the objectives at the beginning of the chapter. These questions reinforce the key points of the chapter.

› Each chapter contains a reference list. Moreover, as previously noted, you will find a "For

More Information" section at the beginning of each of the four parts of the book. We hope that you will use the information in these sections for further reading and exploration.

Instructor Resources

Although the preceding sections have outlined how this new edition will be useful to students, note as well that several items are useful to instructors. (And if you have not read the previous information, please be sure to do so!) This fifth edition is supported by a full array of ancillaries, including an instructor guide, a test package, a presentation package, an image bank, chapter quizzes, and the aforementioned WSG.

› **Instructor guide.** The instructor guide provides a sample syllabus; an explanation of what is included in the WSG, how students should use various WSG activities, and how instructors can use the WSG to prepare for and supplement their classes; an explanation of and a discussion about the importance of critical thinking in sport management; and chapter-by-chapter files that contain lecture outlines, chapter summaries, and additional activities that can be used to supplement the WSG activities.

› **Test package.** The test package includes hundreds of questions in various formats: multiple choice, true–false, fill-in-the-blank, and short answer or essay. These questions are available in multiple formats for a variety of instructor uses and can be used to create tests and quizzes to measure student understanding.

› **Chapter quizzes.** New to the fifth edition are chapter quizzes. These LMS-compatible, ready-made quizzes can be used to measure student learning of the most important concepts for each chapter. Two hundred questions (ten questions per chapter) are included in true–false, multiple choice, and fill-in-the-blank formats.

› **Presentation package plus image bank.** The presentation package includes hundreds of slides that cover the key points of each chapter. Instructors can use these slides as they are presented, but they are also encouraged to modify and add to these slides so that they more fully adhere to specific lecture outlines, class structures, and instructor preferences. The image bank includes all the figures and tables from the book, separated by chapter. These items can be added to the presentation package, student handouts, and so on.

› **Web study guide.** The WSG provides students with many activities that challenge them to think about careers in sport management, demonstrate an understanding of a chapter's content, complete website searches and accompanying essays, thoughtfully consider critical thinking and ethical issues, and test their comprehension of a chapter's main objectives.

All of these ancillaries can be found at www.HumanKinetics.com/ContemporarySportManagement.

A RETROSPECTIVE BY A FOUNDING COEDITOR

The Contemporary Sport Management Family
Janet B. Parks

In her classic novel *To Kill a Mockingbird*, Harper Lee (1960) introduced the axiom "You can choose your friends, but you sho' can't choose your family" (p. 300). Although this notion is generally true, there are exceptions to every rule, and the *Contemporary Sport Management* (CSM) family is just such an exception. In the mid-1980s, as Bowling Green State University (BGSU) colleague Beverly Zanger and I began choosing contributors for an introductory sport management textbook, we were unwittingly sowing the seeds for a professional family that would span several generations. The ties that bound this family together were a common vision of the cultural significance of sport and a collective optimism about the potential of sport management as an academic field of study. Unfortunately, Beverly passed away in 2007, but I know she would join me in expressing pride in the accomplishments of our family and heartfelt appreciation for the time, effort, and expertise that so many family members have shared with us across the life of the book (see "The Contemporary Sport Management Family" sidebar).

The Blue Book

As of the current edition, the *Contemporary Sport Management* family consists of six generations. First, there were the progenitors, the initial members of our family tree. These individuals set the course for the future as they contributed to what we now affectionately call the "blue book,"
which was published in 1990 with the title *Sport and Fitness Management: Career Strategies and Professional Content*.

Before determining the content of the blue book, we consulted with a round table of experts who enthusiastically shared their wealth of knowledge, experience, and suggestions with us. This group included BGSU colleagues Dolores Black, Lynn Darby, Sue Hager, Kathleen Hart, Carol O'Shea, Patricia Peterson, Dean Purdy, Cheryl Sokoll, and Darrell Verney; Christine Brooks and Mike Palmisano of the University of Michigan; and senior vice president for business operations for the Pittsburgh Pirates, Bernard Mullin. Guided by their advice as well as suggestions from our students, we determined the content and invited 23 contributing authors to join us. We chose some authors because they had presented papers at the 1983 sport management curriculum conference held at Bowling Green. Others had distinguished themselves as scholars or sport management practitioners. Rainer Martens, Gwen Steigelman, and June Decker of Human Kinetics (HK) are also considered progenitors because they took a chance on the emerging field of sport management and guided us through the process of producing a book for it. All of the aforementioned individuals helped lay the foundation for a textbook that has since gone through several iterations, with each edition finding its way into the hands of thousands of future sport managers. The progenitors will always be a very special group.

The Contemporary Sport Management Family

As of the current edition, the *Contemporary Sport Management* family consists of the progenitors followed by five more editions. Although many contributing authors wrote chapters for more than one edition, their names and affiliations are listed only in association with the first edition to which they contributed.

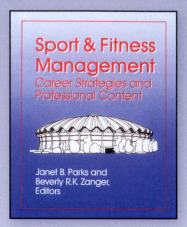

Progenitors

Sport and Fitness Management: Career Strategies and Professional Content (1990)

Coeditors
Janet B. Parks—Bowling Green State University
Beverly R.K. Zanger—Bowling Green State University

Contributing Authors
William L. Alsop—West Virginia University
Robert L. Callecod—Bowling Green (OH) Parks and Recreation Department, director
Allan Chamberlin—Mid-American Conference, sports information director
Annie Clement—Cleveland State University
Joy T. DeSensi—The University of Tennessee at Knoxville
David L. Groves—Bowling Green State University
Dorothy V. Harris—The Pennsylvania State University
Mary Jo Kane—University of Minnesota
JoAnn Kroll—Bowling Green State University
James W. Lessig—Mid-American Conference, commissioner
David O. Matthews—University of Illinois
John McCarthy—International Racquet Sports Association, executive director
Mary Kennedy Minter—Independent training and development consultant
Robert L. Minter—University of Michigan at Dearborn
Robert Moomaw—Bowling Green State University
Crayton L. Moss—Bowling Green State University
Janet B. Parks—Bowling Green State University
Catherine A. Pratt—The Ohio State University
E. Louise Priest—Council for National Cooperation in Aquatics, executive director
Richard J. Quain—Bowling Green State University
M. Joy Sidwell—Bowling Green State University
Eldon E. Snyder—Bowling Green State University
David K. Stotlar—University of Northern Colorado
Michael D. Wolf—International Fitness Exchange, president
Beverly R.K. Zanger—Bowling Green State University

Human Kinetics Acquisitions Editors
Gwen Steigelman
Rainer Martens

Human Kinetics Developmental Editor
June I. Decker

First Generation

Contemporary Sport Management, First Edition (1998)

New Coeditor
Jerome Quarterman—Bowling Green State University

New Contributing Authors
Robertha Abney—Slippery Rock University
Rob Ammon, Jr.—Slippery Rock University
F. Wayne Blann—Ithaca College
Kathy D. Browder—Georgia Southern University

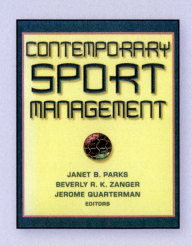

Susan C. Brown—Western Carolina University
Lynn A. Darby—Bowling Green State University
Ted G. Fay—Daniel Webster College
Jay Gladden—University of Massachusetts at Amherst
Stephen M. Horowitz—Bowling Green State University
Linda S. Koehler—University of the Pacific
Vikki Krane—Bowling Green State University
Julie R. Lengfelder—Bowling Green State University
Ming Li—Georgia Southern University
Angela Lumpkin—State University of West Georgia
Mark A. McDonald—University of Massachusetts at Amherst
Jerome Quarterman—Bowling Green State University
William A. Sutton—University of Massachusetts at Amherst

Human Kinetics Acquisitions Editors
Rick Frey
Becky Lane

Human Kinetics Developmental Editors
Andrew Smith
Holly Gilly

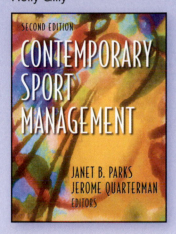

Second Generation

Contemporary Sport Management, Second Edition (2003)

New Contributing Authors
Ketra L. Armstrong—The Ohio State University
Robert Boucher—University of Windsor
Jacquelyn Cuneen—Bowling Green State University
Timothy D. DeSchriver—University of Massachusetts at Amherst
Lawrence W. Fielding—Indiana University
Wendy Frisby—University of British Columbia
Heather Gibson—University of Florida
B. Christine Green—The University of Texas at Austin
Kathryn S. Hoff—Bowling Green State University
Jason Jackson—EyeJax Foundation, president
Stuart M. Keeley—Bowling Green State University
Daniel F. Mahony—University of Louisville
Lori Miller—Wichita State University
Brenda G. Pitts—Georgia State University
Ellen J. Staurowsky—Ithaca College
Clay Stoldt—Wichita State University

Human Kinetics Acquisitions Editor
Amy N. Clocksin [Tocco]

Human Kinetics Developmental Editors
Elaine H. Mustain
Renee Thomas Pyrtel

Third Generation

Contemporary Sport Management, Third Edition (2007)

Retired Coeditor
Beverly R.K. Zanger—Bowling Green State University

New Coeditor
Lucie Thibault—Brock University

New Contributing Authors
Carla A. Costa—The University of Texas at Austin

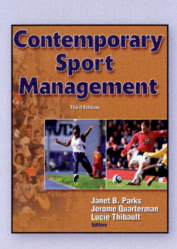

(continued)

Stephen W. Dittmore—East Stroudsburg University
Jess C. Dixon—University of Windsor
Carol Fletcher—St. John's University
David Cruise Malloy—University of Regina
Anita M. Moorman—University of Louisville
David Snyder—State University of New York at Cortland
Lucie Thibault—Brock University

Human Kinetics Acquisitions Editor
Myles Schrag

Human Kinetics Developmental Editor
Elaine H. Mustain

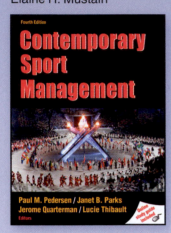

Fourth Generation

Contemporary Sport Management, Fourth Edition (2011)

New Coeditor
Paul M. Pedersen—Indiana University

New Contributing Authors
Jennifer E. Bruening—University of Connecticut
Corinne M. Daprano—University of Dayton
Marlene A. Dixon—The University of Texas at Austin
Sheranne Fairley—University of Massachusetts at Amherst
Eric Forsyth—Bemidji State University
Nicole Fowler—National Basketball Association
Nicole M. Lavoi—University of Minnesota
Paul M. Pedersen—Indiana University
R. Christopher Reynolds—Indiana University
Sally Rea Ross—University of Memphis
Luisa Velez—State University of New York at Cortland
Warren A. Whisenant—University of Miami

Human Kinetics Acquisitions Editor
Myles Schrag

Human Kinetics Developmental Editor
Amanda S. Ewing

Fifth Generation

Contemporary Sport Management, Fifth Edition (2014)

New Contributing Authors
Kathy Babiak—University of Michigan
Coyte G. Cooper—University of North Carolina at Chapel Hill
Andrea N. Eagleman—Massey University
Marion E. Hambrick—University of Louisville
Shannon Kerwin—Brock University
Catherine Lahey—Wasserman Media Group, director of consulting
Tywan G. Martin—University of Miami
Brian P. McCullough—Bowling Green State University
Samuel Olson—University of Louisville
Jezali Ratliff—Wasserman Media Group, senior director of consulting
Cara Wright—Pacers Sports and Entertainment, account executive

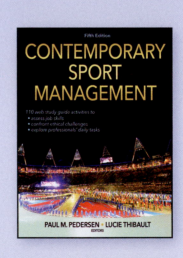

Human Kinetics Acquisitions Editor
Myles Schrag

Human Kinetics Developmental Editor
Amanda S. Ewing

First Edition (1998)

In 1985, when Beverly and I conceived of an introductory sport management text, few resources were available for such courses. Professors typically used materials gleaned from an assortment of articles, books, and personal experiences. It would be two years before the publication of the first issue of the *Journal of Sport Management*, and journals related to sport marketing and law would be even farther down the road. Curriculum standards were in their infancy and program content varied widely. In anticipation of future expansion of this area of study, we envisioned a text that treated sport management as a body of knowledge separate from physical education. Many programs were still housed in physical education departments, though, so some topics related to that field of study also needed to be included.

When the time came for a second edition of the blue book, the professional landscape had changed dramatically. Not only did sport management faculty have more resources than had been available a decade earlier, but programs were beginning to migrate away from physical education into departments of business or into free-standing units where they could focus more on the managerial aspects of sport. Many of the programs that remained in physical education departments were beginning to offer specialized curricula. A particularly important development had been the establishment of curriculum standards by the NASPE–NASSM Joint Committee in 1990 (Zieff, Lumpkin, Guedes, & Eguaoje, 2009).

In response to the changes occurring in sport and in academic programs, Beverly and I broadened the scope of the expertise of the editorial board by inviting our BGSU colleague Jerome Quarterman to join us as a coeditor. As we conceptualized revisions to the blue book, we realized that we were altering it to such an extent that it would be essentially a new product. So with the help of Rick Frey, Becky Lane, Andy Smith, and Holly Gilly at HK, we christened it *Contemporary Sport Management* and conceptualized it as a first edition (1E). We then invited the first generation of contributors, who brought with them a vast amount of knowledge and experience in the burgeoning field of sport (see the earlier sidebar).

Revisions in *CSM* 1E included the addition of more chapters that were directly associated with the management of sport and the elimination of most of the material related to physical education. Along with the other contributing authors, we updated and reorganized much of the content and incorporated new chapters on international sport and sport tourism. Professional profiles made their debut in *CSM* 1E, as did several other features that enhanced the user-friendliness of the book. We added learning objectives for each chapter, and Jerome used those objectives as a framework for our first instructor guide. *CSM* 1E maintained a focus on diversity by including people of all demographic characteristics in every chapter and using inclusive language throughout. This celebration of diversity has remained constant across all editions.

Second Edition (2003)

When Jerome, HK's Amy Clocksin [Tocco], and I began thinking about a second edition of *CSM*, Beverly had retired and was living the dream in Hawaii, where she was involved in other pursuits. Jerome and I were sorry to lose her partnership, but even in her absence, Beverly's ideas, perspectives, and unique vision continued to inform many chapters of 2E.

In accord with our expectations, the sport management programs of the early 21st century had become even more focused on the business of sport and had continued to proliferate at a rapid pace. Moreover, the number of electronic and print resources available to faculty was impressive. With the help of Elaine Mustain and Renee Thomas Pyrtel at HK, we designed the content and ancillaries of 2E to meet the evolving needs of contemporary students. New chapters addressed various aspects of the sport industry, such as the history of the sport business, sport consumer behavior, public relations, and financial aspects of the sport industry. We also incorporated chapters on critical thinking and ethical and legal aspects of sport management as well as sport management research. Most chapters included the authors' perspectives regarding what the future held in store for their particular aspect of sport management. In a very short space of time, technology and the Internet had become an important part of students' lives, so links to a multitude of websites became an important part of *CSM* 2E. Eric Forsyth of Bemidji University created an excellent instructor guide that incorporated technology and contained an enormous amount of information that teachers found helpful.

Third Edition (2007)

In discussing the nature and extent of needed revisions to *CSM* 2E, Jerome and I realized that we needed the assistance of another coeditor. We also wanted to broaden the international scope of *CSM* and knew that a coeditor from a country other than the United States would be helpful. These two considerations led us to invite Lucie Thibault of Brock University to the *CSM* family. Lucie, who was also the editor of the *Journal of Sport Management*, graciously accepted our invitation, and the three of us, along with Myles Schrag, our HK acquisitions editor, set about selecting a third generation of outstanding contributing authors for *CSM* 3E (see the previous sidebar).

As all teachers know, we can learn a lot from students. So, as had been our practice for previous revisions, we asked our students to give us ideas for *CSM* 3E. Omari Aldridge, a BGSU student from Coquitlam, British Columbia, Canada, made the observation that even though *CSM* 2E contained an excellent chapter on international sport and even though we were going to have a Canadian colleague as a coeditor, the next edition needed to include more information about sport around the world. Based on Omari's advice, we conceptualized international sidebars, stories about the management of sport in a variety of countries (see "International Sidebar Contributors"). We also asked the chapter authors to include attention to international sport in their chapters when appropriate.

Another new feature of *CSM* 3E was the inclusion of historical moments in most chapters. These moments were important because sport managers who know about the past are more likely to understand the present and more qualified to plan for the future. Dayton University's Corinne Daprano, who had previous experience assembling time lines for historical events, provided interesting historical moments for most chapters. As had been the case with 2E, the expertise, guidance, and patience of developmental editor, Elaine Mustain, kept *CSM* 3E on track.

Fourth Edition (2011)

As Jerome, Lucie, and I contemplated revisions to *CSM* 3E, we began to think about succession planning for the editorial board. I had retired from teaching in 2004 and had decided that *CSM* 4E would be my final edition as a coeditor. Consequently, in collaboration with Myles Schrag, we enthusiastically invited Indiana University's Paul M. Pedersen onboard as a coeditor. Paul already possessed extensive experience with several forms of publications and, as expected, he did an outstanding job overseeing the production of the fourth edition of *Contemporary Sport Management*.

During the process of selecting contributors for 4E, we became mindful of the need to engage in similar succession planning for chapter authors. Toward that end, we invited several scholars who were relatively new to the academy to author or coauthor chapters. We also encouraged some authors to work with younger colleagues or with their students so that, as retirement took its toll down the road, the younger ones could assume authorship of the chapters (see "The Contemporary Sport Management Family" sidebar).

The college students for whom *CSM* 4E was created had never experienced life without the Internet and were the beginning of a demographic now known as "the connected generation" (Friedrich, Peterson, & Koster, 2011). With assistance from Amanda Ewing, our HK developmental editor, we added a number of electronic ancillaries for students and for faculty. The key update was an online study guide that contained multiple interactive learning experiences. Andrea Eagleman, of Indiana University Purdue University Indianapolis, revised and enhanced the instructor guide, test package, and presentation package, which contained numerous aids, questions, and slides that could be used in the classroom. These electronic resources allowed us to integrate book and electronic content in a more meaningful way than in previous editions.

CSM 4E, our first four-color edition, also saw the reintroduction of chapters on the history of the sport industry and youth and community sport, as well as the addition of a chapter on interscholastic athletics. In recognition of the need for critical thinking skills and an understanding of ethical decision making in all aspects of sport management, we integrated information about those topics into as many chapters as possible. The positive feedback that we had received relative to the international sidebars in *CSM* 3E led us to include that feature once again (see "International Sidebar Contributors").

International Sidebar Contributors

Third Edition

Twenty-three contributors provided 19 sidebars about sport in 12 countries or regions.

Marijke Taks—Western Europe
Jun Oga—Japan
Dwight Zakus—Australia
Allan Edwards—Australia
Karen Danylchuk—Canada
Giorgio Gandolfi—Italy
Bill Gerrard—Europe
Gi-Yong (Win) Koo—Korea
Joanne MacLean—Canada
James Paterson—Australia
Sheranne Fairley—Australia
Hareesh Viriyala—India

Kamini Sharma—Europe
Abel Correia—Portugal
Andy Anderson—El Salvador
John Corlett—El Salvador
James Mandigo—El Salvador
Makoto Nakazawa—Japan
Rosa López de D'Amico—Venezuela
Hilary Findlay—Canada
Lisa Kihl—Australia
Todd Beane—Spain
Babs Surujlal—South Africa

Fourth Edition

Twenty-one contributors provided 20 sidebars about sport in 17 countries or regions.

John Amis—United Kingdom
Hassan Assadi—Iran
Sungho Cho—Korea
Giorgio Gandolfi—Italy
Bill Gerrard—United Kingdom
Morris Glimcher—Canada
Matthew Goltz—Spain
John Harris—Scotland
Anastasios Kaburakis—Greece
Pamm Kellett—Australia
Gi-Yong (Win) Koo—Korea

Sarah Leberman—New Zealand
Li Li Leung—China
Doris Lu-Anderson—Taiwan
Isaac Mwangi Kamande—Kenya
Ricardo João Sonoda-Nunes—Brazil
Toshiyuki Ogura—Japan
John Paton—Canada
Babs Surujlal—South Africa
Marijke Taks—Belgium
Xiaoyan Xing—China

Fifth Edition

Thirty contributors provided 22 sidebars about sport in 19 countries or regions.

Hassan Assadi—Iran
Alina Bernstein—Israel
Veerle De Bosscher—Belgium
Donna de Haan—England
Karen Danylchuk—Canada
Lesley Ferkins—New Zealand
Yair Galily—Israel
Shane Gibson—New Zealand
Morris Glimcher—Canada
John Harris—Wales
Ma Hongjun—China
Isaac Mwangi Kamande—Kenya
Adam Karg—Australia
Elsa Kristiansen—Norway
Reinhard Kunz—Germany

Sanghak Lee—South Korea
Melinda Maika—Canada
Dimitra Papadimitriou—Greece
John Paton—Canada
Pamm Phillips—Australia
Brent W. Ritchie—England
Florian Schnellinger—Germany
Richard Shipway—England
Ricardo João Sonoda-Nunes—Brazil
Babs Surujlal—South Africa
Ilan Tamir—Israel
Victor Timchenko—Russia
Jasper Truyens—Belgium
Yosuke Tsuji—Japan
János Váczi—Hungary

Fifth Edition (2014)

As you learned in "A Letter to Students and Instructors," the editors and contributors to *CSM* 5E have updated the content to reflect the current status of the ever-evolving world of sport management. In examining the lineup of contributors, I was delighted to see that two of our blue book progenitors, Mary Jo Kane and David Stotlar, are still with us. The longevity of service of these two outstanding authors is a perfect example of the staying power of the ties that have always bound our *CSM* family together (see "The Contemporary Sport Management Family" sidebar).

The fifth edition also marks the first voyage of *Contemporary Sport Management* under the leadership of Paul Pedersen and Lucie Thibault as sole coeditors. Not only are Paul and Lucie superstars in sport management teaching and research, but they also possess the work ethic and attention to detail required of editors of academic books. As an added bonus, they have delightful personalities that enrich the lives of all of us who are lucky enough to know them. With these two exceptional scholars at the helm, future editions of *CSM* are guaranteed to have smooth sailing. Bon voyage, Paul and Lucie!

Conclusion

A principle that has guided this book through all of its editions is that students should always be the *raison d'être* for its existence. From the blue book through the current edition, there have been no exceptions to this rule, as the needs of students have always been our first consideration. I am grateful to the students for whom this book was created and to the thousands of them who have used it and helped us improve it since Beverly Zanger and I embarked on this journey almost 30 years ago. I hope they enjoyed learning from it as much as all of us enjoyed creating it.

This retrospective opened with an axiom that *CSM* has defied, and it will close with an adage that *CSM* exemplifies. In act 2, scene I of *The Tempest*, William Shakespeare (1623) gave us the metaphor "what's past is prologue" (p. 9). The *Contemporary Sport Management* family is a shining example of Shakespeare's metaphor at work, as contributors to each edition provided an impressive foundation that served as prologue for editions that followed. It has been my distinct privilege to work with this family. I am humbled by the magnitude of their contributions, proud of what we have accomplished together, and grateful for having had the opportunity to work with them.

References

Friedrich, R., Peterson, M., & Koster, A. (2011). The rise of Generation C. How to prepare for the Connected Generation's transformation of the consumer and business landscape. *Strategy + Business*, 62, 1–10. Retrieved from www.strategy-business.com/media/file/sb62_11110.pdf

Lee, H. (1960). *To kill a mockingbird*. New York, NY: Grand Central Publishing.

Shakespeare, W. (1952). *The tempest. Complete works of William Shakespeare* (pp. 1–22). New York, NY: Books, Inc. (Original work published 1623).

Zieff, S.G., Lumpkin, A., Guedes, C., & Eguaoje, T. (2009). NASPE sets the standard. *Journal of Physical Education, Recreation & Dance, 80*(8), 46–48.

ACRONYMS

AAGPBL: All-American Girls Professional Baseball League

AAHPERD: American Alliance for Health, Physical Education, Recreation and Dance

AASM: Asian Association for Sport Management

AAU: Amateur Athletic Union

ABL: American Basketball League

ACC: Atlantic Coast Conference

AD: athletics director

ADA: Americans with Disabilities Act

AFL: Arena Football League; American Football League (21); also Australian Football League

AL: American League

ASA: Amateur Softball Association (of America)

ASMA: African Sport Management Association

AWSM: Association for Women in Sports Media

AWRA: Australian WomenSport & Recreation Association

BCA: Black Coaches Association (original name); Black Coaches and Administrators

CAA: certified athletic administrator Creative Artists Agency

CAAWS: Canadian Association for the Advancement of Women and Sport and Physical Activity

CABMA: College Athletic Business Management Association

CBA: collective bargaining agreement

CEO: chief executive officer

CFO: chief financial officer

CIAA: Central Intercollegiate Athletic Association

CIAAA: Canadian Interscholastic Athletic Administrator Association

CoSIDA: College Sports Information Directors of America

COSMA: Commission on Sport Management Accreditation

CPA: certified public accountant

CSR: corporate social responsibility

CYO: Catholic Youth Organization

EASM: European Association for Sport Management

EBA: education-based athletics

EPL: English Premier League

ESPN: Entertainment and Sports Programming Network

EAUSF: East African University Sports Federation

FBS: Football Bowl Subdivision

FCS: Football Championship Subdivision

FIFA: Fédération Internationale de Football Association

FSPA: Federation of Sports and Play Associations

GSBA: Global Sport Business Association

HBCU: historically Black colleges and universities

IAAF: International Association of Athletics Federations

ICC: International Cricket Council

IIT: image identification technology

IMG: International Management Group

IOC: International Olympic Committee

IPC: International Paralympic Committee

IPL: Indian Premier League;

ISDPA: International Sport for Development and Peace Association

IT: information technology

KBO: Korea Baseball Organization

KSSM: Korean Society for Sport Management

LPGA: Ladies Professional Golf Association

MLB: Major League Baseball

MLBPA: Major League Baseball Players Association

MLS: Major League Soccer

MNF: *Monday Night Football*

MP: Member of Parliament

N4A: National Association of Academic Advisors for Athletics

NACDA: National Association of Collegiate Directors of Athletics

NAIA: National Association of Intercollegiate Athletics ("the NAIA")

NASPE: National Association for Sport and Physical Education

NASSH: North American Society for Sport History

NASSM: North American Society for Sport Management

NASSS: North American Society for the Sociology of Sport

NBA: National Basketball Association

NCAA: National Collegiate Athletic Association

NFHS: National Federation of State High School Associations

NFL: National Football League

NHL: National Hockey League

NHRA: National Hot Rod Association

NIAAA: National Interscholastic Athletic Administrators Association

NJCAA: National Junior College Athletic Association

NL: National League (of Professional Baseball Clubs)

NSGA: National Sporting Goods Association

NUSF: National University Sports Federation

NWSL: National Women's Soccer League

PGA: Professional Golfers' Association of America

ROI: return on investment

SEC: Southeastern Conference

SGMA: Sporting Goods Manufacturers Association

SFIA: Sports and Fitness Industry Association

SHARP: Sport, Health and Activity Research and Policy

SMA: Sport Marketing Association

SMAANZ: Sport Management Association of Australia and New Zealand

SOCOG: Sydney Organising Committee for the Olympic Games

SRLA: Sport and Recreation Law Association

SSCM: strategic sport communication model

SUNY: State University of New York

TCUs: Tribal colleges and universities

TOP: The Olympic Partner

UAAA: Uniform Athlete Agents Act

UEFA: Union of European Football Associations

UFC: Ultimate Fighting Championship

UN: United Nations

USOC: United States Olympic Committee

VP: vice president

WADA: World Anti-Doping Agency

WASM: World Association for Sport Management

WNBA: Women's National Basketball Association

WPS: Women's Professional Soccer

WSF: Women's Sports Foundation

WSG: web study guide

WTA: Women's Tennis Association

WUSA: Women's United Soccer Association

YOG: Youth Olympic Games

PART I

INTRODUCTION TO SPORT MANAGEMENT

Professional preparation for careers in sport management should be built on a strong conceptual foundation. This opening section provides such a cornerstone as it presents basic—yet important and sometimes overlooked—information and key concepts that prospective sport managers should be well acquainted with. The first three chapters take you through an overview of the field in general, examine professional considerations vital to success in the sport industry, and review key aspects of the history of the field. The last two chapters of this section involve managerial and leadership concepts applied to sport management personnel and sport organizations.

In chapter 1, the editors of this fifth edition—Paul M. Pedersen and Lucie Thibault—provide an overview of the field by introducing sport management as an academic major and a career field. After defining sport and sport management, they delineate the types of sports in the industry, the settings in which sports are found, and the different ways of segmenting the sport industry. Pedersen and Thibault discuss several characteristics of sport-related enterprises that distinguish them from other business pursuits and then describe competencies that are essential for success in sport management. Among the competencies examined is a strategy whereby you can develop critical thinking skills and learn to apply them to issues in sport management. The message of this part of the chapter is that sport managers who can think critically about sport-related issues will be competent, reflective professionals who have the potential to become influential agents of change. The chapter, which includes a section on social media and sport management, concludes with an overview of the opportunities and challenges that sport manag-

ers will face in the future. Among the challenges detailed in this part of the chapter is an extensive examination of ethics, social responsibility, and principled decision making. The sport management professional featured in this chapter is Kalen Irsay, the vice chair and owner of the Indianapolis Colts, an NFL team. In the international sidebar, John Harris (Glasgow Caledonian University, Scotland) examines the administration and hosting of the Ryder Cup, which was staged in Scotland in 2014 for only the second time in the history of the international event.

Chapter 2 contains information that will help you develop a professional perspective on your studies and your career. Sally Ross and Brian McCullough begin by providing a preview of the courses and experiences that you can expect in the preparation program at your college or university. Next, they discuss essential elements of a positive professional perspective—attitude, image, work transition and adjustment, and business etiquette. The authors, who include a section on social media and professional development, give special attention to career planning and management and offer sound advice on finding a career that is compatible with your values, interests, and skills. They close the chapter by offering tips for gathering information about occupations in sport management. Derek Eiler, the managing partner of a boutique brand strategy consulting firm (Fermata Partners), is the profiled sport management professional in this chapter. The international sidebar contains an essay by Israel's Yair Galily (Interdisciplinary Center, Herzliya), Ilan Tamir (Ariel University, Ariel), and Alina Bernstein (The College of Management Academic Studies, Rishon LeZion). Galily, Tamir, and Bernstein discuss how sport can be used to foster peace.

The purpose of chapter 3 is to provide a history of sport businesses and market structures so that you, as a future sport manager, can understand the significant historical influences on the field and develop strategies for your businesses. Lawrence Fielding, Brenda Pitts, and Paul M. Pedersen first present a historical analysis of the commercialization of sport, including the rise of management in sport. Within this part of the chapter, the authors examine the numerous commercialization models of the developmental periods of the sport business industry and present a sidebar on the emergence of social media within it. Fielding, Pitts, and Pedersen then discuss the historical aspects of the sport market. Included in this discussion are key watershed events, ranging from endorsement advertising to increased participation and spectatorship, that caused massive changes in the way that business in the sport industry was (and is) conducted. The professional profile in this chapter is on Donna Lopiano, the former CEO of the Women's Sports Foundation and the current president of Sports Management Resources. Donna de Haan, from the University of Applied Sciences in Amsterdam (the Netherlands), contributed the international sidebar for this chapter. de Haan's sidebar presents a short overview of the history, management, and branding of Wimbledon.

In chapter 4, Kathy Babiak, Lucie Thibault, and Jerome Quarterman define the term *organization* and describe three types of sport organizations—public, nonprofit, and commercial. This discussion is followed by explanations of organizational environment, organizational effectiveness, and organizational structure. The authors, who include a section on social media usage in organizations, present various organizational designs, such as entrepreneurial, diversified, innovative, missionary, and political. The remainder of the chapter addresses organizational strategy, culture, and change. Throughout the chapter, Babiak, Thibault, and Quarterman present research on sport organizations and explain how the research findings apply to real-world situations in organizations. Christy Hammond, the community relations manager for the Detroit Red Wings of the NHL, is the featured sport management professional in this chapter. In the international sidebar, Hassan Assadi, who teaches at the University of Tehran, explains the current state of university sport associations and education in Iran.

Organizational behavior, individual aspects of managerial positions (e.g., manager roles, functions, activities) and leadership, and human resource management in sport organizations are examined in chapter 5. First, Shannon Kerwin, Jerome Quarterman, and Ming Li illustrate three aspects of management—scientific, human relations, and administrative. After detailing managerial processes, functions, classifications, and skills, the authors explain theoretical approaches to the study of leadership, ending the discussion with the integrative concept of managerial leadership. In addition to providing a social media discussion focused on decision making by management, Kerwin, Quarterman, and Li then present decision making, authority, and power aspects associated with management. They conclude the chapter by covering human resource management and organizational diversity. The professional profiled for this chapter is Becky Burleigh, the women's soccer coach at the University of Florida. The international sidebar is an essay about Spyros Louis, the Olympic stadium in Athens, Greece. Dimitra Papadimitriou of the University of Patras contributed the sidebar.

Chapters 4 and 5 are important for aspiring sport managers because such individuals should become familiar with theories of organizational behavior, management, and leadership and should be able to apply these theories in practical settings. Therefore, the last two chapters of this section address the structure and processes of sport organizations and present desirable attributes of managers and leaders in the sport industry. The underlying theme of the two chapters is that managers have a responsibility to themselves, their employees, and their constituents to appreciate and apply theoretical concepts that will improve the effectiveness and efficiency of the workplace as well as the quality of the sport product or experience. The knowledge that is gained from these two chapters, combined with what is presented in the first three chapters, will form the foundation of professional preparation for careers in sport management. The opening five chapters also provide the foundation on which the remaining 15 chapters of the fifth edition of *Contemporary Sport Management* are built.

For More Information

Professional and Scholarly Associations, Institutes, and Organizations

African Sport Management Association (ASMA)

Amateur Athletic Union of the United States (AAU)

American Alliance for Health, Physical Education, Recreation and Dance (AAHPERD)

Asian Association for Sport Management (AASM)

Birkbeck Sport Business Centre

College Athletic Business Management Association (CABMA)

European Association of Sport Employers (EASE)

European Association for Sport Management (EASM)

European Non-Governmental Sports Organisation (EnGSO)

Global Sport Business Association (GSBA)

The H.J. Lutcher Stark Center for Physical Culture and Sports

Institute for Diversity and Ethics in Sport

Institute for International Sport

International Mind Sports Association (IMSA)

International Olympic Committee (IOC)

International Sport Management Alliance

Japanese Association for Sport Management (JASM)

Josephson Institute Center for Sports Ethics

Korean Society for Sport Management (KSSM)

Laboratory for Diversity in Sport

Latin American Association for Sport Management (ALGeDe)

National Sporting Goods Association (NSGA)

North American Society for Sport History (NASSH)

North American Society for Sport Management (NASSM)

Play the Game

Professional Baseball Employment Opportunities (PBEO)

Sporting Goods Manufacturers Association (SGMA)

Sport and Fitness Industry Association (SFIA)

Sport Management Association of Australia and New Zealand (SMAANZ)

Sport Management Council of the National Association for Sport and Physical Education (NASPE)

The Sports Business Institute

World Anti-Doping Agency (WADA)

World Association for Sport Management (WASM)

World Federation of the Sporting Goods Industry (WFSGI)

Professional and Scholarly Publications

Academy of Management Journal

Academy of Management Review

Administrative Science Quarterly

Asian Sport Management Review

Athletic Business

European Sport Management Quarterly

Global Sport Business Journal

Global Sport Management News

Harvard Business Review

International Journal of Sport Management

International Journal of Sport Management and Marketing

International Journal of Sport Management, Recreation, & Tourism

International Journal of Sport Policy and Politics

International Journal of the History of Sport

Journal of Applied Sport Management

Journal of the Philosophy of Sport

Journal of Sport History

Journal of Sport Management

Korean Journal of Sport Management

National Sporting Goods Association (NSGA) Now

SGMA Industry Marketplace

Sport, Business and Management: An International Journal

Sport History Review

Sport in History

Sport Management Education Journal

Sport Management International Journal: Choregia

Sport Management Review

SportBusiness International

Sporting Goods Intelligence

Sporting Traditions

SportsBusiness Daily

Sports Business News

Strategic Management Journal

Street & Smith's SportsBusiness Journal

Sport Management Job Market

AthleticLink

The Field

Game Face

iHire

Jobs in Sports

Malakye

Monster

North American Society of Sport Management

Online Sports

Quintessential Careers

Sports Careers

Sport Business Research Network

Sports Business University

SportsOneSource

Sports Jobs (About.com)

TeamWork Online

Women Sports Jobs

Work in Sports

HISTORICAL MOMENTS

1949 — Baseball business administration offered at Florida Southern University

1957 — Walter O'Malley sent a letter to Dr. James Mason at Ohio University

1964 — Stan Isaacs published *Careers and Opportunities in Sports*

1966 — First sport administration program established at Ohio University

1970s — SMARTS, Sport Management Arts & Science Society, forerunner of NASSM, conceived by University of Massachusetts faculty

1985 — North American Society for Sport Management (NASSM) established

1986 — Inaugural NASSM conference held at Kent State University

1987 — *Journal of Sport Management* (*JSM*) launched

1992 — NASSM Code of Ethics adopted

1993 — European Association for Sport Management (EASM) established

1993 — NASPE–NASSM curricular standards published

1994 — Pitts, Fielding, and Miller's sport industry segment model introduced

1995 — Sport Management Association of Australia and New Zealand (SMAANZ) established

1997 — Meek's economic impact model released

2001 — Li, Hofacre, and Mahony's sport industry model revealed

2002 — Sport Marketing Association (SMA) established

2005 — United Nations proclaimed 2005 the International Year of Sport and Physical Education

2012 — World Association for Sport Management (WASM) formally established

2014 — More than 425 sport management programs established around the globe

1

MANAGING SPORT

Paul M. Pedersen Lucie Thibault

LEARNING OBJECTIVES

› Discuss examples of traditional and nontraditional sporting activities.
› Identify settings in which sporting activities occur.
› Explain ways of organizing the sport industry.
› Discuss unique aspects of sport management and the types of positions available in the field.
› Explain competencies required for success as a sport manager.
› Identify ways in which sport industry stakeholders can effectively use social media.
› Apply critical thinking skills to a problem in sport management.
› Discuss opportunities and challenges facing sport managers of the future.

Key Terms

associated spending
descriptive
discretionary funds
extreme sports
networking
organizational culture

prescriptive
principled decision making
underrepresented groups
workforce diversity

Jackie Robinson, whose 1947 entrance into Major League Baseball (MLB) was portrayed in the widely acclaimed 2013 movie *42*, broke the modern color barrier in the major leagues when he stepped onto the field for the Brooklyn (now Los Angeles) Dodgers Baseball Club. Branch Rickey, the general manager of the team, had carefully selected and groomed Robinson, who went on to a Hall of Fame career. In 1957, the year after Robinson's last at bat, Walter O'Malley (the president and chief stockholder of the Dodgers) anticipated the future growth of organized sport and predicted the need for professionally prepared sport administrators. O'Malley wrote a letter to Dr. James Mason, a faculty member at Ohio University, stating the following:

> *I ask the question, where would one go to find a person who by virtue of education had been trained to administer a marina, race track, ski resort, auditorium, stadium, theater, convention or exhibition hall, a public camp complex, or a person to fill an executive position at a team or league level in junior athletics such as Little League baseball, football, scouting, CYO (Catholic Youth Organization), and youth activities, etc.? A course that would enable a graduate to read architectural and engineering plans; or having to do with specifications and contract letting, the functions of a purchasing agent in plant operations. There would be the problems of ticket selling and accounting, concessions, sale of advertising in programs, and publications, outdoor and indoor displays and related items. (Mason, Higgins, & Wilkinson, 1981, p. 44)*

As a result of that inquiry, Mason and several of his colleagues created a master's-level sport administration program at Ohio University. Inaugurated in 1966, the Ohio program was the first recorded university-sponsored attempt to provide a graduate-level curriculum that specifically prepared students for jobs in a variety of sport-related industries. The idea caught on. According to the North American Society for Sport Management (NASSM), in 2014, there were 429 undergraduate sport management programs, 253 master's programs, and 40 doctoral programs in Africa, Australia, Canada, China, India, New Zealand, Singapore, Taiwan, the United Kingdom (UK), and the United States. In addition to the future sport managers studying in the various programs listed on the NASSM website (see table 1.1), hundreds of college students in other countries, such as Switzerland, Spain, Ireland, the Netherlands, Italy, Belgium, Turkey, Iran, Japan, Greece, and Austria, are also studying sport management. (Refer to chapter 2 for more information on some of the common characteristics of sport management academic programs.)

This chapter represents the first step on your journey toward becoming a sport manager. It includes definitions of basic terms, a discussion of the nature and scope of the sport industry, and explanations of unique aspects of sport management enterprises and careers. You will also learn about desirable sport management competencies and some of the challenges and opportunities that await you as you prepare to take your place among the next generation of sport managers.

Defining Sport and Sport Management

For most of us, sport implies having fun, but it can also be work (for a professional athlete), a means of employment (for a sport tourism director), or a business (for a sport marketing agency). Sport takes many forms. It may include many participants, as in team sports such as soccer and volleyball; two participants, as in dual sports such as tennis and badminton; or one person, as in individual sports such as golf and surfing. Sport includes a combination of these configurations when it involves team competitions, tournaments, or matches in dual sports (wrestling) or individual sports (in-line

Table 1.1   Sport Management Programs in Selected Countries and Regions

Countries, regions	Bachelor's	Master's	Doctoral	Total
Africa	1	1	0	2
Asia	10	11	2	23
Australia	11	3	0	14
Canada	16	8	6	30
Europe	10	22	2	34
India	0	1	0	1
New Zealand	4	1	0	5
United States	377	206	30	613
Total	429	253	40	722

Data from North American Society for Sport Management 2014. Available: www.nassm.com/InfoAbout/SportMgmtPrograms

skating). What criteria qualify games or activities to be classified as sport? Consider, for example, eSports (electronic sports). In 2013, the U.S. government recognized professional video gamers as individual athletes. Thus, certain people who play video games at a high level can now call themselves professional athletes. Dustin Beck, vice president of eSports at Riot Games, had lobbied with others for this designation, and secured it after the government took note "that professional eSports is a full time job for these talented young players, practicing 10–12 hours a day with their teammates and [competing] in regular matches" (LeJacq, 2013, para. 13). Do we classify video gaming as a sport? Is horse racing a sport? What about cycling, water skiing, pocket billiards, or Texas hold 'em poker and other table games? We know that softball, tennis, basketball, ice and field hockey, football, and golf are sports. Are they different from sailing, dog racing, marathoning, and scuba diving? If so, how are they different? If not, how are they similar?

The Council of Europe (2001) defined sport as "all forms of physical activity which, through casual or organised participation, aim at expressing or improving physical fitness and mental well-being, forming social relationships or obtaining results in competition at all levels" (p. 1). Similarly, Pitts, Fielding, and Miller (1994) stated that sport is "any activity, experience, or business enterprise for which the primary focus is fitness, recreation, athletics, and leisure related" (p. 18). According to these definitions, sport does not have to be competitive, nor does it always require specialized equipment or rules; in fact, the broad concept of sport can include activities such as working out, swimming, running, boating, and dancing. For this book, we adopted these broad definitions; consequently, you should interpret the term *sport* to include an expansive variety of physical activities and associated businesses.

Many people who are employed in business endeavors associated with sport are engaged in a career field known as sport management. For instance, Kalen Irsay, the professional profiled later in this chapter, studied sport management as an undergraduate. She is now involved in aspects of management for the Indianapolis Colts of the NFL. The same can be said for the other professionals featured throughout this textbook (e.g., Derek Eiler in chapter 2, Donna Lopiano in chapter 3, Christy Hammond in chapter 4), who are employed in various segments of the sport management field. According to Pitts and Stotlar (2007), sport management is "the study and practice of

Nothing New Under the Sun

Lest we be deluded by the notion that contemporary sport management is markedly different from the ancient art of staging athletic spectacles, let us consider for a moment the following description of the games sponsored in 11 BCE by Herod the Great, king of Judea and honorary president of the Olympic Games:

The games began with a magnificent dedication ceremony. Then there were athletic and musical competitions, in which large prizes were given not only to the winners but also—an unusual feature—to those who took second and third place. Bloody spectacles were also presented, with gladiators and wild beasts fighting in various combinations, and there were also horse races. Large prizes attracted contenders from all areas and this in turn drew great numbers of spectators. Cities favored by Herod sent delegations, and these he entertained and lodged at his own expense. What comes through most clearly . . . is that gigantic sums of money were spent. (Frank, 1984, p. 158)

The success of such an extravaganza relied in all likelihood on the organizational skills of the individuals charged with planning and executing the games. Certainly there was today's equivalent of a general manager, or CEO, to whom all other personnel were responsible. Additionally, assistants who were knowledgeable in economics, accounting, and finance were indispensable if the event was to become profitable. The "business managers" were responsible for obtaining financial support, purchasing equipment (and perhaps even the requisite beasts), furnishing entertainment and lodging for the VIPs, and generally being accountable for the large sums of money that were spent.

Once the financial dimension was secured, there was the challenge of attracting sufficient numbers of contestants and spectators to the games. Enter Herod's "marketing director," armed with unique and unprecedented gimmicks to assure a full complement of participants as well as a full house of onlookers. A new prize structure was devised and, in awarding prizes to musicians as well as athletes, the seeds were sown for the modern spectacle known, among other titles, as the Battle of the Bands. The marketing director must have enlisted the aid of assistants who were responsible for extending invitations, publicizing the games, and keeping records of the day's activities. In the years prior to the printing press, much less the electronic media, informing the public was no small task—to say nothing of offering enticements sufficient to persuade them to journey for days and endure what must have been extremely undesirable traveling conditions. The marketing and promotions people certainly had their hands full!

The parallel[s] could continue—there was a need for crowd control, rules decisions, award ceremonies, and so forth. After all, certain tasks must be performed regardless of the venue in which the event occurs. Now, 2000 years later, we are reminded once again of Solomon's wisdom in proclaiming in Ecclesiastes 1:9 that "there is no new thing under the sun."

Reprinted, by permission, from J.B. Parks and G.A. Olafson, 1987, "Sport management and a new journal," *Journal of Sport Management* 1(1): 1-2

all people, activities, businesses, or organizations involved in producing, facilitating, promoting, or organizing any sport-related business or product" (p. 4). Again, this broad definition includes an incredibly wide variety of sport-related careers.

Sport management is also the name given to many university-level academic programs that prepare students to assume positions in the sport industry. These programs provide two additional sources of confusion regarding vocabulary. First, you might have noticed that many professional preparation programs are titled *sport* management, whereas others are called *sports* management. In our view, people prefer one or the other based on the connotations that the words *sports* and *sport* have for them. To many academics, ourselves included, *sports* implies a collection of separate activities such as golf, soccer, hockey, volleyball, softball, and gymnastics—items in a series that we can count. Conversely, *sport* is an all-encompassing concept. It is a collective noun that includes all sporting activities, not just those that we can place on a list. We have found that students in our classes relate well to the parallel with the different connotations of the words *religions* and *religion*. The word *religions* typically connotes several specific faiths or belief systems—different denominations or sects that we can quantify. *Religion*, on the other hand, is a broad term that we can interpret as a general reverence or faith held by any number of people. A second source of confusion is the fact that many professional preparation programs are titled sport (or sports) management, and others are called sport (or sports) administration. In both instances, we suggest that it would be counterproductive to debate which term is more appropriate. Ultimately, the quality of the curriculum is more important than the title of the program.

Nature and Scope of the Sport Industry

Just as there are several definitions of sport, there are many ways to conceptualize the nature and scope of the sport industry. In the following paragraphs, we will elaborate on three concepts that, in different ways, provide overviews of sport: (1) types of sports, (2) settings in which sports are found, and (3) models of sport industry segments.

Types of Sports

One way to consider the sport industry is to examine the many types of sports that exist. An awareness of the wide diversity of sporting opportunities available to consumers is essential for anyone who anticipates becoming a decision maker in the world of sport. Sport marketers, for instance, must have a good understanding of both traditional and new sports so they can develop effective promotional strategies.

You are already familiar with traditional sports such as baseball, basketball, tennis, golf, American football, swimming, and soccer. You also know that numerous new sports and physical activities have emerged. Pitts and Stotlar (2007) identified the following activities and sports that have appeared on the scene lately: several varieties of aerobics, in-line skating, boogie boarding, snowboarding, snow kayaking, parasailing, ice surfing, mountain boarding, beach volleyball, skydive dancing, street luge, snow biking, ice climbing, the X Games, and indoor soccer.

Several of these new sports are known as extreme (action) sports, and they are becoming more popular. For example, Mawson (2002) reported that people born between 1961 and 1981 demonstrated heightened interest and engagement with action sports such as street luge, motocross biking, bungee jumping, and snow

Canoe polo, which involves kayaking and water polo, is one example of a type of sport. Here, the New Zealand Canoe Polo national squad practices at the Hokowhitu Lagoon in Palmerston North, New Zealand.

bicycling. International sport organizations (e.g., Olympic Games), event organizers (e.g., Riverboarding World Championship 2013 in Indonesia), the mass media (e.g., X Games on ESPN, Dew Tour on NBC), and social media (e.g., Dew Tour on AlliSports.com) have embraced **extreme sports**. Fans even have the opportunity to watch extreme sports 24 hours a day on the Extreme Sports Channel. Younger people are also learning to enjoy extreme sports. In fact, when Bennett, Henson, and Zhang (2003) asked 367 middle school and high school students about their televised sport viewing preferences, more students preferred watching the X Games than the World Series and the soccer World Cup. More students also preferred watching action sports to watching baseball, basketball, ice hockey, and auto racing. More than a decade ago, both Mawson (2002) and Bennett and colleagues (2003) predicted that the popularity of action sports would continue to rise. The same can be said for the heightened interest and participation by adults in ultramarathoning, Ironman racing, endurance racing, and survival sporting events such as England's Tough Guy and Nettle Warrior. Tough Mudder, an obstacle race that had more than 50 scheduled events in 2013, had revenues of US$2 million in 2010 and had projected revenues of US$115 million in 2013 (Grossfeld, 2013). With both the extreme sports and the various endurance races, sport managers of the future should be familiar with these sports and events and should be prepared to make them accessible to consumers as participatory activities and spectator events and through mass media and social media.

Settings for Sporting Activities

Another approach to the sport industry involves examining the many different settings in which sporting activities occur. This approach can provide you with ideas about where to find sites in which sport managers might be needed. The latest edition of the *Sports Market Place Directory* (2013) contains more than 2,000 pages and has over 20,000 updates, contacts, or enhancements covering the following sport-related settings:

> Single sports (professional leagues, teams, organizations)
> Multi-sports (athletic foundations, disabled sports organizations, high school sports, military sports, Olympic sports, professional organizations, sports commissions and conventions/visitors bureaus, sports halls of fame, sports libraries and museums, state games organizations, youth sports organizations)
> College sports (college associations, college athletic conferences, college athletics departments, sport management degree programs)
> Media (newspapers; sports magazines and business directories; sports media production; radio networks and programs, satellite radio, radio stations; sports television, cable, and broadcast networks; pay-per-view television, local and national television programs, satellite television, television stations, sports on the World Wide Web)
> Sports sponsors
> Professional services (executive search services, event planning and services, event security, financial services, marketing and consulting services, technical services, sport agents and attorneys, sports medicine, sport travel services, statistical services, student-athlete recruiting services, ticket services)
> Facilities (arenas and stadiums; auto, equestrian, and greyhound race tracks; facility architects and developers, facility management, facility concession services)
> Manufacturers and retailers (equipment and product manufacturers, software manufacturers, retailers)
> Events, meetings, and trade shows

Sport Industry Segments

A third approach to defining the nature and scope of the sport industry is to create industry models that show the relationships among various segments of the sport industry. Within the various segments of sport management, segmentation models exist that are even more specific. For instance, sport communication—often considered a segment of sport management—has its own segmentation model (Pedersen, 2013; Pedersen, Miloch, & Laucella, 2007). While the strategic sport communication model (SSCM) is detailed in chapter 14, this chapter presents examples of three sport management models, each of which represents a different approach to conceptualizing the sport industry. All three models are useful in showing you interesting and different ways to consider the world of sport.

PRODUCT TYPE MODEL

Pitts and colleagues (1994) developed a segmentation model of the sport industry based on the types of products sold or promoted by the businesses or organizations within them (figure 1.1). The industry segmentation approach is especially useful to sport marketers, who are typically responsible for formulating competitive strategies. Sport marketers can use their understanding of the sport product segments as they make

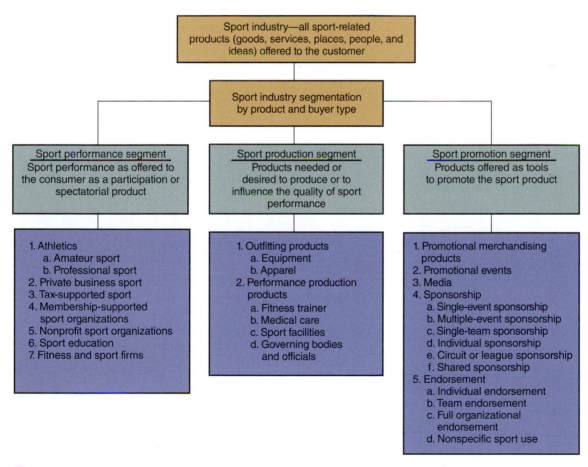

Figure 1.1   Product type model.

Reprinted, by permission, from B.G. Pitts, L.W. Fielding, and L.K. Miller, 1994, "Industry segmentation theory and the sport industry: Developing a sport industry segment model," *Sport Marketing Quarterly* 2(1): 15-24. (Morgantown, WV: Fitness Information Technology, Inc.). © Fitness Information Technology.

decisions such as choosing the segments in which they wish to position their products, selecting the types of marketing strategies to use, and determining whether to create new industry segments.

The model details three product segments of the sport industry: (1) sport performance, (2) sport production, and (3) sport promotion. As shown in figure 1.1, the sport performance segment includes such varied products as school-sponsored athletics, fitness clubs, sport camps, professional sport, and municipal parks sport programs. Examples of products in the sport production segment are basketballs, fencing foils, jogging shoes, sports medicine clinics, swimming pools, and college athletic conferences. The sport promotion segment includes products such as T-shirts, giveaways, print and broadcast media, and celebrity endorsements. Sport marketers can use this product type model to plan marketing strategies, something that you will learn more about in chapter 12.

ECONOMIC IMPACT MODEL

Meek (1997) took another approach to describing the sport industry (figure 1.2). He proposed that the industry could be defined by describing three primary sectors:

1. Sport entertainment and recreation such as events, teams, and individual participants; sports and related recreational activities; and **associated spending**

associated spending— Money spent by sport participants, spectators, and sponsors.

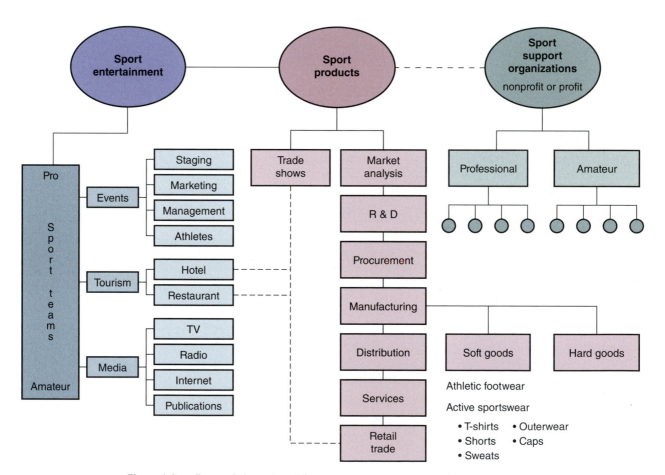

Figure 1.2 Economic impact model.

Reprinted, by permission, from A. Meek, 1997, "An estimate of the size and supported economic activity of the sports industry in the United States," *Sport Marketing Quarterly* 6(4): 15-21. (Morgantown, WV: Fitness Information Technology, Inc.). © Fitness Information Technology.

2. Sport products and services such as design, testing, manufacturing, and distribution of equipment, clothing, and instruments

3. Sport support organizations such as leagues, law firms, and marketing organizations (p. 16)

Meek proposed that his broad definition of sport enabled an analysis of the economic activity of the teams and businesses within each sector and the economic activity associated with sport. You will learn more about sport economics in chapter 15.

SPORT ACTIVITY MODEL

The third model of the sport industry is based on the single characteristic that differentiates the sport industry from all other industries: sport activities, that is, games and events (Eschenfelder & Li, 2007). This model, shown in figure 1.3, defines the sport industry as the firms and organizations that

1. produce sport activities,

2. provide products and services to support the production of sport activities, and

3. sell and trade products related to sport activities.

In the sport activity model, the sport-producing sector is the core of the industry. Six supporting subsectors surround, and overlap with, the activity-producing core. Organizations in these subsectors either (1) provide products and services to the core organizations or (2) sell or trade products related to sport. This model differs conceptually from the other two models in that it places sport at the center and illustrates the dependence of the subsectors on the production of sporting activities.

Unique Aspects of Sport Management

More than three decades ago, Mullin (1980) provided insight into three unique aspects of sport management: sport marketing, sport enterprise financial structures, and sport industry career paths. Mullin's three aspects are just as critical today because they still distinguish sport business from other business enterprises and justify sport management as a distinct area of professional preparation. We add a fourth unique aspect of sport to Mullin's list: the enormous power and influence of sport as a social institution.

Sport Marketing

Sport marketing is unique because the sport product is unlike other products that consumers buy. For example, sport is consumed as quickly as it is produced. It is a perishable product that is not accompanied by any guarantees of customer satisfaction. People who provide the sport experience cannot predict the outcome because of the spontaneous nature of the activity, the inconsistency of events, and the uncertainty surrounding the results. Sport marketers, therefore, face unique challenges.

Sport Enterprise Financial Structures

Most sport businesses are financed differently from other businesses. Typically, the sale of a product or service such as clothing, food, automobiles, or home cleaning finances the business. But with the exception of sporting goods stores, sport enterprises earn a significant portion of revenue not from the sale of a service such as a game, workout, or 10K run, but from extraneous sources such as television rights, concessions, road game guarantees, parking, and merchandise. Intercollegiate athletics and municipal recreation sport programs might generate revenue from student or user fees, private donations, taxes, rentals, or licensing fees. Sport managers continually compete for the

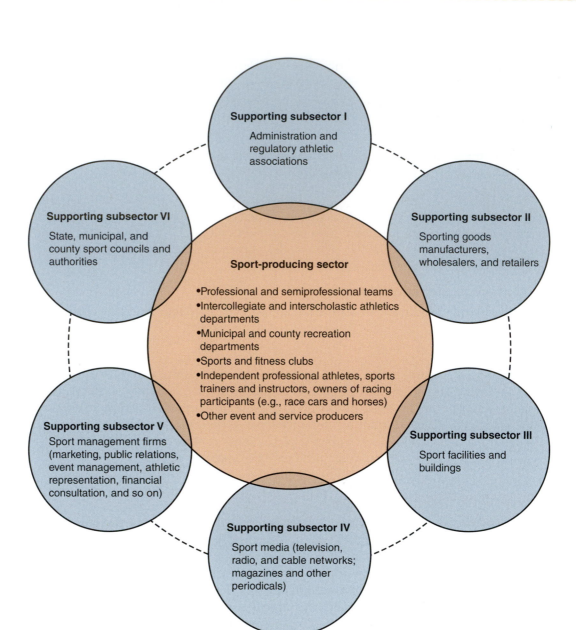

Figure 1.3   Li, Hofacre, and Mahony's sport industry model.

Reprinted, by permission, from M.J. Eschenfelder and M. Li, 2007, *Economics of sport,* 2nd ed. (Morgantown, WV: Fitness Information Technology), 6. © Fitness Information Technology.

discretionary funds— Money left over after necessary expenditures (e.g., rent, food, car payment, insurance) have been made.

discretionary funds of consumers through the sale of items that might or might not be related to the apparent primary focus of the enterprise. Sport also attracts consumers who spend more money outside the sporting arena than they spend on the sport itself (e.g., travel, entertainment, souvenirs, equipment). This unique financial base requires different practices within the sport setting.

Sport Industry Career Paths

Traditionally, many sport management practitioners have been hired from visible groups, such as intercollegiate athletics or professional sport. An example of this phenomenon is the basketball star who becomes a basketball coach and eventually an athletics director. We can find similar career advancement patterns within municipal recreation

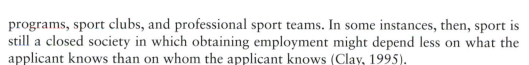

programs, sport clubs, and professional sport teams. In some instances, then, sport is still a closed society in which obtaining employment might depend less on what the applicant knows than on whom the applicant knows (Clay, 1995).

An additional challenge is the assumption that members of **underrepresented groups** do not have the requisite skills for management positions. Arthur Triche, who was the vice president of public relations for the Atlanta Hawks and the first African American public relations director in the NBA, credits volunteering and making contacts (i.e., **networking**) in the sport industry as important steps that he took toward overcoming this obstacle (Clay, 1995). A cautionary note about networking is in order: Mere acquaintance with influential people in the world of sport is not sufficient. Unless your acquaintances have a positive impression of your competence and work ethic, you cannot expect them to assist you in your career. You will read more about networking in chapter 2.

In spite of the advances that have resulted from efforts to diversify the sport management workforce, we have a long way to go before we can claim that sport is truly an equal opportunity environment (Acosta & Carpenter, 2012; *The Racial and Gender Report Card*, n.d.). While there are exceptions (e.g., Big East Conference commissioner Val Ackerman, Baltimore Ravens' general manager Ozzie Newsome), for the most part, professional opportunities for people of color and women continue to lag behind opportunities for White males. Moreover, women and people of color in sport are occasionally subjected to public denigration, as illustrated by comments directed at Jemele Hill. The ESPN columnist shared on social media a racist note she received, and she later added, "I'm called something derogatory on a daily basis" (Tenore, 2013, para. 4). As professionals, you may be in positions of authority in which your sensitivity to cultural inequities can lead to expanded **workforce diversity** and positive changes in the **organizational culture** of the sport industry (Ross & Parks, 2008).

Sport as a Social Institution

Sport is a distinctive social activity that is frequently the basis of a person's social identity (Coakley, 2009). As such, it is a social institution of astonishing magnitude and influence. What other social pursuit is allotted several pages in the daily newspaper, has its own slot on every television and radio news program, has its own cable channels, and creates what appears to be an international withdrawal crisis when members of its workforce go on strike? The sheer power of sport mandates that people who wish to manage it acquire a sound understanding of its historical, psychological, sociological, cultural, and philosophical dimensions.

The General Assembly of the United Nations (UN) publicly recognized the power of sport when—in adopting a resolution titled "Sport as a means to promote education, health, development and peace"—it declared 2005 the International Year of Sport and Physical Education (United Nations, 2004). Further noting the major role that sport can play in promoting the UN goals of peace, dignity, and prosperity, the executive director of the United Nations Environment Programme (UNEP) stated that it is the "cross-cutting, cross cultural nature of sport that makes it such a potentially important influence for good—or for bad." The executive director added, "The way sports events are run, the way sporting goods companies do business, and the way sports stars conduct themselves on and off the field can have profound effects far beyond the financial bottom line" (Toepfer, 2003, para. 9). Clearly, the immense power of sport mandates that sport managers understand the social implications of their actions. Contemporary sport enterprises need well-prepared managers who can make sound management decisions in the context of sport as an exceptionally influential social institution.

underrepresented groups—People who traditionally have not been hired in sport management positions (e.g., women, people of color, people with disabilities).

networking—The building up or maintaining of informal relationships, especially with people who could bring advantages such as job or business opportunities (Microsoft Word online dictionary).

workforce diversity—People of different ages, genders, religions, physical abilities, social classes, sexual orientations, races, ethnicities, and cultures working together in an organization.

organizational culture—Workplace values, norms, and behaviors that produce patterns of behavior unique to an organization.

Sport Management Competencies

Research suggests that sport management competencies are universal, and have remained relatively stable over time (Danylchuk & Boucher, 2003; Horch & Schütte, 2003). Besides emphasizing competencies required for performing traditional tasks such as personnel management and planning, today's sport management organizations and settings place increased importance on communication skills, technological aptitude, and the ability to interact in a global and multicultural society. A couple of the general competency areas that we cover in this chapter are managerial leadership skills and critical thinking skills.

Professional Profile: Kalen Irsay

Title: vice chair/owner, Indianapolis Colts

Education: BS (sport management and marketing), Indiana University-Bloomington (IU)

In 2013, after three years as a vice president of the Indianapolis Colts, Irsay entered her first season as vice chair and owner of this NFL team. Irsay, who grew up with the Colts, is the president of the Indianapolis Colts Women's Organization. She also represents the team at the league owners' meetings. She was born in Indianapolis, where she resides still, and she is on the board of directors for the United Way of Central Indiana. Irsay is also heavily involved with the Indianapolis Humane Society, and she has helped out with their two major fundraisers each year, including being one of their grand marshals for Mutt Strut the past three years. She was also the patron of honor for Down Syndrome Indiana's major fundraiser for two years. The following is a snapshot of her development, education, duties, and insights as a leader in the sport industry.

What have been the key moves, steps, or developments in your career, and how did you arrive at your current position?

When describing how I ended up in my current position, the obvious answer would be that I grew up in a family that has had ownership of the Colts since 1972. But on further inspection, I realize that what led me to where I am today is much more complicated than just growing up in the Irsay family. My grandpa, Robert Irsay, bought the Los Angeles Rams in 1972. Only a few months later, he made a trade with Carroll Rosenbloom for the Baltimore Colts. As we all know, this led to the infamous middle-of-the-night move on March 28th, 1984. When my grandpa passed away in 1997, he left the ownership of the team to my dad, Jim Irsay, who was only 37. I was 9 years old at the time. I guess you could say that the key developments that led me to where I am today started even before I was born.

Growing up, my involvement with the team was kept simple because my parents wanted my two older sisters (Casey Foyt and Carlie Irsay-Gordon) and me to have lives that were as normal as possible. We had allowances and chores. While I was growing up, I worked at my mom's workout studio, as a babysitter, and at a clothing store, and I was constantly involved in volunteering within the community and with the Colts. I mention these minor details because they built the foundation of who I am today. My sisters and I went to every home game as we grew up, and once we were old enough, we were at every single away game as well. In terms of day-to-day interaction with the Colts, we were continually involved in community relation events, but it wasn't until high school that each of us began to interact with the organization in the form of a job or internship. During our high school and college summers, our responsibilities started with the typical odd jobs of making copies, operating the switchboard, running errands, and just getting to know the basics of how the business of an NFL team works and soaking up everything that we witnessed around us.

I cannot describe the steps that led me to my current position without mentioning my alma mater. I enrolled at IU knowing it had one of the best sport marketing and management programs in the country, which I saw

ONE DAY

Go to the WSG and learn more about a typical day in the life for Kalen Irsay. See if she spends her working hours the way you think she does.

firsthand during my four years there. Shortly after I graduated, I threw myself into the business. While my college education and professors had an immense influence on me and definitely heightened my realization that I was and always have been truly passionate about the sport industry, I probably learned more in my first year working full time for the team than I did during my entire time at IU. I say this because in sports, it's gaining real-life experiences within the industry that helps you get a pulse on the sport community. It's all about the opportunities in which you choose to partake. What you take away from each experience enables you to grow as a young professional.

When I first started working full time with the Colts, I had no idea which area I wanted to sink my teeth into first. Therefore, I did what I labeled a mini boot camp, where I spent time with the employees from every department to learn what their jobs entail every month out of the year: anything from our mascot program and community relations to ticketing and radio and TV production. I eventually landed in sponsorship sales with a role as a sponsorship sales account coordinator. Our sales department is made up of sponsorship sales account managers and account coordinators, with each sponsor assigned to one of each. The managers go out and sell to businesses and the coordinators direct coordination of their creative inventory in their contract. Therefore, I work with clients and sponsorship sales account managers on a day-to-day basis in order to coordinate anything from radio spots, television spots, in-stadium permanent and temporary creative elements, private events, hospitality events, player appearances, game-day experiences such as sideline visits, and their personalized community relations programs. The list goes on and on. One of the best aspects about being an account coordinator is that you work with almost every department on a weekly, if not daily, basis.

Although a lot of my time is spend working within sponsorship, over the years my work has led me down many different paths. Some examples of these endeavors include implementing the team's public Colts Women's Club (Blue Ladies), getting involved for a couple years as talent on a local radio station for 5-minute weekly updates throughout the season, and becoming president of our internal Indianapolis Colts Women's Organization (ICWO). Furthermore, in addition to tasks such as participating in the annual owners' meetings, on a daily basis, I am heavily involved in our internal operations within our front office. The tasks involved here range from making changes in salaries and bonuses and interviewing potential employees to conducting other general operations of our organization. Overall, the best way I can think of to describe my start and involvement with the Colts and the NFL as a whole is that football and the industry that revolves around it is truly in my blood; sometimes it feels like it is all I know. Year to year, I'm constantly learning as the landscape of the sport industry forever moves and changes.

What are your current responsibilities and objectives in your job?

My responsibilities can change day to day depending on which hat I am wearing. I can go from interviewing a new hire to coordinating a time for a sponsor to come in and record a new radio spot to planning the next Indianapolis Colts Women's Organization's volunteer opportunity to a meeting where we approve new expenses for our marketing department. Therefore, my main objective is to constantly work toward making the Colts the best team in the NFL from top to bottom. Because the industry is changing every year, in everything we do, we are constantly asking ourselves how we can do better, how we can make our fans' experiences better, and so on. We want to present the best product possible and to be proud of every single element of our organization.

What do you enjoy most about your current job?

My answer to this is threefold. First, I enjoy having the opportunity to work within the NFL. I feel so blessed to work in sport and to be surrounded by a game that I love to my core. Second, I enjoy seeing the city of Indianapolis in a new way every single day. My job responsibilities enable me to continually learn about the city I grew up in. Whether it is learning about a new business, hearing about a new nonprofit, or seeing how Indianapolis' national recognition grows every single year, it makes me proud to call myself a Hoosier. Third, I love that not one day of work is identical to the next.

What do you consider the biggest future challenge to be in your job or industry?

For me, the biggest future challenge in my job would be to overcome the obstacle of the idea of nepotism while being one of the few female executives in the NFL. Yes, my sisters and I were handed this unbelievable opportunity to someday take over the Colts, but I have worked very hard, and I plan to continue to work very hard to prove my worth in an extremely competitive industry. Our mom and dad always taught us to live with as much humility as possible, an ideal I try to live by every day. That's why a common mantra in our lives is "It is amazing the things you can get done when no one cares who gets the credit."

Managerial Leadership Skills

Although competencies required for specific settings vary depending on particular organizations as well as specific assignments, the sport management tasks presented in figure 1.4 provide an overview of industry expectations. Most of the competencies required for these tasks are transferable, which means that you should be able to use them in a variety of vocational settings that include, but are not limited to, sport organizations.

The tasks in the core of figure 1.4 are general sport management responsibilities, those in which all sport managers must be proficient and, to varying degrees, able to perform on the job. For example, regardless of whether you work in a sport club, the front office of a professional sport team, a sport association, or an intercollegiate athletics department, you need to demonstrate competence in writing, speaking, and public relations, as well as in the other tasks presented in the core.

The tasks listed in the clusters branching out from the core reflect distinctions between two types of responsibilities (i.e., organizational management and communication management). Leadership and management skills are necessary for performing tasks in the organization management cluster. Sport managers need good organizational skills to direct and supervise subordinates in settings such as sport clubs, municipal recreation programs, or sport associations for specific populations (e.g., seniors or people with differing abilities); in intercollegiate athletics and professional sport; and in the business aspect of any sport-related enterprise.

In the communication management cluster, written and oral communication skills are of paramount importance. Contemporary sport communication practitioners must also be highly skilled in computer technology related to data storage and retrieval as well as web-based technology (Yu, 2007). Sophisticated communication management competencies and technological adaptability are especially critical in areas such as sport marketing, media relations, sports writing, and social media (thus, the inclusion of a social media sidebar in each chapter of this textbook).

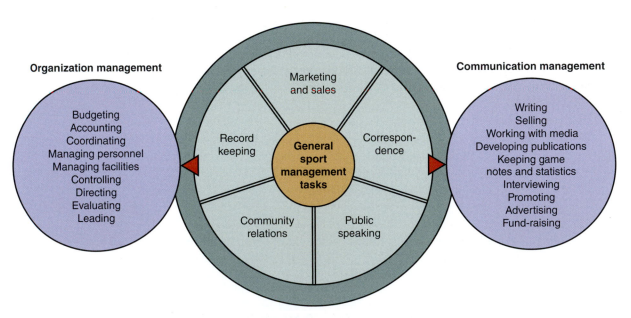

Figure 1.4   Sport management task clusters.

Adapted from J.B. Parks, P.S. Chopra, R.J. Quain, and I.E. Alguindigue, 1988, "ExSport I: An expert system for sport management career counseling," *Journal of Research on Computing in Education* 21: 196-209. By permission of J.B. Parks.

Social Media and Managing Sport

As you will read in each of the following 19 chapters, the sport industry in general and sport managers in particular are increasingly affected—both positively and negatively—by social media. For instance, social media mishaps in sport frequently make the news and hurt sport organizations and affiliated personnel. Such would be the case regarding the attention StubHub received after their ticket broker published a profanity-laced tweet in 2012 or the fallout the Philadelphia Eagles faced in 2013 because of a wide receiver's racist slur, which was captured on a smartphone and subsequently broadcast for the world to watch. While there appears to be a social media mishap on a daily basis in sport, for the most part, sport industry stakeholders have benefitted individually and collectively from the opportunities presented through social media. For instance, fans can interact with like-minded enthusiasts on social networking sites such as Foursquare and Sportlobster. Future sport managers can establish a marketable personal brand through professional and effective usage of Twitter, Facebook, and other social media platforms. Current sport managers can promote themselves, look for growth opportunities, and network through their usage of social media opportunities offered through social networking sites ranging from the popular LinkedIn to the growing, sport-specific Fieldoo. Sport organizations can connect and interact with their stakeholders, engage in source publicity, conduct research, market themselves, engage in cross promotion, and perform damage control through their proper usage of social media platforms ranging from Pinterest and Google+ to Myspace and YouTube. What better way for sport organization social media leaders such as FC Barcelona, Real Madrid CF, Manchester United FC, Chelsea FC, the Los Angeles Lakers, the Ultimate Fighting Championship (UFC), the Dallas Cowboys, and the New York Yankees to market themselves and their products, secure free publicity and exposure, and connect with their millions of fans than by sending a short message on Twitter, pinning a photo to Pinterest, asking a question on Facebook, or posting a video on YouTube? Such opportunities did not exist in the recent past. In each of the following chapters, you can read more about other social media examples and applications in the sport industry.

Although tasks requiring similar competencies appear within one cluster or the other, the clusters are not mutually exclusive. In the scholarly literature, such interrelatedness is explained in Pedersen's (2013) article, which provides research examples illustrating the strategic intersection of management and communication in the sport industry. In practical settings, an example of this would be people employed in media relations. While they belong to the communication management cluster of figure 1.4, they also need to be able to manage and lead personnel (organization management cluster). Conversely, employees in organization management positions need strong communication skills to be successful.

Critical Thinking Skills

An additional competency that sport management students should acquire is the ability to think critically. As Wendy Frisby, a professor at the University of British Columbia and the coauthor of chapter 20, noted, "We want our students to be strong critical thinkers who will make positive contributions to society" (2005, p. 5). Dan Mahony, a professor at Kent State University and the coauthor of chapter 15, added, "Students who have strong critical thinking skills, high levels of quantitative literacy, decision-making skills, and good written and oral communication skills will be able to succeed in almost any job that they choose" (2008, p. 8). Consider, for example, the types of issues that sport managers in the second decade of the 21st century are facing and addressing (or will need to address):

> Should certain protections be implemented to safeguard young athletes from suffering burnout because of high-performance training, intense coaches and parents, and highly competitive situations?

> Should interscholastic athletics be run more as a business (e.g., sponsorship engagement, national television exposure, talent recruitment) and should sport programs be geared for only the talented athletes?
> Should intercollegiate athletes receive salaries?
> Should professional athletes undergo more intensive testing for drugs and should penalties for failed drug tests be increased?
> Should the Confederate flag be flown at sporting events in the United States?
> Should male and female coaches receive equal salaries if they coach the same sport?
> Should an athlete or an employee of a sport organization be retained and given a second chance if guilty of domestic violence? Using recreational drugs? Uttering a racist comment? Carrying an unlicensed firearm? Driving while intoxicated?
> Should athletes in the Olympic Games receive a share of the revenues of the International Olympic Committee?
> Should sport organizations place restrictions on the social media activities of their front-office personnel and affiliated athletes?

As managers, you will need exceptional critical thinking skills to make sound decisions about issues such as these and about additional issues that we cannot even conceptualize today. Sound decisions will not be based on expediency, the easy way out, or on what will cause the least turmoil or make the most money. You are most likely to make sound decisions if you make it a point to work toward principled justifications for your beliefs. Becoming a critical thinker is an important step toward learning to provide such justifications for your decisions.

Ideal critical thinkers possess a particular set of dispositions, or tendencies. We propose that the set of three dispositions summarized by Ennis (2000) is especially useful for the critical thinker to pursue. Thus, according to Ennis, ideal critical thinkers

> care that their beliefs are true and that their decisions are justified; that is, they care to get it right to the extent that it is possible,
> care to present a position honestly and clearly, theirs as well as those of others, and
> care about the dignity and worth of every person.

Note that caring is a central aspect of the critical thinking process. The ideal critical thinker cares enough about what others have to say to make an active attempt to discover and listen to others' reasons and to be sensitive to others' feelings and levels of understanding. An important component of this caring is being truly and seriously open to points of view different from one's own, recognizing that one's own beliefs may not be sufficiently justified. Clearly, achieving this openness is more easily said than done.

What is critical thinking? You probably have encountered the term many times in your daily life and in the classroom. You may also have noticed that when the term is used, its meaning is often unclear. One reason for the confusion is that *critical thinking* means different things to different people. Thus, you must understand the meaning of the term as we are using it in this chapter and in the following chapters. Our definition, an adaptation of definitions that are widely used among scholars who systematically study the concept, should be helpful to you in distinguishing between critical thinking and other kinds of thinking. First, to understand what we mean by the term, you need to understand what we do not mean. Critical thinking is not any of the following:

> Simply thinking—Critical thinking is a special form of thinking. For example, developing a good understanding of something is an important dimension of (just) thinking, but it is quite distinct from critical thinking.

> Negative thinking—To many people, critical thinking does not sound agreeable. It sounds negative. But critical thinkers are not naysayers! Critical thinkers are seeking something positive—as solid a basis for their beliefs as they can find in a world full of uncertainty. Criticisms are simply part of their search for better arguments. In this respect, critical thinking, if practiced appropriately, is positive, caring, and productive.

> Creative thinking—Certain aspects of critical thinking require our best creative efforts, which is one of its appealing components. But critical thinking stresses making evaluative judgments rather than the imaginative leaps associated with brainstorming or generating novel ideas or strategies.

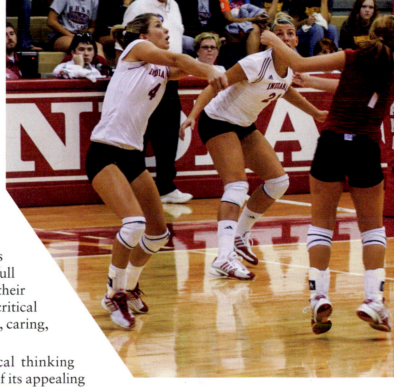

Should these collegiate athletes receive a salary? What are the critical thinking skills needed to argue for and against this question?

CRITICAL THINKING QUESTIONS

We have provided examples of what we do not mean, so what do we mean by critical thinking? A common feature of all critical thinking activity is the systematic evaluation of arguments (i.e., reasons and conclusions) according to explicit standards of rationality—careful thinking that helps us move forward in a continual, ongoing search to improve our opinions, decisions, or judgments. Critical thinking, as we use the term, refers to the following:

> The awareness of a set of interrelated critical questions

> The ability to ask and answer critical questions at appropriate times

> The desire to use those questions and accept their results as a guide to behavior

Central to your success in becoming a critical thinker is having a good understanding of a set of questions that you need to ask to evaluate someone's reasoning. Although there is no single correct set of critical thinking questions, we have selected eight of them in the sidebar "Critical Thinking Questions." The discussion of each question in the sidebar is necessarily brief. For an in-depth discussion of the eight questions, see Browne and Keeley (2007).

Critical Thinking Questions

Question 1: What Are the Issues and the Conclusion?

prescriptive—Concerns about the way the world should or ought to be.

descriptive—Concerns about the way the world is, was, or will be.

You start the critical thinking process by identifying the issue and the conclusion, which will be either **prescriptive** or **descriptive**. Value preferences will have much greater influence over prescriptive conclusions than they will over descriptive conclusions. For example, values will influence the prescriptive conclusion that there should be more African American athletics directors. Conversely, the descriptive conclusion that in 2013 only 18.3% of the NBA league office professional employees were African American will depend on empirical evidence (Lapchick, Hippert, Rivera, & Robinson, 2013).

Question 2: What Are the Reasons?

Reasons are ideas that communicators use to justify their conclusions. To discover reasons, you need to ask, What reasons do the communicators give to support their conclusion? You should decide the merits of the conclusion based on the quality of the reasons.

Question 3: What Words or Phrases Are Ambiguous?

You cannot determine whether you agree or disagree with someone's reasoning if key terms in the reasoning could have more than one meaning and if those different meanings would influence your reactions. For example, in evaluating a coach's success, if you define success as winning percentage, you may reach a different conclusion than if you define success as motivating athletes to achieve their full potential.

Question 4: What Are the Value Conflicts and Assumptions?

Assumptions are ideas that people take for granted. Values are abstract ideas that people see as worthwhile (e.g., honesty, compassion, competition, justice). In many cases, however, values are in conflict, such that embracing one value means rejecting another. The following reasoning example illustrates the influence of value conflicts and value assumptions:

> Conclusion: Sport teams should cease using American Indian symbols and traditions.
> Reason: These practices are inaccurate, disrespectful to American Indians, and offensive.
> Value assumption: The value of human dignity is more important than the value of the right of freedom of expression.

Question 5: What Are the Descriptive Assumptions?

Descriptive assumptions are unstated beliefs about how the world is, was, or will be. You discover these assumptions by asking, What ideas must be taken for granted in order for you to believe that the reason is accurate? The following scenario (Women's Sports Foundation, 2011) illustrates descriptive assumptions:

> Conclusion: Female athletes perform at higher levels when coached by men rather than by women.
> Reason: Teams with male coaches have won more championships than teams with female coaches because female coaches are not as intense and demanding as male coaches.
> Assumptions: Teams coached by women have had the same recruiting resources as teams coached by men; it is acceptable to attribute standard characteristics to all members of a given group; and intense, demanding coaches are more likely to help female athletes reach their potential.

Question 6: Does the Reasoning Contain Fallacies?

Fallacies are mistakes in reasoning that do not seem to be mistakes. The following claim illustrates a fallacy: Either we raise public moneys to finance a sport stadium, or we will have to move the team to another city. This reasoning assumes that only two choices are available. If, however, it is possible to raise private funds to build the stadium, then the reasoning contains a fallacy.

Question 7: How Good Is the Evidence?

Consider the following claims: The graduation rate of nonathletes is higher than the graduation rate of athletes. Title IX has forced several colleges to drop some men's sports. Participation in sport builds good character. To evaluate such claims, ask, How good is the evidence? The greater the quality and quantity of supporting evidence, the more you can depend on it and the more you can legitimately call the claim a fact.

Question 8: What Significant Information Is Omitted?

Communicators who are trying to persuade you are likely to select and use information that supports their conclusion. Thus, you need to ask, What significant information is missing? Some examples of missing information are (a) evidence that supports different conclusions, (b) alternative value assumptions, and (c) identification of the source of the evidence presented. By looking for missing information, you can decide whether you have enough information to judge the communicator's reasoning.

Based on Browne and Keeley 2007.

Future Challenges and Opportunities

Pitts and Stotlar (2007) observed that the world of sport is growing rapidly. This growth is reflected not only in the introduction of many new sports but also in the increasing number of opportunities to participate in sports and activities, an upsurge in the number and variety of sport-related publications and social media platforms, enhanced mass media exposure and source publicity of sporting activities, growth in the number and types of sport facilities and events, increased interest in sport tourism and adventure travel, and the provision of sport-related goods and services for a greater variety of market segments. New amateur and professional sports have emerged, sport opportunities are being offered to a more diverse population, endorsements and sponsorships are on the rise, sport industry education is becoming more prevalent and sophisticated, marketing and promotion orientation is growing in the sport industry, sport managers are becoming more competent, and the globalization of the sport industry is progressing rapidly.

While the continued growth and advances in the field will create numerous job opportunities for aspiring sport managers, the future will also present sport managers with many challenges and opportunities, some that have already emerged and others that we cannot even imagine. In subsequent chapters, you will learn about a variety of such challenges within specific segments of the sport industry. Some challenges will affect all sport managers, irrespective of the segment of the industry in which they are employed. These challenges and opportunities are associated with technology, ethics and social responsibility, and the globalization of sport.

Technology

More than a decade ago, Westerbeek and Smith (2003) provided a hypothetical glimpse into the future with their prediction of a sport scenario in the year 2038. While their predictions (e.g., virtual stadium and police, hologram appearances, cloning, genetic modifications, gene and protection chips) have yet to be realized in accordance to their futuristic presentation, the technology explosion of the past several decades has been mind-boggling, and this is only the beginning! From e-commerce applications to interactivity opportunities, the social media sections in each chapter of this textbook illustrate only one part of this technology explosion in the sport industry. Advances in technology have affected all aspects of the field, from enhanced experiences for spectators in the stands (e.g., Wi-Fi networks in sport facilities to meet fans' smartphone and tablet demands, massive video boards and state-of-the-art sound systems) and at home (e.g., increased usage of HD and 3-D technologies, multiscreen viewing experiences) to better training and care of athletes (e.g., management and editing of training programs, preventive medicine and surgical advancements, fitness activity trackers) and safety of all stakeholders (e.g., protective helmets in football to safer cars, tracks, and methods in auto racing), and sport products (video games, equipment, transportation, logistics, scheduling, manufacturing, etc.), team business, player analytics, research, and the list could go on and on.

Regardless of whether the future will be exactly as Westerbeek and Smith predicted, their scenario does provide food for thought. One notion to consider, however, is that technology is not an end unto itself. It is a means to an end—an innovation that facilitates progress and helps us realize other accomplishments. Take, for instance, the athletic equipment innovations. *Athletic Management* examined the 25 most significant developments in team equipment over the past 25 years (Read, 2013, p. 64). The highest ranked innovation involved the football helmet, which has witnessed advances in its design to reduce the number of concussions in the sport. Read noted, however, that "the best helmet is of little use if it's not properly fitted. Along with increasing training for coaches on the right way to fit a helmet, manufacturers have introduced upgrades that better adapt to the specific shape of each player's head" (p. 65). In addition to helmets, some of the other innovations listed by Read included uniform features and styles, compression apparel, softball and baseball bases, storage systems and laundry supplies, gloves and balls, bats and sticks, protective headgear in lacrosse and other sports, throwing machines, mouth guards, eye and face protection, equipment labeling systems, radar guns, and shoes.

In the future, scientific advances in computers and communication technology will play an increasingly significant role in our society and in sport management. This progress will likely be accompanied by acknowledgment of the human need for high-touch activities, many of which the sport experience can provide. The challenge, therefore, is to become proficient in using technology while remaining aware of the need for human interaction in people's lives and understanding how sport can facilitate such interaction.

Ethics and Social Responsibility

Since there are more opportunities to use the platform of sport for good (e.g., charitable work, sport for development, sustainability awareness) while striving to eliminate illegal and immoral incidences in the sport industry (e.g., cheating, criminal activity), many people are calling for greater accountability on the part of sport managers. In recognition of the need for a heightened focus on ethics and social responsibility in sport, DeSensi and Rosenberg (2003) advised that "being socially responsible is paramount to the execution of one's job" (p. 127). Thus, there are now academic courses offered in this area. For instance, in 2013, The George Washington University launched a 12-course sports philanthropy academic program "tailored to the unique needs of those who work for professional sports teams, leagues, athlete foundations, sport-related companies with an emphasis on corporate social responsibility, nonprofits using sports for social good and those looking to enter the field" (Hunt, 2013, para. 1). Overall, sport managers must deal with a multitude of questions that require an understanding of ethical principles and moral psychology. Consider the following questions:

> How can we best achieve gender, race, and class equity in sport?

> Do professional team owners owe primary allegiance to themselves or to the communities that support the team?

> How can we balance academic integrity with the demands of intercollegiate competition?

> Should athletes sacrifice their health for victory?

> Is winning really the bottom line of sport?

> Is intercollegiate sport an entertainment business for public consumption or an extracurricular opportunity for student development, or both, or something else?

The list is seemingly endless, and no doubt you could add your own concerns to it. Regardless of the question or issue at hand, as DeSensi and Rosenberg (2003) noted, "Developing a social consciousness and being socially responsible assists sport managers with the creation of a sound professional philosophy and subsequent ethical action" (p. 127). In the same vein, Malloy and Zakus (1995) suggested that sport management students should understand the need to "challenge the assumptions, both overt and covert, of sport and society to enable themselves to make ethically sound decisions" (p. 54). The desire and ability to engage in **principled decision making** often distinguishes superior sport managers from their peers.

Now is the time to begin reflecting on ethical concerns because you surely will face them in the years to come. The sidebar "Guidelines for Making Ethical Decisions" contains an approach developed by scholars in the Markkula Center for Applied Ethics at Santa Clara University (*Making an Ethical Decision*, 2009). In subsequent chapters, you will be referred to this sidebar to help you examine ethical concerns in specific sport settings. The guidelines serve well as an introduction to the place of ethics in a sport manager's decision-making process.

We are hopeful that in the future, enlightened sport managers will be aware of their social responsibilities and will deliver their services in ways that reflect this understanding (see the sidebar "Code of Ethics, North American Society for Sport Management" for a listing of NASSM's ethical codebook items covering a sport manager's approach to individual welfare, competency, communication, propriety, integrity, trust, confidentiality, respect, fairness, service, and other canons or principles). For example, sport managers worldwide will be conscious of environmental concerns and will incorporate this understanding into their business practices. Environmental concerns that are important to sport managers include air and water quality, land and water use, waste management, energy management, transportation design and services, accommodation design and services, and facilities construction. Indeed, the United Nations Environment Programme (UNEP) has the following objectives for its Sport and Environment Strategy:

> To promote the integration of environmental considerations in sports

> To use the popularity of sports to promote environmental awareness

> To promote the development of environmentally friendly sports facilities and the manufacture of environmentally friendly sports goods (Toepfer, 2003, para. 5)

Environmental sustainability actions in the sport industry are becoming more prevalent as organizations increasingly recognize the importance and benefits of such initiatives (Ciletti, Lanasa, Ramos, Luchs, & Lou, 2010). While there are numerous possible examples, the international foundation Sustainability in Sport was founded by Gary Neville and Dale Vince in 2012. Neville noted that his organization believes that "sport as an industry must not only grasp the green agenda, but should be leading it" ("Bringing Sustainability," n.d., para. 2). Some of the ways the foundation looks to

principled decision making—Basing decisions on the six pillars of character—trustworthiness, respect, responsibility, fairness, caring, and good citizenship (responsible participation in society) (Josephson Institute of Ethics, 2002).

WEB

Go to the WSG and complete the web search activity by researching environmental issues for sport managers.

Guidelines for Making Ethical Decisions

Recognize an Ethical Issue

1. Could this decision or situation be damaging to someone or to some group? Does this decision involve a choice between a good and bad alternative, or perhaps between two "goods" or between two "bads"?

2. Is this issue about more than what is legal or what is most efficient? If so, how?

Get the Facts

3. What are the relevant facts of the case? What facts are not known? Can I learn more about the situation? Do I know enough to make a decision?

4. What individuals and groups have an important stake in the outcome? Are some concerns more important than others? Why?

5. What are the options for acting? Have all the relevant persons and groups been consulted? Have I identified creative options?

Evaluate Alternative Actions

6. Evaluate the options by asking the following questions:
   - Which option will produce the most good and do the least harm (the utilitarian approach)?
   - Which option best respects the rights of all who have a stake (the rights approach)?
   - Which option treats people equally or proportionately (the justice approach)?
   - Which option best serves the community as a whole, not just some members (the common good approach)?
   - Which option leads me to act as the sort of person I want to be (the virtue approach)?

Make a Decision and Test It

7. Considering all these approaches, which option best addresses the situation?

8. If I told someone whom I respect—or told a television audience—which option I have chosen, what would they say?

Act and Reflect on the Outcome

9. How can my decision be implemented with the greatest care and attention to the concerns of all stakeholders?

10. How did my decision turn out, and what have I learned from this specific situation?

Reprinted, by permission, from *Making an ethical decision*, 2009, Markkula Center for Applied Ethics, Santa Clara University. www.scu.edu/ethics/practicing/decision/making.pdf

promote sustainability in the sport industry are by "seeking to establish eco-standards for all activities relating to the operation of sports clubs" and "using the power of sport to spread information about environmental issues and the need for sustainability to the widest possible audience" (para. 7). In the United States, the Environmental Protection Agency (EPA) provides examples and resources (and the *EPA Green Sports Scorecard*) regarding sustainability efforts in the sport industry ("Green Sports," 2013). As can be seen in the EPA's scorecard and in numerous publicity efforts, many sport entities—ranging from the NFL to intercollegiate athletic departments to NASCAR—are active in their efforts to engage in and promote sustainability efforts.

Additional evidence of future sport managers' sense of social responsibility will include the routine provision of professional childcare services in sport facilities and the targeting of previously untapped and undertapped target markets, such as women and people of differing ages, abilities, and sexual orientations. Sport managers of the future will also recognize the importance of keeping the sport experience accessible to all socioeconomic groups.

Globalization of Sport

The need to understand and appreciate other countries and cultures cannot be overstated (Danylchuk & Boucher, 2003; Thibault, 2009). In recognition of this fact, most chapters of this book contain information on the sport industry in other nations. You can take several steps to prepare yourself to interact effectively in the global community. For example, although students in many countries consider mastery of the English language a basic skill, most students in the United States do not master languages of other countries. Consequently, U.S. students can distinguish themselves from their peers by learning a language other than English. Studying in another country for an extended period and completing courses that focus on other cultures are among the additional steps that you can take to broaden your horizons and enhance the quality of your life. Pursuing this path will also increase your value in the marketplace.

Code of Ethics, North American Society for Sport Management (NASSM)

The following are a few selected canons or principles from NASSM's Code of Ethics. In performing their duties, sport managers should do the following:

> Hold paramount the safety, health, and welfare of the individual in the performance of professional duties.
> Perform services only in their areas of competence.
> Issue public statements in an objective and truthful manner.
> Seek employment only where a need for service exists.
> Maintain high standards of personal conduct in the capacity or identity of the physical and health educator.
> Strive to become and remain proficient in professional practice and the performance of professional functions.
> Act in accordance with the highest standards of professional integrity.
> Respect the privacy of students and clients and hold in confidence all information obtained in the course of professional service.
> Adhere to any and all commitments made to the employing organization. The relationship should be characterized by fairness, non-malfeasance, and truthfulness.
> Treat colleagues with respect, courtesy, fairness, and good faith.
> Relate to the students and clients of colleagues with full professional consideration.
> Uphold and advance the values and ethical standards, the knowledge, and the mission of the profession.
> Take responsibility for identifying, developing, and fully utilizing established knowledge for professional practice.
> Promote the general welfare of society.
> Regard as primary their professional service to others.

Reprinted, by permission, from NASSM (Slippery Rock, PA). Available: www.nassm.com/InfoAbout/NASSM/Creed

Scotland and the Ryder Cup:
Golf Returns Home

By John Harris, Wales
Glasgow Caledonian University, Scotland

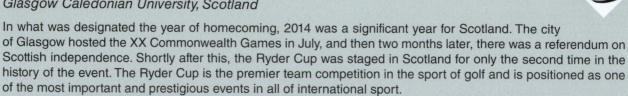

In what was designated the year of homecoming, 2014 was a significant year for Scotland. The city of Glasgow hosted the XX Commonwealth Games in July, and then two months later, there was a referendum on Scottish independence. Shortly after this, the Ryder Cup was staged in Scotland for only the second time in the history of the event. The Ryder Cup is the premier team competition in the sport of golf and is positioned as one of the most important and prestigious events in all of international sport.

The Gleneagles Hotel hosted the 2014 Ryder Cup, only the second time in the history of the event that it was held in Scotland. This photo captures promotional signage in Ireland leading up to the international event.

The Ryder Cup was first staged in 1927, although an unofficial match took place a year prior to that. The trophy was named after the English seed merchant Samuel Ryder, who wanted to see an international competition between the best golfers from Great

The globalization of sport brings with it many benefits. For example, more countries and athletes are participating in international events. Sport is being used as a vehicle that crosses traditional lines of gender, religion, and geographical barriers, and it is bringing people around the world together in a common interest. As you contemplate the positive aspect of the globalization of sport, however, you should understand that some advances in international sport may have come at the expense of poor people in developing countries. As with other issues that have been discussed in this chapter, critical thinking from an ethical perspective will be required to address problems such

Britain and the United States. Honors were shared in the earliest encounters before the United States embarked upon a series of wins to dominate the competition, winning 19 of the first 22 matches. During the 1960s and 1970s, the United States was so dominant of the competition that some expressed concern that the Ryder Cup would cease to exist as it was no longer perceived to be a fair and equal competition. In 1979, the Great Britain and Ireland team (Ireland was added in 1973) was expanded to include players from elsewhere in Europe as a means of making the match more competitive. Since this change to the event, Europe has won the competition nine times and the Ryder Cup has developed into an international media spectacle.

Jointly administered by the PGA of America and the PGA European Tour, the event is a special one as it puts players who usually compete as individuals into a team competition. The 2014 Ryder Cup at the Gleneagles Hotel in Perthshire had a lot to live up to, with the 2013 and 2012 matches both going to the final game and each being decided by a single point. The estimated direct economic impact of the 2014 event was put at 100 million GBP. Many European nations compete for the right to stage the event.

All European Ryder Cup bids must now also have a legacy plan. As part of the Scottish bid to host the event, the ClubGolf program was developed with a commitment to introduce every child in Scotland to the sport of golf before the age of nine. There is a challenge here of course in building a long-term legacy that focuses on inclusion through an event often held at a luxury hotel resort. There was some controversy when the call for volunteers at Gleneagles stated that those chosen to take part would each have to pay £75. The players, golf fans, and armchair sports enthusiasts alike all had September 2014 marked on their calendars. The fact that this installment took place in Scotland, the home of golf, made this international sporting event an even more eagerly anticipated occasion.

International Learning Activity #1

Go to the official website of Ryder Cup 2014 (www.rydercup2014.com) and look at the different ways in which Scotland is promoted on this site. What dominant images of the nation described as "the home of golf" do you see presented here?

International Learning Activity #2

How does the Ryder Cup help promote and celebrate a European identity? How important do you think it is for this European identity to have the United States as opponents in the event?

International Learning Activity #3

The Ryder Cup is one of a number of mega events that has at some point claimed to be the third biggest sporting event in the world. Undertake an Internet search to see what other events have made such a claim, and then outline an argument for putting forward the event that you believe can best claim this title.

as the exploitation of third-world labor in the production of sporting goods, the recruitment and migration of athletes that results in a talent drain on their home countries, the effect of the interrelationships among transnational corporations, media, and sport organizations, and the effect of sport on the environment (Thibault, 2009).

The future will most assuredly bring change. This can be frightening, and is frequently resisted. Progressive sport managers who can anticipate and embrace adaptation will have opportunities to be agents of change who will transform the way that sport is managed. We hope that you will be one of those managers!

Summary

In this chapter, sport is broadly defined as (1) "all forms of physical activity which, through casual or organised participation, aim at expressing or improving physical fitness and mental well-being, forming social relationships or obtaining results in competition at all levels" (Council of Europe, 2001, p. 1) and (2) "any activity, experience, or business enterprise focused on fitness, recreation, athletics, or leisure" (Pitts et al., 1994, p. 18). The sport industry can be conceptualized based on (1) the types of sporting activities that exist, (2) the settings in which sport occurs, and (3) the industry segments into which various sport businesses and organizations can be categorized. Three models of segmentation describe the sport industry: the product type model, the economic impact model, and the sport activity model. Four unique aspects of sport management are sport marketing, the sport enterprise financial structure, career paths, and the power of sport as a social institution. Sport managers should possess general, transferable competencies as well as those specific to organization management and information management and the ability to think critically.

The next generation of sport managers will face challenges associated with technology, ethics and social responsibility, and globalization. Enlightened sport managers of the future will be competent in the technical aspects of their jobs and will be agents of change, both in the management of sport and in the larger society.

Review Questions

1. Name three sports that have emerged in the last few years. How has their emergence affected career opportunities in sport management?

2. List and discuss three sport business settings that might represent job opportunities for sport managers.

3. Describe the models of segmentation that have been applied to the sport industry and provide examples of sport organizations in each segment of each model.

4. Identify three unique aspects of sport management and explain how each makes the sport business different from other businesses.

5. Explain the task clusters into which sport managers' responsibilities can be classified.

6. Define critical thinking and explain the benefits of applying critical thinking skills to important issues in sport management.

7. List the dispositions that critical thinkers should possess and indicate whether you possess each of them. Explain your answers.

8. Define principled decision making and give examples of when and how sport managers need to make principled decisions.

9. Describe opportunities and challenges in technology, social media, ethics and social responsibility, and globalization that all sport managers will face in the future.

References

Acosta, R.V., & Carpenter, L.J. (2012). *Women in intercollegiate sport—a longitudinal, national study: Thirty-five year update 1977–2012.* Retrieved from www.acostacarpenter.org

Bennett, G., Henson, R.K., & Zhang, J. (2003). Generation Y's perceptions of the action sports industry segment. *Journal of Sport Management, 17,* 95–115.

Bringing sustainability to the world of sport. (n.d.). *Sustainability in Sport.* Retrieved from www.sustainabilityinsport.com/about-us

Browne, M.N., & Keeley, S.M. (2007). *Asking the right questions: A guide to critical thinking* (8th ed.). Upper Saddle River, NJ: Prentice Hall.

Ciletti, D., Lanasa, J., Ramos, D., Luchs, R., & Lou, J. (2010). Sustainability communication in North American professional sports leagues: Insights from Web-site self-presentations. *International Journal of Sport Communication, 3,* 64–91.

Clay, B. (1995, February 1). 8 great careers in the sports industry. *Black Enterprise, 25*(7), 158–160, 162, 164, 166.

Coakley, J. (2009). *Sports in society: Issues and controversies* (10th ed.). New York, NY: McGraw-Hill.

Council of Europe. (2001). *The European sports charter* (revised). Brussels, Belgium: Author. Retrieved from www.sportdevelopment.info/index.php?option=com_content&view=article&id=87:council-of-europe-2001-the-european-sports-charterrevised-brussels-council-of-europe-&catid=59:international-documents-&Itemid=82

Danylchuk, K.E., & Boucher, R. (2003). The future of sport management as an academic discipline. *International Journal of Sport Management, 4,* 281–300.

DeSensi, J.T., & Rosenberg, D. (2003). *Ethics and morality in sport management* (2nd ed.). Morgantown, WV: Fitness Information Technology.

Ennis, R.H. (2000). *Super-streamlined conception of critical thinking.* Retrieved from www.criticalthinking.net/SSConcCTApr3.html

Eschenfelder, M.J., & Li, M. (2007). *Economics of sport* (2nd ed.). Morgantown, WV: Fitness Information Technology.

Frank, R. (1984). Olympic myths and realities. *Arete: The Journal of Sport Literature, 1*(2), 155–161.

Frisby, W. (2005). The good, the bad, and the ugly: Critical sport management research. *Journal of Sport Management, 19,* 1–12.

Green sports. (2013). United States Environmental Protection Agency. Retrieved from www2.epa.gov/green-sports

Grossfeld, S. (2013, May 29). 'Tough Mudder' is a grueling test, a growing business. *The Boston Globe.* Retrieved from www.bostonglobe.com/sports/2013/05/28/tough-mudder-grueling-but-growing-business/MsjYrme8Y3b7nW461tVh6L/story.html

Horch, H., & Schütte, N. (2003). Competencies of sport managers in German sport clubs and sport federations. *Managing Leisure, 8,* 70–84.

Hunt, P. (2013, February 22). George Washington University programme in sports philanthropy. *Sports and Development.* Retrieved from www.sportanddev.org/?5334/The-George-Washington-University-academic-programme-in-sports-philanthropy

Isaacs, S. (1964). *Careers and opportunities in sport.* New York, NY: Dutton.

Josephson Institute of Ethics. (2002). *Making ethical decisions.* Retrieved from www.josephsoninstitute.org/MED/MED-intro+toc.htm

Lapchick, R., Hippert, A., Rivera, S., & Robinson, J. (2013). *The 2013 racial and gender report card: National Basketball Association.* The Institute for Diversity and Ethics in Sport. Retrieved from www.tidesport.org/RGRC/2013/2013_NBA_RGRC.pdf

LeJacq, Y. (2013, July 19). Score! Professional video gamers awarded athletic visas. *NBC News: Technology.* Retrieved from www.nbcnews.com/technology/score-professional-video-gamers-awarded-athletic-visas-6C10679998

Mahony, D.F. (2008). No one can whistle a symphony: Working together for sport management's future. *Journal of Sport Management, 22,* 1–10.

Making an ethical decision. (2009). Markkula Center for Applied Ethics, Santa Clara University. Retrieved from www.scu.edu/ethics/practicing/decision/making.pdf

Malloy, D.C., & Zakus, D.H. (1995). Ethical decision making in sport administration: A theoretical inquiry into substance and form. *Journal of Sport Management, 9,* 36–58.

Mason, J.G., Higgins, C.R., & Wilkinson, O.J. (1981). Sports administration education 15 years later. *Athletic Purchasing and Facilities, 5*(1), 44–45.

Mawson, L.M. (2002). The extreme sport challenge for sport managers. *International Journal of Sport Management, 3,* 249–261.

Meek, A. (1997). An estimate of the size and supported economic activity of the sports industry in the United States. *Sport Marketing Quarterly, 6*(4), 15–21.

Mullin, B.J. (1980). Sport management: The nature and utility of the concept. *Arena Review, 4*(3), 1–11.

NASSM. (2013). *Sport management programs.* Retrieved from www.nassm.com/InfoAbout/SportMgmtPrograms

Parks, J.B., Chopra, P.S., Quain, R.J., & Alguindigue, I.E. (1988). ExSport I: An expert system for sport management career counseling. *Journal of Research on Computing in Education, 21,* 196–209.

Parks, J.B., & Olafson, G.A. (1987). Sport management and a new journal. *Journal of Sport Management, 1,* 1–3.

Pedersen, P.M. (2013). Reflections on communication and sport: On strategic communication and management. *Communication & Sport, 1*(1/2), 55–67.

Pedersen, P.M., Miloch, K.S., & Laucella, P.C. (2007). *Strategic sport communication.* Champaign, IL: Human Kinetics.

Pitts, B.G., Fielding, L.W., & Miller, L.K. (1994). Industry segmentation theory and the sport industry: Developing a sport industry segmentation model. *Sport Marketing Quarterly, 3*(1), 15–24.

Pitts, B.G., & Stotlar, D.K. (2007). *Fundamentals of sport marketing* (3rd ed.). Morgantown, WV: Fitness Information Technology.

The racial and gender report card. (n.d.). The Institute for Diversity and Ethics in Sport. Retrieved from www.tidesport.org/racial-genderreportcard.html

Read, D. (2013, August/September). The tools to play. *Athletic Management, 25*(5), 64–68.

Ross, S.R., & Parks, J.B. (2008). Sport management students' attitudes toward women: A challenge for educators. *Sport Management Education Journal, 2,* 1–18.

Sports market place directory. (2013). Amenia, NY: Grey House. Retrieved from www.greyhouse.com/sports.htm

Tenore, M.J. (2013, January 7). Jemele Hill responds to racist letter: 'I'm called something derogatory on a daily basis.' *Poynter.* Retrieved from www.poynter.org/latest-news/mediawire/199688/jemele-hill-responds-to-racist-letter-im-called-something-derogatory-on-a-daily-basis

Thibault, L. (2009). Globalization of sport: An inconvenient truth. *Journal of Sport Management, 23,* 1–20.

Toepfer, K. (2003, December 2). *Sport and sustainable development.* Paper presented at the 5th World Conference on Sport and Environment, Turin, Italy. Retrieved from www.unep.org/Documents.Multilingual/Default.asp?DocumentID=364&ArticleID=4316&l=en

United Nations. (2004). *Resolution adopted by the General Assembly.* Retrieved from http://daccessdds.un.org/doc/UNDOC/GEN/N04/476/80/PDF/N0447680.pdf

Westerbeek, H., & Smith, A. (2003). *Sport business in the global marketplace.* New York, NY: Palgrave Macmillan.

Women's Sports Foundation. (2011). *Coaching—Do female athletes prefer male coaches? The Foundation position.* Retrieved from www.womenssportsfoundation.org/home/advocate/foundation-positions/equity-issues/do_female_athletes_prefer_male_coaches

Yu, C.C. (2007). Important computer competencies for sport management professionals. *International Journal of Applied Sports Sciences, 19*(1), 66–85.

HISTORICAL MOMENTS

- **1924** Auditorium Managers Association founded (renamed International Association of Venue Managers)
- **1966** National Association of Collegiate Directors of Athletics (NACDA) formed
- **1974** First gathering of the Stadium Managers Association held
- **1974** Billie Jean King founded Women's Sports Foundation
- **1978** North American Society for the Sociology of Sport (NASSS) formed
- **1986** First North American Society for Sport Management (NASSM) conference held at Kent State University
- **1987** Sport and Recreation Law Association (SRLA) established
- **1987** Association for Women in Sports Media (AWSM) formed
- **1987** National Association for Sport and Physical Education (NASPE) published curricular guidelines
- **1988** Black Coaches Association (BCA) founded (renamed Black Coaches and Administrators)
- **1994** Sport Management Program Review Council (SMPRC) created
- **1995** Korean Society for Sport Management (KSSM) founded
- **2002** Asian Association for Sport Management (AASM) founded
- **2007** College Sport Research Institute (CSRI) formed
- **2008** Commission on Sport Management Accreditation (COSMA) became official accrediting body of sport management programs
- **2010** African Sport Management Association (ASMA) founded
- **2014** Newly formed Global Sport Business Association (GSBA) held its second conference on a cruise ship

2

DEVELOPING A PROFESSIONAL PERSPECTIVE

Sally R. Ross **Brian P. McCullough**

LEARNING OBJECTIVES

> Describe strategies for positioning yourself to be successful in the competitive field of sport management after graduation.

> Identify where entry-level opportunities exist and outline how to gain experience.

> Recognize the importance of professional preparation, professional attitude, and career planning and management.

> Explain the three components of an undergraduate sport management curriculum.

> Describe how students can secure and optimize their involvement in field experiences.

> Discuss ways in which your personal appearance, work transition and adjustment, and business etiquette and social media habits can enhance your employability and advancement.

> Describe the four stages involved in career planning.

> Identify several resources that are useful in planning a career in sport management.

Key Terms

entrepreneur

etiquette

explicit norms

extracurricular activities

field experience

implicit norms

job content skills

mock interview

values

work ethic

chieving success in most business settings requires specific knowledge, skills, and values that students are expected to begin to acquire as undergraduates. The first step toward developing these essentials to success involves adopting the perspective that you are now more than simply a student. You are a professional. You cannot wait until four years from now to begin to accept the responsibilities of being a professional. Your professors expect you to conduct yourself with professionalism while on campus, and you will gain more from your degree program if you behave as a professional rather than just a student. The level of commitment that you make to sport management as an academic pursuit will influence how you approach your coursework, extracurricular activities, and relationships with fellow students and instructors. Students who develop a professional perspective early on in their academic career will benefit through increased knowledge and opportunities.

The field of sport management is an especially competitive one. Many schools offer a major in sport management, which translates into a large number of graduates each year. In addition, students in majors outside sport management may also be interested in working in sport. What this means is that candidates from a large pool are competing for a finite number of jobs within the sport industry. To achieve success in this competitive environment, students must be willing to put forth a great deal of effort to put themselves in the best position possible.

No matter what type of job you hope to pursue, remember that professionalism begins in the classroom. You must understand and satisfy the requirements and learning objectives of your courses and the expectations of professors. Arrive to class on time, be attentive and prepared, take notes, and show interest. You should also follow the example of professionals and use a day planner, calendar, or organizer in which you can enter assignment due dates, exam dates, work responsibilities, and meetings. Whatever apparatus you use, keep it on hand, update it when necessary, and refer to it often.

Making the decision to develop your professional perspective will allow you to take advantage of resources available to you and dedicate yourself to learning how to develop yourself into a successful professional. This chapter addresses three components of a professional perspective:

> *Professional preparation*—The courses and experiences that you can expect in your undergraduate curriculum and beyond.

> *Professional attitude*—How to present a professional image, follow the fundamentals of business etiquette, develop ethical and critical thinking skills, and enter the world of work and be comfortable and productive there.

> *Career planning and management*—Purposeful steps you can take and helpful resources available to you as you contemplate entering the world of work.

Professional Preparation

Sport management preparation programs exist at the baccalaureate (undergraduate), master's, and doctoral levels. Baccalaureate programs prepare students for entry-level positions in the sport industry. Master's-level education prepares students for more advanced, specialized responsibilities. The doctorate usually emphasizes research. Students who seek the doctoral degree typically wish to become professors or work in some other capacity in a college or university setting.

Currently, you may be enrolled in a sport management undergraduate program, you might be a high school student, or you may be a university student in another major field who wants to learn more about opportunities in sport management. In any case, you will benefit from an explanation of what to expect in sport management curriculum at the undergraduate level. Most undergraduate sport management programs include three components: general education courses, major courses, and field experiences.

General Education

The general education component of the undergraduate curriculum is vital because university graduates should be able to demonstrate understanding and capabilities beyond those acquired in their major courses. As a university graduate, you will be expected to express yourself well, both in writing and in speaking. You should understand and be able to discuss—at least on a topical level—areas such as art, literature, history, and social and physical sciences. With a firm foundation provided by general education courses, you should be able to deal with a changing society that reflects the cultural diversity of our world. Indeed, awareness of other cultures, as well as an understanding and appreciation of them, is essential in addressing the sport management needs of the global community (Chelladurai, 2005). Furthermore, as covered in chapter 1, as a sport manager, you will also be expected to use critical thinking skills that you can acquire and develop in general education courses. As you seek to advance your career, the analytical, critical thinking, and leadership skills developed in general education courses will become even more important.

Major Courses in Sport Management

Desire for consistency and quality in sport management curricula started in 1986 when the National Association for Sport and Physical Education (NASPE) appointed a task force to develop curricular guidelines (Brassie, 1989). Through a joint effort, NASPE and the North American Society for Sport Management (NASSM) served as the program approval agency from 1993 until 2008, when the Commission on Sport Management Accreditation (COSMA) became the accrediting body for sport management curricula.

WEB

Go to the WSG and complete the first web search activity that helps you identify ways two different organizations can help you in your sport management career.

Based on recommendations from these groups as well as published research, this textbook introduces students to areas of study that will prepare them to pursue the rest of the sport management curriculum with enhanced insight and understanding. This book addresses topics in the content areas that have been deemed essential by the accrediting body of sport management education programs (i.e., COSMA). Review the table of contents for an overview of the scope of the sport industry and the range of employment opportunities within sport.

The courses in the sport management curriculum prepare you for a career in one of the many segments of the sport industry. But if you do not enter the sport management field, the course content prescribed in this textbook is sufficiently broad to prepare you to assume positions in a variety of other vocational fields, such as advertising, promotions, sales, and communications.

Keeping up with current events in your field is essential to your academic preparation. Although numerous popular media outlets offer sport stories, the popular media should not be the main source of information for the sport management student. One of the most daunting challenges you may have as you develop in your career is to separate your fandom of various sports or specific teams and your role as a future sport manager. Students studying to be sport managers should subsidize any reading from popular media and fan sites with readings from an assortment of trade and academic journals that specifically address sport management issues. One way to discover the most relevant reading material related to your educational and occupational goals is to pay attention to the publications that your instructors use for assignments. Several chapters of this book discuss relevant publications and professional associations specific to various careers in sport management (for examples of such associations, please refer to the sidebar "Examples of Sport Management Professional Organizations"). Membership in one or more of these associations will offer you opportunities to read publications, attend conferences, and access information exclusive to members. Some organizations have student branches, providing you with opportunities to gain experience in leadership and governance. Sharing ideas and networking with professionals

WEB

Go to the WSG and complete the second web search activity that helps you to research a professional organization of your choice to see how it can help you on your sport management journey.

at all levels will be enjoyable and helpful in your career development. Your instructors can give you advice about which professional organizations will be most helpful to you, both now and in the future.

Additional ways to learn more about your field and gain relevant experience include becoming involved in student activities, gaining on-campus employment, and participating in community service opportunities. Participation in student organizations provides students the chance to assume leadership roles and prepare as future professionals. Student-affiliate chapters of professional organizations, which are often found on campuses that have sport management programs, also provide opportunities to network with professionals, visit sport facilities, and learn about ways to gain work experience in sport settings. Students may wish to pursue community service activities such as volunteering with the Special Olympics, working with recreational sport programs, and assisting in community-sponsored events. Furthermore, numerous jobs are available on most college campuses in sport settings such as the student recreation center, the intramural sport office, and intercollegiate athletics department offices.

extracurricular activities—Opportunities for involvement with clubs, organizations, and sports in which students in a school may participate that are not part of the regular academic curriculum.

Extracurricular activities are an important part of professional preparation because they provide valuable skill practice and opportunities for leadership and development. Furthermore, they have been identified as especially vital to future job success. When employment recruiters were asked to examine résumés of entry-level candidates, academic performance and work experience were found to be important factors in judging potential employees, but **extracurricular activities** were most positively related to the raters' assessments of employability (Cole, Rubin, Field, & Giles, 2007).

Gaining experience through employment is an important part of professional preparation. Work experience provides students with opportunities to build networks, improve organizational skills, establish a greater sense of responsibility, expand skills, learn more about personal strengths and values, and gain self-confidence. Furthermore, in providing advice on how to launch their careers while in college, one career counselor shared a belief that all students should take as many work and volunteer opportunities as possible before graduating (Scheele, 2005).

The National Association of Colleges and Employers (NACE) projects employment trends. The organization's *Job Outlook 2013* found that 71% of employers indicated they prefer to hire new college graduates who have relevant work experience (NACE, 2012).

Field Experiences

field experience—A hands-on learning opportunity in which students gain professional experience in an organization while receiving class credit.

A **field experience** in sport management is typically referred to as an internship, but it may include cooperative work experiences (co-ops) or practicum experiences. A field experience allows students to observe and assist professionals and learn about managerial responsibilities and the scope of the sport organization in which they are employed. Field experience is a common component of the sport management curriculum, and students should expect to be supervised by an on-campus intern coordinator as well as by a professional in the agency providing the experience. Field experiences present excellent opportunities for experiential learning so that students can apply what they have learned in the classroom to a real-life situation, thus connecting the theoretical and conceptual with the practical (Cuneen & Sidwell, 1994; Gower & Mulvaney, 2012). Moreover, as Williams (2003) noted, most sport organizations do not recruit on college campuses or advertise their openings. Consequently, professional opportunities in the sport industry are "part of the 'hidden' job market" (p. 28). Given this reality, practical experience in the professional setting is an essential first step into an environment where you might be seeking employment after graduation.

Research has shown that the best field experiences in sport management are those that require interns to expand their knowledge and learn new skills (Dixon, Cunningham, Sagas, Turner, & Kent, 2005). Many students find that their enthusiasm for the field

Examples of Sport Management Professional Organizations

Adaptive Sports Association

African Sport Management Association

American Alliance for Health, Physical Education, Recreation and Dance

American Sportscasters Association

Asian Association for Sport Management

Association for Women in Sports Media

Athletic Equipment Managers Association

Black Coaches and Administrators

College Athletic Business Management Association

College Sports Information Directors of America

European Association for Sport Management

Global Sport Business Association

International Association for Communication and Sport

International Association of Venue Managers

International Ticketing Association

Latin American Association for Sport Management

National Association of Academic Advisors for Athletics

National Association of Collegiate Directors of Athletics

National Association of Collegiate Marketing Administrators

National Association of Collegiate Women Athletics Administrators

National Association of Concessionaires

National Association of Sports Commissions

National Recreation and Park Association

North American Society for Sport Management

Sport Management Association of Australia and New Zealand

Sport Marketing Association

Stadium Managers Association

World Association for Sport Management

and motivation to excel academically increase because of their internship experience. Students should give themselves sufficient time to prepare and search for a field experience. Preparing a résumé and cover letters and practicing interviewing skills (i.e., engaging in **mock interviews**) are essential. Campus career centers can be valuable sources of assistance in this preparation and may have information about available internships. Additionally, many sport organizations post internship openings on their websites. Your school's internship coordinator may maintain a database of available positions or a list of employers who have provided internships in the past. Your professors can also be a good source of information on planning and preparing for an internship. While internships have been customary in sport management for quite some time, many academic fields have discovered their value. A NACE student survey found that 63.2% of graduating seniors from the class of 2013 reported taking part in an internship or co-op, of which 52.2% were paid and 47.8% were unpaid (NACE, 2013).

mock interview—A practice interview in which you can rehearse your responses to questions that interviewers are likely to ask you.

Professional Profile: Derek Eiler

Title: managing partner, Fermata Partners

Education: BA (sport management), Bowling Green State University

As the managing partner and founder of Fermata Partners, a boutique brand strategy consulting firm in Atlanta, Georgia, Derek Eiler has had the great opportunity to explore the world of true entrepreneurship for the first time in his career. Prior to founding his current firm, he worked for 17 years at The Collegiate Licensing Company (CLC), where he rose from an entry-level position after graduation to eventually run the company from 2007 to 2011 as its managing director. During his first 13 years, CLC was operated as a privately held family business. The company was sold to IMG Worldwide in 2007. Eiler was instrumental in IMG College's aggressive consolidation strategy inside the college marketplace, which eventually led it to make two additional acquisitions to form the nation's largest college athletic marketing and licensing enterprise.

Following the consolidation of the three former companies in the college space (CLC, Host Communications, and ISP Sports) to form IMG College, Eiler made a decision to move on from his role running CLC and start his own firm in Atlanta. In late 2011, Eiler founded the firm along with three of CLC's former senior leaders. Fermata Partners' focus has been on leveraging the company's more than 80 years of combined experience in college athletics, higher education, and trademark licensing to identify and develop undervalued licensed properties in the verticals of sports, entertainment, and corporate brands. In the following interview, Eiler reflects on key steps in his career development and provides some insight on being an **entrepreneur** in a start-up environment.

ONE DAY

Go to the WSG and learn more about a typical day in the life for Derek Eiler. See if he spends his working hours the way you think he does.

entrepreneur—A person who identifies, organizes, and develops a new business venture.

What have been the key moves, steps, or developments in your career, and how did you arrive at your current position?

When I was in high school and at Bowling Green State University, my dream was always to become a sports marketing director in a major university athletic department. Throughout high school and even more so in college, my focus was on achieving this goal by (a) performing well as an undergraduate majoring in sport management, and (b) building a strong portfolio of professional experiences that would rival those of anyone coming out of graduate school (even though I only had an undergraduate degree). The support of a lot of people along the way—coupled with an aggressive focus on internships—allowed me to learn an awful lot about what I might want to do after graduation, as well as what I did not want to do.

Following internships with the University of Michigan athletic department, the Toledo Mud Hens, Special Olympics, and the Bowling Green athletic department, I quickly realized that I wanted to work on the business side of sports, preferably for a smaller company in the private sector.

Through a series of productive informational interviews during my senior year of college, I was connected with the founder of CLC. After being hired in 1993, I found a company and an industry that was enjoyable and poised for strong growth over the next decade. Working underneath great mentors, the professional and personal growth I experienced in my time at CLC was extraordinary. A combination of perseverance, work ethic, and the development of strong leadership skills allowed me to eventually be promoted to lead the company.

In 2011, after the company went through much change and consolidation into IMG Worldwide, the time was right for me to pass the baton in leading CLC. I considered several different options, but ultimately decided to ignite my desire to become an entrepreneur and launch my own firm. It has been a wild ride since our inception in December 2011, but one that has been full of great challenges and amazing new experiences. Starting your own business is one of the highest risks you can ever take, but the rewards are also much greater as a result.

What are your current responsibilities and objectives in your job?

As an entrepreneur, you have to be the ultimate generalist. From raising capital to managing cash flow, and from pitching new business to drafting contracts, it is all hands on deck inside our company. As the managing partner of Fermata Partners, I try to balance most of my time between developing new business and working on existing client projects; however, I never stray too far from minding the shop in managing all of the important business-related tasks involved in building a successful boutique agency.

What do you enjoy most about your current job?
The best part about being an entrepreneur is also the hardest part—you get to choose the direction where you want to steer the business, but the risks are entirely on your shoulders if you are wrong. The ability to pivot quickly and adapt to market conditions is critical, especially in the first 1 or 2 years of any start-up. Much of your eventual direction will be set by where the market sees you fitting in. We have been quite successful in the first 18 months of operation and have built a nice range of consulting clients and licensing clients. We have worked with brands like AS Roma in international soccer and UFC in the United States, and we have multiple projects in the U.S. college athletic space with both athletic departments and major athletic conferences. The diversity of projects has been quite rewarding and has again given me the opportunity to validate and pursue the areas of my career that I enjoy the most.

What do you consider the biggest future challenge to be in your job or industry?
The biggest challenge in my current job is trying to project the future direction of our business. When you are small and nimble, you can react quickly, but big companies have the advantage of being able to see over the horizon a bit more easily. Surrounding yourself with a smart and talented team and aligning with good advisors to help watch out for the company's blind spots is well advised for anyone going down the pathway of starting up a new business.

Advanced Education

As you look toward career advancement and additional responsibilities, you may choose, or be asked by your employer, to pursue a graduate degree. Even now, early in your academic career, you may want to begin thinking about an advanced degree. The first graduate degree after the baccalaureate is the master's. Master's degree programs typically require one or two years of additional study. Doctoral-level education builds on the background gained at the undergraduate and master's levels. It is much more specialized in its focus and is essential for anyone who aspires to be a college professor. In choosing a graduate program, students should consider the location of the program within the university, the industry focus of the program, and the experience and research interests of the faculty.

Some sport management programs are located in departments of physical education or sport management, whereas others are housed within schools of business administration, in departments of kinesiology, or in various other units. Students should make certain that their interests are in line with the offerings of the graduate program. Another important consideration when choosing a graduate program is the industry focus of the program. Some programs are geared toward preparing students for positions in athletic administration within an educational structure (e.g., intercollegiate athletics). Other programs focus on sport management in the private sector (e.g., professional sport) or public sector (e.g., community centers). Graduate programs expect candidates to have high grades, involvement in extracurricular activities, experience in the sport industry, and high scores on entrance exams such as the Graduate Records Exam (GRE) or Graduate Management Admission Test (GMAT). It may behoove you to look at schools in other geographic regions or athletic conferences. Diversifying your academic setting can afford you new experiences and different perspectives of how sport organizations are run.

Utilizing Sport to Foster Peaceful Relations: The Israeli Case

By Yair Galily, Israel
Interdisciplinary Center, Herzliya

By Ilan Tamir, Israel
Ariel University, Ariel

By Alina Bernstein, Israel
The College of Management Academic Studies, Rishon LeZion

In the awards ceremony at the eighth annual Friendship Games, President of Israel Shimon Peres (standing in front of the two large trophies) is awarding the prizes as one of the sidebar authors (Yair Galily) makes an announcement (second from right).

The state of Israel is a home for a widely diverse population from many different ethnic, religious, cultural, and social backgrounds; it is a new society with ancient roots that is still coalescing and developing today. Life in Israel entails constant awareness of and contact with the intractable conflict between Jewish and Arab residents of the area. This historic conflict, together with the painful reality, causes many residents to develop negative attitudes towards the other side. Various agencies, including the education system, have actively tried to counter these negative attitudes by deepening familiarity and encouraging empathy with the other side. Findings of studies conducted in Israel have indicated that even in the hard reality that characterizes this region, education for peace programs involving sporting activities succeed in improving attitudes towards the other side.

Professional Attitude

Planning your future in sport management includes paying attention to one of the most important elements of your portfolio—your professional attitude. Employers commonly share that they cannot teach people to have the mind-set for professional success. Thus, applicants who do not possess this quality are not hired or promoted.

Utilizing sports and other recreational activities to foster peaceful relations and coexistence is an idea that has gained popularity in recent years, particularly in Israel. A variety of recreational coexistence programs are currently being conducted in Israel, ranging from soccer, basketball, martial arts, Ultimate Frisbee, and cricket, to dancing, music, arts, and even cooking.

One example of such a recent event is the eighth annual Friendship Games, which were held in the resort city of Eilat, Israel in June of 2013. Athletes from several different countries and territories came to Israel to participate in a weeklong social and recreational program centered on a basketball tournament. There were male and female teams from Europe, Jordan, and Palestine, as well as Jewish and Arab Israelis. The stated mission of the event is to "create peace in the Middle East and other countries of conflict using sport as a bridge to connect people." The event brings Arab and Jewish Israeli college-age athletes together with peers from other countries in the region and from all over the world to play basketball and participate in other recreational activities. Since its establishment in 2006, teams from Russia, China, Serbia, Jordan, Estonia, Ireland, Greece, Turkey, Palestine, Ukraine, Cyprus, Slovenia, and Israel have played in the tournament. According to the organizers, the event focuses on more than just sports and "introduces the athletes to a healthy respect for religion and culture."

The Friendship Games focuses on more than just the love of sports as the event introduces the athletes to a healthy respect for religion and culture. It is this combination of ingredients that offers the potential for overcoming old wounds and making new bridges in the process of peace. This global initiative aims to use sport as a means to help instill dialogue, tolerance, and ultimately peace among young people in areas experiencing conflict and hostility. Throughout the week all the participants and staff live together in close hotel quarters. This living arrangement gives participants opportunities to meet and share freely over meals, poolside, and in the many public areas. Teams also take part in a dialogue and Q&A with local high school students. Conversations touch on topics such as women in sports, amateur versus professional sports, and athletes as role models.

International Learning Activity #1

Conduct an Internet search for a similar program that utilizes sport to foster peaceful relations. Describe in writing the desirable outcomes of such a program and the obstacles it might face.

International Learning Activity #2

Explore the International Olympic Committee (IOC) website at www.olympic.org/ioc and find the ways in which the IOC is trying to use the Olympic Games to bring people from conflict areas together. Prepare a paper or presentation to inform your fellow students and moderate a discussion about the effectiveness of such an activity.

International Learning Activity #3

While there is a certain theoretical logic to some of the policy assertions about the contribution of sport to foster peaceful relations (among them early beliefs, such as those derived from Allport's "Contact Hypothesis" (1954), which theorize that the interaction of individuals from two different groups can lead to significantly decreased prejudice), several scholars claim that many of the outcomes are, as noted by Kruse (2006), "intriguingly vague and open for several interpretations" (p. 8). Make at least three suggestions on ways to improve or sharpen the message delivered in such programs.

To ensure that you are a competitive candidate, one of the things that you must do is demonstrate a positive attitude in your interviews and on the job (Sukiennik, Bendat, & Raufman, 2008). An enthusiastic and professional attitude will not only enhance your opportunities for employment and advancement but also make you a more pleasant person to be around. That alone is a worthy goal. Furthermore, attitudes are demonstrated by behaviors. The following sections on ethical behavior and critical thinking

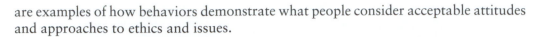

are examples of how behaviors demonstrate what people consider acceptable attitudes and approaches to ethics and issues.

Ethical Decision Making

The professional codes of many sport organizations frequently articulate acceptable behaviors. Professionals in these organizations are expected to adhere to these codes, and those in sport management are no exception. For example, a quick search of the Internet using the phrase "sport code of ethics" will yield more than one million hits. The Institute of Sport Management (2013) sponsors one of those websites. This company, located in New South Wales, Australia, is committed to the development of the profession of sport management. The company's code of ethics and professional conduct as listed on its website notes that "the objectives of the Sport Management profession are to work to the highest standards of professionalism, to attain the highest levels of performance and generally meet the public interest requirement" (para. 2). The website further notes that the objectives require four criteria: credibility, professionalism, quality of services, confidence. Take a few moments to read the Institute's entire code of ethics. After you have examined the code of ethics, refer back to the ethical guidelines presented in chapter 1. In what ways does this sport organization's code of ethics intersect with the guidelines?

You have no doubt witnessed or read about many breaches of ethical behavior, often by high-profile individuals in spheres such as politics, business, and sport. People who have been caught violating social norms and formal laws can face a variety of sanctions. As discussed in chapter 1, understanding how to examine an issue thoughtfully and maintain an ethical demeanor will serve you well in any environment.

To be successful in a classroom or a place of business, individuals must understand expectations and recognize norms that regulate group members. **Explicit norms** are formally communicated rules that govern behavior. In university communities, rules are stated in student policy manuals. In individual classrooms, explicit norms are outlined in the course syllabus and handouts. In a business environment, explicit norms are outlined in documents such as staff handbooks. To gain confidence in any situation, one should review and comprehend an organization's formal policies and procedures.

Seek to understand informal norms, also referred to as **implicit norms**, that serve to "explain the way things happen in an organization" (Harvey & Drolet, 2004, p. 62). These informal norms can be learned, usually by observing other members of the group. As explained by Harvey and Drolet, although these expectations of behavior may be informal, they are extremely important and, in some cases, are more powerful than formal, explicit norms.

An inability to abide by norms, combined with a skeptical view of human behavior and pressure to succeed in college, may influence students to behave unethically in their own lives. Although some students may be willing to compromise ethics and cheat to receive a better grade than they deserve, they are developing habits and behaviors that may seriously jeopardize their future success. Results based on a survey of college students suggest that "if students do not respect the climate of academic integrity while in college, they will not respect integrity in their future and personal relationships" (Nonis & Swift, 2001, p. 71).

Many students, however, have the foresight to understand that ethical behavior while in college will serve them well as they develop their professional aptitude. When

explicit norms—Formally communicated rules that govern behavior of group members.

implicit norms—Unstated or informal rules understood and practiced by members of an organization.

Responsible Group Participation

While taking a college class, you are randomly assigned to a three-person group that is required to research a topic and present to the class. All members of the group will work together for one overall group grade. You have a busy semester, with classes and work and family obligations, and finding a time to meet with other group members is difficult. The way that you approach this assignment may indicate how you perform in the workplace. The following are some questions that you may want to consider as you enter into this group project for the class (keep in mind that you will most likely ask yourself similar questions when engaged in group work as a professional in the sport industry):

> Will you make the effort to find times to meet with group members so that you can play an equal role in the research and presentation?

> Will you avoid them, ignore their e-mails and telephone calls, and give excuses for not getting in touch with them?

> Will you allow the other members of your group to do all the work but take credit for the assignment?

> Will you actively volunteer to take on portions of the assignment, or will you remain silent, hoping that other members will do all the work and let you slide?

preparing for a career after college, students have a responsibility to learn academic content and make good decisions on the road to future success.

As a student, you are confronted with ethical dilemmas on a weekly, if not daily, basis. What are some examples of unethical behavior that you have witnessed as a student in a sport management class? Referring to the guidelines for ethical decision making presented in chapter 1, how might you change your approach to some of the ethical issues that you face (e.g., cheating on a test, plagiarizing an article, forging a signature, explaining an absence to your professor)? How can you apply these guidelines? Why is it important to embrace ethical behavior as a student?

Critical Thinking Skills

Gaining a thorough understanding about issues is an imperative skill for students and professionals alike. As explained in chapter 1, critical thinking skills can assist a person in a quest to seek the truth. When students cultivate and practice critical thinking skills, they are less likely to act or make decisions out of habit. The development of sound critical thinking skills can allow people to thrive in academic and work environments. Mastering academic content is important, as is learning about social situations, ethics, and values. Those who challenge themselves and take the time to think, reflect, and learn give themselves a much better chance to flourish in their personal and professional lives.

Remember the eight critical thinking questions presented in chapter 1? How can you apply those questions and critical thinking to other issues that you may currently be confronting as a sport management student? (For example, should you confront a friend who uses sexist language while taunting a rival school during a tennis match? Should you join or encourage protesters outside the athletics department when school officials consider an increase in student fees to fund a new basketball arena?)

Social Media and Developing a Professional Perspective

Social media can be an effective tool for establishing a professional network, showcasing your accomplishments, applying for your first job, and advancing your career within the industry. As you progress through your undergraduate education, highlight your accomplishments, volunteer opportunities, internships, and employment on various social media outlets (e.g., Facebook, Twitter, Instagram, LinkedIn, Google+, Pinterest, YouTube). Social media sites can allow you to showcase a digital resume that may not otherwise be demonstrated the same way in a traditional resume. Further, as you develop your network, both face-to-face and digitally, updating your social media pages can keep your colleagues up to date on your career. However, networking on social media makes the sport world much smaller. That is, news about your accomplishments or weekend festivities can spread quickly. You should keep in mind that whatever you post or are tagged in on your social media profiles may be accessed by current or future employers (e.g., links, photos, videos, comments, posts, tweets). In fact, a 2009 study (PRNewswire, 2012) showed that 37% of employers check the social media pages of job candidates. Of those companies using social media to evaluate job candidates, 65% check Facebook, 63% use LinkedIn, and 16% check Twitter. Also interesting to note, 15% of the surveyed employers have explicit policies not to use social media websites to evaluate potential employees. Considering this, you should be very cautious regarding the type of content you post, and you should go through your various accounts periodically to see if you need to update privacy settings or if content needs to be deleted. When determining if something should be posted or even deleted, think about how you can tailor your message to your advantage as a potential employee.

Professional Image

When first meeting you, other people rely on your physical appearance to make judgments about you. Mitchell (1998) explained that studies on the initial impression that people make "show that 7% of that impression is based on what a person says, 38% on how he or she says it, and 55% on what the other person *sees*" (p. 10). Although this way of judging you might seem unfair, and although initial impressions can change after someone gets to know you, you can make a first impression only once—so why not make it a good one?

The impression that you make through your physical presentation during interviews and on the job is related less to physical attractiveness than to other factors, all of which are within your control. The following items are among the many aspects of a professional image.

> *Grooming.* Attention to your grooming can pay off as you present yourself to potential employers. Aspects of grooming to consider include care of hair, nails, and teeth, as well as neatness and cleanliness.

> *Attire and accessories.* While in college, you have wide discretion in your choice of clothing and accessories, but as you move into the workplace, you must understand what constitutes appropriate attire. This standard will differ depending on the organization. If you are unsure about what is acceptable attire for your organization, ask your supervisor. Websites on professional dress and business casual dress can be especially helpful.

> *Posture.* Your sitting, standing, and walking posture (body language) convey an impression of your attitude. People will draw different conclusions about the attitude of a person who is slouching as opposed to one who is sitting erect, with feet firmly planted on the floor, or leaning slightly forward to indicate good listening skills, interest, and enthusiasm.

› *Social media.* Believe it or not, your social media page (e.g., Facebook, Twitter, Instagram, LinkedIn) can influence how you are perceived by current or potential employers. You should always be cognizant of what is shown or what you are tagged in on your various social media outlets. You should consider how what you post or what you are tagged in can be perceived by others. Social media content could prevent you from getting an interview or a job. Although there are privacy settings for your accounts, always consider who may be able to see your profile.

Work Transition and Adjustment

Are you ready to face challenges that will present themselves in the workplace? Are you confident in your abilities and competent in your specific job skills? Are you knowledgeable about the social, political, legislative, technological, and economic trends that have influenced your field? Now is the time to begin practicing for life in the work environment. How you enter a new sport organization, approach the challenges of your new position, learn the organizational culture, develop working relationships with bosses and colleagues, participate in departmental and team meetings, communicate your ideas to others, and establish your reputation as an employee will have a major influence on your success. Valuable employees display their professional attitude in the image that they project, in the ways they approach work transition and adjustment, and in their business etiquette. The following sections offer tips on learning your job, understanding organizational culture, demonstrating your work ethic, developing written communication skills, using electronic communication, writing thank-you notes, refining teamwork skills, managing conflict, embracing diversity, being evaluated, and continuing your professional development.

etiquette—A system of rules and conventions that regulate social and professional behavior.

LEARN YOUR JOB

When you start a new job, make sure that you understand what your duties are, what you are expected to do, and how to proceed. Listen carefully to directions and ask for clarification of any instructions that you do not comprehend fully before beginning an assignment. Taking notes as you receive oral instructions is perfectly appropriate to assure understanding and thorough recall of expectations. Set up periodic meetings with your supervisor to confirm and clarify your progress on assignments to ensure that your work is accurate, thorough, and of high quality. In an entry-level or new job, you are not expected to know everything, but you are expected to show interest and actively learn.

UNDERSTAND ORGANIZATIONAL CULTURE

As you will learn in chapter 4, each organization has a unique culture; therefore, new employees must learn what behaviors are expected in the workplace. Employee socialization or onboarding programs are often initiated by management to help employees understand policies and procedures and general ground rules to function on the job (Saunderson, 2012). These expectations are sometimes shared during an orientation or stated in an organization's policy manual. Employees also learn unofficial procedures that have evolved over time by observing the behaviors of others and listening to stories told about the organization at informal gatherings. A clear understanding of expectations is essential to a fast career start. Astute new employees will recognize the importance of learning the organization's rules and guidelines and will distinguish themselves from others by showing their professional maturity (Holton & Naquin, 2001). If you are unclear about expectations within your organization, it is wise to ask for clarification. Kahle-Piasecki (2011) advocated a mentor–mentee relationship between a more experienced employee and a new hire to help increase the mentee's knowledge and productivity and enhance performance.

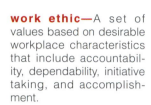

DEMONSTRATE YOUR WORK ETHIC

Demonstrate your commitment to the organization, supervisors, and colleagues by enthusiastically completing all job assignments within the agreed-upon deadlines, keeping your word, offering assistance, and supporting others in achieving the organization's goals. Your attitude toward work can be referred to as your **work ethic**. "Your work ethic is a set of values you work and live by," noted Curtis (1999). "The strength of your work ethic is based on the solidarity of your values" (p. 2). Identifying qualities and characteristics that you admire in others may help you determine your work values. Strive to do the right thing and gain recognition as a valuable member of the organization.

work ethic—A set of values based on desirable workplace characteristics that include accountability, dependability, initiative taking, and accomplishment.

DEVELOP YOUR WRITTEN COMMUNICATION SKILLS

The ability to express thoughts and ideas in writing is one of the most important competencies of a good sport manager. Among the many types of writing that you will have to produce are business correspondence (e.g., memos, e-mail messages, responses to complaints), reports, and technical manuals. Learn to organize your thoughts logically and use grammar and punctuation correctly. Investing time and energy in learning to write well will pay huge dividends when you enter the professional world.

Use Electronic Communication Appropriately   Although e-mail is often used as an informal mode of communication, adherence to the conventions of good business writing is expected in business-related e-mail messages. Good judgment regarding the content of e-mail messages is essential. Use capitalization and punctuation in e-mails and make sure you use the spellchecking function. Proofread e-mails for errors and to ensure that the tone is professional and appropriate. This can be practiced when sending e-mails to your instructors. Always use formal titles (e.g., Dr., Ms., Mr., Professor), use an appropriate greeting, and keep your correspondence professional. A number of excellent websites address the proper uses of e-mail and provide tips for composing electronic business correspondence (search using keywords *netiquette* or *e-mail etiquette*).

Thank Others   Take the opportunity to express gratitude to anyone who provides you with information or her or his time. A good practice to follow is to send your thanks within 24 hours of a social or business contact or event. You may send a personal letter of thanks; in many cases, a well-composed e-mail will be appropriate. Making a habit of thanking people who help you will go a long way toward establishing your reputation as a professional.

REFINE YOUR TEAMWORK SKILLS

The ability to participate as a valuable member of a team is imperative in any work setting. Tasks and assignments often utilize the talents of a work team, which is a group of people working in relationship with one another to accomplish a task or solve a problem. To be an effective team member, you need to develop skills along several dimensions, including commitment to the task, communication, collaboration, confrontation, consensus building, and caring and demonstrating respect for other team members. Remember to be prompt and provide complete and quality work or feedback in an agreed-upon time frame.

Learn to Manage Conflict   Conflict is energy among groups of people or individuals; it is not about winning or losing. Conflict is an opportunity to acknowledge and appreciate our differences. Carney and Wells (1995) noted that workplace differences or conflicts are most likely to occur "when workers are under pressure, when their responsibilities are not clear, or when their personal expectations or needs are violated." They added that situations involving conflict "offer ideal opportunities for clarifying personal differences and for team building" (p. 179). If you disagree with a colleague, supervisor, or customer, express yourself without being unpleasant. When handled in a mature, positive way, conflict can be healthy.

Embrace Diversity   Appreciate and celebrate diversity of gender, race, religion, sexual orientation, ability, age, and so on. Do not engage in racist, ageist, or sexist behaviors, and let others know, tactfully, that you do not appreciate such behaviors. Seek to understand and respect the history, values, understandings, and opinions of others. Being inclusive is the right thing to do, and it can benefit an organization's bottom line as well. A study by the National Urban League (2005) suggested that "investments in the area of diversity are by no means being made at the expense of productivity. In fact, it is likely that the effective diversity practices—exemplary leadership and management practices—also result in productivity gains" (p. 15).

Assess Performance   As a new professional, you should welcome the evaluation process, recognizing that the aim of constructive criticism is to improve your performance. Expect to be involved in setting goals that will challenge your learning process. Your progress will be measured on a recurring basis so you and your supervisor can identify appropriate professional development activities to help you perform to the best of your ability. Be prepared to discuss your specific needs for development and strategies to improve your job performance. The most important question to ask your supervisor is, What should I be doing to improve my job performance?

CONTINUE YOUR PROFESSIONAL DEVELOPMENT

As the concept of a successful career continually changes in our global sport marketplace, personal flexibility and the ability to adapt to change become even more important. Underlying the assumption that professionals can be flexible and can adapt to change is the concept of lifelong learning. Your professional education is just beginning, and it will continue throughout your life.

You should make an early commitment to lifelong learning, both formal and informal, so that you can continue to grow professionally and personally. Participation in business and professional associations (as noted earlier, some examples are listed in the sidebar "Examples of Professional Organizations") increases your knowledge and expands your network of associates throughout your career. A well-developed career network is vital to your professional advancement. Your network members can provide information, guidance, support, honest feedback, and access to career opportunities. Interaction with sport management colleagues is stimulating and allows you to grow professionally and contribute to your field.

ACTION

Go to the WSG and complete the Learning in Action activity that helps you identify appropriate workplace decorum.

Business Etiquette

The academic environment is clearly a helpful setting for learning and practicing manners to increase the professionalism that students bring into the sport industry. In interviews with 15 managers from five sport organizations in Northern California, Lilienthal (2004) sought to identify the professional behavior the managers expected of their new or young employees. She found that almost all the managers had recurring issues with employees' unprofessional behavior with regard to dress code and courtesy. The managers believed that classroom and workplace training in professional etiquette would be helpful. A more recent survey by York College of Pennsylvania (Moltz, 2009) revealed that business leaders and human resource executives believe many college graduates fail to exhibit appropriate levels of professionalism and workplace etiquette. As you prepare for a career in sport management, we encourage you to consider the following reminders of good manners:

> *Telephone.* Answering the telephone in a professional manner includes clearly identifying yourself and your organization or department; giving each caller your full attention; restating important information to check for understanding and accuracy; projecting a tone that is cheerful, natural, and attentive; ending the conversation with agreement on what is to happen next; and following up appropriately. When leaving your phone number on someone's voice-mail system, speak distinctly and at a reasonable speed. Remember to leave your name, phone number, and a brief message so that the caller will be prepared when she or he returns your call.

> *Voice-mail messages.* Refrain from leaving inappropriate greetings for callers, especially during times when you are searching for an internship or professional employment. Busy callers do not appreciate long messages, silliness, or loud music in the background.

> *Language.* Practice being inclusive in spoken and written language rather than using gender-biased or racially biased language. In the workplace of the 21st century, employees will interact with managers, clients, and customers who are women, people of color, or people from other cultures. Mastery of inclusive language is a good way to demonstrate your sensitivity to such concerns and to create a more pleasant workplace (Parks, Harper, & Lopez, 1994).

> *Meeting participation.* Expected behavior in business meetings may vary by organizational culture, but general conventions include being prepared, arriving approximately 10 minutes early, silencing or turning off cell phones, staying on task, participating openly, giving your full attention through active listening, and encouraging others to participate and offer their ideas. Refrain from checking e-mail or other social media sites on your computer, tablet, or phone.

> *Dining etiquette.* Many business meetings and interviews include a meal, and prospective employers, customers, and other business associates will judge your table manners. You will be more comfortable when you know what to expect. First, be prepared to engage in light conversation. Appropriate topics include current events, sports, and the arts. On the other hand, politics, religion, and sex are taboo topics. Although alcohol is never appropriate at a business lunch in the United States, know your organization's policy on alcohol at business functions or follow your host's lead.

> *International experiences.* From an international perspective, good manners can be defined in various ways. Communicating with and relating to people from other cultures requires that you learn the protocols, courtesies, customs, and behaviors of those cultures. To avoid embarrassment, investigate the customs prevalent in other countries before traveling there and before entertaining international visitors.

> *Introductions and greetings.* The host is responsible for introducing those who are meeting for the first time. When making an introduction, use the name of the most senior person first and introduce everyone else to him or her. As a general rule of respect, do not use a person's first name until invited to do so. Regardless of your gender, stand when being introduced to others. When shaking hands, both women and men should expect to use a firm grip. Grasp the person's entire hand, not just the fingers, and adjust your grip to the state of health and physical strength of the person whom you are greeting.

> *Office etiquette.* Many organizations today use dividers rather than walls, so you may find yourself working in a small space with a number of coworkers. Be conscious of their need for privacy and a quiet workplace. Be cautious in your use of music players, speakerphones, and other devices that can be distracting in a small work space.

> *Romantic relationships.* The office is not an appropriate place to engage in flirting or in more overt forms of affectionate behavior. Often, employee handbooks address issues of dating and romantic relationships in the workplace. Furthermore, be aware of your actions because others can perceive flirtatious behavior as sexual harassment (Pedersen, Osborne, Whisenant, & Lim, 2009).

A positive, professional attitude—as reflected in your professional image, work habits and behavior, and business etiquette—is essential to your future success. Do not underestimate the roles that enthusiasm and a positive self-image play in creating a successful professional attitude.

Career Planning and Management

To thrive in the second decade of the 21st century, employees will need to assume responsibility for their own career planning and management. Gone are the days when college graduates could expect to find a job directly after graduation and spend their entire careers working for one organization. You will make multiple career and job choices throughout your life span. Estimates are that U.S. workers will change career fields 3 to 5 times and switch jobs as many as 10 times during their working lives. Although frequent job changes will become the norm, you can achieve employment security by continuing to develop new skills through lifelong learning and by assuming personal responsibility for managing your career.

Career Decision Steps

The complex process of making career decisions involves four stages: self-awareness, occupational exploration, decision making, and career implementation. Career planning can be fascinating because you will gain new insights about yourself as well as knowledge about the variety of career options available to you. The following steps will help you in your career planning. You do not have to complete them in the order presented, and you may need to repeat a step or two as you gain new information about yourself and your career options or encounter obstacles or barriers.

> *Self-awareness* entails identifying and understanding your personal and work values, interests, abilities, aptitudes, personality traits, and desired future lifestyle.

> *Occupational exploration* entails taking a broad look at career fields and researching specific sport management occupations, work environments, and employers that may be a match with your unique career profile as identified through your self-assessment.

> *Career decision making* is the process of consciously analyzing and weighing all information that you have gathered about yourself, various sport management occupations, and career paths. At this stage, you will make a tentative career decision, formulate educational and vocational goals, and develop plans to achieve them. The more you learn about yourself and the world of sport management, the better and more realistic your educational and career choices will be.

> *Career implementation* involves sharpening your job search skills. You will learn to prepare an effective résumé and cover letter, identify sources of job leads, present yourself professionally in interviews, evaluate and accept a job offer, and adjust to a new position.

Career planning is not a single, once-in-a-lifetime event. You are continually developing new interests, knowledge, and skills through your coursework, leisure activities, volunteer experiences, summer and part-time jobs, and internships. Throughout your career, you may be motivated to reevaluate your options when changes in duties or work conditions of a job cause you to become less satisfied with it. Each time you face a career or job change, you will go through the career planning stages.

Your college career center offers services and programs to help you develop career goals, find the right academic and experiential programs to achieve those goals, and gain employment after graduation. Career counselors can be extremely helpful in providing guidance and direction in assessing your vocational interests, identifying skills, writing résumés and cover letters, preparing for interviews, developing a professional portfolio, and conducting the job search.

It will be helpful to you if you keep a portfolio, or collection of your work, as evidence of what you have done and, by implication, what you will be able to do as a professional. Although portfolios may be a bound collection of work completed during each semester in the program, Gentile (2010) suggested keeping work in an electronic portfolio. Regardless of format, the portfolio would include various projects and assignments from a myriad of sport management courses. Although time consuming to develop, portfolios are valuable to students in providing examples of skills and knowledge. Furthermore, in the process of creating portfolios, students will have an opportunity to reflect on their competencies and proficiencies.

Volunteering at sporting events can help you decide if a career in sport management is for you.

Values

Your values are fundamental to career planning, and they indicate what you consider most important in your life. Zunker (2009) stated that a value can be defined as simply as "something that is important or desirable to you" (p. 16). Many factors contribute to your process of learning what you value. These include, but are not limited to, cultural background, family influences, educational opportunities, religious and spiritual experiences, friends, and peers. In an analysis of a computer-based career guidance system (SIGI) that provides clarification of values, Zunker explained that eight values are currently being used in this system: high income, prestige, independence, helping others, security, variety, leadership, and leisure. The choices that you make about your occupational life need to be in harmony with your basic values and belief systems; otherwise, you will not find personal satisfaction in your job.

values—Indicators of what you consider most important or desirable (Zunker, 2009).

You should seek an occupation and jobs that will enhance, strengthen, and support the values that you consider important. For example, high school coaches may possess values different from those of sport entrepreneurs. The coaches may demonstrate the value that they place on facilitating the physical, mental, and moral development of young people, whereas sport entrepreneurs may demonstrate the value that they place on providing a high level of financial security for family members.

Interests

Interests are activities that you enthusiastically engage in and find enjoyable, and subjects that arouse your curiosity or hold your attention. Interests are an integral part of your personality, and are related to your values. Throughout your life, your personal experiences shape your interests. These interests often lead to competencies in the same areas. When your occupation matches your interests, you experience greater job satisfaction. If you have difficulty identifying or articulating your interests, you might want to seek the assistance of a career counselor at your university career center. Using interest inventories, career counselors can help you assess your measured interests and match those interests with appropriate occupations.

Skills

A skill is the developed aptitude, ability, or personal quality needed to perform a task competently. The three basic types of skills are job content skills, functional skills, and adaptive skills. **Job content skills** are the specialized knowledge or abilities needed to fulfill a specific job responsibility. Knowing the rules of basketball is an example of a job content skill for a basketball referee. Functional skills are general abilities that transfer to many jobs or situations. For example, the referee uses functional skills to make quick, accurate decisions and to resolve player conflicts that occur on the court. Adaptive skills are personal attributes or personality traits. In our example, the referee must remain calm and poised under stressful conditions.

job content skills—The specialized knowledge or abilities needed to fulfill specific job duties.

Information for Occupational Success

Because our global economy is becoming more competitive, skills such as critical thinking and problem solving, communication, collaboration, and creativity and innovation will become even more important to organizations in the future. According to the American Management Association's (AMA) 2010 Critical Skills Survey, the majority of managers surveyed agreed that job applicants are assessed in skills and competencies related to communication (80.7%), critical thinking (75.7%), collaboration (62.6%), and creativity (60.4%) during the hiring process. Knowing which skills are required to be successful in today's workplace is a good starting point for assessing your level

Sport Management Career Resources

Please refer to the lists in each textbook part opener for additional resources

Online Resources

Academic Jobs Today

Blue Fish Jobs

Canada's Sport Information Resource Centre

Career Voyages

CareerBuilder.com

CareerOneStop

Chronicle of Higher Education: Jobs

ESPN Careers

First Job in Sports

Game Face

HigherEdJobs

Jobs in Sports

Major League Baseball Careers

Monster.com

National Alliance of Intercollegiate Athletics: NAIA Careers Center

National Alliance of State Broadcasters Associations

National Association of Collegiate Directors of Athletics: Job Center

National Communication Association

National Hockey League: NHL Hockey Jobs

NBA Career Opportunities

NCAA Market

Nike, Inc.

Occupational Outlook Handbook

The Official Sports Industry Job Board

Professional Baseball Employment Opportunities

Sports Careers

Sports Careers Institute

SportJobMatch.com

Sports Sales Combine

TeamWork Online

Women Sports Careers

Work in Sports

Book Resources

American Kinesiology Association. (2011). *Careers in sport, fitness, and exercise*. Champaign, IL: Human Kinetics.

Devantier, A.T., & Turkington, C.A. (2006). *Extraordinary jobs in sports*. New York, NY: Facts on File.

Field, S. (2010). *Career opportunities in the sports industry* (4th ed.). New York, NY: Ferguson.

Freedman, J. (2013). *Dream jobs in sports management and administration*. New York, NY: Rosen.

Heitzmann, W.R. (2003). *Opportunities in sports and fitness careers*. Boston, MA: McGraw-Hill.

Niver, H.M. (2013). *Dream jobs in sports marketing*. New York, NY: Rosen.

Robinson, M.J., Hums, M.A., Crow, R.B., & Phillips, D.R. (2001). *Profiles of sport industry professionals: The people who make the games happen*. Gaithersburg, MD: Aspen.

Sports market place directory. (2013). Amenia, NY: Grey House.

Stevens, C.A. (2010). *Career with meaning: Recreation, parks, sport management, hospitality, and tourism*. Champaign, IL: Sagamore.

Wells, M., Kreutzer, A., & Kahler, J. (2010). *A career in sports: Advice from sports business leaders*. Raleigh, NC: Author.

Wong, G.M. (2013). *The comprehensive guide to careers in sports* (2nd ed.). Burlington, MA: Jones & Bartlett Learning.

of skill attainment. After you have identified the skills that you possess and to what degree you have them, you can develop a plan for enhancing your level of those most pertinent to your career goals.

By using a systematic approach, you will be able to compare occupations and make decisions that are compatible with your values, interests, skills, personality, and desired future lifestyle. For each occupation that you are considering, gather the following information: the nature of the work, work setting and conditions, educational and personal qualifications required, earnings, employment outlook and competition, methods of entering the occupation, opportunities for advancement, opportunities for exploring the occupation, related occupations, and sources of additional information. (For a listing of online sources that may be useful in your research, refer to the sidebar "Sport Management Career Resources.")

Another way of collecting data is through a computerized career information system. Most career centers provide an interactive, web-based career guidance and education planning system, such as FOCUS V2 (Career Dimensions, 2010), that helps students with important career planning tasks, including (1) understanding their interests, work values, personality, skills, and educational preferences; (2) identifying and discovering how their personal qualities relate to occupations; and (3) narrowing their options by interactively exploring and analyzing occupations. Another computer-aided counseling system, SportJobMatch.com, is a career guidance website geared toward students who are interested in sport management. The website offers an opportunity for students to complete a survey that provides results that can help them determine a career path within the sport industry. The website also provides information about job-related duties and opportunities that exist in the field of sport management.

Interviewing employees on site is an excellent way to gain additional information about jobs and work environments. Most sport managers are willing to help eager college students learn about the field. Through informational interviews, you can gain an insider's view on a sport management job, obtain referrals to other professionals, and create a network of contacts.

Practice asking questions and having a conversation with a friend before you meet with the professional. Next, identify a sport manager to interview and call to arrange an appointment. When meeting with this manager, practice your professionalism. Wear business formal or business casual attire, and be prepared to ask a variety of questions about how you can prepare to enter the occupation and be a successful professional. Remember to take notes. After the interview, send a thank-you letter within 24 hours.

Summary

Three elements necessary for success in sport management are professional preparation, professional attitude, and career planning and management. You can find sport management professional preparation programs at the bachelor's, master's, and doctoral levels. The typical undergraduate curriculum consists of general education courses and major courses, along with field experiences that give you opportunities to apply in sport settings what you learn in the classroom. Master's and doctoral programs will be more specific to your career goals should you wish to pursue an advanced degree.

Professional attitude is reflected in your personal appearance (e.g., hygiene, posture, self-confidence), adjustment to the workplace (e.g., academic preparation, writing skills, dependability, ethics, work habits), and business etiquette (e.g., telephone, e-mail, thank-you letters). Recruiters evaluate professional attitudes during interviews and employers evaluate them in performance appraisals.

Career planning consists of self-awareness (e.g., values, interests, skills), occupational exploration (i.e., gathering information from a variety of sources), career decision making, and career implementation. College career centers can provide valuable guidance and direction, including directing you to a multitude of resources (see the "Sport Management Career Resources" sidebar) and helping you create an electronic portfolio.

Review Questions

1. How can professional preparation, a professional attitude, and career planning and management contribute to your success in sport management?

2. List the three components of your undergraduate sport management curriculum. Which elements within each component fulfill the content requirements of the COSMA accreditation standards?

3. Define field experiences. How do they benefit students, employers, colleges and universities, and society?

4. How would you outline an effective plan for finding an optimal field experience in sport management?

5. According to *Job Outlook 2013* (NACE, 2012), what skills and competencies will you need for a successful career in sport management? Explain how you plan to acquire these skills and competencies while in college.

6. List important elements of personal appearance, work transition and adjustment, and business etiquette. What does your conduct reveal regarding your personal perspective on each?

7. In your own words, how would you explain the four stages involved in career planning?

8. What are some print and electronic resources that you could use in seeking employment in sport management?

9. In what ways can social media platforms be utilized in your professional development and personal brand in the sport industry?

References

Allport, G.W. (1954). *The nature of prejudice*. Reading, MA: Addison-Wesley.

American Management Association. (2010, April). Critical skills survey: Executives say the 21st century requires more skilled workers. Retrieved from www.p21.org/storage/documents/Critical%20Skills%20Survey%20Executive%20Summary.pdf

Brassie, P.S. (1989). Guidelines for programs preparing undergraduate and graduate students for careers in sport management. *Journal of Sport Management, 3*, 158–164.

Career Dimensions. (2010). *FOCUS V2: A career & education planning system*. Retrieved from www.focuscareer2.com

Carney, C.G., & Wells, C.F. (1995). *Discover the career within you* (4th ed.). Pacific Grove, CA: Thomson Brooks/Cole.

Chelladurai, P. (2005). *Managing organizations for sport and physical activity: A systems perspective* (2nd ed.). Scottsdale, AZ: Holcomb Hathaway.

Cole, M.S., Rubin, R.S., Field, H.S., & Giles, W.F. (2007). Recruiters' perceptions and use of applicant resume information: Screening the recent college graduate. *Applied Psychology, 56*, 319–343.

Cuneen, J., & Sidwell, M.J. (1994). *Sport management field experiences*. Morgantown, WV: Fitness Information Technology.

Curtis & Associates. (1999). *Work culture*. Kearney, NE: Author.

Dixon, M.A., Cunningham, G.B., Sagas, M., Turner, B.A., & Kent, A. (2005). Challenge is key: An investigation of affective organizational commitment in undergraduate interns. *Journal of Education for Business, 80*, 172–180.

Gentile, D. (2010). Teaching sport management: A practical guide. Sudbury, MA: Jones and Bartlett.

Gower, R.K., & Mulvaney, M.A. (2012). Making the most of your internship: A strategic approach. Champaign, IL: Sagamore.

Harvey, T.R., & Drolet, B. (2004). *Building teams, building people* (2nd ed.). Lanham, MD: Scarecrow Education.

Holton, E.F., III, & Naquin, S.S. (2001). *How to succeed in your first job: Tips for college graduates*. San Francisco, CA: Berrett-Koehler.

Institute of Sport Management. (2013). *Code of ethics*. Retrieved from http://ismhome.com/main/code-of-ethics-and-professional-conduct

Kahle-Piasecki, L. (2011). Making a mentoring relationship work: What is required for organizational success. *Journal of Applied Business and Economics, 12*(1), 46–56.

Kruse, S.E. (2006, October). *Review of kicking AIDS out: Is sport an effective tool in the fight against HIV/AIDS?* Oslo, Norway: Norwegian Agency for Development Cooperation.

Lilienthal, S. (2004, June). *Professional etiquette of sport management students: Investigating employer perceptions*. Paper presented at the annual conference of the North American Society for Sport Management, Atlanta, GA.

Mitchell, M. (with Corr, J.). (1998). *The first five minutes: How to make a great first impression in any business situation*. New York, NY: Wiley.

Moltz, D. (2009, October 23). Are today's grads unprofessional? *Inside Higher Ed*. Retrieved from www.insidehighered.com/news/2009/10/23/professionalism

National Association of Colleges and Employers. (2012, November). *Job outlook 2013: Special report*. Retrieved from www.unco.edu/careers/assets/documents/NACEJobOutlookNov2013.pdf

National Association of Colleges and Employers. (2013, June 19). Class of 2013: Majority of seniors participated in internships or co-ops [press release]. Retrieved from www.naceweb.org/press/releases/internship-co-op-participation.aspx?referal=pressroom&menuid=273

National Urban League. (2005). *Diversity practices that work: The American worker speaks*. Retrieved from www.nul.org/sites/default/files/Diversity_Practices_That_Work_2005.pdf

Nonis, S., & Swift, C.O. (2001). An examination of the relationship between academic dishonesty and workplace dishonesty: A multi-campus investigation. *Journal of Education for Business, 77*(2), 69–77.

Parks, J.B. (executive producer), Harper, M.C. (writer), & Lopez, P.G. (director). (1994). *One person's struggle with gender-biased language: Part 1* [Videotape]. (Available from WBGU-TV, Bowling Green State University, Bowling Green, OH 43403.)

Pedersen, P.M., Osborne, B., Whisenant, W.A., & Lim, C. (2009). An examination of the perceptions of sexual harassment by newspaper sports journalists. *Journal of Sport Management, 23*, 335–360.

PRNewswire. (2012, April 12). Thirty-seven percent of companies use social networks to research potential job candidates, according to new CareerBuilder survey. *PRNewswire*. Retrieved from www.prnewswire.com/news-releases/thirty-seven-percent-of-companies-use-social-networks-to-research-potential-job-candidates-according-to-new-careerbuilder-survey-147885445.html

Saunderson, R. (2012). Onboarding recognition. *Training, 49*(2), 60, 62.

Scheele, A. (2005). *Launch your career in college: Strategies for students, educators, and parents*. Westport, CT: Praeger.

Sukiennik, D., Bendat, W., & Raufman, L. (2008). *The career fitness program: Exercising your options* (9th ed.). Upper Saddle River, NJ: Pearson/Prentice Hall.

Williams, J. (2003). Sport management internship administration: Challenges and chances for collaboration. *NACE Journal, 63*(2), 28–32.

Zunker, V.G. (2009). *Career, work, and mental health: Integrating career & personal counseling*. Los Angeles, CA: Sage.

HISTORICAL MOMENTS

- **1862** William H. Cammeyer began charging admission to baseball games
- **1869** Cincinnati Red Stockings became first all-professional baseball team
- **1872** Yale played Columbia in first intercollegiate football game with admission charge
- **1876** Spalding opened Baseball and Sporting Goods Emporium (Chicago)
- **1898** Golf ball patent established
- **1910** Philadelphia Athletics' Connie Mack introduced low-cost producer concept to professional sport
- **1919** Babe Ruth's autographed model bat number one seller for Hillerich & Bradsby Company
- **1940** First college basketball doubleheader was broadcasted (NBC)—Pittsburgh v. Fordham and NYU v. Georgetown
- **1951** First live, coast-to-coast broadcast of a sporting event was televised (NBC)—college football, Duke v. Pittsburgh
- **1953** Major League Baseball Players Association (MLBPA) formed
- **1961** Sports Broadcasting Act allowed leagues to negotiate one television contract for all their teams
- **1964** CBS bought 80% of Yankees and became first media outlet to own pro team
- **1966** Roberta Gibb became the first woman to run the Boston Marathon; the following year, Kathrine Switzer became the first woman to run it with a race number
- **1983** NBA salary cap instituted
- **1999** NHL Canadian teams petitioned federal government for financial aid
- **2002** NBA luxury tax system implemented
- **2005** Manchester United bought by American Malcolm Glazer
- **2010** United States Supreme Court rejected the NFL's request for broad antitrust law protection
- **2012** After strategic planning, the Sporting Goods Manufacturers Association (SGMA), founded in 1906, made various organizational adjustments, including changing name to the Sports & Fitness Industry Association (SFIA)
- **2013** First women's UFC bout held
- **2013** Valued at US$3.3 billion, Real Madrid named most valuable sport franchise by *Forbes*

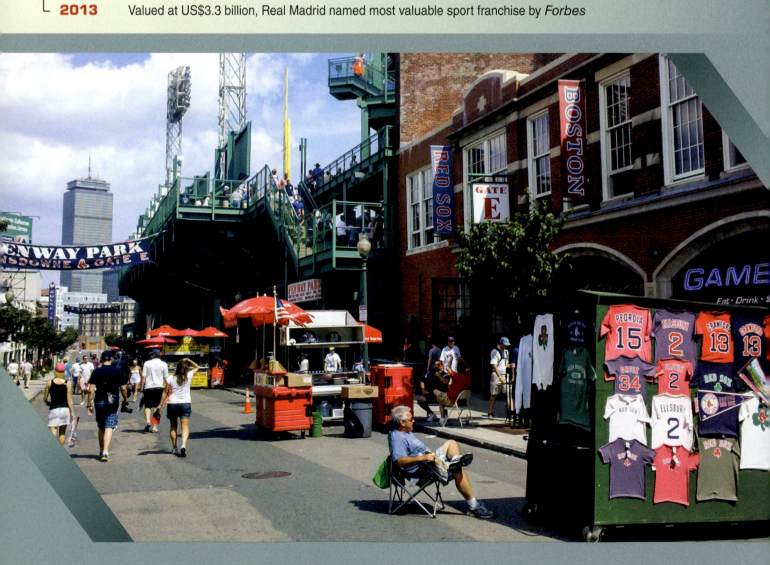

3

HISTORICAL ASPECTS OF THE SPORT BUSINESS INDUSTRY

Lawrence W. Fielding \ **Brenda G. Pitts** \ **Paul M. Pedersen**

LEARNING OBJECTIVES

> Identify the major business and market structures that allowed people to develop various historical sport businesses.

> Explain how the sport business industry evolved through the work of several influential people and companies.

> Discuss the influence of technology, marketing, and travel on the sport business industry.

> Understand the importance of communication (e.g., new and social media) to sport stakeholders and organizations.

> Identify the ways in which the sport business industry has been influenced by significant social, cultural, economic, and legal issues.

> Detail how an understanding of the history of sport businesses and market structures can help today's sport managers develop strategies for their businesses.

Key Terms

age of organization

Battle of the Sexes

decentralized
  organization

distribution

diversification

emotive advertising

market share

reason-why
  advertisements

vertical integration

watershed events

In 2013, the Real Madrid Football Club surpassed Manchester United not for the championship of the Union of European Football Associations (UEFA), but for the crown of most valuable franchise in the sport industry. According to *Forbes* (Badenhausen, 2013), Los Blancos (Real Madrid's nickname dating back to the first decade of the 20th century) is valued at US$3.3 billion, followed by fellow UEFA Champions League franchises Manchester United (US$3.165 billion) and Barcelona (US$2.6 billion). The New York Yankees (US$2.3 billion), Dallas Cowboys (US$2.1 billion), New England Patriots (US$1.635 billion), Los Angeles Dodgers (US$1.615 billion), Washington Redskins (US$1.6 billion), New York Giants (US$1.468 billion), and Arsenal Football Club (US$1.326 billion) round out the top 10 most valuable teams. Examples of other notable franchises are the Boston Red Sox in 11th place valued at US$1.312, Formula One's Ferrari in 21st place valued at US$1.15 billion, and the Chicago Cubs of MLB. Holding the 31st spot on the list of most valuable sports franchises, the Cubs—valued at US$1 billion—are one of the eight original teams of the National League, founded in 1876.

Albert Goodwill (A.G.) Spalding was a pitcher for the Chicago team in that inaugural NL season. That same year, Spalding opened a retail sporting goods store in Chicago a few doors down from the Chicago White Stockings (now known as the Chicago Cubs). His store, the Baseball and Sporting Goods Emporium (Spalding & Brothers), sold baseball products to professional baseball teams and department stores. As a famous pitcher and a player–coach with the White Stockings, Spalding intended to capitalize on his baseball reputation and coaching position. Ten months later, his company, Spalding & Brothers, Inc., reported a profit of US$1,083 ("Once Upon a Time," 1947). Today, Spalding, one of the top four sporting goods companies in the United States, manufactures all types of sporting goods equipment, from portable basketball backboards to innovative electronic referee whistles. The firm—which pioneered the development of brand recognition in sporting goods through athlete endorsements and continues such promotional activity today with sports superstar endorsers ranging from Olympians Misty May-Treanor and John Hyden to professional athletes Mark Ingram and Paul Pierce—is part of a sporting goods industry that sells more than US$59 billion worth of goods each year (National Sporting Goods Association, 2013).

Franchises such as Real Madrid, manufacturers such as Spalding, and athlete endorsers such as May-Treanor are part of a sport business industry that annually produces, advertises, and sells billions of dollars in sport products and services. This chapter provides brief historical sketches in the development of the sport business industry in the United States. Because of the size and diversity of the industry, this chapter will cover only selected historical developments. Besides being able to find information in hundreds of sport history books, you can read about some historical aspects of the sport business industry not covered in the following pages by referring to some of this textbook's other chapters that include various aspects of history (e.g., chapter 7 includes a discussion of the historical aspects of interscholastic athletics; in chapter 6, you can read about the historical developments of community and youth sport participation). You can also refer to the sidebar, "Rise of Management in Sport," which looks at some of the eras in sport management and the origination dates of a few select sport organizations and activities.

Historical Aspects of Commercialization in Sport

This section examines the developmental periods as well as the early commercialization models of the sport business industry. The developmental periods start with the later 19th century and involve issues of urban population growth, consumer demands, modernization, and entrepreneurship. This is followed by an overview of sport business industry commercialization models, especially those associated with the sporting goods segment of the sport industry.

Developments

Numerous commercialization models have surfaced throughout the developmental periods of the sport business industry. The decade of the 1870s is a good starting point for the discussion of these commercialization models because by this time, several developments were underway that made the emergence of the sport business industry possible. The urban population had grown large enough to support this new industry. At the same time, changes in response to the urban populace's demand for sport made sustainable commercialization of sport possible; the urban practice of buying sport entertainment had by this time become firmly entrenched. Various sports had become quite popular, making sport products and services viable for sustained commercial success (Rader, 2009). The process of modernizing sport, begun in harness racing, horse racing, and baseball before 1870, experienced exponential growth after 1870 (Adelman, 1986). The modernization process included the specialization of athletic skill, the development of effective organizational structures to present and control sport, the standardization and routinization of the sport product, and an educated citizenry ready to learn about and follow sport in newspapers and popular magazines. The development of the sport business industry was also aided during the last quarter of the 19th century by the growth of per capita income that left consumers with discretionary funds to spend on sport and entertainment.

Technology also influenced the beginnings of a viable sport business industry after 1870. It is difficult, for example, to imagine the development of the sport business industry without railroads to transport teams and distribute products or the telegraph to report scores and solidify business deals. By 1870, all major Eastern and Midwestern cities were interconnected by rail and telegraph. Technological developments in the newspaper press and printing industry also helped spread information about sport to an increasingly interested middle class.

Finally, by the decade of the 1870s, the United States had produced a group of entrepreneurs knowledgeable about the sport business industry and eager to exploit its opportunities. During the last quarter of the 19th century, new firms organized to exploit opportunities in the leisure experience market. Sport entrepreneurs concentrated on developing techniques and processes to produce products and experiences for a growing leisure market. They also invented and experimented with methods of promoting and selling sport.

Models

Numerous commercialization models in the sport business industry developed over the last few decades of the 19th century. Several early commercialization models were associated with the sporting goods segment of the sport business industry. Between 1880 and 1890, 79 companies began to produce sporting goods products. Some of these companies had formed much earlier, such as Draper & Maynard, which organized in 1841 to manufacture men's gloves. The company converted to sporting goods and began to manufacture hunting gloves and baseball gloves during the 1880s. Other companies, such as the Weed Sewing Machine Company, changed completely. In 1878, Weed began the production of bicycles. Still others, such as B.F. Goodrich and the Narragansett Machine Company, added the manufacture of sport equipment to their other product lines. B.F. Goodrich began the production of golf balls during the 1880s, and the Narragansett Machine Company added gymnastic equipment to its product line in 1885.

Rise of Management in Sport: Eras and Select Organizations*

Era	Year	Example organization*
Rise of Organized Sport (Before 1840)	776 BCE	Olympic Games
	1735	Royal Burgess Golfing Society of Edinburgh
	1754	Royal and Ancient Golf Club of St Andrews
Owner/Manager (1840-1870)	1845	Knickerbocker Base Ball Club of New York
	1860	The Open Championship (British Open)
Field Manager/Team President (1870-1900)	1876	National League of Professional Baseball Clubs (NL)
	1894	International Olympic Committee (IOC)
	1894	American Jockey Club
	1894	United States Golf Association (USGA)
	1895	American Bowling Congress (ABC)
Team President/Field Manager/ Business Manager (1900-1920)	1900	International Cycling Union
	1903	Tour de France
	1904	International Federation of Association Football (FIFA)
	1904	American Automobile Association (AAA)
	1906	National Collegiate Athletic Association (NCAA)
	1916	Women's International Bowling Congress (WIBC)
	1916	Professional Golfers' Association of America (PGA)
	1917	National Hockey League (NHL)
	1919	Triple Crown Horseracing
General Manager (1920-1950)	1920	National Football League (NFL)
	1921	World Boxing Association (WBA)
	1944	Sports Car Club of America (SSCA)
	1948	National Association for Stock Car Auto Racing (NASCAR)
	1950	Ladies Professional Golf Association (LPGA)
	1950	Formula One (F1)
Management Team (1950-1980)	1951	National Hot Rod Association (NHRA)
	1955	United States Auto Club (USAC)
	1958	Canadian Football League (CFL)
	1954	Rugby League World Cup
	1973	Women's Tennis Association (WTA)
	1977	United States Boxing Association (USBA)
	1978	Championship Auto Racing Teams (CART)
	1979	Entertainment and Sports Programming Network (ESPN)

Era	Year	Example organization*
Conglomerate/Subsidiary Team Management (1980-Present)	1986	International Floorball Federation
	1987	Arena Football League (AFL)
	1987	National Lacrosse League (NLL)
	1992	Premier League (EPL)
	1993	Ultimate Fighting Championship (UFC)
	1993	Major League Soccer (MLS)
	1995	X Games
	1996	Women's National Basketball Association (WNBA)
	1997	American National Rugby League
	1998	Women's Premier Soccer League (WPSL)
	2008	Indian Premier League (IPL)
	2013	FOX Sports 1
	2013	National Women's Soccer League

*Current name (various organizations had previous names or evolved/merged from other orgs).

ACTION

Go to the WSG and complete the four activities associated with "Rise of Management in Sport: Eras and Select Organizations."

Some companies began with the express objective of producing sport equipment. For example, the Nelson Johnson Manufacturing Company was established in Chicago in 1883 to produce tubular skates. The John Gloy Company was established two years later in Chicago to manufacture gymnastic equipment. Some firms were transplanted to U.S. soil to produce sporting goods. Two companies, Slazenger and Bancroft, arrived from England in the early 1880s to produce tennis rackets. Several other firms were established to distribute and sell sporting goods. These new firms competed directly with hardware stores, which began the distribution of sporting goods during the 1870s, and department stores and mail-order houses, which began to sell sporting goods during the 1880s. Each new entrant into the sport business industry helped to popularize sport, thus developing and expanding the market.

A.G. Spalding & Brothers is an excellent example of the growth and success of the sporting goods industry during the 1880s. The Spalding firm is one of the first and certainly the most successful of the early sporting goods firms. The diversification of Spalding during the last quarter of the 19th century provides insight into the development of the industry. Spalding's experiments in marketing goods and services provide evidence of the state of the art in the late 1800s and early 1900s. Spalding & Brothers was the first modern sport business enterprise, and many other companies copied its techniques, methods, and attitudes.

The success of Spalding & Brothers resulted from four interrelated developments within the firm: (1) vertical integration, (2) diversification, (3) the development of a modern management system, and (4) the promotional skills of A.G. Spalding himself. As noted in the chapter introduction, Spalding & Brothers began in 1876 as a retail store. By the next year, however, the firm had initiated its practice of **vertical integration** by wholesaling sporting goods from the same store. By 1884, Spalding had established wholesale centers in Chicago and New York to coordinate service for Eastern and

vertical integration—A company's expansion by moving forward or backward within an industry; expansion along a product or service value chain. The opposite of vertical integration is horizontal integration. Horizontal integration occurs when a company adds new products and services to its organizational structure.

Wimbledon: Managing a Quintessential English Brand

By Donna de Haan, England
University of Applied Sciences, Amsterdam, The Netherlands

Wimbledon is the home of the All England Lawn Tennis and Croquet Club, and for two weeks in June every year the club hosts a tournament that has become one of the most iconic hallmark events in the global sporting calendar and is synonymous with English summertime: at best, brief periods of sunshine interspersed with cloud cover and frequent rain stopping play! Wimbledon is a unique event that has managed to retain its quintessential Englishness, upholding long traditions of players only being allowed to wear white, players having to bow to a royal box, the use of traditional grass courts (the only tournament of the four Grand Slam tennis events to be played on grass courts), and the serving of strawberries and cream (where else in the world is a fruit so integral to the experience of sport?). From a sport business perspective Wimbledon offers a unique insight into brand management.

Britain's Andy Murray, a favorite amongst the 2013 Wimbledon crowd, defeats Taiwan's Lu Yen-Hsun on Court One in the second round of the tournament. Murray went on to win the tournament, ending Britain's 77-year wait for a men's Wimbledon champion.

The Club

Wimbledon was originally home to the All England Croquet Club, which was founded in 1868 and moved to the Worple Road ground, which was the original site of Wimbledon, in 1870. As with most organized sport in England during this time, croquet was seen as a sport only suitable for the British gentry and was associated with those of elite social status, played by families whose estates had extensive lawns or those wealthy enough to join croquet clubs. In 1877 the inaugural Lawn Tennis Championship was held in order to raise funds to repair the club's pony-drawn roller, which was used to maintain the lawns of the club, and remains as a monument in the grounds today, and the club changed its name to the All England Croquet and Lawn Tennis Club. Gradually, interest in croquet declined, and was superseded

Western markets. During the 1890s, Spalding added additional wholesale centers to cover the North and South. By the beginning of the 20th century, Spalding was producing sporting goods equipment in 15 plants in the United States and 5 plants overseas. Vertical integration meant that Spalding could benefit from economies of scale and scope, thus more effectively coordinating the manufacture and distribution of sporting goods. This approach directly influenced the sale of Spalding products in local stores. Vertical integration allowed the company to control resale prices.

by the popularity of tennis. By the end of 1882 the word *croquet* was removed from the club's title, only to be reinstated in 1899 after a brief resurgence of the sport. The club has retained the title of the All England Lawn Tennis and Croquet Club ever since.

The Championships

To some extent the branding of the championships is synonymous with the traditions of the club. Uniquely transcending the handicap of heritage, which could have formed barriers with regards to the development of the sport through the attraction of new fans, players, and supporters, Wimbledon has instead embraced tradition in a way that has cultivated a unique sport brand. Unlike most 21st century sporting events, Wimbledon promotes itself as a clean event devoid of sponsors, although it does have several key suppliers. For example, there were 14 official suppliers for the 2013 Championships. Therefore, when visiting the event or when watching coverage of the Championships, fans are exposed to very few brands. While spectators may notice the brand Slazenger on the balls, or Rolex on the clocks, the predominant brand is that of Wimbledon itself. Despite the fact that the Championships is simply a two-week single-sport event, the Wimbledon brand has grown into a cultural icon, inextricably linked to the traditions of an English 19th century sports club. The brand is British to the core yet international in its appeal.

Wimbledon organizers work hard to retain their clean branding strategy and often have to fend off ambush marketing attacks as companies offer commercially branded free goods such as sun hats, umbrellas, and water bottles to those waiting to enter the tournament. In order to deal with this, the protocol is to either temporarily confiscate those items which are believed to be part of an ambush marketing campaign, or refuse entry to spectators who are not prepared to surrender such items. Spectators are perfectly entitled to leave any such items at Left Luggage and collect them at the end of the day.

International Learning Activity #1

Watch footage of a recent Wimbledon tournament and try to identify as many brands as you can, then go to the official Wimbledon website (www.wimbledon.com), click on the link Official Suppliers and have a look at the list of key suppliers. Did you pick up on all of them in the footage?

International Learning Activity #2

As with the Olympic Games, in terms of marketing and sponsorship, Wimbledon is seen as a clean event. Through your own experience and through research, identify an event which could be seen as the opposite of this (a heavily sponsored event with numerous brands associated with it) and write a brief paper outlining the similarities and differences between the two events from a marketing perspective.

International Learning Activity #3

The Wimbledon tournament includes competitions for gentlemen's and boys' singles, doubles and wheelchair doubles, ladies' and girls' singles, and mixed doubles. Since 2007 Wimbledon has offered equal prize money to both the male and female champions. In 2012 the prize money for the gentlemen's and ladies' singles champion was £1,150,000, for the mixed doubles it was £92,000 (per pair) and for the wheelchair doubles it was £8,000 (per pair). With regards to equality in sport, what is the significance of the prize money as outlined above?

Diversification was another key to the company's success. Spalding began by selling baseball equipment. Its largest contract was with one of the baseball clubs in Chicago, the White Stockings. Within two years, Spalding & Brothers was selling fishing equipment, ice skates, and croquet equipment. During the 1880s, Spalding expanded into football, soccer, boxing, track and field, tennis, boats, canoes, and a variety of sport clothing, uniforms, and shoes. In the early 1890s, Spalding produced the first basketball for James Naismith (the inventor of the game of basketball) and helped to introduce

diversification—The act of adding new products to the company's product mix, thus diversifying the company's product offerings.

golf equipment into the U.S. market. Spalding employees were hired out to communities interested in constructing golf courses. By the mid-1890s, Spalding had become a leading contender in the burgeoning bicycle market, producing and marketing bicycles and bicycle accessories. Before the end of the 19th century, Spalding manufactured nearly everything that the sport enthusiast might want or require to improve sport performance or pleasure, diversifying its offerings to meet the growing demand for sport equipment by middle-class consumer participants.

Spalding & Brothers also influenced market demand for sport products in a variety of ways. The company's Library of Sports helped to expand interest and demand for sporting equipment by providing knowledge about and training in particular sports. Spalding used popular sport figures to discuss sports rules and to provide instruction in how to develop sports skills. Spalding advertisements promoted the benefits of sport for participants, helping to popularize the motives for active involvement. Spalding promotions also motivated active participation in more direct ways. The company donated trophies for tournaments, track meets, regattas, bicycle races, baseball contests, and league championships. Spalding staff members offered lessons and training for beginners as well as more advanced players and provided advice on the construction of facilities. Spalding employees taught local consumers about club organization and management of tournaments and contests. These services helped to expand local markets, brought goodwill to the company, and promoted Spalding products.

The purpose of Spalding & Brothers' promotions was not just to expand the market for sport equipment, but also to hawk its products. Hence, when Spalding received the contract to publish the *National League Official Rules,* the name of the rule book was changed to *Spalding's Official National League Rule Book,* and it advertised Spalding sporting goods equipment. When Spalding obtained the rights to produce the official baseball for the National League, the firm quickly announced to the baseball consumer that only Spalding could produce the real thing. Realizing the significance of being the official producer, Spalding tried to outdistance rivals by declaring its status as the official producer of footballs and soccer balls as well as golf, tennis, and track and field equipment. Spalding's pioneering use of professional and popular athletes as endorsers of the company's products resulted in the development of the unique aspect of brand recognition in sporting goods. Spalding's promotional slogans, such as "First make sure it's Spalding and then go buy," further established brand identity. Spalding helped to establish the power and popularity of reason-why advertising during the 1880s and negative advertising during the 1890s.

Other sporting goods entrepreneurs learned from Spalding & Brothers about **decentralized organization** and successful management techniques. Spalding was the first sporting goods firm to become a multiunit enterprise, a process that began almost immediately for the company. When A.G. Spalding purchased the Wilkins Manufacturing Company in 1878, he knew little about the manufacture of baseball bats, croquet mallets, ice skates, or baseball uniforms. To overcome this problem, Spalding retained Wilkins' staff and employees. He used the holdover employees from Wilkins to train his Spalding staff. When Wilkins sold his interest in the company three years later, Spalding had a trained administrative staff ready to take over and run the business. Spalding used the same approach when diversifying into the manufacturing of other sporting goods products. The company adopted the same approach in the development of its retail and wholesale distribution networks. Instead of searching for new employees to manage newly acquired or developed retail and wholesale outlets, Spalding hired managers away from the competition. In some instances, the acquired firm was allowed to keep its own name and to continue business as it had before the merger.

WEB

Go to the WSG and complete the web search activity that helps you compare a relatively new entrant in the sport business industry with one of the first modern sport business enterprises.

decentralized organization—The act of developing separate divisions, subcompanies, or departments that focus on certain tasks or products of the company and can be run autonomously.

A.G. Spalding was a pioneer in the sport business industry whose name can still be seen on sporting goods used today.

By 1894, Spalding had established two separate divisions, one in the East with headquarters in New York City and the other in the West with headquarters in Chicago. Each division was further subdivided into major activities: manufacturing, retail, and wholesale. These subdivisions were further subdivided into departments organized around sport categories (e.g., golf department, tennis department). Departments organized and administered their own functional activities such as accounting, purchasing, and advertising. To coordinate activities across divisions and departments, Spalding developed overarching functional departments. The marketing department, for example, coordinated advertising, product promotions, and markdown sales promotions nationwide. A top-level management department observed, standardized, and coordinated management techniques in each of Spalding's retail stores. This matrix organizational design proved highly effective and efficient. It gave Spalding a distinct advantage in management and proved to be an asset in the preparation of future top managers for the company. Both Julian Curtis and C.S. Lincoln, future presidents of the company, came through this system in the last decades of the 19th century.

Just as sporting goods entrepreneurs in the 1800s learned their trade from model companies such as Spalding & Brothers, entrepreneurs in the intercollegiate athletic system benefited from observing student-athletes and student organizers. Some of the best examples of these entrepreneurs can be found in the early years of intercollegiate football.

Historical Aspects of the Sport Market

watershed events—Events or developments in an industry that cause significant changes throughout the industry.

Over the years in the sport business industry, **watershed events** have caused massive changes in the way that business is conducted. These events have led to new ways of doing activities (e.g., manufacturing) and new strategies and techniques for achieving business success. Although several watershed events illustrate such changes in the sport business industry, the bicycle craze of the 1890s probably provides the most instructive historical example. In 1890, 27 firms manufactured bicycles, and sales competition was relatively low. The safety bicycle, invented in England in 1887, had not had much of an effect on the U.S. market. The pneumatic tire, invented in 1889, was just beginning to be widely used. Beginning developments in ancillary industries were under way. Dunlop, B.F. Goodrich, Goodyear, Penn Rubber Company, and a few others were beginning to manufacture bicycle tires. Miscellaneous bicycle parts such as bells, seats, and lamps were just beginning to make inroads into consumer markets. Top-grade bicycles sold for US$150. Medium-grade bicycles, introduced for the first time in 1890, sold for around US$100. Bicycles were sold primarily through hardware stores, although a few specialty shops and sporting goods stores sold bicycles. Distribution was targeted toward the larger cities in the East and Midwest. **Reason-why advertisements** attempting to convince potential customers about the importance of the bicycle for fun, health, fitness, and self-development were placed predominantly in trade magazines. Promotions included trade shows, instructional books, and essay and poster contests.

reason-why advertisements—Advertising that tells consumers why they should buy a certain product.

All of this changed during the 1890s. By 1898, 312 companies were manufacturing bicycles and bicycle parts. Rapid technological improvements in the safety of the bicycle between 1890 and 1895 led firms to emphasize the need for consumers to purchase a new model each year. When technologies faltered after 1895 and the bicycle remained virtually the same from year to year, bicycle manufacturers resorted to stylistic changes so that consumers would think that it was necessary to purchase a new model each year. Bicycle sales skyrocketed after 1893, but so did competition among an ever-expanding number of firms that produced bicycles. Competition spread quickly to ancillary industries as new entrants vied for **market share**. Bicycle sundries (e.g., seats, bells) also experienced a boom period between 1893 and 1898, prompting the emergence of new firms in the industry. Competition forced bicycle prices down. In 1898, top-grade bicycles could be bought for US$75, middle-grade bicycles for US$40, and low-grade bicycles for US$20. Secondhand bicycles sold for as little as US$3.

market share—Ranked position in a market determined by the percentage of a company's product sales in that market. For instance, if only three companies produce and sell basketball shoes, the company that sells the most shoes to the most consumers is considered to hold the number one market share in that product market.

The increase in competition forced bicycle firms to change the way that they did business. Beginning in 1893, firms stressed marketing and tried to meet customer needs in a variety of new ways. Firms emphasized brand equity and tried to establish entry barriers, protect against price cutting, and move bicycles through distribution channels more quickly. To accomplish these objectives, bicycle firms advertised extensively, moving into the top 10 industries in advertising volume during the 1890s. Systematic advertising became the rule as bicycle companies planned advertising campaigns across a 6- to 12-month period. Advertising agencies became the principal planners of advertising copy. Sophisticated reason-why advertising and **emotive advertising** became

emotive advertising—Advertising that attempts to appeal to consumers' emotions.

commonplace. Firms developed slogans and trademarks to help establish brand-name recognition. Advertisers trotted out the established themes of fun, health, fitness, and self-improvement that were accepted parts of sport participation ideology. They also created new advertising themes to place the bicycle in the mainstream of American social movements and perceived individual needs and wants.

During the last years of the 19th century, the bicycle became at once an engine of democracy, an escape from the bonds of technology and industrialization, a tool promoting freedom for women, a moral elevator and developer for youth, and an agent for training young men. Advertisers used popular middle-class magazines and newspapers to sell bicycles. Bicycle firms began to use sales records to test advertising effectiveness. Bicycle firms employed traveling salesmen, former athletes, and former bicycle racing stars to visit local shops and hawk company products. These same traveling salesmen taught locals how to organize bicycle clubs, hold and administer bicycle races, arrange and coordinate bicycle parades and bicycle cross-country runs, and establish and direct bicycle tour routes. Traveling salesmen also helped to establish training facilities. Some of these, such as Spalding's Bicycle Training School in New York City, became famous. Most were local affairs, however, unrenowned beyond city limits. These services increased participation and improved company sales. They were part of the firm's attempt to increase or protect market share.

Bicycle firms further promoted brand equity by organizing racing teams, which were quite popular and received extensive newspaper coverage during the 1890s. Bicycle firms used them to document the supposed superiority of their specific bicycle models. Firms sponsored bicycle races and bicycle tours, as well as other athletic events, in their attempts to bring their company names and products before the public eye. By the end of the decade, endorsements

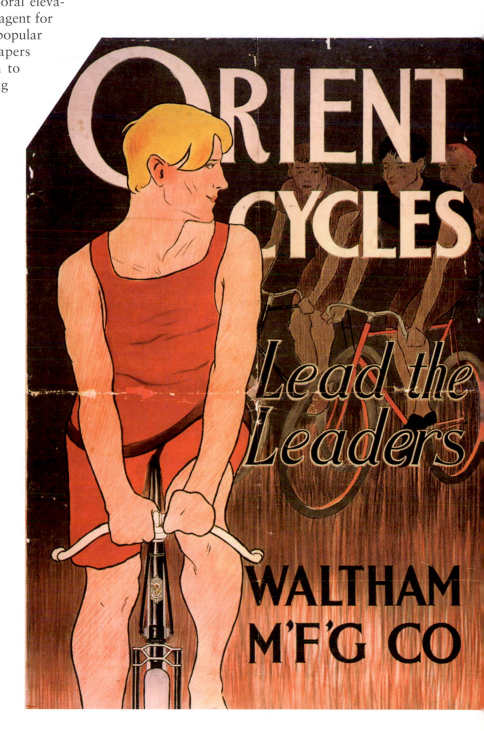

As bicycle technology changed, manufacturers needed to change how they advertised their product, as shown in this advertisement from the mid-1890s.

by prominent figures who either raced or rode bicycles became a common selling technique.

The bicycle craze motivated many firms to enter the industry (Fielding & Miller, 1998). New entrants were successful because the demand increased each year. Demand for bicycles and bicycle accessories amounted to a product value of US$2,568,326 in 1890. Perceptive observers were well aware that demand was running well ahead of supply between 1890 and 1895. Bicycle prices remained high through 1896, and 1895 was a banner year for profits. But as the decade progressed, supply caught up to and exceeded demand. By 1898, product value had increased to US$31,915,908, but profits had dropped, and perceptive observers knew as early as 1897 that supply exceeded demand. Falling profits after 1895 were the immediate result of the intensity of competition that increased exponentially each year from 1892 through 1898. After 1898, price wars occurred frequently, replacing more solidly based marketing and promotion efforts, as firms, alarmed at shrinking profits, sold below cost to unload surplus. Despite such efforts, end-of-the-year bicycle inventories increased every year after 1897, and profits declined each year after 1895. By 1897, net earnings were less than half what they had been in 1896. Bicycle prices dropped steadily after 1895. Production costs increased slightly, while selling costs skyrocketed. In the eyes of many 1899 observers, the bicycle industry was ready for a crash. The collapse happened gradually but was in full force by 1901. By 1909, only 94 companies remained in the bicycle industry.

The bicycle craze and the crash that followed it served (and still serve) as examples for members of the sport business industry. It influenced thinking about business and business strategy in three key areas. First, it raised questions about how firms coped with the uncertainty created by intense competition. Overproduction and price cutting became watchwords in the sport industry. The need to curb intense competition for the good of the industry became a precept. Second, the influence of the bicycle advertising message, promoting sport in general, convinced sport firms of the necessity of promoting all kinds of sport. Third, the bicycle craze influenced marketing strategy. Successful bicycle companies employed a variety of marketing techniques in an integrated marketing strategy. Marketing strategy emphasized brand equity. Marketing techniques integrated advertising, sponsorship, and endorsements and included organizing participation through the development of local clubs and local activities, the use of traveling salesmen, and promotion through trade shows. The sport marketing mavericks from the bicycle industry had demonstrated the importance of testing for advertising success, market segmentation and market research, and the use of specialized agencies to develop and implement advertising and promotions. Perhaps far more important, the bicycle craze taught manufacturers the necessity of helping local dealers with advertising through national campaigns linked to local advertising and promotional efforts.

Although the first decade of the 20th century was tough on the bicycle segment of the sport business industry, numerous sports were becoming more popular and witnessing tremendous growth (read the critical thinking section at the end of this chapter for more about the growth and popularity of sport at this time). The popularity and growth were particularly true in baseball, tennis, golf, football, basketball, fishing, target shooting, and roller skating. At this time, the number of firms that manufactured sport equipment increased, as did the number of sporting goods sold. The *Sporting Goods Dealer* (*SGD*), a trade journal that provided monthly marketing reports, reported that firms selling sporting goods had tripled during the decade ("Retail

Sporting Goods," 1907). The *SGD* periodically reported on what it called the "golf and tennis boom" during the decade. Equipment sales for these sports increased each year during the decade. Companies manufacturing or selling baseball equipment reported brisk business throughout the decade. Companies that made protective equipment for football, such as Rawlings Sporting Goods, reported accelerating sales each year. The roller-skating craze of 1906 through 1908, prompted by the building of outdoor skating facilities in several large cities, created a demand for roller skates. Equipment sales indicated that many people were participating in sport.

The growth of sport participation as evidenced by the increase in sporting goods sales during the decade was influenced by the drive to organize sport participation during the **age of organization** (the decades of the 1880s and 1890s). For example, YMCAs began to organize and market sport during this period, helping to create a youth sport market by the turn of the century. The United States Lawn Tennis Association (USLTA), organized in 1881, promoted tennis for both men and women by sponsoring national tournaments during the 1890s. The United States Golf Association (USGA) offered similar opportunities for men and women golfers. As Betts (1974) explained, the National Canoe Association (1880), National Croquet Association (1882), and United States Skating Association (1884) all promoted participation and organized sport opportunities for men and women before 1900. The American Bowling Congress (ABC), organized in 1895, promoted and helped organize bowling clubs for both men and women. Men's intercollegiate athletic organizations multiplied during the 1870s, 1880s, and 1890s, codifying rules of play and organizing and administering intercollegiate contests in such diverse sports as football, soccer, track and field, cross country, baseball, and rowing (Smith, 1988). Their efforts helped to popularize sport participation and prompted participation after college. Women's colleges offered sport opportunities during the 1880s and 1890s. Women learned the joys of participation in gymnastics, basketball, golf, tennis, field hockey, and track and field. When they left college, women took with them a desire to continue to participate in sport. In addition to offering opportunities for athletic participation, just over a half century later, institutions of higher education began offering women and men opportunities to study sport management.

age of organization—A period of time, the 1880s and 1890s, during which companies began to organize and market sport to specific markets, such as youth.

Segmentation

By the turn of the 20th century, perceptive observers within the sport business industry saw opportunities to make money by selling participation opportunities, charging spectators admission to watch others perform, and selling equipment for players to improve performance. The segmentation of sport marketing commenced as sport business leaders recognized that the market for sport participants, sport audiences, and sport equipment purchasers was segmented.

The largest of these segments was the growing number of White male middle-class sport enthusiasts in U.S. cities. This was the key segment for financial success. Middle-class consumers far outnumbered spenders in other segments in the market, and they had the money to buy participation opportunities, tickets to games and matches, and high-priced equipment to perform. Other market segments could be ignored, but firms that overlooked the needs and wants of middle-class men did so at their peril. Astute observers of the sport scene were also aware of the second important segment—the developing youth market. Periodically, readers of the *SGD* were informed about the necessity of catering to the American boy for two important reasons. First was the

Professional Profile: Donna Lopiano

Title: president and founder, Sports Management Resources

Education: PhD, University of Southern California

Currently, as the president and founder of Sports Management Resources, a consulting firm that specializes in helping sports organizations solve integrity, growth, and development challenges, Dr. Donna Lopiano has had a tremendous career as one of the nation's top leaders for girls and women in sport at every level. From 1992 to 2007, Dr. Lopiano was the CEO of the Women's Sports Foundation (WSF) in the United States, where she built an internationally respected education, research, and public policy organization. While in that highly respected position, Dr. Lopiano secured award funds of more than US$50 million in cash grants and educational materials, expanded the WSF endowment from US$1 million to US$4 million, worked as a driving force behind the award-winning GoGirlGo! educational curriculum that has reached more than 625,000 girls since 2001, repeatedly led national efforts to strengthen Title IX legislation and its enforcement, and served as a leading expert and national spokesperson on gender equity issues. She was recognized as being among the 100 most influential sports educators in America by the Institute for International Sport, the 100 most influential people in sports by *Sporting News*, and the 50 most influential people in college sports by *College Sports*.

Dr. Lopiano prefaced that highly influential period of time with a post as the director of intercollegiate athletics at the University of Texas at Austin, from 1975 to 1992. During that time, Dr. Lopiano developed what many believe to be the premiere women's athletics program of that time. While she was there, all eight sports were consistently ranked in the top 10 in Division I. She also grew the budget from a mere US$57,000 in 1975 to more than US$4 million with 34 endowed academic scholarships, reveled in 18 national championships in six different sports, and saw 51 individual sport national champion athletes, 57 Southwest Conference championships, and 395 All-American athletes, of whom dozens were Olympians and world champions. Further, 90% of the women athletes from her tenure exhausted their athletic eligibility and received a baccalaureate degree. Previously, from 1971 to 1975, she held the position of assistant director of athletics and head coach of men's and women's varsity teams at Brooklyn College of The City University of New York (CUNY), while at the same time serving as an assistant professor of physical education.

Dr. Donna Lopiano has been a major force in girls and women's athletics and sports in the United States and around the world. The following is a snapshot of Dr. Lopiano's current duties and insights as a leader in the sport industry.

ONE DAY

Go to the WSG and learn more about a typical day in the life for Donna Lopiano. See if she spends her working hours the way you think she does.

What have been the key moves, steps, or developments in your career, and how did you arrive at your current position?

After leaving the Women's Sports Foundation in 2007, I decided that I wanted to run my own business, since I had never done that before—I had always worked for someone else. I thought that I had enough experience and credentials to establish a consulting practice. I also wanted to make a move that could continue into my retirement years, continuing to work at a pace I could set, and to teach one course a semester as an adjunct professor, as I have done most of my life. I am currently teaching at Southern Connecticut State University.

What are your current responsibilities and objectives in your job?

At my business, Sports Management Resources, I help nonprofit sports organizations and educational institutions solve integrity, growth, and development challenges. I serve as an expert witness in Title IX and Title VII lawsuits. I am also a speaker—I still do 10 to 20 public lectures per year. As an adjunct professor, I teach sports management students. I have always loved to teach. I now finally have the control of my schedule (which you don't have when working for someone else) to do more volunteer work, so now I am (1) helping a nonprofit organization get started to address the issue of sexual abuse in sport, (2) serving as a member of a group of college faculty members pursuing NCAA and collegiate athletics reform, and (3) helping nonprofit women's funds produce strategic plans.

What do you enjoy most about your current job?

I enjoy the variety and magnitude of challenges I encounter in my SMR work, especially the two years I spent in the Middle East helping an educational sport organization and learning the nuances of a complex culture. I always enjoy teaching—changing the way people think, making them more questioning and thoughtful decision-makers conscious of moral obligations. Also, helping organizations that can't afford to hire me to do their good and important work, changing women's lives for the better, and pursuing a lifelong interest in orchestrating NCAA reform.

What do you consider the biggest future challenge to be in your job or industry?

The biggest challenge is working on structural and legislative reform of the NCAA to control costs, commercial pressures, and reduce misconduct.

fact that the participation rate for boys was up and that an increasing number of boys purchased sport equipment. Second, entrepreneurs realized that today's youth participant would become tomorrow's adult participant. Brand recognition and brand loyalty began in adolescence. White upper- and middle-class women constituted a third major segment in the sport market, particularly for specific sports. Marketers were interested in enticing women to participate and purchase golf and tennis equipment, fishing equipment, bicycles, and athletic wear.

Promoters experimented with methods of reaching the various market segments. One of the most successful experiments was store window advertising. Window displays, it was argued, attracted consumers who were not yet aware of what they needed. Window displays informed consumers about new developments in equipment technology, introduced new sport equipment, taught people about sport, and educated them about the benefits of participation. Window displays attracted attention and sold Americans on sport. Another way to attract attention and advertise a sport product was by using famous athletes as product endorsers.

Endorsement Advertising

Athlete endorsements today are commonplace, as evidenced by deals between Lionel Messi and adidas, Serena Williams and Nike, Candace Parker and Gatorade, Lewis Hamilton and Mercedes, Rafael Nadal and Richard Mille, Danica Patrick and Tissot, LeBron James and McDonald's, Aaron Rodgers and State Farm, Yani Tseng and Adams Golf, and Tiger Woods and a host of companies and products. Such endorsements commenced years ago. For example, in 1917, J.H. Hillerich signed George Herman Ruth, otherwise known as Babe Ruth, to a contract, allowing the sporting goods company Hillerich & Bradsby (H&B) to use Ruth's autograph on its Louisville Slugger bats. Two years later, the Babe Ruth–autographed Louisville Slugger was the leading seller for H&B, outdistancing the sale of any other bat sold in America. The contract with Ruth had cost H&B US$100 and a set of golf clubs—probably the most lucrative deal (for a company) in endorsement contract history.

Using an athlete's name to sell a product, particularly a sporting goods product, was not a novel idea in 1917. Hillerich had signed Honus Wagner, Hall of Fame shortstop for the Pittsburgh Pirates, to a similar deal back in 1905. Before 1910, Hillerich signed Ty Cobb and Napoleon Lajoie, both future Hall of Famers, to endorsement contracts. Wagner, Cobb, and Lajoie were chosen to endorse Louisville Slugger bats because they were expert hitters. They were excellent choices for a baseball bat company whose slogan was "the bat that gets more hits." Hillerich was using men who knew about bats, because they used them to make a living, to sell his product. This message, endorsed by the best hitters in professional baseball, sold bats. The connection was obvious.

Indeed, the connection between experts and professionals and consumers had been made before. As mentioned earlier in this chapter, Spalding employed the idea back in the 1880s to sell baseballs. In an attempt to increase sales, bicycle manufacturers took Spalding's endorsement ideas a step further during the 1890s. Spalding chose experts from an existing professional league. Bicycle manufacturers had to create the professional league first and then sign experts to endorsement contracts. Successful professional bicycle racers endorsed bicycles and bicycle tires for companies willing to pay top dollar for their allegiance. The arms and ammo industry applied similar techniques at the turn of the century to attract buyers. Experts told less-skilled participants what products to use to improve skill, accuracy, and overall performance. Advertisers used endorsements by experts to symbolize product quality and to establish brand-name recognition. Product endorsements by experts attracted consumers who wanted to improve performance in some way. Endorsements linked participant performance to product quality.

Hillerich & Bradsby (H&B) has used athlete endorsements for decades, including a deal that allowed the company to use Babe Ruth's autograph on its Louisville Slugger bats.

Hillerich & Bradsby—through Ruth, Cobb, Wagner, Lajoie, and others—took the matter a step further. Ruth was more than simply an expert who informed consumers about bats. Ruth was a personality, a hero, a human interest story, a style to be copied. He was an icon, symbolizing a certain type of individuality and style. Ruth was larger than life. Indeed, vocabulary was created to describe him (e.g., people spoke of "Ruthian feats" to communicate heroic accomplishments). Consumers purchased the Ruth-autographed bat not just to improve their batting average or hit more home runs. They wanted to be like the Babe. Consumers' desire to copy the Ruthian style and mode meant that Babe Ruth endorsements could be used to sell not only baseball bats but also candy bars and other products unrelated to athletics.

Competition and Cooperation

The First World War (1914–1918) increased the attractiveness of the sporting goods industry for companies seeking long-term profitability in at least three important ways. First, military training programs that introduced and trained soldiers in sport brought a new source of revenue to the industry. Second, the war had an immediate effect on the sale of sporting goods equipment at home because the demand for all kinds of athletic equipment increased. Third, the belief that sport would nurture and develop manly traits was further solidified by the war. Throughout the war, the military promoted sport as a means of training soldiers and developing better citizens. Local and state governments recognized the benefits of sport and the resultant demand for facilities. Similarly, physical education became a mandatory part of the educational curriculum, and school and college athletic programs flourished. The war functioned as a catalyst for the growth of sport during the 1920s.

Established members of the sporting goods industry were confident that demand would continue to increase after the war. This anticipation of postwar demand for sporting equipment had three important consequences. First, it led to improved manufacturing techniques. To meet the demand, manufacturers were determined to improve production facilities, increase manufacturing efficiency, and produce at full capacity. Second, several companies converted existing production capability to the manufacture of sporting goods after the war. Many of these new entrants were powerful competitors with significant capital and the ability to make large commitments to advertising and promotions to facilitate brand identity. These new entrants significantly increased the supply of sporting goods equipment. The third result was the expansion of the type of outlet in which sporting goods were distributed. The attractiveness of the sporting goods industry for investment and profit encouraged new entrants into the wholesale and retail trades. Sporting goods products began to be distributed through nontraditional outlets (e.g., drugstores, clothing stores). **Distribution** practices were further altered when many of the new jobbers and wholesalers eliminated the retailer and dealt directly with schools, industrial leagues, sport clubs, and community recreation associations. These new distributors frequently offered discounts, rebates, and gifts to generate goodwill and secure sales. Established manufacturers and traditional jobbing houses turned to direct sales to remain competitive. Improvements in manufacturing techniques meant that the supply of sporting goods products increased significantly. The proliferation of sporting goods distribution outlets meant that sporting goods were more readily available to consumers. Increased supply and improved distribution resulted in both lower prices for consumers and greater competition among industry members.

Because of the new entrants into the marketplace, leaders in the sporting goods industry soon realized that the industry had become highly competitive and consequently unprofitable. The supply of sporting goods products exceeded demand as early as 1925, increasing the intensity of competition as companies vied for consumer dollars. The cost of doing business increased, and profits plummeted. To survive, manufacturers resorted to ruinous competitive practices such as price cutting. But as the industry moved into the 1930s, sporting goods leaders realized that cooperative efforts were needed to curb competition. Presidents and vice presidents of the large successful firms started the movement for cooperation, the primary vehicle for which was trade associations. Cutthroat competition decreased as industry leaders shared customer credit information, discussed solutions to common problems, talked about industry profitability, exchanged information about demand, and in general cooperated among themselves. These practices increased the individual and collective knowledge about the sporting goods industry. Competitors gained better understanding about the effects of competitive strategy on industry members and overall profitability. Cooperative efforts were used to increase market size and to gain better understanding of the industry.

The abundance of sporting goods products and distribution outlets during the 1920s meant that sport equipment was widely available to a public whose interest in sport was growing steadily. As detailed by Lewis (1973), public policies begun during the First World War and expanded during the 1920s helped to influence this growing demand in

distribution—The manner in which a sport industry product or service moves from the producer or manufacturer to the consumer; distribution channels and outlets are the individual people (e.g., jobbers, dealers, salespeople, brokers) and companies (e.g., wholesalers, retailers) involved in the process of getting the product to the end user (O'Reilly & Seguin, 2009).

Roone Arledge, Televised Sport, and Entertainment

Finding sports on television at any time of the day is not difficult to do with the rise of televised sport programming overall and the proliferation of sport-focused television networks (Pac-12 Network, NBC Sports Network, Longhorn Network, Fox Sports 1, Golf Channel, and so on). The seemingly ubiquitous sport broadcast content available today is a result of a relationship between television and sport that commenced decades ago. Along with the increases in sporting goods, distribution outlets, and participation opportunities in the first half of the 20th century came the arrival of televised sport, starting with a college baseball game in the late 1930s, a variety of sport broadcasts (e.g., Gillette Cavalcade of Sports) in the 1940s, and popular niche broadcasts such as roller derby and wrestling in the 1950s.

In 1960, Roone Arledge proposed to ABC executives a new plan for covering football games. The application of his plan revolutionized how sports were televised during the remainder of the 20th century. Arledge wanted to bring the TV viewer to the game, to get the audiences emotionally involved. He wanted viewers at home to experience the game as though they were at the stadium. Even if they were not football fans, reasoned Arledge, they could still enjoy the game. Bringing the consumer to the game required developing a new method for covering the game. Arledge increased the number of cameras from 3 to 9 and then to 12 or more. He introduced instant replay. To bring the action up close and personal, he used handheld and isolated cameras. Split screens and other technical devices helped the viewer experience the atmosphere of the game. To help duplicate the live atmosphere, Arledge used directional and remote microphones to capture the sounds of the game and crowd.

Arledge believed that televised sport was in the commercial entertainment business. Television programs survived only if they could draw higher ratings, support more advertising dollars, and generate greater corporate profits. The same was true for televised sport. This requirement meant that televised games had to attract a variety of viewers. Arledge realized that the casual viewer and the sometimes fan were far more important than the avid football consumer. The reason was simple: There were more of them. These folks required more than just sport to be entertained. Arledge believed that the participants in a sport contest were the essence of entertainment. People, he thought, watched sports to be entertained by people performing. Sport viewing was experiential. Therefore, Arledge sought to extend the entertainment value of sport beyond the game itself.

Arledge's lessons on improving sport entertainment were copied by others. For instance, the 1970s ushered in the age of the mascot. Later in that decade, the success of the Dallas Cowboys cheerleaders prompted other teams to add cheerleaders to extend the entertainment value of the game. Additional ways that sport was tailored to appeal to more followers included exploding scoreboards, artificial grass, extended schedules and playoff systems, and rule changes to make games more action packed and exciting (Rader, 1984; Roberts & Olsen, 1989).

several ways. During the war, Army and Navy officials used sport for both training and recreation, giving thousands of young men opportunities to play and watch sport. Their extensive use of sport did much to popularize sport and to legitimize sport programs as part of public policy. As part of the war effort, the War Camp Community Service began public recreation programs in hundreds of communities. After the war, local communities continued these programs, providing opportunities for participation at public expense. Between 1920 and 1930, the number of public recreation departments more than doubled. Community expenditures on public recreation increased sixfold during the 1920s. The notion that the provision of facilities and programs was public responsibility became firmly entrenched in the public mind. The war effort also encouraged the inclusion of sport instruction and the development of athletics programs in high schools and colleges throughout the nation. From the 1920s through the 1940s, states passed laws requiring physical education. By 1948, only English classes had a higher enrollment in the public school system than physical education classes.

Increased Participation and Spectatorship

World War II severely curbed the production of sporting equipment, especially goods made from rubber, leather, wood, cotton, and petroleum. Many sporting goods companies attempted to stockpile raw materials. This action proved fruitless because government policy curbed production of sport equipment regardless of material supplies. Rationing was the rule of civilian life during this time. Many sporting and

Brand Equity and Intercollegiate Athletics: Updating the Formula for Success

The University of Notre Dame football team came into prominence in 1913 after an upset win over the heavily favored Army. A century later, the Fighting Irish were seeking their 12th title only to be routed by the University of Alabama in the 2013 BCS National Championship Game. While they lost to the Crimson Tide in 2013, the upset victory over the Army a century earlier commenced their domination of sports headlines in the ensuing years. Between 1918 and 1930, Notre Dame football grew from an informal Saturday afternoon game to a national phenomenon. Knute Rockne, the head coach during this period, developed and applied a formula for the commercial success of big-time intercollegiate football. Because of his actions, Notre Dame football became a highly recognizable and distinguished name that consumers associated with value. Therefore, his formula produced brand equity.

The four dimensions of brand equity are brand loyalty, brand awareness, perceived quality, and brand associations or brand image (Aaker, 1991). Rockne created brand loyalty by developing a following. This loyalty was brought about by the creation of a winning tradition, the arrival of star players who both represented and drew on the school's diverse customer base, and the establishment of an athletic culture at the university.

Rockne's formula included brand awareness, which, besides the three developments listed earlier, included such novel actions as the hiring of Archie Ward to be a student press assistant (Littlewood, 1990). Ward received tuition in return for promoting Rockne, Notre Dame football, and the team's stars.

Following Ward, Francis Wallace and George Strickler had the same promotional assignments.

The development of perceived quality was also part of Rockne's formula. Besides the promotional work of the student press agents, Rockne understood the importance of self-promotion. His hiring of Christy Walsh, the first sport agent, helped to establish a perception of quality for Rockne and his program. For instance, Walsh got Rockne to participate in various activities (e.g., after-dinner speech circuit, radio broadcasts, movie contracts, endorsements) that helped develop his image as an intelligent, ethical, and entrepreneurial football coach.

The development of brand associations was the final part of Rockne's formula. During the 1920s, Notre Dame football developed several linkages in consumer minds. The players became the Fighting Irish. The Fighting Irish became synonymous with football excellence as established by a winning tradition. Notre Dame football also became synonymous with Knute Rockne, the charismatic and technically brilliant leader of the Fighting Irish. Although representing Catholics, Notre Dame football also stood for the acceptance of diversity (the new melting pot).

Overall, the creation of brand equity meant that the Fighting Irish became associated with a set of values in the minds of consumers. Those values translated into a solid nationwide fan base that prompted financial success for Notre Dame football (Oriard, 2001; Sperber, 1993; Watterson, 2000).

leisure activities and events were suspended, terminated, or affected in other ways. The prestigious Wimbledon championships were suspended from 1940 through 1945. Many male professional athletes were called into military duty, leaving many men's sports with less-skilled players. College and high school sport programs were cut back or eliminated altogether.

Other forms of amateur sports, however, flourished during the war. In both military life and civilian life, sport participation became a matter of policy. Inductees into the army and the navy had to be trained. Sport, including highly competitive athletic events, became part of this training as a matter of military policy. The military tried to coerce every soldier and every sailor into the sporting life. Military leaders advised civilian authorities to adopt similar policies as part of the war effort. When the war ended in 1945, hundreds of thousands of men and women returned home to the United States. Both the military policy to use sport as part of training and as a recreational activity and the corporate business policies to organize civilian sport participants helped create sport enthusiasts. Postwar Americans went looking for entertainment and leisure as sport participants and as spectators. The sport industry responded to the desires of these new sport enthusiasts in other ways. Because of the growing popularity of men's football, a new professional football league began in 1946 and survived for three seasons before merging with the NFL for the 1950 season. In 1949, the men's Basketball Association of America merged with the National Basketball League to become the NBA. The end of the decade was a boom period for professional sports.

The late 1940s saw the modern color barrier broken in professional sport when—as can be seen in the widely acclaimed 2013 movie *42*—Jackie Robinson signed with the Brooklyn Dodgers in 1945. Robinson was followed by Larry Doby, who signed with Cleveland in 1946. Both would play in the major leagues during the 1947 season. In 1946, professional football saw Marion Motley and Bill Willis join the Cleveland Browns and Kenny Washington and Woody Strode play for the Los Angeles Rams. In 1949, Indiana University All-American George Taliaferro became the first African American drafted by the NFL. The following year, professional basketball integrated when Chuck Cooper joined the Celtics and Sweetwater Clifton left the Harlem Globetrotters for the New York Knicks. Several factors influenced the integration process. It was, at least in part, a response to the pressure for integration in the military during World War II. Part of it was also a question of ethics and values and of changing attitudes. Part of it was economics. African Americans constituted a large, untapped, and inexpensive talent pool. During the decades that followed, team owners became aware that African American talent often meant the difference between financial success and failure, particularly in the 1950s and 1960s as a new breed of owners took control of professional sports. Bill Veeck, an innovator who introduced new techniques to sport managers, was one of the best examples of this new breed of owners and promoters.

The military policy of coercing people into the sporting life was directed toward all soldiers and sailors. The military developed sport programs to meet the needs of women. World War II brought substantial numbers of women into the army, navy, and coast guard. Athletic competition became part of the training program for women, which copied the men's program. Women were encouraged to participate in competitive athletics programs in volleyball, archery, basketball, bowling, tennis, table tennis, swimming, badminton, and softball. Women's military teams also took on civilian teams.

ACTION

Go to the WSG and complete the fifth Learning in Action activity, which will test how well you know your history of the sport business industry.

Women had been competing in industrial leagues since World War I. The 1930s had witnessed a great deal of expansion in women's industrial leagues, particularly softball leagues. World War II brought more women into more sports. Society's attitude toward the participation of women in sports began to change. An example is the women's professional baseball league. To address the sport entertainment desires of the American public, the All-American Girls Professional Baseball League (AAGPBL) was begun. Made famous by the movie *A League of Their Own*, the AAGPBL enjoyed success from 1943 to 1954. The league was the idea of Philip K. Wrigley, owner of the Wrigley chewing gum company and the Chicago Cubs, who thought that men's baseball would have to stop during the war. Although the AAGPBL is the most well-known women's baseball league, the historical record shows that women played baseball long before then—in colleges in 1866 and on professional women's teams in 1867. At its peak in 1948, 10 teams played in the AAGPBL, and more than one million fans watched them play. The AAGPBL, along with other societal changes in the United States, helped bring about the beginning of a positive change in thinking toward women in sport.

Over the succeeding decades, sport participation rates for women grew dramatically. For example, between 1968 and 1980, high school girls' sport participation increased by more than 500%. Participation by women collegians increased nearly as much. The feminist movement of the late 1960s and 1970s prompted tremendous growth in the women's market for sport and sport products. The fitness boom of the 1970s and 1980s also influenced women's interest. Increased participation by women was also a matter of public policy (i.e., Title IX), and the increased opportunities translated into increased sales. Sporting goods manufacturers, distributors, and retailers strove to do their bit for public policy by selling sport shoes, sport equipment, and sport apparel and by promoting participation opportunities for women athletes.

Women's sports grew exponentially, becoming more popular than ever at every level and every age. The new notion of the female athlete changed before our eyes. The 1960s and 1970s had provided an all-out assault on sexism and the traditional notions and limitations of genderized and sexualized roles. Now, with legislation and the women's rights movement making progress, women in sport charged ahead. But the rights of women in sport would be resisted by societal strongholds that clung to old traditions. Not until the 1990s would women in sport in the United States become comfortable with their muscularity and approach equality in pay to men. Along the way, it took Title IX, several lawsuits, and a series of events to reach this point (please read this chapter's professional profile on Dr. Donna Lopiano for some insight into the history and influence one woman in particular has had on intercollegiate athletics and girls and women's sport overall). The 1973 Billie Jean King defeat of Bobby Riggs in tennis, dubbed the **Battle of the Sexes**, helped. Five years later, the Women's Professional Basketball League (WBL) made history by becoming the first such professional league. The league lasted three years, folded, started again and went another three years, folded, and then repeated this sequence a few more times. Today, the WNBA, WTA, and other women's professional sports leagues and intercollegiate athletics programs are so popular that they have commercial value and major corporate support. They have become mainstays in the sport business industry. Overall, the 1990s (known as the decade of the woman athlete) through well into the second decade of the 21st

Battle of the Sexes— A tennis match in 1973 between Billie Jean King and Bobby Riggs. King's much-heralded victory over Riggs represented a key triumph over sexism and provided a significant historical lesson on exceeding sexist expectations and assumptions (Nelson, 1994).

century have witnessed increased interest in women's sports and increased participation by women in athletic competitions, ranging from mixed martial arts, extreme sports, and boxing to football, soccer, and basketball. The sport industry—including media outlets such as ESPN with its *Nine for IX* documentary series (table 3.1)—celebrated the 40th anniversary of Title IX in 2013.

Critical Thinking in the History of the Sport Business Industry

PORTFOLIO

Complete the critical thinking portfolio activity in the WSG, consulting as needed the "Critical Thinking Questions" sidebar in chapter 1.

This critical thinking section relates to the section "Historical Aspects of the Sport Market" in this chapter. Reflecting on the business of sport during the first decade of the 20th century, P.R. Robinson, president of the New York Sporting Goods Company, concluded that it had been a good decade. Robinson noted tremendous growth in the popularity of sport, particularly in baseball, tennis, golf, football, basketball, fishing, target shooting, and roller skating. Even the business panic of 1907, remarked Robinson, had not hurt the sport industry. "When general trade is down," he said, "people have more time to devote to sports." Looking to the future, Robinson saw only good times for the sport business industry. As times became better, he concluded, the demand for high-priced sporting equipment would increase because people would want to perform more effectively (Robinson, 1909).

Table 3.1   **Documentaries in ESPN's *Nine for IX***

Documentary	Director(s)	Topic
Venus VS.	Ava DuVernay	Venus Williams and equal prize money
Pat XO	Lisa Lax and Nancy Stern Winters	NCAA Division I winningest coach Pat Summitt
Let Them Wear Towels	Annie Sundberg and Ricki Stern	Equal access for female sports journalists
No Limits	Alison Ellwood	Competitive free diver Audrey Mestre
Swoopes	Hannah Storm	College, Olympic, and pro champion Sheryl Swoopes
The Diplomat	Jennifer Arnold and Senain Kheshgi	Figure skater Katarina Witt and the Cold War
Runner	Shola Lynch	Mary Decker's running exploits, pursuits, and challenges
The 99ers	Erin Leyden	Legacy of 1999 World Cup win by U.S. women's soccer team
Branded	Heidi Ewing and Rachel Grady	Play and image double standard faced by women in sports

Adapted from *Nine for IX,* 2013, espnW. Available: http://espn.go.com/espnw/w-in-action/nine-for-ix/

Social Media and Historical Aspects of the Sport Business Industry

Young sport management readers may not remember a time when social media did not have a seemingly ubiquitous influence on the sport industry. However, a search of the leading trade magazines for sport industry practitioners will reveal the entrance of various social media platforms into the field's dialogue. While an online keyword search of social media mentions in the *Street & Smith's SportsBusiness Journal* is not going to reveal every article published, the results of the searches on the publication's website do provide a glimpse into the recent rise of social media and its influence on the sport industry. For instance, Myspace was first mentioned in November of 2005, when a columnist reported in passing "a recent Internet acquisition binge" by News Corp., noting that "these are boom times for owners of online media assets" (Bernstein, 2005, para. 10). Since that first mention back in 2005, there have been more than 95 subsequent *SBJ* entries (e.g., articles) that mentioned the website. The following year, 2006, included the first *SBJ* mentions of Facebook and YouTube. Facebook was mentioned in January of 2006 (more than 550 subsequent articles that mentioned Facebook were present at the last check) when a leading marketer provided an opinion column, noting that "Social networking sites already bind our kids together. . . MySpace.com and Facebook.com are driving a new dot-com boom, which could offer disciplined marketers an avenue to speak to the elusive teen and young adult segment. Look for these sites to get into the advertising and sponsorship game. . . . On a blogging-related note: This new citizen journalism is added incentive for teams and athletes to stay clean or face the consequence of public embarrassment, and accountability is good for everyone" (Lynch, 2006, para. 2). Two months after this came the first *SBJ* mention of YouTube. This social media site (which has since been mentioned in more than 250 *SBJ* entries), was highlighted in a piece titled "What lies ahead on the sport media landscape." The article noted that consumers, who now have "more choices than ever when it comes to new media platforms" ("Predictions," 2006, para. 1) also have access to online video-sharing websites.

While more than 890 *SBJ* entries (e.g., articles) mention Twitter, the first time the journal mentioned the social media platform was in September of 2008 in the last sentence of a writer's sponsorship article (Smith, 2008). The staff writer was examining the exposure, merchandise sales, and online traffic success experienced by M&M's with the candy's sponsorship of NASCAR driver Kyle Busch. The driver was having success on the track, and one way that M&M's was trying to capitalize on the sponsorship was through Twitter. Only two months after their first mention of Twitter, *SBJ* mentioned the social networking site LinkedIn for the first time. While the site has been mentioned only 28 times overall by *SBJ*, its first mention was in an article about social networking and how this site "caters to job recruiters and professionals looking to network with colleagues" (Donohue, 2008, para. 5). Another social media site is Pinterest. This social media photo website has only been mentioned a total of 16 times on *SBJ*, with the first mention in February of 2012 when the author—Peter Stringer, the director of interactive media for the NBA's Boston Celtics—labeled it "the latest craze!" Stringer noted that Pinterest "and any other digital marketing platform a team controls should be driving fans where they belong: into a team's database" (Stringer, 2012, para. 13). As you can see from these select searches, social media platforms have only been a part of sport industry dialogue in the last 5 to 10 years. Despite this short and early history, social media has quickly become a powerful and seemingly ubiquitous influence.

Ethics in the History of the Sport Business Industry

Beginning in 1927, Frank Bradsby, president of the Chamber of Commerce of Sporting Goods Manufacturers (later renamed the Sporting Goods Manufacturers Association [SGMA] and then renamed the Sports & Fitness Industry Association [SFIA]), led a concerted effort to develop a code of ethics for sporting goods manufacturers. Bradsby was prompted to lead the fight for a code of ethics by several industry-wide trade practices that hurt the image of the industry and curbed profits. Key among these unethical practices were price cutting, selling below cost, tying contracts, giving hidden rebates or discounts to secure sales, commercial bribery, piracy of trademarks,

PORTFOLIO

Complete the ethical issues portfolio activity in the WSG, consulting as needed the "Guidelines for Making Ethical Decisions" sidebar in chapter 1.

brand names, and athletic endorsements, piracy of the term *official*, misbranding of products relative to grade, quality, and guarantees, and interference with existing contracts. Through the auspices of the SGMA, Bradsby was able to enlist several sporting goods industry leaders (including Julian Curtis of Spalding Brothers; H.B. Canby of Crawford, McGregor & Canby; E. Goldsmith of Goldsmith Sons; and L.B. Icely of Wilson Sporting Goods). Between 1927 and 1930, leaders in the SGMA established a set of ethical trade practices for sporting goods manufacturers. These practices were endorsed by the entire membership of the SGMA at the industry-wide meeting in 1930 in Sulfur Spring, Virginia.

Summary

This chapter provided sketches of some of the significant developments that took place starting in the 19th century and described the foundation for the development of the sport business industry in the United States. The key events, innovations, and entrepreneurs presented here are only a few of the myriad activities and people who have played some crucial roles in the development and history of sport management. The sketches provided in this chapter are useful because history offers many lessons relevant to your studies and career in the sport business industry.

Review Questions

1. What are some of the ways that the history of the sport business industry can be helpful to a sport management executive today?

2. How has commercialization affected the sport industry over the years, and how is it currently influencing the industry?

3. What are some events that have significantly influenced and changed the sport industry?

4. How have advances in manufacturing processes influenced the growth of the sport industry?

5. What are some advances in technology and communication (e.g., social media) that have influenced the development of the sport industry?

6. What factors have affected the growth and development of participatory, spectator, and professional sports for girls and women?

7. How have historical developments related to endorsement and sponsorship marketing affected the sport industry?

References

Aaker, D.A. (1991). *Managing brand equity.* New York, NY: Free Press.

Adelman, M.L. (1986). *A sporting time: New York City and the rise of modern athletics, 1820–70.* Urbana, IL: University of Illinois Press.

Badenhausen, K. (2013, July 15). Real Madrid tops the world's most valuable sports teams. *Forbes.* Retrieved from www.forbes.com/sites/kurtbadenhausen/2013/07/15/real-madrid-tops-the-worlds-most-valuable-sports-teams

Bernstein, A. (2005, November 7). CBS sees big possibilities for CSTV. *Street & Smith's SportsBusiness Journal.* Retrieved from www.sportsbusinessdaily.com/Journal/Issues/2005/11/20051107/Media/CBS-Sees-Big-Possibilities-For-CSTV.aspx?hl=myspace&sc=1

Betts, J.R. (1974). *America's sporting heritage 1850–1950.* Reading, MA: Addison-Wesley.

Donohue, S. (2008, November 17). How it works: Primer for social networking. *Street & Smith's SportsBusiness Journal.* Retrieved from www.sportsbusinessdaily.com/Journal/Issues/2008/11/20081117/SBJ-In-Depth/How-It-Works-Primer-For-Social-Networking.aspx?hl=linkedin&sc=1

Fielding, L.W., & Miller, L.K. (1998). The ABC trust: A chapter in the history of capitalism in the sporting goods industry. *Sport History Review, 29*(1), 44–58.

Lewis, G. (1973). World War I and the emergence of sport for the masses. *Maryland Historian, 4,* 109–122.

Littlewood, T.B. (1990). *Arch: A promoter, not a poet: The story of Arch Ward.* Ames, IA: Iowa State University Press.

Logan, L. (2013, April 3). Inside the second running boom. *Competitor.com.* Retrieved from http://espn.go.com/sports/endurance/story/_/id/8930050/endurance-sports-women-running-explosion

Lynch, M. (2006, January 9). My crystal ball shows trends to watch in '06. *Street & Smith's SportsBusiness Journal.* Retrieved from www.sportsbusinessdaily.com/Journal/Issues/2006/01/20060109/Opinion/My-Crystal-Ball-Shows-Trends-To-Watch-In-06.aspx?hl=facebook&sc=1

National Sporting Goods Association. (2013, June 26). *Sporting goods market report shows 7% increase in sales during 2012.* Mount Prospect, IL: Author.

Nelson, M.B. (1994). *The stronger women get, the more men love football: Sexism and the American culture of sports.* New York, NY: Harcourt Brace.

Nine for IX. (2013). *espnW.* Retrieved from http://espn.go.com/espnw/w-in-action/nine-for-ix

Once upon a time: Turning back the pages of Spalding's first ledger. (1947). *Sporting Goods Dealer, 96,* 128–130.

O'Reilly, N., & Seguin, B. (2009). *Sport marketing: A Canadian perspective.* Toronto, Ontario, Canada: Nelson.

Oriard, M. (2001). *King football: Sport & spectacles in the golden age of radio & newsreels, movies & magazines, the weekly & the daily press.* Chapel Hill, NC: University of North Carolina Press.

Predictions: What lies ahead on the sports media landscape. (2006, March 27). *Street & Smith's SportsBusiness Journal.* Retrieved from www.sportsbusinessdaily.com/Journal/Issues/2006/03/20060327/SBJ-In-Depth/Predictions-What-Lies-Ahead-On-The-Sports-Media-Landscape.aspx?hl=youtube&sc=1

Rader, B.G. (1984). *In its own image: How television has transformed sports.* New York, NY: Free Press.

Rader, B.G. (2009). *American sports: From the age of folk games to the age of televised sports* (6th ed.). Upper Saddle River, NJ: Prentice Hall.

Retail Sporting Goods Dealers' Association. (1907). *Sporting Goods Dealer, 17,* 14.

Roberts, R., & Olsen, J. (1989). *Winning is the only thing: Sports in America since 1945.* Baltimore, MD: Johns Hopkins University Press.

Robinson, P.R. (1909, January). Trade prospects for 1909. *Sporting Goods Dealer, 20,* 31–32.

Smith, M. (2008, September 8). M&M's in sweet grove with Busch. *Street & Smith's SportsBusiness Journal.* Retrieved from www.sportsbusinessdaily.com/Journal/Issues/2008/09/20080908/This-Weeks-News/Mms-In-Sweet-Groove-With-Busch.aspx?hl=twitter&sc=1

Smith, R.A. (1988). *Sports & freedom: The rise of college athletics.* New York, NY: Oxford University Press.

Sperber, M. (1993). *Shake down the thunder: The creation of Notre Dame football.* New York, NY: Henry Holt.

Stringer, P. (2012, February 27). Moving beyond like: How one team monetized Facebook base. *Street & Smith's SportsBusiness Journal.* Retrieved from www.sportsbusinessdaily.com/Journal/Issues/2012/02/27/Opinion/Peter-Stringer.aspx?hl=pinterest&sc=1

Watterson, J.S. (2000). *College football: History, spectacle, controversy.* Baltimore, MD: Johns Hopkins University Press.

HISTORICAL MOMENTS

- **1910** Classical management school of thought emerged
- **1911** Taylor's *Principles of Scientific Management* presented productivity improvement strategies
- **1917** *Administration Industrielle et Générale* by Fayol proposed 14 principles of management
- **1920s** Follett promoted power sharing, employee participation, and negotiations in organizations
- **1938** Barnard's *Functions of the Executive* focused on roles of executives in organizations
- **1940s** Systems theory proposed cross-disciplinary problem solving (e.g., mathematics, statistics, engineering)
- **1950s** Total quality management movement, focused on quality assurances, emerged
- **1964** Big Ten Conference on Body-of-Knowledge Project implemented
- **1975** *Administrative Theory and Practice in Physical Education and Athletics* published by Zeigler and Spaeth
- **1980** "Sport Management: The Nature and Utility of the Concept" by Mullin, published in *Arena Review*, discussed sport management as a unique profession
- **1982** Peters and Waterman published groundbreaking management book *In Search of Excellence*
- **1984** *Sport Management Curricula: The Business and Education Nexus* edited by Zanger and Parks
- **1990** *The Fifth Discipline* by Senge detailed the concept of the *learning organization*, which focused on gaining competitive advantage through training organization members to think critically and creatively
- **1997** Slack published *Understanding Sport Organizations: The Application of Organization Theory*
- **2001** *Good to Great: Why Some Companies Make the Leap . . . and Others Don't*, by Collins, examined companies that achieved a sustained competitive advantage
- **2008** In *On Competition*, Porter discussed value creation and sustainability and compiled his thinking on strategy and management
- **2009** Chelladurai released third edition of *Managing Organizations for Sport and Physical Activity*
- **2013** Memphis Grizzlies, Green Bay Packers, Pittsburgh Penguins, and Arizona Diamondbacks ranked by *ESPN The Magazine* as top professional sport franchises in their respective leagues

4

MANAGEMENT CONCEPTS AND PRACTICE IN SPORT ORGANIZATIONS

Kathy Babiak \ **Lucie Thibault** \ **Jerome Quarterman**

LEARNING OBJECTIVES

> Identify concepts of management theory and understand how these concepts can help leaders and executives better manage their sport organizations.

> Define *organizational environment* and describe its influence on sport organizations.

> Demonstrate an understanding of organizational effectiveness and explain how it is measured in sport organizations.

> Discuss the structure and design of sport organizations.

> Describe the importance of strategic planning, organizational culture, and organizational change.

> Explain the importance of critical thinking in management concepts and practice in the sport industry.

> Detail the role ethics and social responsibility play in the management of sport.

> Explain how new media platforms such as social networking applications affect sport industry organizational issues.

Key Terms

demography
economies of scale
economies of scope
effectiveness
efficiency
environment

organization
organizational culture
organizational design
organizational structure

GET A JOB

Continue on your journey in sport management by going to the web study guide (WSG) at www.HumanKinetics.com/ContemporarySportManagement. Check out the job opportunities and consider the skills and experiences that can help you succeed in sport management.

We are surrounded by organizations. Most of us were born in hospitals. We have been and continue to be educated in schools. We regularly shop for goods and services in stores, and we are protected by organizations (e.g., fire departments, police departments). Even in death, we rely on organizations. Organizations associated with sport also surround us. Most children are introduced to active participation in sport and develop sport skills through schools. Children often stay involved in sport through physical education courses, intramural activities, and interschool competitions in the education system. They may also take advantage of community sports organized by local governments and nonprofit sport clubs. For highly skilled, competitive athletes, opportunities are available in college and university sport programs, amateur sport organizations, and professional sport organizations.

Other types of organizations provide us with opportunities for passive participation in sport. For example, media organizations keep us informed about sport in various ways (e.g., the Internet, television, radio, magazines, newspapers). We may attend sport competitions at our community gathering spaces, in school facilities, and in professional sport venues. Anyone who consumes sport either actively or passively will be exposed to many different types of organizations.

In the first issue of the *Journal of Sport Management,* Earle F. Zeigler (1987) wrote that sport and physical activity over the previous 100 years had "blossomed into a large and complex enterprise that demands a multitude of good managers" (p. 10). Slack and Parent (2006) emphasized this point by noting that "increased amounts of discretionary income, a heightened awareness of the relationship between an active lifestyle and good health, and a greater number of opportunities to participate in sport have all contributed" (p. 3) to the rapid growth and increasing diversity of the sport industry.

Publications such as *Street & Smith's SportsBusiness Journal, Sports Business Daily,* and *Sport Business International* consistently report on the financial and economic state of high-profile sport around the world. Sport business information is also a central part of broadcasts on networks such as ESPN and Fox News in the United States, TSN in Canada, or the BBC in Britain. Clearly, in most industrialized nations, the sport sector plays an important role in the national economy as well as in the country's social and cultural fabric.

Given the importance of the sport sector in society, sport leaders and managers must understand management concepts and organizational structures and processes so that they can adopt and implement the best managerial and organizational practices. In this chapter, we apply management concepts and practices to the broad sport industry. We provide illustrations, exercises, and activities to help you understand how sport organizations function. First, we define the term *organization* and describe three different types of sport organizations. Then we address major topics that are central to understanding how organizations are structured and how they operate. This chapter provides only a basic introduction to management concepts and practice applied to sport organizations. As you progress through your professional preparation program, you will have opportunities to learn much more about them.

Organization Defined

organization—Social entity created to coordinate the efforts of individuals with the intent to achieve goals.

Daft (2010) defined **organizations** as "social entities that are goal-directed, are designed as deliberately structured and coordinated activity systems, and are linked to the external environment" (p. 11). Coordinated actions lead to the creation of social entities (i.e., organizations) in which people work collectively to achieve goals. In essence, people work collectively because achieving goals is often easier when working together rather than working independently. Shown in figure 4.1 is an organizational chart for a fictitious professional baseball club. Here it is conceptualized that a variety of people and groups work collectively. One person would almost certainly be unable to perform all the tasks and responsibilities required for the baseball organization to achieve its goals and objectives. By working collectively, however, organizations can achieve economies of scale and economies of scope.

According to Daft (2010), **economies of scale** represent savings that originate from the mass production of goods and services (i.e., increasing the scale of operations). As an organization produces more goods and services, it can realize savings by buying raw material in larger volume and by maximizing the use of specialized labor or machinery in producing, distributing, and selling these products and services. Economies of scale can result in improved efficiencies within an organization. A greater volume of production and distribution, for example, would enhance the skills of employees in carrying out those tasks. For example, if your sport marketing agency occasionally undertakes market research for professional sport franchises, it will realize economies of scale when it starts to undertake additional market research contracts for other sport organizations. The agency will already have developed the survey tools needed for market research. Refining those tools takes less time than developing them from scratch. In addition, as the employees of the agency undertake more market research contracts from various clients, they will become more knowledgeable, competent, and comfortable with conducting market research.

economies of scale—Savings originating from the mass production of goods and services.

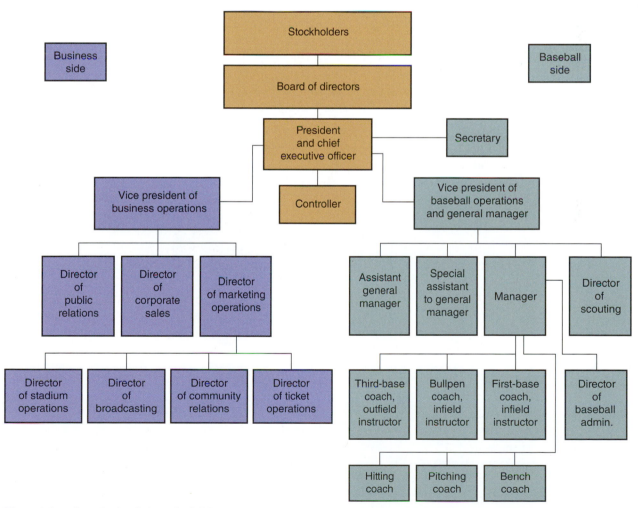

Figure 4.1   Organizational chart of a fictitious professional baseball club.

economies of scope— Maximization of resources used throughout an organization.

Economies of scope represent savings originating from the maximization of resources used throughout the organization. Scope refers to "the number and variety of products and services a company offers" and the market it serves (Daft, 2010, p. 213). An organization that has a large scope will be better equipped to realize economies by being able to service more clients in more markets. For example, International Management Group's (IMG) global presence (more than 130 offices in 25 countries) provides the company with a definite advantage over other marketing, representation, and sport event organizations. IMG's scope allows the organization to service more clients around the globe without expending considerable resources because it is already well established in many countries. In this way, IMG maximizes its resources.

Organizations are vehicles to achieve goals. In their quest to achieve goals, organizations secure inputs and transform them into outputs, like this:

$$\text{Inputs} + \text{Transformation} = \text{Outputs}$$

Organizations obtain inputs such as financial resources, human resources, raw materials, expertise, and knowledge from the external environment. They then transform those inputs through technology (e.g., through the use of machinery or digital platforms) and through the skills and abilities of employees to produce outputs, such as goods and services sought by consumers. An organization also produces other outputs, such as dividends for shareholders and salaries for employees (Jones, 2010).

There are three types of sport organizations: public, nonprofit, and commercial.

The United States Olympic Committee (USOC) is an example of a nonprofit sport organization. The USOC headquarters are in Colorado Springs, Colorado, and there are three U.S. Olympic Training Centers, including this complex in Chula Vista, California.

> *Public organizations.* The entities that make up this type of organization include federal and state government agencies or units as well as regional and local government departments responsible for the delivery of recreation and sport programs and the maintenance of sport fields, arenas, swimming pools, and parks. The National Park Service, Boston's department of parks and recreation, and the Kansas City Sports Commission and Foundation are examples of public sport organizations.

> *Nonprofit organizations.* In the case of nonprofit organizations (also referred to as volunteer or voluntary organizations), volunteer executives are responsible for the operation and management of the organizations. They may hire paid staff to assist in carrying out day-to-day operations, but the volunteer executives are ultimately in charge of making decisions and setting the strategic directions for the organizations. For example, the United States Olympic Committee (USOC), the International Olympic Committee (IOC), and the U.S. Ski and Snowboard Association are all nonprofit organizations. A number of sport-related charities are also nonprofit organizations, including team-linked foundations (Detroit Tigers Foundation of MLB), athlete charities (Tony Hawk Foundation), and stand-alone sport-related foundations such as the Women's Sports Foundation or Right to Play. In these organizations, volunteer executive members, often referred to as members of the board of directors or executive committee, make policy decisions about the direction of the sport or charity efforts and often rely on paid staff to implement and evaluate those policies.

> *Commercial organizations.* The main goal of commercial organizations is to make a profit. Professional sport teams are commercial organizations. For example, the New Jersey Devils (NHL), Manchester United (English Premier League), and the Boston Celtics (NBA) are commercial organizations. Sport equipment manufacturers are commercial organizations as well (e.g., Wilson, Under Armour, lululemon athletica). Other examples include sport retailers such as Dick's Sporting Goods and Foot Locker. In addition, organizations that offer sport or sport-related services, such as private golf clubs, downhill ski and snowboard resorts, fitness clubs, tennis and racket clubs, bowling clubs, and bungee-jumping and wall-climbing facilities, also typically operate as commercial organizations. Finally, sport broadcast and media companies (e.g., ESPN, Comcast SportsNet (NBC Sports) as well as companies who own and manage sport facilities and events (AEG Worldwide) are all commercial, for-profit businesses.

In the following pages, we introduce a number of management concepts and practices that apply to all three types of sport organizations. These concepts include organizational environment, effectiveness, structure and design, strategic planning, culture, and change.

Organizational Environment

In the quest to achieve goals, organizations must deal with their environments. Environments can be turbulent and uncertain. To address these uncertainties, leaders of organizations devise strategies to divide labor by area of expertise so that the most qualified employees are in appropriate roles. Organizations also use technology to support the ongoing production of goods and services. Additionally, organizations can manage the external environment by exerting power and control over other organizations (Daft, 2010). For example, executives of professional sport organizations may exert some control over local government officials by requesting a share of the revenues from concessions and parking of the city-owned stadium.

All organizations operate in an environment. As Daft (2010) explained, the **environment** is composed of "all elements that exist outside the boundary of an organization and have the potential to affect all or part of the organization" (p. 140). The environment can be divided into two categories: general and specific. The general environment includes elements that may not have a direct effect on the day-to-day operations of the organization but may nonetheless influence the organization. Elements in the general environment include the economy, technology, politics, social and cultural forces, and demography.

environment—All elements outside the boundary of the organization that have the potential to affect all or part of the organization.

> Economic conditions affect the way in which a given organization operates. How does inflation affect the organization? For example, do fans purchase high-priced tickets for sport events when inflation rates are high? How do interest rates affect the organization's ability to acquire the inputs necessary for the fabrication of its products?

> Technology has a powerful effect on most organizations. For example, how do computers, software, cellular phones, and the Internet help the organization reach more consumers, maintain more accurate records of inventory, communicate with suppliers, and monitor purchasing patterns? How does technology help the organization develop more (and better) products?

> The political climate is another element of the general environment. As an example, the development of the North American Free Trade Agreement (NAFTA) between the United States, Canada, and Mexico in the 1990s has facilitated trade among the three countries over the past few decades.

demography—Involves the examination of populations, including such elements as size, births, deaths, migration, and aging.

> Social and cultural forces as well as **demography** may affect the organization. The age structure of the population, the level of education, and the standard of living are examples of social, cultural, and demographic elements.

Stakeholders play an important role in an organization's environment (Freeman, 2010). The specific environment, or task environment, includes stakeholders internal and external to the organizations. Freeman (1984) defined stakeholders as individuals or groups that can affect or be affected by the organization or business. These can include "customers, employees, management, owners and stockholders, unions, creditors, suppliers, community, and the government" (Daft, 2010, p. 21). More specifically, as people create organizations, they can determine what goals they will seek to achieve, how the organizations will be structured, and what processes will be used in the organizations' operations. All of these activities affect and are affected by stakeholders such as managers, suppliers, partners, or shareholders. Conversely, through their rules, processes, and structural elements, organizations can also influence the behavior of employees.

Even within the specific environment, there are primary stakeholders (i.e., those who engage in economic exchanges with an organization or business) and secondary stakeholders (i.e., those who affect or are affected by the actions and practices of the business or organization). Here are some important questions about elements of the specific environment:

> Who are the consumers? What are their preferences?

> Who are the suppliers? How easy is it for the organization to acquire its resources from suppliers? Does the organization deal with labor organizations or unions for its workforce?

> Who is the competition? Nike, adidas, New Balance, and Asics are all competitors of Puma. But does Puma have other competitors? What about nonsport shoe manufacturers? What about clothing manufacturers that also produce leisure wear?

> What role does the government play in the environment? The government might be an element of the specific environment through its imposition of legislation and guidelines for the treatment of employees and consumers. Organizations must also provide details to government agencies for taxation purposes.

Clearly, the environment significantly influences and represents a major source of uncertainty for an organization. As a result, leaders and managers of organizations must understand the environment and carefully monitor its effects on the organization.

Professional Profile: Christy Hammond

Title: community relations manager, Detroit Red Wings

Education: BA (sport management); BA (communication studies), University of Michigan

Christy Hammond is third from the left, holding the award.

ONE DAY

Go to the WSG and learn more about a typical day in the life for Christy Hammond. See if she spends her working hours the way you think she does.

In her role with one of the most popular NHL teams, Christy Hammond engages with local nonprofits, players, coaches, team executives, corporate sponsors, the media, and members of the local community to both help those in need and achieve the business objectives of the Detroit Red Wings and the team's corporate partners. Hammond's job requires strong organizational, communication, and interpersonal skills—all of which she puts to the test during every game of the season and beyond.

What have been the key moves, steps, or developments in your career, and how did you arrive at your current position?

Internships helped me open the door to achieving my position here at the Red Wings. In my first internship during my sophomore year, I worked with the *Michigan Hockey* publication, writing articles about youth ice hockey. During that year, I also interned on game nights for the Plymouth Whalers of the Ontario Hockey League. I began as an intern working at the Red Wings during my junior year. I started in the public relations department for my first stint; then in my senior year, I did an internship at the Red Wings with public relations and new media. I was also the student assistant for media relations in the University of Michigan athletic department during their ice hockey games, and I helped out as a student assistant at the University of Michigan football games. By the end of my time as a student, I was logging 35 to 65 hours a week on internships in addition to taking 18 credits a semester. Needless to say, my social life was not the same as that of my classmates! After I graduated, I was fortunate that a community relations coordinator position opened up in the Red Wings' public relations department. After 1.5 years in that position, I was promoted to community relations manager, my current title.

What are your current responsibilities and objectives in your job?

The community relations staff has different responsibilities than our charitable arm (the Red Wings Foundation), whose mission is to grow the sport of ice hockey by holding fundraisers and carrying out programming (i.e., Learn to Skate) to offer opportunities for children and youth in the Detroit area to play hockey. The community relations staff handles all other charitable initiatives or programs that do not focus on growing the sport of ice hockey. That is what I manage. I plan, coordinate, and oversee team events such as the MI Wings Community Tour, where a day before training camp, two groups of four players stop at hospitals, military bases, and elementary schools as they make their way to Traverse City (5 hours north of Detroit) for training camp. My job requires me to oversee logistics for all of our initiatives such as in game collections (smoke detectors, mittens, canned foods) to help our charitable partners. I also oversee bigger game-night initiatives such as Breast Cancer Awareness Night, Military Appreciation Night, and our Wings for Wishes event, where we partner with the Make-A-Wish Michigan. I also help coordinate High School Journalist Day, which I actually participated in myself when I was in high school. That experience was what made me want to go into community relations.

In addition to game-day events and activities, I work closely with players who are interested in developing charitable programs. Two players on the Red Wings have their own foundation. Six players and our head coach have charity ticket programs. These efforts have grown and evolved since I have been at the Wings. I help them figure out what cause they want to support, and then I work with the player and charities to find how to best implement the program.

My overarching objective in this position is to engage in initiatives that have a positive influence on the community as well as to develop something that could generate publicity and connect the fans with our team and corporate partners through our community programming.

What do you enjoy most about your current job?

My job is so rewarding—this is really my dream job. One of the things I love most is the tangible influence I can see that the team, players, and staff have on the community and our fans. It is a creative and challenging

(continued)

Professional Profile: Christy Hammond *(continued)*

role, and it's very important for the organization. For example, a player approached me once with the idea of helping kids who had lost a parent because he had lost a parent when he was a teenager. He wanted to do something to help grieving kids. I put together a proposal with various options (ticket program, visits at events, meet and greets). In the span of a couple of weeks, we narrowed down the scope, I recommended a nonprofit organization to work with, and we worked out pricing, timing, goodie bags, and so on. I really got to see the effect this effort had on kids and on the athlete. It is a great feeling.

And one final perk of working for a professional sport team? I injured my knee in high school, and have since had 13 surgeries, and I'll need another soon. This place has an awesome ice machine!

What do you consider the biggest future challenge to be in your job or industry?
I think a future challenge, particularly with community relations, is to really balance the community impact. We want to do good locally and throughout the state, but we also need to balance our business goals, our corporate partner goals, and our community partner goals. We want to ensure that we are truly influencing the community with strong programs, because this is a value that the Red Wings feel is important. We do not want it to come across as simply a corporate ploy.

Organizational Effectiveness

effectiveness—The extent to which goals are achieved.

efficiency—The extent to which goals are achieved using the fewest possible resources.

The **effectiveness** of an organization is the extent to which it achieves its goals. A related term, **efficiency**, refers to the achievement of goals using minimum resources. For example, the 2004 Athens Olympic Games were effective because members of the organizing committee achieved their objectives. But did the organizers achieve efficiency? In other words, did they achieve their objectives using the fewest possible resources? Given that members of the organizing committee went down to the wire with the construction of facilities and the training of human resources in advance of the Olympic Games, they were not efficient. They achieved their objectives, but they had to spend more resources (i.e., invest more money than budgeted for facility construction) to ensure the completion of the facilities before the Opening Ceremonies. In sum, effectiveness focuses on *results*, while efficiency focuses on *activities*.

Efficiency implies the minimal use of resources to produce outputs (ratio of inputs to outputs). As a result, concepts of cost–benefit, return on investment (ROI), and budget compared with number of customers served are assessed to evaluate efficiency. As you can see, achieving effectiveness is easier than achieving efficiency. In fact, most managers and leaders of organizations rarely achieve efficiency.

Evaluating Organizational Effectiveness

Ultimately, managers and leaders want to ensure that the goals set out for the organization are met. Assessing organizational effectiveness, however, is not always this simple. Consequently, a number of approaches should be considered to evaluate organizational effectiveness (Jones, 2010). Traditional approaches include the goal approach, the resource-based approach, and the internal process approach. Contemporary approaches include the competing-values approach and the stakeholder approach (Daft, 2010).

> *Traditional approaches.* The goal approach focuses on the outputs side of the organization. The organization is considered effective if it achieves its organizational goal (e.g., maximizing profits, winning the game, successfully teaching sport skills to students, healing patients) (Daft, 2010; Yuchtman & Seashore, 1967). The resource-based approach focuses on the inputs side of the organization. With this approach, the

effectiveness of an organization is assessed by its ability to acquire resources from the external environment in order to transform them into outputs. The logic behind this approach is that without inputs or the ability to acquire them, an organization will be unable to produce outputs (Daft, 2010). The internal process approach focuses on the transformation side of the organization—the ability to process the inputs while considering the internal well-being of the organization. Focusing on the transformation of inputs into outputs helps ensure the organization's stability and long-term survival (Daft, 2010). While traditional approaches contribute to our understanding of effectiveness, they lack nuance and acknowledgement of the complexity of the environment in which the organization operates (e.g., acquisition of various types of resources, multiple measures of success or effectiveness) (Yuchtman & Seashore, 1967). Thus, a more multidimensional set of criteria must be considered. More contemporary approaches provide this perspective (Daft, 2010).

> *Contemporary approaches.* Two approaches are included in this section: competing values and stakeholders. Instead of focusing on single parts of the organization (i.e., inputs, transformation, or outputs), the competing-values approach combines elements of all traditional effectiveness approaches by focusing on the value dimensions of focus and structure. The dimension of focus is represented on a continuum from internal to external, whereas the dimension of structure is represented on a continuum from stability to flexibility. An internal focus means that the organization values the well-being of its employees, whereas an external focus values the well-being of the organization. A stable structure would favor a task-oriented approach, and a flexible structure would favor change and innovation in the organization (Quinn & Rohrbaugh, 1981). With the competing-values approach, the assessment of your organization's effectiveness will be based on your values with respect to the dimensions of focus and structure. In this approach, as a leader or manager, you acknowledge that the assessment or interpretation of organizational effectiveness depends on who you are, what interests you represent, and what values you favor for your organization. The stakeholder approach is based on the premise that several groups, entities, and other organizations have an interest in the focal organization. Various stakeholders will assess organizational effectiveness differently. For example, employees in an organization might not judge effectiveness in the same manner that executives in the organization do or that customers do. For instance, suppliers may judge the organization's effectiveness by the volume of raw materials that they acquire and sell annually, whereas shareholders may consider the value of the shares as their measure of organizational effectiveness. Furthermore, customers may judge effectiveness by the quality and price of the product they purchased, and employees may consider wages and benefits when they evaluate organizational effectiveness.

Those who subscribe to the stakeholder approach and the competing-values approach believe that the organization must consider the values and interest of the various groups, or stakeholders, in the organization and consolidate these interests and views to achieve effectiveness (Daft, 2010). As explained by Daft, the stakeholder and the competing-values approaches address the complexities involved in determining whether an organization is effective.

Effectiveness in Sport Organizations

Several sport management researchers have investigated the concept of organizational effectiveness. Wolfe and Putler (2002) examined the perceptions held by various stakeholders (e.g., faculty members, student-athletes, potential students, university students, members of the athletics department, and alumni) about the priorities of intercollegiate athletics programs. These priorities included win–loss record, graduation rates, violations, attendance, gender equity, number of teams, and finances. In a subsequent study, Wolfe, Hoeber, and Babiak (2002) investigated how perceptions of effectiveness differed according to the values of various intercollegiate athletics stakeholders. In a different context, Papadimitriou (2001) evaluated the effectiveness of Greek sport organizations from the athletes' perspectives. Her results showed that athletes perceived their sport organizations' effectiveness to be low because the following factors were poorly addressed: interest in the athletes, long-term planning, caliber of the board, sport science support, and internal and external liaisons. The athletes, as one group of stakeholders of the sport organizations, had different opinions about the sport organizations' levels of effectiveness than did the leaders of those organizations, another group of stakeholders. Shilbury and Moore (2006) examined the competing-values approach in Australian nonprofit sport organizations whose funding from government is dependent on measures of organizational effectiveness, yet which operate in a more commercialized environment. Their aim was to operationalize the competing-values approach to measure the effectiveness of national sport organizations (NSOs). Their findings indicated that important measures of effectiveness in these organizations included productivity, planning, flexibility, and stability.

Organizational Structure

organizational structure— A formal system of task and authority relationships that control how people coordinate their actions and use of resources to achieve organizational goals (Jones, 2010, p. 7).

Jones (2010) defined **organizational structure** as a "formal system of task and authority relationships that control how people coordinate their actions and use of resources to achieve organizational goals" (p. 7). When addressing the topic of organizational structure, we usually refer to formal organizations, or what we typically see when we examine an organizational chart. As noted earlier in the chapter, figure 4.1 provides an example of a formal organization for a fictitious professional baseball organization. Note, however, that every organization also has an informal dimension. Figure 4.2 illustrates how formal and informal relationships operate simultaneously within a fictitious sport organization. The solid lines illustrate the official relationships in the formal organization, and the dashed lines illustrate the informal relationships among employees who have lunch together on a regular basis and discuss everything from sports to company politics. These latter relationships are not officially acknowledged in the structure of the organization, but are likely to either compete with or support the formal organization. Although the formal organization cannot control informal relationships, encouraging a positive organizational culture, a topic discussed later in the chapter, will increase the likelihood of mutual support.

Dimensions of Organizational Structure

Organizational theorists generally agree on three major dimensions of structure: specialization, standardization, and centralization (Daft, 2010; Jones, 2010). Specialization concerns the division of labor, or the extent to which tasks and duties are divided into separate roles (Daft, 2010). According to Daft, when specialization is high, employees carry out a limited range of tasks and duties, and when specialization is low, individual employees carry out a wide range of tasks. The dimension of specialization is tied to the concept of complexity. There are three levels of complexity: vertical, horizontal, and spatial.

> Vertical complexity is evidenced by the number of levels that exist between the top executive in the organization (i.e., president, chief executive officer) and the lowest positions and units in the hierarchy (i.e., support positions and departments). The more levels there are, the more vertically complex the organization is. For instance, The Ohio State University Athletic Department has

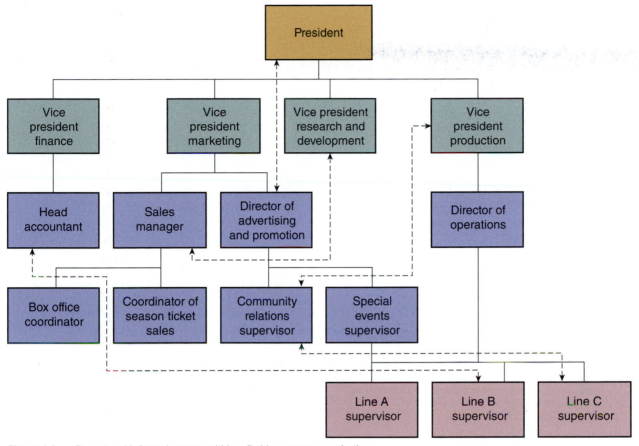

Figure 4.2   Formal and informal groups within a fictitious sport organization.

several levels (e.g., executive associate athletic director, senior associate athletic director, associate athletic director) between the athletic director (Associate Vice President Gene Smith) and lower athletic department positions, indicating a high degree of vertical complexity.

› Horizontal complexity is shown in the number of units that exist across the organization. The NBA's organizational structure has more horizontal complexity with an array of business units, including NBA Entertainment, the WNBA, the NBA Development League, and the Global Merchandising Group, all with different business functions.

› Spatial complexity refers to the number of geographical locations in which an organization operates. An organization situated in a number of locations would be considered spatially complex relative to an organization operating in a single location. For example, the UEFA (Union des Associations Européennes de Football), which includes 53 national football (soccer) associations, is more spatially complex than the CONCACAF (Confederation of North, Central American, and Caribbean Association Football), which has 40 national football associations, or the CONMEBOL (Confederación Sudamericana de Fútbol), which comprises 10 national football associations.

Standardization is another dimension of structure. In organizational theory literature, the terms *formalization* and *standardization* are often used interchangeably because high levels of formalization result in standardization. Formalization refers to "the amount of written documentation in the organization" (Daft, 2010, p. 15), such as job

ACTION

Go to the WSG and complete the Learning in Action activity that tests your understanding of sport management organizational structures.

Organizational Structure Makes a Difference

According to Daft (2010), 11 organizational dimensions exist. These are then categorized into the two broad areas of structural dimensions and contextual dimensions. Daft explained and provided examples of these dimensions. Structural dimensions refer to the labels that describe the "internal characteristics of an organization" (p. 15). The six types of structural dimensions are formalization, specialization, hierarchy of authority, centralization, professionalism, and personnel ratios. The contextual dimensions, he noted, "characterize the whole organization" (p. 15). The five types of contextual dimensions are size, technology, the environment, goals, and strategies.

A study in sport management examined the relationship of three structural dimensions (i.e., specialization, formalization, and centralization) and job satisfaction in the context of intercollegiate athletics (Cunningham, 2006). Specialization refers to the extent to which sport organizations can be vertically different (i.e., the number of layers in a sport organization) and horizontally different (i.e., roles specialized for specific people). Formalization refers to the number of written rules, procedures, written records of employee performance, and job descriptions. Lastly, centralization refers to the hierarchical level of people who have authority to make a decision.

Associate and assistant athletics directors of NCAA Division I member institutions were surveyed to examine the extent to which the relationships between the three selected elements of organizational dimensions noted earlier were mediated by job satisfaction. The statistical analyses revealed that the relationship of formalization was partially mediated by job satisfaction and that the relationship between centralization and organizational commitment was fully mediated by job satisfaction. Although the study did not examine all 11 types of organizational dimensions (e.g., hierarchy of authority, professionalism, personnel ratios, size, technology, environment, goals), the results of the study did demonstrate that of the three organizational dimensions (i.e., formalization, specialization, and centralization) examined in the study, each has a significant effect on subsequent employee work outcomes in the sport industry.

descriptions, policies, procedures, and regulations. This documentation is often used to control employees' behaviors and activities. A high degree of formalization leads to a high degree of standardization because employees who face similar situations will be expected to act in a similar fashion (Daft, 2010). The National Collegiate Athletic Association (NCAA), for example, has a high degree of formalization in its guidelines, policies, procedures, and regulations regarding intercollegiate athletic activities in American universities.

Centralization is the third dimension of organizational structure. This concept refers to "the hierarchical level that has authority to make a decision" (Daft, 2010, p. 17). When leaders and managers at the top of the hierarchy handle the decision-making activities, the organization is considered centralized. When decision making is delegated to levels throughout the organization, the organization is decentralized.

Typically, organizations are not completely centralized or decentralized. Some decisions in the organizations may be centralized (e.g., hiring and firing of employees, establishing the strategic direction of the organization), whereas other decisions may be decentralized (e.g., purchasing of organizational supplies, marketing strategies for products and services). Several factors affect whether decisions are centralized or decentralized:

> The cost (i.e., organizational resources) of the decision to the sport organization—The greater the cost, the more centralized the decision will be.

> The timing (how much time a sport manager has to make the decision)—The more urgent the decision, the more decentralized it will be.

› The qualifications of employees—The greater the number of expert employees involved throughout the sport organization, the more decentralized the decision will be.

Relationships Among the Dimensions of Organizational Structure

Specialization and standardization are interrelated. For example, high levels of specialization are typically associated with high levels of standardization. In other words, the greater the number of roles in the organization, the more formalized the organization will be (e.g., more job descriptions, more policies and procedures). In the same way, when an organization has a small number of roles, standardization will be low.

The relationship between standardization and centralization is not as easy to predict. Research in organizational theory has failed to demonstrate a consistent relationship between the two dimensions. As reported by Slack and Parent (2006), research in sport management has not examined the relationship between standardization and centralization. Similarly, research in sport organizations has not analyzed the relationship between specialization and centralization or the relationship between complexity and centralization. In situations where specialization and complexity are high and thus where roles, tasks, and duties within the organization are narrowly defined, one would expect decentralization of decision making. With low levels of specialization and complexity, one would expect centralization of decision making within the organization.

WEB
Go to the WSG and complete the first web search activity, which asks you to examine and explain the organizational structure of three sport organizations.

Organizational Design

Jones (2010) defined **organizational design** as the process by which leaders "select and manage aspects of structure and culture" (p. 9) so that the organization can undertake its various activities and achieve its objectives. The concept of organizational culture is addressed later in this chapter. For the moment, however, consider organizational design as the structural configurations that leaders use to arrange their organization's activities and operations so that it can reach its goals.

Mintzberg conducted extensive work on organizational design. In a 1979 study, he outlined different design configurations for various types of organizations based on the nature of their operations. A sporting goods organization in the business of manufacturing running shoes will be designed differently from a sport marketing agency or an event management business. Mintzberg based his designs on the interplay among five major parts of the organization that have been simplified as the following:

› Top management, which represents the leadership within the organization

› Middle management, which represents the managers who are between the leadership of the organization and the employees who are directly involved with the production of goods and services

› Technical core, which represents the group of employees responsible for the production of goods and services

› Administrative support staff, which represents the employees who provide a support function in the organization

› Technical support staff, which represents the employees who provide technical and technological support to assist in the production of goods and services and the introduction of innovative practices to enhance existing goods and services or create new ones

Based on the relevance and importance of these five parts of the organization, various designs are proposed. Mintzberg (1979) identified several designs, among them

organizational design— Process by which leaders select and manage aspects of structure and culture of the organization.

the simple structure, the machine bureaucracy, and the professional bureaucracy. Subsequently, new designs have been added to reflect emerging realities for organizations. Among these new designs are entrepreneurial, innovative, missionary, and political designs.

The simple structure is typically a suitable design for small organizations that have only two major parts, top management and the technical core. Simple structures are characterized by low levels of specialization and standardization and high levels of centralization. A small sport club that operates at the local level might have a simple structure.

Machine bureaucracy is a design appropriate for sporting goods manufacturers that have high levels of specialization, standardization, and centralization. In the machine bureaucracy design, all parts of the organization identified by Mintzberg are important—top management, middle management, technical core, administrative support staff, and technical support staff.

The professional bureaucracy is characterized by an important technical core and administrative support staff along with a limited technical support staff, middle management, and top management. This design would be appropriate for national sport organizations in which professionals (e.g., coaches, sport psychologists, professional administrators) are responsible for the products or services. Decentralization and high levels of specialization and standardization are also characteristics of this design.

Entrepreneurial organizations have a simple design. With a minimal number of staff, the organization initially has little need for specialization and standardization because the top of the organization coordinates much of the work. As outlined in Sack and Nadim (2002), Starter Corporation, a licensed sport apparel business now owned by Nike, was initially structured as an entrepreneurial organization.

Innovative designs allow greater flexibility than the bureaucratic design while providing decentralization not found in entrepreneurial organizations. Organizations featuring an innovative design emphasize a climate of creativity for the experts responsible for developing the product or the service. As a result, the power in the organization resides in the experts, who might be allowed to work in creative teams or on special projects. A marketing agency or ad agency with several accounts could exhibit an innovative design.

A missionary organization is designed around its ideology. After employees become indoctrinated into the organization and identify strongly with the organization's ideology, they have the freedom to make decisions. In her research of organizational designs of organizing committees for the Olympic Games (OCOGs), Theodoraki (2001) found evidence of this missionary design.

Organizations with political designs are extremely flexible. They have no definite mechanisms of coordination. Typically, organizations that are temporarily created use this design so that they can address challenging transitions. An organization bidding to host a major sport event such as a World Cup or international championship, for example, might be designed as a political organization since it addresses needs to secure resources (e.g., funding, facilities, volunteers) and support in the hopes of hosting an event. Table 4.1 outlines the structural profiles of Mintzberg's organizational designs that are discussed in this chapter.

Structure and Design of Sport Organizations

Several sport management scholars have investigated or provided an overview (e.g., Slack & Parent, 2006) of the structure and design of various sport organizations. For example, Theodoraki (2001) applied Mintzberg's organizational design theories to OCOGs. She explained how the organizational design of OCOGs changed over time.

Table 4.1   Characteristics of Organizational Designs and Their Structures

Mintzberg's design types	Specialization or complexity	Formalization or standardization	Centralization
Simple structure	Low	Low	High
Machine bureaucracy	High	High	High
Professional bureaucracy	High	High	Low
Entrepreneurial	Low	Low	High
Innovative	High	Low	Low
Missionary	Low	High	Low
Political	High	Low	Undetermined

Mintzberg 1979; Slack and Parent 2006.

The committees are created seven years before the Olympic Games take place, immediately following the IOC's decision about which bid city will host the Olympic Games. These organizations have a life span of eight years and are typically dismantled one year after hosting the Olympic Games. According to Theodoraki, OCOGs initially display a simple structure, Mintzberg's most basic design. She noted that OCOGs eventually display characteristics of the missionary design during the hosting of the Olympic Games and in the year following. In other words, as the members and employees of the OCOG become indoctrinated and socialized into the organization, they start to work collectively toward the organizational goals without the need for high levels of formalization or centralization.

Strategy

The managers and leaders of organizations use strategies, or plans, to cope with the environment. A plan refers to a course of action or a direction in which to move the organization from one point to another. The development of a plan involves the following four steps:

1. Identifying the goals, objectives, and mission of the organization—The strategy must be congruent with the goals, objectives, and mission.
2. Determining the strategic objectives—This step involves assessing what the organization wants to achieve with the strategy, and it includes the SWOT analysis. As you will learn in chapter 12, a SWOT analysis consists of an assessment of the strengths and weaknesses of the organization and the opportunities and threats emanating from the organization's environment.

3. Identifying the resources required to implement the strategy—Without adequate resources, the organization will find it difficult to implement the strategy.

4. Establishing a timeline for implementing the strategy and identifying milestones to assess whether the organization is on target to achieve its objectives (Jones, 2010).

Organizations undertake the process of developing a strategy to gain a competitive advantage, or edge, over other organizations. They may achieve this advantage by acquiring scarce resources. For sport organizations, scarce resources may be financial resources, sponsorship opportunities, media visibility, participants or athletes, clients, members and fans, market share, equipment, or facilities. In turn, access to these resources might lead to success in sport competitions or greater profit because of increased fan attendance at games or increased sales of sporting goods. Strategies are extremely important for leaders and managers because they outline the major direction and activities of the organization for the future. As such, strategies serve as the road maps for the organization.

Olberding (2003) investigated the strategies of 33 Olympic sport organizations in the United States. He examined the following elements: each organization's competitive position relative to other U.S. sport organizations, the domestic sport programs, the level of participation in the sport in the country, the costs involved in taking part in the sport, the level of visibility of the sport, the extent to which the sport was entrenched in the grass roots, the opportunities for competitions in the sport, and the new programs being developed within the organization. Using the framework developed by Thibault, Slack, and Hinings (1993) for Canadian sport organizations, Olberding found that U.S. sport organizations used similar strategies (i.e., enhancers, refiners, innovators, and explorers).

Ferkins and Shilbury (2012) explored strategic capability in NSOs. In particular, they were interested in factors that constrained or enabled strategic function. They identified four dimensions that were considered integral to a strategically able board: capable people (human resources), frame of reference (objectives and plan), facilitative board process (practices and structures), and facilitative regional relationships (partnerships).

Some research on strategy has focused on the development of partnerships (also known as interorganizational relationships or strategic alliances) with other organizations as a strategy to retain or gain a competitive advantage. All types of sport organizations (i.e., public, nonprofit, and commercial) are increasingly involved in alliances with other organizations to capitalize on opportunities and access more resources; to increase programs, services, and products offered to members or clients; and to reduce uncertainty.

In the context of sport, several researchers have applied the work of Oliver (1990) on the organizational motives behind the creation of partnerships. Oliver uncovered six motives leading organizations to collaborate: asymmetry, reciprocity, necessity, legitimacy, efficiency, and stability.

> Asymmetry refers to an organization's choice to enter into partnerships to exercise power over, and control of, another organization or its resources.
> Reciprocity refers to the creation of partnerships to achieve common or mutual goals or activities.
> Necessity refers to partnerships created to respond to legal obligations or regulations set by another organization (e.g., government).
> Legitimacy refers to the creation of partnerships to provide credibility or enhance its reputation, image, or authority.

> Efficiency refers to the need for an organization to improve its input–output ratio. As a result, partnerships may be created to decrease the cost of raw materials needed for producing goods and services.

> Stability refers to the development of partnerships to reduce uncertainty and increase predictability for the organization.

These six motives for partnership creation were featured in the works by Babiak (2007) and Turner and Shilbury (2008, 2010). Babiak studied a training center for high-performance elite athletes and its network of partnerships to achieve its goal of providing the best possible training environment for these world-class athletes. The training center's motives for developing partnerships with other nonprofit organizations, with public organizations, and with private commercial organizations were varied, but these alliances all contributed to the center's strategy to enhance the training environment of the athletes. On a different topic, Turner and Shilbury examined the development of partnerships between clubs of the Australian Football League and the National Rugby League with broadcasters. They found different motives for clubs to undertake strategic alliances with broadcasters. Furthermore, the authors discussed the effect of broadcasting technologies on the establishment of partnerships. Given the increasing importance of broadcasters for sport organizations (e.g., for access to much-needed resources), further studies addressing the relationships between sport leagues and clubs with media are imperative.

Organizational Culture

Edgar Schein (1985), one of the pioneers of research into culture in organizations, defined organizational culture as "a pattern of basic assumptions—invented, discovered, or developed by a given group as it learns to cope with its problems of external adaptation and internal integration" (p. 9). Schein explained that organizations consider this set of assumptions valid and as a result promote them to new members as the appropriate and correct way to act in the workplace. Jones (2010) defined organizational culture as "the set of shared values and norms that controls organizational members' interactions with each other and with people outside of the organization" (p. 179).

Culture manifests itself in different ways throughout organizations. These manifestations include stories and myths, symbols, language, ceremonies and rites, physical setting, and symbolic artifacts. Stories and myths are narratives that may be based on truth, fiction, or a combination of the two. Symbols consist of events, objects, or acts that convey meanings for the organization. Organizational logos, slogans, and mission statements are symbols. Language refers to the terminology and jargon that organizational members use to communicate with each other. Ceremonies and rites include social events and award and recognition events that leaders organize. These events often reinforce organizational values. Physical setting includes the office space and objects found in the organization. Artifacts are items found in the organization's physical setting. Photographs of past successes or ceremonies, banners, copies of past marketing campaigns, and displays of awards, achievements, and products are examples of artifacts that could be evident in the physical setting. The setting and these artifacts are representative of the organization.

Colyer (2000) investigated organizational culture in nonprofit Australian sport organizations. Her findings revealed the existence of "tensions between two of the main groups of people (employees and volunteers) in sport organizations" (p. 338). She explained that if leaders were to draw cultural profiles of their organizations, they would become aware of tensions and could develop strategies to change the culture and thus enhance organizational effectiveness. She also discussed the presence of subcultures—an important element in any examination of an organization's culture.

organizational culture— Set of shared values and norms that controls organizational members' interactions with each other and with people outside the organization.

WEB

Go to the WSG and complete the second web search activity, which asks you to look for NASSM abstracts related to organizational culture.

University Sport in Iran: Opportunities and Threats

By Hassan Assadi, Iran
University of Tehran

The number of university sports in Iran has been growing, especially in the last decade. Sports in universities can be divided into two categories. The first category is based on university students' sports participation within or between universities, sports at the national and international levels, and sport for all. The second category is based on sport as a field of study at universities.

Wrestling is a popular sport in Iran. In this photo, Iranians in the Azadi sports complex enthusiastically watch an international wrestling competition.

In Iran, university students' involvement in sports is managed by the following units: student sport associations and physical education departments in universities. These departments work under the supervision of the physical education general department of science, within the science, research, and technology ministry; although they are independent, they are financially supported by the general department. They organize intra-university and national sport events and competitions and hold national Universiade competitions biennially. The National University Sports Federation (NUSF), which was founded by the science, research and technology ministry, plays a role at an international level although it is supported by the sport and youth ministry and the National Olympic Committee. The NUSF organizes national

Other studies have focused on the values held in sport organizations. Because values are central to an organization's culture, they are often the focus of research. Milton-Smith (2002) discussed the scandals, corruptions, and controversies involving the IOC in the late 1990s and early 2000s. He explained how concerns about the Olympic Games mirror concerns about the movement toward globalization. Concerns regarding "winning at any price; commercial exploitation by MNCs [multinational corporations]; corruption; intense national rivalry; [and] the competitive advantage of advanced nations" were identified (p. 132). In analyzing the case of the Sydney 2000 Olympic sport teams in all public and private universities. The best result achieved by Iran was 11th place (with a total of eight medals) during the 2009 Universiade Games (organized by the International University Sports Federation). Iran was particularly successful in taekwondo, weightlifting, wrestling, shooting, and volleyball. Although the development of sport for all for university students is a priority in the ministry's 2020 strategic plans, more resources are invested in athletes and championships. The university system within the sport studies and physical education fields has been growing so fast in Iran that the unequal ratio of supply and demand for sport services in the next decade will become a challenge.

Physical education, as a field of study, has been qualitatively and quantitatively growing at universities in recent years, although there have been some challenges. Firstly, many universities have founded physical education and sport studies so that 31 provinces now have physical education undergraduate degrees at their universities. Secondly, there are many graduate physical education and sport studies degrees. The area of physical education and sport studies includes a number of programs: general physical education, sport physiology, kinesiology, sport management, development and motor learning, sport injury, and sport biomechanics. Each program has its own set of courses. For example, sport management features the following courses: sport economics and marketing, facility management, sport media, sport events, management of sport organizations, and sport tourism. The growth of physical education and sport studies within universities demonstrates the value that society attaches to higher education generally and to youth's fascination with physical education and sport studies specifically. The growth of physical education faces challenges, however. For example, there is a high professor–student ratio, meaning that there is one professor for 20 to 40 students at different universities. The next challenge is the rank of the professors; at the moment, of the country's professors, 74.5% are assistant professors, 23% are associate professors, and 2.5% are full professors. Another challenge is the lack of work opportunities for graduates. The main concern for the students is to find work related to their field of study. It seems that sport studies and physical education in universities should be modified to some extent so that they are better adapted to the work requirements of organizations in the community and so that graduates can gain the necessary administrative and executive skills. In summary, it can be noted that Iran has a balanced position in university sport activities, although the main challenge with respect to management is the interaction between university sport organizations. In the next decade, attention should be devoted to the voluntary movement in sport and sport for all.

International Learning Activity #1

Consider your university's involvement in sport for all and elite sport. In your opinion, what should be the priority for university sport? Explain your answer.

International Learning Activity #2

Can hosting a championship event in interuniversity competition lead to improvements or benefits for university sport? Also, do university students in your country care about participating actively in sport activities and becoming involved as volunteers in sport? Discuss your answers.

International Learning Activity #3

Can a variety of physical education curricula and courses meet the sport and physical education needs of society and financially increase work opportunities for graduates? Why or why not?

Games, he drew on the values espoused by the Olympic Movement and demonstrated how members of the IOC and members of the Sydney Organising Committee for the Olympic Games (SOCOG) violated those values. According to Milton-Smith's analysis, the IOC and SOCOG compromised values such as honesty, transparency, objectivity (i.e., avoiding conflict of interest), fairness, dignity, and loyalty. Although it was not the purpose of his work to discuss the organizational culture of the IOC or the SOCOG per se, Milton-Smith explained that the leadership of the IOC cultivated a culture of excess while overlooking questionable and unethical practices of its members. In other words, the Olympic ideals and the core values of the Olympic movement were used as marketing tools to showcase the IOC, but they were never translated into the culture of the organization.

A more recent study on culture in professional sport examined the culture transformation process undertaken by owners and general managers (Frontiera, 2010). Frontiera considered the link between culture and performance and the influence a leader can have on supporting or changing the culture of a professional sport team. His findings revealed that leaders were able to recognize a dysfunctional culture manifested in cultural artifacts such as substandard facilities and win–loss records. Competing values were also espoused by members of the organization (i.e., "selfishness, placing too much emphasis on monetary profit and minimizing the value of players" (p. 76). Leaders in these professional sport teams made efforts to change the existing dysfunctional culture in their own ways by articulating a clear vision for the team or organization, expressing their values clearly, changing personnel, hiring and developing employees, and engaging in explicit communication. Frontiera concluded that cultural understanding is essential for sport leaders to guide and direct the organization in a way that achieves its goals.

Organizational Change

Organizational change is defined as "the process by which organizations move from their present state to some desired future state to increase their effectiveness" (Jones, 2010, p. 270). To remain competitive, relevant, and viable, organizations constantly undergo change. Several frameworks have been developed to study organizational change. In the following pages, we will feature two frameworks.

The first framework is identified as the organizational life cycle or the model of organizational growth. This framework is an adaptation of Greiner's (1972) work on the various stages of evolution and revolution that an organization undertakes as it grows and of the work of Quinn and Cameron (1983) on the life cycle of an organization. Figure 4.3 provides a graphic illustration of the evolution and revolution stages as an organization grows. There are four stages of growth for organizations (i.e., entrepreneurial, collectivity, formalization, and elaboration), and each of these stages is punctuated by a crisis (i.e., need for leadership, need for delegation with control, need to deal with too much red tape, and need for revitalization). These stages and crises are briefly described in the next paragraphs.

> *Entrepreneurial stage.* This stage is based on the vision of the founder of the organization. The founder is investing her or his energies in all aspects of the organization (e.g., management, technical production, marketing, delivery of products or services) to ensure that the organization survives and grows. As a catalyst for progression toward the next growth stage, the organization typically undergoes a crisis identified as *need for leadership.* During this crisis, the founder becomes overwhelmed with the quantity of work involved and with the increasing responsibilities that she or he holds within the organization. As a result, the founder who created the organization needs help.

> *Collectivity stage.* In this stage, the leadership crisis has been addressed. The organization is now developing clear goals and establishing its direction. Functional areas, departments, and a hierarchy of authority are created to help divide and assign the work to newly hired employees. Also, formal communication mechanisms are being developed to help in the coordination of the work to be achieved and to address the rapid growth experienced by the organization at this stage. For progression into the next stage, the organization in the collectivity stage will go through a crisis termed *need for delegation with control.* During this crisis, lower-level employees are limited in their ability to make decisions autonomously. As they gain experience

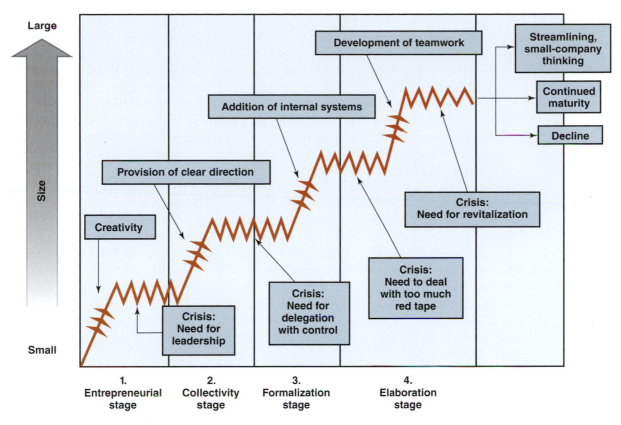

Figure 4.3 Stages of organizational development.

Adapted from Greiner 1972; Quinn and Cameron 1983.

and expertise in their functional areas, they become increasingly frustrated with the strong top-down leadership. During this crisis, leaders develop coordination and control mechanisms within the organization and provide employees with some level of autonomy and decision-making power.

› *Formalization stage.* During this stage, rules and procedures are developed. Job descriptions are created, and communication becomes more formal. Top management executives invest their time in strategic planning and allow middle management the responsibility of managing the operations. During this stage, decentralized units may be created and incentive systems for managers may be introduced to enhance the effectiveness of the organization. As the organization increases its levels of formalization and standardization, the crisis of *too much red tape* will surface. With systems and high levels of formalization in place, middle management may begin to experience some constraints in their ability to do their work within the organization. Specifically, too much bureaucracy may paralyze employees and stifle innovation. The organization is large and complex, and will require adjustments to reach the next stage.

› *Elaboration stage.* To address the increasing red tape, leaders and managers within the organization undertake collaboration and teamwork. This collaboration occurs across different hierarchical levels, departments or divisions, and functions. Leaders, managers, and employees work together to solve problems. During this stage, formal systems may be simplified in favor of more collaboration among leaders, managers, and employees. As the organization matures, its crisis woes will be the *need for revitalization.* Renewal may be needed as the organization's alignment with its environment becomes askew. A streamlining of operations may be necessary for the organization to respond better to a changing environment. Also, innovations provide the organization with new energy and spirit.

The various stages involved in an organization's life cycle help us understand the changes that organizations go through as they develop and mature. As reviewed in the previous paragraphs, this life cycle is punctuated with challenges and crises along the way. If leaders respond to these crises, they can lead the organization to success.

Another framework for studying organizational change is the contextualist approach developed by Pettigrew (1987, 1990). The contextualist approach acknowledges that change does not take place in isolation or in a brief time. Understanding change is important, but it must be accomplished over a long term by considering three elements: content, context, and process. To acquire a full understanding of change, one must first examine the content of change, which is best done by answering the question, What changed? The next element of Pettigrew's framework is the context of change. The focus is on answering the question, Why did the change occur? Context includes two sections: the inner context and the outer context. Inner context consists of internal elements at play within organizations, such as strategy, culture, and the structure of organizations. Outer context refers to general political, economic, and social forces at work within the organizational environment. After content and context of change have been uncovered, the process of change needs to be examined. The process of change is concerned with answering the question, How has change occurred? In uncovering the process of change, leadership is often a key component because change agents often contribute to the adoption of change within the organization. By answering the what, why, and how, leaders are in a better position to understand change in their organizations.

A few studies have applied Pettigrew's contextual approach to organizational change to the sport context. Specifically, Cousens, Babiak, and Slack (2001) investigated changes in the NBA over a 17-year period, focusing on the relationship marketing approach adopted by the league. The scholars discussed the relevance of Pettigrew's approach to understand the need to foster relationships within and outside the NBA. In another example of Pettigrew's work applied to the context of sport, Caza (2000) examined the adoption of innovative practices in a Canadian provincial sport organization. His investigation looked at the extent to which organizational members were receptive to the implementation of two initiatives. Caza found that Pettigrew's framework was useful in understanding challenges related to the implementation of innovations in the sport sector.

Thibault and Babiak (2005) also used Pettigrew's framework to investigate changes in Canada's sport system. They were specifically interested in examining how and why the Canadian sport system changed to accommodate greater involvement from athletes. They found that increased representation by athletes on decision-making boards of sport organizations, greater funding of athletes, the creation of national sport training centers, and the creation of a forum for athletes to resolve conflicts between themselves and sport organizations or coaches all contributed to an athlete-centered sport system. Thibault and Babiak were able to understand the nature of the change that had occurred in light of the context in which Canada's sport system operated. They were also able to examine the leadership role assumed by change agents to bring about the adoption of more athlete-centered change in the sport system.

Critical Thinking in Sport Organizations

Critical thinking is important in sport organizations. As introduced in chapter 1, sport leaders, managers, and employees with critical thinking skills are better able to solve problems, make informed decisions, and develop comprehensive plans and strategies

Social Media and Management Concepts and Practice in Sport Organizations

Social media and networking platforms, such as social network applications (e.g., Twitter, Facebook, LinkedIn), blogs, social tagging, wikis, and microblogs, are being adopted by sport organizations at a rapid rate. However, the implications of social media on organizational practices have not yet been broadly explored. These new technologies have the potential to alter organizational processes in profound ways, since they are a set of communication tools with a possible influence on organizational processes that is different from traditional computer-mediated technologies. Some have argued that social media has the potential to advance organizational performance (effectiveness) and to improve organizational processes (efficiency) (Treem & Leonardi, 2012). Communication through social media facilitates the exchange of a broader scope and type of information, sometimes bypassing formal structures and channels. It may also influence communication of thoughts and ideas, affecting values and possibly shaping organizational culture. Treem and Leonardi explore how new media differs from other forms of traditional computer-mediated communication (e.g., e-mail, teleconferencing). They argue that social media communication benefits organizations because it affords visibility, persistence, editability, and association. The use of social media in organizations may influence and alter knowledge sharing, socialization (formal and informal connections), and power processes in organizations. Treem and Leonardi identified "three types of information or actions that are made visible through the use of social media in organizations: (a) work behavior, (b) metaknowledge, and (c) organizational activity streams" (p. 150). For example, information about work behavior becomes more readily accessible and easier to find, and is shared more easily across organizational boundaries. The visibility of social media provides metaknowledge and data about people who work for the organization (i.e., they share information about their skills and interests). It also allows employees to orient themselves appropriately in the company because they are informed about what is happening around them. The information shared on social media platforms is also persistent—that is, it does not disappear after a user has logged off (like instant messaging or video conferencing). This may foster the development of a common ground in communication settings and in the transmission of complex ideas. Finally, social media allows for more extensive associations across various levels of the organizational structure, creating social capital and building community and bridges between employees. In sport organizations, social media is being used to communicate with external constituents. However, little work has investigated how social media affects internal organizational operations in different types of sport organizations.

for the organization. Given the constant flux in the environment, sport managers must adopt a critical thinking approach whereby they can analyze and evaluate information, facts, evidence, assumptions, ideas, and implications.

Numerous sport management scholars have expounded on the importance of developing critical thinking skills. For instance, Boucher (1998) explained that "a true measure of whether [sport management] graduates are truly prepared is *not* the courses listed on their transcripts but whether they have been educated to *think* intelligently and *make decisions* about issues they will face in the dynamic world of managing a sport enterprise" (p. 81). Similarly, Harris (1993) urged sport management educators to give greater emphasis to students' development of critical and reflective competencies. She surmised that such an emphasis would prepare professionals who would be able to "free themselves from traditional ways of identifying and solving problems, [and] to look at problems from new perspectives" (p. 322). In the same vein, Edwards (1999) suggested that critical reflection should receive more attention than it currently receives in sport management so that we can find "new, less oppressive, and more just ways of creating and managing sport" (p. 79). Furthermore, Frisby (2005) proposed that sport management educators become "versed in critical social science theories" so that they can help students become "strong critical thinkers who will make positive contributions

PORTFOLIO

Complete the critical thinking portfolio activity in the WSG, consulting as needed the "Critical Thinking Questions" sidebar in chapter 1.

to society" (p. 5). The clear implication of all these suggestions is that, as the managers of the future, you will need exceptional thinking skills to make the necessary decisions to deal effectively and responsibly with the myriad challenges that you will encounter. For instance, sport managers will have to make difficult decisions as they address issues regarding where limited funds are invested (e.g., in high-performance sport or sport for all). Thibault (2009) applied critical thinking to her analysis of globalization and sport and encouraged academics and practitioners to consider the "inconvenient truths" of globalization for those without power. This type of critical perspective may allow for different and more effective and appropriate organizational decisions to be made.

Ethics in Sport Organizations

Besides applying critical thinking skills, sport organization employees, managers, and leaders will also need to act ethically. In recent years, several ethical issues have surfaced in the context of sport. For example, incidents involving drugs and cheating in sport, violence in sport, overtraining of children involved in high-performance sport, eating disorders among athletes, recruitment violations within intercollegiate athletics programs, corruption in decision making, athlete hazing, and questionable behaviors from athletes, coaches, and referees on and off the court or field have all had an effect on sport and sport organizations. As mentioned in the section on organizational culture, the Milton-Smith (2002) study of unethical practices by the members of the IOC and OCOG led to serious negative repercussions for both organizations. Although rules, procedures, and codes of ethics were developed within these organizations, those responsible for upholding the standards of the organizations did not respect them. Managers and leaders of sport organizations are constantly facing situations, events, and issues that challenge their ability to make ethical decisions.

An extension of ethical considerations in sport organizations is the broader framing of corporate social responsibility (CSR). Carroll (1999) identified four dimensions of CSR: economic, legal, ethical, and discretionary. His view was that in being socially responsible, organizations should engage in behaviors that serve the organization financially, but that are also within the boundaries of the law and morally ethical (an obligation to do what is right and fair), as well as being good corporate citizens by contributing to the community and improving the quality of life of those affected by the organization's activities. Porter and Kramer (2006) extended these concepts to consider the role of social responsibility as being a source of competitive advantage for organizations and that the capacity exists for companies to maximize their social agendas and, at the same time, advance their business agendas. In this way, ethics and social responsibility are now being woven into the fabric and strategy of many organizational activities. In sport, these efforts are being examined by several authors from many different perspectives, including environmental responsibility (Pfahl, 2011; Polite, Waller, Spearman & Trendafilova, 2012), community involvement and relations (Babiak & Wolfe, 2009), fan and customer perspectives (Walker & Kent, 2009), and philanthropy (Tainsky & Babiak, 2011). The next chapter provides more details on managers' and leaders' involvement in ethical decision making.

PORTFOLIO

Complete the ethical issues portfolio activity in the WSG, consulting as needed the "Guidelines for Making Ethical Decisions" sidebar in chapter 1.

Summary

The organizational theory topics covered in this chapter—management concepts, organizational environment, effectiveness, structure and design, strategy, culture, and change—are all important to consider and monitor. Left unchecked, problems in these areas can reduce the effectiveness of a sport organization and, ultimately, lead to its demise. Note that these topics are interrelated. For example, the structure and design of the sport organization may affect, or be affected by, the culture of that organization. Similarly, the ability to develop and implement a strategy or to cope with change may affect, or be affected by, the structure and design of the sport organization.

These interrelationships take on even more complexity with consideration of the roles that people play in the development and management of organizations in the sport industry. The following chapter addresses the topic of individuals and their roles in organizations.

Review Questions

1. How would you define the term *organization*? What are three types of sport organizations?

2. What is the difference between effectiveness and efficiency? What is the best approach to the study of organizational effectiveness?

3. Select one sport organization. How would you describe its structure using the three structural dimensions featured in this chapter?

4. What organizational design would be most appropriate for a sporting goods manufacturer? For a sport marketing agency? For an organization bidding for the right to host a major international event?

5. What is the difference between the general environment and the specific environment?

6. Why would sport organizations choose to develop strategies?

7. What are some possible ways that stakeholders can influence sport organizations?

8. In what ways can some organizational cultures be positive for a sport organization? In what ways can other cultures be negative for a sport organization?

9. How could you use Pettigrew's contextual approach to study change in a sport organization of your choice?

10. Describe how some sport businesses view corporate social responsibility as a strategic practice.

11. Describe how new media platforms (e.g., social networking applications) affect organizational issues in the sport industry described in this chapter (e.g., effectiveness, structure, and strategy).

References

Babiak, K. (2007). Determinants of interorganizational relationships: The case of a Canadian nonprofit sport organization. *Journal of Sport Management, 21,* 338–376.

Babiak, K., & Wolfe, R. (2009). Determinants of corporate social responsibility in professional sport: Internal and external factors. *Journal of Sport Management, 23,* 717–742.

Barnard, C.I. (1938). *The functions of the executive.* Cambridge, MA: Harvard University Press.

Byers, T., Slack, T., & Parent, M. (2012). *Key concepts in sport management.* London, UK: Sage.

Boucher, R.L. (1998). Toward achieving a focal point for sport management: A binocular perspective. *Journal of Sport Management, 12,* 76–85.

Carroll, A.B. (1999). Corporate social responsibility: Evolution of a definitional construct. *Business and Society, 38*(3), 268–295.

Caza, A. (2000). Context receptivity: Innovation in an amateur sport organization. *Journal of Sport Management, 14,* 227–242.

Chelladurai, P. (2009). *Managing organizations for sport and physical activity: A systems perspective* (3rd ed.). Scottsdale, AZ: Holcomb Hathaway.

Collins, J. (2001). *Good to great: Why some companies make the leap . . . and others don't.* New York, NY: Harper Business.

Colyer, S. (2000). Organizational culture in selected Western Australian sport organizations. *Journal of Sport Management, 14,* 321–341.

Cousens, L., Babiak, K.M., & Slack, T. (2001). Adopting a relationship marketing paradigm: The case of the National Basketball Association. *International Journal of Sports Marketing and Sponsorship, 2,* 331–355.

Cunningham, G.B. (2006). Does structure make a difference? The effect of organizational structure on job satisfaction and organizational commitment. *International Journal of Sport Management, 7,* 327–346.

Daft, R.L. (2010). *Organization theory and design* (10th ed.). Mason, OH: South-Western, Cengage Learning.

Edwards, A. (1999). Reflective practice in sport management. *Sport Management Review, 2,* 67–81.

Fayol, H. (1917). *Administration industrielle et generale.* Paris, France: Dunod & Pinat.

Ferkins, L., & Shilbury, D. (2012). Good boards are strategic: What does that mean for sport governance? *Journal of Sport Management, 26,* 67–80.

Freeman, R.E. (1984). *Strategic management: A stakeholder approach.* Boston, MA: Pitman.

Freeman, R.E. (2010). *Strategic management: A stakeholder approach.* New York, NY: Cambridge University Press.

Frisby, W. (2005). The good, the bad, and the ugly: Critical sport management research. *Journal of Sport Management, 19,* 1–12.

Frontiera, J. (2010). Leadership and organizational culture transformation in professional sport. *Journal of Leadership and Organizational Studies, 17*(1), 71–86.

Greiner, L.E. (1972). Evolution and revolution as organizations grow. *Harvard Business Review, 50*(4), 37–46.

Harris, J.C. (1993). Using kinesiology: A comparison of applied veins in the subdisciplines. *Quest, 45,* 389–412.

Jones, G.R. (2010). *Organizational theory, design, and change.* Upper Saddle River, NJ: Prentice Hall.

Milton-Smith, J. (2002). Ethics, the Olympics and the search for global values. *Journal of Business Ethics, 35,* 131–142.

Mintzberg, H. (1979). *The structuring of organizations.* Englewood Cliffs, NJ: Prentice Hall.

Mullin, B.J. (1980). Sport management: The nature and utility of the concept. *Arena Review, 4,* 1–11.

Olberding, D.J. (2003). Examining strategy content in U.S. Olympic sport organizations. *International Journal of Sport Management, 4,* 6–24.

Oliver, C. (1990). Determinants of interorganizational relationships: Integration and future directions. *Academy of Management Review, 15,* 241–265.

Papadimitriou, D. (2001). An exploratory examination of the prime beneficiary approach of organizational effectiveness: The case of elite athletes of Olympic and non-Olympic sports. *European Journal of Sport Management, 8,* 63–82.

Peters, T., & Waterman, R. (1982). *In search of excellence: Lessons from America's best-run companies.* New York, NY: Warner.

Pettigrew, A.M. (1987). Context and action in the transformation of the firm. *Journal of Management Studies, 24,* 649–670.

Pettigrew, A.M. (1990). Longitudinal field research on change: Theory and practice. *Organization Science, 1,* 267–292.

Pfahl, M. (2011). Strategic issues associated with the development of internal sustainability teams in sport organizations: A framework for action and sustainable environmental performance. *International Journal of Sport Management, Recreation, and Tourism, 6*(C), 37–61.

Polite, F.G., Waller, S., Spearman, L., & Trendafilova, S.A. (2012). Social accountability and responsibility in sport: An examination of the National Collegiate Athletic Association. *Sport Science Review, XX*(1-2), 111–135.

Porter, M.E. (2008). *On competition. Updated and expanded edition.* Boston, MA: Harvard Business School.

Porter, M.E., & Kramer, M.R. (2006). Strategy and society: The link between competitive advantage and corporate social responsibility. *Harvard Business Review, 84*(12), 78–92.

Quinn, R.E., & Cameron, K. (1983). Organizational life cycles and shifting criteria of effectiveness: Some preliminary evidence. *Management Science, 29,* 33–51.

Quinn, R.E., & Rohrbaugh, J. (1981). A competing values approach to organizational effectiveness. *Public Productivity Review, 5*(2), 122–140.

Sack, A.L., & Nadim, A. (2002). Strategic choices in a turbulent environment: A case study of Starter Corporation. *Journal of Sport Management, 16,* 36–53.

Schein, E.H. (1985). *Organizational culture and leadership.* San Francisco, CA: Jossey-Bass.

Senge, P. (1990). *The fifth discipline: The art and practice of the learning organization.* New York, NY: Doubleday/Currency.

Shilbury, D., & Moore, K.A. (2006). A study of organizational effectiveness for national Olympic sporting organizations. *Nonprofit and Voluntary Sector Quarterly, 35*(1), 5–38.

Slack, T. (1997). *Understanding sport organizations: The application of organization theory.* Champaign, IL: Human Kinetics.

Slack, T., & Parent, M.M. (2006). *Understanding sport organizations. The application of organization theory* (2nd ed.). Champaign, IL: Human Kinetics.

Tainsky, S., & Babiak, K. (2011). Professional athletes and charitable foundations: An exploratory investigation. *International Journal of Sport Management and Marketing, 9*(3/4), 133–153.

Taylor, F.W. (1911). *The principles of scientific management.* New York, NY: Harper.

Theodoraki, E.I. (2001). A conceptual framework for the study of structural configurations of Organising Committees for the Olympic Games (OCOGs). *European Journal for Sport Management, 8,* 106–124.

Thibault, L. (2009). The globalization of sport: An inconvenient truth. *Journal of Sport Management, 23,* 1–20.

Thibault, L., & Babiak, K. (2005). Organizational changes in Canada's sport system: Toward an athlete-centred approach. *European Sport Management Quarterly, 5,* 105–132.

Thibault, L., Slack, T., & Hinings, C.R. (1993). A framework for the analysis of strategy in nonprofit sport organizations. *Journal of Sport Management, 7,* 25–43.

Treem, J.W., & Leonardi, P.M. (2012). Social media use in organizations: Exploring the affordances of visibility, editability, persistence, and association. *Communication Yearbook, 36,* 143–189.

Turner, P., & Shilbury, D. (2008). Broadcasting technology and its influence on sport broadcaster inter-organisational relationship formation. *International Journal of Sport Management and Marketing, 3,* 167–183.

Turner, P.E., & Shilbury, D. (2010). The impact of emerging technology in sport broadcasting on the preconditions for interorganizational relationship formation in professional football. *Journal of Sport Management, 24,* 10–44.

Walker, M., & Kent, A. (2009). Do fans care? Assessing the influence of corporate social responsibility on consumer attitudes in the sport industry. *Journal of Sport Management, 23,* 743–769.

Wolfe, R., Hoeber, L., & Babiak, K. (2002). Perceptions of the effectiveness of sport organisations: The case of intercollegiate athletics. *European Sport Management Quarterly, 2,* 135–156.

Wolfe, R., & Putler, D. (2002). How tight are the ties that bind stakeholder groups? *Organization Science, 13,* 64–80.

Yuchtman, E., & Seashore, S.E. (1967). A system resource approach to organizational effectiveness. *American Sociological Review, 32*(6), 891–903.

Zanger, B.K., & Parks, J.B. (Eds.). (1984). *Sport management curricula: The business and education nexus.* Bowling Green, OH: School of Health, Physical Education, and Recreation, Bowling Green State University.

Zeigler, E.F. (1987). Sport management: Past, present, future. *Journal of Sport Management, 1,* 4–24.

Zeigler, E.F., & Spaeth, M. (1975). *Administrative theory and practice in physical education and athletics.* Englewood Cliffs, NJ: Prentice Hall.

HISTORICAL MOMENTS

- **1917** Frank Calder named first president of the NHL
- **1920** Kenesaw Mountain Landis appointed first commissioner of MLB and Jim Thorpe appointed first president of the American Professional Football Association (now NFL)
- **1946** Maurice Podoloff appointed president of the Basketball Association of America (now NBA)
- **1962** Marvin Miller became first executive director of Major League Baseball Players Association (MLBPA)
- **1984** David Stern named NBA commissioner; retired in 2014
- **1986** Anita DeFrantz became first American woman and first African American on the International Olympic Committee (IOC)
- **1992** Donna Lopiano became executive director of the Women's Sport Foundation; served until 2007
- **1998** Bud Selig named MLB commissioner and Sepp Blatter elected president of FIFA
- **2001** Jacques Rogge elected president of the IOC
- **2003** Myles Brand became National Collegiate Athletic Association (NCAA) chief executive officer (CEO) and served until his death in 2009
- **2005** Valerie Ackerman became first female president of USA Basketball; served until 2008
- **2006** Roger Goodell named NFL commissioner
- **2007** Tonya Antonucci named Women's Professional Soccer (WPS) commissioner; served until 2010
- **2008** Jerry Reese became first African American NFL general manager to win the Super Bowl
- **2009** Riccardo Fraccari voted into office as president of the International Baseball Federation (IBAF)
- **2010** Scott Blackmun became CEO of the United States Olympic Committee (USOC)
- **2011** Laurel J. Richie appointed president of the WNBA; Peter Dawson named president of the International Golf Federation (IGF) for a two-year term
- **2012** With the most wins (1,098) of any men's or women's NCAA basketball coach, Pat Summitt announced her retirement as head coach of the female basketball program at the University of Tennessee
- **2013** Thomas Bach elected ninth president of the IOC
- **2014** Adam Silver became fifth commissioner of the NBA

5

MANAGING AND LEADING IN SPORT ORGANIZATIONS

Shannon Kerwin \ Jerome Quarterman \ Ming Li

LEARNING OBJECTIVES

> Define organizational behavior and its application to the sport industry.
> Differentiate between the terms *management* and *leadership*.
> Define managerial skills, theoretical approaches to management, and levels of management in sport organizations.
> Understand the components of the contingency theory of leadership.
> Understand the full range of leadership model.
> Understand the concepts of decision making, authority, and power.
> Identify and understand the principles of human resource management.
> Understand the importance of diversity, ethics, and ethical leadership in the workplace.
> Explain the critical role that theory plays in the management of people within sport organizations.

Key Terms

behaviors centered on employees

behaviors centered on tasks

directive leadership style

ethical leaders

leadership

management

participative leadership style

GET A JOB

Continue on your journey in sport management by going to the web study guide (WSG) at www.HumanKinetics.com/ContemporarySportManagement. Check out the job opportunities and consider the skills and experiences that can help you succeed in sport management.

Whereas the previous chapter deals with structural, design, and environmental features of sport organizations, this chapter introduces and examines the roles that individuals play within those organizations. Thus, this chapter is about organizational behavior. Organizational behavior is defined as the study of individuals and groups in organizations (Robbins & Judge, 2008). According to Schermerhorn, Hunt, and Osborn (2008), organizational behavior "is a multidisciplinary field devoted to understanding individual and group behavior, interpersonal processes, and organization dynamics" (p. 5).

This chapter addresses a number of topics related to people in the sport management workplace. Management functions and skills are also introduced, followed by an examination of leadership and leaders relative to the skills of the sport manager, their followers, and the sport context. The concepts of decision making, authority, and power are then explained. Human resource management, including recruitment and selection of employees, orientation, training, and performance evaluation of these employees, is explained next. The chapter concludes with discussions of diversity and ethics in the sport workplace and the relevance of critical thinking in managing and leading people in sport organizations.

Theoretical Approaches to Management

management—The process of working with and through individuals and groups to accomplish organizational goals.

The success of sport organizations ultimately depends on how effectively managers apply their management and leadership skills. Hersey, Blanchard, and Johnson (2008) provided one of the most comprehensive definitions of **management** as "the process of working with and through individuals and groups and other resources (such as equipment, capital, and technology) to accomplish organizational goals" (p. 7). Numerous theoretical approaches to management and managing people in organizations have been developed. We classify these approaches into three basic types: scientific management, human relations management, and the process approach (also known as administrative management). In the following paragraphs, we summarize these approaches.

Scientific Management Approach

Early theorists believed that the primary responsibility of managers was to increase workers' output. Frederick Taylor (1911) developed this approach, in which the major concern was to scrutinize the performance of individual workers. The key was that workers who produced more than others would receive greater rewards. This approach advocated paying people by the number of units produced or sold rather than by the length of time (e.g., hours) that they worked. In the sport industry, this approach is best illustrated when employees work on a commission basis. For example, a game-day salesperson might earn a commission based on the number of programs sold. The sport manager working under such conditions would focus primarily on how effective each individual game-day salesperson was in selling game programs. The scientific management approach considers pay and working conditions to be the most important factors in increasing a worker's performance.

Human Relations Management Approach

The human relations approach grew out of studies conducted at Western Electric's Hawthorne, Illinois, plant during the late 1920s and early 1930s (Mayo, 1933). Mayo's research on more than 20,000 employees found that when employees believed they were important, they became more cohesive and productive. The researcher's conclusion was that managers' concern for workers would lead to higher rates of job satisfaction, which would result in better performance and higher productivity (Staw, 1986).

Process Approach to Management

The process approach has been the predominant theoretical framework used in the study and practice of management in recent times. Unlike the scientific and human relations management approaches, the process approach focuses on managing the organization as a whole entity. Using the process management approach, we review various management functions assumed by managers.

Management Functions

The process approach to management uses a set of ongoing, interactive activities—known as the underlying processes of management—to accomplish the goals and objectives of organizations, departments, or work units. Such processes were first introduced more than six decades ago as POSDCORB (Gulick & Urwick, 1937). POSDCORB is the acronym for planning, organizing, staffing, directing, coordinating, reporting, and budgeting. The original seven processes have since been reduced to five functions: planning, staffing, organizing, directing, and controlling and evaluating (Jones & George, 2009). Figure 5.1 illustrates that these underlying processes flow in all directions and that decisions made in each component affect all other components. Ultimately, all the processes revolve around the manager's actions and decisions.

In sport organizations, the management process typically starts with planning and ends with controlling and evaluating. Managers might engage in the activities in various sequences, and sometimes they perform several activities simultaneously as they carry out the responsibilities of their jobs. The element common to all the processes, whenever they are performed, is decision making. Table 5.1 provides definitions of each function, as well as examples of how the general manager of a private sport club might practice them. The concepts of decision making, authority, and power are covered later in this chapter. We now proceed to a discussion of the classifications of managers.

Classifications of Managers

Although all managers have formal authority for organizing, directing, and controlling the work activities of others, managers possess different degrees of authority. In the hierarchy of an organization, managers are usually classified as top level, middle level, or supervisory level. Examples of titles of managers at these different levels in three types of sport organizations are shown in table 5.2.

> *Top-level managers.* The number of managers in this group is small. Also known as executive or senior-level managers, they have the most power and authority. They are usually responsible for the entire organization or a major part of it.

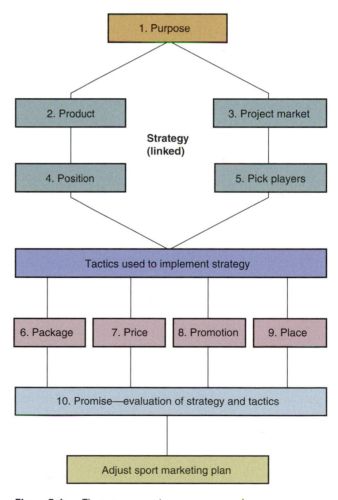

Figure 5.1   The management process approach.

Table 5.1   **Management Process of a General Manager in a Private Sport Club**

Underlying process	Definition	Example
Planning	Developing and implementing goals, objectives, strategies, procedures, policies, and rules to produce goods and services in the most effective and efficient manner	The general manager of a private sport club predicts the increase in enrollment at the start of the new year and arranges for the facility to be open 18 hours per day instead of 15 hours per day.
Staffing	Recruiting, selecting, orienting, training, developing, and replacing employees to produce goods and services in the most effective and efficient manner	The general manager advertises the positions: three teaching pros, one maintenance person, and one administrative assistant. The general manager then holds interviews, checks references, makes job offers, and selects the staff needed for the golf program.
Organizing	Arranging resources (e.g., human, financial, equipment, supplies, time, space, information) to produce goods and services in the most effective and efficient manner	After conducting an assessment, the general manager establishes a work unit for teaching golf at the club. The general manager appoints a full-time coordinator who will coordinate three teaching pros and a new golf course with an adequate budget.
Directing	Influencing members (e.g., subordinates, peers, supervisors) as individuals and as groups to produce goods and services in the most effective and efficient manner	The general manager encourages the golf teaching pros to prepare weekend course packages for local executives who have expressed an interest in learning golf skills.
Controlling and evaluating	Evaluating whether the employees are on task and making progress toward achieving the goals and adhering to the guidelines and standards for producing goods and services in the most effective and efficient manner	After 3 months, the general manager monitors the progress of the new golf program with the pros and discusses ways to make the program more attractive to potential new members.

> *Middle-level managers.* Also known as administrative-level managers, these people are usually selected by top-level managers. They are, therefore, accountable to top-level managers and responsible for the employees who are below them in the hierarchy. The managers at the middle level are, in general, responsible for (1) managing a department or unit that performs an organizational function, and (2) ensuring that the assigned tasks are done efficiently. To their subordinates, middle-level managers are the source of information and solutions to problems because they know the technical side of the products and services. Middle-level managers are unique because they must be both leaders and followers. They are connected to supervisors and to subordinates, both of whom are also managers.

> *Supervisory-level managers.* These managers, also known as first-line managers or supervisors, report to middle-level managers and are responsible for the employees who work in their units. The employees for whom these managers are responsible can be classified as operatives or technical specialists. Supervisory managers have the least amount of authority. They are primarily responsible for a single area in a work

Table 5.2   Selected Titles for Managers at Different Levels in Three Typical Sport Organizations

Levels of management	Professional baseball organization	Investor-owned health and fitness club	Intercollegiate athletics program
Top-level managers (executive or senior level)	President Chief executive officer (CEO) Vice president of business operations Vice president of baseball operations	Owners General managers Regional director of corporate wellness Regional director of health promotion	Board of trustees University president Vice president for athletics Athletics director (AD) Senior associate AD
Middle-level managers (administrative-level)	Director of public relations Director of corporate sales Director of marketing operations Team manager Director of scouting	Site manager of corporate wellness Site manager of health promotion	Associate AD Director of development
Supervisory-level managers (first line)	Director of stadium operations Director of broadcasting Director of community relations Director of baseball administration	Coordinators (supervisors) of aerobics, fitness, golf, pro shop, weight training	Assistant ADs Sports information director Coordinator of athletics training Marketing director Academic coordinator Director of event operations Manager of ticket sales Director of compliance Equipment manager

unit, division, or department, in which they supervise the work of the operatives or technical specialists. Their job is to communicate with, inspire, and influence their subordinates to get the job done in the most effective and efficient way. Supervisory managers represent the contact point between the technical specialists (operatives) and middle-level managers.

Managerial Skills

Within each classification of manager addressed in the previous section, an individual will possess certain managerial skills that aid in the performance of day-to-day management tasks. As noted by Katz (1974), the skill sets of effective administrators can be broken down into three categories: conceptual skills, human relations skills, and technical skills. Interestingly, the amount of each skill required by a manager may change from organization to organization, and may fluctuate as well with the level of management (Katz, 1974). Further, managerial skills do not function in isolation in that most managers may display multiple managerial skills at any given time. A summary of the link between each managerial skill category and the levels of management is found in table 5.3.

Table 5.3   **Linking Managerial Skills to Levels of Management in the United States Olympic Committee (USOC)**

Managerial skills	Definition	Link to levels of management
Conceptual skills	Possesses the ability to see the organization as a whole Effectively uses analytical, creative, and initiative skills Aids in planning and organizing processes of managers Most often linked to top-level managers	Top-level managers (e.g., the CEO of the USOC) analyze the state of high-performance sport in the United States to determine a long-term athlete development plan.
Human relations skills	Possesses the ability to work with people (i.e., interpersonal skills) Effectively uses communication and listening skills Aids in planning, staffing, organizing, directing, and controlling/evaluating processes of managers; each process requires interaction with people Most often linked to all three levels of manager	Top-level managers (e.g., the CEO of the USOC) must communicate with each chief officer when planning the budget for each Olympic year. Middle-level manager (e.g., the chief communications and public affairs officer) must communicate with the managing director of information technology (IT) to ensure a plan is in place for the effective utilization of Twitter for the upcoming Olympic Games. Supervisory-level managers (e.g., the managing director of IT) must work closely with members of his/her research team to evaluate the most effective use of Twitter for the upcoming Olympic Games.
Technical skills	Can perform a job based on the job requirements Effectively uses skills (e.g., computer, IT) required for a given position Aids in completing everyday operational tasks Most often linked to supervisory-level managers	Supervisory-level managers (e.g., the research team within the IT department at the USOC) must have the computing skills to work with research software and statistics associated with collecting data from potential Olympic Games consumers.

A manager's conceptual skills help to identify the root cause of problems rather than simply stating the symptoms of an issue. For instance, in an effort to redirect an unmotivated corporate culture, the CEO of the USOC may use his or her human relations skills to communicate with each of the chief officers to develop an understanding of the factors that influence the USOC's corporate culture. Rather than diagnose and label the symptoms (e.g., poor productivity, low morale) of the issue, the CEO would use his or her conceptual skills to see the big picture and create solutions for the betterment of the USOC as a whole.

A manager's human relations skills help in leading, motivating, and developing cohesion among employees. Within sport organizations, managers at all levels must work with a variety of employees, including paid staff, volunteers, and interns. Thus, effective human relations skills are an essential component to the daily operations of sport managers.

A manager's technical skills are directly associated with everyday tasks on the job. For instance, the chief financial officer (CFO) of the USOC must possess technical skills associated with budget management, management of internal and external audits, and financial planning. More specifically, he or she must also possess human relations skills when communicating with and directing supervisory-level managers responsible for preparing budgets using their technical skills in computer programs such as Microsoft Excel and PeopleSoft.

Leadership

Hersey and colleagues (2008) defined **leadership** as influencing people to work individually or collectively toward the achievement of a goal. As explained in previous pages, these same authors have defined management as working with individuals and groups while using other resources (e.g., time, money, equipment, facilities) to achieve the goals of an organization. The roles of leaders and managers have both similarities and differences. For example, both roles involve people working with other people. The roles are different with respect to the ways in which leaders and managers accomplish the objectives. Managers are often leaders, but not all leaders are necessarily managers. The term *leader* is broader than the term *manager* because people need not be in management positions to be leaders. Depending on the situation, all employees of the organization can act as leaders. Any time a person influences the behavior of others, regardless of the reason, that person is demonstrating leadership. For example, a sport management intern might have special skills using a specific computer software program to create complex video presentations. When that intern assists the controller or director, she or he is taking the lead during that time. Conversely, when employees in an organization rely on others for direction or guidance, those others are acting as leaders, even if they are not in official decision-making positions. As dynamic and often complex structures, organizations in the sport industry require managers who are skilled in both management and leadership.

Like management, leadership is also conceptualized as an interactive process. The primary goal of leadership is to exert influence on individual and group behaviors, toward the leader's goals, the organization's goals, or both. Although the terms *manager* and *leader* are sometimes used interchangeably, the two concepts are not the same. When people function as managers, they are primarily focused on efficiency and *doing things right*. When people function as leaders, they are concerned with effectiveness and *doing the right things*. Differences between management and leadership are further elaborated in table 5.4, which shows that managers cope with complexity in the workplace and that leaders cope with change.

> **leadership**—The process of influencing the activities of an individual or group in an effort to achieve a goal in a given situation.

WEB

Go to the WSG and complete the web search activity, which will help you identify the traits of various sport industry leaders.

Table 5.4   Comparative Summary of the Management–Leadership Dichotomy

Management (coping with complexity)	Leadership (coping with change)
Planning and budgeting—Setting goals for the future, establishing procedures for achieving the goals, and allocating adequate resources to effectively achieve the goals.	*Setting a direction*—Developing a vision of the future and strategies for producing the changes needed to achieve the vision.
Organizing and staffing—Creating an organizational structure for accomplishing the plan, staffing the organization with qualified workers, delegating responsibility for carrying out the plans, and constructing a system to monitor implementation.	*Aligning people*—Communicating the new direction to those who can create coalitions that understand the vision and are committed to its achievement.
Controlling and problem solving—Monitoring results in some detail, both formally and informally, by means of reports, meetings, and other tools; identifying deviations; and then planning and organizing to solve the problems.	*Motivating and inspiring*—Keeping people moving in the same direction, despite confronting major obstacles, by appealing to basic but often untapped human needs, values, and emotions.

Adapted from Kotter 1990.

Based on the distinction between managers and leaders, it is important for sport leaders to recognize the characteristics of effective leaders and determine which characteristics are present (or can be developed) within the human resources of their sport entity. Table 5.5 outlines the characteristics of successful leaders.

Sport management scholars also conceptualized leadership and managerial behaviors as a unified concept. Soucie (1994), for example, suggested that management and leadership are qualitatively different and that each complements the other, resulting in more effective and efficient sport managers. Quarterman (1998) provided further support for this notion when he noted in his study that NCAA conference commissioners used both management and leadership skills, depending on the given situation.

Contingency Theory of Leadership

As noted previously, leaders differ from managers in their ability to cope with change. When dealing with change, it is important for sport leaders to examine themselves, their followers, and the leadership context. Specifically, Fiedler's (1963) contingency theory suggests the most effective style of leadership is dependent on the situation or context. In this theory, leadership is multidimensional in that it includes (a) the leaders' traits, power or influence, and goals, (b) their followers' expectations and values, and (c) the leadership context, defined by organizational complexity and task uncertainty. The following subsections provide detail for each of these elements of the contingency theory of leadership. Figure 5.2 illustrates the connection between each element and highlights the interaction that occurs between them during the leadership process.

LEADERS

Within contingency theory, leaders are responsible for introducing and managing change. In order for leaders to be successful, they must possess some form of power over their followers to ensure buy-in and commitment to change. Whether this power comes in the form of charisma, superior knowledge or experience, or an individual's position in the organizational hierarchy, this power provides a leader with the ability to influence the actions of followers toward personal and organizational goals. In essence, the leader's goal is to influence others to follow him or her on a certain path

Table 5.5 **Characteristics of Successful Leaders**

They trust their subordinates.	A good leader makes use of employees' energy and talent. The key to a productive relationship is mutual trust.
They develop a vision.	Employees want to follow a visionary leader. They want to know where they are going and why.
They keep their cool.	Leaders demonstrate their mettle in crisis and under fire. They inspire others to remain calm and act intelligently.
They are experts.	Employees are much more likely to follow a leader who radiates confidence, is intuitive, and continues to master the profession.
They invite dissent.	A leader is willing to accept and integrate a variety of opinions.
They simplify.	Leaders focus on what is important and reach elegant, simple answers to complex problems by keeping the details to themselves.
They encourage risk.	Leaders encourage employees to take chances, readily accept error, and not fear failure.

Adapted from Labich 1988.

(designated by the leader), which ultimately leads to the end-state goal. For instance, the commissioner of the NFL strives to create change (goal) toward diversity and racial equality (end-state goal) within the NFL head office. The commissioner uses his place in the organizational hierarchy (position power) and legal expertise (legitimate power) to lead his followers through this change. Further description of sources of power will appear later in this chapter.

FOLLOWERS

An important element within Fiedler's (1963) contingency theory is the interactive relationship between leaders and followers. Followers (or subordinates) are a vital component to the change process; however, they are often overlooked in favor of a leader-centered focus. Specifically, alignment between the followers' expectations and values and the leader's goals significantly influence the effectiveness of the change process. Specifically, within our example regarding the hypothetical diversity-change initiative within the NFL, the executive group within each NFL team (i.e., the followers) would have (1) expectations of what diversity in the NFL should look like and (2)

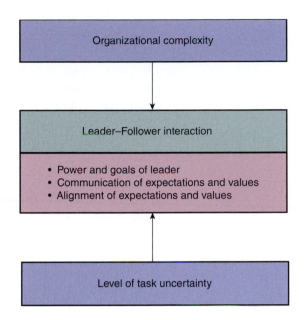

Figure 5.2 The interactive process associated with the contingency theory of leadership.

Adapted from Lorsch 2010.

personal values associated with how the change process should unfold. As such, in order for effective change to occur around the end-state goal of racial equality, the commissioner must actively align his or her goals and power with each executive group member's expectations and values. This may become a tall task for leaders when organizations have a number of layers with multiple leader–follower dyads. This potential complexity highlights the essential elements of communication and alignment within the leadership process.

CONTEXT

Within the leadership context, contingency theory (Fiedler, 1963) suggests that organizational complexity and task uncertainty will guide the leadership style that is most appropriate (and effective) when it comes to coping with change. *Organizational complexity* consists of the size of the organization or group within which leaders and followers operate, and the location of the workspace. In terms of size, the larger the organization, the larger the number of leader and follower goals and expectations to manage. Specifically, in a large sport organization like FIFA, the president and executive office would have to coordinate efforts with thousands of followers within their member associations in order to effect change. Following the tenets of contingency theory, the president must ensure that expectations and values of each member association were communicated and aligned with the leader's goals. This becomes more complex when a leader examines the location of FIFA and must coordinate (for example) member associations across the globe. Thus, the larger the organization and the greater the distance between a leader and their followers, the harder it is for leaders to match their power and goals with each follower's values and expectations. As such, larger sport organizations may require multiple leaders with complementary power and change goals to coordinate multiple followers.

Task uncertainty is a contextual factor that influences leaders' ability to cope with change in their sport organizations. As noted by Fiedler (1963), tasks can range from

Professional Profile: Becky Burleigh

Title: head coach, women's soccer, University of Florida

Education: BA (biology), Methodist University; MS (exercise science), Georgia State University

As the head coach of the women's soccer team at the University of Florida (UF), Becky Burleigh has focused her attention on developing her players as leaders and active citizens within the community. Her leadership development program highlights core competencies required of leaders and followers on her team, manages these competencies with active communication between leader and followers, and teaches consideration of each other's expectations and values. This commitment to leadership development and management of values has made Coach Burleigh's team one of the most successful programs in the country, both on and off the field of play. Coach Burleigh applies the tenets of the contingency theory of leadership into her daily routine by constantly assessing her own goals, communicating with followers, and aligning the values and expectations of all individuals involved with her team. She self-reflects and develops her own capacity to cope with change as a leader. The following is a snapshot into her role as a leader in the sport industry.

ONE DAY

Go to the WSG and learn more about a typical day in the life for Becky Burleigh. See if she spends her working hours the way you think she does.

What have been the key moves, steps, or developments in your career, and how did you arrive at your current position?

I became a head coach at Berry College in Rome, Georgia right out of college. I graduated in May and took the job at Berry College in June at the age of 21. My only coaching experience prior to that was as a coach at the state and regional levels. I left Berry College after 5 years and two NAIA National Championships and came to UF, where I have been head coach for 18 years. Here, I would be classified as a middle-level manager, since I lead my coaching staff, trainers, and team, but I ultimately answer to the director of athletics at UF.

What are your current responsibilities and objectives in your job?

Similar to the manager of a department, I am responsible for all facets of the women's soccer program at UF. I manage a team of 25 to 30 women, two full-time assistants, a full-time trainer and strength coach, and a volunteer coach. My team plays in the Southeastern Conference (SEC) in the NCAA, where the goal (and expectation) each year is to win the conference and compete for a national championship (the team has won 12 SEC titles and one national title under my leadership). In addition to the on-field play of my players, I am dedicated to managing my players' academic and social lives as college students. I am committed to a leadership development program, which requires a significant time commitment from leaders and followers but provides a strong culture and identity for the team.

What do you enjoy most about your current job?

I enjoy the relationships that come from spending four years with players, as well as watching them have a lot of growth in development both on and off the field in that time. I also love competing and taking a team that is different every year through the challenges that each new season brings. I enjoy the task uncertainty that comes with the turnover of players and the addition of new personalities to their team culture each year.

What do you consider the biggest future challenge to be in your job or industry?

The biggest future challenge is recruiting in our sector of the sport industry. As leaders, we are required to recruit players way too young. This results in many problems. Most players commit to a school as early as their sophomore year in high school, which is a lot of pressure for women at such a young age.

routine and repetitive (certain) to innovative, novel, and nonrepetitive (uncertain), thus describing the level of uncertainty within a task. Implicit in this distinction is an analysis of the leadership style that may appropriately lead followers through change. For example, on the one hand, a foreman within the front lines of Nike's manufacturing division may be required to lead employees through a shift in production line techniques. This change process requires motivating followers directly connected to a very routine and certain daily task. In this case, a more directive leadership style may be appropriate, where followers are expecting guidance and structure and employees have little (if any) input in planning and decision making.

On the other hand, when a marketing manager with adidas asks her subordinates for a new and creative marketing strategy to target girls and women in their new fall marketing campaign, the leader may find a more participative leadership style most effective. This would involve the marketing manager seeking employee involvement in the planning and decision making of the campaign. With task uncertainty, followers may expect flexibility and autonomy, which would promote innovation and creativity through change.

As a sport leader, it is imperative that the workplace context be assessed to determine which leader style is most appropriate for the situation. The next section details the full range of leadership models, highlighting effective leader behaviors attached to leadership theory.

Leadership Styles

Over the years, several approaches to the study of leadership have been developed. Among the most common approaches are (1) theories that attempt to explain why some people are good leaders and others are not and (2) models that represent observed patterns of effective leadership that can be learned. Leadership approaches have identified specific traits and characteristics held by leaders (e.g., honesty, integrity, self-confidence, cognitive abilities), behaviors assumed by leaders (i.e., behaviors centered on tasks, behaviors centered on employees, or behaviors centered on both tasks and employees), and leadership based on situations (i.e., as discussed in the previous section, where different situations call for different leadership styles). The following paragraphs focus on specific leadership behaviors outlined in the full range of leadership model. This model includes transactional, laissez-faire, and transformational leader behaviors. As you progress in your sport management curriculum and study leadership in more depth, you will discover additional leadership theories and models. You will also learn that some leader behaviors overlap categories and defy neat classifications. Nonetheless, a brief discussion of this model will provide you with a basic understanding of current thought regarding leadership in organizations.

Full Range of Leadership Model

Bass and Avolio (1994) developed the full range of leadership model based on research investigations of a variety of leader behaviors. An overview of this model, which includes transactional, laissez-faire, and transformational leader behaviors, is presented in table 5.6. As shown in this table, the transactional leadership style implies an exchange between leaders and followers whereby they agree on the types of performances that will lead to reward or punishment for followers (Bass & Riggio, 2006). Transactional leadership includes three types of reinforcement behaviors: contingent reward, active management by exception, and passive management by exception. In contingent reward, leaders attempt to be clear about their expectations of followers. When followers' performances are satisfactory, leaders can provide rewards, such as praise or an increase in pay. When followers' performances are unsatisfactory, leaders can respond with notification of the inadequacies and, ideally, with additional clarification. Management by exception (MBE) is a more negative approach. Adherents to this leadership style ascribe to the "If it ain't broke, don't fix it" philosophy (Bass & Riggio, 2006, p. 4). MBE-active leaders keep track of followers' performances. When

directive leadership style—Leaders function where employees have little (if any) input in planning and decision making.

participative leadership style—Leaders seek employee involvement in project planning and decision making.

ACTION

Go to the WSG and complete the first Learning in Action activity, which asks you to describe sport organizations in terms of their connection to contextual factors influencing leadership style within contingency theory.

behaviors centered on tasks—Primarily concerned with the technical or formal aspects of jobs and considering followers primarily as the means for accomplishing the organization's goals.

behaviors centered on employees—Primarily concerned with interpersonal relations, meeting personal needs of followers, and accommodating personality differences among followers.

Olympic Complex "Spyros Louis" in Athens, Greece: When the Obvious Is Not Obvious

By Dimitra Papadimitriou, Greece
University of Patras, Rion-Patras

For more than three decades the Olympic Stadium Spyros Louis in Greece has hosted many major sporting and entertainment events, but now it faces a battle for survival and threats for privatization.

The Olympic Stadium Spyros Louis, or simply OAKA, is part of a large complex of sport facilities located in the municipality of Marousi, in the broad area of Athens, Greece. The stadium was originally built in 1982 and named after Spyros Louis, the first winner of the marathon of the 1896 inaugural Athens Olympic Games.

The stadium has hosted several major events including the 1982 European Championships in athletics, the 1997 World Championships in athletics, the 1991 Mediterranean Games, two football finals for the UEFA Champions league (1994, 2007) and the 1987 UEFA Cup Winners' Cup final. Until recently it also remained the home ground of major and historical football clubs (i.e., AEK, Panathinaikos) in the Athens area. However, one of the most unique events hosted in this stadium was the 2005 Acropolis Rally, the first-ever Fé-

followers make mistakes, the leaders take corrective action. MBE-passive leaders do not monitor followers' performances. Rather, they wait passively and make corrections only when mistakes occur.

The second leadership style in table 5.6 is characterized as nontransactional. In reality, the nontransactional approach is not a leadership style at all because the people who use this approach are extremely passive. They avoid all forms of leadership. They neither monitor nor correct their followers. Consequently, this style is the least effective.

dération Internationale de l'Automobile (FIA) World Rally event to be staged in a stadium, which resulted in a great success. The stadium has been also extensively used for hosting major music concerts, with pop and rock superstars such as Madonna, U2, Pyx Lax, the Red Hot Chili Peppers, and Bon Jovi performing on the stage, most of them achieving sold-out ticket records of over 70,000 attendants.

After an extensive renovation just before the 2004 Olympic Games, the stadium hosted the opening and the closing ceremonies of the Games, along with the athletics events and the final of the Olympic football tournament. In its current form, the capacity of the stadium is 69,618 seats. One of its landmarks is the roof designed by Santiago Calatrava, the world-renowned Spanish architect. The Olympic Complex is owned by the Greek state and run by a nonprofit organization that is largely subsidized by the state. A board of directors consisting of nine members appointed by the government is responsible for running the stadium along with the executive director and 220 largely underskilled employees.

Over the last few years, the Olympic Stadium has been used extensively by local football clubs, which recently had no other choice but to drop out of these stadium usage deals due to the economic crisis. This left behind damages to the facility from fan riots and added to the stadium's mounting debt. Today the complex faces deep financial problems as it largely depends on state support, which is literarily in a free fall, with a 50% drop in public subsidies between 2011 and 2013 because of the effects of the five-year government economic crisis. In the same vein, major past customers of the stadium (clubs) face their own difficulties in convincing owners to spend money on football and basketball teams.

Interestingly, one of the top teams views its departure from OAKA as a major relief and most importantly as a challenge to find new opportunities for alternative markets and revenue generation. The leading team recently announced plans to develop new areas of the market relevant to sport tourism with quality programs and the creation of two new Olympic-themed museums. They also plan to open up the surrounding areas and some of the facilities to more promising markets such as tourists, businesses, and families by redesigning and repositioning the usage options for these facilities in new markets. As the daily battle for survival becomes acute in OAKA and the threats for privatization take center stage for a series of public assets, the OAKA president, Mr. P. Galaktopoulos (a wrestling Olympic medalist in 1968) stressed that "it is about time to turn a new page in the activities of this world-known complex." As the complex's leader, he is expected to successfully carry out the unenviable task of leading the stadium out of the toughest years the country has faced.

International Learning Activity #1

Search for similar stadiums in your country or abroad that are linked to previous Olympic Games. Go back at least six Summer Olympic Games and prepare a table with the main features of these stadiums as today (e.g., name, capacity, owner, operator, staffing, construction cost, innovations, major activities hosted, major accomplishments). Compare these features and identify common or different operational patterns.

International Learning Activity #2

Pick a major sport facility you know well and identify the major sources of revenue it has developed so far. Consider the importance of each one of these resources toward the achievement of facility's goals. Discuss how complex it is for the facility management to combine all these sources of revenue. Also, why might the facility want to cut back on some of these sources? Weigh the pros and cons.

As shown in table 5.6, the third type of leader behavior is the transformational style (Yukl, 2012). Transformational leaders practice the four *I*s: idealized influence, inspirational motivation, intellectual stimulation, and individualized consideration (Avolio, Waldman, & Yammarino, 1991). They are trustworthy, encouraging, risk taking, and considerate. They raise their followers' consciousness about the importance of outcomes and explain how followers can reach those outcomes by placing organizational interests ahead of self-interests.

Table 5.6   **Brief Overview of the Full Range of Leadership**

Leadership behaviors	Transactional style
Contingent reward	Gives followers a clear understanding of what is expected of them; arranges rewards for satisfactory performance
Management by exception (active)	Monitors followers' performances and takes corrective action when mistakes are observed
Management by exception (passive)	Waits for mistakes to be made and then corrects them
	Nontransactional style
Laissez-faire	Avoids leadership; is inactive
	Transformational style
Idealized influence	Serves as a good role model; can be trusted to do the right thing
Inspirational motivation	Encourages the optimism and enthusiasm of followers
Intellectual stimulation	Encourages followers to consider new ways of looking at old methods and problems
Individualized consideration	Gives personal attention to followers; listens to them; serves as a coach or mentor

Adapted from Bass 1985; Bass and Avolio 1994.

Although most leaders engage in the full range of leadership styles, they do so to differing degrees. Many studies in a variety of organizations have suggested that the leaders who were most effective used the transformational style most frequently, the transactional style occasionally, and the nontransactional (laissez-faire) style rarely, if at all (Bass & Avolio, 1994; Bass & Riggio, 2006).

No matter the leadership style, one of the most challenging areas that you will encounter in your first management position is exercising authority over subordinates, especially your former colleagues. On the one hand, most often, newly promoted managers must distance themselves from their former colleagues and friends and thus contend with being lonely at the top (well, not really the top, but closer to the top than before being promoted). On the other hand, the promotion brings the rewards of elevated status, higher salary, and additional opportunities to make important contributions to the organization as well as to subordinates. Specifically, promotion brings the opportunity to lead through (and cope with) change.

Decision Making, Authority, and Power

The identification and understanding of the contingency theory of leadership is a perfect segue into a discussion of decision making, authority, and power. Leaders and managers are consistently required to make important decisions for the welfare of the organization and its employees. In most cases, strategy decisions—big and small—involve change on some level within a sport organization. In the following section, we introduce the steps involved in decision making and discuss the concepts of authority and power.

Decision Making

Decision making involves a series of steps. Although authors may disagree on the number of steps, researchers agree on the essence of these steps. For the purposes of our discussion, we present six steps:

1. *Defining or framing the problem.* What is the problem or issue that requires a decision? Does the manager fully understand all that is involved in addressing this problem? For example, if a sport team needs a new stadium, the organization must be in a position to explain the problem (e.g., the current facility is poorly designed and does not meet the needs of the franchise, players, and fans).

2. *Identifying criteria for decision.* What criteria must be considered before making the decision? For example, is time of the essence in making the decision about the need for a new stadium (for the next season)? Is there a cost issue to consider? What is the budget for this facility? Are other organizations involved in this decision (e.g., local government, corporate sector, developer)?

3. *Developing and evaluating alternatives.* For every problem or issue, various alternatives may be available. Alternatives may include what type of facility will be built (e.g., Should the facility cater to the sport only? Should it be designed to host other sports or other types of events? What will the seating capacity be? What design will be used?) and where the facility will be located (e.g., city center, suburb).

4. *Selecting an alternative.* Which alternative will be selected? Which alternative best responds to the problem identified in step 1 and the criteria identified in step 2? The decision is made at this step.

5. *Implementing the alternative.* This step involves implementing the decision selected in step 4. Determining who needs to be involved in implementing the decision and how this decision can best be implemented must be established during this stage.

6. *Evaluating the effectiveness of the decision.* Did the decision lead to the intended outcomes? Was it the right decision? Was it the best decision given the circumstances? What were the final costs of building the stadium? Is the stadium in a location that is easily accessible to sport fans?

Decisions are an integral part of the activities that leaders, managers, and employees undertake in their day-to-day work. These people must consider all factors involved in the decision and make the decision within the parameters set out by leaders and by the circumstances. Some decisions are easier to make than others. Decisions involving significant resources—time, personnel, financial resources (as the construction of a stadium would involve)—typically take more time to make than decisions involving few resources. In addition, note that decisions involving several people and groups (sometimes beyond the confines of the organization) may take more time because various resources, interests, and values may require more negotiation to reach a decision. Although the process of decision making may appear rational and consensual, power may also be part of this process. In the next section, we present the concept of power and discuss various sources of power.

ACTION

Go to the WSG and complete the second Learning in Action activity regarding the use of social media in decision making.

Social Media and Managing and Leading in Sport Organizations

With social media becoming the foundation for modern communication in sport organizations, sport leaders now find themselves in a position where they must adopt new online habits to ensure two-way communication with sport consumers. With relationship marketing (i.e., connecting with individual consumers through Twitter and Facebook) on the rise, sport leaders are increasingly engaging consumers in the decision-making process to ensure that they establish and maintain high-quality relationships. For example, when attempting to decide on the facility maintenance required in a professional hockey team's arena, the general manager may utilize Facebook to involve fans in the process. The following are selected steps from the decision-making process outlined in this chapter that demonstrate how leaders may use social media in this context:

> *Defining or framing the problem.* The general manager recognizes that the team's arena is aging, and may not meet the needs of the current fan base. Because a new stadium is not financially viable, management decides to engage their consumers in the problem-framing process. In this case, social media can be used to help identify potential problem areas within their current facility. Facebook may be used as a forum to present a question to its franchise's online "friends" or followers. For instance, a post within the group could state, "For those who have attended recent games in our facility, what could be improved within the facility to ensure an enhanced sporting experience?" Further, information could be solicited in real time, where fans are asked to comment on their experience within the arena in the moment through Facebook posts. This may provide a foundation for defining key problem areas within the arena that are most relevant to fans.

> *Identifying criteria for decision.* When monitoring real-time posts on Facebook, management can track the frequency and quality of comments regarding specific aspects of arena functionality. The people submitting the posts can also be tracked. Specifically, questions can be asked: Are the people posting comments season ticket holders? Are they first-time attendees? The criteria for choosing the appropriate arena maintenance option can be tied to information originating from key stakeholder groups directly identified on the social media website (i.e., Facebook).

> *Evaluating the effectiveness of the decision.* Finally, Facebook offers access to real-time evaluations of the effectiveness of decisions made by leaders regarding arena maintenance. For example, following a decision to add additional concession stands with more food options within given sections of an arena, the general manager directs Facebook followers to log on to their mobile devices and "like" adjustments that they have experienced. The feature on Facebook also allows fans to add comments where displeasure may arise and share favorable adjustments with their Facebook friends. This may result in unofficial promotion of facility maintenance, which may increase the return in investment by showcasing the focus that management has on growth and change within the organization.

Power and Its Sources

As noted within the contingency theory of leadership, power is an important element when assessing the effectiveness of leaders in coping with change. Power is sometimes defined as the ability to influence others. It has also been defined as control over resources. Individuals within organizations may have power from various sources, ranging from the organizational to the personal. Among the organizational sources, we find legitimate power, reward power, and coercive power. Among the personal sources of power, we find referent, expert, and informational power. In the following paragraphs, we review these sources of power, starting with organizational sources.

Legitimate or positional power is the first source. This source of power comes from the leadership or management position that a person holds in the hierarchy (i.e., top-level manager, middle-level manager, and supervisory-level manager). Managers hold a legitimate source of power as long as they occupy the position. Furthermore, they have power only in the organization in which they hold a senior position.

Another organizational source of power is reward power. For this source, the person in the organization who provides rewards to employees has power. In most cases, an individual with legitimate power may also have reward power. Examples of rewards include raises in wages or performance bonuses, promotions, desirable assignments, and training opportunities. Rewards need to be considered valuable by others for the person who gives them to have power.

Coercive power is another source of power. The person in the organization who provides sanctions, punishments, or threats to employees has power. Reprimands, demotions, and decreased access to resources are examples of sanctions and punishments. This source of power is often perceived as problematic because it operates in the negative sphere. As in the case of reward power, this form of power is also often tied to legitimate forms of power.

Let us now review the personal sources of power starting with referent power. This source of power stems from charisma, charm, and appeal. Referent power is based on people's perception of the person with power because of personality characteristics, respect, and admiration. The person with power does not have to do anything to deserve it. Note that this source of power can be abused. For example, someone who is charming and likeable but lacks integrity and honesty may rise to power and then use it for evil.

Another source of personal power is expert power. This source is based on knowledge and skills that are perceived as valuable in a particular situation. Generally, people are willing to listen to the advice and judgment of the expert. The ideas of an expert are often considered more valuable than the opinions of people with legitimate power.

The last source of power, which was subsequently added to the original list developed by French and Raven (1959), involves information. Although this source of power is along the same lines as expert power, the difference is that the person with the power has access to information (not expertise). Access to this information may be a result of the position held in the organization. For example, the support staff of organizational leaders may be privy to valuable information (e.g., promotions, demotions, terminations, budget cuts). Office location may be another circumstance in which a person can have access to information (e.g., by overhearing information that may be considered valuable). Relationships with other people in the organization may be another way in which information can be accessed. In the growing age of social media, it is also important to note that information can be accessed more readily than ever before. As such, it is important to understand the ease of information access (24 hours a day, 7

As commissioner of the NFL, Roger Goodell has power and authority.

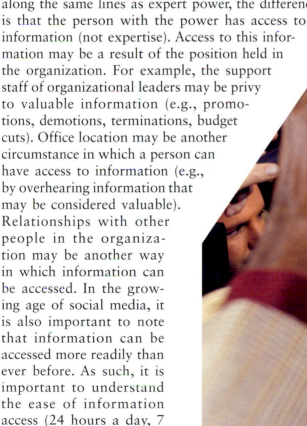

days a week) that employees have and the potential ramifications associated with bridging the power gap between those with information and those without in our sport organizations.

When considering these sources of power, note that people often rely on more than one source of power. Recognize as well that organizational sources of power can be revoked by the organization (e.g., the person in the power position can be demoted or terminated) but that personal sources of power can be held for long periods (in the case of referent power, potentially forever). When exercising power, the ultimate goal is to influence others (e.g., subordinates, peers); people who exercise power will typically rely on the source that is most likely to achieve this goal.

Distinction Between Power and Authority

The literature on organizations has often addressed authority and power as two distinct concepts. Authority is defined as the power to enforce rules and to expect subordination from those who have no authority. In terms of French and Raven's (1959) sources of power, authority would fall under legitimate power. Those with legitimate power in organizations have authority.

Power is often perceived at the individual level of analysis where organizational actors, through various sources (e.g., position, personality, resources), have power that can be exercised in decision-making processes. In the absence of such sources of power, influencing decisions in the organization is difficult. Lukes (1974) suggested that power can be viewed beyond the individual level of analysis. He argued that although human behaviors are visible manifestations of power, dimensions of power in organizations are less visible. These involve collective actions and social interactions among people, including "subjective and real interests" and "observable (overt or covert) and latent conflict" (p. 25).

Human Resource Management

One of the most basic activities of sport industry leaders and managers is to plan the needs of their particular sport organizations in terms of the labor force. How many people need to be hired to achieve the objectives of the sport organization? What jobs will these human resources perform within such an organization? What special training will they require to do their jobs better? How will the quality of their work be evaluated at the end of the year? Human resource planning may also involve making difficult decisions (e.g., firing employees if necessary). As such, human resource management is an important responsibility for sport leaders and managers.

Several elements should be considered in the management of human resources. The most basic step before hiring people is to determine what human resources are needed and in what role. After leaders and managers have established the need for more employees in the organization, they will be involved in the recruitment and selection of personnel (Schwind, Das, & Wagar, 2007).

Recruitment involves the development of job ads posted in various outlets (e.g., websites, trade publications, professional journals, newspapers) to generate interested and qualified applicants. On each job ad, a position title, along with a summary of work responsibilities and required qualifications, will be outlined. Recruitment may also entail active involvement of leaders and managers, who may contact potential candidates they know to inform them of the position and encourage them to apply. After applications are received, a screening of potential candidates takes place, and the

ACTION

Go to the WSG and complete the third Learning in Action activity, which asks you to build a job description around a vacancy within the sport industry.

selection process follows. Selecting the right candidates involves reviewing résumés or curricula vitae, interviewing the candidates, and verifying their references. Social media provides managers and leaders with an additional forum to check the character, experience, and connections of applicants. This provides employers with more informational power during the selection process.

After the right person has been hired, a process commences whereby this person is introduced to the operations and practices in the organization. This process is often called orientation. During the orientation, new employees are introduced to coworkers. They become familiar with the organization and their work environment. Policies, procedures, and the employee handbook will be presented to new employees so that they can become familiar with the operations within the workplace (Schwind et al., 2007). During this stage, new employees are often provided with a resource person who can answer their questions. Orientation is an important process in human resource management because it allows full integration of employees into the workplace.

As new employees become integrated into the workplace, they may from time to time require specialized training so that they can be better prepared for their work within the organization. Training may include workshops about new procedures or new computer software or courses to improve sales and promotion skills. Training is always part of a strategy to enhance the effectiveness of both the individual and the organization. New skills acquired during training may also serve to motivate employees and lead to their satisfaction as they learn new elements and apply this learning in their work. Training may also lead to employees' mobility within the organization. As employees become better prepared, their responsibilities in the workplace may change or increase, and these employees may be called on to undertake new roles in the organization (e.g., working with different clientele).

Another important area to consider in human resource management is performance appraisal, or the evaluation of an employee's performance in the workplace. The work of each employee in the organization should be assessed on a regular basis (typically, once a year). This evaluation serves many purposes: to improve performance, to adjust compensation, to establish career plans and development for employees, to determine training needs, to assess deficiencies in staffing and job designs, and to assess organizational and environmental challenges affecting employees (Schwind et al., 2007). In a formal meeting, the manager and employee have an opportunity to review the employee's performance during the previous year. This discussion may entail a self-assessment on the part of the employee and an assessment from the manager. Strengths and weaknesses of the employee may be discussed and areas of improvement and strategies to meet productivity targets and performance expectations may be developed. The employee may be asked to propose areas in which the manager could improve to create a better work environment. Performance appraisals are important because people are the most important resource of an organization. Within the sport industry, the appraisal provides leaders and managers with an opportunity to enhance human resources in the sport organization.

Organizational Diversity

Leaders and managers of sport organizations are working with an increasingly diverse workforce. Although some may believe that the existence of diversity in the workforce is not important, others understand that a diverse workforce represents an advantage for organizations. A diverse workforce can better respond to consumers' needs and can provide consumers with better goods and services. Diversity can also improve organizational effectiveness by improving managerial decision making. Diversity, therefore, is an important resource for organizations.

Diversity can represent variations in age, gender, race and ethnicity, religion, sexual orientation, socioeconomic status, and ability. Managing diversity in organizations can be challenging, but leaders should not be deterred from ensuring that the workplace is diverse. Although managing diversity effectively is good for business (Jones & George, 2009), diverse employees are often subjected to unfair treatment. Jones and George identified three factors that may lead managers and employees to treat diverse employees unfairly:

> Biases: systematic use of information about others that leads to inaccurate perceptions
> Stereotypes: inaccurate beliefs about characteristics of groups of people
> Overt discrimination: denying diverse individuals' access to opportunities and outcomes

Dass and Parker (1999) proposed four strategies that leaders use to manage organizational diversity: reactive, defensive, accommodative, and proactive. Leaders usually adopt reactive strategies when they do not value diversity. In some cases, reactive strategies have been used to maintain and protect the status quo. Although reactive strategies are often used to resist diversity in the workplace, a reactive strategy may be appropriate in some cases. For example, the Ladies Professional Golf Association (LPGA) Tour might consider using a reactive strategy if male golfers wanted to join a tournament.

Defensive strategies typically emerge from a discrimination and fairness perspective. In this context, leaders are interested in leveling the playing field for members of diverse groups. Legislation (e.g., affirmative action policies, equal opportunity for employees) may force organizations to adopt this strategy.

With the adoption of accommodative strategies, leaders have embraced the notion that a diverse workforce is beneficial for the organization. Differences are celebrated. This strategy ensures that a diverse workforce results in access to more consumers, often from diverse groups.

The last strategy, proactive, represents a more ingrained perspective about diversity in organizational activities compared with accommodative strategies. Proactive strategies originate from the idea that educating managers and employees of the organization will result in the complete adoption of diversity. In this case, diversity is central to the core operations of the organization. Ideally, all leaders would choose to adopt the proactive strategy.

To protect diverse employees, equal employment opportunity initiatives and affirmative action programs have been developed in the United States. Matton and Hernandez (2004) conducted a study of the successes and challenges of diversity and compliance initiatives in 10 organizations. The authors examined training, goal setting and targets for gender and race, equal employment opportunities and affirmative action initiatives, and mentoring and succession planning. Their findings revealed that several factors in the organization favored the success of diversity initiatives:

> Leadership: commitment, passion for diversity, and sustained involvement from the leaders in the organization
> A diversity or compliance professional: creation of a position within the organization and the hiring of a strong person to implement diversity efforts in the workplace

How to Improve Organizational Diversity in Sport Organizations

To address diversity-related issues in organizations, a sport organization needs to value diversity at both the managerial and organizational levels, and to promote and increase diversity through initiatives and actions.

Why do sport organizations need to improve their organizational diversity? Although this chapter examines this question in some detail, some specific answers follow. First, the population is diversifying, racially and ethnically; cultural diversity is a fact of life in today's society and will also be present tomorrow. Second, a sport organization can function more smoothly and be more beneficial to society if a set of stakeholder rights and responsibilities can be established and applied meaningfully (Carroll & Hannan, 2000). Furthermore, there is a strong relationship between a commitment to diversity and organizational effectiveness (Wheeler, 2003). Therefore, understanding diversity is a crucial ability, if not a requisite, for managers to succeed in their business dealings.

Building diversity in sport organizations is not simple. It is a multiphase process. According to scholars in diversity research (Carnevale & Stone, 1994), organizations need to improve their organizational diversity with strategies in several areas.

Area I: Governance
> Reexamining its mission statement to determine whether a diversity element is present
> Ensuring that the bylaws of the association refer to the inclusion of all individuals

Area II: Strategic Planning
> Aggressively tracking trends in the sport industry relative to diversity and disseminating the information to stakeholders
> Identifying the diversity issues in the sport organization
> Establishing meaningful goals by adding inclusiveness as one of the sport organization's key goals
> Strengthening management commitment and ensuring that inclusiveness receives organizational attention

Area III: Communication and Promotion
> Adding a periodic diversity column or feature to the in-house organizational newsletter
> Developing a communication and promotion plan that builds awareness of the sport organization's diversity initiatives among employees, customers, and other stakeholders

Area IV: Membership Involvement
> Infusing diversity elements into the sport organization's management structure

Work-Family Conflict Among NCAA Coaches

Dixon and Bruening conducted a two-part study (Bruening & Dixon, 2007; Dixon & Bruening, 2007) that examined role conflict experienced by women NCAA Division I coaches in balancing their work and family responsibilities. Multilevel factors (e.g., individual, organizational, and sociocultural) have been found to affect the conflict between work and family roles. For the first part of their research, the authors investigated these multilevel factors and examined the extent to which they affected NCAA female coaches. In the second part, the authors focused on the consequences of this conflict and on the mechanisms developed by coaches to manage the work–family conflict. Forty-one coaches took part in online focus groups.

In the first part of the study, coaches identified a number of elements that contributed to the conflict that they experienced between their coaching and family responsibilities along three factors: individual, organizational, and sociocultural. Among individual factors, the coaches identified their competitive drive (their expectation to experience success in both coaching and motherhood), the importance that they attributed to both family and work (and trying to balance the need to spend more time with family with the need to spend more time at work), and being far from extended family (few close family members at hand to help with childcare, with emergencies, and with travel plans) as all contributing to this work–family conflict. Among organizational factors, the coaches identified the number of work hours, the travel obligations associated with the job, and the level of autonomy in the coaching job (coaches felt pressured, usually by the administration, to spend face

(continued)

How to Improve Organizational Diversity in Sport Organizations *(continued)*

time in the office during regular work days). From the perspective of sociocultural factors, coaches identified the male-dominated nature of the workplace, women's typical home and family responsibilities, and society's expectations of mothers.

In part two of the study, Bruening and Dixon reported on the mechanisms used by the coaches to deal with the stress of addressing the work–family conflict. These mechanisms included stress release (e.g., playing with their children, getting a massage, retail therapy), self-awareness, organization and time management, sacrificing some aspects of work, and support networks (e.g., family, friends, staff, assistant coaches). Coaches also discussed organizational strategies in place to help them manage the conflict. These strategies included flexibility with work hours, family-friendly policies, and family-friendly culture in the workplace.

> Employee involvement: the role of employees in communicating with leaders and informing, assisting, and recruiting diverse employees
> Ties to performance evaluation and reward system: connection to performance evaluations and rewards to middle managers and diversity officers to encourage them to meet their diversity goals
> Availability and communication of data: information allowing leaders and employees in the organization to monitor patterns, problems, and opportunities for diversity in the organization

Matton and Hernandez (2004) noted that the organizational culture was among the challenges associated with the successful implementation of diversity initiatives. Organizational culture was also tied to the difficulty that some organizations had in generating buy-in from current employees and middle managers. Specifically, it is increasingly important to develop a culture of diversity in order to embrace diversity in the sport workplace. For example, people who work within contexts with a culture of similarity tend to expect that their colleagues will behave in a similar fashion and possess similar values (Doherty & Chelladurai, 1999). Alternatively, a culture of diversity is one where individual differences are seen as strengths and unique values are appreciated (Doherty & Chelladurai, 1999). Cunningham (2007) suggested that a culture of diversity can be embraced by leaders using several strategies. For instance, proactive management tactics (e.g., orientation and training) could be introduced to promote core departmental values surrounding embracing the functionality of diverse values. These values associated with diversity can then be incorporated into planning and organizing organizational tasks and evaluating personnel.

Achieving diversity initiatives is extremely difficult when an organization's culture and employees are not open to diversity. In 2006, the *Journal of Sport Management* featured a special issue on the topic of diversity in the sport industry. In their introductory article for this special issue, guest editors Cunningham and Fink (2006) discussed the major diversity issues facing sport organizations. These issues include differences in the quality of the work experience for employees who are judged to be different. Elements of power, inequality, and conflict often emerge in the workplace. Some studies on the work experiences of employees have focused on the effect of diversity on organizational commitment and turnover (e.g., Cunningham & Sagas, 2004). Other studies have investigated the issue of diversity from the perspective of consumption patterns (e.g., Armstrong, 2002; Armstrong & Stratta, 2004).

These studies and several others clearly suggest that diversity can promote the success of organizations. If a sport organization does not have strategies in place to embrace a diverse workforce, consumers, members, and clients may choose to buy their products and services from a competing organization that better understands their interests and responds more effectively to their needs. Using a hand analogy, Chelladurai (2005) clearly demonstrated the value of diversity in the workplace—all the fingers of the hand are different, but each plays an important role, particularly in concert, to open a door, to give a handshake, to hold things, to throw a ball, and to write a note.

Critical Thinking in Sport Managing and Leading

As introduced in chapter 1, critical thinking skills are important for the management of human resources in the sport industry. Leaders and managers should base their decisions and actions on rational, factual, and objective information. Caring about others and considering their opinions, concerns, and interests are important elements for the critical thinker. Steps discussed in decision making and the management of human resources in the workplace offer good strategies to ensure a systematic evaluation of alternatives based on objective criteria to enhance the well-being of employees in the workplace and as such attain the objectives of the organization. Critical thinking ensures sound reasoning about appropriate decisions and behaviors surrounding the most important resource in organizations—people.

Ethics in the Leadership of Sport Organizations

Employees, managers, and leaders are expected to act ethically as they undertake their duties and responsibilities within the sport organization. Unfortunately, as many incidents in the recent past have demonstrated, people in organizations do not always act ethically. In a study on ethical decision making and practical morality for compliance officers of U.S. university athletics departments, Kihl (2007) demonstrated that these sport leaders drew from various sources to make ethical decisions. The sources included their personal moral codes; professional codes of conduct; and their organization's standards, rules, and procedures. Decisions made often involved a manager's ability to balance these three sources. To illustrate the challenges of decision making, a modified version of the scenario presented by Kihl is detailed in the next paragraph.

The scenario involves the International Basketball Federation (FIBA) and its decisions related to an under-18 world basketball game. Because of agreements with organizational sponsors and the television company broadcasting the game, the leaders of FIBA wanted to abide by their policy to plan a game time optimal for reaching the largest audience. Therefore, the leaders decided to go with an 11:00 p.m. local start for the final contest of the tournament. Besides adhering to the prior television and sponsorship agreements, a late start produced the most potential global viewers for the television broadcast. An increase in potential viewership would provide the opportunity for the organization and its stakeholders to reap the economic benefit (e.g., increased revenue through ad sales). But the coaches and leaders of the teams involved believed that the late start could negatively affect the players' performance. Thus, they disagreed with the organizational policy.

This scenario, which is frequently played out in the sport industry (e.g., agreements between television companies and universities regarding the start of college football games), highlights the often conflicting and competing values and interests of the various stakeholders involved in sport. These varying values and interests lead to important

PORTFOLIO

Complete the critical thinking portfolio activity in the WSG, consulting as needed the "Critical Thinking Questions" sidebar in chapter 1.

PORTFOLIO

Complete the ethical issues portfolio activity in the WSG, consulting as needed the "Guidelines for Making Ethical Decisions" section in chapter 1.

challenges that managers and leaders must carefully consider in making the best (i.e., most ethical) decisions.

Ethical leadership may be an appropriate strategy to help thwart unethical behaviors within sport organizations. Brown and Treviño (2006) suggested that **ethical leaders** are characterized "as honest, caring, and principled individuals who make fair and balanced decisions" (p. 597). In this light, sport leaders must frequently communicate with their followers about ethics, set clear ethical standards, and use rewards and punishments to see that those standards are followed. Sport leaders must also proactively communicate, reinforce, and make decisions with consideration of the effect of those decisions on the organization and its stakeholders.

ethical leaders—Honest, caring, and principled individuals who make fair and balanced decisions.

Summary

People play an important role in sport organizations. This chapter provides an overview of some of the concepts involved in the management of these people and the relevance of leadership in guiding their activities toward the achievement of organizational goals. As outlined in the chapter, management and leadership are two distinct yet complementary functions. Management refers to the process of working with, and through, individuals and groups to accomplish organizational goals. Leadership is the process of influencing individual and group behavior for some desired result.

Contemporary management theorists have cited five underlying functions that guide the concept of management: planning, staffing, organizing, directing, and controlling and evaluating. Managers in sport organizations commonly use three basic skills: conceptual, human relations, and technical. In this chapter, the roles of top-level, middle-level, and supervisory-level managers are explained and connected to specific managerial skills. Conceptual skills are often exercised by top-level managers where communication and planning are needed to assess the big-picture within a sport organization. Human relation skills are an integral component of top-level, middle-level, and supervisory-level managers, since managers at each level are required to interact with people on a daily basis. Finally, supervisory-level managers require technical skills in that specific skills related to their role must be present in order for effective operation. For instance, the front line manager of the concession area at the local hockey arena must have technical knowledge and skill with the cash register computing system in order to effectively manage subordinates.

Several theories have been developed to explain leadership. This chapter briefly covers the contingency theory of leadership. It also covers leader traits and behaviors and focuses on a more contemporary leadership model—the full range of leadership model.

As part of their responsibilities, managers and leaders are constantly involved in making decisions. Steps in decision making include defining or framing the problem, identifying criteria for the decision, developing and evaluating the alternatives, selecting an alternative, implementing the alternative, and evaluating the effectiveness of the decision. The concepts of power and authority are integral to decision making. Power is defined as the ability to influence others or as control over resources. Power can originate from different sources—organizational and personal. Organizational sources of power include legitimate, reward, and coercive power. Personal sources of power include referent, expert, and informational power. Authority is defined as the power to enforce rules and to expect subordination from those who have no authority. Collectively, decision making, power, and authority are important concepts for managers and leaders to understand and carefully wade through to achieve the goals of the sport organization.

Human resource management is about addressing the needs of the sport organization in terms of its labor force. More specifically, recruitment and selection of employees, their orientation within the organization, their training, and the appraisal of their performances within the workplace are all important. The management of human resources also includes addressing diversity and ethical behavior in the organization. Diversity can represent variation in age, gender, race and ethnicity, religion, sexual orientation, socioeconomic status, and ability. Managing diversity in organizations can be challenging, but leaders should not be deterred from ensuring that the workplace is diverse. In addition, diversity management may connect directly to ethics in the leadership of sport organizations in that leaders are influenced by sources of ethics, including their personal moral codes; professional codes of conduct; and their organization's standards, rules, and procedures. Each source contributes to the ethical outcome of a leader's decision-making process.

Review Questions

1. What are three theoretical approaches to management and managing people in sport organizations?

2. What are the three managerial skills of sport managers? What are the levels of management typically associated with each managerial skill?

3. What is the difference between management and leadership? Explain the distinction using examples from sport organizations.

4. What are the essential components of the interactive process associated with the contingency theory of leadership?

5. What are the major features of the full range of leadership model?

6. What steps are involved in the decision-making process?

7. What is the difference between power, authority, and leadership? Provide an example of each.

8. What are the sources of organizational power? What are the sources of personal power? How do these sources of power affect decision making?

9. What elements are involved in the management of human resources? How can diversity enrich the operations and effectiveness of sport organizations?

10. What is ethical leadership? What sport organizations may benefit from ethical leadership?

References

Armstrong, K.L. (2002). An examination of the social psychology of Blacks' consumption of sport. *Journal of Sport Management, 16,* 267–288.

Armstrong, K.L., & Stratta, T.M.P. (2004). Market analyses of race and sport consumption. *Sport Marketing Quarterly, 13,* 7–16.

Avolio, B.J., Waldman, D.A., & Yammarino, F.J. (1991). Leading in the 1990's: The four I's of transformational leadership. *Journal of European Industrial Training, 15,* 9–16.

Bass, B.M. (1985). *Leadership and performance beyond expectations.* New York, NY: Free Press.

Bass, B.M., & Avolio, B.J. (1994). *Improving organizational effectiveness through transformational leadership.* Thousand Oaks, CA: Sage.

Bass, B.M., & Riggio, R.E. (2006). *Transformational leadership* (2nd ed.). Mahwah, NJ: Lawrence Erlbaum Associates.

Brown, M.E., & Treviño, L.K. (2006). Ethical leadership: A review and future directions. *The Leadership Quarterly, 17*(6), 595-616.

Bruening, J.E., & Dixon, M.A. (2007). Work-family conflict in coaching II: Managing role conflict. *Journal of Sport Management, 21,* 471–496.

Carnevale, A.P., & Stone, S. (1994). Diversity: Beyond the golden rule. *Training & Development, 48*(10), 22–39.

Carroll, G.R., & Hannan, M.T. (2000). *The demography of corporations and industries.* Princeton, NJ: Princeton University Press.

Chelladurai, P. (2005). *Managing organizations for sport and physical activity* (2nd ed.). Scottsdale, AZ: Holcomb Hathaway.

Cunningham, G.B. (2007). *Diversity in sport organizations* (2nd ed.). Scottsdale, AZ: Holcomb Hathaway.

Cunningham, G.B., & Fink, J.S. (2006). Diversity issues in sport and leisure. *Journal of Sport Management, 20,* 455–465.

Cunningham, G.B., & Sagas, M. (2004). Racial differences in occupational turnover intent among NCAA Division I-A assistant football coaches. *Sociology of Sport Journal, 21,* 84–92.

Dass, P., & Parker, B. (1999). Strategies for managing human resource diversity: From resistance to learning. *The Academy of Management Executive, 13*(2), 68–80.

Dixon, M.A., & Bruening, J.E. (2007). Work-family conflict in coaching I: A top-down perspective. *Journal of Sport Management, 21,* 377–406.

Doherty, A.J., & Chelladurai, P. (1999). Managing cultural diversity in sport organizations: A theoretical perspective. *Journal of Sport Management, 13,* 280–297.

Fiedler, F.E. (1963). *A contingency model for the prediction of leadership effectiveness.* Champaign, IL: University of Illinois Press.

French, J.R.P., & Raven, B. (1959). Bases of social power. In D. Cartwright (Ed.), *Studies in social power* (pp. 150–167). Ann Arbor, MI: University of Michigan Press.

Gulick, L., & Urwick, L. (1937). *Papers on the science of administration.* New York, NY: Institute of Public Administration.

Hersey, P., Blanchard, K.H., & Johnson, D.E. (2008). *Management of organizational behavior: Leading human resources* (9th ed.). Upper Saddle River, NJ: Prentice Hall.

Jones, G.R., & George, J.M. (2009). *Contemporary management* (6th ed.). Toronto, Ontario, Canada: McGraw-Hill Ryerson.

Katz, R.L. (1974). Skills of an effective manager. *Harvard Business Review, 52,* 90–102.

Kihl, L.A. (2007). Moral codes, moral tensions, and hiding behind the rules: A snapshot of athletic administrators' practical morality. *Sport Management Review, 10,* 279–305.

Kotter, J.P. (1990). What leaders really do. *Harvard Business Review, 68*(3), 103–111.

Labich, K. (1988). The seven keys to business leadership. *Fortune, 118*(9), 58–62, 64, 66.

Lorsch, J.W. (2010). A contingency theory of leadership. In N. Nohria & R. Khurana (Eds.), *Handbook of leadership theory and practice* (pp. 411–429). Boston, MA: Harvard Business Press.

Lukes, S. (1974). *Power: A radical view.* London, UK: Macmillan.

Matton, J.N., & Hernandez, C.M. (2004). A new study identifies the "makes and breaks" of diversity initiatives. *Journal of Organizational Excellence, 23,* 47–58.

Mayo, E. (1933). *The human problems of an industrial civilization.* New York, NY: MacMillan.

Quarterman, J. (1998). An assessment of the perception of management and leadership skills by intercollegiate athletics conference commissioners. *Journal of Sport Management, 12,* 146–164.

Robbins, S.P., & Judge, T.A. (2008). *Organizational behavior* (13th ed.). Upper Saddle River, NJ: Prentice Hall.

Schermerhorn, J.R., Hunt, J.G., & Osborn, R.N. (2008). *Organizational behavior* (10th ed.). Hoboken, NJ: Wiley.

Schwind, H.F., Das, H., & Wagar, T. (2007). *Canadian human resource management: A strategic approach* (8th ed.). Toronto, Ontario, Canada: McGraw-Hill Ryerson.

Soucie, D. (1994). Effective managerial leadership in sport organizations. *Journal of Sport Management, 8,* 1–13.

Staw, B.M. (1986). Organizational psychology and the pursuit of the happy/productive worker. *California Management Review, 2,* 40–53.

Taylor, F.W. (1911). *The principles of scientific management.* New York, NY: Harper.

Wheeler, M.L. (2003). Managing diversity: Developing a strategy for measuring organizational effectiveness. In M.J. Davidson & S.L. Fielden (Eds.), *Individual diversity and psychology in organizations* (pp. 57–75). West Sussex, UK: Wiley.

Yukl, G. (2012). *Leadership in organizations* (8th ed.). Upper Saddle River, NJ: Prentice Hall.

PART II

SELECTED SPORT MANAGEMENT SITES

The sport industry offers a wide variety of career opportunities to aspiring sport managers. The purpose of the chapters in this section is to introduce you to six sites within the sport industry where job possibilities exist for you. These six sites—community and youth sport, interscholastic athletics, intercollegiate athletics, professional sport, sport management and marketing agencies, and sport tourism—are representative of settings in which you could find careers in sport. Keep in mind, however, that these sites do not constitute a complete inventory of sport-related job possibilities. If you take advantage of the additional resources included in the reference lists in each chapter and the "For More Information" section in each of this book's part openers, you will discover many more opportunities available to you in the world of sport.

Sport management in community and youth settings is the topic of chapter 6. In their chapter, Marlene Dixon and Jennifer Bruening present an overview of the operational, strategic, and sociocultural aspects involved in the design and delivery of sport at the youth and community levels. First, the authors illustrate a few historical aspects of community and youth sport and examine the size and scope of this segment of the sport industry. Dixon and Bruening, who include in their chapter various examples as well as a social media application, conclude with an analysis of the managerial challenges and unique offerings associated with community and youth sport. Tiffany Patterson is the featured sport industry professional for this chapter. Patterson is the executive director of the TownLake YMCA in Austin, Texas. The international sidebar—written by Elsa Kristiansen of the Norwegian School of Sport Sciences in Oslo—is about Norway's unique approach regarding the development and protection of young athletes.

In chapter 7, Warren Whisenant, Eric Forsyth, and Tywan Martin discuss interscholastic athletics, a segment of the sport industry that is often overlooked, yet offers numerous career opportunities. The authors first examine the historical and governance foundation of interscholastic athletics. Next, they detail the structural and operational differences for high school sports affiliated with public and private educational institutions. After identifying the careers available at all levels of interscholastic athletics, Whisenant, Forsyth, and Martin discuss key issues facing interscholastic athletics such as administrator certification, budgetary constraints, and parental involvement. The authors conclude their chapter with sections on critical thinking, ethical considerations, and social media applications in interscholastic athletics. The sport industry professional profiles for this chapter are on Claude Grubair and Bruce Whitehead. Grubair is the director of athletics at the Ransom Everglades School in Coconut Grove, Florida, and Whitehead is the executive director of the National Interscholastic Athletic Administrators Association (NIAAA). In addition to these practitioner features, the chapter also includes two international sidebars. The first is a Canadian perspective of high school sports. The authors of the sidebar are two Canada-based leaders, Morris Glimcher and John Paton. Glimcher is affiliated with the Manitoba High Schools Athletic Association and Paton works for the Alberta Schools' Athletic Association. The second international sidebar is by Jasper Truyens and Veerle De Bosscher, from Vrije Universiteit Brussel (VUB). These authors examine the governance and organization of youth and school sports in Belgium.

Intercollegiate athletics is the topic of chapter 8. Ellen Staurowsky and Robertha Abney first present an overview of the history of intercollegiate athletics in the United States. They then describe several governing bodies associated with intercollegiate athletics and discuss unique financial aspects of college sport. The authors—who provide a sidebar on social media and intercollegiate athletics—conclude their chapter by examining various administrative positions and related responsibilities within intercollegiate athletics departments and governing bodies. Gene Smith, the associate vice president and the director of athletics at The Ohio State University, is the featured professional in this chapter. In the international sidebar, Isaac Mwangi Kamande of Strathmore University (Nairobi) examines the development, management, and challenges of university sport in Kenya.

In chapter 9, James Gladden and William Sutton define professional sport and discuss its history and growth in the United States. The authors address the unique characteristics of professional sport, including its governance structure and labor-management issues such as antitrust legislation, collective bargaining, free agency, salary caps, and player drafts. The significant influences of television and the new media—including a social media sidebar pertaining to professional sport—are also presented, as is a discussion of the major revenue sources (e.g., gate receipts, sponsorship opportunities, and television rights fees) for professional sport teams. After describing the challenges future leaders in professional sport will face, Gladden and Sutton conclude their chapter with a discussion of the various employment categories associated with professional sport. The professional profile for this chapter is on Jeff Ianello, who is a vice president with the NBA but at the time the interview was conducted was the senior vice president for sales and service with the Phoenix Mercury (WNBA) and Phoenix Suns (NBA). The international sidebar addresses the relationship marketing approach and revenue opportunities in Australian rules football. Adam Karg from Deakin University in Melbourne, Australia contributed this essay.

Catherine Lahey, Jezali Ratliff, and William Sutton are the authors of chapter 10. There, they define sport management and marketing agencies and present valuable information about the major functions (e.g., strategic planning, sponsorship engagement, licensing solicitation, event operations, contract negotiations, marketing activation, financial planning, and research) performed by these sport organizations. The authors then differentiate among four types of agencies—full-service, general, specialty, and in-house—and explain the evolution of each. In addition to their sidebar focused on sport agency oversight of social media accounts, the authors conclude their chapter by discussing career opportunities and unique challenges facing sport management and marketing agencies. The sport industry practitioner featured in this chapter is AJ Maestas, the founder and president of Navigate Research. In the international sidebar, János Váczi—a deputy mayor of Budapest—discusses the unique sport system in Hungary.

Chapter 11 addresses the unique aspects of and career opportunities affiliated with sport tourism. Heather Gibson and Sheranne Fairley first describe tourism and its industry and then explain the intersection of tourism and sport. The authors provide a thorough explanation of the different types constituting the industry: active sport tourism (e.g., traveling to participate in physical activities), event sport tourism (e.g., traveling to watch sporting events), and nostalgia sport tourism (e.g., traveling to sport museums or halls of fame). This chapter, which includes a sidebar (written by Ashley Schroeder) on social media's influence on sport travel and tourism, concludes with a discussion of the sociocultural, economic, and environmental effects of sport tourism. In addition to a feature on Alex Alston, who is now working for SMG but at the time of the interview was the executive director of the Tulsa Sports Commission, this chapter has two international sidebars. The first—by Brent Ritchie (University of Queensland) and Richard Shipway (Bournemouth University)—examines perceptions of tourism development regarding the 2012 London Olympic and Paralympic Games. In the second international sidebar, Deakin University's Pamm Phillips discusses opportunities for participation, economic benefit, and tourism affiliated with skate parks and facilities in Australia.

Understanding the wide variety of career opportunities available in the sport industry will enable you to plan your professional life more realistically. The chapters in this section focus on sport industry settings involving amateur sport (e.g., community, youth, interscholastic, and intercollegiate), professional sport, agencies, and sport tourism. Rather than concentrating only on the chapters that address the careers in which you are currently interested, we hope that you will study the material in each of these six chapters and reflect on the possibilities that each site may hold for you. Who knows? As you learn more about the possibilities that exist, you may develop new interests and revise your career goals!

For More Information

Professional and Scholarly Associations, Institutes, and Organizations

1A Athletic Directors' Association

Adventure Sports

American Association of Adapted Sports Programs

Athletes for Education (AFE)

Athletes CAN, the association of Canada's national team athletes

Canadian Sport Tourism Alliance

Canadian Tourism Commission

Centre for Tourism and Leisure Management

Coalition on Intercollegiate Athletics

College Sport Research Institute

Committed to Green Foundation

The Drake Group

Federation of Sports and Play Associations (FSPA)

International Alliance for Youth Sports

International Sports Heritage Association (ISHA)

International University Sports Federation

Josephson Institute Center for Youth Ethics

National Alliance for Youth Sports

National Association for Athletics Compliance (NAAC)

National Association of Academic Advisors for Athletics (N4A)

National Association of Collegiate Directors of Athletics (NACDA)

National Association of Collegiate Women Athletics Administrators (NACWAA)

National Association of Intercollegiate Athletics (NAIA)

National Association of Sports Commissions

National Association of Sports Officials

National Christian College Athletic Association (NCCAA)

National College Players Association (NCPA)

National Collegiate Athletic Association (NCAA)

National Federation of State High School Associations (NFHS)

National Interscholastic Athletic Administrators Association (NIAAA)

National Junior College Athletic Association (NJCAA)

National Operating Committee on Standards for Athletic Equipment (NOCSAE)

Travel Industry Association of America

World Sport Publishers' Association (WSPA)

World Tourism Organization

World Travel and Tourism Council

Youth Sport Trust

Professional and Scholarly Publications

Academic Athletic Journal

Annals of Tourism Research

Applied Research in Coaching and Athletics Annual

Athletic Business

Athletics Administration

Chronicle of Higher Education

College Sports Business News

Current Issues in Tourism

Diverse: Issues in Higher Education

High School Journal

Interscholastic Athletic Administration

Journal for the Study of Sports and Athletics in Education

Journal of Community Psychology

Journal of Contemporary Athletics

Journal of Hospitality, Leisure, Sport and Tourism Education (JoHLSTE)

Journal of Issues in Intercollegiate Athletics

Journal of Leisure Research

Journal of Sport & Tourism

Journal of Travel and Tourism Marketing

Journal of Vacation Marketing

Leisure Sciences

Leisure Studies

Managing Leisure

National Aquatics Journal

New Directions for Youth Development

NISR Journal of Sport Reform

Polish Journal of Sport and Tourism

Sporting News

SportsBusiness Daily

Sports Illustrated

Sports Travel

Street & Smith's SportsBusiness Journal

Tourism Recreation Research

Youth & Society

Visions in Leisure and Business

HISTORICAL MOMENTS

- **1844** Young Men's Christian Association (YMCA) founded
- **1858** Ladies Christian Association founded (term *YWCA* first used in 1866)
- **1888** Amateur Athletic Union (AAU) formed
- **1898** Canadian Amateur Athletic Union (CAAU) formed
- **1906** Federated Boys Clubs in Boston formed; later renamed Boys and Girls Clubs of America
- **1914** Police Athletic League (PAL) began in New York City
- **1929** Pop Warner Football began
- **1939** Little League Baseball began
- **1961** Fitness and Amateur Sport Act passed in Canada
- **1964** American Youth Soccer Organization (AYSO) founded
- **1978** Amateur Sports Act of 1978 adopted by United States Congress
- **1981** National Alliance for Youth Sports (NAYS) founded
- **2002** Canadian Centre for Ethics in Sport released a report specifically addressing issues in youth sport
- **2003** International Alliance for Youth Sports (IAYS) established
- **2006** United States Olympic Committee created Multi-Sport Organizations Council (MSOC)
- **2009** President Barack Obama established White House Office of Olympic, Paralympic, and Youth Sport
- **2013** ESPN examined issue of kids in sports on its website, in an issue of *ESPN The Magazine*, on television, at a town hall meeting, and through social media #KidsInSports
- **2013** First Lady Michelle Obama launched *Let's Move!* Active Schools program
- **2014** Nanjing, China hosted the second Summer Youth Olympic Games (YOG)

COMMUNITY AND YOUTH SPORT

Marlene A. Dixon   Jennifer E. Bruening

LEARNING OBJECTIVES

- Define community sport and youth sport.
- Identify different sectors and key providers of sporting opportunities at the community and youth levels.
- Identify and explain challenges regarding access to youth and community sport.
- Explain key challenges in managing youth and community sport and propose solutions for those challenges.
- Differentiate the outcomes and goals associated with various types of sport offerings and the management implications thereof.
- Identify the social media influences and career opportunities available within youth and community sport.

Key Terms

community sport

multi-sport organization (MSO)

national regulatory association

professional human resource management (HRM) model

quality of life

social capital

sport-based youth development (SBYD) model

sport league

sport tournament

volunteer sport organization (VSO)

youth sport

GET A JOB

Continue on your journey in sport management by going to the web study guide (WSG) at www.HumanKinetics.com/ContemporarySportManagement. Check out the job opportunities and consider the skills and experiences that can help you succeed in sport management.

many people around the world have participated in sport in their communities either as children or as adults, or perhaps throughout their lives. Because of familiarity with this sport structure, participants may tend to think that their experiences are similar to the experiences of most participants in other localities in North America or around the world. In so doing, however, they may take for granted the unique organizational and structural challenges surrounding the management of community and youth sport. This chapter introduces the history of community sport in North America as well as its current forms. It also presents an overview of some of the operational, strategic, and sociocultural challenges and opportunities inherent in the design, delivery, and future direction of youth and community sport.

Origins of Community Sport

The history of sport in North America is difficult to condense because it varies widely by place of residence, gender, social class, race and ethnicity, and family background. In other words, not everyone's experience in sport was the same. But some general trends in this sport history can help us understand the place of community sport in our society and the way that **community sport** is organized and delivered today.

community sport—Organized physical activity that is based in community, school, and local sport organizations.

In North America, sport and games were part of communities and cultures long before the arrival of Europeans. Emerging histories of native communities in North America showed rich and varied traditions of sport and physical contests. The contests ranged from the races, wrestling, and rites-of-passage contests of the North American Dene and Inuit peoples, to moose-skin ball of the Athapaskan women, to perhaps the most influential game, lacrosse, among the Iroquoian, Algonquian, Sioux, Chickasaw, Choctaw, and Cherokee nations (Morrow & Wamsley, 2005). In native communities, sport and contests often served the purposes of training youth for adult experiences; displaying the strength, skill, and prowess of community members; or celebrating the culture and religion of the community. Although much of the original meaning and symbolism of community sport from these native peoples has been lost or redefined, they have had a lasting influence on the structure, form, and meaning of community sport in North America.

Before the 1800s, European North Americans rarely engaged in physical contests that could be labeled as sports as we know them today (Rader,

Native American communities participated in many forms of sports and games, as illustrated in this engraving showing native youths shooting arrows, throwing balls at a target placed on a tall pole, and running races.

2009). Much time was spent simply surviving and establishing new towns, cities, and industries. The folk games played at this time were usually simple and had no written rules; they were legitimated by custom and often changed to fit the circumstances of play (e.g., space or time available). In the early 1800s in rural Canada and America, these games often sparked contests between citizens or towns that formed the basis of early sport experiences. For example, fishing, hunting, snowshoeing, rowing, archery, throwing, running, and rail-splitting were activities that could be contested between men, often serving as a source of pride and identity for the family or village (Morrow & Wamsley, 2005; Rader, 2009).

At the same time, a sporting fraternity of sorts emerged in urban centers such as New York, Philadelphia, Montreal, and Toronto where men would gather to play sports and wager on billiards, horse racing, prize fighting, or footraces. For example, the Great Race of 1835 offered a prize of $1,000 to anyone who could run 10 miles in less than an hour. More than 20,000 spectators watched as one man, Henry Stannard, a farmer from Connecticut, finished in 59 minutes and 48 seconds (Rader, 2009). In Canada, curling contests, races, and hunting contests between fur traders and frontiersman thrived through local taverns and military garrisons (Morrow & Wamsley, 2005). The races and spectacles continued across the continent, yet sport remained largely unorganized and unregulated.

In the early 1800s, however, voluntary sport clubs emerged for sports such as curling, rowing, cycling, snowshoeing, quoits, cricket, track and field, and baseball. These clubs were mostly the domain of upper- and middle-class men who could afford the time and membership dues required to belong to the sporting clubs. Contests were arranged first within clubs for the benefit of the club members and then later between clubs. The sponsoring club provided the rules, the facilities, the prize money, and the social events surrounding the contests. For example, the Montreal Curling Club, established by the Scots in 1807, organized the first curling contests in North America exclusively for the benefit of its 20 elite citizens (Morrow & Wamsley, 2005). The Montreal Snowshoe Club, Montreal Bicycle Club, and Montreal Lacrosse Club also served as important clubs for the early foundation of regulated amateur sport in Canada. In the United States, the New York Athletic Club (established in 1850) built the first cinder track for track and field and sponsored the first national amateur track and field championship in 1876. This club also sponsored the first national amateur championships for swimming (1877), boxing (1878), and wrestling (1878). The various sport clubs in the United States and Canada represented the beginning of a larger sport movement in the countries that spread both in types of sport offered and the delivery and governance thereof. As sport clubs expanded, battles ensued over who would provide and regulate community sport, and who would define its guiding principles.

In the early 1900s, sport and physical activity continued to grow. In the United States, for example, under the presidency of Theodore Roosevelt, local, state, and national funding was committed to the growth of parks and recreation facilities and spaces, and the Playground Association of America (which eventually became the National Parks and Recreation Association) was born. At this time, parks and recreation activities were more focused on play and leisure, not necessarily on organized sport. Sport was in the domain of private clubs, schools, and the Amateur Athletic Union (AAU), which represented the United States in international competition. After World War II, much debate occurred during the ensuing decades about America's lack of prominence in international sport, which led to the passage of the Amateur Sports Act in 1978 and the creation of national sport governing bodies (e.g., USA Swimming, USA Track and Field). These governing bodies have been given the task of sport development in the United States, and they govern U.S. representation in international sport, but they do not necessarily have enforcement powers to become the sole sport providers or governors of amateur sport within the country.

In Canada, the governance of community sport took a slightly different route. The formation of the Canadian Amateur Athletic Union (CAAU) in 1898 gave Canada a unified structure for the regulation of amateur sport. This body also "vowed to advance and improve all sports among amateurs and stated an even loftier goal, that is, to encourage systematic physical exercise and education in Canada" (Morrow & Wamsley, 2005, p. 76). The CAAU, along with the passage of the Fitness and Amateur Sport Act of 1961, has kept Canada's sport and recreation systems more coordinated and unified than those in the United States. Thus, in Canada sport is delivered on a local level but typically is coordinated under the auspices of the national governing body (i.e., a **national regulatory association**).

national regulatory association—A national sport governing body that makes eligibility and playing rules and sponsors competition according to its rules.

In summary, the history of North American sport in the 19th and 20th centuries has highlighted the emergence of two very different community sport systems in the United States and in Canada. Neither system is superior, and both present challenges to sport managers in the design and delivery of community-level sport. For example, although many parks and recreation centers in the United States have adopted sport programming, debate continues to this day about whether sport is complementary or contradictory to the mission and goals of parks and recreation, which often creates ongoing tension over the meaning and purpose of public recreation centers. This debate is not seen in Canada (or in most other countries in the world). In the United States, furthermore, because no single body governs amateur sport, sport structures and systems vary widely across states, cities, and local communities. In Canada, although sport is seemingly more uniform and coordinated, some sport organizations struggle for more control and voice in their local sport governance. Today, community sport in North America is a widely varying experience that offers both challenges and opportunities to sport managers.

Youth Sport History

As Americans began to understand the effect of children's social interactions and activities on their development, organized sport emerged as a means to provide interactions, friendships, and learning experiences transferrable to life outside these activities. Since the late 19th century when the Young Men's Christian Association (YMCA) began offering boys competitive sporting opportunities (Koester, 2000; Marten, 2008), sport has been a part of the landscape for children. The Boys Clubs also began in the 1800s with a mission of providing safe spaces for boys to play. The charter was expanded in 1990 to represent its current participants as the Boys and Girls Clubs (Halpern, 2002). The Young Women's Christian Association (YWCA) began in 1866, although sport programming today exists at only about 24% of its U.S. facilities (Hopkins, 1951; Murphy, 2005).

Other notable beginnings include the Police Athletic League (PAL), Pop Warner Football, the Catholic Youth Organization (CYO), and Little League. The PAL, created in 1914 in New York City, had the goal of providing safe places to play for children who lived in the city. Pop Warner Football, started in 1929, is still the only youth football organization that requires participants to maintain academic standards. The CYO commenced in 1930, followed by Little League Baseball (1939) and Little League Softball (1974). The Canadian Royal Legion began in the 1940s with the Foster Fathers Program for boys left fatherless by World War II. The program originated as an effort to teach boys leadership skills through sport. This philosophy, as evidenced by the focus on boys in these original youth sport organizations, is supported by Howard Chudacoff's (2007) history of children at play in the United States. The historian traces the origins and evolution of community-based youth sport from the male-centered model aimed at building character and preparing young boys and men for their futures in the workplace. Over time, community-based **youth sport** has evolved to include more girls, particularly after the passage of Title IX in 1972 and its enforcement beginning in the 1980s. Today, in the United States, close to 20 million children of both genders between the ages of 6 and 16 participate in organized sport (Coakley, 2009).

Organized youth sport has a broad definition in North America, ranging from the community organizations highlighted earlier to both interscholastic and club programs. The variations on sport that exist on a town, region, state or province, and national level are grounded in both the philosophy and the financial situation of the specific location. Shortly after the turn of the century, the Canadian Centre for Ethics in Sport (2002) released a report that specifically addressed issues in youth sport. The results included discussion that the increasing economic influence of youth sport, particularly at the club level of competition, and the "Americanization of sport" (p. 1) are leading youth sport away from its beginnings as a means to educate children and build leaders and turning it into a source of revenue and entertainment. With the growing privatization and specialization of organized youth sport (Coakley, 2009; Engh, 1999), some community-based teams and leagues are finding themselves with fewer participants from which to draw.

Consider a recent development in youth basketball in the United States that speaks to the issues discussed in the Canadian Centre's report. The National Collegiate Athletic Association (NCAA) is stepping into the youth arena because of its concern that school-based basketball is not as essential to children as it once was. The club system had taken over the role of developing young basketball players; according to the NCAA, it was missing the educational and sportsmanship aspects that the organization believes are necessary. So, in 2009, the NCAA announced an initiative to provide more structure to the club system. The NCAA added that although the organization wishes to have a positive influence on all children who participate in nonscholastic basketball, a second aspect of the initiative is to identify and develop elite players (Brown, 2009) who could eventually play at NCAA institutions.

youth sport—Organized physical activity for children and adolescents offered through schools, community organizations, or national sport organizations.

Job Opportunities in Youth Sport

Two organizations are highlighted in this sidebar. First, Up2Us (www.up2us.org) is a growing association currently composed of around 600 member organizations from across the United States. The goal of Up2Us is to bring together community sport programs that share common missions emphasizing the health, life skills, and social change benefits of sports. One function of the coalition is to share opportunities for jobs that exist at its member organizations in order to assist in expanding the workforce for youth sport programs.

Next, an example of an Up2Us member organization is Playworks. Playworks is a nonprofit that focuses on low-income schools by providing opportunities for play with the aim of fostering a positive environment for both learning and teaching. The organization, which had anticipated bringing its "power of play" to 380 schools in 2013, has set out to rescue recess at schools across the country. The youth sport organization hires city directors, among other staff, who are responsible for managing all aspects of their programs in a particular city. Part of their duties includes the implementation of the Playworks comprehensive school-based programming at as many as eight schools per year. The city director is Playworks' senior staff person in a particular city, and oversees up to 11 staff people in the first year of operations and then builds the staff each year moving forward.

Service Learning through UConn's Husky Sport

Bringle and Hatcher (1995) collected multiple definitions of service learning across disciplines and across universities. From these definitions, they derived three general characteristics of service learning on college campuses:

1. It meets the needs of the communities in which it takes place.
2. It includes both reflection and academic learning.
3. It develops or accentuates students' interest in and understanding of community life.

The Husky Sport program at the University of Connecticut uses a service learning model to expose students to an urban community in need of nutrition, life skills, and sport and physical activity opportunities for its children. The UConn students mentor the community children in these areas during both in-school and after-school hours at nine sites (five schools, one recreational center, and three community programs) in one neighborhood. Visit the website (www.huskysport.uconn.edu) to learn more about service learning and the Husky Sport program.

The NCAA initiative is but one example of the ongoing tension in youth sport in North America. In youth sport, should the focus be education or elite sport development? Who should govern youth sport? Who has access to the various kinds of sport opportunities? Remember that throughout the history of North American sport, not everyone has agreed on the purpose or process of youth sport, which continues to present significant challenges to sport managers in this context.

Definition of Community Sport

In defining community sport, we take a broad approach wherein community sport is conceptualized as organized physical activity that is based in community, school, and local sport organizations. Thus, this definition—drawn from the work by Stewart, Nicholson, Smith, and Westerbeek (2004)—encompasses both recreational and competitive sport but does not include exercise and fitness facilities or programs. Further, community sport may, but does not necessarily have to, culminate in high-performance sport that takes place at the college, professional, Olympic, national, or international level. The following sidebar provides examples of community sport organizations mentioned throughout this chapter.

Emphasis on the Participant

In professional sport (see chapter 9), management's concerns are often focused on people as spectators and consumers of sport for entertainment. In contrast, the emphasis in community sport is on people as participants. Therefore, management's concerns in this area focus on continuing to attract new participants and keeping them involved in the programs, as well as the types of programs or sports offered, the time and place of activities, the organization and delivery of programs, and cost and pricing considerations. Concern for the financial performance of the organization coincides with a focus on high-quality service as well as sport development. By keeping participant needs and wants central, managers can ensure the short- and long-term viability of their organizations. In terms of youth community sport, in particular, these needs and wants include participation and education on the rules and strategies of the game as well as the related social and ethical development of the children (Hedstrom & Gould, 2004; Larson, Walker, & Pearce, 2005; Le Menestrel & Perkins, 2007).

Benefits of Sport Participation

Numerous benefits are associated with sport participation. Some of these positive aspects include physical benefits, improved family well-being, a sense of community, and increased social capital for families and other groups. Although much focus has been placed on physical benefits, the broader benefits to individuals, families, and communities have sometimes been overlooked (Chalip, 2006; Dixon, 2009).

QUALITY OF LIFE

The physical benefits of sport participation include increased cardiovascular health, decreased stress, and increased functioning of the musculoskeletal system (U.S. Department of Health and Human Services, 1996). One benefit of sport participation for children specifically is helping to maintain a healthy weight; sport participation can reduce weight in obese children (Stanford University Prevention Research Center, 2007).

In addition, people who participate in recreation and sport report better concentration, task persistence, disposition, and analytical ability. These gains can lead to higher work productivity and lower absenteeism. People also report psychological benefits of participation such as increased self-esteem and social belonging (Dixon, 2009; Koltyn & Schultes, 1997). Children, in particular, benefit from being physically active through sport. Physical activity improves psychological health and helps cognitive, physical, social, and emotional development. Sport participation and physical

Sampling of Community Sport Organizations in North America

YMCA	City of Burbank Youth Sports
YWCA	American Softball Association
Police Athletic League	United States Volleyball Association
Little League Baseball and Softball	Girls on the Run (GOTR)
The Royal Canadian Legion	United States Field Hockey Futures
Catholic Youth Organization	United States Youth Soccer
Pop Warner Football and Cheerleading	Amateur Athletic Union
Women's Sports Foundation	United States Swimming
GoGirlGo!	YMCA of Greater Toronto
National Alliance for Youth Sports	Sugar and Spikes Softball Club
International Alliance for Youth Sports	Husky Sport
Canadian Fitness Tax Credit	Playworks
Lakewood (CO) Recreation Department	Up2Us
Hartford (CT) Recreation Department	U.S. Olympic Committee
United States Tennis Association	Blaze Sports America
West Suburban YMCA, Newton (MA)	Fitzgerald Youth Sports Institute

quality of life—The degree of well-being felt by an individual or a group of people.

activity can delay the onset of many chronic diseases (Government Accountability Office, 2006; Stanford University Prevention Research Center, 2007). Overall, there is general agreement that sport participation can positively affect a person's **quality of life** and that childhood physical activity through sport increases the likelihood of maintaining an active lifestyle as an adult.

Note, however, that these benefits are not experienced universally or to the same degree across all groups. In 2008, the Women's Sports Foundation (WSF) published findings revealing that a gender gap continues to be present in youth sport participation and that the percentage of girls from both urban and rural communities participating in sport is disproportionate to that of boys. Additionally, the data show that interest in being physically active in both sport and exercise results not from biological inheritance but rather from the opportunity and encouragement of influential people in a child's life. The WSF also reports that physical education classes, indicative of other sport and exercise participation, are even further unequal on the basis of both gender and geography. Urban girls, rural girls, and low-income boys and girls, in that order, are underrepresented as students in school physical education classes. More positively speaking, girls have expanded their participation to include a larger variety of sports and activities than boys do, although boys' sports tend to fall more often under the umbrella of school or community sport. Lastly, according to the data, girls have a shorter time frame in which to participate than boys do. Girls typically start later (i.e., age 7.4 compared with 6.8 for boys) and exit organized sport sooner, usually during middle school (i.e., between the ages of 12 and 14) (Sabo & Veliz, 2008).

FAMILY LIFE

Benefits of sport participation extend beyond the individual because they include improved family well-being. Families report a greater sense of belonging and increased bonds through sport and recreation participation (Henderson & Hickerson, 2007). Many parents report enjoyment from participating in recreational activities with their children, in coaching their children's sport teams, or in attending sporting events together with their families (Dixon, 2009). Children's athletic participation was associated with higher levels of family satisfaction (Government Accountability Office, 2006; Sabo & Veliz, 2008).

SENSE OF COMMUNITY AND SOCIAL CAPITAL

social capital—Contextual characteristics of communities that describe how people develop trust and social ties. Social capital is also described as the glue that holds communities together.

Finally, sport participation can create a sense of community and create **social capital** for families and other groups of people (Putnam, 2000). Social capital could be defined as a "contextual characteristic that describes patterns of civic engagement, trust, and mutual obligation among individuals" (Cuskelly, Hoye, & Auld, 2006, p. 8), or more simply as the glue that helps communities stay together (Badcock, 2002). People who participate in sport together along with those who volunteer together to deliver a community sport program develop social networks, shared norms, and understandings that can lead to greater cooperation and cohesiveness in a community. Chalip (2006) maintained that one of the main outcomes that legitimizes sponsoring sport at its various levels is community development and the building of social capital within and across communities.

Size and Scope of Community Sport

Although counting the exact number of people in North America who participate in sport is difficult, recent reports indicate that sport participation in general continues to grow in both the United States and Canada and that millions of people in both countries participate in sport at both the recreational and competitive levels. The Canada Survey of Giving, Volunteering, and Participating ("Canada," 2012) reports that 1.53 million

Canadians aged 15 or older volunteered for sport organizations that served participants of all ages in their communities. In the United States, recent data from the Sporting Goods Manufacturers Association (2012) show trends and actual participant numbers in a myriad of sports ranging from billiards and darts to waterskiing. Table 6.1 reports the most popular participant sports in 2012. For example, 16.7 million Americans aged 6 and above participated in basketball at least 13 times over the past year, and 24.8 million played at least once. Bowling had more than 11 million regular participants, baseball had 9.4 million, and another 6.4 million played outdoor soccer on a regular basis. Some of the fastest growing sports over the past five years (2007–2011) in the United States include traditional triathlon (90% increase), nontraditional or off-road triathlon (69% increase), high-impact aerobics (34% increase), running (18% increase), and lacrosse (12.8% increase). Sports that report declining participation include billiards and pool (40% decrease), darts (35.6% decrease), touch football (28.5% decrease), wrestling (27.5% decrease), and cheerleading (26.8% decrease). Individual conditioning and exercise have also seen strong gains in participant numbers over the past five years. For example, participation in yoga has increased 36%, participation in elliptical training has increased 24.75%, trail running participation has increased by 27%, and group stationary cycling (spin class) participation has increased by 24%. It is not clear, however, whether these people also participate in sport or have shifted from sport to exercise.

Table 6.1   **Most Popular Sports (Based on Participation Numbers) in the United States**

Sport	Number of core participants
Basketball	16.7 million
Bowling	11.5 million
Baseball	9.4 million
Yoga	9.8 million
Soccer (outdoor)	6.4 million
Table tennis	5.6 million
Softball (slow pitch)	4.5 million
Martial arts	3.9 million
Volleyball (court)	3.9 million
Football (tackle)	3.8 million
Mountain biking	3.7 million
Football (touch)	3.1 million
Flag football	2.8 million

Note: A core participant is one who participates in the sport 13 or more times in a given year. Respondents may participate in more than one core sport. Includes community and school providers.

Adapted from Canada 2012; Sporting Goods Manufacturers Association 2012.

Thus, in the United States, most traditional sports continue to have strong participation rates, indicating a continued demand for community sport offerings. But sport managers should note trends in increasing or decreasing demand so that new sports can be added or old programs dropped if they are no longer relevant to sport consumers.

Types of Community Sport Organizations

This section examines types of community sport organizations in North America. We first examine Canadian sport organizations before turning our attention to sport organizations in the United States. Although the two sport systems have some similarities in the ways that community sport is designed and structured, there are also distinct differences.

Although sport is offered through primary and secondary schools and in colleges and universities in Canada, community sport is almost exclusively offered through local and regional sport clubs (Cuskelly et al., 2006). These club-sport offerings are in addition to recreational sport (e.g., outdoor sports) and exercise and fitness (e.g., yoga, aerobics) opportunities in both public (e.g., community centers) and private health clubs in Canada (e.g., Goodlife Fitness Clubs). Community sport clubs, also known as **volunteer sport organizations**, or **VSOs**, provide myriad sport opportunities including curling, hockey, cross-country skiing, basketball, and soccer. Typically, these organizations work in conjunction with a network of organizations including their provincial and national counterparts (e.g., a local soccer club will be a member of the provincial soccer association, and this provincial association will be a member of the Canadian Soccer Association). This network of organizations oversees and governs the various elements of the sport system. VSOs are all nonprofits run by volunteers. In this system, therefore, it is not unusual for a sport participant to serve in some volunteer capacity for the organization (Cuskelly et al., 2006).

In the United States, sport at the community level is offered through a wide range of organizations, both public and private. Private facilities include organizations such as the YMCA and YWCA, in which sport is one of many programs or services offered. Participants pay membership dues to join the organization and receive access to the programs and facilities. A paid staff manages the organization and provides the services. Community sport is also provided at private country clubs, which typically offer sports such as swimming, golf, and tennis. Sport is also offered at private, for-profit clubs such as soccer centers and running clubs. Again, in this model, members usually pay a fee in exchange for the opportunity to play in the club's sport leagues, receive professional training or coaching, and have access to the organization's facilities. As the number of private sport organizations continues to grow in the United States, sport management students have found more employment opportunities in community sport. (See the sidebar "Career Opportunities: Austin Sports and Social Club" for more information.)

Community sport in the United States is also offered through public entities such as schools and parks and recreation facilities and programs. Unlike in most countries throughout the world in which sport for school-aged children is sponsored by community organizations, in the United States, youth sport is not only offered by public schools but is often considered central to the middle and high school experience (Hartmann, 2008). In school-sponsored sport, communities pay taxes to support the schools, which then provide the coaches and sport opportunities. In some school settings (e.g., Texas), coaches are also expected to teach an academic subject, whereas in other settings (e.g., Colorado, Ohio) coaches can be part-time professionals hired only to coach. As noted earlier, sport opportunities through the public schools are largely subsidized by local tax dollars. Some schools, however, now charge a participation fee to students to help offset costs of providing the sports. For more information on such arrangements, see chapter 7 ("Interscholastic Athletics").

volunteer sport organization (VSO)—Nonprofit local sport organization that provides organized sport opportunities for community members. VSOs are governed and supported through volunteer management and coaching.

Career Opportunities: Austin Sports and Social Club

The Austin Sports and Social Club (www.austinssc.com) was founded in 2005 to provide sporting opportunities for adults in the Austin, Texas metropolitan area. The club has since expanded operations to San Antonio and Dallas. In the beginning, the club was owned and operated by a single person who maintained the office, organized the leagues, and hired part-time officials to manage the games. As the club has expanded, opportunities have grown for administrative positions such as financial officer, website manager, league coordinator, and tournament coordinator. These people work to promote the club and manage team entries, progress, and so on. One critical position that has been created is director of market research. This person explores the needs of people in the target markets so that the sports offered in the club meet those needs. This person also explores possibilities for new markets and confirms that the population of interested members is viable to support an expansion. Finally, this person works with sponsors to ensure that the club reaches the appropriate target market so that sponsors achieve the desired results from their contributions. Other positions are more directly involved with the sports themselves. One person manages all the officials, which involves recruitment, training, and scheduling. Another person is in charge of facilities and scheduling. This person works with public recreation facilities to lease playing fields for the club and to keep the fields safe and clean. Thus, positions are available for marketing, finance, operations, and risk management.

Also important to note as a type of community sport organization is the **multi-sport organization (MSO)**. For instance, the Multi-Sport Organizations Council (MSOC) is a multi-sport organization arm of the United States Olympic Committee ("Multi-Sport," 2013). The goal of the MSOC is to facilitate the growth of the current number of national organizations (34) that promote multi-sport participation and provide more opportunities for international, national, and grassroots participation and competition.

multi-sport organization (MSO)—Composed of, involving, or accommodating several sports.

Publicly supported parks and recreation centers also offer sport and recreation opportunities at the community level. These centers are usually supported financially by a combination of local tax dollars and user fees, depending on the governmental unit involved. People who live within the tax district are able to participate in the program or use the facilities at a discounted rate, and some programs are limited only to people who live within the defined tax district (so that the taxpayers are also the beneficiaries of the programs). For example, the City of Lakewood, a suburb of Denver, Colorado, provides sport and recreation facilities and programs for its citizens. They offer everything from pay-as-you-use recreation facilities to organized **sport leagues** for participants aged 5 and older. From a management perspective, public parks and recreation facilities operate much like private clubs—with paid management and operations staff, although many still rely heavily on volunteer coaches for the delivery of their youth and adult organized sport programs. An example of a different model would be that in the city of Hartford, Connecticut. Hartford's six recreation centers as well as its four swimming pools are open to residents of the city at no cost. The city also provides free swimming lessons at these pools to its residents, space permitting. Children in Hartford are also eligible for free, eight-week summer camps at one of the city's parks. The free camps include transportation to and from any of the city's recreation centers. In most cases, children can participate in any structured program offered at the city's recreation centers at no cost. A nominal charge for basketball leagues is the exception. The city, whose residents have a much lower average socioeconomic status (SES) than those in Lakewood, subsidizes these programs rather than tapping its citizens for additional fees.

sport league—An organization that exists to provide ongoing regulated competition in a specific sport.

Yet another example of how models of community sport opportunities are managed comes from Canada. In 2005, then Member of Parliament (MP) Stephen Harper, now

Regulations of Children's Sport in Norway

By Elsa Kristiansen, Norway
Norwegian School of Sport Sciences, Oslo

Children are engaged in sports because they enjoy it, and the phrase *sport for all* embraces what sport should offer children. However, this is more than a slogan in Norway; through unique regulations of activities in voluntary sport organizations, the aim is to protect the youngest athletes from the negative consequences of elite sport. Decades of discussion replaced sport organizations' focus on talent spotting with physical activity within a safe environment. As a result, competitive sport disappeared from the schools in the 1970s and local sport clubs took over the responsibility under supervision of the Norwegian Confederation of Sports (later named the Norwegian Olympic and Paralympic Committee and Confederation of Sports, NIF). Sport within the school system continues to emphasize pedagogical objectives. As a result, a competitive high school sport system, as found in the United States, is almost nonexistent in the Norwegian context.

Young Norwegian athletes display their awards from a regional swimming competition.

Today, the NIF serves as an umbrella organization for sport at all levels in Norway and has over two million memberships (out of five million Norwegians). The NIF organizes the 54 national sport federations, 19 regional confederations, approximately 366 sports councils and also 11,793 clubs. The NIF is in charge of elite sport, with the aim of creating Olympic winners, as well as recreational sport for all age groups. No matter the level or aim of the sport organization, the NIF requires that all the different federations implement

the prime minister, proposed a tax break for families who enrolled their children in organized sport (Leitch, Bassett, & Weil, 2006). The strategy of the proposal, packaged with a child-care and general sales tax credit, was to provide economic relief, particularly to middle-class citizens, and to encourage children to be active in sports. The proposal went into effect in 2007. Children under the age of 16 were eligible in certain sports, and children under the age of 18 who had disabilities were also eligible. Although the motivation of the Canadian government was to promote physical activity and fitness through this legislation, it has been criticized because only certain activities qualify for the tax credit and, after their marginal tax rate is taken into account, families do not actually receive the initial amount of the credit (C$500 per child) (Taber, 2008).

child protection measures. The children's rights were first developed as guidelines, but recent influence by the United Nations resulted in these becoming mandatory regulations. The provisions are today absolute rules which must be complied with, obeyed, and enforced in sports.

The NIF created a development plan to ensure the learning of a wide array of movements for all children. The youngest, from ages 5 to 7, should play and do a variety of activities. At the age of 6, they are allowed to participate in local competitions, preferably in their own club. From ages 7 to 10, exploration and training with different physical activities will provide a good foundation for subsequent movement training. The different sports should adapt the activities to the children's level of development. Learning fundamental skills is prioritized from ages 10 to 12, and at this age children are also allowed to pursue an in-depth focus on one or a few sports in order to ensure a good foundation of techniques. At the age of 11, lists of results, tables, and rankings may be used for the first time, and the children may participate in regional competitions in Norway, Scandinavia, or North Calotte, where there is no need to meet a qualifying standard. In 2007 the regulations were modified to allow children to compete at national and international championships from the year they turned 13 (for further reading on regulation of children's sport see Skirstad, Waddington, and Säfvenbom, 2012).

Do the kids benefit from these restrictions? Local sport leaders are aware of the regulations, but it does not mean that all coaches follow them. Representatives from sports where early specialization is needed (gymnastics, figure skating, diving) argue against them, as they believe systematic and specialized training must be allowed and enforced. Historically, Norway has never dominated sports that require such training. At the grassroots level, these aims and goals are embraced, as they serve as an alternative to the elite sport thinking of children colored by the media's focus. The win at all costs mentality is postponed a few years in Norway.

International Learning Activity #1

Norway achieved its worst result since 1984 in the 2012 Summer Olympic Games, and there are voices arguing that the increasing number of sports participation is of no significance as long as the country does not develop talent early enough. Do you think that these restrictions and regulations may be a hindrance for the development of Olympic winners?

International Learning Activity #2

In the United States, UK, and other European countries, there is a greater acceptance of identifying talent early and emphasizing competition than in Norway. Early specialized training organized by a short-term profit focus can lead to lack of motivation, lower achievement rates, dropout and, at worst, burnout. How should Norwegian sport be organized for talented youths in order to create future winners?

International Learning Activity #3

Many children today are too sedentary and in poor physical condition, and obesity and poor motor skills are becoming more prevalent as a result. How should community sport be organized in order to combat these negative developments?

Management Challenges

Community sport presents a unique challenge concerning management because its structure and delivery system is varied and nonprescriptive (Cuskelly et al., 2006). That is, some organizations are highly professional, using paid staff to govern, manage, and deliver the sport offering. Others are loosely organized, informal volunteer groups that form more of a cooperative coalition to provide sport for themselves and a small network of community members. In many cases, the community sport organization is governed by a volunteer board of directors that sets policy for the organization. The board's wishes are carried out by a paid executive director who employs a small paid staff and a larger cadre of volunteers, especially volunteer coaches. Although volunteers have long been a mainstay of community sport delivery, pressure is increasing to make sport programs more professional because of legal issues and government policy. Such a circumstance can create tension in management styles between professional, standardized, and clearly defined procedures and volunteers' desire to have freedom over their volunteer experience (Cuskelly et al., 2006). Still, most experts agree that volunteers are a critical component of community sport, and managing volunteers is essential to organizational functioning and survival.

professional human resource management (HRM) model—A model that describes scientific methods for staffing, training, developing, and managing human resources. Although well suited for paid employees, it does not often fit for volunteers.

Although a **professional human resource management (HRM) model** can sometimes be a hindrance in completely volunteer-run sport organizations, it can be helpful in providing guidelines, structure, and accountability for community sport organizations (Meijs & Karr, 2004). Establishing HRM procedures and guidelines for worker (paid or volunteer) recruitment, selection, training, and development can help organizations streamline program delivery and make better transitions as people come and go through the organization. The basic HRM functions and their relationship to volunteer management are described next.

Personnel management begins with planning, a task that involves examining the organization's strategies, goals, and resources. As the organization's managers plan their programs and services, they can then begin to think through their personnel needs to deliver the programs. In planning for volunteers, organizational managers may ask the following questions: Does the organization have the resources to provide paid personnel, or will it rely on volunteers? What work will be performed by volunteers, and what activities will receive compensation? How many volunteers will be necessary to perform essential functions? Where will volunteers be recruited? How many hours will volunteers need to commit? What skills or training will volunteers need? How can we ensure participant safety (e.g., child protection laws) and privacy protection (e.g., participants' personal information that can be accessed by volunteers)?

After these questions are answered, the organization can develop a plan for recruiting and selecting volunteers and paid personnel. Recruitment can involve informal word-of-mouth contacts, advertisements, or broader search mechanisms. In local communities, volunteers are often the members themselves or parents of members. For example, a player on an adult soccer club team may volunteer to organize the league's schedule and book fields through the local community center. Selection of volunteers involves completing background checks (to ensure child safety) and matching volunteer skills and desires with organizational needs.

Next, volunteers often need to undergo training and development to understand the organization's goals, policies, and procedures and to become competent and successful in their volunteer duties. Much training is focused on volunteer coaches because they are often at the forefront of sport delivery, and participant experience in sport largely depends on the quality of coaching (Wiersma & Sherman, 2005). If children, in particular, do not enjoy their sport experience, they are unlikely to continue to participate. Coach training should include ethical standards, proper child safety (if coaching children), education in the particular sport coached in terms of techniques and tactics, and education in motivation and behavior management (Cuskelly et al., 2006).

Quality HRM is essential to community sport delivery. Although volunteers in particular need guidelines and training to ensure a quality experience for themselves and the participants, community sport managers must also ensure that volunteers enjoy the experience and see it as valuable and worthwhile. Procedure should not be taught at the expense of experience.

Professional Profile: Tiffany Patterson

Title: executive director, TownLake YMCA in Austin, Texas

Education: BS, Texas A&M University; MA (nonprofit administration), University of San Francisco

In her position as executive director, Tiffany Patterson focuses her attention on developing her staff and forging connections with other influential community leaders in the Austin area. Ultimately, her goal is to make a difference in the Austin community by providing programs and services that will help people increase their quality of life. To achieve this goal, she works with a knowledgeable and caring staff. Together with her branch managerial team, she problem solves on branch issues and shares best practices for running successful programs that focus on helping those in the community to realize their own goals. Patterson also reaches out to partners in the community who have the same vision of increasing individuals' quality of life through sport, physical activity, and healthy living. As an executive director, she faces the challenge of organizing, motivating, connecting, and ultimately being a leader not only in her branch, but also in the community. The following is a brief insight into her role as an influential leader in the sport and fitness industry community.

ONE DAY

o to the WSG
nd learn more
bout a typical day
the life for Tiffany Pat-
rson. See if she spends
er working hours the way
ou think she does.

What have been the key moves, steps, or developments in your career, and how did you arrive at your current position?

The road leading me to my current position started in 1995 when I received my bachelor of science degree from Texas A&M University in College Station, Texas. After graduating from Texas A&M, I moved to San Francisco, California to take a summer job at a YMCA as a camp counselor. I thought living in San Francisco for the summer working as a camp counselor would be a great way and place to spend my summer. After that summer, however, I was hooked at the YMCA and continued working in San Francisco at different YMCA branches for 15 years. I gradually moved up the management chain during that time, starting as an after-school coordinator and camp unit director to middle school coordinator to teen program director to community program director, a position I had for 6 years. From community program director, I was promoted to associate executive director of the Marin YMCA in San Rafael, California. After 2 years in this position, I accepted the position of executive director of the Richmond District YMCA in San Francisco. During this time as executive director in San Francisco, I completed my master's. My Texas roots finally pulled me back home, though. In 2010, I accepted my current position.

What are your current responsibilities and objectives in your job?

As an executive director of a YMCA branch, I am responsible for a number of tasks that fall into three categories: operations, staff development, and fundraising. On the operational side of my job, I am responsible for overseeing the daily assignments at my branch. These tasks include items like meeting with members to provide customer satisfaction, monitoring new membership growth and retention trends, and checking the facilities to ensure safety and quality. Regarding staff development, I meet regularly with my managerial team to problem solve and share best practices for keeping the branch on track for reaching their strategic goals. I also help set strategic short- and long-term goals for the branch. Finally, I spearhead the fundraising efforts for the branch. To raise funds I reach out to current members and also connect to other community-centric organizations that support the YMCA's mission.

What do you enjoy most about your current job?

I love this position because every day is different. Naturally, I have regular meetings with other executives and my own managerial team, and spend a considerable amount of time answering e-mails and making phone calls. However, the position continually challenges me to meet new people and forge new connections with wonderful individuals in the community who are all working to make a positive difference in the world. My job's dynamic environment and the autonomy to face challenges in my own way provide me with fulfillment and enjoyment.

What do you consider the biggest future challenge to be in your job or industry?

There are significant challenges on the horizon for the community fitness and sport industry. I view fighting obesity (which is meeting pandemic levels) as a major challenge, one that I feel neither I nor the YMCA can tackle alone. I believe the fight is possible, however. By collaborating with other caring partners, I know that positively affecting the quality of life of individuals is possible. Through this group effort, I will be able to play an influential role in facing the challenge of obesity.

Adult Community Sport Offerings

Community sport opportunities in North America are often provided through three basic structures: classes, leagues, and tournaments. Classes are defined as instructional sessions that enhance the skill or fitness level of the participants. For example, people may want to participate in golf classes (individual or group) to enhance their golf skills for either recreational or competitive play.

Leagues are organized forms of ongoing competition in a given sport. They may be as simple as a few teams at a community recreation center that play each other on a rotating basis, or as complex as a professional sport league (e.g., the Pacific Baseball League in Mexico, National Football League in the United States, or the Canadian Hockey League). Leagues define the playing season, rules, and participant eligibility, and usually provide a system to determine a champion. Although usually thought of in terms of team sports (e.g., soccer, basketball, hockey), leagues can also be formed for primarily individual sports (e.g., golf, tennis, archery).

Tournaments are organized forms of sport that usually extend over several days or weeks, starting with a large pool of participants and narrowing down to an eventual champion. Again, these can be as simple as a local three-on-three basketball charity fundraiser to as complex as the annual US Tennis Open Championships. For example, the United States Tennis Association (USTA) sponsors tournaments around the country nearly every weekend. The tournaments are managed and sponsored by local tennis clubs, or facilities, but are conducted under USTA rules and regulations.

Youth Sport Offerings

Community youth sport offerings and the rate at which children take advantage of those offerings vary by demographic factors (e.g., socioeconomic status, race, and ethnicity), cognitive and behavioral factors (e.g., attitudes, family influences, beliefs, perceptions, social influences, sedentary behaviors), and community factors (e.g., general safety, built environment, availability of venues for sport, school-based sport) (Government Accountability Office, 2006). These factors are important to consider when planning, implementing, and managing youth sport. Organized activities affiliated with youth sport are typically structured as classes, as instructional leagues, as competitive leagues, and through after-school programs.

Classes

Youth sport classes can range from beginning sport instruction at facilities such as community recreation centers to organizations such as the YMCA or YWCA. From a young age, even infancy in the case of swimming lessons, children can enroll to learn skills, rules, and strategies with an emphasis on enjoyment. The classes can be sport specific or composed of a variety of sports, emphasizing development. For instance, the West Suburban YMCA in the Boston suburb of Newton, Massachusetts, offers a program called Super Sports for children ages 4 through 9. In the seven-week program, children play a different sport each week. Typically, the offerings include kickball, soccer, Wiffle ball, basketball, floor hockey, flag football, and an occasional game of dodgeball or capture the flag to facilitate the children's learning of sports while maintaining a fun environment.

Instructional Leagues

The goal of instructional leagues is to provide information and knowledge to children as they begin to play sports or are introduced to new sports. Youth sport programs build basic motor skills (e.g., eye–hand coordination, footwork, balance) and provide

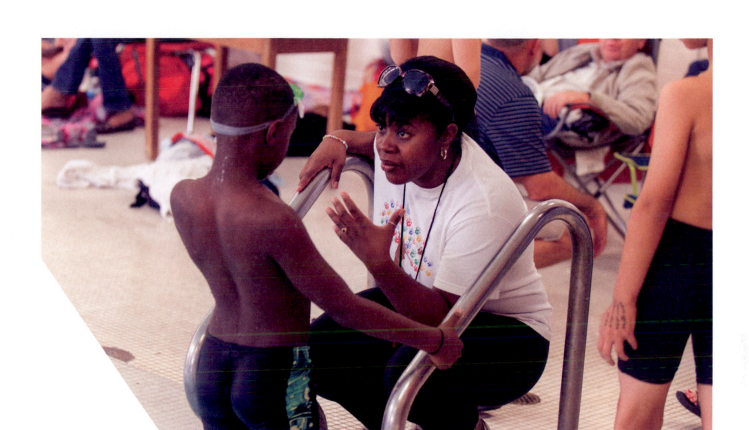

children positive instruction in the basic skills, rules, and strategies associated with a specific sport. Children are also provided with the opportunity to scrimmage or play the sport to put into practice what they have learned. At the younger levels, most leagues have at least an instructional component. Others are strictly instructional, with no scores or standings being kept.

In Burbank, California, the city recreation department provides instructional children's leagues for several sports (e.g., soccer, baseball, softball, volleyball, flag football). The philosophy of both the offerings and the instruction is based in several national models. The city of Burbank is a member of the National Alliance for Youth Sports (NAYS), which adheres to the provision of positive and safe sports and activities for children. The city does this through its application of the NAYS national standards for youth sports to its coaches, officials, administrators, and young athletes. In addition, the parents of participants complete the Parents Association for Youth Sports (PAYS) orientation program to assist them in understanding how sport plays a role in the development of their children. Specifically, Burbank's softball league offers noncompetitive tee ball divisions for grades K through 2 and then transitions into competitive leagues for grades 3 through 8. The instructional league provides motor skill and fundamental development and concludes the season with its annual jamboree, during which children participate in a parade and skill events to highlight what they have learned during their season.

Competitive Leagues

After children enter third grade in Burbank, they transition into competitive spring and fall leagues guided by Amateur Softball Association (ASA) standards and rules. Children

Children can learn basic movement and athletic skills through various youth sport organizations, classes, and leagues.

can continue in the competitive leagues until they graduate from high school and enter adult leagues. These ASA national standards and rules provide the structure for what is still a positive environment, with quality instruction that adds the competitive aspect of standings and the opportunity to enter the ASA district **sport tournament** and progress to a national championship. The ASA has more than 90 national championships, starting with fast pitch for ages 10 and under. Annually, more than 40,000 players from children to adults participate in ASA national championships.

Similar to the ASA model, other competitive sports progress from the local level to national championship events. The United States Volleyball Association (USVBA) sponsors junior leagues beginning at 10 years of age and under. At the younger levels, more emphasis is given to instruction and development; at the older levels, the emphasis shifts to competition. Teams play at local and regional tournaments. Based on finishes at those events, they can qualify for national tournaments and even the Junior Olympic Championships. USAV also sponsors outdoor leagues (e.g., Junior Beach Programs) and a Junior Beach Tour. Other examples of youth club sport opportunities include the United States Field Hockey Futures, the Amateur Athletic Union (e.g., track and field, basketball, gymnastics), and United States Swimming. The Youth Olympic Games (YOG) is a newcomer in international youth sport competition (Hanstad, Parent, & Kristiansen, 2013). It hosted its inaugural event in Singapore in 2010, followed by events in Innsbruck (2012) and Nanjing (2014).

After-School Programs

Historically, after-school programs have been viewed as beneficial to children for the personal enjoyment that they experience, the safety and supervision provided, the academic enrichment and improvement in social skills that may occur, and the emphasis on physical health and fitness (Afterschool Alliance, 2008). The hours immediately after school ends are considered a crucial time in the development of children (Bruening, Dover, & Clark, 2009; Noam, 2002). But according to the *America After 3pm* report (Afterschool Alliance, 2008), only 11% of children in the United States in grades K through 12 are in after-school programs of any kind. Typically, younger children are more likely to be enrolled in after-school programs than older ones are; as many as 66% of participants are from grades K through 5. The number drops to 15% for grades 5 through 8. Furthermore, as many as 11% of children in grades K through 5 are identified as taking care of themselves after school with no adult presence. In particular, African American and Hispanic youth spend more time unsupervised than other children do, so the demand for after-school programs is much higher in those families.

In the United States, public schools provide the largest number of general after-school programs. YMCAs and Boys and Girls Clubs are within the top five of providers of after-school programs even when sports are not specified in the rankings. For example, the YMCA of Greater Toronto offers after-school programs for children in grades K through 8 at more than 125 facilities across the metro area, making it the largest provider of after-school programs and care for children in Canada. Through these programs, children receive affordable after-school care centered on healthy character development and team building with the benefits of the facilities and trained staff of the YMCA.

Other private and nonprofit organizations also offer after-school sports programming. Like the YMCA, this programming typically uses sport as a means to learning larger life lessons. Such programming subscribes to the **sport-based youth development (SBYD) model**.

For example, The Fitzgerald Youth Sport Institute in Boston provides programs focusing on physical activity and programming. The program reports that it has served more than 14,000 children and has created more than 1,600 new sport and recreation opportunities since 2009. The unique approach of the Fitzgerald Youth Sport Institute

sport tournament— A competition involving a relatively large number of competitors. It can be offered over a set period at a single venue or can be a set of matches or competitions that culminate in a single champion.

sport-based youth development (SBYD) model— Programs that use sports in general, or a particular sport, to facilitate learning and life skill development.

is to build relationships between community health centers and families who are eligible to use their facilities. Health professionals and researchers develop programming that emphasizes physical activity as a means to improve the health of the children in the communities. Sport programming paired with life skills training and healthy development initiatives are the means to achieve Fitzgerald's goal of widespread change, not just in the Boston area but in urban communities regionally, nationally, and internationally.

Critical Thinking in Youth and Community Sport

In a city-league 18-and-up flag football game, the Badgers and the Titans meet to determine which one will advance to the league championship game. The teams faced each other earlier in the season, and the game was close and competitive. In particular, the wide receivers and defensive backs of the two teams played a rough game against each other. As the current game is nearing the end of the first half, the Badgers' defensive back is called for a passing interference foul against the Titans' receiver. At the beginning of the second half, the Titans' receiver makes a remark to his opponent in response to the foul call. The tension continues between the two players throughout the remainder of the game until, as the horn sounds to end the game with a 21-14 victory for the Badgers, the Titans' receiver runs at the Badgers' defensive back and shoves him forcibly from behind so that he falls to the ground. The Titans' player runs off the field to join the rest of her team on the sidelines. The Badgers' player is visibly injured.

Ethics in Community and Youth Sport

One issue that has become increasingly difficult for sport managers to control is that of positive sportsmanship among participants, parents, and fans during and after athletic contests. Consider the case of a recent basketball game between Jefferson High School

WEB

Go to the WSG and complete the web search activity, which asks you to research five organizations that use a sport-based youth development model to provide sport opportunities.

PORTFOLIO

Complete the critical thinking portfolio activity in the WSG, consulting as needed the "Critical Thinking Questions" sidebar in chapter 1.

Social Media and Community and Youth Sport

Social networking technologies are beginning to influence the ways community sport organizations market to, interact with, and engage with program participants. One YMCA branch in Austin, Texas utilizes the social networking site Rallyhood.com for logistical and communication purposes. This website allows the YMCA youth sport director to set up individual team pages. Within the secure team pages, parents, youth, and coaches from a certain team can privately share photographs with each other, discuss the logistics for game transportation and snacks, and send messages to each other regarding potential changes to practice times or games. Coaches can utilize the team page to upload documents such as season schedules. This particular social networking site is even more convenient for users because it is available as an application for mobile devices. Those who fully use the team site enjoy increased logistical clarity and communication transparency. Tasks that used to be completed by e-mail or over the phone can now be done smoothly through the team's social network site, which the entire team can enjoy.

Although there are many potential benefits for participants who utilize the social networking site, one drawback is that not all participants adopt the system. When this happens, the youth sport director must communicate redundantly (that is, sharing the information both over e-mail and through Rallyhood.com so that no one misses important announcements). As a result, some participants feel that the Rallyhood site is unnecessary, and adoption rates decrease. Social media is becoming more popular for use in community sport settings as managers see the potential benefits. However, it should be noted that community sport organizations do not yet fully depend on social media technologies for marketing, communicating, and organizing their sport opportunities.

PORTFOLIO

Complete the ethical issues portfolio activity in the WSG, consulting as needed the "Guidelines for Making Ethical Decisions" sidebar in chapter 1.

and Washington High School. The students of Jefferson High School come predominately from wealthy, White families. Students at Washington High School come mostly from middle or lower socioeconomic class, non-White families. The two high schools are separated geographically by only 10 miles (16 km). These factors contribute to the rivalry between the two schools. In the most recent varsity basketball game between the two schools, Jefferson High School had a commanding lead going into the final minutes of the game. When they realized their ensuing victory, the fans from Jefferson High School began yelling derogatory names at the Washington High School players based on their perceived race, ethnicity, and socioeconomic status. The Washington High School players were frustrated. They knew they had tried their hardest and were proud of their effort on the court, even though it resulted in a loss. However, they also felt embarrassed, discouraged, and ashamed as a result of the fans' comments.

Summary

Youth and community sport in North America are offered in a variety of settings including schools, private sport clubs, and public recreation centers. The different types of sport structures create various management challenges including access, management of volunteers, financial viability, and conflicts over the mission and goals of the organization.

Although sport participation continues to grow in both Canada and the United States, participation opportunities vary widely based on geography and gender; rural areas and girls still lag behind in access to sport participation. Individuals, families, and communities benefit from sport and physical activity participation. These benefits include improved physical and psychological health, increased family time together, and increased social capital. Because sport can be beneficial, sport managers should identify ways to attract and retain participants in the local community.

Youth and community sport opportunities also take a variety of forms, ranging from instructional classes to after-school programs to competitive tournaments and leagues. Understanding the structure and goals of a participation opportunity helps managers determine the organizational needs and strategies for meeting those needs among the various constituents. Sport managers in this sector must continually monitor participant needs and wants so that they can provide the kinds of sports and formats that serve their community best.

Review Questions

1. How would you define youth and community sport?
2. What are the various sectors of youth and community sport?
3. What are the goals and outcomes associated with each youth and community sport sector?
4. What are some key providers to the youth sector? To the community sector?
5. How is access to youth and community sport a complex issue in different communities?
6. What challenges exist in managing youth and community sport? How would you meet those challenges?
7. What career opportunities within youth sport can you identify? Within community sport? Which opportunities are most attractive to you and why?
8. How has social media influenced the work of sport managers in the various sectors of youth and community sport?

References

Afterschool Alliance. (2008). *America after 3pm: A household survey on afterschool in America key findings.* Retrieved from www.afterschoolalliance.org/documents/AA%203%20pm_Key_Findings.pdf

Badcock, B. (2002). *Making sense of cities: A geographical survey.* London, UK: Arnold.

Bringle, R., & Hatcher, J. (1995). A service learning curriculum for faculty. *Michigan Journal of Community Service Learning, 2,* 112–122.

Brown, G. (2009, January 9). NCAA and NBA look to change youth basketball culture. *NCAA News.* Retrieved from www.ncaa.org/wps/ncaa?ContentID=43661

Bruening, J.E., Dover, K.M., & Clark, B.S. (2009). Preadolescent female development through sport and physical activity: A case study of an urban after-school program. *Research Quarterly in Exercise and Sport, 80,* 1–18.

Canada survey of giving, volunteering and participating. (2012). Ottawa, Ontario, Canada: Volunteer Canada.

Canadian Centre for Ethics in Sport. (2002). *Public opinion survey on youth and sport: Final report.* Ottawa, Ontario, Canada: Decima Research.

Chalip, L. (2006). Toward a distinctive sport management discipline. *Journal of Sport Management, 20,* 1–21.

Chudacoff, H. (2007). *Children at play: An American history.* New York, NY: New York University Press.

Coakley, J. (2009). *Sport in society: Issues and controversies* (10th ed.). New York, NY: McGraw Hill.

Cuskelly, G., Hoye, R., & Auld, C. (2006). *Working with volunteers in sport: Theory and practice.* London, UK: Routledge.

Dixon, M. (2009). From their perspective: A qualitative examination of physical activity and sport for working mothers. *Sport Management Review, 12,* 34–48.

Engh, F. (1999). *Why Johnny hates sports: Why organized youth sports are failing our children and what we can do about it.* Garden City Park, NY: Avery.

Government Accountability Office. (2006). *Childhood obesity: Factors affecting physical activity.* GAO-07-260R. Washington, D.C.: Author.

Halpern, R. (2002). A different kind of child development institution: The history of after-school programs for low-income children. *Teachers College Record, 104,* 78–211.

Hanstad, D.V., Parent, M.M., & Kristiansen, E. (2013). The Youth Olympic Games: The best of the Olympics or a poor copy? *European Sport Management Quarterly, 13,* 315–338.

Hartmann, D. (2008). *High school sports participation and educational attainment: Recognizing, assessing, and utilizing the relationship.* Retrieved from www.la84foundation.org/3ce/HighSchoolSportsParticipation.pdf

Hedstrom, R., & Gould, D. (2004). *Research in youth sports: Critical issues.* East Lansing, MI: Institute for the Study of Youth Sports.

Henderson, K.A., & Hickerson, B. (2007). Women and leisure: Premises and performances uncovered in an integrative review. *Journal of Leisure Research, 39,* 591–610.

Hopkins, C.H. (1951). *History of the YMCA in North America.* New York, NY: Association Press.

Koester, M. (2000). Youth sports: A pediatrician's perspective on coaching and injury prevention. *Journal of Athletic Training, 35,* 466–470.

Koltyn, K., & Schultes, S. (1997). Psychological effects of an aerobic exercise session and a rest session following pregnancy. *Journal of Sports Medicine and Physical Fitness, 37,* 287–291.

Larson, R., Walker, K., & Pearce, N. (2005). A comparison of youth-driven and adult-driven youth programs: Balancing inputs from youth and adults. *Journal of Community Psychology, 33,* 57–74.

Leitch, K., Bassett, D., & Weil, M. (2006). *Report of the expert panel on the children's fitness tax credit.* Ottawa, Ontario, Canada: Canadian Department of Finance.

Le Menestrel, S., & Perkins, D. (2007). An overview of how sports, out-of-school time, and youth well-being can and do intersect. *New Directions for Youth Development, 115,* 13–25.

Marten, J. (2008). A new view of the child: Children and youth in urban America, 1900–1920. *Romanian Journal of Population Studies, 1,* 67–81.

Meijs, L., & Karr, L. (2004). Managing volunteers in different settings: Membership and programme management. In R. Stebbins & M. Grahem (Eds.), *Volunteering as leisure/leisure as volunteering* (pp. 177–193). Wallingford, UK: CABI.

Morrow, D., & Wamsley, K. (2005). *Sport in Canada: A history.* Toronto, Ontario, Canada: Oxford University Press.

Multi-Sport Organizations. (2013). United States Olympic Committee. Retrieved from www.teamusa.org/About-the-USOC/In-the-Community/Partner-Programs/Multi-Sport-Organizations.aspx

Murphy, K.P. (2005). Hallelujah lads and lasses: Remaking the Salvation Army in America, 1880–1930; Making men, making class: The YMCA and workingmen 1877–1930. *Labor, 2,* 112–114.

Noam, G. (2002). Youth development and after-school time. *New directions for youth development, 94,* 1–2.

Putnam, R. (2000). *Bowling alone: The collapse and revival of American community.* New York, NY: Simon & Schuster.

Rader, B.G. (2009). *American sports: From the age of folk games to the age of televised sports* (6th ed.). Upper Saddle River, NJ: Prentice Hall.

Sabo, D., & Veliz, P. (2008). *Go out and play: Youth sports in America.* East Meadow, NY: Women's Sports Foundation.

Skirstad, R., Waddington, I., & Säfvenbom, R. (2012). Issues and problems in the organization of children's sport: A case study of Norway. *European Physical Education Review, 18*(3), 309–321.

Sporting Goods Manufacturers Association. (2012). *2012 sports, fitness and leisure activities topline participation report.* Washington, D.C.: Author.

Stanford University Prevention Research Center. (2007). *Building "generation play": Addressing the crisis of inactivity among America's children.* Palo Alto, CA: Author.

Stewart, B., Nicholson, M., Smith, A., & Westerbeek, H. (2004). *Australian sport: Better by design? The evolution of Australian sport policy.* London, UK: Routledge.

Taber, J. (2008, September 29). Harper offers tax credit for children's arts programs. *The National,* p. A13.

U.S. Department of Health and Human Services. (1996). *Physical activity and health: A report of the surgeon general.* Atlanta, GA: U.S. Department of Health and Human Services, Centers for Disease Control and Prevention, National Center for Chronic Disease Prevention and Health Promotion.

Wiersma, L., & Sherman, C. (2005). Volunteer youth sport coaches' perspectives of coaching education/certification and parental codes of conduct. *Research Quarterly for Exercise and Sport, 76,* 324–338.

HISTORICAL MOMENTS

- **1888**   Massachusetts established the Interscholastic Football Association
- **1904**   Georgia became the first state to establish a high school athletics association
- **1921**   Midwest Federation of State High School Associations founded
- **1971**   National Conference of High School Directors of Athletics established
- **1974**   *Interscholastic Athletic Administration* magazine launched
- **1977**   National Interscholastic Athletic Administrators Association (NIAAA) formed
- **1979**   Minnesota Adapted Athletics Association (MAAA) founded first high school athletics conference for students with disabilities
- **1981**   National Federation Interscholastic Coaches Association (NFICA) formed
- **1982**   National High School Sports Hall of Fame established
- **1990**   National Federation Interscholastic Spirit Association (NFISA) formed
- **1993**   Robert F. Kanaby named the National Federation of State High School Associations (NFHS) executive director
- **1996**   American Association of Adapted Sports Programs (AAASP) founded—first interscholastic athletics governing body for students with physical or visual impairments
- **1996**   Becky Oakes named first female president of the NFHS
- **2005**   Athletics participation topped 7 million for first time
- **2008**   NFHS developed its National High School Spirit of Sport Award
- **2009**   NIAAA established Quality Program Award
- **2010**   Bob Gardner named NFHS fifth executive director
- **2011**   Proposed amendment allowing NFHS to sanction national championships in cross country and golf defeated
- **2011**   Interscholastic athletic contests banned by the National Collegiate Athletic Association (NCAA) from being televised on school- or conference-owned TV networks
- **2012**   NIAAA launched national public service announcement campaign with NFHS
- **2013**   NFHS partnered with PlayOn! Sports to develop a high school sports network

7

INTERSCHOLASTIC ATHLETICS

Warren A. Whisenant \ Eric W. Forsyth \ Tywan G. Martin

LEARNING OBJECTIVES

> Identify the historical and governance foundations of interscholastic athletics.
> Explain the differing critical views of the role that interscholastic athletics plays in society.
> Discuss the operational differences between public and private schools.
> Explain the benefits and restraints of athletics departments that are centralized and of those that are dispersed.
> Identify careers available in interscholastic sports at the national, state, district, and local levels.
> Explain the unique and similar issues that face athletics directors at private schools and public schools.
> Discuss the associations related to interscholastic athletics at the national and state levels.

Key Terms

athletics administrator

athletics director

centralized organizational structure

decentralized organizational structure

interscholastic athletics

interscholastic sport governance

National Federation of State High School Associations

National Interscholastic Athletic Administrators Association

private schools

public schools

state athletics or activity associations

GET A JOB

Continue on your journey in sport management by going to the web study guide (WSG) at www.HumanKinetics.com/ContemporarySportManagement. Check out the job opportunities and consider the skills and experiences that can help you succeed in sport management.

nterscholastic athletics is a segment within the sport industry that seems to draw the least amount of attention within the realm of sport management studies and academia. Scholars have tended to focus their research agenda toward collegiate and professional sport. Students entering the profession also tend to envision themselves as being key players within a Division I athletics department, working in the front office of a professional sport team, or even working as an agent negotiating multimillion dollar contracts. The attention toward those segments is understandable considering the dominant national media exposure of the professional and collegiate segments within the sport industry provided by cable outlets such as Fox Sports and ESPN. If the lead story on SportsCenter dealt with a rift between the Bulldogs' athletics director and head football coach, viewers would expect to see a story involving Greg McGarity and Mark Richt from the University of Georgia, not Paula Gonzalez and Kevin Brewer at McAllen High School (McHi) in McAllen, Texas. A story concerning the job security of the head coach of the Cowboys would draw attention to Dallas, not LaBelle High School in Hendry County, Florida. The many issues facing interscholastic administrators seldom draw widespread attention or interest.

Although the national media may not cover high school athletics, this segment of the sport industry should not be overlooked in terms of growth, career opportunities, and economic impact. The U.S. Bureau of Labor Statistics (2012) suggested that the employment opportunities within sport and entertainment were expected to grow roughly 16% from 2010 to 2020, exceeding the growth rate of many other occupations. A significant portion of that growth will occur in the more than 24,000 athletics departments at the high school level, both public and private. Employing more than 300,000 coaches and administrators, as a business segment, **interscholastic athletics** contributes over US$15 billion to the sport industry in the United States.

The potential influence interscholastic athletics administrators have over the lives of young adults can be significant. Almost 7.7 million of the 14.8 million (52%) high school students who attended public schools during the 2011–2012 school year participated in athletics. As such, interscholastic administrators have a deep responsibility and obligation to meet a wide range of needs to their constituents, the youth of America. For many kids, the manner in which their schools' athletics programs are managed and delivered will shape their perceptions about success and failure, organizational fairness, and other social norms. Although sport management professionals at both collegiate and professional levels are typically tasked with delivering a quality entertainment product for their fan base, interscholastic athletics administrators play an important role in the educational and social development of the students who are involved with their school's athletic program. High school athletics also plays a role in the community by providing sports entertainment and serving as a prominent source of community well-being.

interscholastic athletics— Combination of sport offerings whereby boys and girls can elect to participate in athletics at the high school level.

Arrival of Interscholastic Athletics

The first intercollegiate athletics competition can be traced back to August 3, 1852, when Harvard and Yale matched their crew teams on the waters of Lake Winnipesaukee in New Hampshire (Dealy, 1990). The details of the first interscholastic athletics competition are less certain. But students from various public and private high schools in Massachusetts formed the Interscholastic Football Association in 1888 (Hardy, 2003). As such, it may well have been among those Boston-area schools that the first interscholastic athletics competition occurred. At the turn of the century, interscholastic sport had become the largest sector in the entire sport enterprise (Robinson, Hums, Crow, & Phillips, 2001). No other level of sport has as many participants, sport teams, or athletics programs as interscholastic sport does. In addition, each school and each state provides an array of sporting options to meet the interests of their students. Both traditional sports and niche sports are offered across the country. A sampling of the sports offered by schools can be found in following sidebar.

Governance of Interscholastic Athletics

Individual state associations started developing and giving interscholastic athletics a more formalized governance structure in the early 1900s. The associations developed broad and sport-specific standards, rules, and policies. The first state to establish a high school athletics association was Georgia in 1904 (Georgia High School Association, 2013). During the early years when state associations were being established, colleges, universities, nonschool clubs, and promoters were organizing many interscholastic athletics competitions. As a result, little attention was given to the eligibility rules that were being established by the state high school athletics associations (*NFHS Handbook*, 2012–13).

List of Most Popular School-Sponsored Sports for Both Boys and Girls

Traditional Sports

Baseball	Softball
Basketball	Swimming and diving
Competitive spirit squads	Tennis
Cross country	Track and field
Football	Volleyball
Golf	Wrestling
Soccer	

Niche Sports

Adapted floor hockey	Indoor track and field
Alpine skiing	Judo
Badminton	Kayaking
Bowling	Lacrosse
Canoeing	Skiing
Crew	Orienteering
Dance and drill team	Power lifting
Decathlon	Riflery
Equestrian	Rodeo
Field hockey	Sailing
Flag football	Skiing
Gymnastics	Snowboarding
Heptathlon	Synchronized swimming
Ice hockey	Water polo

High School Sport— The Canadian Perspective

By Morris Glimcher, Canada
Manitoba High Schools Athletic Association

By John Paton, Canada
Alberta Schools' Athletic Association

More than 800,000 student-athletes, 55,000 volunteer teacher coaches, and 3,250 schools are part of School Sport Canada (SSC). The Canadian system operates as a school-based model in which promoting good sportsmanship and ethical behavior is a key objective.

School Sport Canada (SSC) represents interscholastic sports for 10 provinces as well as two territories throughout Canada.

The Canadian philosophy is that school athletics are complementary to the curricular programs. Teachers are encouraged to contribute to the school in capacities such as coaches, supervisors, choir leaders, student council advisors, and other roles. All Canadian school coaches are volunteers. Depending on the province, 60% to 80% of these volunteer coaches are teachers, but this number is declining. As a result, schools and school athletics associations must deal at times with differing philosophies of teacher versus nonteacher coaches regarding issues such as playing time, cut policies, focus on winning, recruiting, and athletic eligibility.

After concerns were raised regarding the welfare of student-athletes, representatives from Illinois, Indiana, Iowa, Michigan, and Wisconsin met to discuss common concerns arising out of collegiate and nonschool publicity of high school athletics contests. As a result of this historic meeting that took place in May 1920, the Midwest Federation of State High School Athletic Associations (MFSHSA) was created

In Canada, most schools and school districts do not have paid athletic directors (ADs). Some schools are able to structure timetables to give a teacher a few slots each week to look after the many athletic issues. This practice is more common in urban areas than in rural areas. Many schools have a physical education coordinator who looks after the curriculum as well as the interschool sport programs.

Although Canada does not have legislation similar to Title IX, gender equity has always been a high priority, and the school athletics programs reflect that position. Litigation relating to school athletics typically occurs in relation to eligibility matters, and is done through the provincial court system. In some cases, Provincial Human Rights Commissions have dealt with concerns raised by parents and schools, and school athletics associations have modified eligibility policy to comply with their decisions.

Adequate financial support for athletics is not assured because the budgets are school based. Where booster clubs exist, they may contribute to a variety of school programs, not just athletics. Most students pay a participation fee that ranges from C$50 to C$300, or more, per sport. Local school sport sponsorships are necessary to keep costs affordable for participants.

Coaches' certification programs are not mandatory for schools in Canada, but many programs are available to coaches. The Coaching Association of Canada (CAC) offers courses to coaches, and the CAC has partnered with the SSC on a specific coaching in schools module that teaches them the basics on topics such as ethical decision making, dealing with parents, and understanding provincial athletic association rules. In 2012, the SSC launched an online coach education website, www.schoolcoach.ca, modeled initially on the NFHS online initiative from the United States. Some provinces have mandated a degree of involvement in this program.

The SSC and the Canadian provinces and territories have positive relationships with the NFHS and the National Interscholastic Athletic Administrators Association (NIAAA) in the United States. Because there is much commonality in what athletics administrators do, the SSC works positively with and between provincial, state, and national organizations to offer the best opportunities for student-athletes. Sometimes resources are shared, and at other times cross-border (i.e., province to province or province to state) athletics competitions are organized.

Most recently, Canada has launched a national association for school athletic directors, the Canadian Interscholastic Athletic Administrator Association (CIAAA, www.ciaaa.ca), building on several years of lead work and development by the Alberta Interscholastic Athletic Administrators Association, Canada's first AD association. Canada has many opportunities to share ideas and philosophies among provinces and territories and with the United States. It is all part of the educational process of school sport.

International Learning Activity #1

Visit the School Sport Canada (SSC) website as well as the National Federation of State High School Associations (NFHS) website. Browse each one and determine what differences and similarities exist between the Canadian organization and the U.S. organization.

International Learning Activity #2

Identify similarities and differences between the interscholastic athletics system in Canada and the interscholastic athletics system in your country. Note the instances in which you prefer the Canadian system and those in which you prefer the system in your country. Construct a table of the most salient features for each system in the two countries. Which features do you prefer and why?

International Learning Activity #3

Think back to the school sports you participated in while you were growing up. Explain how your school sports system was funded, staffed, and managed. How does this compare to the Canadian sport system? What are the benefits and drawbacks of each system?

in 1921. The mission of the federation was "to protect the athletic interests of high schools belonging to the various state associations and to promote pure amateur sport" (*NFHS Handbook*, 2012–13, p. 17). This mission still applies today. Not long after the formation of the MFSHSA, other state high school associations began expressing an interest in joining.

Interest grew nationally, and by 1923, it was fitting to change the name to the National Federation of State High School Athletic Associations. By 1930, there were 28 state athletics associations establishing membership. Ten years later, the state athletics association membership had grown to 35. In 1969, all 50 state associations and the association for the District of Columbia had become members of the national association. By the 1970s, selected fine arts activities were sanctioned by the national federation, which thereby dropped *athletic* from its name entirely. Today, the National Federation of State High School (NFHS) Associations consists of 22 additional members outside the United States. Associations are located in Bermuda, Guam, St. Croix, St. John and St. Thomas, 10 provinces and three territories in Canada, and seven affiliated associations for defense, forensic, and music (*NFHS Handbook*, 2012–13). Additional information on each state, including a recap of the history, mission, and beliefs of each state association, may be found on the websites of the individual state associations. Summaries of three state associations and the national association follow.

National Federation of State High School (NFHS) Associations—This national governing body provides leadership for the administration of education-based interscholastic sport and nonsport activities.

Florida High School Athletic Association

The Florida High School Athletic Association (FHSAA) was founded in 1920 by a group of 29 high school principals. During its nine-decade history, the association has shown steady growth, and currently has almost 800 member schools. For its first 77 years in operation, the association served as a voluntary governing body. Not until 1997 did the Florida State Legislature recognize the association as the official governing body for interscholastic athletics in Florida. The principal aim is to promote, direct, supervise, and regulate high school athletics programs. The association's members are committed to the ideal and belief that education does not begin or end in the classroom but continues outside the classroom. The association asserts that through their participation in interscholastic athletics, high school student-athletes also learn teamwork, sportsmanship, and citizenship as they become future leaders ("Florida High School Athletic Association," 2013).

Minnesota State High School League

The Minnesota State High School League (MSHSL) was organized in 1916 as the State Interscholastic Athletic Association. In 1929, the association broadened its scope by including nonsport activities. The inclusion of speech and debate under the association's domain led to a name change to the Minnesota State High School League. The MSHSL's principal aim is to provide educational opportunities for students through athletics and nonsport programs and to provide leadership and support for its nearly 500 member schools ("*Minnesota State High School League*," 2013).

University Interscholastic League

The University Interscholastic League (UIL) governs the largest number of high school athletes in the nation. Since its inception in 1909, the UIL has provided leadership and guidance to public schools in Texas and has become the largest interschool organization of its kind in the world. The UIL provides oversight to the state's high school extracurricular activities associated with academics, athletics, and music. The organization "is dedicated to offering character-building, educational competition to member school students in Texas" (*University Interscholastic League*, 2013, p. 3).

National Federation of State High School Associations

The NFHS was founded in 1920 to serve as the national leadership organization for high school sport and fine arts activities. Its principal aim is to support academic achievement,

Professional Profile: Claude Grubair

Title: director of athletics, Ransom Everglades School

Education: BA (history and political science), University of Miami (Florida)

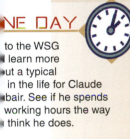

NE DAY
to the WSG
learn more
ut a typical
in the life for Claude
bair. See if he spends
working hours the way
think he does.

Claude Grubair has served as the athletic director at Ransom Everglades School since 1999. Ransom was established in 1903 in Coconut Grove, Florida, along the shores of Key Biscayne Bay. Located on two campuses, Ransom Everglades is a coeducational, college preparatory school for grades 6 through 12. Athletics plays an integral role in the students' education process, with 93% of the 1,075 students participating on at least one of the school's 26 teams. In addition to the high level of student involvement, 90% of the school's teams are coached by faculty members who have an average tenure of 18 years, with 71% possessing a master's degree or higher.

What have been the key moves, steps, or developments in your career, and how did you arrive at your current position?

After I graduated from UM, my original plan was to attend law school. While waiting to apply to law school, I helped my father in his electronics store. It didn't take long before I knew that retail sales was not for me. A short time later, an old coach from high school called me to tell me that there was an open position as an assistant athletic director (AD) and coach at a local private school. The coach suggested that I apply for the position. That was the start of my career as an administrator in interscholastic athletics. I worked there for 5 years. I feel extremely lucky to have worked for a gentleman with more than 35 years of experience as an AD. Then I had an opportunity to teach and become the assistant athletic director here at Ransom, and I took it. When I got here, I worked for a female AD for 2 years. Their two management styles were completely different. His was very organized and structured, while her style was very fluid. I learned a great deal from both ADs. She left after 2 years, and he was promoted to director of athletics. I am convinced that the unsolicited call from my high school coach came not because I knew him, but because the coach knew me—he called because of my personal reputation.

What are your current responsibilities and objectives in your job?

My duties and responsibilities are very typical of those of other athletic directors. My time is split between general administrative duties and meetings with the school's administrators and faculty, direct reports and coaches, student-athletes, administrators from other schools, competition officials, and parents. I am responsible for ensuring the students have the best equipment, facilities, and coaches available. That requires me to dedicate considerable time to designing and overseeing the construction of new facilities and to fundraising to pay for those facilities. As student interests change over time, I feel I have to be willing to introduce new sports to the program. And as new sports are added, I must ensure the athletes have qualified coaches, the proper equipment, and the best possible facilities, with the goal to be competitive shortly after a sport is introduced.

What do you enjoy most about your current job?

Despite the long hours, I derive my greatest enjoyment from changing the lives of the kids who participate in the school's athletic program. The kids learn the importance of teamwork, dedication, commitment, and the feeling of success when they win, and they also learn when they are not successful. My job allows for constant renewal as new kids enter the school and move on after graduation. Every year is different.

What do you consider the biggest future challenge to be in your job or industry?

Perhaps our biggest challenge, looking ahead, is adapting to the changes in parental involvement. More and more I see parents not in the role as cheerleader or their kid's biggest fan, but in the role of manager. I think administrators will need to focus more time on the parents, since many of them seem to be interfering with their kid's sporting experience by pushing for sport specialization and for their kids to play on without regard to injury, as well as not allowing their kids to experience failure.

good citizenship, and equitable opportunities for boys and girls in high schools (as well as middle schools) by enhancing interaction among its member state associations. The national organization is also dedicated to developing and maintaining the playing rules for athletics contests at the high school level. Through its member state associations, the NFHS serves approximately 19,000 high schools and approximately 11 million participants in high school activities, nearly 7.7 million of whom are participating in athletics (*NFHS Handbook*, 2012–2013). Table 7.1 lists the year in which each state association joined the national federation.

Table 7.1   **State Associations and Year Joining the National Federation of State High School Associations**

Association	Year	Association	Year
Alabama	1924	Montana	1934
Alaska	1956	Nebraska	1924
Arizona	1925	Nevada	1939
Arkansas	1924	New Hampshire	1945
California	1940	New Jersey	1942
Colorado	1924	New Mexico	1932
Connecticut	1926	New York	1926
Delaware	1945	North Carolina	1949
DC	1958	North Dakota	1923
Florida	1926	Ohio	1924
Georgia	1929	Oklahoma	1924
Hawaii	1957	Oregon	1931
Idaho	1926	Pennsylvania	1924
Illinois	1920	Rhode Island	1952
Indiana	1924	South Carolina	1947
Iowa	1920	South Dakota	1923
Kansas	1923	Tennessee	1925
Kentucky	1941	Texas	1969
Louisiana	1925	Utah	1927
Maine	1939	Vermont	1945
Maryland	1946	Virginia	1948
Massachusetts	1944	Washington	1936
Michigan	1920	West Virginia	1925
Minnesota	1923	Wisconsin	1920
Mississippi	1924	Wyoming	1936
Missouri	1926		

Value of Interscholastic Athletics Programs

According to the NFHS (2013), three central premises indicate the value of offering interscholastic activities: (a) athletics support the academic mission of schools, (b) athletics are inherently educational, and (c) athletics foster success in later life. Many of the supporters of high school sport draw on these attributes to promote the importance of athletics in the educational mission of public and private schools.

Athletics Support the Academic Mission of Schools

When compared with the general student population with regard to several components (e.g., grade-point averages, attendance, dropout rates, discipline), student-athletes tend to exceed students who do not compete in interscholastic athletics programs. Therefore, athletics should be viewed as an extension of a good educational program.

Athletics Are Inherently Educational

Through athletics participation, students learn such things as teamwork, the value of fair play, winning and losing, the benefits associated with hard work, self-discipline, self-confidence, and skills to handle competitive situations. Parents, guardians, and the public typically expect schools to instill such qualities in students during their years in high school.

Athletics Foster Success in Later Life

By collecting exit surveys of participants at the state level, the NFHS has documented the successes of student-athletes over the years, including such markers as attending college, earning a degree, and having a higher socioeconomic status within society. Note that nonathletes also attend institutions of higher education, receive degrees, and attain prominent status within their respective communities. Overall, however, the professional success rate is higher for those who participated in interscholastic athletics programs than for those who did not.

Conflicting Views

Some people, however, hold conflicting views of the value in offering interscholastic sport programs within the education setting. Scholars such as Coakley (2009) and Sage and Eitzen (2013) present a critical perspective with respect to interscholastic sports and its place within society. Some critical views include the following:

> Participation in athletics programs distracts students from their academics.
> Athletics programs distort educational values within the school culture.
> Athletics programs turn students into passive spectators.
> Many injuries are associated with athletics competitions.
> Athletics goals are unrelated to educational goals.
> Athletics programs deprive educational programs of resources needed to survive.
> Athletics programs create too many additional pressures on student-athletes.
> Student-athletes tend to be privileged over other students.
> Athletics prepare students to be disciplined cogs in the industrial world.

Regardless of the lens through which you view high school sport, its presence is well entrenched within the American school system. Although athletics departments and participation rates grew throughout the 1900s, sports were not readily accessible to all students until the early 1970s. Not until the passage of Title IX legislation did girls earn equal access to the sport experience.

Participation Numbers

Title IX of the Educational Amendments of 1972 was a landmark legislation that banned sex discrimination in public and private schools. The act, covered in chapters 8 ("Intercollegiate Athletics") and 17 ("Legal Considerations in Sport Management"), applies to the activities of educational institutions that receive federal funding. At the time of its passage, fewer than 8% of the 3.9 million student-athletes participating in interscholastic athletics were girls (see table 7.2). At the end of the 2011–2012 school year, girls accounted for 41.5% of the 7.7 million high school students playing sports. Some critics of the application of Title IX to sport have argued that to be compliant with the legislation, boys' sports were cut, thus diminishing opportunities for boys to participate in sport. That position may be disputable because, as indicated in table 7.2, the number of boys participating in high school sport is at an all-time high, at nearly 4.5 million.

Texas continues to have the most participants (with 808,806 athletes, or 10.5% of all the high school athletics participants in the United States). The remaining top 10 states are California (781,912 athletes), New York (389,475 athletes), Illinois (346,896 athletes), Ohio (333,349 athletes), Pennsylvania (317,869 athletes), Michigan (308,080 athletes), New Jersey (259,219 athletes), Florida (257,282 athletes), and Minnesota (238,363 athletes). In rank order, the 10 most popular sports in terms of the number of programs for boys are basketball, track and field, baseball, football, cross country, golf, soccer, wrestling, tennis, and swimming and diving. For girls, the 10 most popular sports in terms of the number of programs are basketball, track and field, volleyball, softball, cross country, soccer, tennis, golf, swimming and diving, and competitive spirit squads (*NFHS*, 2013a).

Operating Models

centralized organizational structure—An operational model whereby all decisions are controlled by a central administration unit and carried down through the chain of command within an organization.

decentralized organizational structure—An operational model whereby respective units of an organization are given autonomy to control and carry out decisions, although each unit is expected to operate within the organization's guiding principles.

private schools—Schools that operate on moneys received through various forms of funding and giving (e.g., personal, religious, corporate).

One of the most challenging aspects of managing any organization is establishing an organizational structure that best fits the needs of the organization's employees (e.g., teachers, coaches, officials, administrators) and constituents (e.g., parents, students, athletes). One significant consideration when structuring an athletics department is the size of the school district. Small districts or private schools—such as Newfound Area School District in New Hampshire, which serves seven cities and has approximately 1,400 students, one high school, and two middle schools, or Storm Lake Community Schools in Iowa, which has approximately 2,000 students, one high school, and one middle school—have a **centralized organizational structure**. Centralized structures tend to have vertical reporting relationships often characterized as a chain of command (figure 7.1 illustrates the difference between a centralized and a **decentralized organizational structure**). The athletics director (AD) may work at the high school and report to the high school principal while overseeing the athletics administrative duties for the entire district. The AD may also serve as a coach, a teacher, or even the high school principal. In a centralized structure, the AD typically hires all the district's coaches and has a campus coordinator at each middle school to oversee daily athletics administrative duties. This type of structure is most often used by **private schools**. For larger school districts—such as the Miami–Dade County Public Schools, which has more than 345,000 students in over 100 high schools and middle schools, or the Houston Independent School District, which has more than 203,000 students and over

Table 7.2   **Participation Among Boys and Girls Since the Enactment of Title IX**

Year	Boys	Girls	Year	Boys	Girls
1971–72	3,666,917	294,015	1993–94	3,472,967	2,130,315
1972–73	3,770,621	817,073	1994–95	3,536,359	2,240,461
1973–74	4,070,125	1,300,169	1995–96	3,634,052	2,367,936
1975–76	4,109,021	1,645,039	1996–97	3,706,225	2,474,043
1977–78	4,367,442	2,083,040	1997–98	3,763,120	2,570,333
1978–79	3,709,512	1,854,400	1998–99	3,832,352	2,652,726
1979–80	3,517,829	1,750,264	1999–2000	3,861,749	2,675,874
1980–81	3,503,124	1,853,789	2000–01	3,921,069	2,784,154
1981–82	3,409,081	1,810,671	2001–02	3,960,517	2,806,998
1982–83	3,355,558	1,779,972	2002–03	3,988,738	2,856,358
1983–84	3,303,599	1,747,346	2003–04	4,038,253	2,865,299
1984–85	3,354,284	1,757,884	2004–05	4,110,319	2,908,390
1985–86	3,344,275	1,807,121	2005–06	4,206,549	2,953,355
1986–87	3,364,082	1,836,356	2006–07	4,321,103	3,021,807
1987–88	3,425,777	1,849,684	2007–08	4,372,115	3,057,266
1988–89	3,416,844	1,839,352	2008–09	4,422,662	3,114,091
1989–90	3,398,192	1,858,659	2009–10	4,455,740	3,172,637
1990–91	3,406,355	1,892,316	2010–11	4,494,406	3,173,549
1991–92	3,429,853	1,940,801	2011–12	4,484,987	3,207,533
1992–93	3,416,389	1,997,489	2012–13	4,490,854	3,222,723

Data from National Federation of State High School Association 2013.

80 high schools and middle schools—a centralized athletics department would not be feasible or manageable. In these mega athletics programs, administrative responsibilities are often decentralized through a matrix management template. This type of structure allows dual reporting relationships. The district might have a district athletics director who coordinates athletics activities within the district with staff level authority in the schools and school-based athletics directors who report directly to the school principals for implementing the district programs. These high school ADs would most likely supervise feeder school campus coordinators as well as one or more assistant ADs and a business manager.

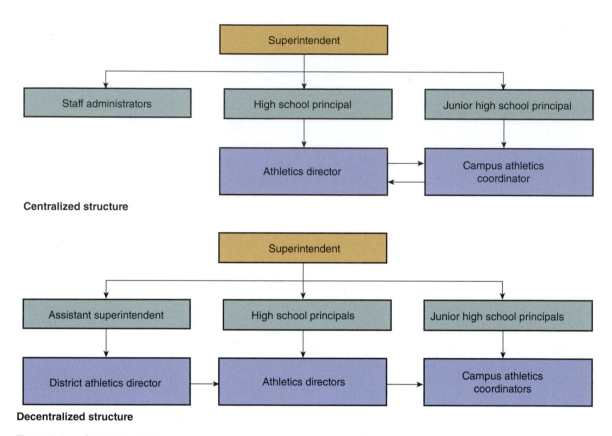

Figure 7.1   Organizational structures: centralized structure and decentralized structure.

Although athletics budgets may differ from school to school, the primary expenses tend to be similar. Most budgets will be composed of the following categories: salaries and benefits, equipment, supplies, transportation, professional development, awards, and other miscellaneous costs. Typically, insurance and facility costs are held back at the district level for **public schools.** ADs at private schools or smaller public school districts may also be responsible for facility expenditures. School budgets allocated to athletics vary greatly from 1% to 3% of operating budgets to as much as 8%. As operating costs continued to rise during the 2008–09 school year, the economic downturn across the country had a detrimental effect on overall school funding and, in turn, on athletics. The primary source of funding for most school districts is through property tax assessments. Because the economy grew throughout the 1990s and into 2007, property values increased, providing additional revenues to school districts. In 2008, however, when the real estate market collapsed, many school districts and athletics departments found themselves with significant revenue shortfalls. The Miami–Dade school district, for example, reported an estimated operational deficit in excess of US$200 million, requiring spending cuts in all facets of the education system, including athletics.

ADs across the country were forced to adapt to the decline in revenues and stretch their budgets to meet the growing needs of student-athletes. Numerous options were available to ADs. Although some programs drastically reduced the number of contests in which their athletes competed, others eliminated sports completely, particularly in

public schools—Schools that operate on moneys received largely through local property taxes.

middle schools. Additional attempts to resolve funding concerns included replacing some individual contests or matches with tournaments, implementing pay-to-play policies, reducing the frequency of uniform purchases, increasing fundraising activities, and seeking greater support from booster clubs. Athletics administrators have also reduced transportation costs by restricting competition to schools in proximity to the home school, discontinuing courtesy bus service to transport parents to and from away events, and scheduling contests on the same nights for both the boys' team and the girls' team or the varsity and junior varsity teams so that teams could travel together.

Unlike public schools, which derive most of their funding from district property tax revenues, private schools rely on donations, tuition allocations, or participation fees. When faced with budget issues, private schools can raise tuition or seek donations from companies or individuals. Because public schools tend to be public bureaucracies, ADs must operate within a rigid bureaucratic structure. Private schools tend to be leaner in their management structure, allowing greater flexibility in making decisions.

Careers in Interscholastic Athletics

Career opportunities in high school sport cover a wide array of disciplines at the grassroots level. The nature of the job requires professionals to work long and often irregular hours. Typically, practices and competitive events occur outside the regularly scheduled school day, taking place in late afternoons, evenings, and weekends.

Besides positions in coaching, in officiating, and as athletics directors, people are needed in administrative support, as coordinators at the middle school and junior high level, and in various associate athletics director positions to oversee facilities and transportation, event management, and business operations. Beyond the school district level, professionals play a large role in interscholastic sport governance and in the management of the various state and national professional associations. A brief list of full-time professional positions available in interscholastic athletics with their common job accountabilities follows.

interscholastic sport governance—High school athletics competition that is governed by state athletics or activity associations.

Positions Within Professional Associations

> *Executive director.* This person serves as the chief executive officer (CEO) for an association. As the CEO, she or he is accountable for the daily operations of the organization. This person supervises the staff, carries out the agenda of the organization's membership and officers, and oversees the organization's legal affairs and legislative interests.

> *Chief financial officer.* The CFO is accountable for all financial transactions of the organization affiliated with interscholastic athletics. The financial transactions include business operations, payroll, and accounts payable. Besides overseeing the various transactions required, the CFO prepares all financial reports and the annual operating budget.

> *Director of media relations and marketing.* The person who holds this position serves as the public liaison for the interscholastic athletics organization. Besides maintaining a website, this person oversees sponsorships and other revenue-generating ventures such as broadcasting rights, licensing, and merchandising.

> *Director of membership services.* Professionals who hold this position maintain the interscholastic athletics membership database. Furthermore, they manage services and benefits for the membership as well as lead the interscholastic athletics association's membership recruitment efforts.

Professional Profile: Bruce Whitehead

Title: executive director, National Interscholastic Athletic Administrators Association (NIAAA)

Education: MS (mathematics), Purdue University; certified master athletic administrator (CMAA)

Bruce Whitehead is the executive director for the NIAAA. The road to this pinnacle position has been a long and exciting one. After completing his education, Bruce became a high school math teacher and coach. Only eight years into his career, he was asked to serve as athletic administrator. He agreed to the request and filled the position for the next 25 years. After serving as an educator and athletics administrator at the district level for 33 years, he became aware of an opening at the NIAAA. With the many years of experience he gained as an athletic administrator at the district level as well as from serving at the state and national levels on various committees, he applied for and was chosen as an assistant director with the national association in 2001. Just three years later, in 2004, he was hired as the executive director of the NIAAA. His career has evolved into a leadership position with the national organization that serves interscholastic athletics administrators through the United States, Canada, and other affiliates. His position requires many common skills, including leadership, organization, financial expertise, relationship building, and oral and written communication skills. The following are his comments about his career and the interscholastic athletics segment of the sport industry.

ONE DAY

Go to the WSG and learn more about a typical day in the life for Bruce Whitehead. See if he spends his working hours the way you think he does.

What have been the key moves, steps, or developments in your career, and how did you arrive at your current position?

I began my career as a math teacher and coach at Crawfordsville High School in Crawfordsville, Indiana. After eight years, I became the director of athletics at Crawfordsville. I was elected to the Indiana Interscholastic Athletic Administrators Association board of directors, and served as president of the IIAAA. Later in my career, I was elected to three terms on the Indiana High School Athletic Association board of directors. While on the IHSAA board, I chaired the study committee that made a recommendation in 1995 to move Indiana team sports from a single-class system to a multiple-class system. The recommendation was approved by the board, and Indiana moved to a multiple-class system for team sports in 1997. I was selected to the NIAAA resolutions committee in 1988, becoming chair of that committee in 1991. In 1995, I was asked to serve as secretary of the NIAAA board of directors. In 2001, after 33 years at Crawfordsville High School, serving 25 of those as the director of athletics, I retired and went to work for the NIAAA as an assistant to the director. In 2004, the director at that time announced his retirement. I applied for and was hired by the board of directors as the new executive director. I assumed that position in January of 2005 after working for the NIAAA for 3.5 years.

What are your current responsibilities and objectives in your job?

The NIAAA has approximately 8,500 individual members and 52 state associations as organizational members. It has evolved into an organization that provides resources and support for the individual athletic administrators as well as for the state associations. In addition, we continually promote the value of education-based athletics to all entities. My tasks include keeping the organization focused on our mission, networking with other individuals and organizations with a similar mission to that of the NIAAA, and envisioning where the association should be going in the future.

What do you enjoy most about your current job?

I most enjoy the opportunity to influence the professional life of athletic administrators in a positive manner and to provide them with resources and support that assist them in performing their job. I also enjoy the opportunity to interact with people and to help develop new and exciting programs.

What do you consider the biggest future challenge to be in your job or industry?

There are two big immediate challenges in education-based athletics (EBA). The first is providing a safety net for new athletic administrators that will support them and keep them in the profession longer than three years. The turnover rate of athletic administrators is far too high, and we must make every effort to reduce it. The second is the preservation of education-based athletics. EBA faces many threats today, including pay-to-play and challenges in the courts and club programs, just to name a few. We must continue to promote EBA for the quality program it is and for its valuable benefits to the students and to the future of this country.

Positions at the Local School Level

> *Athletics director.* An **athletics director (AD)** serves as the school's senior administrator for athletics. The primary function is to provide the leadership and management of the interscholastic athletics program. In research that we have conducted, we found that ADs spend the greatest amount of their time (39%) engaged in traditional managerial activities. They deal with human resource issues for 27% of their time. The balance of their time is spent engaged in either communication-based activities (24%) or networking (10%). The AD position calls for extensive levels of interaction with students, parents, coaches, faculty, and members of the community. Specific duties and responsibilities include the following:

> Prepare a master budget for capital expenditures and ongoing operations of each school-sponsored sport
> Ensure that all sport programs operate within the guidelines (e.g., eligibility) established by the appropriate governing bodies
> Coordinate and schedule use of all athletics venues
> Hire all officials, coaches, trainers, and athletics department support staff
> Oversee the scheduling of all athletics events
> Provide oversight to athletics booster club activities and fund-raising activities
> Ensure compliance of the athletics program with Title IX

Most ADs begin their careers as teachers or coaches. Although in the past ADs tended to hold two positions (i.e., AD and coach), at larger schools, the AD has become more of an administrator, with no additional coaching or teaching duties. At most smaller schools, however, the AD continues to have multiple collateral duties in addition to athletics administrative activities. The credentials required for ADs vary from state to state and between public and private schools. Typically, the minimum qualifications for the position in a public school system are a bachelor's degree and a valid teaching certificate. Additional requirements may include a master's degree in education administration, educational leadership, or sport administration. In some states, such as Texas, a mid-management certification may also be required. Private schools have the flexibility to waive teacher certification and other credentials. The **National Interscholastic Athletic Administrators Association (NIAAA)** provides professional certification and development for athletics administrators through its leadership training program. The organization ("*NIAAA*," 2014, para. 1; *Whitehead & Blackburn, 2013*) noted that the program was developed in 1996 to

> promote the professional growth and prestige of **athletics administrators**,
> provide an opportunity for athletics administrators to participate in the nation's largest professional organization whose activities are directed exclusively to high school and middle school athletics administrators,
> provide education programs as a resource tool for athletics administrators, and
> promote quality in all programs conducted at the national, state, and local level.

The organization has four levels of certification: the Registered Athletic Administrator (RAA), Registered Middle School Athletic Administrator (RMSAA), the Certified Athletic Administrator (CAA), and the Certified Master Athletic Administrator (CMAA).

Job titles that share similar duties with varying levels of responsibility include associate and assistant athletics director and campus coordinator. Many ADs also serve as coaches or teachers or have additional collateral duties. For example, in Texas, while studying AD job announcements, Whisenant (2005) found that approximately

athletics director (AD)—A high school senior administrator in charge of providing leadership and management of the school's interscholastic athletics programs.

National Interscholastic Athletic Administrators Association—This organization, known as the NIAAA, is a national governing body that serves as a liaison between individual state high school athletics associations and state athletics administrator associations.

athletics administrator—A person who provides administrative support to the school's various athletics programs.

WEB

Go to the WSG and complete the web search activity, which helps you answer the following question: What conclusions can be drawn with regard to the representation of women in leadership roles in high school athletics?

73% of the advertised AD positions also required the person to serve as the head football coach. Because men outnumber women as coaches and often the AD must also coach, men hold approximately 86% of the AD positions across the United States (Whisenant, 2003).

> *Athletics business manager.* The business manager often oversees a wide range of activities including the implementation of the athletics budget and all business-related affairs of the athletics department. Specific duties and responsibilities include the following:

> Monitor expenditures and budgets
> Negotiate contracts and oversee departmental purchases
> Develop, prepare, distribute, and interpret the financial data for the department and each sport team
> Perform other duties as assigned by the athletics director

People in this role are often required to have a strong grasp of accounting principles and procedures and to be proficient with computers and financial software and able to interpret numerical data. Because the athletics business manager serves in a staff position reporting directly to the athletics director, she or he should have strong interpersonal and communication skills that allow effective exchange of information with coaches and other athletics department personnel.

> *Coach.* Most coaches are full-time teachers who coach part time either for the love of the game or to supplement their income. Coaches are responsible for the following:

> complying with the rules and regulations governing interscholastic athletics and their specific sport
> teaching appropriate fundamentals and techniques, rules, and strategies of the sport
> scheduling practices and competitions
> supervising student-athletes while they participate in school-sponsored activities
> teaching fair play and other appropriate social behaviors
> ensuring player safety and responding to player injuries
> maintaining school equipment, uniforms, and facilities
> maintaining effective communications with parents and booster clubs.

The credentials required to coach vary between public and private schools. A couple common qualifications, however, are knowledge of the assigned sport and previous coaching experience. Most public schools hire full-time teachers from their own faculty to serve as coaches. Such individuals will hold a bachelor's degree and have a valid teaching certificate. If the school is unable to find a suitable coach within its full-time faculty, a person from outside the school may be hired as a part-time employee to coach a sport. Some states require some type of coaching certificate to coach, whereas others do not. Both the National High School Athletic Coaches Association and the NFHS Coaches Association actively engage in professional development activities for high school coaches and have established and recognized certification programs.

Most states provide certification through their own state coaches association. For example, in Texas, the Texas High School Coaches Association (THSCA) provides a professional development certification (PDC) program for coaches. The basic qualifications include an undergraduate bachelor's degree and active membership in the THSCA. Requirements for certification are to *(a)* attend a minimum of eight PDC lecture hours at the THSCA's annual coaching school, *(b)* hold current CPR and AED certifications, and *(c)* have a current first aid certificate. The certification is valid for a two-year period. Private schools have the flexibility to waive teacher certification and other credentials.

> *Athletics trainer.* Athletics trainers (ATs) are usually the first medical personnel on the scene when a sport-related injury occurs. Because their primary duty is to prevent and treat injuries, their work day is often longer than that of most other personnel in the athletics department. Before and after practice or competitive events, they treat the athletes' injuries, provide rehabilitation treatment, and apply protective devices to help prevent injuries. For those ATs who are also teachers, the typical work week may exceed 60 hours. An AT's primary responsibilities include such aspects as providing athletic training services to student-athletes, being accessible at all sporting events in the event of an injury, and serving as a liaison between the school district, physicians, student-athletes, and parents.

Because ATs deal with the physical and psychological well-being of the athletes, the credentials required to work at public and private schools are similar. Athletics trainers should have a bachelor's degree and a certification from the National Athletic Trainers Association (NATA). They must also be certified in first aid and CPR before becoming certified as athletics trainers by the NATA.

> *Officials.* Although most of the positions noted previously are full-time positions, officiating in interscholastic athletics is a part-time job. Most states require officials to register with the state's governing agency and pass a competency exam. States also have minimum age requirements, and state interscholastic athletics supervisors conduct a background check to ensure that the prospective official is of sound moral character.

Issues Facing Interscholastic Athletics

In 2009, the headline "School Sport Now a Luxury" was printed in the *Minneapolis-St. Paul Star Tribune* (Millea, 2009, p. B1). Being eliminated from the team has a whole different meaning as school districts struggle during the current economic crisis. Athletics administrators across the country have made hard decisions to keep their athletics programs afloat. Reducing game contests, cutting back on transportation and equipment, eliminating teams, and raising participation fees are just a few decisions that have been made by administrators to curtail budgets. In a study conducted by Forsyth (2007, 2012, 2013), athletics administrators identified several challenging issues that face high school athletics.

Experienced and Certified Athletics Administrators

Matching an athletics administrator's responsibilities to the person chosen to fill a vacancy has been a recurring challenge. According to the executive secretary of the Minnesota Interscholastic Athletic Administrators Association, an administrator's position that becomes vacant is often filled internally by a coach who does not have the necessary knowledge or experience (P. Veldman, personal communication, March 30, 2009). As noted earlier, to help bridge this gap, the NIAAA developed the certified athletics administrator program to assist athletics administrators in their new role. This program consists of leadership training courses that include content such as supervision and decision making, management strategies and organizational techniques, marketing and promotions, budget and finance, mentoring and problem solving, assessing programs and personnel, legal issues, field and equipment management, and contest

Governance and Organization of Youth and School Sports: A Case Study of Belgium Athletics

By Jasper Truyens, Belgium
Vrije Universiteit Brussel (VUB), Brussels

By Veerle De Bosscher, Belgium
Vrije Universiteit Brussel (VUB), Brussels

As sport in Belgium is assigned to regional governments, financial and organizational means for sport participation are assigned to different governments and organizations (both at the regional and local level). Even though this organizational heterogeneity is often a point of dispute, multiple organizations succeed in the development of several events that bring children in contact with sport and ways to participate in sport clubs. Not surprisingly, schools play a vital role in this, as they are a breeding ground for sporting talents. This case study provides a brief description of different events and organizations in athletics (track and field), as it is one of the most popular sports in Flanders, Belgium.

A young Flemish girl participates in the Vlaamse veldloopweek in Belgium.

management (Whitehead & Blackburn, 2013). Certification, however, is often not mandated by school principals or district superintendents. Those wishing to pursue a career as an athletics administrator need to take it upon themselves to obtain the necessary credentials to succeed in this complex but exciting position.

Budgetary Constraints

Although some athletics departments may account for as much as 8% of their schools' operating budgets, the NFHS (2013b) reported that most athletics departments receive

During every third week of September, national and local sport organizations in Flanders work together on the organization of the Vlaamse veldloopweek ("week of cross country"). During this week, schools, track and field clubs, the local authority sports services and the track and field federation (Vlaamse Atletiekliga) organize a local cross country competition for students between 6 and 18 years old. Through the coordination of national sport organizations like Bloso (national sport agency) and SVS (the national school sport organization), local clubs and sport services receive specific guidelines for the organization and promotion of this national event. The ultimate purpose of this event is to involve children and young adolescents in physical activity and running. Through different sideline events in schools and during the competition (bike run, a team marathon, and so on), children are encouraged to enjoy running. In 2012, a total of 219,866 students participated in one of the competitions organized in 282 different cities. More than 86% of all cities in Flanders participate in a cross country competition. Belgian decathlete Hans Van Alphen, who placed fourth at the 2012 London Olympics and won the 2012 IAAF World Combined Events Challenge, is the national representative for these cross country competitions, which have taken place for the past 25 years.

The program Sterren van Morgen ("stars of tomorrow") was launched by the Flemish minister of sport in 2007. Similar to the school sport competitions, athletics clubs and the CrossCup (a competition of cross country events for top level athletes) took the lead to attract young children to the sport of athletics. Various athletics clubs, which received additional financial support, organized a total of 30 different local competitions. These youth events provide clubs the opportunity to scout additional talents and select athletes to participate in four youth competitions during CrossCup competitions.

Both the SVS and the athletics federation organize a one-day indoor athletics event for younger children. In accordance to the Fun in Athletics program of the IAAF, children are exposed to athletics via specific games within a team competition format. While the SVS organizes this one-day event for almost 800 students in the area of Ghent, the athletics federation also organizes this type of competition for young members of athletics clubs.

The cooperation between regional and local organizations as highlighted here should support children's participation in athletics. It is thought that athletics clubs and physical education teachers could use these events to improve children's long-lasting participation in sport.

International Learning Activity #1

Which organizational role should schools fulfill in extracurricular sporting activities for young children? What role should physical education teachers, parents, and local sports clubs play in the sport development of school children and teens?

International Learning Activity #2

What is the value of interscholastic sport activities in terms of talent identification? What is the value in terms of supporting socially vulnerable youth?

International Learning Activity #3

Should schools provide students with a wide range of sport activities or focus on only one specific sport? What are the benefits and drawbacks of these two options for the sport participants, organizers, and stakeholders?

only 1% to 3% of the total allocation given to schools. Many schools throughout the Midwest, South, and West receive even less. For example, the NFHS promotional brochure *The Case for High School Athletics* illustrates how some school districts have allocated their budgets:

> Chicago's public schools education budget was US$4.6 billion, and activity programs received US$36.2 million, which amounts to one-seventh of 1%.

> Charlotte-Mecklenburg's public schools education budget was US$1.2 billion, and activity programs received US$4.7 million, which amounts to one-third of 1%.

> Seattle's public schools education budget was US$339.7 million, and activity programs received US$3.2 million, which amounts to one-ninth of 1%.

Although the millions of dollars allocated to high school athletics appear to be a substantial amount to support programs, these figures and percentages fail to represent the true operating costs, particularly as costs continue to escalate year after year. The budgets allocated for athletics fail to keep pace with the annual rising costs. The result requires athletics programs to continue working with less (Forsyth, 2012).

An example of the effects of rising costs would be the Albuquerque public school (APS) district in New Mexico. According to the budget director for APS, in 1985, the total education budget for the school district was US$247.7 million and the athletics department received US$2.4 million (T. Osborn, personal communication, March 30, 2009). Five years later, when the total APS education budget rose to US$279.7 million, the portion allocated to the athletics department decreased to just over US$2 million. After 10 years, the total education budget almost doubled to US$554.7 million, whereas the athletics department continued to decline to about US$1.8 million. APS athletics went from receiving nine-tenths of 1% of the total education budget to three-tenths of 1% during this 10-year period. Working with less meant that by 1995, APS lost 24 athletics teams and 62 coaching positions. Student participation also decreased substantially. Since 2007, the APS overall operational budget has been US$1 billion plus. From 2004 to 2008, money allocated for APS athletics ranged between two-tenths and five-tenths of 1% of the overall budget. Over the last five years (2009–2013), money allocated for APS athletics ranged between two-tenths and three-tenths of 1%. For the 2014 school year, the overall APS operational budget was projected to be US$1.3

As high school sport faces more and more issues, making a team and having an opportunity to compete are no longer certainties.

billion, of which APS athletics was to receive US$5 million, or three-tenths of 1% (G. Harris, personal communication, June 5, 2013).

Coach Turnover and Exiting

Another challenging issue is retaining coaches. In many school districts throughout the country, up to 50% of coaches are not licensed teachers (Forsyth & Olson, 2013a). Whether they are full-time teachers or not, many coaches leave after just a couple years on the job. Athletics administrators are finding it more difficult to retain coaches as problems arise with athletes, parents, and fans, adding to the daily personal demands on coaches' time. Under the NFHS umbrella, the National Coaches Association (NCA) has taken initiatives to help athletics administrators retain coaches through its coaches' education and training program. Some of those initiatives are developing positive relationships with parents or guardians and administrators, dealing with challenging personalities, understanding the fundamentals of coaching in specific sports, safety, and first aid, and so forth. Unfortunately, these initiatives are not mandatory for coaches to complete. Likewise, those wishing to pursue a career in coaching need to take the initiative to pursue the necessary education and training so that they can handle problems that may arise on the job.

Recruitment and Retention of Officials

When it comes to challenging issues with interscholastic sport officials, athletics administrators typically find that the issues are the same as those with their coaches: A shortage exists, and recruiting and retaining quality officials is extremely time consuming. Surveys conducted by the National Association of Sport Officials (NASO) sought to gain (a) the views of high school state association executive directors ("NASO Officials," 2001) and (b) the views of officials ("Accountability," 2003). The results give a glimpse into why recruiting and retaining officials is challenging:

› Ninety percent of executive directors reported a shortage of qualified officials.
› Seventy-six percent reported lack of fair play by spectators as being the reason that officials quit.
› Sixty-eight percent reported lack of fair play by participants as being the reason that officials quit.
› Forty-nine percent of officials reported lack of respect shown by athletes, coaches, and spectators.

The NASO is committed to helping athletics administrators improve their recruitment and retention of sport officials through consultant programs, newsletters, and magazines, website services, officiating resources, and performance evaluations. Those wishing to become practicing interscholastic sport officials need to take advantage of NASO's offerings and expertise by their own initiative.

Participation Options

Although participation rates have consistently increased from year to year for boys and girls (refer to table 7.2), the athletes' commitments to their schools' athletics program have become another challenge. More students are electing to compete on nonschool athletics teams as well. By competing on a school-sponsored team and a non-school-sponsored team at the same time, athletes are faced with demands from two coaches. Students become torn between their commitments to both teams, and some end up choosing to compete on the non-school-sponsored team only. The reason for this decision is that nonschool programs such as those associated with AAU and the Junior Olympics often have traveling teams and year-round competitions. Such opportunities entice athletes to choose their nonschool athletics program over their school athletics program. Rather than forcing an athlete to choose, representatives from both school and nonschool programs should work together for the student-athlete's well-being.

Fair Play

Many of the ugly issues apparent in college and professional sport are appearing in high school gyms. Students and parents must be constantly reminded that competition is just a game rather than a war. Fair play is as much a concern for fans as it is for athletes. Because fans and players view poor sport behavior on TV (in collegiate and professional sports), enforcing fair play expectations at the prep level has become extremely difficult. The need to teach fair play through high school sport is apparent.

The NFHS is trying to combat poor sporting behavior issues through its program "Citizenship and Asset Building Through Athletics." Also, the NIAAA offers specific courses titled "Student Centered Educational Athletics" and "Coach Centered Educational Athletics" in its certified athletics administrator program curriculum. Perhaps these character-building models are being practiced. At a Texas high school girls' basketball contest, a private school beat a public school by a score of 100-0. After reflecting on the victory, representatives from the winning school not only apologized for the blowout (there are no mercy rules in Texas for such mismatches) but also tried to have the game forfeited ("*School Seeks*," 2009). While representatives from both schools appear to have learned a great deal from this experience, similar blowouts continue to happen in other states; for example, in December of 2012, the score for an Indian high school girls' basketball game was 107-2.

Transfers

Historically, Minnesota permitted open enrollment for high school student-athletes, allowing them to participate at the school of their choice. That changed at the beginning of the 2007–2008 school year, when the MSHSL executive board voted to discontinue open enrollment, with the exception of waivers for special circumstances. Many parents and student-athletes did not agree with this new policy, so they took their complaints to their local legislators. Before legislators could attempt to overrule the new policy, the MSHSL conducted a public relations push through the media to explain their rationale for the change. The tactic, according to the executive director of the MSHSL, inevitably won favor and the legislators' efforts ended (D. Stead, personal communication, March 30, 2009).

state athletics or activity associations—Governing body that sets rules and policies for high school sport eligibility, competitions, and state championship tournaments.

Most **state athletics or activity associations** require a waiting period for transfers to be eligible to compete. Transfers often are athletically motivated (Smith, 2005). Many say that private schools have an unfair advantage over public schools, because private schools recruit athletes and eligibility rules do not apply to transfers who attend private high schools (Popke, 2006). Athletes and parents have stretched the truth to the breaking point to bring about transfers; changes of address, divorces, separations, illnesses, and the like have been claimed, although later it was found out that none of those had occurred.

Parents

According to Bruce Whitehead, executive director for the NIAAA (and a professional who is profiled in this chapter), handling parent issues has become very time-consuming for both athletic administrators and coaches (Forsyth, 2007; Forsyth & Olson, 2013b). Let's take a closer look at some of those issues as identified by Forsyth (2013):

> Parents are reluctant to give coaches full responsibility to coach their team as they deem necessary.

> Parent groups want a voice in decisions being made on behalf of sport programs.

> Parents feel their sons and daughters are entitled to play and receive special treatment, given the amount of time and money they have provided.

> Parents are living through the athletic successes of their sons and daughters, which can adversely cause more stress on the athletes' desire to succeed.

> Coaches are finding it difficult to make supportive connections with parents.

Future athletic administrators and coaches will need to devote resources and time in communicating and developing supportive relationships with parents as concerns such as these continue to surface within interscholastic athletic programs. In the end, it is paramount that parents understand that athletics is not separate from education, but is rather an integral part of their children's education.

Media in Interscholastic Sports

An area that continues to be a growing concern is the presence of the media in interscholastic sports. The marketplace is fertile ground for media organizations to secure live content, since rights fees to televise live high school contests are significantly less expensive than the media rights for many professional sport leagues and major collegiate sport offerings. The recent ruling by the NCAA to ban school- and conference-owned networks (e.g., Sooner Sports TV, SEC Network) from showcasing high school games and events (Leibsohn, 2013) has arguably opened the door for other media conglomerates (e.g., ESPNU, FOX Sports Network) to acquire the rights to televise interscholastic sports. In fact, the opportunity to feature high school sports has caught the attention of the NFHS. The national high school governing body has a planned launch of an NFHS Network, which is projected to have revenues of US$100 million a year in approximately five years from the network's commencement date (Smith, 2013). While the NFHS will own a majority of the network, there are still unsolved issues such as revenue sharing among the organization's members, sport coverage beyond football and basketball, and whether girls' sports will be afforded similar network coverage as boys' sports, to name only a few. Thus, the NFHS should work closely with each state's high school governing body to ensure the presence of an equable and fair system that benefits all constituents.

These issues challenge administrators to adapt to a constantly changing environment involving school policies and the rules governing sport. Each issue is often unique in the minds of the people involved, so the administrator must be consistent when dealing with them. Coaches, parents, players, officials, and members of the community all may have a sense of involvement, which the administrator must balance.

Critical Thinking in Interscholastic Athletics

Balancing the needs and interests of the student-athletes and the educational mission of a high school often requires the athletics administrator to reach some form of compromise. If the decision is fair and ethical, all the affected constituents should be satisfied or at least willing to accept the decision. Maintaining fairness in the decision-making process, involving the associated parties with some degree of participation in the process, and treating everyone with dignity and respect throughout the process will often result in acceptance of the decision. The following paragraphs present two issues that require critical thinking by athletics administrators.

Social Media and Interscholastic Athletics

The presence of social media (e.g., Facebook, Twitter, Instagram, Vine) in sport has arguably changed the sport landscape forever. While professional and collegiate leagues, teams, and athletes utilize various social media platforms to keep fans current with the latest breaking news, jury reports, product information, and the like, interscholastic athletic programs are also finding a tremendous amount of utility in social media outlets as well. Coaches across the country at the high school level use social media for a variety of reasons that include up-to-the-minute scores, results, practice and game schedules, cancellations, inspirational quotes, and communication with parents. Similar to other sport levels, the immediacy of social media has become critically important to many involved with interscholastic sports. In addition, social media allows communication to take place much more easily in large groups. The process is much different than the antiquated phone-chain communication of the past (Hunn, 2012).

Even though many people have found tremendous value in social media within interscholastic sports, some in the field have raised concerns about high school athletes' use of the powerful media. A number of schools prohibit direct communication between coaches and student-athletes through social media platforms. In fact, some schools have gone as far as instituting a designated e-mail system for coaches and student-athletes to engage in cyber communication. The other ominous concern is the unfortunate reckless way that student-athletes use social media. Countless stories exist of how high school athletes have abused social media to taunt an opposing team, bully fellow schoolmates, use offensive and graphic language, and post incriminating photographs that jeopardize their eligibility. While social media brings many positives, coaches and other athletic administrators are extremely hesitant about embracing these new forms of mass communication at the interscholastic level.

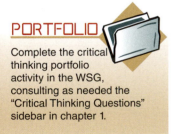

PORTFOLIO

Complete the critical thinking portfolio activity in the WSG, consulting as needed the "Critical Thinking Questions" sidebar in chapter 1.

Proponents of high school sport stress the importance of athletics as an extension of the classroom learning experience. As covered earlier in this chapter, sport offers some unique benefits that are certainly laudable. For example, many argue that participation in sport builds character, teaches teamwork, and encourages fair play. Participants learn the rewards of hard work, self-discipline, and self-confidence. Participation often improves social adaptability. Students involved in extracurricular activities often have lower dropout rates, higher attendance rates, higher grade-point averages, and fewer discipline problems in school. Furthermore, students engaged in extracurricular activities are often less likely to use drugs or become teen parents. Using the critical thinking questions from chapter 1, examine the argument that through the benefits offered by participation, athletics is an extension of the classroom learning experience.

Yet another critical thinking exercise could involve the monetary aspect of interscholastic athletics. For example, we noted earlier in the chapter that because of declining property values, many communities and school districts face revenue and budget shortfalls. Many schools have embraced outsourcing as a means of controlling their expenses. Typical services being provided by private sector companies include school transportation, food services, custodial services, and substitute teachers. Why not expand the services to athletics? Schools could outsource their athletics departments either to one company or to a variety of private club sports. Another option might be to provide vouchers so that kids could play the sport that they prefer in a club-sport setting year-round.

Ethics in Interscholastic Athletics

As issues arise in interscholastic athletics, appropriate resolutions require high school administrators to make decisions consistent with the goals and aspirations of their programs, teams, and various stakeholders. The various options to be considered require constant consideration to ensure that ethical conduct is maintained. Three examples of the myriad issues that require ethical reasoning in interscholastic athletics follow.

Department Action and School Mission

One junior high school had the following as its mission statement:

> *ABC Junior High School is committed to creating and maintaining an environment whereby each student is given the opportunity and encouragement to grow intellectually, physically, emotionally, and socially in order to assume a responsible role in today's ever-changing world. Students, teachers, parents, and the community will work collaboratively so that all students will achieve a quality education.*

The school's enrollment was approximately 1,100 students (55% girls and 45% boys). The athletics department at the school fielded six football teams each fall. Three teams were for seventh-grade boys, who practiced in the morning before school. The other three teams were for eighth-grade boys, who practiced in the afternoons after school. Each team had a roster of approximately 45 boys. No teams cut players, so all boys who wanted to play could be on a team. For the girls, the major fall sport was volleyball. The school had one girls' volleyball team that had a roster of 12 girls. More than 200 girls tried out for the team each fall.

Funding Interscholastic Athletics

As noted earlier in this chapter, athletics administrators face difficult decisions to keep their athletics programs afloat during times of economic hardships. The money is simply not available to operate athletics programs at their current capacity. Therefore, athletics administrators are trying to make reductions that will have the least negative effect on their schools and programs. One direction that athletics administrators may take to support their programs is to market talented athletes.

Let's consider a prediction made by sport marketers. Because of the growth of national and regional television outlets looking for sport programming and the money that those outlets can offer, Mullin, Hardy, and Sutton (2014) predicted that such enticements "will begin having a noticeable effect on top-tier high school athletics programs, which will schedule athletics contests on a national scale and 'rent' athletes for one- or two-year terms to become attractions" (p. 455). These scholars wonder whether talented high school athletes will be more motivated to transfer to showcase their abilities, whether booster clubs will become more motivated to raise funds on the talents of selected athletes rather than the athletics programs and their purpose, and whether the marketing of athletes might trickle down to high school, middle school, and even youth programs.

Prayer and Praise

Throughout collegiate, professional, and Olympic sports, in reverence to their faith, athletes often

PORTFOLIO

Complete the ethical issues portfolio activity in the WSG, consulting as needed the "Guidelines for Making Ethical Decisions" sidebar in chapter 1.

While athletics administrators often face economic challenges, one possible revenue stream is the selling of officially licensed merchandise. Here, endorsed high school gear for a local team is displayed on the clothing racks in a national sporting goods store.

pray and express praise for their achievements. At times, people have expressed their discontent with such actions. But for the most part, athletes have been allowed to express their gratitude. However, at the high school level, athletes are being discouraged in expressing these types of celebrations. Let's take a look at two examples that have appeared in the media; unsportsmanlike conduct and excessive celebration.

> *Unsportsmanlike conduct.* In a high school football game in the state of Washington, after a running back crossed the goal line, he knelt down on one knee, briefly bowed his head, and then pointed a finger towards the sky. Seeing the referee approaching, the player stood up and presented the ball to the referee. As a result of the running back's celebration, the referee then pulled a yellow flag for unsportsmanlike conduct (KOMO News, 2010).

> *Excessive celebration.* During a high school track event in Texas, after the anchor for a boys 4 x 4 100 meter team crossed the finished line, he raised a hand to his ear and pointed his finger towards the sky. As a result of the anchor's celebration, the team was disqualified from competing in the state championships. The track officials based their decision on excessive celebration (NewsCatcher31, 2013).

Although interpretation of athletics bylaws can be confusing, future athletics administrators and coaches will need to be aware and understand their respective state association bylaws, as well as make sure their athletes understand the bylaws in reference to expressions of prayer and praise.

Summary

This chapter has provided an overview of interscholastic athletics, which is one of the largest, yet relatively understudied, segments of the sport industry. From a human development and sociological perspective, high school athletics affects 50% of all high school students. As a segment of the sport industry, interscholastic athletics contributes billions of dollars to the economy and provides full-time and part-time jobs for more than half a million people. School-sponsored athletics programs shape or influence, in some form, the lives of more than 14 million people (e.g., students, family members, coaches, administrators) in the United States. Although supporters and detractors may have differing views of the role that interscholastic athletics should play in the educational process, both would agree that athletics is tightly woven into the culture and society of the United States.

Review Questions

1. In what year did high school sport governance begin, and why was a governing body needed?
2. How has the passage of Title IX affected participation rates in high school sport?
3. What are the major operational differences between public school and private school athletics departments?
4. In relation to other levels of sport competition, where does interscholastic athletics rank in size and scope?
5. What are some of the underlying factors that caused interscholastic sport to become part of the educational system?
6. What are some of the perceived benefits that students receive by participating in interscholastic sport programs?

7. How are career paths similar and different at the national, state, district, and local levels?

8. What are some of the ways the media (e.g., social media, national broadcasts of high school basketball) have affected interscholastic athletics? What future changes do you see in terms of the media's influence at the high school level?

9. Which of the nine listed issues facing interscholastic athletics do you consider the most pressing or important? Explain your answer.

References

Accountability in officiating survey. (2003). National Association of Sports Officials. Retrieved from www.naso.org/surveys/Acct.Survey.pdf

Coakley, J. (2009). *Sports in society: Issues and controversies* (10th ed.). New York, NY: McGraw-Hill Higher Education.

Dealy, F.X. (1990). *Win at any cost*. New York, NY: Carol.

Florida High School Athletic Association. (2013). *About the FHSSA*. Retrieved from www.fhsaa.org/about

Forsyth, E. (2007). *Current issues surrounding interscholastic sports: Survey report*. Indianapolis, IN: National Interscholastic Athletic Administrators Association.

Forsyth, E. (2012). Contemporary issues surrounding interscholastic sports: Finance issues. *Interscholastic Athletic Administration, 31*(1), 16–18.

Forsyth, E. (2013). Contemporary issues surrounding interscholastic sports: Parents issues. *Interscholastic Athletic Administration, 39*(3), 16–17.

Forsyth, E., & Olson, J. (2013a). Closing. In M. Blackburn, E. Forsyth, J. Olson, & B. Whitehead (Eds.), *NIAAA's guide to interscholastic athletic administration* (pp. 361–368). Champaign, IL: Human Kinetics.

Forsyth, E., & Olson, J. (2013b). Introduction. In M. Blackburn, E. Forsyth, J. Olson, & B. Whitehead (Eds.), *NIAAA's guide to interscholastic athletic administration* (pp. ix–xvi). Champaign, IL: Human Kinetics.

Georgia High School Association. (2013). GHSA homepage. Retrieved from www.ghsa.net

Hardy, S. (2003). *How Boston played: Sport, recreation, and community, 1865–1915*. Knoxville, TN: University of Tennessee Press.

Hunn, C. (2012, March 24). Social media provides benefits, potential pitfalls in high school sports. *The New Haven Register*. Retrieved from www.nhregister.com/articles/2012/03/24/sports/high_school/doc4f6e58fd1a7cb266999428.txt

KOMO News [KOMOcommunities]. (2010, November 30). *Running back penalized for gesture to God* [Video file]. Retrieved from www.youtube.com/watch?v=xIi2H4zMZW8

Leibsohn, B. (2013). Analysis of the NCAA rule prohibiting a school- or conference-owned television. *Marquette Sports Law Review, 23*(2), 434–454.

Millea, J. (2009, January 19). School sports now a Minnesota luxury? *Minneapolis-St. Paul Star Tribune*, p. B1.

Minnesota State High School League. (2013). History of the Minnesota State High School League. Retrieved from www.mshsl.org/mshsl/aboutmshsl.asp?page=2

Mullin, B.J., Hardy, S., & Sutton, W.A. (2014). *Sport marketing* (4th ed.). Champaign, IL: Human Kinetics.

NASO officials shortage survey results. (2001). National Association of Sports Officials. Retrieved from www.naso.org/surveys/shortage.html

NewsCatcher31. (2013, May 4). *High school track team disqualified from state championships* [Video file]. Retrieved from www.youtube.com/watch?v=P9wlFwhtWOU

NFHS. (2013a). *2012–13 high school athletics participation survey*. Indianapolis, IN: National Federation of State High School Associations. Retrieved from www.nfhs.org/content.aspx?id=3282

NFHS. (2013b). *The case for high school activities*. Indianapolis, IN: National Federation of State High School Associations. Retrieved from http://www.nfhs.org/content.aspx?id=8936

NFHS handbook. (2012–2013). Indianapolis, IN: National Federation of State High School Associations.

NIAAA. (2014). NIAAA certification program. Retrieved from www.niaaa.org/niaaa-programs/niaaa-certification-program

Popke, M. (2006). Public notice: Schools in Kentucky claim unfair advantages for private schools. *Athletic Business, 30*(4), 106–110.

Robinson, M., Hums, M., Crow, R., & Phillips, D. (2001). *Profiles of sport industry professionals: The people who make the games happen*. Gaithersburg, MD: Aspen.

Sage, G.H., & Eitzen, D.S. (2013). *Sociology of North American sport* (9th ed.). New York, NY: Oxford University Press.

School seeks to forfeit 100–0 win. (2009). Retrieved from http://highschool.rivals.com/content.asp?CID=903780

Smith, L. (2005). A tough game: Dealing with athletically motivated transfers. *Athletic Management, 17*(6), 26–33.

University Interscholastic League. (2013). *Character Attitude Responsibility Ethics (C.A.R.E.): Sportsmanship and UIL athletics*. Retrieved from www.uiltexas.org/files/athletics/manuals/sportsmanship-manual.pdf

Smith, M. (2013, June). PlayOn!, high school group planning national network. *SportsBusiness Journal, 16*(11). Retrieved from www.sportsbusinessdaily.com/Journal/Issues/2013/06/24/Media/High-school-TV.aspx

U.S. Bureau of Labor Statistics. (2012). *Occupational employment projections to 2020*. Retrieved from www.bls.gov/opub/mlr/2012/01/art5full.pdf

Whisenant, W. (2003). How women have fared as interscholastic athletic administrators since the passage of Title IX. *Sex Roles, 49*(3/4), 179–184.

Whisenant, W. (2005). In Texas it's football: How women have been denied access to the AD's office. *International Journal of Sport Management, 6*, 343–350.

Whitehead, B., & Blackburn, M. (2013). Professional foundations. In M. Blackburn, E. Forsyth, J. Olson, & B. Whitehead (Eds.), *NIAAA's guide to interscholastic athletic administration* (pp. 19–35). Champaign, IL: Human Kinetics.

HISTORICAL MOMENTS

1852 First intercollegiate sport competition held: Yale–Harvard Regatta

1906 Intercollegiate Athletic Association of the United States (IAAUS) formed; name changed to National Collegiate Athletic Association (NCAA) in 1910

1912 Central Intercollegiate Athletic Association (CIAA), oldest Black athletic conference, founded

1935 First presentation of Heisman Trophy took place

1939 First NCAA men's basketball championship game held: University of Oregon beat Ohio State University, 46-33

1942 Eddie Robinson became head football coach of Grambling State University; retired in 1997 with 408 wins, 165 losses, and 15 ties

1951 Walter Byers appointed first executive director of NCAA

1971 Association for Intercollegiate Athletics for Women (AIAW) formed; disbanded in 1982

1973 NCAA split its membership into Divisions I, II, and III

1987 NCAA levied "death penalty" on SMU football program because of repeat violations of NCAA rules

1989 Knight Commission formed by the Knight Foundation in response to scandals in college sports

1994 Equity in Athletics Disclosure Act (EADA) established

1998 Bowl Championship Series (BCS) established

2002 CBS TV signed rights deal with NCAA for US$6 billion. The network, along with Turner Broadcasting, signed a new 14-year deal in 2010 for US$10.8 billion

2009 Pat Summitt reached 1,000 career wins; became all-time wins leader in NCAA basketball history

2010 Mark Emmert named fifth CEO of the NCAA

2012 NCAA imposed sanctions—including a US$60 million fine, vacated wins, lost scholarships, and other penalties—on Penn State

2013 Six active student athletes joined former UCLA basketball player Ed O'Bannon and other plaintiffs in their lawsuit suing the NCAA and seeking compensation for the use of their names and likenesses

2014 College Football Playoff (CFP) officially began after powerhouse football programs in Division I had responded to legal threats and created the system two years earlier

8

INTERCOLLEGIATE ATHLETICS

Ellen J. Staurowsky Robertha Abney

LEARNING OBJECTIVES

> Define intercollegiate athletics.
> Demonstrate an understanding of the events surrounding the development of intercollegiate athletics.
> Describe the purposes of intercollegiate athletics governance organizations.
> Identify key administrative personnel within intercollegiate athletics departments.
> Identify the roles and responsibilities of personnel working in intercollegiate athletics departments.
> Discuss several current challenges and social media issues facing intercollegiate athletics administrators.
> Identify key associations, organizations, and publications related to intercollegiate athletics.

Key Terms

academic progress rate (APR)

Equity in Athletics Disclosure Act (EADA)

executive search firm

HBCUs

licensing royalty

outsourcing

senior woman administrator (SWA)

tribal colleges and universities (TCUs)

ticket operations

ticket scalping

GET A JOB

Continue on your journey in sport management by going to the web study guide (WSG) at www.HumanKinetics.com/ContemporarySportManagement. Check out the job opportunities and consider the skills and experiences that can help you succeed in sport management.

From the intrigues of the College Football Playoff to March Madness, college sport occupies a prominent place not only within the sport culture of the United States but also within broader society. ESPN's annual coverage of President Barack Obama's NCAA men's tournament bracket ("Barack Obama," 2013) and the national media coverage of his attendance at the Syracuse vs. Marquette men's basketball game in March of 2013 illustrate the point vividly ("President Obama," 2013).

Whether one is the Leader of the Free World or just an average citizen of Fan Nation, the fate of favored and favorite teams is the subject of much attention. Bloggers churn out speculation as to which team will come out on top and which shoe company has reached an agreement with which university for a multiyear, big-money sponsorship deal. Fans, as avid in their watchfulness as those following the stock market, fervently monitor the prospects of high school recruits on Rivals.com while following coaches on Twitter. Through sport media coverage, which relies on multimedia platforms including television, radio, print, and web-based publications, players and coaches become celebrities, and the games themselves entertain millions of fans around the country.

There is much more to college sport than meets the eye. The financial stakes are high, as evidenced by the 13-year, US$10.8 billion agreement that the National Collegiate Athletic Association (NCAA) reached with CBS and Turner Broadcasting in 2010 for the broadcast rights to the men's Division I basketball tournament, which expanded to 68 teams in 2011 (Sandomir & Thamel, 2010). In turn, the College Football Playoff agreed to a 12-year television deal with ESPN for US$7 billion, which will yield more than US$585 million per year (Matuszewski, 2013). Of equal importance are the reputations of the schools that sponsor these athletics programs. The purpose of this chapter is to provide an overview of contemporary U.S. college athletics and to create a snapshot of what goes on behind the scenes. After reading this chapter, you should have a better understanding of the organizations that govern and regulate college sport, the way that college athletics programs operate, and the kinds of careers that you might wish to pursue in this segment of the sport industry.

Origins of Intercollegiate Athletics Governance

According to most historical accounts, college sport as we have come to know it started with a challenge that would "test the superiority of the oarsmen" of Harvard University and Yale University (Veneziano, 2002, para. 1). Harvard prevailed in a 2-mile (3.2 km) race proposed by executives from the Boston, Concord, and Montreal Railroad as a way of boosting tourism and travel. According to Edes (1922), "The race was supposed to be a frolic and no idea was entertained of establishing a precedent" (p. 347). As much of a lark at it appears to have been, the event held in 1852 may have been more significant than quaint depictions suggest. Democratic presidential nominee Franklin Pierce, who would eventually win the White House later that same year, attended, as did other dignitaries who would play an important role in pre–Civil War America as lawyers, politicians, and educators.

The fact that the students brokered the deal with the Boston, Concord, and Montreal Railroad, however, reflects how times have changed. During the latter half of the 1800s, college sport was essentially run by students, sometimes as social occasions, at other times as highly competitive contests, and often as a form of protest against boring recitations and a curriculum that did not match their aspirations and goals. By the early part of the 1900s, a shift toward professional coaches, overspecialization, and an emphasis on winning against perennial rivals was well underway. As Harvard football coach Bill Reid would document in his diary in 1905, coaches of the age were negotiating with faculty to keep players eligible, developing strategies to subvert an inquisitive press, and clashing with college presidents over the role of sport on college campuses (Smith, 1994).

Prompted by deaths and charges of brutality in college football, President Theodore Roosevelt hosted two White House conferences on football in 1905. Roosevelt summoned coaches, faculty, and alumni representatives from Harvard, Yale, and Princeton universities to the conference. The purpose of the conference was to encourage the representatives to carry out both the letter and the spirit of the football rules. Roosevelt's decree led to the formation of the Intercollegiate Athletic Association of the United States (IAAUS), which was officially constituted on March 31, 1906, and became known as the NCAA in 1910 (Crowley, 2006).

National Collegiate Athletic Association (NCAA)

The NCAA is the largest and most influential college sport governing body in the United States. Its membership includes more than 1,287 colleges and universities, conferences, and sport organizations. NCAA rules and regulations focus on amateurism, recruiting, eligibility, playing and practice seasons, athletically related financial aid, championships, and enforcement ("*Composition*," n.d.).

The NCAA membership is separated into three competitive divisions, generally referred to as Divisions I, II, and III (see figure 8.1). Several factors determine the divisional classification for NCAA member institutions. These include the number of sports sponsored, the type of sport sponsored (team or individual), the size of the athletics department budget, attendance at games and seating capacity in stadiums and arenas, and whether the program offers athletics grants-in-aid. Among football-playing institutions in Division I, subdivisions formerly referred to as Division I-A and I-AA are now referred to as the Football Bowl Subdivision (FBS) and the Football Championship Subdivision (FCS).

The divisional structure within the NCAA is a reflection of how the association has grown and changed over time. At its inception in 1906, the NCAA had 28 members. Expansion in the 1950s and 1960s led to the creation of what were then called the University and College divisions. The three-division system in place within the NCAA arose in the 1970s as the membership continued to expand and become increasingly diverse. By 2007, overall membership had increased from 665 to 1,288. To control membership so as to ensure delivery of quality championships and other services, the NCAA implemented a series of moratoriums on the acceptance of new members during the past two decades, the most recent one ending in 2011 (Sander, 2011). Division III experienced the greatest influx of new schools, and approximately 20 Division II institutions have sought reclassification at the Division I level. In summary, as more institutions become NCAA members, questions regarding how to manage that growth arise as well (Copeland, 2007). Numerous questions linger.

At present, Division III is the largest of all three divisions, comprising 40% of the NCAA membership. Given the variety of institutions represented within Division III, will the policies governing playing and practice seasons, awarding of financial aid, recruiting, and academic eligibility adequately address the concerns of those members, or will a point come when there will be a divisional split among Division III schools? How will Division II, viewed by some institutions as a stepping-stone to Division I, retain membership in a way that allows it to remain competitively viable? And will Division I be able to mediate the interests of approximately three dozen institutions attempting to move from a lower division to Division I in the next few years while effectively managing the interests of the division's constituents?

Other National Governing Bodies

Established in 1940, the National Association of Intercollegiate Athletics (NAIA), located in Olathe, Kansas, is composed of 291 member institutions. The NAIA is open to four-year and upper-level two-year colleges and universities in the United States and

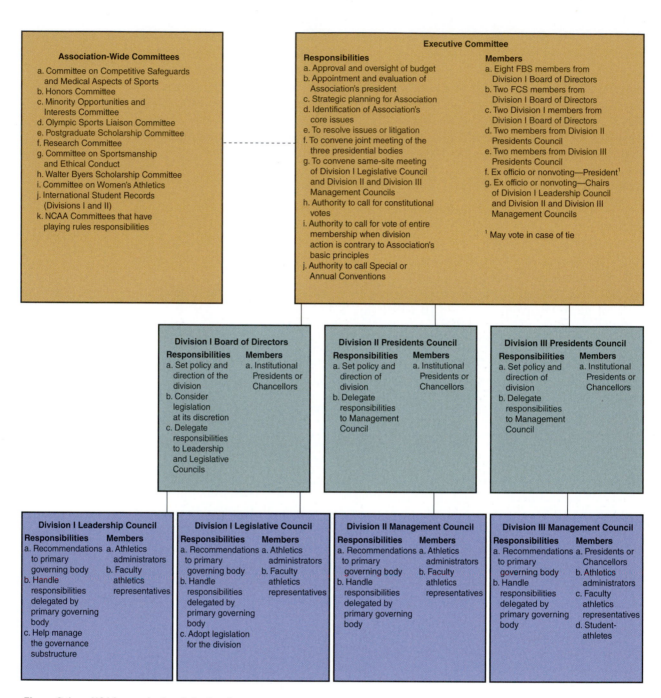

Association-Wide Committees

a. Committee on Competitive Safeguards and Medical Aspects of Sports
b. Honors Committee
c. Minority Opportunities and Interests Committee
d. Olympic Sports Liaison Committee
e. Postgraduate Scholarship Committee
f. Research Committee
g. Committee on Sportsmanship and Ethical Conduct
h. Walter Byers Scholarship Committee
i. Committee on Women's Athletics
j. International Student Records (Divisions I and II)
k. NCAA Committees that have playing rules responsibilities

Executive Committee

Responsibilities

a. Approval and oversight of budget
b. Appointment and evaluation of Association's president
c. Strategic planning for Association
d. Identification of Association's core issues
e. To resolve issues or litigation
f. To convene joint meeting of the three presidential bodies
g. To convene same-site meeting of Division I Legislative Council and Division II and Division III Management Councils
h. Authority to call for constitutional votes
i. Authority to call for vote of entire membership when division action is contrary to Association's basic principles
j. Authority to call Special or Annual Conventions

Members

a. Eight FBS members from Division I Board of Directors
b. Two FCS members from Division I Board of Directors
c. Two Division I members from Division I Board of Directors
d. Two members from Division II Presidents Council
e. Two members from Division III Presidents Council
f. Ex officio or nonvoting—President[1]
g. Ex officio or nonvoting—Chairs of Division I Leadership Council and Division II and Division III Management Councils

[1] May vote in case of tie

Division I Board of Directors

Responsibilities

a. Set policy and direction of the division
b. Consider legislation at its discretion
c. Delegate responsibilities to Leadership and Legislative Councils

Members

a. Institutional Presidents or Chancellors

Division II Presidents Council

Responsibilities

a. Set policy and direction of division
b. Delegate responsibilities to Management Council

Members

a. Institutional Presidents or Chancellors

Division III Presidents Council

Responsibilities

a. Set policy and direction of division
b. Delegate responsibilities to Management Council

Members

a. Institutional Presidents or Chancellors

Division I Leadership Council

Responsibilities

a. Recommendations to primary governing body
b. Handle responsibilities delegated by primary governing body
c. Help manage the governance substructure

Members

a. Athletics administrators
b. Faculty athletics representatives

Division I Legislative Council

Responsibilities

a. Recommendations to primary governing body
b. Handle responsibilities delegated by primary governing body
c. Adopt legislation for the division

Members

a. Athletics administrators
b. Faculty athletics representatives

Division II Management Council

Responsibilities

a. Recommendations to primary governing body
b. Handle responsibilities delegated by primary governing body

Members

a. Athletics administrators
b. Faculty athletics representatives

Division III Management Council

Responsibilities

a. Recommendations to primary governing body
b. Handle responsibilities delegated by primary governing body

Members

a. Presidents or Chancellors
b. Athletics administrators
c. Faculty athletics representatives
d. Student-athletes

Figure 8.1 NCAA organizational chart and governance structure.

Canada. With an emphasis on academic achievement, the NAIA is also dedicated to respect, integrity, responsibility, servant leadership, and fair play. In 1948, the NAIA was the first national organization to offer postseason opportunities to Black student athletes. It was also the first national organization to sponsor both women's and men's intercollegiate athletics. In 1980, it became the first to offer athletics championships for women's sports. Historically Black institutions were voted into the NAIA in 1953.

At its most powerful in the early 1970s, the NAIA had a membership of 588 institutions and was considered a realistic competitor of the NCAA. The relationship today, however, is markedly different. As Wolverton (2008) pointed out, "In sports lingo, they're David and Goliath—one a struggling organization few people have heard of, the other a money-making machine whose teams vie for championships on national television" (para. 1). Speculation abounds about the future of the NAIA. There are rumors that the NCAA may buy out the NAIA, whereas others argue that there is still a niche for NAIA schools on the college sport landscape. Nevertheless, in 2008, shortly after the NCAA backed away from creating a fourth division, NCAA leaders pursued discussions with the NAIA more earnestly to explore relaxing NCAA ratings that deter member schools from playing against NAIA competitors. They have also engaged in discussions on cost-sharing initiatives to reduce health insurance costs and other administrative expenses. A proposed partnership between the NCAA and the NAIA would result in the creation of an NAIA eligibility clearinghouse that would be run through the NCAA's Eligibility Center (Dannelly, 2009). While some of those initiatives had been fulfilled, the most recent prediction is that the NAIA will continue to lose membership, dropping to a level of 250 to 270 by the year 2016 (Dannelly, 2011a).

Another organization that governs intercollegiate athletics is the National Christian College Athletic Association (NCCAA). Incorporated in 1968 and located in Greenville, South Carolina, the NCCAA focuses on "the maintenance, enhancement, and promotion of intercollegiate athletic competition with a Christian perspective" (NCCAA, 2013, para. 1). The NCCAA has a membership of just under 113 institutions in two divisions. Division I consists of 70 Christian liberal arts (CLA) institutions, and Division II consists of 43 CLA and Bible colleges (National Christian College Athletic Association, 2014). Describing the comparison between the NCCAA and the NAIA and the NCAA, a board member commented, "The NCAA and, on a smaller but increasing level, the NAIA, are the leaders in the media saturated collegiate sports culture. That fills a necessary void within our culture but that is not the mission of the NCCAA. Using the tool of intercollegiate athletics to further the work of Christ, while creating and funding corporate service opportunities for our membership, is our #1 priority" (Dannelly, 2011b).

Although the NAIA does provide a membership option for two-year institutions, governance of intercollegiate athletics within two-year institutions is managed primarily by four organizations: the American Indian Higher Education Consortium Athletic Commission (AIHEC—36 schools representing 1,000 athletes), the National Junior College Athletic Association (NJCAA—525 schools representing approximately 60,000 athletes), the California Community College Athletic Association (CCCAA—107 schools representing 27,000 athletes), and the Northwest Athletic Association of Community Colleges (NWAACC— 35 schools representing 3,780 athletes) ("CCCAA," 2013; "What is the NWAACC?", 2013; "NJCAA," 2013; Staurowsky, 2009). Nearly half of all two-year institutions offer intercollegiate athletics programs to their students (Staurowsky, 2009).

The state of California, with an extensive community college system that educates more than 25% of the entire U.S. two-year student population, has long been committed to supporting athletics participation at the two-year level ("*Commission*," n.d.). In 1929, the California Junior College Federation was founded, creating a single administrative entity for establishing policies and rules governing athletics participation among its member institutions (Winters, 1982). Emerging out of the Golden Age of Sports (1920–1930), athletes from California's community college system rose to distinction in sports such as track and field. When the NCAA refused to allow community college programs to compete in its track and field championship in 1937 (Winters, 1982), the NJCAA was conceived in Fresno, California, and became a functioning organization in 1938.

Although **tribal colleges and universities (TCUs)** may be members of the COA, the NAIA, the National Intercollegiate Rodeo Association (NIRA), or the NJCAA, the AIHEC created the Athletic Commission in 2003 to formalize and govern AIHEC

tribal colleges and universities (TCUs)—The 37 tribal institutions of higher education (www.aihec.org) in the United States and Canada.

Development of University Sports in Kenya

By Isaac Mwangi Kamande, Kenya
Strathmore University, Nairobi

The management of university sports in Kenya falls under the auspices of Kenya Universities Sports Association (KUSA). This is an umbrella organization that has membership from both private and public universities in Kenya. By virtue of universities subscribing to KUSA, Kenyan universities are also members of the East African University Sports Federation (EAUSF), the Federation of African University Sports (FASU) and the International University Sports Federation (FISU).

Kenyan Universities Rugby teams competing in the Kenya Rugby Union Premier League. University sports in Kenya have grown to the point where university teams take part in the top leagues in the country.

Sports in Kenyan universities have seen a steady growth due to various factors. One of the main contributing factors is the increase in the membership of KUSA as a result of a government policy that created a new commission in charge of higher education. The Commission of Higher Education has approved the accreditation of more universities as well as university colleges, which in turn has increased the membership in KUSA.

In 2013, the Kenyan government introduced the Sports Act 2013, which aimed at streamlining the management of sports in Kenya. Under the Sports Act, all sports organizations were supposed to ensure compliance with the provisions in this legislation. KUSA, being a membership multi-sport organization, therefore had to revamp its activities as well as align its constitution to be compliant with the act.

intercollegiate sporting events (Talahongva, 2009). This commission oversees the running of the AIHEC men's and women's basketball tournaments as well as other events throughout the year (Korby, 2013; Woodenlegs, 2009).

One of the common features in all these associations, with the exception of the AIHEC, is that, at one time, they governed only male sports. Before these associations incorporated women's sports into their rules and championships structures, the Association for Intercollegiate Athletics for Women (AIAW) was established by female physical educators from colleges and universities in 1971 (Wilson, 2013). During its 10-year existence, the AIAW provided many opportunities for female athletes, coaches, and

In line with the new developments as stipulated in the Sports Act and in order to increase geographical representation, university sports in Kenya are divided into zones with the Nairobi, Coast, Central, and Western conferences. The conferences take part in leagues within their geographical regions and then select the best teams in each discipline to compete in the National Championships. In addition, universities take part in the KUSA Games, which are organized in an Olympic format. This competition is held every two years.

Through the conference leagues, tournaments, national championships, and the KUSA Games, teams are identified to represent the country in international competitions. Kenya took part in the World University Games in Shenzhen, China in 2011 and subsequently also fielded a team during the Summer Games in Kazan, Russia in 2013, in which a Kenyan athlete won a silver medal in athletics.

Many universities in Kenya, especially the newly created ones, face challenges in terms of facilities for sports. University administration tends to give priority to academic infrastructures at the expense of sports facilities. This means that athletes are not able to train and compete at world-class standards, especially at the elite level. Lack of proper sports facilities coupled with limited financial allocations for most university sports departments is a major setback in running university athletic programs.

The university academic calendar is another major hindrance in the management of sports in Kenya. Most universities are yet to embrace a culture where sports are given a priority. This means that there is little time set for training. Universities in Kenya need to adopt new and innovative ideas of boosting sports performance in academic institutions, like earning credits through participation in sports.

Some universities have embraced the idea of sports scholarships, which are awarded to students who are talented in sports. This has boosted performance, especially in teams that take part in national leagues and represent the country in international competitions like the Olympics and World Championships. Many Kenyan athletes have been travelling abroad to countries like the United States, Canada, Japan, and China on sports scholarships. This new program will help in identifying talent locally and molding athletes within Kenyan universities.

International Learning Activity #1

Conduct an online search for university sports in Kenya, as well as in another country (other than the United States) of your choice. Find and compare the various sport offerings for the two countries. How do each country's history, culture, and traditions influence the sports that are most prevalent within its universities?

International Learning Activity #2

Identify similarities and differences between the intercollegiate athletics system in Kenya and the intercollegiate athletics system in the United States. Note the instances in which you prefer the Kenyan system and those in which you prefer the U.S. system. In each case, give reasons for your preference.

International Learning Activity #3

Think about the intercollegiate sport system in your home country as well as the system in place in Kenya. What are the major challenges that each system encounters? How are these similar or different, and what internal and external factors contribute to these challenges?

administrators. The organization also offered several national championships, many of which received television coverage. Eventually, however, the NCAA and other college sport governing bodies expanded their structures to include women's athletics. This was met with resistance from the AIAW. In 1980, the move by the NCAA to sponsor women's championships for the first time was viewed as a hostile takeover of the AIAW. In recounting the history, Hosick (2011) wrote, "The 1981 [NCAA] Convention actions on the question known as the governance plan are seen alternately as the best thing that ever happened to women's athletics or a takeover from which women's athletics never fully recovered" (n.p.). Dr. Christine Grant, a former AIAW president and women's athletics director at the University of Iowa said, "We were fighting for our lives. And we lost. It was a very difficult and emotional situation" (Hosick, 2011). As a measure of how times change, Dr. Grant became a well-respected and admired leader within the NCAA, receiving the president's Gerald R. Ford Award. In giving the award to Dr. Grant, then NCAA president Myles Brand stated, "Christine is a pre-eminent and passionate leader who represents an entire class of pioneers that broke through barriers to the benefit of women's sports." He added that "she and others did the heavy lifting that has afforded college women athletes the opportunities they enjoy today, and her courage and character have made her a role model for today's student-athletes and athletics administrators alike" ("Big Ten Pioneer," 2006, para. 3).

Athletic Conferences

Picture the scene: the Palmer House in Chicago, 1895. Seven university presidents from the Midwest are talking about problems in college football and baseball, contemplating how to prevent athletes for hire not enrolled as full-time students from playing for or against their teams. With a motion to restrict "eligibility for athletics to bona fide, full-time students who were not delinquent in their studies," a conference that would later become the Big Ten was formed ("Big Ten History," 2013, para. 3).

In many respects, the work of a conference is much like it was when the Big Ten was founded. The basic function of a conference is to establish rules and regulations that support and sustain a level playing field for member institutions while creating in-season and postseason competitive opportunities. As Grant, Leadley, and Zygmont (2008) pointed out, however, "In the modern era, they also negotiate television contracts and distribute the proceeds and any other revenue they agree to share" (p. 41). With the exception of a few institutions that opt to remain independent, the vast majority of colleges and universities seek membership in conferences that will enhance the prestige and status of their programs and provide competition with peer institutions that are similarly situated financially, academically, geographically, and philosophically.

Although no official agency classifies conferences into major, mid-major, and small-college categories, fans as well as sportswriters routinely use these designations. Thus, the Atlantic Coast Conference (ACC), Big Ten, Big 12, Pacific-12 (Pac-12), and Southeastern Conference (SEC) are recognizable as major power conferences. From year to year, there is some flexibility in the designation of NCAA Division I conferences on the basis of power, influence, and ratings; nevertheless the mid-major list typically includes American Athletic, America East, Atlantic 10, Atlantic Sun, Big Sky, Big South, Big West, Colonial, Conference USA, Horizon League, Ivy Group, Metro Atlantic, Mid-American, Missouri Valley, Mountain West, Northeast, Ohio Valley, Patriot League, Southern, Southland, Southwestern Athletic, Summit League, Sun Belt, and West Coast conferences.

The distinction between major and mid-major for Division I conferences, however, is the dividing line between those that have automatic bids in the BCS and those that do not. When understood in this way, the decision-making process behind the college sport enterprise becomes clearer. For example, within the NCAA committee structure, representatives of each of the BCS conferences with automatic bids have guaranteed seats on the Division I board of directors, and seven seats are available to the remaining 20 conferences ("NCAA Division I," n.d.).

As power and money continue to influence the college sport environment, the governance structure in place today is likely to change in the not so distant future. In January of 2014, NCAA Division I members agreed in principle to give greater decision making autonomy to leaders in the power five conferences. The details of this concept are being worked out as of this writing (Schroeder, 2014).

With billions in new dollars generated by television contracts, the landscape for the most powerful and lucrative NCAA Division I programs has gone through an unprecedented period of volatility. Long-standing conference relationships have been broken up as athletic programs in the elite tier of college sport seek market share and position, leading to discussions about whether athletic programs with the very best football teams will leave the NCAA and form a superconference of their own or remain in the NCAA under a new structure that accommodates the wealthiest and most powerful schools (Farrey, 2013; Griffin, 2013).

This lock on decision making fueled some of the investigations between 2006 and 2013 on the part of members of the U.S. Congress into the business practices of the BCS, which some allege may be anticompetitive in nature and in violation of antitrust regulations.

Despite the high profile of NCAA FBS and FCS conferences, most conferences are more familiar at a regional and local level. The Eastern College Athletic Conference (ECAC), for example, is the largest conference in the United States, distinctive because of the fact that its 300 members from 16 states include schools associated with NCAA Divisions I, II, and III ("*Membership*," n.d.).

In turn, the Central Intercollegiate Athletic Association (CIAA) and the Mid-Eastern Athletic Conference (MEAC) have a different history when compared with major conferences. The CIAA is the nation's oldest Black athletic conference, founded in 1912. Today, the membership of the CIAA and the MEAC are composed exclusively of historically Black colleges and universities (**HBCUs**). As low-resource institutions, HBCUs have often been adversely affected by NCAA policies that call for greater investments in personnel to support compliance efforts as well as specialized academic athletic support facilities (Gayle, 2013). To illustrate the significance of this issue, 11 of the 17 athletic programs identified by the NCAA as having programs that failed to meet new academic requirements under the APR (academic progress rate) were members of MEAC and Southwestern Athletic Conferences.

HBCUs—Historically Black colleges and universities (e.g., Alabama State University, Albany State University, Bethune-Cookman College, Florida A&M University, Grambling State University, Howard University, Tuskegee University).

College Sport Finance

The college sport industry is like any other sector of the sport industry worldwide. Those expecting to work in it, whether in the capacity of an athletic director or even as a coach, must be aware of the financial considerations that drive the business. An easy way to begin to gain an understanding of the revenue streams that contribute to a college or university athletics budget is to go to reports filed in compliance with what is called the **Equity in Athletics Disclosure Act (EADA)**. To determine whether spending on men's and women's intercollegiate athletics programs is equitable and in conformance with Title IX of the Education Amendments Act of 1972, the EADA requires institutions receiving federal financial assistance to submit a report documenting expenditures for each fiscal year. This information is publicly available on a website (www.ope.ed.gov/athletics) hosted by the U.S. Department of Education Office of Postsecondary Education. The database is searchable, so you can look up individual institutions, institutions by division and association, or institutions by athletic conference.

Being able to determine the difference between the capacity of an athletics department to generate revenue versus turn a profit is an important skill for an athletics administrator. According to EADA data for the 2011–2012 academic year, Ohio State University brought in nearly US$142 million in revenue, and the University of Texas at Austin generated just over US$163 million. More important, the revenue generated by OSU and UT exceeded their expenses, in both cases by several million dollars.

Equity in Athletics Disclosure Act (EADA)—Provides public information about the spending patterns of athletics departments in terms of men's and women's programs. Information about EADA may be found at www.ope.ed.gov/athletics.

Most athletics programs, however, are not profitable. In 2006, OSU and UT were 2 of just 19 schools that turned a profit (Weinbach, 2007). Depending on the year and the comprehensiveness of the analysis, the number of schools that generate revenue in excess of expenses may be as low as 10 (Zimbalist, 2007). A 2013 study by *USA Today* of college sport finances revealed that out of 228 NCAA Division I institutions, only 7 (Louisiana State, Nebraska, Ohio State, Oklahoma, Penn State, Purdue, and Texas) were truly self-supporting, meaning those programs did not receive subsidies in order to balance their books (Berkowitz, Upton, & Brady, 2013). An NCAA report on revenues and expenses for Division I intercollegiate athletics programs for the academic year 2010–2011 (Brown, 2012) revealed the following (all money amounts in US$):

> Of 1,100 institutions across all three divisions, only 23 Division I programs reported generating revenue in excess of overall athletics expenses.

> There is a large gap in the capacity of programs in Division I to generate revenue—the median reported revenue is $38 million, with some schools generating almost $150 million.

> The largest total expense for a Division I program was $130 million, with the median gap between the top and bottom quartiles being in excess of $60 million.

> In Division II programs offering football, the largest generated net revenue was $9.7 million, while the median generated net revenue was $618,000. The largest reported expense was $18.6 million, with the median expense being $972,200.

For Division III football playing institutions, the median total expense for athletic programs increased by nearly 85% from approximately $1.5 million in 2004 to about $2.86 million in 2011.

Intuition leads many outside observers of college sport to believe that spending more money will lead to greater program success. But in a 2009 study of FBS athletics financing, only the top programs (those ranked in the top 25 in recent years) realized a benefit from spending more. Despite the trend to award multiyear, multimillion dollar contracts to head coaches of football and men's and women's basketball, the researchers found no significant relationship between winning and high coaching salaries (Hosick, 2009).

Table 8.1 **Revenues and expenses in 2012 for NCAA Division I institutions**

	FBS	FCS	Division I—no MFB
Generated revenues	$40,581,000 ($4.2 million to $163.3 million)	$3,750,000 ($705,000 to $19.3 million)	$2,206,000 ($454,000 to $15.6 million)
Total revenues	$55,976,000 ($11.3 million to $163.3 million)	$13,761,000 ($2.6 million to $44.6 million)	$12,756,000 ($1.5 million to $33.8 million)
Total expenses	$56,265,000 ($10.8 million to $138.3 million)	$14,115,000 ($4.6 million to $44.9 million)	$12,983,000 ($3.5 million to $33.8 million)
Net generated revenue	−$12,272,000 (−$44.1 million to $32.7 million)	−$10,219,000 (−$2.7 million to −$27.3 million)	−$9,809,000 (−$2.8 million to −$24.6 million)

An ongoing concern regarding the financial model in place for college sport is whether it is sustainable over the long term and whether the rate of expenditures for athletics are appropriate given the degree to which institutions of higher learning are struggling to control escalating costs in the face of declining state support, limited endowment income, and rising tuition prices that are passed along to students. For athletic departments that rely on budgets primarily funded through tuition dollars and student fees,

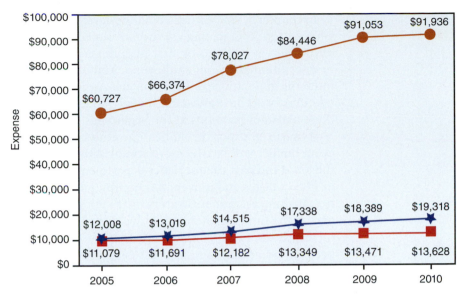

Figure 8.2   Academic and athletic spending in Football Bowl Subdivision.
Used with permission from the Knight Commission on Intercollegiate Athletics.
Available: http://knightcommission.org/images/pdfs/2010data/fig_1a_fbs_2010.pdf

some question the investment in athletics when academic programs are not funded to the degree they should be. According to the Delta Project in a report for the Knight Commission in 2013, athletic departments spend three to six times more to educate an athlete than institutions spent to educate the average student. Median spending per athlete among FBS institutions was US$92,000 per year. Median spending per student was less than US$14,000 at those same institutions.

From a gender equity perspective, these reports can offer insight into potential problems as well as existing shortfalls. For example, as Grant (2009) pointed out, "It is clear that the athletic budgets of men's basketball and football at many institutions in the Football Bowl Subdivision (FBS) are increasing at an alarming rate" (para. 1). After comparing data from the NCAA's financial reports for 2004 and 2006, she found that spending on men's sports increased during that two-year span by 14% compared with an increase of just 6% for women's sports. Additionally, 78% of men's athletics budgets are consumed by football and men's basketball.

Finally, depending on the division, the issue of whether a program is profitable is an important philosophical issue as well as a monetary one. In NCAA Division III, for example, athletics programs are intended to encourage participation, with a focus on the athletes' experience, not spectator appeal. As a consequence, the Division III infrastructure is not designed to generate revenue. The question for Division III institutions then becomes how much to invest in varsity athletics programs and how to justify those investments.

WEB

Go to the WSG and complete the web search activity, which asks you to investigate how equitably your institution is spending resources on men's and women's athletics programs.

Intercollegiate Athletics Administrators

As a student, you may want to find a definitive answer to the question of what athletics administrators do. To some degree, athletics administrators resemble managers in other business settings and industries. They must be able to execute the fundamental managerial functions of planning, organizing, staffing, directing, coordinating, reporting, and budgeting. The sections that follow will expand on the types of management positions found in intercollegiate athletics programs and conferences and outline general responsibilities associated with each position.

In chapter 5, you learned about top-level (i.e., senior) managers, middle-level (responsible to top-level managers; oversee supervisory and technical personnel) managers, and supervisory-level, or first-line, managers (report to middle-level managers and oversee nonmanagerial employees). You can find all three types of managers in most intercollegiate athletics departments. An important point to remember is that many administrators have assistants. Novice athletics administrators often pursue and occupy these assistant positions at the beginnings of their careers.

As a rule, the more prominent the athletics department is, the larger the annual operating budget will be; the more complex the organizational structure is, the larger the full-time and part-time athletics department staff will be. Thus, administrators working in FBS colleges and universities occupy positions with narrowly defined responsibilities. In contrast, administrators in athletics departments in Division II, in Division III, and at the junior and community college levels may be responsible for a wider array of responsibilities. Consequently, people employed in those settings might have to perform other duties, such as teaching in sport-related areas, coaching, or working in an area related to student life.

The size of the school and the scope of the athletics department are not the only factors that can affect the approach that athletics administrators take to their jobs. Most of what we know about intercollegiate athletics management today pertains to traditionally White institutions. Although management functions overlap significantly in every athletics department, we cannot assume that what we know about intercollegiate athletics management, based on that information, can be uniformly generalized and applied to HBCUs, such as Tennessee State, Mississippi Valley State, Howard, South Carolina State, Florida A&M, Tuskegee, and Grambling State universities. In fact, historically Black colleges are among the nation's leaders in FCS football attendance (Johnson, 2009).

The notion that not all athletics programs fit the dominant model of college sport management is borne out not only by the HBCUs but also by women's college athletics programs. Located in small liberal arts institutions and governed by the rules of Division III, the women's athletics programs in schools such as Smith, Bryn Mawr, Mount Holyoke, and Mills colleges employ management models that are consistent with single-sex women's education institutions. Because of the variability of the college sport marketplace, no two positions are identical nor are the job titles used to describe them the same. As you explore careers in college sport, spend some time reading position descriptions to gain a better understanding of job expectations and requirements.

Director of Athletics

An athletics director (AD) assumes oversight of numerous areas within the athletics department. Some of these, depending on the structure of the department, may include budget and finance, facilities, risk management, television contracts, compliance with laws and regulations of national and conference governing bodies, academic progress of college athletes, communication with the media, scheduling, marketing games and other events, corporate sponsorships, ticket sales, community relations, alumni relations, campus relations, fundraising, and personnel management, including the hiring and termination of coaches. A definitive answer to the question of what ADs do is elusive, however, because of the unique nature of athletics departments and how they are structured within specific colleges and universities. On one hand, the business of college sport is big business. As Dave Hart (vice chancellor and director of athletics at the University of Tennessee) noted, the job of an AD "is now much like that of a CEO. I don't know where else you find the complexity that exists with the job of an athletics director today" ("Q&A," 2008, para. 20).

Villanova University director of athletics Vince Nicastro acknowledged the growing business demands associated with his position, estimating that he spent at least half of his time dealing with issues related to budget, finance, and human resources (Robinson, 2009). Being able to execute what famed entrepreneur Donald Trump refers to as the art of the deal is an essential skill for an athletics director (Harris & Lowry, 2008).

At the same time, an athletics director at a Division III institution or junior college, with responsibility for a budget of perhaps US$3 million, faces different job demands and responsibilities. In many respects, the difference in these situations resembles the distinction between a major corporation and a locally owned business. Both require managerial skills and experience, but the demands on the leaders of the enterprises vary markedly.

Candidates for AD positions are increasingly scrutinized in terms of their business credentials and recruited because of them. Six of the seven athletics directors hired by Pac-12 schools during the past five years had business or fundraising backgrounds (Henderson, 2013).

The stature and status of the athletics director role on campus is changing. The role has been significantly elevated to warrant the use of **executive search firms** (Schoffel & Henry, 2013). Once used by institutions to fill major positions such as chancellors, presidents, and provosts, college and university administrators are now turning to executive search firms to identify and vet qualified athletics administrators for open positions. The average fee a firm charges to run a search for an athletics director or coach in a major sport has been estimated at US$75,000. In recent years, questions have been raised about the value of going through a search firm to help in the hiring process. While search firms that handle athletic department personnel recruitment typically charge less on average than firms that handle hiring for other higher education executives, the timeline for athletic department hiring is typically much shorter (Heitner, 2013).

executive search firm—An organization that identifies talented administrators for positions such as college presidents, chancellors, provosts, athletics administrators, and coaches.

Not surprisingly, when asked about qualities that they find most important when hiring athletics directors, college presidents across all three divisions identified a solid foundation in budget and finance along with skills in management and leadership, marketing, and communication (Schneider & Stier, 2005). A key element of success for ADs who wish to move up the ranks is mastering the art of networking (Whisenant & Pedersen, 2004).

Associate or Assistant Athletics Director

Associate and assistant ADs are clearly middle-level managers. These titles generally represent either the level of administrative responsibility assigned to the person in the role or the level of seniority and experience that the person has. In many respects, the associate or assistant AD supports the AD in achieving the overall mission of the department by working closely with the AD and overseeing specific areas, such as marketing, fundraising, event management, facilities management, or athletics communications. In large athletics departments, several people are designated as associate or assistant ADs. Senior associates usually serve as the second in command within an athletics department and assume responsibility for the overall operation of the department in the absence of the AD. As mentioned previously, to determine what people in these positions do, you have to read their job descriptions or speak with them directly.

First-Line Managers

First-line managers are responsible for specific work groups in the athletics department. These managers typically report to an associate or assistant AD. Many of these positions have emerged, or have been expanded, only within the past two decades.

Professional Profile: Gene Smith

Title: associate vice president and director of athletics, The Ohio State University

Education: BA (business administration), University of Notre Dame

ONE DAY

Go to the WSG and learn more about a typical day in the life for Gene Smith. See if he spends his working hours the way you think he does.

If there is a prototype for the 21st century athletics director, Gene Smith might well be it, since he is recognized as "one of the most powerful people in collegiate sport" ("Gene Smith," 2013, para. 1). He has received numerous honors and awards for his national leadership and service. In 2013, he was honored with the NAAC Organizational Leadership Award, which honors organizational leaders who have demonstrated outstanding commitments to promoting compliance of NCAA rules within their organization and on a national level. He has served (including a year as chair) on the NCAA Men's Basketball Committee, and has been recognized as the 2010 Carl Maddox Sports Management Award recipient (awarded for effective managerial practices in the sport industry) and *Street & Smith's SportsBusiness Journal* Athletic Director of the Year. Just a few of the many ways in which Smith has been recognized include the John L. Toner award (for exhibiting outstanding administrative ability and dedication to intercollegiate athletics and college football in particular), *Black Enterprise Magazine's* 50 most powerful African Americans in college sports, and the Black Coaches & Administrators (BCA) athletic administrator of the year. Smith's service to the profession is also very extensive, including presidencies of the Division 1-A Athletic Directors Association and the National Association of Collegiate Directors of Athletics (NACDA). He has served in various other capacities as well, including on distinguished boards such as the National Football Foundation Honors Court, the NCAA Division I Administration Cabinet, the President's Commission Liaison Committee, the NCAA Management Council, the NCAA Football Rules Committee, the NCAA Committee on Infractions, and the NCAA Executive Committee. Smith is responsible for providing the vision for and overseeing one of the largest and most successful university athletic programs in the United States. In his role, he must demonstrate command of an array of organizational management skills in running a Football Bowl Subdivision (FBS) athletic department that is a member to the Big Ten Conference. The department sponsors 36 fully funded varsity sports. Under his leadership, OSU's sports teams and individual athletes have continued to regularly compete for conference and national championships and awards. He has additional oversight responsibility for a recently created business advancement division of OSU, which includes the Schottenstein Center, Nationwide Arena, Blackwell Hotel, Drake Union, Fawcett Center, and trademark and licensing ("Gene Smith," 2013).

You can follow Smith on Twitter (@OSU_AD) and read more about his career advancement and current activities as follows and in the WSG.

What have been the key moves, steps, or developments in Smith's career, and how did he arrive at his current position?

Smith attended Chanel High School, where he distinguished himself in football, basketball, and track and received the football team's most valuable player award. He then went to the University of Notre Dame and was a defensive end for the Irish, including being a member of the team's 1973 national championship. Smith transitioned from player to coach at Notre Dame and was an assistant coach on the 1977 national championship team. Following his coaching experience, Smith chose to make a career move, becoming a marketing representative for IBM, a decision that would eventually lead to his positions as the director of athletics at Eastern Michigan University, Iowa State University, and Arizona State University. In 2005, he was appointed the eighth director of athletics at The Ohio State University. Three years after his appointment as athletics director, he was promoted to assistant vice president and director of athletics. Currently, his title is associate vice president and director of athletics ("Gene Smith," 2013).

What are his current responsibilities and objectives in his job?

Smith leads an athletic department with a staff of 340 and a US$140 million budget. The mission of the department is to ensure that the roughly 1,000 Buckeye athletes have an environment in which to be academically, athletically, and developmentally successful.

What does he enjoy most about his current job?
Smith enjoys seeing athletes graduate and become champions.

What does he consider the biggest future challenge to be in his job or industry?
Smith believes that financing the enterprise and adjusting to the ever-changing culture of the student are the biggest future challenges to the sport management industry.

Positions include academic coordinator, business and finance manager, compliance officer, development and public relations director, event and facility manager, marketing and promotions director, sports information director, ticket manager, senior woman administrator, and equipment manager. Brief descriptions of these jobs follow.

ACADEMIC COORDINATOR

According to the National Association of Academic Advisors for Athletics (N4A), fewer than 10 full-time academic advisors for athletes existed in 1975. As of 2013, the N4A had a membership of more than 1,300 (Pignataro, 2013). This phenomenal growth resulted from the passage of NCAA bylaw 16.3.1, which requires all Division I programs to offer academic support and tutoring services to athletes, and the existence of the Academic Enhancement Fund Program, which allocates US$62,438 per year to each Division I athletics program in support of academics.

Athletics academic advisement services assist athletes in addressing the dual and sometimes conflicting demands of being both a student and an athlete. As with all areas that we have addressed, the structure of these offices and the range of services that they provide can vary from one institution to another. In general, athletics academic offices assist athletes in the broad areas of admission, academic orientation, academic standards, registration, financial aid, housing, and student life. The academic coordinator monitors the academic activities of athletes and maintains records on their academic progress. To do their jobs effectively, academic coordinators work closely with coaches, faculty, the compliance officer, and other administrators.

To address concerns about academic progress and performance among athletes in Divisions I and II, the NCAA adopted a series of rules and initiatives during the past decade. In brief, these include the following:

> Freshman eligibility standards for Division I are 16 core high school courses, a sliding scale for test score and grade-point average; for Division II, the standards are 14 core courses, minimum SAT of 820 or an ACT sum score of 68, and a minimum GPA of 2.0 (NCAA Eligibility Center, 2008)

> Academic progress rate, more commonly referred to as the APR

> The 40/60/80 rule, which requires athletes, by the end of the second year, to have completed at least 40% of their degree, by the end of the third year, at least 60%, and by the end of the fourth year, at least 80%

academic progress rate (APR)—According to the NCAA, this is a measure of how successful athletics programs on individual campuses are in ensuring that college athletes make appropriate progress toward their degrees.

In the case of the APR, penalties for failure to meet the threshold standards of 900 to 925 per team range from public warning to loss of scholarships to restricted membership in Division I. The academic support staff members associated with athletics departments play a key role in helping athletes remain eligible and in assisting programs to meet APR requirements ("NCAA backgrounder," n.d.).

People interested in working as athletics academic advisors need to understand the business of college sport and the regulations that affect athletes. They must be equally familiar with the processes of social adaptation and human development, academic performance assessment, and career guidance strategies. In large athletics programs, the athletics academic support services staff might include several academic counselors, mentors, and tutors, some of whom are undergraduate and graduate students.

BUSINESS AND FINANCE MANAGER

The business and finance manager for an intercollegiate athletics department recommends and implements policies, procedures, and methods of accounting that ensure strict compliance with sound business practices in accordance with the rules and regulations of the institution, the conference, and the national governing body. Brown (2008) noted, "Presidents, athletics directors and other campus leaders rely on business managers a great deal for athletics budget projections, comparisons with peer groups and other trend analyses that give those leaders more information on which to base decisions" (para. 9). He added that business managers are also typically responsible for the business processes of accounting and reporting, contract management, human resources, purchasing, travel, and ticketing operations.

The professional organization for this group of athletics department personnel is the College Athletic Business Management Association (CABMA). With athletics spending progressing at a rate that is three times that of spending overall on college and university campuses (Brown, 2007), greater emphasis has been placed on finding ways to reduce expenses. Business managers have been called on to contribute in significant ways to implement what the NCAA refers to as the dashboard indicator project. This project allows schools to compare budget information that will better inform decision making about athletics spending.

COMPLIANCE OFFICER

Compliance with NCAA regulations is not solely the responsibility of the person designated in an athletics department to serve as the compliance officer or coordinator. It is technically a shared responsibility among all parties who come in contact with the athletics program, including the AD, coaches, current athletes, prospective athletes, boosters, and alumni, as well as representatives from various campus offices (e.g., admission, financial aid, residence life, health services). The process of compliance in its contemporary form evolved in the 1990s in conjunction with the development of the NCAA program certification process.

Broadly stated, the role of compliance coordinators is to develop educational processes that help everyone directly or indirectly involved with the athletics program understand and comply with the rules of the institution, the conference, and the national governing body. The span of responsibilities to which compliance officers may be assigned includes assessment of student initial eligibility, continuing eligibility, and transfer eligibility, as well as adherence to regulations that govern athlete recruitment. Because of the complexity of rules, compliance coordinators often have the task of developing and implementing record-keeping methods to demonstrate that compliance in various areas is monitored. Much of this record keeping is done with computer software programs. Compliance officers play a crucial role in the formulation of compliance reports that institutions must submit to the NCAA on a regular basis.

Those interested in working in the compliance area must be detail oriented and have an exhaustive understanding of NCAA and conference rules and regulations, along with the management and communication skills necessary to explain these rules and regulations effectively. Although a law degree is not a requirement for this type of position, the nature of the job lends itself to someone with this kind of interest and background.

DEVELOPMENT AND PUBLIC RELATIONS DIRECTOR

Depending on the institution, the process of raising money from friends of an athletics program is called athletics fundraising, development, or advancement. Athletics fundraising organizations may be called fan clubs, booster clubs, friends associations, alumni clubs, or athletics foundations. Athletics development officers are responsible for raising funds to support various aspects of the athletics department by identifying and implementing fundraising projects and cultivating potential and current donors.

In athletics fundraising, several basic principles apply. The fundraiser wants to encourage people who donate to the program to continue to donate and ideally to donate more over time, while searching out and contacting new donors to expand the program's financial base. The importance of development efforts to college athletics programs cannot be underestimated; alumni and booster contributions often involve both individually and collectively millions of dollars in support. The fundraiser position requires a combination of marketing, management, and media relations skills.

One extremely important element in this area is vigilance with regard to the donors involved with the program. The potential for rules violations in this area has proved to be high. Donors and friends of athletics programs may offer athletes under-the-table payments, improper gifts, and other benefits that violate NCAA rules. Athletics development officers are required to show the steps that they take to educate friends of the program about rules and regulations that govern athletics programs so as to avoid problems in this area.

EVENT AND FACILITY MANAGER

In recent years, a marked expansion of athletics facilities on college campuses has occurred. Because of limitations of space and resources, athletics departments must find ways to use facilities to serve the multiple needs of campus constituencies and generate income through the rental and use of multipurpose facilities for special events, such as concerts. The position description for an event and facility manager reflects this trend. Facility scheduling, maintenance, improvements, and contest management are the major duties assigned to event and facility managers. Because many people use athletics facilities for many different activities, facility and event managers must be attentive to the reduction of risk and liability while finding ways of being user-friendly by creating as much availability and accessibility as possible. One of the major responsibilities of the event and facility manager is game management for home athletics events. This task entails arranging for appropriate levels of security at games; hiring, training, and supervising ushers; marking and lining fields and courts; making arrangements for ticket sellers and ticket takers; managing the time schedule of the game, including such things as the national anthem, bands, and halftime shows; and attending to the needs of game officials. A more detailed description of event and facility management is presented in chapter 16.

MARKETING AND PROMOTIONS DIRECTOR

In the summer of 2001, the University of Oregon bought a 10-story billboard in New York City's Times Square that displayed a picture of its Heisman Trophy nominee, quarterback Joey Harrington. The cost of that billboard was a tidy US$250,000—a quarter of a million dollars! Although the amount of money invested in the Harrington campaign was exceptionally high, the promotion itself was not unusual; schools routinely invest thousands of dollars in the promotion of their Heisman candidates. Marketing and promoting the contemporary college athletics program happen at all levels. They are motivated by the need to generate interest in the program through enhanced visibility, increased attendance, and expanding revenue streams. Marketing and promotions directors may be responsible for promoting ticket sales for individual games, nonrevenue sports, season packages, and championship events, along with a complete line of apparel, fan support merchandise, and items for retail sale by direct mail and through the university's bookstore and concessions area. Marketing and promotions directors are also responsible for identifying potential corporate sponsors, developing sponsorship proposals, and ensuring that proposals are implemented according to agreements reached with sponsors (Irwin, Sutton, & McCarthy, 2008). In an age in which product branding, merchandising, and licensing (i.e., **licensing royalty**) have become integral parts of the marketing of intercollegiate athletics programs, marketing and promotions directors must have a comprehensive understanding of trademark licensing and be familiar with trademark principles, terms, and definitions used in trademark law (Pitts & Stotlar, 2007). A division of the world's leading sport marketing firm, IMG College is devoted to marketing college sport. Its efforts are inspired by the awareness that more than 173 million people, nearly half of whom are female, comprise the largest fan base of any sport entity (Janoff, 2012). Arguably the most visible way college sport is marketed is through the advertising done in conjunction with the NCAA's men's basketball tournament. From 2003 to 2012, with national TV ad spending from 266 companies for the tournaments were US$5.9 billion, with spending in 2012 exceeding US$1 billion ("Kantar Media," 2013).

Traditionally, the job of marketing an athletics program at the college and university level has been done in-house. During the past two decades, however, the marketing function within athletic departments has expanded. At the same time, in an effort to maximize existing revenue and access new revenue streams, Division I athletics departments are **outsourcing** their marketing to firms that specialize in college sport marketing. Companies

licensing royalty—The earnings paid to the sport property, or licensor (e.g., athletics department), by a licensed manufacturer in return for the right to produce and sell merchandise bearing a logo or other mark associated with its sports program (Irwin, Sutton, & McCarthy, 2008).

outsourcing—In the context of this chapter's section on the marketing of college programs, it refers to the use of outside sport marketing firms to maximize revenues for athletics programs.

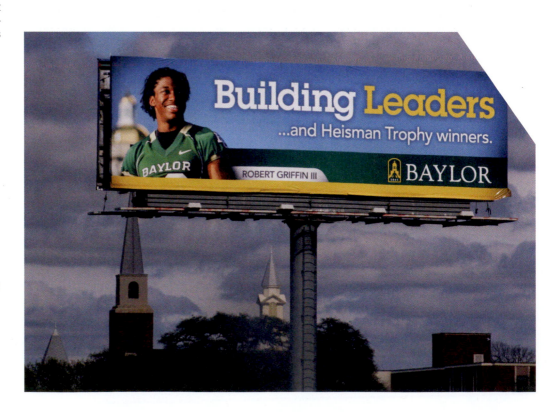

The marketing of a university sometimes involves alums of the intercollegiate athletics program, such as Baylor University's promotion of its affiliation with one of its former student-athletes, current professional quarterback Robert Griffin III.

such as CBS Collegiate Sports Properties, IMG College, the Collegiate Licensing Company (a subdivision of IMG), Learfield, and Nelligan purchase rights to college properties and share the revenue from the sale of those properties with athletics departments.

SPORTS INFORMATION DIRECTOR

Sports information directors (SIDs)—also referred to as athletics communications specialists, college athletic communicators, sport publicists, and college sport public relations directors—are responsible for both technical and management functions. As a public relations practitioner, a sports information director must be adept at developing an array of publication materials, including media guides, press releases, recruiting brochures, game programs, feature stories, and newsletters. They also do the background work (e.g., research, interviews with coaches and players) to support those publications.

John Humenik, executive director of the College Sports Information Directors of America (CoSIDA) argues that the college sport industry needs to reconceptualize the role of media relations professionals. Although the title *information director* refers to a person "who is involved mostly in keeping stats, preparing basic news releases, working on publications, setting up interviews and managing the press box," according to Humenik, the title *communications director* refers to a person who "is viewed more in a strategic and visionary capacity" (Stoldt, 2008, p. 460). Besides executing the technical demands of the job, sports information directors are also responsible for managing budgets, organizing events, and supervising personnel. Successful sports information directors need to have excellent writing and research skills, a firm understanding of mass communication and media technologies, an awareness of and ability to appeal to internal and external audiences, and a capacity to maintain a calm demeanor while working in high-stress, high-pressure situations. Practicing sports information directors offered this advice for students who want to pursue careers in this field: "Get as much writing experience as possible," "Gain as much experience as possible as an undergraduate," "Be prepared to work long hours," and "Plan on a career with little pay and little appreciation, but also plan on it being a lot of fun" (Hardin & McClung, 2002, p. 38). In an age of new and social media, college athletic communications is changing. Those in management roles are more likely to spend time working on blogs and in social media, where monitoring environmental issues, issues management, and strategic messaging are key responsibilities (Stoldt & Vermilion, 2013).

TICKET MANAGER

The primary responsibilities of the ticket manager are coordinating all **ticket operations**, designing the ticketing plan, and accounting for all money expended and received for tickets. Responsible for a major area of revenue generation and customer service, ticket managers are called on to assist in setting the price of tickets, determining staffing, ensuring that ticket distribution is handled in a secure manner, and understanding state laws that pertain to **ticket scalping** (Reese, 2003; Reese, 2013). A major resource for the ticket manager is the International Ticketing Association (INTIX). Members of INTIX include an array of businesses and organizations in sport and entertainment fields around the world (e.g., amphitheaters, ballet and opera companies, festivals, sport teams, state fairs, theaters, universities). Ticketing software and hardware development workers, ticket agents and printers, and Internet-based ticketing companies also belong to INTIX. This organization sponsors an annual conference as well as an intensive certification program to help people in the industry stay current on trends and techniques to provide the best service possible to consumers.

SENIOR WOMAN ADMINISTRATOR (SWA)

When you read biographies of people working in intercollegiate athletics, you may come across the term **senior woman administrator (SWA)**. The term is not a position title per

ticket operations—Process by which tickets are distributed to customers (season ticket holders and fans), coupled with attention to a high level of customer service (Reese, 2003).

ticket scalping—Selling a ticket for a price in excess of the price printed on the ticket.

senior woman administrator (SWA)—The highest ranking female administrator involved in the management of an NCAA institution's intercollegiate athletics department.

se. In Divisions I and III, it designates "the highest ranking female administrator involved with the management of a member institution's intercollegiate athletics program" (NCAA, 2008, p. 18). At the Division II level, it refers to a member of the institution's senior management team (Brown, 2009). The purpose of the SWA concept is to ensure that women have a role in the decision-making process in college sport and that women's interests are represented at the campus, conference, and national levels.

Research about SWAs reveals that 79% of Division I SWAs serve in some administrative role within their departments, occupying assistant, associate, or senior associate athletics director positions (Claussen & Lehr, 2002). Tiell noted (as cited in Brown, 2009) that in Division II, more than half of those designated as SWAs did not have jobs that positioned them to be members of the department's senior management team, and in Division III, 47% of SWAs were not members of a senior management team.

The intention of the SWA designation to integrate women in the decision-making process of athletics departments has not been realized. Comparison between the perceptions of athletics directors and SWAs regarding the role of SWAs in decision making at the senior management level reveals a disconnect. Noting that the role of the SWA was adopted at a time when athletic programs for men and women were separate, Hoffman (2010) reports that the SWA role has not been effective in advancing the interests of women in athletic administration, and has left women with the challenge of having to be super performers in order to get promoted or be hired.

Whereas ADs perceived that SWAs were instrumental in advancing the interests of the athletics department, SWAs perceived that they encountered barriers because of the limits placed on their assignments or authority (Claussen & Lehr, 2002; Tiell & Dixon, 2008). Many SWAs are not satisfied with the level of participation that they have in operations, budgeting, capital outlay, salary considerations, media broadcast contracts, and sponsorship and advertising (Grappendorf, Pent, Burton, & Henderson, 2008).

Although some SWAs are assigned sole responsibility for women's athletics programs and teams, the range of responsibilities assigned to SWAs can encompass all that goes on in a coeducational athletics department. SWAs have been found to perform roles and tasks that are gender neutral, meaning that they have administrative assignments that support both men's and women's programs. According to McDermott and Lynch (2008), SWAs should contribute to decision making in the following areas: program supervision, budget management, fundraising and marketing, compliance and governance, human resource management, gender equity monitoring and implementation, and advocacy for women within the athletics program. In recent years, steps have been taken to designate an SWA within athletics conferences as well.

EQUIPMENT MANAGER

Intercollegiate athletics equipment managers who are certified by the Athletic Equipment Managers Association (AEMA) perform various tasks such as purchasing and fitting equipment, inspecting and preserving uniforms, and establishing an accountability system (e.g., inventory, reconditioning, storage, cleaning) of equipment and garments. As with all other positions mentioned in this chapter, an equipment manager's job includes a significant management component. As Dale Strauf (2002), equipment manager at Cornell University noted, "Equipment managers play a major role in the decision-making process for all aspects of equipment administration" (para. 2). Effective communication with top-level, middle-level, and other first-line administrators is essential. Since 1991, AEMA has promoted a certification program for equipment managers to ensure a high standard of performance and professional preparation. According to Dorothy Cutting at the AEMA (personal communication, June 27, 2014), in 2014, there were more than 1001 members and 585 certified athletics equipment managers in the United States.

Administrators in Governing Bodies

Recent research on the profiles and career paths of conference commissioners suggests that some distinctly different skill sets and backgrounds may set commissioners apart from other athletics administrators. As a case in point, conference commissioners appear to be more likely to hold degrees in journalism and communication while exhibiting a broader range of experiences. A pattern similar to that seen in individual school settings is the underrepresentation of women and minorities in conference offices (Davis, 2008).

As can be seen in table 8.2, conference commissioners in all NCAA divisions perform their duties within three major role classifications: interpersonal, informational, and

Table 8.2   **Adaptation of Mintzberg's Managerial Roles for Intercollegiate Athletic Conference Commissioners**

Role	Description of role	Examples
Interpersonal		
Figurehead	Performing ceremonial duties on behalf of the conference	Welcoming dignitaries, greeting visitors, participating in groundbreaking ceremonies
Leader	Influencing subordinates to get the work done at the conference office	Conducting performance evaluations, acting as a role model in the workplace, praising an employee for doing a good job
Liaison	Maintaining a network of outside contacts to gather information for the conference	Attending meetings with peers, listening to the grapevine, participating in conference-wide meetings
Informational		
Monitor	Perpetually scanning the environment for information that may prove useful to the conference	Lobbying for information at an NCAA meeting, staying in contact with other commissioners by telephone, reviewing the athletics literature
Disseminator	Transmitting information received by individuals or groups outside the conference	Sending information to coaches and athletics directors, having a review session on NCAA rules with the athletics directors
Spokesperson	Transmitting information to individuals or groups outside the conference	Speaking at community and professional meetings, briefing the state legislature about athletics
Decisional		
Entrepreneur	Searching for new ideas and implementing changes for the betterment of the conference	Initiating a new marketing concept for increasing revenue, bringing new technology to the conference
Disturbance handler	Making decisions to deal with unexpected changes that may affect the conference	Resolving a conflict among member institutions, dealing with changes in game schedules
Resource allocator	Making decisions concerning resource use—people, time, money, space—for the conference	Making a decision about a tournament site, adding or deleting a sport program
Negotiator	Bargaining with individuals, groups, or organizations on behalf of the conference	Negotiating a television contract, negotiating with vendors

Reprinted, by permission, from J. Quarterman, 1994, "Managerial role profiles of intercollegiate athletic conference commissioners," *Journal of Sport Management* 8: 131-132.

Social Media and Intercollegiate Athletics

Most intercollegiate athletic departments, programs, teams, and stakeholders have been affected by social media. "I definitely think that social media have been a game-changer all across the sports landscape," noted ESPN's Danny Kanell. "No matter what position you're in—whether you're a player, a coach or a broadcaster like [me]" (Elfman, 2013, para. 2). The benefits of social media for an intercollegiate athletics program can be vast. Opportunities to connect with loyal fans, deliver information, and generate revenue all yield positive results for athletics administrators. The benefits of social media are tempered, however, by the challenges. Speaking at the IMG Intercollegiate Athletics Forum in December of 2012, Duke University director of athletics Kevin White discussed the power social media has to influence the lives of coaches, athletic administrators, and athletes. He said, "When somebody gets foreclosed on because of social media, there are unfortunately times where you are driven to make a decision that perhaps 10 or 20 years ago without that social media you would allow it to ferment a little longer and hopefully you could find a way out of a rough and back into the fairway" (Elfman, 2013, para. 7). Staying in front of mass movements calling for coach and athletics director firings, being aware of fans from opposing teams manipulating information about players to disrupt focus and create negative media attention, and managing the celebrity status that comes with being in the public view are all challenges that intercollegiate athletic administrators face now and will continue to face well into the future.

decisional (Quarterman, 1994). These functions are similar to those of an AD, except that ADs act on behalf of a university, whereas commissioners act on behalf of member institutions. The organizational chart in figure 8.1 identifies additional positions in the NCAA.

Critical Thinking in Intercollegiate Athletics

PORTFOLIO

Complete the critical thinking portfolio activity in the WSG, consulting as needed the "Critical Thinking Questions" sidebar in chapter 1.

Are college sports compatible with the goals of higher education? This is a question posed by Kirk Hanson, director of the Markkula Center for Applied Ethics at Santa Clara University, and his colleague, Matt Savage. What do you think? Before answering the question, watch a debate hosted by Intelligence Squared between writers Buzz Bissinger and Malcolm Gladwell versus former NFL player, attorney, writer, coach, and broadcaster Tim Green and sportswriter Jason Whitlock (Hanson & Savage, 2012). The debate focused on the question of whether college football should be banned.

Ethics in Intercollegiate Athletics

In recent years, the financial stakes in college sport have risen rapidly. In 2009, IMG struck a deal with The Ohio State University that guaranteed the Buckeyes US$110 million over 10 years (Berkowitz, 2009). In turn, the NCAA itself in 2009 reorganized the seating plan for the Men's Final Four to accommodate tens of thousands more ticket buyers, resulting in a US$7 million increase in gate receipts (Wieberg & Berkowitz, 2009).

Although corporate entities capitalize on the games played by college athletes, using their performances and likenesses to market everything from television air time to jerseys to video games, the athletes themselves are prevented from receiving compensation beyond the limits of their scholarships. As a study released by the National College Players Association in 2013 documented, athletics scholarships do not cover the full cost of attendance because of NCAA regulations. As a result, even athletes on full scholarship often have to cover an average financial shortfall of US$3,285 per year, meaning that over five years, a full scholarship athlete will have a debt of approximately US$16,425 (Huma & Staurowsky, 2013).

Although the NCAA argues that its rules of amateurism protect athletes from commercial and professional exploitation, the question of how the NCAA defines the term *exploitation* has been raised by the Knight Commission on Intercollegiate Athletics (2009). As commercial interests in college sport have escalated, so too has the possibility increased that college athletes will start to seek more compensation for the work that they do.

Summary

Intercollegiate athletics has come a long way from the days when students ran their own practices, devised their own training programs, and negotiated the terms of the contests in which they played. As the business of college sport continues to expand, job opportunities for aspiring young professionals are no longer limited to college campuses. Students can look to media outlets (e.g., CBS Sports, CSTV, Fox College Sports, the Big Ten Network, the SEC Network, ESPNU), new and emerging media, as well as numerous sport marketing firms (e.g., IMG College Division) to find work. The overall structure of intercollegiate athletics extends far beyond the bounds of the FBS, through to local community colleges. Although the challenges are different, numerous opportunities to work in college sport exist in institutions as varied as tribal colleges, NCAA Division III institutions, and NCCAA schools.

An examination of intercollegiate athletics reveals that the leaders of tomorrow must be prepared to face challenges ethically and to exercise critical thinking skills in examining what has become standard operating procedure. Intercollegiate athletics has the potential to be a valuable asset to institutions of higher learning and to the students who participate in it. At the same time, to be blind to the persistent problems that have plagued the college sport enterprise is to endanger its future and the future of those who work in it. Thus, students are uniquely positioned to devise new ways of addressing old problems. In this sense, the intercollegiate athletics system is in your hands. What will you make of it?

Review Questions

1. What role did President Theodore Roosevelt play in the development of college sport in the United States?

2. What was the relationship between the NCAA and the NAIA in the 1970s? How has that relationship changed today?

3. How do FBS conferences exert influence and control over decision making within the NCAA?

4. Why is the ECAC such an unusual conference?

5. How many Division I athletics departments make a profit?

6. What is the relationship between winning and high coaching salaries, at least according to one study noted in the chapter?

7. Why is there concern about the rate of spending in men's sports at the Division I level compared with the rate of spending in women's sports? On average, what percentage of Division I men's sport budgets are consumed by football and men's basketball?

8. What possible penalties may be assessed to a school if a team fails to meet the APR standards?

9. What are the possible rules violations that athletics development officers need to be aware of, and how do they try to reduce the likelihood that those violations will occur?

References

Barack Obama picks winner. (2013, March 20). *ESPN.com*. Retrieved from http://espn.go.com/mens-college-basketball/tournament/2013/story/_/id/9073386/ncaa-tournament-2013-president-barack-obama-fills-bracket

Berkowitz, S. (2009, May 1). IMG jolts campus scene to give schools a cash boost. *USA Today*. Retrieved from www.usatoday.com/sports/college/2009-04-01-img-cover_N.htm

Berkowitz, S., Upton, J., & Brady, E. (2013, July 1). Most NCAA Division I athletic departments take subsidies. *USA Today*. Retrieved from www.usatoday.com/story/sports/college/2013/05/07/ncaa-finances-subsidies/2142443

Big Ten history. (2013). Retrieved from www.bigten.org/trads/big10-trads.html

Big Ten pioneer to receive prestigious Ford Award. (2006, October 25). Retrieved from www.bigten.org/genrel/102506aad.html

Brown, G. (2008, May 2). A look at the role business managers play in intercollegiate athletics. *NCAA News*. Retrieved from http://fs.ncaa.org/Docs/NCAANewsArchive/2008/association-wide/cabmaqa%2B-%2B05-02-08%2Bncaa%2Bnews.html

Brown, G. (2009, January 21). GLIAC strengthens role of league SWAs. *NCAA News*. Retrieved from http://fs.ncaa.org/Docs/NCAANewsArchive/2009/Division+II/gliac_strengthens_role_of_league_swas_01_21_09_ncaa_news.html

Brown, G. (2012, October 9). NCAA report reveals consistent financial allocation among DI schools. Retrieved from www.ncaa.org/wps/wcm/connect/public/NCAA/Resources/Latest+News/2012/October/NCAA+report+reveals+consistent+financial+allocation+among+DI+schools

Brown, G.T. (2007, October 22). Division I budget trends get dashboard treatment. *NCAA News*. Retrieved from http://fs.ncaa.org/Docs/NCAANewsArchive/2007/Division+I/division%2-Bi%2Bbudget%2Btrends%2Bget%2Bdashboard%2Btreatment%2B-%2B10-22-07%2B-%2Bncaa%2Bnews.html

CCCAA Commission on Athletics. (2013). Retrieved from www.cccaasports.org/about.asp

Claussen, C.L., & Lehr, C. (2002). Decision making authority of senior woman administrators. *International Journal of Sport Management*, 3, 215–228.

Commission on Athletics. (n.d.). California Community College Athletic Association. Retrieved from www.coasports.org/COA.pdf

Composition and sport sponsorship of the membership. (n.d.) 2012-13 composition. Retrieved from www.ncaa.org/about/who-we-are/membership/composition-and-sport-sponsorship-membership

Copeland, J. (2007, December 17). A simple question, a difficult answer. *NCAA News*. Retrieved from http://fs.ncaa.org/Docs/NCAANewsArchive/2007/Association-wide/a%2Bsimple%2Bquestion,%2Ba%2Bdifficult%2Banswer%2B-%2B12-17-07%2B-%2Bncaa%2Bnews.html

Crowley, J. (2006). *In the arena: The NCAA's first century*. Indianapolis, IN: NCAA.

Dannelly, J. (2009, February 24). *The future of the NAIA: Part 3 of 3 [Blog post]*. Retrieved from www.collegefanz.com/blogs/jasondannelly/2009/02/24/the-future-of-the-naia-part-3-of-3

Dannelly, J. (2011a). Future of the NAIA. *The Senior Reports*. Retrieved from www.theseniorreports.com/naiafuture.htm

Dannelly, J. (2011b, April 11). NCCAA: 2011 and beyond. *The Senior Reports*. Retrieved from www.theseniorreports.com/nccaa.htm

Davis, G.K. (2008). *NCAA athletic conference commissioners profiles and career paths*. Unpublished master's thesis. Raleigh, NC: North Carolina State University.

Delta Cost Project at American Institute for Research. (2013). *Academic spending versus athletic spending: Who wins?* Washington, D.C.: Knight.

Edes, G. (1922). *The annals of the Harvard class of 1852*. Cambridge, MA: Author.

Elfman, L. (2013, January 23). Social media's undeniable impact on college sports. *Diverse Education*. Retrieved from http://diverseeducation.com/article/50932

Farrey, T. (2013, June 20). After TV deals, battle was inevitable. *ESPN.com*. Retrieved from http://espn.go.com/college-sports/story/_/id/9404803/why-ed-obannon-antitrust-lawsuit-was-inevitable-ncaa-why-face-challenge

Gayle, T. (2013, June 18). Alabama State University failure symbolic of HBCU struggles. *Huffington Post*. Retrieved from www.huffingtonpost.com/2013/06/18/alabama-state-university-failure-symbolic-of-hbcu-struggles_n_3458824.html

Gene Smith. (2013). Retrieved from www.ohiostatebuckeyes.com/genrel/gene_smith_204956.html

Grant, C. (2009, February 23). Football Bowl Subdivision athletics budgets increase at alarming rate. *Sport Management Resources*. Retrieved from www.sportsmanagementresources.com/node/207

Grant, R.R., Leadley, J., & Zygmont, Z. (2008). *The economics of intercollegiate sports*. Mountain View, CA: World Scientific.

Grappendorf, H., Pent, A., Burton, L., & Henderson, A. (2008). Gender role stereotyping: A qualitative analysis of Senior Woman Administrators' perceptions regarding financial decision making. *Journal of Issues in Intercollegiate Athletics*, 1, 26–45.

Griffin, T. (2013, May 30). Another NCAA subdivision for large schools discussed at Big 12 meetings. Retrieved from www.chron.com/sports/college/article/Another-NCAA-subdivision-for-large-schools-4563685.php

Hanson, K., & Savage, M. (2012, August). Ethics in college sport. Retrieved from www.scu.edu/ethics/publications/submitted/college-sports-ethics.html

Hardin, R., & McClung, S. (2002). Collegiate sports information: A profile for the profession. *Public Relations Quarterly*, 47(2), 35–40.

Harris, A., & Lowry, J. (2008). The powerful negotiator. *Athletic Business*, 102–107.

Heitner, D. (2013, June 22). Are executive search firms worth the cost to college athletic departments? *Forbes*. Retrieved from www.forbes.com/sites/darrenheitner/2013/06/22/are-executive-search-firms-worth-the-cost-to-college-athletic-departments

Henderson, J. (2013, June 6). Business as unusual for ADs: Job description now has corporate, fundraising tones, as Pac-12 bosses know. *The Denver Post*. Retrieved from www.denverpost.com/ci_23469459/business-unusual-ads

Hosick, M.B. (2009, May 1). Board tackles financial issues. *NCAA News*. Retrieved from www.ncaa.org/wps/ncaa?ContentID=49508

Hosick, M.B. (2011, February 2). Equal opportunity knocks. *The NCAA News*. Retrieved from www.ncaa.com/news/ncaa/2011-02-02/equal-opportunity-knocks

Hoffman, J.L. (2010). The dilemma of the senior woman administrator (SWA) role in intercollegiate athletics. *Journal of Issues in Intercollegiate Athletics*, 3, 53–75. Retrieved from web.ebscohost.com/ehost/pdfviewer/pdfviewer?vid=3&sid=e7cc6cbe-dc2f-493e-9d1d-85d9ded15b47%40sessionmgr12&hid=24

Huma, R., & Staurowsky, E.J. (2013). *The $6 billion heist: Robbing college athletes under the guise of amateurism*. Retrieved from www.ncpanow.org/news_articles?id=0050

Irwin, R., Sutton, W., & McCarthy, L. (2008). *Sport promotion and sales management* (2nd ed.). Champaign, IL: Human Kinetics.

Janoff, B. (2012, November 15). IMG College helping marketers reach college sports fans across venues and platforms. *Broadcasting & Cable*. Retrieved from www.broadcastingcable.com/article/490428-IMG_College_Helping_Marketers_Reach_College_Sports_Fans_Across_Venues_and_Platforms.php

Johnson, G.K. (2009, February 11). Football attendance continues to rise amid economic uncertainty. *NCAA News*. Retrieved from www.ncaa.org/wps/ncaa?ContentID=45320

Kantar Media releases March Madness advertising trends report. (2013, March 6). *KantarMedia.com*. Retrieved from http://kantarmediana.com/intelligence/press/2013-march-madness-advertising-trends-report?destination=node%2F24%2Fpress

Knight Commission on Intercollegiate Athletics. (2009, February). *2009 NCAA Convention—Future of commercial activity*. Retrieved from www.knightcommission.org/index.php?option=com_content&task=view&id=263

Knight Commission on Intercollegiate Athletics. (2013, January 16). College athletic departments spend three to six times more per athlete than their institutions spend to educate each student. Retrieved from www.knightcommission.org/recent-news/794-january-16-2013-college-athletic-departments-spend-three-to-six-times-more-per-athlete-than-their-institutions-spend-to-educate-each-student

Korby, T. (2013, March 21). AIHEC tribal event more than basketball. *Pine Journal*. Retrieved from www.pinejournal.com/event/article/id/29024

Matuszewski, E. (2013, April 24). College Football Playoff will replace Bowl Championship Series. *Bloomsberg Businessweek*. Retrieved from www.bloomberg.com/news/2013-04-23/college-football-playoff-to-replace-bowl-championship-series.html

McDermott, E., & Lynch, M. (2008, April). *Enhancing the role of the SWA*. Paper presented at the 2008 NCAA Gender Equity & Issues Forum, Boston, MA.

Meleney, M. (2009, February 16). President's message. *N4A News*. Retrieved from www.nfoura.org

Membership benefits. (n.d.). Eastern College Athletic Conference. Retrieved from www.ecac.org/membership/index

National Christian College Athletic Association (NCCAA). (2014). About us. Retrieved from www.thenccaa.org/sports/2012/6/20/GEN_0620123640.aspx

National Collegiate Athletic Association (NCAA). (2008). *2008–2009 NCAA Division I manual*. Indianapolis, IN: Author.

NCAA backgrounder on academic reform. (n.d.). Retrieved from www.ncaa.org/wps/ncaa?ContentID=339

NCAA Division I [homepage]. (n.d.). Retrieved from www.ncaa.org/

NCAA eligibility center. (2008, May 7). NCAA freshman-eligibility standards quick reference sheet. Retrieved from www.ncaa.org/wps/wcm/connect/af238a804e0b869285bcf51ad6fc8b25/Quick_Reference_Sheet_for_IE_Standards-5-2-08.pdf?MOD=AJPERES&CACHEID=af238a804e0b869285bcf51ad6fc8b25

NJCAA marketing opportunities. (2013). Retrieved from www.njcaa.org/marketing.cfm

Pignataro, J. (2013). N4A president: Dear colleague message. Cleveland, OH: National Athletic Academic Advisors Association. Retrieved from www.nacda.com/nfoura/presidentscorner.html

Pitts, B.G., & Stotlar, D.K. (2007). *Fundamentals of sport marketing* (3rd ed.). Morgantown, WV: Fitness Information Technology.

President Obama attends game. (2013, March 30). *ESPN.com*. Retrieved from http://espn.go.com/espn/print?id=9115607&type=story#

Q&A with Dave Hart Jr. (2008, May 29). *Athletic Management*. Retrieved from www.athleticmanagement.com/2008/05/qa-with-dave-hart-jr.html

Quarterman, J. (1994). Managerial role profiles of intercollegiate athletic conference commissioners. *Journal of Sport Management*, 8, 129–139.

Reese, J. (2003). Ticket operations. In U. McMahon-Beattie & I. Yeoman (Eds.), *Sport and leisure: A service operations approach* (pp. 167–179). London, England: Continuum.

Reese, J. (2013). *Ticket operations and sales management*. Morgantown, WV: Fitness Information Technology.

Robinson, M. (2009). SMQ profile/interview: Vince Nicastro. *Sport Marketing Quarterly*, 18, 3–5.

Sander, L. (2011, September 18). Students' dream of big-time sports unnerve a wary faculty. *The Chronicle of Higher Education*. Retrieved from https://admin.xosn.com/attachments1/114725.pdf?DB_OEM_ID=5800

Sandomir, R., & Thamel, P. (2010, April 22). TV deal pushes NCAA closer to 68 team tournament. *The New York Times*. Retrieved from www.nytimes.com.

Schneider, R.C., & Stier, W.F. (2005). Necessary education for the success of athletics directors: NCAA presidents' perceptions. *Sport Journal*, 8(1). Retrieved from www.thesportjournal.org/article/necessary-education-success-athletics-directors-ncaa-presidents-perceptions

Schoffel, I., & Henry, J. (2013, June 27). A.D. search firm picked: Committee set to meet. *Tallahassee.com*. Retrieved from www.tallahassee.com/article/20130627/FSU02/306260030/A-D-search-firm-picked-committee-set-meet

Schroeder, G. (2014, January 17). Analysis: At NCAA convention, Div. I path becomes clearer. *USA Today*. Retrieved from www.usatoday.com/story/sports/college/2014/01/17/ncaa-convention-division-i-governance-debate-autonomy/4594249/

Smith, R. (1994). *Big-time football at Harvard 1905: The diary of Coach Bill Reid*. Urbana, IL: University of Illinois Press.

Staurowsky, E.J. (2009). Gender equity in two-year college athletic departments: Part II. *New Directions for Community Colleges*, 147, 63–73.

Stoldt, G.C. (2008). Interview with John Humenik, executive director of the College Sports Information Directors of America. *International Journal of Sport Communication*, 1, 458–464.

Stoldt, G.C., & Vermilion, M. (2013). The organizational roles of college athletics communicators: Relationship to use and perceptions of social media. *Journal of Intercollegiate Sport*, 6, 185–202.

Strauf, D.L. (2002, October 28). Days of the "towel jockey" are long gone. *NCAA News*. Retrieved from www.ncaa.org/wps/ncaa?key=/ncaa/ncaa/ncaa+news/ncaa+news+online/2002/editorial/days+of+the+_towel+jockey_+are+long+gone+-+10-28-02

Talahongva, P. (2009). Counting coups on the courts. *Tribal College Journal*, 20(3), 14–20.

Tiell, B., & Dixon, M.A. (2008). Roles and tasks of the Senior Woman Administrator (SWA) in intercollegiate athletics: A role congruity perspective. *Journal for the Study of Sports and Athletes in Education*, 2(3), 339–361.

Veneziano, J. (2002). *America's oldest intercollegiate athletic event*. Retrieved from www.hcs.harvard.edu/~harvcrew/Website/History/HY

Weinbach, J. (2007, October 19). Inside college sports' biggest money machine. *Wall Street Journal*. Retrieved from http://online.wsj.com/article/SB119275242417864220.html

What is the NWAACC? (2013). Retrieved from www.nwaacc.org/marketing/demographics.pdf

Whisenant, W.A., & Pedersen, P.M. (2004). The influence of managerial activities on the success of intercollegiate athletic directors. *American Business Review*, 22(1), 21–26.

Wieberg, S., & Berkowitz, S. (2009, May 1). NCAA, colleges pushing the envelope with sports marketing. *USA Today*. Retrieved from www.usatoday.com/sports/college/2009-04-01-marketing-cover_N.htm

Wilson, A.S. (2013). *A saga of power, money, and sex in women's athletics: A presidents' history of the Association for Intercollegiate Athletics for Women (AIAW)*. (Doctoral dissertation, University of Iowa). Retrieved from http://ir.uiowa.edu/etd/2661/

Winters, M. (1982). *Professional sports: The community college connection*. Los Angeles, CA: Winmar.

Wolverton, B. (2008, May 23). 2 athletics associations consider joining forces. *Chronicle of Higher Education*. Retrieved from http://chronicle.com/weekly/v54/i37/37a01501.htm

Woodenlegs, T. (2009, March). CDKC Warriors head to AIHEC tourney. *Tseokeameehese*, p. 2. Retrieved from www.cdkc.edu/March%20Newsletter.pdf

Zimbalist, A. (2007, June 18). College athletics budgets are bulging but their profits are slim to none. *Street & Smith's SportsBusiness Journal*, p. 26.

HISTORICAL MOMENTS

1903	First Major League Baseball (MLB) World Series held
1917	National Hockey League (NHL) established
1919	Black Sox scandal in MLB erupted
1920	American Professional Football Association formed, later renamed the National Football League (NFL)
1920	Negro National League formed
1934	First Masters Golf Tournament held
1941	Ted Williams compiled .406 batting average, the last time an MLB player hit over .400 for a season
1946	Basketball Association of America (BAA), forerunner of National Basketball Association (NBA), formed
1947	Jackie Robinson became first African American to play in modern MLB
1950	Ladies Professional Golf Association (LPGA) founded
1967	Super Bowl I held at the Los Angeles Memorial Coliseum—AFL v. NFL World Championship Game
1989	Pete Rose banned from baseball
1995	Cal Ripken broke Lou Gehrig's record of playing in 2,130 consecutive games
2006	Effa Manley became the first woman elected to the National Baseball Hall of Fame
2009	Martin Brodeur won 557th career game; attained NHL career wins record
2011	Ultimate Fighting Championship (UFC) debuted on Fox TV Network
2012	MLB's San Diego Padres and Los Angeles Dodgers purchased for US$800 million and US$2 billion, respectively
2013	Andy Murray became the first British tennis player in 77 years to win the men's singles Wimbledon title
2014	Jason Collins, center for the Brooklyn Nets, played his first game as the NBA's first openly gay player
2014	New Jersey and New York worked together to host NFL's Super Bowl XLVIII at MetLife Stadium

PROFESSIONAL SPORT

James ("Jay") M. Gladden \ William A. Sutton

LEARNING OBJECTIVES

> Define, explain, and discuss the development of professional sport.

> Describe the unique facets of professional sport, including its governance and the labor–management relationship on which professional team sports depend.

> Document the significance of the relationship between media—including new and social media—and professional sport.

> Describe the major revenue sources for a professional sport team.

> Identify the types of employment opportunities available in this segment of the sport industry.

> Apply ethical reasoning and critical thinking skills to issues in professional sport.

Key Terms

collective bargaining

labor

league think

LED signage

local television contracts

luxury tax

management

salary caps

sponsorship

virtual signage

GET A JOB

Continue on your journey in sport management by going to the web study guide (WSG) at www.HumanKinetics.com/ContemporarySportManagement. Check out the job opportunities and consider the skills and experiences that can help you succeed in sport management.

Professional sport is any sport activity or skill for which the athlete is compensated. Compensation can be in the form of salary, bonuses, reimbursement for expenses, or any other type of direct payment. The activity that the athlete performs can be a team sport such as basketball, a dual sport such as tennis, an individual sport such as figure skating or skateboarding, or a sport entertainment performance such as World Wrestling Entertainment (WWE). A representative list of some professional sports in North America includes the following:

Baseball
Basketball
Billiards
Bodybuilding
Bowling
Boxing
Curling
Football
Golf
Hockey
Horse racing
Ice skating

Mixed martial arts
Motocross
Racquetball
Rodeo
Skateboarding
Skiing
Snowboarding
Soccer
Surfing
Tennis
Triathlon
Volleyball

Major events such as the Super Bowl involve much more than the highly publicized on-field competition since there are many tangential activities (e.g., business endeavors, promotional efforts, networking opportunities, social and fan engagement) surrounding such professional sport events.

Professional sport events such as the Ultimate Fighting Championship (UFC), Super Bowl, World Series, Masters Golf Tournament, Indianapolis 500, U.S. Open Tennis Championships, Kentucky Derby, and X Games now occupy the heart of North

American sport. Although the preceding list mentions both team sports and sports featuring the individual, this chapter concentrates on professional team sport because of its profound economic effect and the number of job opportunities available in this segment of the sport industry. Professional sport exemplifies sport at its highest level of performance, and it generates the majority of coverage devoted to sport through the print, electronic, and new media.

As packaged events, professional team sports (e.g., men's and women's football, men's and women's ice hockey, men's and women's soccer, men's baseball, women's softball, men's and women's basketball) provide considerable entertainment and pleasure for spectators. As such, demands on the three principals that form the professional sport industry—labor, management, and governance—are complex, diverse, and ever changing. Labor aggressively continues to protect and procure additional resources for its membership, which is made up of the professional athletes. Management, or the owners of professional teams, is trying to win back some leverage and control lost to labor over the past few decades. Finally, governance, made up of the professional sport leagues, attempts to regulate, but not completely control, both labor and management. In professional team sport, governance is the league structure that exists to oversee both the competitive and business elements of the sport.

Historical Aspects of Professional Sport

Professional sport can be traced to ancient Greece where, beginning with the Olympic Games in 776 BCE, a class of professionals in sport known as athletai existed. These athletai were well-paid men recruited from mercenary armies and trained exclusively for brutal competition (Freedman, 1987). In exchange for competing and winning, athletai often received remuneration in the form of prizes and money.

Although baseball is often considered America's national pastime, it was not the first sport that professionals played. Boxers, jockeys, and runners were paid for their prowess during the early and mid-19th century. Baseball, however, was the first team sport to employ professionals. In 1869, the Cincinnati Red Stockings became the first professional baseball team. Their appearance was closely followed in 1871 by the National Association of Professional Base Ball Players (NAPBBP), the first professional sport league (Rader, 2009). In 1876, William Hulbert formed the National League, the precursor to MLB as we know it today.

A recognized professional league in another sport did not form until after the turn of the 20th century. In 1917, the NHL emerged after the National Hockey Association of Canada Limited suspended its operations. This was closely followed in 1921 with the creation of the NFL. The National Basketball League (NBL), founded in 1937, was the first professional basketball league. In 1949, the NBA resulted from a merger between the NBL and the Basketball Association of America (BAA) (Staudohar & Mangan, 1991).

Inclusion (and Exclusion) in Professional Sport

Although professional team sport has been in existence for more than 100 years, only in the past 80 years have professional sport opportunities become available to many minority segments of the American population. Professional sport opportunities were segregated until 1947, when Jackie Robinson broke baseball's modern color line with the Brooklyn Dodgers. The National Colored Baseball League was founded in 1887 as an outlet for African American baseball players who were not allowed to play in the all-White major leagues. This league failed because of lack of attendance. But in 1920, the Negro National League was formed. This league and others, such as the Eastern Negro League and Negro American League, afforded players such as Satchel Paige,

labor—A collective group of athletes in team sports who unionize so that they can bargain collectively with the league owners (i.e., management). Labor is typically represented by a union head in negotiations with management.

management—When referring to the collective bargaining process, management refers to the collective group of ownership that is negotiating with the players, or labor. Management is typically represented by a league commissioner, who is technically an agent for the owners, in negotiations with labor.

Josh Gibson, and even Robinson an opportunity to play professionally (*Negro League Baseball*, 2003). In addition, most owners, club managers, reporters, and umpires in the Negro leagues were also African American.

Professional sport outlets for women have arisen only in the past 80 years. In the 1940s, the first women's professional league, the All-American Girls Professional Baseball League (AAGPBL), was formed. Created in 1943 in response to decreased player quality in MLB during World War II and the popularity of women's amateur softball, the AAGPBL played 11 seasons before folding in 1954 because of poor management (Browne, 1992). Since 1954, a number of other women's professional leagues have operated, mainly in the sport of basketball.

In the mid-1960s, women began playing semipro tackle football, and by the 1970s, teams were competing in Ohio, New York, Michigan, and Pennsylvania. In 1974, the Women's Professional Football League (WPFL) was established with teams in Dallas, Fort Worth, Columbus, Toledo, Los Angeles, and Detroit. During the ensuing years, a number of leagues emerged as women expressed interest and ability in tackle football. Examples of these women's professional football leagues include the Women's American Football League (WAFL), American Football Women's League (AFWL), United Football League, Independent Women's Football League (IWFL), National Women's Football Association (NWFA), Women's Football League, Women's Spring Football League, and Women's Football Alliance (WFA).

The past two decades have seen a resurgence of interest in women's professional sport. In 1996, two women's professional basketball leagues were formed: the American Basketball League (ABL) and the WNBA. The ABL played over two seasons before folding because of financial difficulties, which were at least partially because of competition from the NBA-sponsored WNBA. In June 1997, the Women's Professional Fastpitch (WPF) softball league began. During the summer of 2001, the Women's United Soccer Association (WUSA) began play, but it folded in 2003 because of financial difficulties. In 2009, Women's Professional Soccer (WPS) marked the second formal attempt for women's soccer. While this second attempt was unsuccessful as well, ceasing operations in 2012, the inaugural season of the National Women's Soccer League (NWSL) occurred in 2013.

Unique Aspects of Professional Sport

Four aspects of professional sport distinguish it from other industries: interdependence, structure and governance, labor–management relations, and the role of the electronic and new media.

Interdependence

league think—Pioneered and most effectively implemented by the NFL, this term represents the notion that teams must recognize the importance of their competition and share revenues to ensure that their competitors remain strong.

The central premise that differentiates professional team sport from any other business is the need for teams to compete and cooperate simultaneously (Mullin, Hardy, & Sutton, 2014). In other words, the teams depend on one another to stage the games that constitute the product. In his classic work on the NFL, *The League*, David Harris (1986) described this unique situation as **league think**. When teams function together collectively, some teams sacrifice the potential for higher revenue in the interest of league stability. For example, the Dallas Cowboys and Oakland Raiders typically sell a disproportionate amount of NFL-licensed merchandise. This money, however, is pooled and shared equally among all 32 NFL teams. The presence of the Cowboys and Raiders in the collective bargaining agreement (CBA) increases the revenue generated for all NFL member teams. Because of their location in large television markets, the New York Giants and Chicago Bears function in much the same way during television negotiations. The key is that all members make sacrifices and concessions for the long-term benefit and growth of the league.

Although major professional sport leagues differ in the extent to which they share revenues, each league pools its revenues to some extent. For example, NFL teams all share equally in their national media contracts (e.g., cable, satellite, network), and they cannot negotiate separate local media contracts, whereas baseball teams share only their national contracts and keep all revenue from their local agreements. These local agreements can vary significantly in the amount of revenue produced. Large-market teams (clubs located in heavily populated cities that have the potential to negotiate lucrative local media contracts), such as the New York Yankees, have local broadcast packages that are significantly larger than those of small-market teams (clubs in midsize or smaller markets whose potential for local media contracts is not that high), such as the Kansas City Royals. Over the past 15 years, the disparity in local media revenues has created significant discrepancies in the amount of money that MLB teams are able to pay their players. Such revenue disparities led MLB to implement a **luxury tax** on teams that had the highest payrolls. Teams with disproportionately high payrolls pay a tax to MLB, and the collected luxury tax money is then shared among teams with lower payrolls.

luxury tax—Device used to tax the teams that spend the most (or spend too much as defined by the CBA) on player payroll; those taxes are then shared with teams that do not have high payrolls.

Structure and Governance

Each professional sport has its own structure and system of governance, typically referred to as the league office, which usually involves the following components:

› League commissioner
› Board of governors or committee structure composed of the team owners
› A central administrative unit that negotiates contracts and agreements on behalf of the league and assumes responsibility for scheduling, licensing, record keeping, financial management, discipline and fines, revenue-sharing payments, marketing and promotional activities, developing and managing special events, and other functions such as coordinating publicity and advertising on behalf of the teams as a whole

For example, MLB is composed of 30 teams situated in two leagues (National and American—see table 9.1). Each league consists of three divisions (i.e., East, Central, and West). The MLB commissioner is responsible for representing the interests of all

Table 9.1   Organization of Major League Baseball

National League East	National League Central	National League West	American League East	American League Central	American League West
Atlanta Braves	Chicago Cubs	Colorado Rockies	Baltimore Orioles	Chicago White Sox	Houston Astros
Miami Marlins	Cincinnati Reds	Los Angeles Dodgers	Boston Red Sox	Cleveland Indians	Los Angeles Angels of Anaheim
Washington Nationals	Milwaukee Brewers	San Diego Padres	New York Yankees	Detroit Tigers	Oakland A's
New York Mets	Pittsburgh Pirates	San Francisco Giants	Tampa Bay Rays	Kansas City Royals	Seattle Mariners
Philadelphia Phillies	St. Louis Cardinals	Arizona Diamondbacks	Toronto Blue Jays	Minnesota Twins	Texas Rangers

parties associated with professional baseball. These parties include owners, players, fans, television networks, corporate sponsors, host cities and venues, and the minor leagues. Contrast this organizational structure with mainstream business. For example, no authority governs the actions of candy manufacturers Hershey's and Mars in their attempts to make money.

Baseball is unique in having an extensive minor league system, which provides an elaborate way of preparing players to participate in the major leagues. Each major league team has at least four affiliate teams in the minor leagues. As long as they meet certain standards in terms of the size of their facilities, owners of minor league teams can enter into contractual relationships with major league clubs whereby the minor league team becomes an affiliate of a major league team. The cultivation of minor league systems is increasingly popular among the other major professional sport leagues. For example, the NBA Development League commonly referred to as the "D League," began play in 2001. In 2013, the league had 17 teams playing in 13 states. The purpose of the league is to provide a training ground for players, referees, coaches, front-office personnel, and other operational staff who want to prepare for a possible career in the NBA. Each D-League team has one or more NBA affiliates. For example, the Bakersfield Jam is affiliated with both the Los Angeles Clippers and the Golden State Warriors. The 2013 champion, the Rio Grande Valley Vipers, has an affiliate relationship with the Houston Rockets.

Labor–Management Relations

Five unique circumstances and conditions are present in the labor–management relationship in North American professional sport: baseball's antitrust exemption, collective bargaining, free agency, salary caps, and player draft. Some aspects are the opposite of common, traditional business practices and philosophies. But the participating parties consider such idiosyncrasies essential to preserving the financial stability of the professional sport product. The following sections examine each element and explain its uniqueness and significance to professional sport.

BASEBALL'S ANTITRUST EXEMPTION

Perhaps the most exceptional condition in professional sport is MLB's exemption from the rules and regulations of the Sherman Antitrust Act. This antitrust legislation was created to prohibit companies from dominating their respective markets in interstate commercial activity, thus creating a monopoly in which consumers have only one product choice rather than several. As a result of the U.S. Supreme Court's ruling in the *Federal Base Ball Club of Baltimore, Inc. v. National League of Professional Base Ball Clubs* (1922), MLB was granted an exemption to antitrust law. In its decision, the court deemed that baseball was local in nature, did not involve the production of a tangible good, and thus was not subject to interstate commerce law. In effect, this ruling granted MLB the right to undertake strategies that would prevent the establishment of competitive leagues. This exemption gives professional baseball team owners significant leverage over the cities in which they operate. In some cases, owners have threatened to leave their host cities if new stadiums are not built. Although MLB's exemption from antitrust regulations has been challenged on several occasions, the courts have not overturned the decision.

COLLECTIVE BARGAINING

Workers involved in interstate commerce, which includes all professional team sport (except MLB because of its antitrust exemption), are covered by the National Labor Relations Act (NLRA). The NLRA provides three basic rights that are at the center of labor relations policy in the United Sates: (1) the right to self-organize, form, join, or assist labor organizations, (2) the right to bargain collectively through agents of one's own choosing, and (3) the right to engage in concerted activities for employees' mutual aid or protection (Staudohar, 1989). In professional team sport, the NLRA provides players the right to join a union, to have a basic player contract (establishing a minimum salary, benefits, and working conditions) negotiated collectively by union representatives, and to strike or conduct other activities that help achieve objectives. The term **collective bargaining** is used because all active league players are in the bargaining unit and thus form a collective unit (labor) for negotiating and bargaining with the owners (management). Teams join as a league in bargaining with the players union so that in each league the negotiated contract applies to all teams uniformly. Some of the issues that are subject to collective bargaining include salary (minimum and maximum), drug testing, and discipline procedures.

FREE AGENCY

Free agency is the ability of players, after fulfilling an agreed-upon (through a CBA) number of years of service with a team, to sell their services to another team with limited or no compensation to the team losing the players. Thus the terms *free agent* and *free agency* have evolved to signify the relative freedom that all professional team sport players have to move from one team to another. Professional team sport, however, still imposes significant restrictions on its labor. For example, players do not immediately become free agents. Instead, free agency is a negotiated item in the CBA of all professional team sport leagues. The CBA recognizes the investment that the team has incurred in developing the player, while also recognizing the fair market value of the player in the open market. Thus, the CBA provides free agency after the player has played an agreed-upon (by both labor and management) number of years.

The implementation of free agency in the mid-1970s had a profound effect on the economics of professional sport. After professional athletes gained the freedom to negotiate with the highest bidder, their salaries escalated astronomically. In 1976, when the players first earned the right to become free agents, the average salary in professional baseball was US$46,000. In 2012, the average salary in MLB was US$3.44 million, which represented a 4% increase over 2011 (CBS Sports, 2013). Similar salaries exist in the other men's major professional sport leagues (i.e., NHL, NFL, and NBA), while the average salaries for women's professional sport teams are currently much lower. For example, the average WNBA salary in 2012 was US$72,000, with the maximum salary being US$105,000. The heightened power of the players' unions and increased salaries of players contributed to an increase in labor stoppages in the professional

collective bargaining— Process used to negotiate work terms between labor and management. All active league players are in a bargaining unit and thus form a collective unit (i.e., labor) for negotiating and bargaining with the owners (i.e., management).

Organizations will sometimes try unique strategies to entice the athlete to stay. Here, the Los Angeles Lakers placed a billboard and used social media (#STAYD12) in the team's attempt to keep Dwight Howard, who eventually spurned the team and signed with the Houston Rockets.

sport leagues. With player salaries continuing to rise, owners of professional sport teams are facing the challenge of generating sufficient revenue to match those increased costs. Such concerns have led owners to take an increasingly tough stance during collective bargaining negotiations. Because of management–labor salary disputes, work stoppages have become a frequent occurrence.

SALARY CAPS

With the onset of free agency in the 1970s, players who became unrestricted free agents (those who had fulfilled the terms of their contracts) were able to sign with the highest bidder or whomever they chose. Consequently, spending on player salaries increased significantly, particularly among teams with greater resources. In response, salary caps that set a ceiling on player payrolls were created to protect the owners, essentially from themselves, from overbidding for talent. Salary caps are agreements collectively bargained between labor and management that establish a league-wide team payroll threshold that cannot be exceeded in most cases. The salary cap is typically set using a percentage of league gross revenues as a starting point. Pioneered by the NBA in 1983 and implemented for the 1985–86 season, the salary cap guarantees that players will receive an established percentage of all gross revenues. The initial NBA salary cap established this percentage at 53%, the 2005 CBA set it at 57%, and the latest CBA, implemented in 2011, sets the percentage between 49% and 51% over the 10-year agreement.

Salary caps ensure parity between large- and small-market teams as well as between owners whose resources may vary considerably. In addition to the NBA, the NFL, the NHL, and MLS have all adopted a salary-cap structure; of the four major professional sport leagues in the United States, only MLB does not have a cap. The NBA salary cap is referred to as a soft cap, meaning there are exceptions where the team can exceed the salary cap such as the Bird rule, where the team can offer a contract of five years at maximum value to retain their free agent, whereas another team attempting to sign that player may only sign that player to a four-year contract. Thus, when Dwight Howard signed as a free agent with the Houston Rockets in 2013, he accepted a four-year contract for a total amount of US$30 million less than the Los Angeles Lakers had offered him (Amick, 2013).

The NFL and NHL both operate with hard salary caps, meaning there are no exceptions to the collectively bargained cap amount. The consequence of a hard cap is that higher paid veteran players are often released (contracts terminated) in lieu of keeping a younger player who commands less salary because of his tenure. The hard cap is much more stringent and understandably much less acceptable to players and their labor unions.

A luxury tax, defined earlier in the chapter, is also an attempt to ensure competitive balance. The luxury tax in professional sports is a surcharge put on the aggregate payroll of a team to the extent to which it exceeds a predetermined guideline level set by the league. The ostensible purpose of this tax is to prevent teams in major markets with high incomes from signing almost all of the more talented players and hence destroying the competitive balance necessary for a sport to maintain fan interest. The money derived from the tax can be divided among the teams that play in the smaller markets, presumably to allow them to have more revenue to devote toward the contracts of high-quality players. In the case of MLB, it is used by the league for other predefined purposes, such as investing in international player development and in domestic player development, such as the minor leagues (Dietl, Lang, & Warner, 2010). In both the NBA and MLB, teams that have payrolls in excess of the salary cap must pay the luxury tax, but they are not permitted to share in the distribution of the tax revenue.

In North America, MLB has implemented the luxury tax system. The NBA also has a luxury tax provision; its utility is somewhat limited by the fact that the league also

salary caps—Agreements collectively bargained between labor and management that establish a league-wide team payroll (i.e., salaries, bonuses, and incentive clauses) threshold that cannot be exceeded in most cases. The salary cap is typically set using a percentage of league gross revenues as a starting point.

has a salary cap provision. The hard salary cap of the NFL and the NHL has prevented any need for a luxury tax arrangement (Andreff & Szymanski, 2006).

PLAYER DRAFT

In accordance with the principles of league think, the player draft aims to be an equitable system for distributing new talent among all league members. The draft provides each professional sport league with a mechanism for the teams with poor records to have an advantage over teams with winning records in acquiring talented new players. Through the draft, teams voluntarily agree to restrict competition for new talent. As a result, the team that drafts a player determines the player's destination and salary. Phenomena such as the player draft do not exist in other areas of the labor market. Imagine a scenario in which top sport management graduates were restricted as to whom they could work for and where they could work by an annual draft held by sport businesses throughout the country! Collective bargaining agreements in men's basketball and men's football have sought to limit the number of rounds of the draft. This limitation results in fewer players getting drafted and more players becoming free agents to sign with any team that offers them a contract.

Role of the Electronic and New Media

The electronic and new media—network television, cable and satellite television, terrestrial and satellite radio, and the Internet—play a critical role in driving the popularity of professional sport and generating additional revenue for associated teams. As we are in the second decade of the 21st century, new media sources such as satellite television and the Internet could be the next important horizons in broadening the reach of professional team sport and the enhancement of league revenue streams.

IMPORTANCE OF TELEVISION

No single factor has influenced the popularity of sport, the escalation in player salaries, free agency, and the growth and increase of corporate involvement in professional sport more than television. TV has helped elevate professional sport beyond competition and athleticism into the realm of entertainment. *Monday Night Football* (MNF), which is now on ESPN, was a pioneering effort to package professional sport as entertainment. Although there were popular televised spectacles for other sports (e.g., boxing, roller derby, bowling), the prime-time extravaganza of *MNF* sought to reach more than just traditional football fans by adding analysis, commentary, special guests, additional camera angles, video replays, graphics, and highlights to enhance the event and broaden its appeal to women and other nontraditional viewing groups (Roberts & Olson, 1995). Concurrent with the success of *MNF*, the ultimate TV sport spectacle, the Super Bowl, was created. Born from the rivalry and merger of the NFL and the American Football League (AFL), the Super Bowl has become one of the most successful televised events of all time, viewed by millions around the world.

Leagues associated with professional sport need TV for three reasons. First, as already discussed, the leagues and member teams receive significant revenue outlays from network, satellite, and cable TV agreements. Second, TV enhances the enjoyment associated with watching professional sport events. Third, TV helps increase the amount that teams and leagues can charge for sponsorships because of the increased exposure that it provides.

Emerging Sources of Media Coverage

Imagine that you grew up in Chicago and now live on the East Coast. Because of where you were raised, you are an ardent follower of the Chicago professional sports teams (the Bulls, Red Stars, Bears, Sky, Cubs, Fire, White Sox, and Blackhawks). Unless these

WEB

Go to the WSG and complete the first web search activity, which will help you investigate how *Monday Night Football* has affected many areas of professional sport.

teams make the playoffs, however, you are rarely able to follow your team through radio or cable television broadcasts. Millions of fans worldwide face this dilemma. But solutions are becoming increasingly available to such fans. Most notably, satellite television and the Internet have greatly increased the access of sport fans to a full menu of sport events.

Satellite technology and satellite television providers such as DirecTV have worked with the leagues to create packages whereby the average sport fan can access any game during the season either by paying an up-front fee for season-long access or by subscribing (paying a one-time fee) on a game-by-game basis. For example, in 2013, for US$299, owners of a satellite television system received NFL Sunday Ticket, which provided them access to all regular season games. Satellite radio provider Sirius/XM also allows displaced fans an opportunity to follow their favorite teams on a regular basis for a monthly fee. The Internet is affording fans a higher level of access to games of interest. Increasingly, the right to stream live games or other team- and league-related content directly to tablets and cellphones are a significant part of media rights negotiations. Fans can now listen to and view various online sporting events and broadcasts, sometimes even using their smartphones to do so! For example, in the scenario described earlier, the Chicago fan living on the East Coast could watch every Cubs game on MLB.com.

Revenue Sources for Professional Sport Teams

Revenue sources for sport organizations are discussed in more detail in chapter 15. We will discuss here some unique aspects of revenue generation in professional sport.

Media Contracts

local television contracts—Agreements made between professional teams and local television stations and regional sport networks. These agreements provide teams with additional media revenue beyond what they receive from the national television contract.

The details of the national media contracts for a variety of professional sport leagues are presented in chapter 15 (see table 15.2). One major distinction is found with respect to media revenues in professional sport. Namely, MLB, the NBA, and the NHL all permit their member teams to negotiate local television contracts for regular season games, whereas the NFL does not. This arrangement results in great disparity in revenue among teams. For example, the Yankees generate significantly more income from the local television contract with the Yankees Entertainment and Sports (YES) Network than do the Pittsburgh Pirates through their agreement with Root Sports.

The dollar amounts presented in chapter 15 (see table 15.2) may evolve in the future. The leagues have been successful in increasing the total rights fees paid in recent negotiations, in part because the leagues have been able to discover (and subsequently charge for) new ways to deliver game video and associated content. However, the future ability to increase rights fees may be lessened as a result of the following factors:

> Each league now has its own network (e.g., MLB Network, NHL Network) from which to broadcast games; hence, the leagues are becoming limited competitors as well as partners. The leagues may seek to increase the inventory offered by their own networks, which could decrease the rights fees generated from outside sources.

> Sponsorship dollars that are a large part of television rights were diminished by the economic crisis of 2008–2010. Corporate sponsors are now more discerning than ever in deciding if and how to spend their marketing dollars.

> Leisure and entertainment offerings have never been more fragmented and diverse. Additionally, alternative delivery options (e.g., smartphones, tablets) are changing the way people consume live sporting events.

Social Media and Professional Sport

Social media can be an invaluable tool for driving the popularity of a professional sports team. Although you might not think of it immediately, such efforts can actually be led by the owner. No, owners do not actually play in the games, but they can be positive and visible figures associated with the team by demonstrating an interest in the fans.

A great example of this is Jim Irsay, owner of the NFL's Indianapolis Colts. Irsay regularly uses Twitter (@ JimIrsay) to promote various aspects of the team he owns. In one three-week period in the summer of 2013, Irsay used Twitter (his preferred social media tool) to promote a Colts season-opening concert, a 5K run sponsored by the Colts, the date of the 2013 season's first practice, and the next location for the Colts' travelling fan festival. In all four cases, Irsay promoted ways for his more than 250,000 followers to become engaged with the Colts. Irsay, who is known for having a fun-loving personality, also regularly runs contests where he gives money away to Twitter followers who answer such questions as which hip he had replaced! In all cases, Irsay uses Twitter and social media to communicate with fans of the Colts in the hope that he will be able to develop more fans and deeper connections for his franchise.

Gate Receipts

As late as 1950, gate receipts and concessions accounted for more than 92% of the revenue of professional teams (Gorman & Calhoun, 1994). With the increasing importance of media revenues, professional sport teams have become less reliant on gate receipts, although they remain the major source of revenue for NHL and MLS teams as well as minor league baseball. In addition, gate receipts have historically been the most important source of revenue for newer professional leagues such as the WNBA. The home team retains the majority of the gate receipts, but to varying degrees, depending on the league, a portion of the gate receipts is given to the league (to cover their operating expenses) and a portion of the proceeds may be given to the visiting team. This is not to say that gate receipts are not of consequence to MLB, the NBA, and the NFL. For example, in 2012, the Yankees grossed an estimated US$330 million in gate receipts and premium seat sales (Badenhausen, 2013). Table 9.2 provides a sampling of attendance information from a variety of professional sport leagues.

Table 9.2 **Attendance Information from Select Professional Sport Leagues***

League	Average attendance	Percent of capacity	Number of teams at 90% of capacity or greater
NFL (2012)	67,394	95.4%	25 out of 32
NBA (2012–13)	17,274	90.8%	18 out of 30
NHL (2012–13)	17,768	96.9%	25 out of 30
MLB (2012)	30,362	71.3%	5 out of 30
MLS (2008)	18,807	85.7%	7 out of 19
WNBA (2008)	7,457	72.1%	1 out of 12

Adapted from *Street & Smith's SportsBusiness Journal* and *Sports Business Daily*.

NFL Turnstile tracker, January 7, 2013, *Street & Smith's SportsBusiness Journal*, p. 12; NBA Turnstile tracker, April 29, 2013, *Street & Smith's SportsBusiness Journal*, p. 15; NHL Turnstile tracker, May 6, 2013, *Street & Smith's SportsBusiness Journal*, p. 13; MLB Turnstile tracker, October 8, 2012, *Street & Smith's SportsBusiness Journal*, p.5; MLS Turnstile tracker, May 4, 2009, *Street & Smith's SportsBusiness Journal*, p. 12; WNBA Turnstile tracker, September 22, 2008, *Street & Smith's SportsBusiness Journal*, p. 17.

Licensing and Merchandising Revenues

Licensing revenues are generated when leagues and teams grant merchandise and apparel manufacturers the right to use their names and logos. In return for that right, the leagues and teams receive a royalty (i.e., a percentage of the selling price) for each item sold by the manufacturers. These agreements have been an increasingly lucrative source of revenue for professional teams. Licensing programs, administered by the league offices, distribute the revenue equally among the teams. Domestic licensing revenues, however, have begun to plateau as the market for such merchandise has become saturated. The ability to continue to increase licensing revenues depends partly on the growth and demand for league-licensed video games and the demand for league-licensed products overseas. Although leagues continue to seek new opportunities for revenue growth, this revenue stream appears to have leveled off over the last dozen years.

Sponsorship

Consider for a moment the magnitude of these sponsorship agreements (Leuty, 2013):

> › Farmers Insurance has committed to paying US$600 million for a proposed football stadium in Los Angeles.

> › Citigroup is paying US$400 million over 20 years so that the New York Mets baseball stadium and site of the 2013 All-Star Game could be called Citi Field.

> › Barclays PLC is paying $200 million over 20 years to name the basketball arena in Brooklyn, New York, the Barclays Center.

sponsorship—The acquisition of rights to affiliate or associate directly with a product or event for the purpose of deriving benefits related to that affiliation or association (Mullin, Hardy, & Sutton, 2014).

Given Mullin, Hardy, and Sutton's (2014) definition of **sponsorship**, these associations and affiliations could be quite lucrative.

Most leagues and teams have more than 100 sponsorship agreements in place, and they are always looking for more. Revenue per agreement has dropped in recent years, putting more pressure on teams and leagues to find additional sponsors to make up the revenue shortfall. The benefits provided to sponsors often include signage that is visible in the sport venue as well as on television (local broadcasts only). The demand for signage location visible to both attendees and television viewers has led sport marketers to seek new and innovative display techniques such as rotational signage (stationary signage placed on scoreboards and around the playing surfaces that rotates the advertisements

A stadium vendor sells licensed merchandise and souvenirs at an Oakland Athletics game in Oakland, California.

shown, usually in 15- to 30-second intervals), **LED signage** (much more visual computer-generated signage that can be animated and is typically found above the lower bowl and below the upper bowl in arenas and stadiums), and **virtual signage** (also computer-generated but imposed over an existing space, such as the wall behind home plate on telecasts during baseball games).

Future Challenges Facing Professional Sport

As teams in professional sport move to the future, they face a variety of challenges (and opportunities), many of which are discussed in this chapter. Although the challenges are too many to enumerate in this section, we have isolated four major challenges that professional teams face in the future: maintaining reasonable labor–management relations, developing new revenue streams, managing new technology, and dealing with globalization.

> *Maintaining labor–management harmony.* First, given the history of acrimony between the players (labor) and the owners (management), and the history of work stoppages (i.e., strikes or lockouts), a continual challenge for professional sport will be ensuring that the games go on. As evidenced by the NHL lockout that cancelled the entire 2004–05 season and subsequent NHL work stoppage in 2012, accomplishing this goal is not always easy. Although typically a variety of issues create tension between labor and management, the most visible conflict is associated with the owners' desire to manage costs, mostly tied to players' salaries. At the same time, the players are seeking their fair share of the ever-increasing revenues generated by teams and their owners. For this reason, labor disputes are likely to keep occurring.

> *Developing new revenue streams.* The increased salaries of professional athletes affected the business of sport. To fund continued increases, team owners are looking for new revenue streams or ways to enhance existing revenue streams. Technological advances, such as the virtual signage and satellite television opportunities examined earlier, have already provided significant new revenues to leagues and teams. Such quests for revenue enhancement are likely to continue in the future, and technology will probably be involved. Think for a minute about how our world is shrinking because of technology. Professional sport crosses international barriers with increasing regularity.

In fact, globalization, along with branding of a sponsor name on team uniforms, is the largest revenue frontier yet to be crossed by sport teams and leagues based in the United States (with the notable exception of Canada, which serves as a permanent host to teams in all of the major U.S.-based team sports with the exception of the NFL). By globalization, we currently mean any or all of the following activities:

> Sales and distribution of broadcast and other media rights outside of their country of origin

> Merchandise sales occurring outside of the country of the respective team identified on the merchandise

> Corporate partnerships that can be activated outside of the country of origin of the corporate entity

> Exhibition contests, regular season games, and tours played outside of the continental United States and Canada by U.S.–based professional leagues and teams and also by college conferences and their respective teams

> Extending social media content outside the national boundaries of the country of origin producing the content

LED signage—Signage located in the arena bowl and primarily found on the fascia below the upper bowl. This signage is computer generated and has the capability to add sound, animation, and other visual effects to present a colorful eye-catching message. LED (light-emitting diode) signage is usually sold in 30-second increments, with a predetermined number of rotations per game.

virtual signage—Signage that is generated by digital technology and placed into a sport event telecast so that it appears as though the sign is part of the playing surface or adjacent to the playing surface.

Fostering the People:
Membership as a Revenue Source in Australian Sport

By Adam Karg, Australia
Deakin University, Melbourne

For corporate sport organizations such as professional teams, revenue is generated from a range of sources, including media and broadcast deals, match day or ticketing sales, and commercial sources such as sponsorship and licensing. In different markets, the proportion each contributes can differ based on market orientation, commercial strategy, or the brand equity of the team or sport. Under a relationship marketing approach, high volumes of season ticket holders (STHs) are emerging as an increasingly valuable component within this revenue mix. This is particularly the case in Australia, where STHs (also referred to as members) provide substantial portions of the revenue collected by teams each year, as well as a range of other benefits.

Hawthorn fans react on the final siren after winning the AFL premiership.

Australian rules football, a sport indigenous to Australia, has seen particular success in developing STH strategies as part of its business strategy. The Australian Football League (AFL), currently made up of 18 professional teams or *clubs*, is Australia's largest professional sport league. In 2012, it attracted a cumulative attendance total of over 7 million. Its average match attendance consistently ranks it within the top five professional football leagues globally. In 1987, the 14 AFL clubs had around 70,000 members in total. Currently, over 700,000 people—or around 1 in 32 Australians—are members of an AFL club. What is especially unique in the case of the AFL is that 9 of the 18 clubs are based in the city of Melbourne, Australia's second largest city. Considering this market, 1 in 10 Melbournians are members of an AFL club.

Within this density of appeal, the make-up and size of team member bases can differ. In multiple sports, Australian teams have been able to convert between 5% and 25% of their fans to membership, often across a suite of products. As such,

Most of the activities described in the preceding list, as well as those in the following, are already occurring throughout Europe and other continents primarily in the sport of football (or, as we refer to it in the United States, soccer). Globalization by professional teams in the United States over the next 10 years or so is projected to mean all of the activities previously listed, plus some or all of the following:

the membership product provides opportunities to engage fans and build relationships with them, while generating and cultivating a continuing revenue stream (STH renewal rates of over 85%, or in some cases over 90%, have been seen in recent years). Of course, for the revenue stream to be sustainable, clubs and the league have had to constantly rethink and improve their approach to customer service and service quality, investing heavily in centralized and club specific services and research to understand best practice STH management.

The value of this investment has been significant, though, with membership comparable to other major revenue streams for the case of the AFL. While the value of membership to clubs may not yet reach the contribution of the recent AFL broadcast deal that nets the sport over US$235 million a year, its contribution to teams' overall revenue is comparable to the total contribution of sponsorship within the sport, which has recently been valued at around US$120 million to US$140 million.

The AFL's successful approach in converting and engaging a high volume of consumers to membership continues to deliver financial and additional rewards to teams and the sport. More recently, STH or membership is becoming an increasing focus in the strategies of other sports and teams, including cricket, rugby union, rugby league, and soccer. Membership-type subscription products are also emerging for different properties such as the Australian Open Grand Slam tennis tournament and for largely overseas-based teams such as the Australian-owned International ProTour professional cycling team, Orica Green Edge.

International Learning Activity #1

Apart from the revenue created by STHs or members, there are a range of other advantages that member bases provide for sport organizations such as professional teams. List and discuss these, including any influence they might have on other revenue streams gathered by corporate sport organizations.

International Learning Activity #2

Research the season ticket products offered by a sport team in your local market. What features and innovations are present in the way these products are developed, serviced, and marketed? What suggestions could you make to improve the STH product or experience for your researched organization?

International Learning Activity #3

Teams convert fans to season ticket holders at different rates across different sports. What might some of the barriers be to fans becoming STHs, and how might these barriers be overcome by organizations? Additionally, there are reasons why STH do not renew their ticket. Develop a list of these potential reasons and some strategies the club could implement to arrest churn, or lapsed member, rates.

International Learning Activity #4

Given technological advancements and the increasing quality of the at-home experience, media-dominant consumers are emerging in many markets, which may threaten the ongoing attractiveness of the season ticket. As such, consumers may make trade-offs between the media experience and live or stadium-based products, including season tickets. Given this, how might the season ticket product be adapted to maintain relevance for these consumers?

> Sanctioned competitions involving U.S. teams and non–North American professional teams competing in a meaningful league contest that involves standings and records

> A championship event in which the winner is truly acknowledged and accepted as the World Champion

› *Meeting technology challenges.* The same technologies that have helped spread the popularity of professional sport and increase revenues have also created the most competitive entertainment and leisure landscape ever. Twenty-five years ago, people could access four or five TV channels. Today, they can access hundreds of channels and choose from a wide variety of entertainment without leaving their homes. Further, think about all the other leisure options that compete with the consumption of sporting events. Video games, movies, numerous outdoor activities, e-mail, texting, social media, and other activities occupy people's time as never before. Couple this with the fact that new sports and sporting genres such as action sports appear to be here to stay, and you can clearly see how fiercely professional teams have to compete for consumers' attention and money. This competition is likely to continue in the future. Technology will also present challenges to the traditional business models employed by professional sport. For example, digital video recorders (DVRs) such as TiVo allow people to consume sporting events and shows at their leisure and view them more quickly because they can skip through commercials. This practice may significantly affect the broadcast advertising models that are currently in place. Similarly, the streaming of video content to handheld devices such as cell phones creates a new way for athletes, teams, and leagues to deliver broadcasts. While this potentially creates a new opportunity for revenue generation, the challenge is to determine what consumers want and how to provide it. Further, at the league level, the emergence of such new sources of revenue will challenge traditional league revenue-sharing concepts.

WEB

Go to the WSG and complete the second web search activity, which shows you how emerging technology can help you find information and view sporting events.

› *Dealing with globalization.* New technologies are also helping spread professional sport across international boundaries. Thanks to this, Japanese fans can watch Yu Darvish play for MLB's Texas Rangers and Spanish fans can watch Ricky Rubio play for the NBA's Minnesota Timberwolves. Similarly, new means to facilitate the spread of sport across international boundaries are emerging every day. The NFL has played exhibition and regular season games in Mexico City, London, Toronto, Tokyo, and Berlin. In 2013, two regular season games were played abroad in Wembley Stadium. Similarly, MLB has held season-opening games in other countries, as has the NBA. MLB has been an integral part of the World Baseball Classic, which was played in 2006, 2009, and 2013. The NBA sent the Orlando Magic and the Cleveland Cavaliers to China in 2007 to participate in the China Games, and the 2013–14 NBA preseason included eight games in Brazil, the Philippines, Spain, England, Turkey, and China. These efforts have been geared toward increasing the global popularity of the sports as a way to generate more revenue. One obvious decision facing the leagues is whether to put a professional team outside North America. This issue raises several challenges, such as how to deal with cultural differences and account for exchange rates. At a league-specific level, NFL Europe, the NFL's former development league that played games in the spring and summer, was never profitable, and its long-term viability was always in question. These issues are just a few of the challenges facing professional sport in the future.

Career Opportunities in Professional Sport

Like any business, a professional sport organization constantly attempts to upgrade its efficiency through its personnel. In searching for new employees, management often looks to sport management and administration programs, to other professional sport organizations, and to people working in the corporate sector who may have skills essential to the sport industry.

Common Categories of Work Responsibility

The types and existence of positions in professional sport organizations vary from team to team and sport to sport. For example, MLB teams, because of their extensive minor league systems, employ more people in player personnel than do teams in the NBA or the NFL. In addition, minor league organizations (e.g., International Hockey League [IHL], East Coast Hockey League [ECHL]) typically employ fewer people than do major league organizations (e.g., NHL, MLS). This section highlights positions that may be available within any professional sport organization. Major professional sport teams typically have several executives on board:

› Chief executive officer (CEO) or chief operating officer (COO)—responsible for the day-to-day functioning of the entire organization, both on the field (performance) and off the field (revenue generation)

› Chief financial officer (CFO)—responsible for the organization's accounting and financial planning

› Chief marketing officer (CMO)—responsible for coordinating the marketing mix among communications, ticket sales, and corporate sponsorship and partnership sales

› General counsel—responsible for overseeing all legal matters associated with the team including, but not limited to, player contracts, liability issues, and marketing contracts

› General manager—typically responsible for acquiring, developing, trading, and releasing talent, as well as creating a development system for young players

Beyond these executive positions, jobs with professional sport teams typically fall into two categories:

1. Player personnel positions
2. Business positions

PLAYER PERSONNEL POSITIONS

Numerous jobs focus on player personnel. These jobs involve putting the best possible team on the field or court. Descriptions of these jobs follow. Before you examine the individual jobs on this side of the professional sport organization, recognize the difficulty and competitiveness associated with these positions. Because many of the positions require intricate knowledge of the sport, being a former athlete, or even a former professional athlete, in the particular sport may be a prerequisite for success.

› *Player personnel.* This department is involved in identifying, evaluating, and developing potential and current players. In baseball, this department would also be involved in observing players assigned to the minor leagues. Typical jobs in this area include being a scout, in which researching potential draft picks and upcoming opponents are central responsibilities. The pinnacle position within the player personnel side of the organization is typically the general manager position. The general manager is the final decision maker on drafting and trading decisions.

› *Medical, training, and team support.* These people assume responsibility for the physical (and sometimes mental) preparation and readiness of the players. Responsibilities include medical care, treatment of injuries, rehabilitation, dental care, nutrition, strength training and conditioning, career counseling, and after-care programs.

› *Coaching staff.* This group concentrates on all activities occurring between the lines. In other words, these professionals are primarily concerned with coaching, managing, and training the players on their rosters.

Professional Profile: Jeff Ianello

Title: vice president, team marketing and business operations, National Basketball Association

Education: BS (sport management), University of Massachusetts Amherst

In November of 2013, Jeff Ianello assumed a league vice president position in the team marketing and business operations (TMBO) department of the NBA. Previously, as a senior vice president with the NBA's Phoenix Suns and WNBA's Phoenix Mercury, Ianello had a leadership position that kept him active and involved throughout the year. Just over a decade ago, Ianello graduated with a sport management degree and took his first position in the sport industry as a sales consultant for the now New Orleans Pelicans. Because of his work ethic, interest and success in sales, education, and business acumen (as you can see from his answers in the following interview, which was conducted when he was with the Suns and Mercury), the league VP has methodically, yet quite impressively, moved up in professional basketball. The basic principles he has learned over the years and the tutelage he has received from his mentors have helped him become one of the top producers on a senior level and someone who has ascended to inside sales manager, director of sales and development, senior director of sales, team VP, senior VP, and now league VP. Jeff is a native of New York and an alum of the University of Massachusetts Amherst. After you read more about him in this Q&A, you are encouraged to follow him on Twitter at @Jeff_Ianello.

ONE DAY

Go to the WSG and learn more about a typical day in the life for Jeff Ianello. See if he spends his working hours the way you think he does.

What have been the key moves, steps, or developments in your career, and how did you arrive at your current position?

Toward the end of my senior year of college, I had little idea where my career was going to begin. I had learned that breaking into the world of sport was going to be difficult. Every job I was being interviewed for was a sales position. (In retrospect, I realized that companies were seeking help in sales because they always need people who can produce revenue.) Ultimately, I was recommended for an entry-level ticket sales program with the NBA's Hornets, who were just moving from Charlotte to New Orleans. The job entailed selling season tickets as well as ticket packages and group sales. If not for the relationships and advice that my professors had given me, I would not have been recommended for the position, nor would I have accepted it.

My first month as an inside sales (IS) representative for the New Orleans Hornets (now the New Orleans Pelicans) was a roller-coaster ride. Sales consultants recommended by the NBA were sent in to train the staff of 10 new hires. Considering that I had minimal sales experience, the consultants' word was gospel to me. After training, we were thrust into the fire of making sales calls. We did most of this by phone, attempting to contact decision makers at businesses, with an occasional face-to-face appointment mixed in. I quickly rose to the top of my inside sales class. After six months in New Orleans, I accepted a job as a season ticket account executive on the senior staff with the Phoenix Suns. Two years later, I moved into the IS manager role. In 2007, I was promoted to the position of director of sales and development, and two years later, I became the senior director of sales. Then, in 2010, I moved into the position of vice president for sales. Two years later I became the vice president for sales and service (suites). My latest advancement came in 2013 when I became the senior vice president for sales and service. (As noted above, Ianello is now a league vice president).

What are your current responsibilities and objectives in your job?

My position involves overseeing all aspects of ticket sales, retention, and premium/suite sales and retention. I spend the majority of my time internally with my boss and with the managers and staff who report to me. As such, I am the manager of a department of approximately 60 sales and service professionals, including managers and support staff. I also lead the planning of our new SixthMan Membership platform (more than just a season ticket holder) and I develop strategy and implementation of secondary markets, brand integrity, and strategy. Furthermore, I implement a robust training and development curriculum, as well as oversee a strong sales process.

What do you enjoy most about your current job?

I most enjoy the day-to-day challenge of being the best in class. Along with this, I also enjoy helping people develop, both in skill sets and career growth. Why sales? What about it is so attractive to me that it is hard to imagine myself working in any other field? First, it provides a highly competitive, fast-paced environment in which productivity is rewarded. Literally every phone call or face-to-face appointment provides a unique challenge. Learning to deal with different personalities and becoming more adept at countering a wide variety of objections has helped me grow as a professional. Another benefit is that the harder I work and the better I become at my craft, the greater the financial reward. More specifically, the great thing about ticket sales is that it offers a path for career growth. Those who are successful can pursue opportunities in premium sales (suites leasing), sponsorship, and management.

What do you consider the biggest future challenge to be in your job or industry?

The biggest future challenges I see involve determining how technology supports the sport industry and finding the correct content balance in game for our members.

> *Player education and relations.* People in these positions are typically responsible for educating players on issues like financial management, substance abuse, nutrition, image management, and additional higher education. Other responsibilities may include working as a liaison between the team and players with respect to player appearances in the community.

> *Video support staff.* Responsibilities of the video support staff include producing and editing videos, purchasing and maintaining video hardware and software products, supervising and coordinating satellite feeds, and coordinating all broadcasting that originates at the home facility. The video support staff also is responsible for filming games and maintaining the team's library of game films and player-evaluation videos.

> *Stadium and facility staff.* This group is responsible for the maintenance, upkeep, and repair of the playing surface. They are also responsible for preparing the team's offices, locker rooms, training facilities, practice facilities, and playing fields. In terms of playing surfaces and related areas, these people are the liaisons between the venue management team and the professional franchise.

BUSINESS POSITIONS

Unlike the player personnel side of the organization, the business side does not have any control over team performance issues. But people in these positions play an important role in the organization because they are responsible for generating revenue, marketing the product, developing a fan base, and working with customers and other stakeholders.

> *Ticket sales.* One of two types of sales representatives within the organization, ticket salespeople typically focus on selling season tickets, partial season tickets, and group tickets. They target not only individual ticket purchasers but also groups and corporations that can buy either a larger number of tickets or expensive season tickets. Working in ticket sales is a good first position in professional sport. Many openings are available in this area because teams must sell a large number of tickets to maximize team revenues.

> *Corporate sales.* In contrast to those who primarily sell individual tickets, corporate salespeople target corporations exclusively. They may sell corporate sponsorships, luxury suites, or club seats.

Case Study

The phone rang in Tonya Mertz's apartment. A senior in the sport management program at Smithson University, Tonya was hoping that this would be a return phone call about an internship for summer.

"Hi, Tonya, this is Kristin Carter of the Raleigh Flyers. I'm calling to offer you an internship in our community relations department. Your responsibilities will include assisting with all of our charitable efforts and events in the community. Your background working in the community with your team at Smithson is what convinced us that you were right for this internship. What do you think?"

"Ms. Carter, I am flattered by your offer," said Tonya. "Would it be possible to think about this over the weekend?"

"No problem, Tonya. I will look forward to hearing your response on Monday," concluded Carter.

Tonya was excited as she hung up the phone. As a four-year starter on the Smithson basketball team, Tonya's career had just ended. Knowing that she was not quite good enough for the WNBA, Tonya decided to parlay her passion for basketball into a career in professional basketball. This opportunity with the Flyers could provide the start she was looking for. The phone rang again.

"Hello, Tonya. This is Paul Butterworth of the Topeka Trackers [a new team in the NBA Development League]. I'm calling to offer you an internship position in marketing. As you know, we are a new organization. So, while this is an internship, we are poised to integrate you into the workings of our ticket sales, corporate sales, and promotions efforts."

Tonya was surprised, but she collected herself enough to say, "Wow, Mr. Butterworth, that sounds great. But would you mind if I took the weekend to think about it?"

"No problem, Tonya. I will wait for your call on Monday." With that, Butterworth hung up.

Tonya did not know what to do. She was stunned. Five minutes ago, she was all but headed for the Raleigh-Durham area. Now another company was offering her an internship. What should she do?

Based on what you learned in this chapter and in chapter 2 and what you can garner from outside research, consider the following questions:

1. What does Tonya need to consider before making a decision?
2. What are the advantages and disadvantages of each opportunity?
3. What are the opportunities for growth with each opportunity?

› *Game experience.* Responsibilities for these positions focus on enhancing the experience of people who attend games. Specific tasks may include overseeing the music, video boards, and public address messaging during a game. Opportunities in this area have increased as stadiums and arenas have become more sophisticated and as teams have increasingly focused on providing an entertaining experience both on and off the field, court, or ice.

› *Advertising.* Responsibilities in advertising include designing and writing advertising copy and identifying, securing, and placing advertisements in a variety of media. The sport organization may handle this responsibility in-house or outsource it to an advertising agency that specializes in ad creation and placement.

› *Promotions.* Like the game experience area, the field of promotions offers increasing opportunity as organizations focus on providing an optimal experience to spectators. Responsibilities typically include overseeing all promotional activity that occurs on the field of play or in the stands during the game.

› *Community relations.* This department may be part of the public relations or marketing department. The community relations staff is responsible for creating and administering grassroots functions, such as clinics and other charitable events that the team sponsors. Staff members are also responsible for implementing league-wide programs, such as the NBA's Read to Achieve program.

> *Media relations.* This department is involved in assisting and working with the media by providing information necessary for game coverage and publicity. This job includes ensuring that the needs of the media are met at every sporting event. People in media relations positions are also often involved with overseeing the team's social media activities as well as being responsible for all publications, such as media guides, yearbooks, and game programs.

> *Database marketing coordinator.* People in this area focus on building databases of information about the team's customers so that the team can more effectively serve its customers and better meet their needs. This position may also include overseeing the marketing research efforts of the professional sport organization.

> *Hospitality coordinators.* Hospitality coordinators are responsible for the game-related needs of corporate clients, club seat holders, and luxury box owners. This responsibility includes coordinating the provision of food, beverages, and any other special needs (e.g., Internet connection) required by corporate clients.

> *Ticketing.* This department may or may not include the ticket sales staff. Ticketing personnel manage the ticket inventory. They are responsible for ticket distribution, printing, accounting, game-day box office sales, complimentary tickets, and the financial settlement for the visiting team.

Critical Thinking in Professional Sport

Assume that you work for a major professional sport league that is establishing a league-controlled cable network (e.g., NBA TV, MLB Network, NFL Network, NHL Network). The success of these networks depends on your ability to (a) gain distribution through all the cable carriers (e.g., Comcast) and (b) attract enough viewers to be able to sell advertising during programming at a price that will generate a profit. Central to meeting this goal is the quality and attractiveness of the programming offered on the network. Although you can control rebroadcasts of your games, your past practice has been to sell the rights to televise your games to networks and cable channels. That said, if you carried live games, you could sell the advertising in-house (using league resources) and attract a broad audience interested in watching your games. You are now approaching the point where you need to decide whether you allow the networks and cable channels to use the current content (e.g., games) and how much you offer them so that you can use the live games to attract viewers.

Ethics in Professional Sport

The topic of professional athletes' use of performance-enhancing drugs has been at the forefront of conversations about professional sport for the better part of the last 20 years (including 2013 controversies involving sprinter Tyson Gay, baseball players such as Alex Rodriguez and Ryan Braun, and a host of other notable athletes). Interestingly, the collective bargaining process (CBA) has played an important role in this issue. Taking MLB as an example, some argue that management was aware that the gaudy batting statistics posted after 1995 were due to the use of steroids or other illegal supplements and that management ignored this circumstance because of the marketing benefits that accrued from high-scoring games, record-breaking performances, and more towering home runs than ever. Finally, in the past decade, management sought to implement a drug-testing program. Yet this issue is part of the CBA. Therefore, the Major League Baseball Players Association (MLBPA) was not willing initially to agree to a drug-testing program unless management was willing to give concessions in other areas of the collective bargaining process (e.g., more flexibility with free agency, lessening of the luxury tax). Further, the MLBPA could argue that they were acting in the

ACTION

Go to the WSG and complete the Learning in Action activity, which tests how well you remember some of the key terms and their definitions used in this chapter.

PORTFOLIO

Complete the critical thinking portfolio activity in the WSG, consulting as needed the "Critical Thinking Questions" sidebar in chapter 1.

PORTFOLIO

Complete the ethical issues portfolio activity in the WSG, consulting as needed the "Guidelines for Making Ethical Decisions" sidebar in chapter 1.

best interests of their players to resist a drug-testing program. Not until the last five years did societal and governmental pressure become so significant that both labor and management agreed on a drug-testing program. Even then, the program was enacted only after a year of confidential testing whereby the volume of positive drug tests had to exceed a certain level for a program to be implemented.

Summary

Professional sport is a large part of the entertainment, social, political, economic, legal, and cultural fabric of North America. The continued growth of the media and related technology, particularly television and the Internet, ensures that professional sport is prevalent and highly accessible, regardless of the demographic characteristics of its audience. Because of this accessibility and prevalence, the importance of the roles that labor, management, and governance play often seem out of balance when compared with their roles in other forms of business. For the most part, reserve clauses, free agency, league think, and antitrust exemptions exist only in the context of professional sport. These concepts are not essential in conducting the traditional activities of mainstream business operations, but they appear to be essential to the survival of the business of professional sport. Further, these concepts will be crucial for those involved in new professional sport leagues, such as the NWSL, to understand if they are to be successful. By understanding the unique limitations and opportunities of professional sport as well as the revenue sources and the influence of the media, you will be able to appreciate the career challenges and possibilities in the field.

Review Questions

1. Since 1850, what have been the three most significant developments affecting the growth of professional sport?

2. How is the management of professional sport different from the management of Microsoft?

3. Why is league think important to professional sport?

4. How have cable television media rights deals entered into by teams such as the Los Angeles Dodgers and Texas Rangers affected the teams, the league, fans, and professional sports? What are two or three recent television rights deals that have been signed? What do you see are the advantages and disadvantages of such deals for the various stakeholders involved?

5. Can professional sport continue to grow its revenues? Identify the revenue sources that can be enhanced.

6. What would you consider to be three future challenges that the professional sport segment of the sport industry will face?

7. What are the two general categories of jobs within a professional sport organization? What are four ways in which the explosion of social media opportunities and platforms has affected the professionals involved in the two general categories?

References

Amick, S. (2013, July 5). Dwight Howard will join Houston Rockets. *USA Today*. Retrieved from www.usatoday.com/story/sports/nba/2013/07/05/dwight-howard-houston-rockets-contract-decision-los-angeles-lakers/2492347

Andreff, W., & Szymanski, S. (2006). *Handbook on the economics of sport*. Cheltenham, UK: Edward Elgar.

Badenhausen, K. (2013, July 15). Real Madrid tops the world's most valuable sports teams. *Forbes*. Retrieved from www.forbes.com/sites/kurtbadenhausen/2013/07/15/real-madrid-tops-the-worlds-most-valuable-sports-teams

Browne, L. (1992). *Girls of summer*. Toronto, Ontario, Canada: HarperCollins.

CBS Sports. (2013, July 16). MLB salaries. Retrieved from www.cbssports.com/mlb/salaries/avgsalaries

Dietl, H., Lang, M., & Werner, S. (2010). The effect of luxury taxes on competitive balance, club profits, and social welfare in sports leagues. *International Journal of Sport Finance*, 5(1), 41–51.

Federal Base Ball Club of Baltimore, Inc. v. National League of Professional Base Ball Clubs, 259 U.S. 200 (1922).

Freedman, W. (1987). *Professional sports and antitrust*. New York, NY: Quorum.

Gorman, J., & Calhoun, K. (1994). *The name of the game: The business of sports*. New York, NY: Wiley.

Harris, D. (1986). *The league: The rise and decline of the NFL*. New York, NY: Bantam.

Leuty, R. (2013, May 9). *San Francisco Business Times*. Top 10 stadium, arena naming rights deals. Retrieved from www.bizjournals.com/sanfrancisco/blog/2013/05/stadium-naming-rights-deals-49ers-levis.html

Mullin, B.J., Hardy, S., & Sutton, W.A. (2014). *Sport marketing* (4th ed.). Champaign, IL: Human Kinetics.

Negro League Baseball. (2003). *Negro League Baseball: Timeline of events in professional black baseball*. Retrieved from www.negroleaguebaseball.com/timeline.html

Rader, B.G. (2009). *American sports: From the age of folk games to the age of televised sports* (6th ed.). Upper Saddle River, NJ: Pearson/Prentice Hall.

Roberts, R., & Olson, J. (1995). *Winning is the only thing: Sports in America since 1945*. Baltimore, MD: Johns Hopkins University Press.

Staudohar, P.D. (1989). *The sports industry and collective bargaining*. Cornell, NY: ILR.

Staudohar, P.D., & Mangan, J.A. (1991). *The business of professional sports*. Urbana. IL: University of Illinois Press.

HISTORICAL MOMENTS

1921	Sport agents arrived—Christy Walsh began ghostwriting columns for Babe Ruth
1960	Mark H. McCormack started International Management Group (IMG)
1972	Host Communications founded
1985	Joyce Julius and Associates, a sponsorship measurement agency, formed
1995	First Summer X Games held (first called Extreme Games)
1996	Hit movie *Jerry Maguire*, centered around a fictional sport agent, released
1998	Bill Duffy founded BDA Sports Management, focusing on representation of basketball talent
1999	SFX Sports Group and Octagon founded
2004	Ted Fortsmann acquired IMG after founder McCormack's death in 2003
2005	Women's Tennis Association (WTA) signed US$88 million six-year title sponsorship deal with Sony Ericsson—largest sponsorship deal in the history of women's sport
2007	Through acquisitions of Host Communications and The Collegiate Licensing Company, IMG formed IMG College
2009	Women's National Basketball Association (WNBA) Phoenix Mercury signed US$1 million team jersey sponsorship deal
2010	Agencies Velocity Sports & Entertainment and Vivid Marketing joined to lead creation of new agency, Team Epic
2012	Global agency, Wasserman Media Group, made history representing #1 picks in NFL, NBA, MLB, and MLS drafts
2013	Music mogul Jay-Z partnered with Creative Artists Agency (CAA) to form Roc Nation Sports, a talent representation firm

10

SPORT MANAGEMENT AND MARKETING AGENCIES

Catherine Lahey \ Jezali Ratliff \ William A. Sutton

LEARNING OBJECTIVES

> Describe the inception, evolution, and mainstreaming of sport management and marketing agencies.
> Explain the role, scope, and influence of sport management and marketing agencies as they relate to the business of sport.
> Differentiate between the types of agencies to determine which are most appropriate for particular tasks and assignments.
> Appraise career opportunities associated with sport management and marketing agencies.
> Examine the critical skills needed and ethical issues associated with the work of agencies in the sport industry.
> Detail the key challenges facing agencies in the sport industry in the second decade of the 21st century.

Key Terms

client	inventory
downsizing	solicitation
entitlement	turnkey
gatekeepers	value added
grassroots programs	venue

GET A JOB

Continue on your journey in sport management by going to the web study guide (WSG) at www.HumanKinetics.com/ContemporarySportManagement. Check out the job opportunities and consider the skills and experiences that can help you succeed in sport management.

client—Sport-related person, brand, property, media company, or concept represented by a sport management and marketing agency.

venue—A facility or site where a special event or sport activity takes place.

A sport management and marketing agency is a business that acts on behalf of an entity involved in the sport industry. This sport-related entity, commonly referred to as a **client**, can be a person, a corporate brand, a media company, a property (e.g., event, team, university, **venue**), or even a concept. Actions an agency may undertake on behalf of their clients include representation, negotiation, sales, licensing, marketing, management, strategy, and measurement. Ultimately, an agency bears a responsibility to protect and uphold the best interest of its individual clients.

The role of sport management and marketing agencies has evolved significantly in a relatively short period of time. In the early 1900s, as professional sports grew increasingly prominent and athletes began to be compensated for endorsing products, sport agents began to emerge. Early agents, like Christy Walsh and Charles C. Pyle, represented professional athletes' interests in public relations, in contract negotiations, and in seeking endorsements and other revenue streams. These individualistic athlete–agent pairings continued until the 1960s when the late Mark H. McCormack founded the International Management Group (IMG)—the first agency dedicated to representing professional athletes. McCormick's vision opened the door for the establishment of many new sport-focused agencies. Over time, changes to the sport marketplace have led sport management and marketing agencies, including IMG, to evolve their scope and expertise beyond just athlete representation. This evolution will only continue, evidenced by the fact that many agencies that were once solely focused on sport now deal in complementary lifestyle activities like fashion, entertainment, and leisure.

The purpose of this chapter is to provide an overview of sport management and marketing agencies and to introduce career opportunities within this rapidly evolving segment of the sport industry. The chapter sheds light on the unique and multifaceted nature of agencies by outlining their key functions and then classifying the many agencies into three categories: full service, general, and specialty. Examples of each type of agency will help delineate the similarities and differences. In addition, the chapter addresses in-house groups, such as those within properties and corporate brands, whose functions commonly overlap with those of agencies. After providing insight into career opportunities, the chapter concludes by providing examples of challenges and ethical issues facing sport management and sport marketing agencies.

Sponsorship and licensing solicitation—one of the functions of sport management and marketing agencies—can include working on behalf of a professional athlete to secure endorsement opportunities, personal appearances, product placements, book contracts, and video games.

Functions of Sport Management and Marketing Agencies

Sport management and marketing agencies perform a vast scope of functions for the four key stakeholder groups (i.e., talent, properties, corporate brands, and media companies). The degree of specialization necessary to serve each stakeholder group is extensive. Although an agency might perform several or perhaps only one function, some agencies, such as IMG and Wasserman Media Group, perform all of them. Table 10.1 outlines the main functions that sport management and marketing agencies undertake for their four main client groups.

> *Strategic planning and management.* Agencies provide consultative services to clients regarding business, marketing, and promotional decisions in order to best meet their objectives. One of the most common functions of sport management and marketing agencies, regardless of their size or scope, is consulting about solicitation and securing corporate sponsorships. According to the *IEG Sponsorship Report*, corporations were expected to increase global sponsorship spending by 4.2% in 2013, for a total of US$53.3 billion, a considerable increase since 2009 when total global spending was at US$44 billion. Although many properties (e.g., teams, sport events, festivals) handle these functions in-house, most seek outside assistance in determining value and identifying and obtaining appropriate sponsors. Similarly, corporations and other potential sponsors often employ a sport management and marketing agency to identify properties that may assist them in achieving their corporate goals and objectives. The Wasserman Media Group's Global Consulting Division, as detailed on the agency's website, "develops strategies that drive measureable marketing success for some of the world's preeminent brands and properties in over 80 countries around the globe" (Wasserman Media Group, 2014).

Table 10.1   **Major Functions Sport Management and Marketing Agencies Perform for Clients**

Function	Talent	Property	Corporate brand	Media company
Strategic planning	X	X	X	X
Sponsorship and licensing solicitation	X	X		
Event creation, management, marketing	X	X	X	X
Contract negotiation	X	X	X	X
Marketing activation	X	X	X	X
Content development	X	X		
Financial or investment planning	X			
Research and evaluation	X	X	X	X

> *Sponsorship and licensing solicitation.* The agency works on behalf of the client to sell rights, assets, or other inventory for commercial benefit. For a professional athlete, this may involve securing endorsement opportunities (e.g., adidas' endorsement deal with Derrick Rose of the NBA), personal appearances, product placements, book contracts, movie and television roles, interviews and feature stories, video games, and so on. For a rights holder, this may mean that the agency assists in the sale of the property's marquee inventory (e.g., an entitlement) or consults on the best way to package sales assets in order to derive maximum value.

entitlement—Associating the name of a sponsor with the name of an event or facility in exchange for cash or other considerations (e.g., the AT&T Cotton Bowl Classic).

> *Event creation, management, and marketing.* The growth of sport television over the past few decades, the proliferation of sport networks and channels, and the development of new satellite, digital, and mobile technology have led to fiscally rewarding opportunities to create compelling content through the creation of new events. Examples of emergent ways in which sport managers have capitalized on these opportunities include sport leagues (e.g., Major League Lacrosse), an increase in the number of college football bowl games, and a wider array of collegiate basketball doubleheaders. Some television entities such as ESPN, ESPNU, Fox Regional Sports Networks, and Turner Broadcasting have created events to fill their inventory. In addition to new events, many sport organizations now hire outside agencies to manage, activate, and market their current events. Event management and marketing agencies are involved in activities such as golf and tennis tournaments, festivals, bowl games, and other sport and lifestyle special events. Event management may involve any of the following areas: tournament operations, hospitality and entertainment, sponsorship and ticket sales, licensing and merchandising, television production, public relations, and promotion.

inventory—The assets that a sport property has to sell, including not only its quantity but also its characteristics and traits.

> *Contract negotiation.* Contract negotiation involves representing a client in contract discussions, which could be between player and team, corporate sponsor and a sports team, product and endorser, or many other parties. Contract negotiation processes are typically highly sensitive, requiring a deep knowledge of the sport marketplace and a honed skill set. For athletes in particular, perceived contract negotiation skills are one

Maximizing Sports Sponsorships as Part of a 360 Marketing Strategy

As corporate sport sponsorship continues to grow in popularity among both large and small companies, so have the rights fees and media commitments associated with traditional sponsorships. This heightened investment has created a stronger need for companies and their agencies to continually justify sports investments internally to leadership and externally to shareholders to demonstrate strong return on investment (ROI) through how they leverage the rights and assets granted in the partnership. While some may think that this just requires stronger measurement on the back end of a company's sponsorship activation, the maximization actually starts in the planning and negotiation stages.

Over the last few decades—and often at the urging of their sports agencies—companies have started to shift sponsorship from being one tool in their marketing toolbox to a central driver and thematic that benefits all elements of their company's marketing mix. Instead of creating stand-along programs solely focused on sports fans, companies are using sports as their total market campaign and sports agencies as leaders of cross-functional agency teams. This has been seen recently by brands such as P&G, which shifted its entire marketing mix (media, point of sale, digital, public relations, and social media) over to its Olympic-themed "Thank You, Mom" campaign during the 2012 London Olympic Games.

of the most important factors when deciding on agency representation. Agencies are also often incentivized in contract negotiation processes with a compensation structure that is linked to the final financial terms of the agreement that is being negotiated.

> *Marketing activation.* A frequently overlooked function of a sport management and marketing agency is that of creating, arranging, and managing hospitality management services. Hospitality management services include, but are not limited to, transportation and other logistical issues, menu and food service planning and management, corporate sponsor entertainment, special auxiliary event creation and management, housing, and awards, gifts, and recognition programs. As with most events and activities, the type and scope of these services vary greatly according to the event. In the United States, the Super Bowl is one of the most coveted destinations for hospitality packages in all of sport because of geographic location, appeal, and ticket demand. Corporations reward their best sales personnel, thank their highest volume customers, and court new clients through invitations to this mega event. The Super Bowl offers a prestigious opportunity to achieve these objectives. Agencies such as Party Planners West (PPW) arrange transportation, accommodations, meals, auxiliary events such as cruises, golf tournaments, and postevent parties, gifts, and spouse programs (Conrad, 1995). Grassroots programs build a following for a product, service, or organization. Although they may not pay immediate benefits, they contribute to long-term growth by creating interest among potential consumers. Most **grassroots programs** are aimed at children and adolescents who may or may not be consumers of the product, service, or organization in question but who possess the qualities, abilities, and potential to become consumers in the future. Grassroots programs often involve participants in activities and events that are held at local sites, which could be thousands of miles or kilometers from the headquarters of the sponsoring organization. These local events and activities are often targeted to certain demographic groups and ethnic markets. For example, Major League Baseball's RBI Program focuses on inner-city youth and the NBA's Basketball Without Borders is a global program that targets youth.

> *Content development.* The growth and proliferation of cable, satellite, digital, mobile, and pay-per-view have created many opportunities and outlets for developing and producing programming. Host Communications (which was acquired by IMG in 2007) and Raycom Sports are agencies that have been involved in packaging rights fees for college football and basketball and the subsequent sales of these rights to networks such as CBS, NBC, ABC, ESPN, and TBS. Traditional sport management and marketing agencies have recognized the opportunities that television presents and have aggressively moved to capitalize on them.

> *Financial planning.* The highly specialized service of planning involves accountants, financial planners and advisors, and investment specialists and portfolio managers. Few sport management and marketing agencies specialize in financial planning and management. IMG offers this service as part of its client management services. Several of IMG's clients have benefited well enough from the investing and planning services that they have started their own companies or have entered limited partnerships with IMG to create new ventures. The success of both Arnold Palmer and Jack Nicklaus in creating their own companies and ventures is testament to the performance of IMG in discharging its fiscal planning duties. But except for IMG and a few others, sport management and marketing agencies usually contract financial and investment services out to reputable financial planners and accountants whose primary function is related not to sport but to fiscal management and planning.

> *Research and evaluation.* Evaluation and documentation are critical factors in determining the success of the various types of sport management and

grassroots programs— Programs targeted to people at the primary level of involvement, usually participants rather than spectators.

downsizing—Becoming a smaller organization by reducing personnel or departments, often because of a change in the mission or direction of the organization.

value added—The perception, by the consumer, of added or augmented product or service benefits.

ACTION
Go to the WSG and complete the Learning in Action activity, which will test your understanding of the different types of sport management and marketing agencies.

solicitation—Requesting support or assistance on behalf of a sport property from a potential sponsor.

marketing programs discussed throughout this chapter. Several concepts (e.g., **downsizing, value added**) stress a high degree of relevance and accountability, for both the sport organization and the agency or program delivering the services. One such example is the concept of reengineering, whereby a sport organization changes its structure or philosophy to capitalize on existing opportunities. Another concept, postevent impact analysis, involves research conducted (usually by a third party but commissioned by a sponsor or the event itself) after the event ends to determine the effect that the event had on the sponsor's product (i.e., image, awareness, or sales) or on the community in general (e.g., economic growth through spending associated with the event). Research, through mail and on-site surveys, personal interviews and focus groups, pre- and postevent impact analyses, and other methods, is essential to assist the decision maker in justifying a program's cost, value, and relevance to the client. Most corporations involved in sponsorship or licensing activities perform some type of assessment, either through an in-house department or by contracting with an agency that offers research and evaluation services. The research agency selected is typically not involved in the sponsorship and licensing sales process to ensure that it does not have a stake in the findings. Thus, the research agency selected should be a specialist in evaluating sponsorship and licensing programs or perhaps in sport consumer behavior. Joyce Julius and Associates, Performance Research, and Navigate Research are examples of research or consulting companies that specialize in such services. The type of research to use and the best agency to employ will vary with the scope and magnitude of the event, whether the event is televised, the types of sponsorship and licensing activities that take place at the event, the budget, and the commitment of the organization to undertake a sound research approach.

Types of Sport Management and Marketing Agencies

The preceding sections cover the vast array of functions that sport management and marketing agencies perform on behalf of their clients. We now explore the agencies themselves. Numerous organizations categorize themselves as sport management and marketing agencies, and even more in-house groups exist whose functions often overlap with those of true agencies, such as state sport commissions, sport sponsorship departments within corporate brands, or divisions of leagues such as NBA Properties, Inc. If these quasi-agencies, which are explored later in this section, were included, the total number of sport management and marketing agencies would exceed 3,500.

Sport management and marketing agencies vary in size, budget, type of clientele, and scope of services. Some agencies provide a broad array of services across all four of the previously mentioned key stakeholder groups, while others may be more closely focused, catering to only a single one of these groups or specializing in a specific function such as measurement or activation. Given the wide range of potential differences, both prominent and subtle, it is helpful to categorize agencies into three basic types: full service, general, and specialty. Table 10.2 provides a concise overview of some top sports management and marketing agencies with more illustrative examples of each of the three main types of agencies contained later in the chapter.

Full-Service Agencies

Full-service agencies offer the greatest breadth of functions, touching all or most of the four key stakeholder groups. On a daily basis, a full-service agency handles core functions like strategic planning, sponsorship solicitation, event management, contract

Table 10.2   **Top Sport Management and Marketing Agencies**

Agency	Type	Founded	Key clients	Key offices
Creative Artists Agency (CAA)	Full service	1975	*Talent:* Chris Paul, Dwyane Wade, Robert Griffin III, Ryan Howard, Shaun White, Sidney Crosby, Cristiano Ronaldo, Jim Rome, Michael Wilbon *Properties:* Madison Square Garden, New York Yankees, FC Barcelona *Brands:* RBS, Best Buy	Los Angeles, CA; New York, NY; Chicago, IL; St. Louis, MO; London; Stockholm
International Management Group (IMG)	Full service	1960	*Talent:* Rafael Nadal, Venus Williams, Peyton Manning, John Madden, Tom Coughlin, Joe Mauer, Danica Patrick, Bob Costas *Properties:* American Airlines Center, Rose Bowl *Brands:* GE, Johnson & Johnson, Coca-Cola, Allstate *Media:* World's largest independent distributor of sports programming	New York, NY; Cleveland, OH; Winston-Salem, NC; London; Hong Kong
Octagon (rebranded from Advantage International in 1999)	Full service	1983	*Talent:* Michael Phelps, Stephen Curry, Jimmie Johnson, Marshawn Lynch, Bill Cowher *Brands:* BMW, Sprint, MasterCard, Johnson & Johnson, AB InBev, The Home Depot *Properties:* Targa Tasmania, SAS Championship	Los Angeles, CA; Chicago, IL; New York, NY; Charlotte, NC; London; Moscow; Paris; Sydney
Wasserman Media Group	Full service	2002	*Talent:* Andrew Luck, Yu Darvish, Hanley Ramirez, Derrick Rose, Pau Gasol, Rickie Fowler, Brittney Griner, Travis Pastrana, Abby Wambach *Properties:* America's Cup, NFL, NBA *Brands:* Nationwide Insurance, Pepsi, Verizon *Media:* BBC, British Telecom, ESPN	Los Angeles, CA; New York, NY; Miami, FL; Carlsbad, CA; Raleigh, NC; Toronto; São Paulo; London; Singapore
16W Marketing	General	2000	*Talent:* Cal Ripken, Jr., Howie Long, Phil Simms, Hakeem Nicks *Brands:* Fanatics, Nike	Rutherford, NJ

(continued)

Table 10.2 (continued)

Agency	Type	Founded	Key clients	Key offices
GMR Marketing	General	1979	**Brands:** MillerCoors, Lowe's, Humana, FX **Properties:** NFL, Comcast, SPEED	New Berlin, WI; Charlotte, NC; Chicago, IL; Los Angeles, CA; New York, NY; São Paulo; Toronto; Singapore; London
Premier Partnerships	General	2003	**Properties:** Rose Bowl, NBA, MLS **Brands:** Avis, Honda, Herbalife, Pizza Hut	New York, NY; Santa Monica, CA
Team Epic (Velocity Sports & Entertainment/Vivid Marketing)	General	2010	**Properties:** USOC **Brands:** FedEx, AT&T, JPMorgan Chase, Samsung, P&G, Toyota	Norwalk, CT; Chicago, IL; Atlanta, GA; San Francisco, CA; Charlotte, NC; New York, NY; Cincinnati, OH; London
Excel Sports	Specialty	2002	**Talent:** Tiger Woods, Tyson Chandler, Paul Pierce, Blake Griffin, Deron Williams, Lance Lynn, Mark Teixeira, Zack Greinke	New York, NY; Los Angeles, CA
Joyce Julius & Associates	Specialty	1985	**Properties:** ESPN Regional, Chicago Bulls, Roush Fenway Racing, NHRA **Brands:** Aflac, Chick-fil-A, Dollar General, NAPA, Sprint	Ann Arbor, MI
Millsport (sport-focused practice of The Marketing Arm)	Specialty	1975	**Brands:** AT&T, Pepsi, Dove, Hilton, Walmart	Dallas, TX; New York, NY; Los Angeles, CA; Chicago, IL; Greenwich, CT; Charlotte, NC
Momentum Worldwide	Specialty	1987	**Brands:** American Express, Coca-Cola, Kraft, Microsoft, Subway	New York, NY; Atlanta, GA; Chicago, IL; Detroit, MI; Los Angeles, CA; Toronto; São Paulo; London; Dubai; Tokyo
Navigate Research	Specialty	2006	**Properties:** NFL, MLS, AEG, USOC **Brands:** AAA, Liberty Mutual, Best Buy, Farmers Insurance	Chicago, IL; Scottsdale, AZ

negotiation, marketing activation, and research and evaluation for multiple clients. In order to support this diversity of clients and functions, full-service agencies tend to have multiple divisions and be the largest of the sport management and marketing agencies. For example, divisions of Wasserman Media Group include global media, consulting, team sports, golf, global football, action and Olympic sports, digital, and multicultural. In addition to traditional sport services roles like agents and consultants, full-service agencies employ in-house attorneys, accountants, sales personnel, public relations personnel, creative personnel, and management information services personnel. These employees function together to tackle all aspects of a client's sport management and marketing needs. Interestingly, even when an agency offers a full range of services, some clients, particularly large corporate brands, elect to employ multiple agencies that must then work together in the brand's best interest. This creates an environment of both collaboration and competition among agencies.

In addition to Wasserman, other full-service agencies include IMG, Octagon, and now Creative Artists Agency, which has recently made a strong push to expand its scope of services beyond its core competency of talent management. An examination of IMG, the first true global sport management and marketing agency, provides an excellent overview of a full-service agency.

IMG, the first completely dedicated sport marketing agency, was initially created by McCormack to represent the interests of golfer Arnold Palmer. As times changed and marketing forces such as television gained greater influence on the sport scene, the roles of sport marketing agencies expanded to include managing not only athletes, but other sport properties and events. IMG was on the leading edge of this shift, and owes much of its early success to visionary recognition of the opportunities that the Golden Age of Sport Television (1958–1973) offered.

The diversity of IMG's endeavors reflects the company's unprecedented success over its life span. Today, IMG represents not only athletes, corporations, and world-class sporting events, but also performing artists, writers, fashion models, speakers, resorts, and cultural institutions. Additionally, IMG holds the position of largest independent distributor of sports programming worldwide. Most recently, it has made a significant mark in the world of college athletics programs, under the umbrella IMG College, which is further explored later in the chapter. These evolutions have shaped IMG into the largest sport marketing agency in the world, with 3,500 employees in 30 countries (IMG, 2013b). IMG's breadth across the key stakeholder groups is evident based on its businesses related to client management, event and corporate marketing, event management, and media. Examining each of these businesses is essential to comprehending the scope and magnitude of IMG and the scale of functions that a full-service agency performs on behalf of clients in the interest of driving revenue.

CLIENT MANAGEMENT

In serving talent, IMG's client management activities encompass contract negotiation, personalized strategic planning, endorsement marketing, corporate and resort affiliation, personal appearances, broadcasting, publishing, licensing, and merchandising (IMG, 2013a). Because of the size and scope of IMG, as well as the many relationships that it has constructed during the past four decades, IMG may enjoy an advantage over competitors in attracting clients and providing services. Below is a partial listing of key IMG sport clients:

Annika Sörenstam (golf)	Cam Newton (football)
Arnold Palmer (golf)	Danica Patrick (motorsports)
Bill Self (basketball coach)	Eli Manning (football)
Bob Costas (broadcaster)	John Madden (broadcaster)

LaDainian Tomlinson (football)   Rafael Nadal (tennis)
Lindsey Vonn (skiing)   Sasha Cohen (figure skating)
Luke Donald (golf)   Steve Nash (basketball)
Maria Sharapova (tennis)   Tom Coughlin (football coach)
Michelle Wie (golf)   Venus Williams (tennis)
Novak Djokovic (tennis)   Victor Cruz (football)
Peyton Manning (football)

In addition to representing sport personalities, IMG is also extremely active in fashion and entertainment representation, showing how the core competencies gained through sport can lead to revenue generation in other industries. Clients outside of sports include platinum selling musicians Justin Timberlake and Taylor Swift and a lengthy list of international models including supermodels Gisele and Kate Moss.

One key to successful client management is to have satisfied, highly successful, and visible clients involved heavily in both on-field and off-field activities. The success of the clients ensures successful negotiations and endorsements, and the visibility helps attract new clients, creating a cyclical effect. Given the labor unrest in professional sport in the second decade of the new millennium, having a broad client base that ensures income, stability, and diverse sports or activities is integral for those companies who count talent representation among their core services.

EVENT MANAGEMENT AND MARKETING

With property clients, IMG is involved in creating, developing, and managing sport and lifestyle activities and events. The company also manages licensing, sponsorship, and broadcast rights for many of the oldest and most distinguished events on the international sport and event calendar. These events have included Wimbledon, the Australian Open, the World Championship of Women's Golf, the Snowboarding World Championships, and Escape from Alcatraz Triathlon. In addition to traditional major sports opportunities, IMG has also created a niche with more grassroots activities like high school sports through the IMG Academies, including lending significant expertise to management and creation of youth athletic events like the annual Under Armour Combines. Given the diverse nature and varying demands of these properties, as well as the combination of rights, duties, and obligations associated with these events, the complexity of the event management and marketing industry is understandably high. With more than 50 years of expertise over almost every event and property type, IMG is able to seamlessly lend guidance and add value to event management and marketing clients, both large and small.

CORPORATE MARKETING

Given IMG's vast expertise and relationships in all channels of global sport, consulting corporate brands on their sport marketing presence is a natural extension. IMG offers clients a proprietary process, referred to as IMG ICON Engineering, to identify, create, and execute sport marketing platforms (IMG, 2013c). Within this process, IMG functions include identifying opportunities, negotiating relationships, developing messaging, executing events, and measuring results. IMG is known throughout the sport industry for its strength in marketing platforms around the Olympics, having assisted brands like GE, Johnson & Johnson, and Volkswagen in connecting with consumers through the shared passion point of sports.

MEDIA

IMG boasts the distinction of being the largest independent distributor and producer of sport programming in the world. Each year, IMG distributes more than 20,000 hours of television content worldwide and also produces over 21,000 hours of television programming and 30,000 hours of radio programming (IMG, 2013d). The acquisition of Host Communications (now branded IMG College), which is further discussed later in this chapter, also added a new facet to IMG's media portfolio. In the area of media, IMG brings value to clients by

1. serving as an advisor and consultant to rights holders,
2. negotiating the sale of television rights,
3. creating and producing television series and events for sale or distribution, and
4. handling the distribution of programming.

This integrated approach coupled with years of expertise in the space makes IMG highly sought after by sports properties and broadcast rights holders alike.

FUTURE OF IMG

Internal leadership changes within the last 10 years have been a major factor for IMG, and the biggest changes are likely still to come. Following McCormack's death in 2003, the firm Forstmann Little & Co. bought IMG for US$750 million in 2004 (Saitto, Soshnick, & Fixmer, 2013). After the death of Forstmann Little cofounder Ted Forstmann, industry speculation began about a possible sale of IMG. The intent to sell, and sell quickly, was confirmed in 2013 by IMG Sports President George Pyne, who stated that he found it "reasonable to say" that the sale would take place in the not too distant future. The likely asking price is around US$2 billion for an all cash purchase. Steve Horowitz, a partner at sports investment bank Inner Circle Sports, states that a "new owner has an opportunity to grow a business based on solid financials in an exciting world, which should encourage a lot of bidders to look at the business" (Mickle, 2013). While there has been strong speculation about possible purchasers—from other major agencies looking for immediate, large-scale growth opportunities to investments funds, holding companies, and even individuals—much about the potential sale is still unknown. What is certain is that any purchase of a sport management and marketing agency as central and storied as IMG is sure to have a ripple effect on the entire sport industry.

General Agencies

General agencies are those that fall between the expansive scope of work performed by full-service agencies and the narrow scope of work undertaken by specialty agencies. Some of these agencies may have the objective of becoming full service over time, while others find themselves best suited for their current offerings with no intention of significant growth. Examples of generalist agencies include GMR Marketing, Team Epic, which was formed in 2010 by the merger of Velocity Sports & Entertainment and Vivid Marketing, and 16W Marketing. An overview of 16W Marketing, led by partners Steve Rosner and Frank Vuono, provides an example of the scope of functions and services undertaken by a generalist agency:

› Athlete, coach, and broadcasters provide representation for all off-field and off-court business and marketing endeavors, including licensing, endorsements, broadcaster contract negotiation, media placement, promotions, speaking engagements, and personal appearances. The company specializes in seeking ownership for athletes and celebrities and gaining equity positions with affiliated companies to provide mutual incentives to grow.

› Corporate consulting and property marketing include comprehensive strategic planning and implementation of integrated marketing programs for consumer products or service corporations, online or e-commerce fulfillment companies, manufacturers, retailers, and sport and entertainment management organizations. Services include

Professional Profile: AJ Maestas

Title: founder and president, Navigate Research

Education: BA (finance), University of Washington; MBA (sports business), W.P. Carey School of Business, Arizona State University

In 2006, AJ Maestas and a cofounder launched Navigate Research, then Navigate Marketing, to address an area of opportunity in the sport industry—the increasingly pressing need for accountability and accuracy in measurement of return on investment (ROI). In the years since, he has guided Navigate to a position of industry leadership in the area of sponsorship research, particularly in custom analytics and measurement. Throughout the course of his career, he has worked with sponsors, agencies, and rights holders across the sport landscape to measure the value of media, media equivalents, hospitality, promotions, and sponsorship ROI. His professional and personal experience includes working with the leagues and properties of the NFL, NBA, MLB, NHL, AVP, NASCAR, IRL, Champ Car, and NCAA. Beyond the office, he is a member of the board of Big Brothers Big Sisters of Metropolitan Chicago and is a frequent speaker at sport industry events. He has also served as an adjunct or visiting professor at ASU, Columbia University, Northwestern University, Ohio University, and NYU. The following is a snapshot of his role as a leader in the sport industry.

ONE DAY

Go to the WSG and learn more about a typical day in the life for AJ Maestas. See if he spends his working hours the way you think he does.

What have been the key moves, steps, or developments in your career, and how did you arrive at your current position?

Prior to launching Navigate Research, I built my sponsorship and measurement expertise in roles as senior manager at IEG, a Chicago-based sponsorship consultancy, and as director of marketing communications at rEvolution, a sport marketing agency also based in Chicago. Prior to working on the agency side, I worked for Yellow Roadway Corporation, supporting their sports investments. Getting a sport-specific MBA was likely the catalyst that led me here; I went to ASU back when they had a program.

What are your current responsibilities and objectives in your job?

As president at Navigate, I'm accountable to Navigate employees and to our current and future clients. My major responsibilities include the following:

> Guiding the entire Navigate team to success and growth, particularly through talent acquisition and retention

> Managing and assuring execution of sales strategy and client communication

> Driving revenue for Navigate through proactive outreach and their existing client base

> Providing custom solutions for sponsorship executives to measure and quantify the success of their marketing partnerships in the sports and entertainment landscape

What do you enjoy most about your current job?

The people—our team, our clients, and friends in the industry. Most people enter sport business because of a passion for the product or service you work with every day, but it has been the people with those same passions and interests who make my day-to-day job a true joy. I can honestly say that I love my job.

What do you consider the biggest future challenge to be in your job or industry?

The business of sports and entertainment is maturing at a rapid pace. You must grow and evolve fast or you will be left behind. At Navigate, we have a culture of continuous improvement. Without that, we wouldn't be in business.

turnkey—A program or product that the vendor executes without further involvement from the client.

sponsorship negotiations and evaluation, value-added media packages, licensing, merchandising, and cross-promotional ties.

> Hospitality and event management includes **turnkey** hospitality, event and experience management, promotional coordination, and licensing and merchandising, both on-site and at retail for top sport and entertainment events ("16W Marketing," n.d.).

A comparison between 16W Marketing and IMG shows distinct similarities in services and functions, but one can see the differences that exist in scale and in the stakeholder groups targeted.

Specialty Agencies

As the category name suggests, a specialty agency is one that specializes in a specific type of services or caters to a specific stakeholder clientele. Some agencies, such as Excel Sports, focus solely on talent representation, while some, such as Millsport, focus on consulting corporate brands about their sport marketing platforms. Other agencies (e.g., Joyce Julius & Associates, Navigate Research) do not focus on a single stakeholder group, but rather on a specific function—research and measurement.

Founded in 1985, Joyce Julius & Associates measures and evaluates branding in all forms of media. Using a combination of technology and employee expertise, the company is able to provide properties, corporate brands, and media rights holders with an extremely detailed evaluation of the value of their marks within a particular broadcast or over the course of a lengthier platform (see the sidebar "*Sponsors Report* and the NTIV Analysis" for additional insight into this methodology). Given how specialized, time-consuming, and potentially costly it is to produce this type of detailed research, other agencies are also often major clients of research and measurement focused agencies. IMG, Millsport, and Octagon have all been clients of Joyce Julius & Associates. As technology improves, other agencies may push to bring this capability in-house, whether through acquisition or organic capability growth, rather than continuing to outsource to specialty agencies.

In-House Groups

With a firm understanding of the different types of agencies and their functions, it's also important to recognize groups with functions similar to those of agencies and the influence they may have on the businesses of traditional sport management and marketing agencies. One such group is the internal sport or sponsorship department of corporate

Sponsors Report and the NTIV Analysis

The services provided by Joyce Julius and Associates are among the most used and reputable in the sport industry (Liberman, 2005). Through the company's primary products—*Sponsors Report* and the National Television Impression Value (NTIV) Analysis—Joyce Julius and Associates arguably sets an industry standard. *Sponsors Report* is a publication that focuses on the value of the exposure received directly from national television broadcasts. Value is determined by calculating clear, in-focus exposure time during the broadcast. Exposure time is the amount of time given to logos, signage, displays, and audio mentions during the broadcast. Clear, in-focus exposures are the ones that television viewers can readily see. Joyce Julius & Associates identifies these exposures using what is called image identification technology (IIT) powered by Magellan, with supplementary checks and insight from their trained staff. Exposures are measured and converted to advertising costs per 30 seconds for the actual advertising costs on that specific broadcast. Joyce Julius has also recently added an additional layer of analysis, a proprietary methodology called Recognition Grade, that accounts for the quality and prominence of a given logo. The popularity of this type of analysis is growing rapidly, and it is widely sought out by brands to track the value of their sport spends and by properties and broadcasters to solidify the value of their sales assets. Given this demand, competition has arisen in the marketplace through competitors specializing in sport measurement, such as Repucom, and through traditional agencies working to add this component to their overall scope of services.

gatekeepers—Individuals or groups responsible for controlling the flow of proposals or solicitations to the decision maker.

brands (e.g., AB InBev, MasterCard), which may be responsible for sport functions on behalf of the products and divisions of the parent company. These departments have only one company to answer to—themselves—and often function as **gatekeepers** in reviewing opportunities presented to them by other entities like agencies, properties, and media broadcasters. Besides performing this gatekeeping function, these groups work with other units of the corporation, such as brand or product managers, advertising departments, public relations departments, and community affairs departments, to create or implement sport and lifestyle programming in order to achieve corporate objectives. Some corporations elect to solely rely on an internal department for all agency functions, but the majority of companies, particularly the largest and most active brands in sport, retain one or more agencies that work in daily collaboration with the internal team.

Professional league departments may also serve many functions that overlap with those of agencies. Each professional sport league and most sport properties have departments that drive their marketing, promotional, and sales efforts. For example, NBA Events and Attractions, an NBA division, markets and promotes the NBA as a holistic product through special events and activities such as NBA Jam Session, the NBA Draft, and international tours and activities. NBA Events and Attractions personnel work with the marketing departments of individual teams to promote the growth and development of the league itself. In many cases, these departments, along with their respective corporate partnership divisions, are charged with creating and implementing the activation programs that corporate partners have purchased as part of their sponsorship or licensing agreements. To do so, these personnel must understand the uniqueness and complexities of each team's market and must be prepared to assist teams in maintaining their identity while promoting the image of the whole league. Without an internal department to act as this central, collaborative body, an agency might be retained to serve this purpose.

Ultimately, sport management and marketing agencies work in close collaboration with these in-house groups in order to achieve the client's objectives; however, the continued growth of these groups does pose a potential threat to agencies. This issue is further considered in the next section of this chapter.

Careers in Agencies

The following section provides an overview of careers in sport management and marketing agencies and some of the challenges agencies face in the current sport landscape. Careers in this segment of the sport industry are diverse, requiring a wide range of skills and abilities. Furthermore, insourcing, mergers and acquisitions, and labor unrest in professional sport leagues have created added levels of uncertainty for those employed by agencies.

Careers in sport management and marketing agencies are challenging and varied. While breaking into the sports industry as a whole may seem daunting, agencies provide opportunities at every experience level, and they often look to hire team members with varied backgrounds who can complement their current employee base. For entry-level positions, agencies may prefer some sport marketing experience; however, agencies are more focused on the candidates' potential, which is generally determined by their level of preparedness for the interview, eagerness to contribute and be part of a team, flexibility to work off-hours and weekends, and perceived demeanor or cultural fit

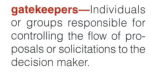

WEB

Go to the WSG and complete the web search activity, which helps you discover current or upcoming internship or part-time employment opportunities with top sport management and marketing agencies.

within the organization as a whole. For mid-level and more senior positions, agencies tend to bring in experienced people from other sports industry segments who have a network in place that can be used to benefit current clients or generate new clients over the long term.

Given the large number of sport management and marketing agencies, it is important to understand the functions and types of agencies so that you can seek employment with those that are most relevant to your skill set and desired career path. For example, if you are interested in working with brands on their sports sponsorships, an agency well known for consulting or event management will likely have more of the opportunities you desire. Likewise, if you want to become a certified player agent, you should consider large full-service agencies or specialty agencies that strictly manage talent. Lastly, if you are unsure of your desired career path within sports, agencies (both large and small) can be a great first step to gain significant breadth of experience in a relatively short amount of time.

In terms of educational background, a business degree with a marketing background is preferable. A sport management degree, with several electives in business, is also desirable. An advanced degree in business, law, or sport management is an advantage for applicants, particularly those seeking senior level positions.

Clearly, the sport management and marketing agency segment of the sport industry is diverse and contains both generalists and specialists. Although the personnel in larger sport management and marketing agencies are more likely to function as specialists as they advance in the organization, those employed in smaller agencies must have a variety of skills and knowledge to perform their duties effectively. Skills essential to working in sport marketing and management agencies can be classified as organizational, technical, and people. Essential skills under each classification are provided in figure 10.1.

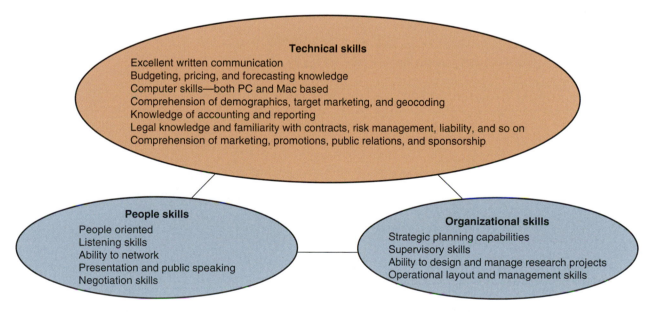

Figure 10.1   Organizational, technical, and people skills essential for sport management and marketing agency personnel.

Hungary: A Small Country With a Unique Sport Management System

By János Váczi, Hungary
Deputy Mayor of Budapest XII District, Budapest

Dániel Gyurta is collecting another Olympic gold for Hungary.

Hungary has a unique sport system. Its roots go back to the 1970s, when the ruling communist government deliberately picked and positioned certain Olympic sports to enhance the country's image. Because of Hungary's small size and economy, it was obvious that Hungarians could no longer be competitive in Europe's dominating and gradually growing business-driven sport of soccer. Therefore, sport politicians and administrators consciously selected to focus on lesser-known international sport disciplines where they thought success could be achieved relatively easily at low costs and in a less competitive environment. Fenc-

Challenges Facing Agencies

Although the sport management and marketing agency segment of the sport industry is growing in number of firms and job opportunities, agencies face many complex challenges in the second decade of the 21st century. These challenges are similar to those encountered by advertising agencies, public relations firms, creative firms, and other enterprises that rely closely on client bases for their revenue. Some prominent challenges are outlined here:

ing, swimming, kayaking, wrestling, gymnastics and modern pentathlon federations, clubs, and athletes received a great deal of government attention and support. The results of this were shiny Olympic medals and growing national pride. In fact, Hungary, despite its small size, has been one of the best performing nations at the Summer Games. When basing medal counts on GDP, size, or population, Hungary is almost a world leader.

In addition to Hungary's small individual sports, one team sport, water polo, became a dominating factor on the international sport scene. With a total of nine Olympic gold medals, including three consecutive wins between 2000 and 2008, some have begun to call water polo the national sport of Hungary. With a unique sport system, however, a unique sport management model has also developed. Small individual sports and water polo in an undeveloped market have been unable to work and operate based on marketing or business principles. Because of the weak market and lower popularity of these sports, the Hungarian government stepped in as the main financial player, and these Olympic events are almost solely state or government supported. As the western world is drifting toward a sports structure where everything is media, marketing, or business driven, Hungary created its own system that relies mostly on government funds.

Two years ago, new legislation deepened the state's role in sports financing. Five so-called spectator sports were selected (soccer, basketball, handball, water polo, and ice hockey) and a scheme was developed that local companies could allocate their company tax to support teams, federations, youth development, and facilities of these five sports. In addition to this, 16 sport federations were selected to receive direct support from the government to prepare for the next Olympic Games. While these measures significantly increased the available funds, they also undermined any possible transformation or shift toward a modern, competitive, marketing or business-oriented local sports market.

The only exemption where some signs of change or business approach are seen is soccer. Although the national team has not been to the Euro or the World Cup for almost 30 years, the management philosophy of clubs is slowly changing, while more and more local and international owners and businessmen consider Hungarian soccer as a long-term investment. Still, Hungary has a long way to go before its team reaches the number one status in Europe again.

International Learning Activity #1

The United Kingdom completely revitalized its sport financing after a disappointing performance at the 1996 Olympic Games. Conduct an Internet search to find out how the UK restructured its financing and compare it to the Hungarian system described earlier.

International Learning Activity #2

The Champions League is the most lucrative European sport product organized by the UEFA. Find out how much the winning team made and list the various sources the money came from. Sometimes it's not the overall winner of the Champions League who makes the most money after the series. Explain why this can happen.

International Learning Activity #3

Conduct an online search for the highest earning international athletes of the past year. Check the same list that was issued five years ago. See if there are changes of sports or if new trends are emerging. Find a list of your own country's best earners and make a comparison to see the regional differences.

› *Uncertainty in client base.* As a segment of the sport industry with a strong reliance on clients, whether athletes, corporate brands, properties, or broadcast entities, many decisions that directly affect sport management and marketing agencies fall well outside their control. An athlete may simply decide to select new representation. A corporate brand may elect to step back from sports due to a wholesale strategy shift or because the new CEO doesn't believe in spending in sports. For properties and media entities, agency work is often temporary, discontinued as specific projects come to completion.

This has the potential to distinctly affect not only bottom-line revenue at agencies, but also the employee bases who generally work as individuals or teams focused on a specific client. Should that particular client no longer exist, those employees can be more vulnerable than their counterparts at other types of companies in the sport industry. While agencies work hard to put themselves in a favorable position and positively influence these factors, they ultimately cannot control them. Given this uncertainty, sport management and marketing agencies are particularly motivated to provide an exceptional level of service to existing clients while constantly seeking out new ones. Similar concerns created by the economic marketplace are explored in greater detail in the economic challenges section that follows.

› *In-house versus outsourcing.* After benefiting from high-level performance by a sport management and marketing agency for several years, clients may believe that they know the functions that the agency performs and decide to dismiss the agency to bring that function in-house. As with the uncertainty challenge mentioned previously, the agency may then have to cut personnel and budgets due to losing the account. Often in these situations, the agency will also lose a key staff member or members, as the client may hire individuals for the in-house team given their expertise and familiarity with the organization. This practice is becoming more prevalent in professional sport leagues, such as the NBA and NHL, and in collegiate athletics departments due to the need to reduce costs like agency fees while maximizing revenues that are perceived to be driven from inside the organization. By bringing sponsorship, licensing, and broadcasting in-house instead of outsourcing them to agencies or hiring an outside agency to perform functions on their behalf, organizations believe that they will have more control and generate more income while cutting the expense of agency fees. For a more detailed examination of outsourcing, refer to the critical thinking section later in this chapter.

› *Conflicts of interest.* With the growth of full-service agencies, the potential for conflicts of interest has increased. Firms such as Wasserman Media Group represent a wide variety of clients across the sport landscape including leagues, teams, athletes, events, corporate brands, and media companies. With such a broad client base, it is inevitable that the interests of some of these parties will occasionally come into conflict. For example, an agency may be under contract with both a free-agent basketball player and several NBA teams, resulting in a potential conflict of interest. Or perhaps an agency represents two corporate clients with a small subset of overlapping products or interests. Additionally, as noted earlier in this chapter, agencies often create and own events in which their athletes participate. Each of these scenarios presents a potential conflict of interests and subsequent ethical and business questions for agency leadership. Fundamentally, agencies bear the responsibility to mitigate these issues and act in good faith to all parties involved, while also remaining mindful of the charge to maximize agency profits. Often, a distinct separation of divisions within agencies, particularly large, full-service agencies, serves as a built-in check and balance against potential conflicts of interest of this nature.

› *Mergers and acquisitions.* Agencies have traditionally grown organically in size and scope, but the current trend is toward growth through aggressive mergers and acquisitions. Three firms that have used this growth strategy are WMG, IMG, and Octagon. Since 2005, WMG has acquired SFX Sports, OnSport, Reich & Katz baseball representation, RAM Sports and Entertainment (UK), SportsNet, Arn Tellem's athlete management business, and Champion Sports Group. These acquisitions have helped WMG quickly achieve full-service status and emerge as a global leader among sport management and marketing agencies. Regarding IMG, as noted earlier in the chapter, this agency acquired Host Communications in 2007, which now operates as a division of IMG College. Lastly, Octagon, as a division of advertising conglomerate Interpublic Group, expanded rapidly by acquiring firms such as Advantage International; Flammini

Group, an Italian motor sports producer; CSI, a large UK-based television rights and production firm; Koch Tavares, a Brazilian sports agency; and IMS Sports, an agency that represents action sports athletes. Octagon now represents more than 900 athletes and manages over 13,000 events annually (Octagon, 2013). The acquisitions strategy allows agencies to reach critical mass quickly and provide a full range of services to clients, while strengthening their appeal to new prospective clients. A downside of this strategy is the challenge of assimilating existing companies into the overall culture of the agency. Agencies that succeed with an acquisition strategy tend to be those that mitigate this risk by making culture and adaptability a critical factor in the selection process well before merging the new group into the parent organization.

› *Labor unrest.* After the resolution of the NHL's labor issues in 2013, the major sport leagues seem to be back on track. During labor unrest and lockouts, employment at properties (e.g., leagues, teams) can be uncertain as properties look to cut costs during non-revenue-generating periods. For agencies, labor unrest can mean both opportunities and challenges. During a lockout, talent management agents will often maintain their staff in numbers but refocus their efforts to marketing and endorsements where there is still opportunity for the athlete to generate revenue. Without a collective bargaining agreement (CBA) in place, athletes may actually have more endorsement opportunities, since they can temporarily endorse brand categories not typically allowed by their league or team (e.g., alcohol, tobacco, spirits).

› *Economic challenges.* Sport management and marketing agencies also face a unique set of economic challenges. To remain competitive and profitable, the agencies in the sport industry must find ways to mitigate or conquer major economic challenges in the marketplace, particularly those listed as follows.

> The banking and automotive industries are just beginning to emerge from challenging years of pushing to improve their business models and satisfy a high level of accountability and public scrutiny, often resulting in a significant reduction in sponsorship spend. Companies in these industries have traditionally been reliable, large-scale spenders on sport sponsorship, and their reductions have had a ripple effect across the sport landscape.

> Beyond specific sectors, the generally weakened economy has resulted in increased overall budget scrutiny, with many companies implementing cost-cutting measures. With cost becoming the distinct area of focus, this has resulted in a move back to evaluation by quantitative ROI models and away from more qualitative return on objective (ROO) and return on experience (ROE) models. In some cases, this has created a hard strategy shift away from sponsorship and toward traffic-building ideas and couponing, thereby eliminating the need for a sport management and marketing agency.

> As economic conditions constrict the total pool of potential sport-related stakeholders and the funds they may dedicate to sport, it is increasingly imperative that the sport management and marketing agency become more creative in terms of activation and more responsible in terms of accountability and results.

> Sport management and marketing agencies and their clients will need to become more focused on creating business solutions using marketing platforms. These platforms must be structured for cost efficiency while amplifying marketing impact.

> Corporate brands and category segments that have been significantly restricted in sport, such as alcohol purveyors, are now back in play. Agencies must identify new opportunities for products and brands that have limited or no previous sport marketing experience.

> Sport management and marketing agencies must become more nimble in making quick adjustments to capitalize on new and emerging opportunities and markets. The time available to wait and react is limited.

> Sport products such as sponsorships and premium seating (e.g., suites) may be sold in different incremental offerings (e.g., monthly, quarterly) than they were in the past. Agencies must be able to visualize how to use sport in a more constricted time basis that might lead to a better ROI and expanded marketing opportunities.

> New revenue models featuring revenue sharing may become more common because of the economy. Agencies may garner less up-front money, with deals structured for more of an upside in terms of revenue sharing. This approach will require different strategies and forms of accountability and documentation.

> As deal terms contract and contract amounts decrease, sport management and marketing agencies will need to expand their client bases or the breadth of their offerings in order to assure financial stability. This will be a particular challenge, especially for smaller agencies, giving the competitiveness of the marketplace.

> Global connectivity of sport has grown and will continue to grow exponentially. Sport management and marketing agencies must become well versed in global thinking, with a strong understanding of different cultures. This knowledge will provide them with an accurate way of assessing international marketing opportunities and the best chance of experiencing success outside the United States. Looking to the future, global experience and knowledge will be a requirement for assuring financial viability.

Critical Thinking in Agency Activities

For more than two decades, collegiate athletic departments have made a common practice of outsourcing their rights fees in several areas, most notably in the area of radio and television rights fees, but also in the area of their corporate partnerships. Purchasing the rights fees from collegiate athletic departments was a practice developed by Host Communications, which originated in Lexington, Kentucky, in 1972. The company was acquired by IMG in 2007 to form IMG College.

Social Media and Sport Management and Marketing Agencies

With the growth and mainstreaming of social media, fans have been introduced to a much closer relationship with the athletes, coaches, and broadcasters they have long adored from afar. Now more than ever, industry talent has an outlet to express their opinions, thoughts, and life moments without interference from traditional media. However, with this new access has also come an overwhelming responsibility to be mindful of what, when, where, and how one posts, tweets, and so on. This ripple effect has caused leagues, teams, and governing bodies to institute new rules regarding the nature and timing of how their entities and employees may interact with social media. For instance, the National Football League (NFL) modified its social media policy to restrict any postings by players or coaches from 90 minutes prior to a game until after postgame interviews have ended. From a talent perspective, athletes have realized that they must be responsible with their social media presence, but that a strong following can lead to incremental revenue through digital endorsements. Most full-service agencies such as Octagon or Wasserman now employ teams of digital experts to assist the athletes they represent in creating and managing their social media feeds, leading to greater endorsement opportunities and media exposure for those athletes.

These rights fees, which can be limited to a single college or university or an entire conference, can include all or multiple elements of the following services: corporate sponsorships, radio and television programs, publishing, printing, creative design, marketing, Internet, national advertising and signage sales, and numerous lifestyle and event marketing platforms ("IMG to Acquire," 2007). Most recently, IMG College has expanded these services to include ticket sales, a space they share with other agencies like Learfield and the Aspire Group. The reasons for the popularity of service outsourcing are multifaceted:

> It ensures a guaranteed, fixed revenue stream to the university or league regardless of team performance, the economy, or other influential factors. The outsourced agency, in essence, assumes the revenue risk previously held by the university.

> It eliminates the in-house groups that universities and leagues would have to employ to handle these functions. This can save costs by reducing head count for athletics departments that are not equipped to structure the types of compensation and benefit packages necessary to secure these specialized groups of sales employees.

> Outsourcing allows athletics directors and departments to focus on their core business—athletes, teams, facilities, fundraising, and the university.

> It creates economies of scale by aggregating inventory to allow agencies to uniquely bundle and package content in order to garner a premium price.

In 2009, IMG College entered into a record US$110 million agreement with The Ohio State University for rights to the university's athletic inventory. This contract is the largest ever in this marketing area and is even more impressive because it does not include any TV rights (which are owned by the Big Ten Conference) except the coaches' television shows. The deal also excludes the current licensing agreement with Nike, which will continue to be managed in-house (Smith, 2009). IMG's rights include corporate sponsorships and stadium and arena signage, on-site marketing, coaches' endorsements and television shows, publishing rights, and a partnership with Radio Ohio, the broadcast company that has held the Buckeyes' radio rights since 1984.

According to then senior associate athletics director Ben Jay, "My concern, with the economy, is how many of our sponsorship deals were going to get renewed." Jay added, "How many of those sponsors are going to be looking for a reduction" (Smith, 2009, para. 15). The 10-year agreement gave OSU peace of mind on both accounts. Conversely, the length of the agreement provided IMG College sufficient time to develop its relationships, grow the business, and generate revenue. When asked why the Buckeyes, one of the last programs to continue to keep its rights in-house, were willing to make such a significant change, OSU athletics director Gene Smith stated, "When you project our revenue in future years, IMG's bid is almost double what we were looking at had we kept the rights in-house" (Smith, 2009, para. 16).

Only time will tell if IMG College can make the partnership successful by not only meeting the obligations and expectations of this agreement, but also generating enough profit to justify the record-breaking rights fee. Needless to say, IMG College's competition and potential future clients will be watching with great interest.

PORTFOLIO

Complete the critical thinking portfolio activity in the WSG, consulting as needed the "Critical Thinking Questions" sidebar in chapter 1.

Ethical Issues in Sport Management and Marketing Agencies

In 2009, NBA team owners reversed a long-time ban on courtside advertising by spirits brands in an effort to increase revenue during the current economic downturn. Before this decision, alcoholic spirits signage was limited to premium clubs and related signage that was not on camera during telecasts. The NBA decision followed those of MLB, the NHL, and NASCAR in allowing spirits advertising within camera view.

This ownership vote opens new revenue sources for all NBA teams that have observed the ban on such advertising since 1991. According to Chris Granger, then senior vice president of team marketing and business operations for the NBA, "We are always trying to find ways to drive more revenue and this falls in line with that." Granger added, "We are working too on what other opportunities will exist" (Lombardo & Lefton, 2009, para. 5).

Over the past decade, various ad restrictions at sport properties regarding formerly off-limit categories have been loosened. For example, casino resorts are a fixture at many big sport venues and on sports telecasts, as are state lotteries. Then principal of WMG Gary Stevenson stated, "I don't have an issue with this because I don't see a lot of difference between hard liquor and beer when it comes to advertising" (Lombardo & Lefton, 2009, para. 12).

Given the state of the global economy, what comes next? Will tobacco be given consideration under a set of narrow and restrictive guidelines for messaging? Will electronic cigarettes grow to become a new major category in the sport sponsorship landscape? One thing that remains clear is that as some categories and businesses cut back on their sport spending, those revenues need to be replaced. Will other categories emerge or existing categories grow to fill that gap? This is a key question for sport management and marketing agencies.

PORTFOLIO

Complete the ethical issues portfolio activity in the WSG, consulting as needed the "Guidelines for Making Ethical Decisions" sidebar in chapter 1.

Summary

A sport management and marketing agency is a business that acts on behalf of a sport-related stakeholder, commonly referred to as a client. The four major stakeholder groups are talent, properties, corporate brands, and media companies. Although agencies were initially formed to represent athletes, they have evolved to serve myriad functions, such as strategy, representation, negotiation, sales, licensing, marketing, management, and measurement, for all sport stakeholders. Sport management and marketing agencies and the sport industry groups that perform similar functions can be classified into the following major categories:

> Full-service agencies (e.g., IMG, Wasserman, Octagon)—provide a full range of services performed by in-house personnel across multiple stakeholder groups

> General agencies (e.g., 16W Marketing, GMR Marketing, Team Epic)—provide a variety of services to clients, but are not involved in all potential agency functions or with all stakeholder groups

> Specialty agencies (e.g., Millsport, Joyce Julius & Associates)—specialize in providing particular types of services or serving a particular stakeholder group

> In-house groups (e.g., NBA Events and Attractions)—departments of existing companies that perform many agency-like sport marketing functions on behalf of the products or divisions of the parent company

Careers in sport management and marketing agencies are challenging and varied. Agencies provide opportunities at every experience level and often look to hire team members with varied backgrounds who can complement their current employee base. Lastly, sport management and marketing agencies face several current challenges—uncertainty in client base, in-house versus outsourcing, conflicts of interest, mergers and acquisitions, and labor unrest—as well as economic uncertainty and ethical issues that affect their daily operations.

Review Questions

1. What are the functions performed by sport management and marketing agencies?

2. Why is research and evaluation a crucial role performed by sport management and marketing agencies?

3. How are specialty agencies different from full-service sport management and marketing agencies?

4. What are some of the benefits of bringing functions such as sponsorship in-house instead of outsourcing to sport management and marketing agencies?

5. Founded in 1960, IMG benefited from being the first and best-known sport management and marketing agency. What events affected the competitive situation faced by IMG? With recent changes, what is the current situation for this sport management and marketing agency?

6. What are some examples of how you can apply ethical decision making and critical thinking skills to the activities of sport management and marketing agencies?

7. What are the most pressing challenges facing agencies in the second decade of the 21st century?

References

16W Marketing. (n.d.). 16W Marketing, LLC. Retrieved from http://16wmktg.com

Conrad, E. (1995, January 10). NFL experience: Super Bowl-related bazaar will be running right next to JRS. *Sun Sentinel*, p. 10.

IMG. (2007, November 12). IMG to acquire Host Communications. *Marketwire*. Retrieved from www.marketwired.com/press-release/img-to-acquire-host-communications-nasdaq-tcmi-791612.htm

IMG. (2013a). IMG homepage. Retrieved from http://img.com/home.aspx

IMG. (2013b). About us. Retrieved from http://img.com/about-us.aspx

IMG. (2013c). Services: Consulting. Retrieved from http://img.com/services/consulting.aspx

IMG. (2013d). Services: Media Production. Retrieved from http://img.com/services/media-production.aspx

Liberman, N. (2005, September 26). Agencies roll out new measurement tools as sponsors seek to justify their investments. *Street & Smith's SportsBusiness Journal*, p. 23.

Lombardo, J., & Lefton, T. (2009, January 19). NBA cans ban on liquor ads. *Street & Smith's SportsBusiness Journal*, p. 1.

Mickle, T. (2013, April 8). Pieces in place for IMG sale; who are the likely bidders? *Street & Smith's SportsBusiness Journal*, p. 1.

Octagon. (2013). Who we are: By the numbers. Retrieved from www.octagon.com/who_we_are/by_the_numbers

Saitto, S., Soshnick, S., & Fixmer, A. (2013, May 2). Forstmann said to choose Morgan Stanley, Evercore for IMG sale. *Bloomberg*. Retrieved from www.bloomberg.com/news/2013-05-02/forstmann-said-to-choose-morgan-stanley-evercore-for-img-sale.html

Smith, M. (2009, March 30). Ohio State lands $110M deal. *Street & Smith's SportsBusiness Journal*, p. 1.

Wasserman Media Group. (2014). Home: Consulting. Retrieved from http://wmgllc.com

HISTORICAL MOMENTS

- **1897** First Boston Marathon held
- **1912** Inaugural Calgary Stampede held
- **1936** Sun Valley Ski Resort opened
- **1939** National Baseball Hall of Fame dedicated
- **1963** Pro Football Hall of Fame opened
- **1975** First General Assembly of World Tourism Organization held in Madrid, Spain
- **1978** First Ironman Triathlon held
- **1987** First National Senior Olympic Games held in St. Louis, Missouri
- **1992** National Association of Sports Commissions (NASC) founded
- **1997** ESPN Wide World of Sports Complex opened—originally called Disney's Wide World of Sports
- **2001** First World Conference on Sport and Tourism held in Barcelona, Spain
- **2006** FIFA World Cup hosted in Germany
- **2008** Beijing Summer Olympic and Paralympic Games held
- **2010** Vancouver Winter Olympic and Paralympic Games held
- **2010** First FIFA World Cup hosted on the African continent by South Africa
- **2011** Germany hosted 2011 FIFA Women's World Cup
- **2012** London hosted the Summer Olympic Games and Paralympic Games
- **2013** *SportsTravel* noted sport-related travel annually generates over 47 million room nights
- **2014** Sochi Winter Olympic and Paralympic Games held; Brazil hosted FIFA World Cup

11

SPORT TOURISM

Heather Gibson Sheranne Fairley

LEARNING OBJECTIVES

> Explain tourism and the tourism industry.

> Describe the intersection between sport and tourism.

> Distinguish among the three types (i.e., active, event, and nostalgia) of sport tourism.

> Discuss the sociocultural, economic, and environmental effects of sport tourism.

> Detail issues in sport tourism that involve critical thinking, ethical decision making, and technological (e.g., social media) application.

> Understand the basic premises of sustainable development and how they relate to sport tourism.

Key Terms

casuals

convention and
   visitors bureau
   (CVB)

destination image

displacement effect

leverage

psychic income

seasonality

sports commission

synergy

time switchers

GET A JOB

Continue on your journey in sport management by going to the web study guide (WSG) at www.HumanKinetics. com/ContemporarySportManagement. Check out the job opportunities and consider the skills and experiences that can help you succeed in sport management.

Over the past couple decades, sport-related travel has received increasingly more attention from both academics and the sport and tourism industries. In fact, sport tourism has been touted as the fastest growing sector in the global travel and tourism industry. In support of such a sport-travel contention, an industry study showed that in 2011, there were 23.9 million sports visitors in the United States (Schumacher, 2012), while a study by Humphreys (2008) found that in 2005, Americans spent a total of 797.2 billion hours attending sports events, or nearly 9.5 hours per person per year. Moreover, two of the world's most influential agencies for sport and tourism, the International Olympic Committee (IOC) and the United Nations World Tourism Organization (UNWTO), have cooperated since 1999 and recognized the mutually beneficial relationship that sport and tourism can have as a tool for sustainable economic growth.

Sport-related travel stretches back over the centuries. The Greeks traveled to take part in the ancient Olympic Games from as early as 900 BCE, and the Romans regularly staged popular sport competitions that drew large crowds of spectators from various localities (Coakley, 2009). In recent years, the term *sport tourism* has become widely used to describe this type of travel and involvement, and sport-related travel has gradually become a specialized sector of the sport and tourism industries. Sport tourism as defined by Gibson (1998a; 1998b) encompasses three main types of travel and sport participation:

> Active sport tourism, a trip in which the tourist takes part in a sport such as golf

> Event sport tourism, a trip in which the tourist watches a sport event such as the Super Bowl

> Nostalgia sport tourism, a trip in which the tourist visits a sport-themed attraction such as the Baseball Hall of Fame in Cooperstown, New York

The purpose of this chapter is to explore the relationship between sport and tourism, examine the three types of sport tourism, and recognize some of the environmental, economic, and sociocultural effects of sport tourism within a framework of sustainable development. The intent is to provide future sport managers with an understanding of the symbiotic (i.e., mutually beneficial) relationship between sport and tourism and to present some of the issues related to this growing industry.

Tourism and the Tourism Industry

In the first decade of the 21st century, the tourism industry experienced some rocky times. Economic uncertainty, the terrorist attacks of September 11, 2001, the bombing of a nightclub in Bali (Indonesia), the SARS outbreak in Asia and Canada, and the swine flu epidemic in 2009 all affected the confidence of the traveling public. Despite the increased risks associated with travel, people have returned to it again in even greater numbers. In 2012, the UNWTO reported that international tourism receipts generated US$1,075 billion and that travel is the largest and fastest growing industry in the world (World Tourism Organization, 2013, p. 3).

The enormous size of the tourism industry is partly attributed to the range of services and products associated with it, from airlines to rental cars, cruise ships to bus tours, campsites to five-star resorts, and theme parks to national parks. Indeed, Goeldner and Ritchie (2011) proposed that any definition of tourism must include four components:

1. Tourists
2. Businesses that provide goods and services for tourists
3. The government in a tourist destination
4. The host community or the people who live in the tourist destination

WEB

Go to the WSG and complete the web search activity, which has you research and compare the government sport tourism strategies of at least two countries.

This chapter is dedicated in memory of Jack Hughes, executive director (1997-2013) of the Gainesville Sports Commission (GSC) and a former president of the National Association of Sports Commissions. Jack was a pioneer in sport tourism. His legacy will live on through all of the students who interned or volunteered at the GSC over the years and in the communities he inspired to develop sport tourism initiatives. We would like to thank Megan Axelsen (University of Queensland) for her assistance with the revision of this chapter.

The travel and tourism industry also encompasses a wide range of traveler types—leisure travelers, business travelers, those visiting friends and relatives, and those traveling for a range of other reasons. The World Tourism Organization (1994) developed a standardized definition of tourism to alleviate some of the inconsistencies that had been occurring around the world in measuring tourism: "Tourism comprises the activities of persons traveling to and staying in places outside of their usual environment for not more than one consecutive year for leisure, business and other purposes" (p. 9).

If tourism constitutes the "activities of persons traveling," it would follow that tourists are the people who actually do the traveling outside their home communities. At the simple level, this is correct, but the defining characteristic of a tourist is not just the travel component. Attributes also include the reason or the motivation for the trip, the length of the trip, and even the distance traveled.

In terms of motivation or reason for the trip, Cohen (1974) argued that people who travel for leisure are tourists and that business travel is a related but separate segment of the travel industry. In the realm of sport tourism, it makes sense to adopt the idea that a tourist is a leisure traveler because most sport-related trips constitute our everyday understanding of leisure as occurring outside of work, activity that is freely chosen and enjoyable (Roberts, 2006). Consequently, examples of a sport tourist would be someone who travels to play golf, to watch a favorite team play football, or to visit a sport hall of fame.

Defining Sport Tourism

Most existing definitions of sport tourism distinguish between two types of behavior: active, in which a person travels to take part in a sport, or passive, in which a person travels to watch a sport (Standeven & De Knop, 1999). Redmond (1991) recognized the growing popularity of sport-themed destinations, such as sport halls of fame, cruises in which tourists have the opportunity to meet their favorite sport personalities, and sport stadiums as tourist attractions. Like Redmond, we argue that this type of sport tourism constitutes a third type of behavior—one motivated by nostalgia or a chance to pay homage to a sport personality or stadium associated with a great team or event. This third type is called nostalgia sport tourism.

Thus, the working definition of sport tourism for this chapter will be "leisure-based travel that takes individuals temporarily outside of their home communities to participate in physical activities [active sport tourism], to watch physical activities [event sport tourism], or to venerate attractions associated with physical activities [nostalgia sport tourism]" (Gibson, 1998b, p. 49).

Active Sport Tourism

The first type of sport tourism is travel to take part in sport, or active sport tourism. With a growing focus on active living, more people are choosing to be active while on vacation (Fluker & Turner, 2000). Research from the U.S. Census Bureau (2012) indicates that in 2009, Americans spent US$10.38 billion on participation sport travel. A number of recent trends might explain the increased popularity of active sport vacations. These trends include an increase in the range of sports offered to include nontraditional sports such as mountain biking and snowboarding, the fact that more people are choosing to take active sport vacations, and a growing awareness of active vacations around the world (Mintel Oxygen, 2006). A review of some of the specific types of active sport tourism illustrates the growth in opportunities for the active sport tourist.

ADVENTURE TOURISM

Some of the activities we include as active sport tourism, such as skiing, mountain biking, and hiking, can also be classified as adventure tourism. Adventure tourism has been "defined as travel outside a person's normal environment for more than 24 hours and not more than one consecutive year. A trip may be classified as an 'adventure' trip if it involves two of the following three elements: (1) interaction with nature or (2) interaction with culture or (3) a physical activity" (Adventure Travel Trade Association et al., 2011, p. 5). The physical and sportlike nature of these activities shows the crossover between active sport tourism and what is called adventure tourism. Adventure tourism is gaining in popularity. One tourism brochure published by the Adventure Travel Trade Association and associates (2011), in referring to a study into the adventure travel market in the United States, notes that more than one-fourth of travelers engage in adventure activities while on vacation. The same study also estimated the international adventure tourism industry to be worth US$89 billion.

Adventure tourism also encompasses a variety of experiences—some travelers seek what has been termed hard adventure, while others seek soft adventure. This continuum from soft to hard adventure begins with mild adventure at one end of the scale and progresses to hard adventure at the other extreme; it also involves differing degrees of challenge, uncertainty, setting, familiarity, personal abilities, intensity, duration, and perceptions of control (Swarbrooke, Beard, Leckie, & Pomfret, 2003; Tsaur, Lin, & Lui, 2013). Soft adventure travel activities include camping, canoeing, and wildlife viewing, while mountain biking, whitewater rafting, and hang gliding are examples of hard adventure (Schneider & Vogt, 2012).

An emerging niche sector within adventure and sustainable tourism is philanthropic adventure tourism. It is described as adventure tourism that raises money for charitable initiatives, for example, long-distance, multiday cycling or hiking events (Coghlan & Filo, 2013). Lyons and Wearing (2008) suggested that adventure philanthropy participants "blend the voluntary act of fund-raising with the more hedonic pleasures of a packaged adventure tour" (p. 151).

CRUISES

Sport-themed cruises, part of the cruise industry since the 1990s, provide opportunities for both nostalgia sport tourism and active sport tourism. For example, Royal Caribbean ads show groups of men playing golf on board the ship and a mother indicating that she had taken a spinning class. The invention of the golf simulator has been credited with creating

Cruise ships often offer nostalgia sport tourism and active sport tourism opportunities, including on-board options such this rock climbing wall.

a close relationship between golf and the cruise industry. Many cruise ships such as the *Queen Mary 2* have multiple golf simulators on board. In addition to on- and off-board golf offerings, adventure activities are also increasingly incorporated into cruise-line excursion itineraries (Adventure Travel Trade Association et al., 2011).

AMATEUR SPORTS

Amateur sport events, which encompass both active tourism and event sport tourism, have grown in recent years (Kaplanidou & Gibson, 2010). Such events are held in a wide range of sports, including road running, triathlon, archery, cycling, soccer, volleyball, swimming, and rugby. Some of these events are multi-sport competitions that are targeted at various population segments. For example, the Junior Olympics holds regional and national events for young athletes, the Special Olympics has events for people with mental disabilities, and the Transplant Games are for participants who have undergone transplant surgery. Since 1987 when the first National Senior Games Association (2013) competition was held, thousands of athletes aged 50 and older have participated at local, state, and national levels in a variety of sports.

Many community organizations host amateur sports events that attract not only local residents but also competitors from outside the community (Gibson, Kaplanidou, & Kang, 2012). While major events such as the New York Marathon and Boston Marathon are internationally recognized for having professional and amateur runners race side by side, lesser-known events also have the ability to attract competitors from all over the world. For example, the Manchester Road Race—a Thanksgiving Day run in Manchester, Connecticut—attracts runners from as far away as Europe and Africa.

GOLF AND SKIING

Over the past century, two of the most popular forms of active sport tourism have been golf and snow sports, notably alpine, or downhill, skiing. The United States has 25.7 million golfers (age 6 and over) and 15,619 golf courses, many of which are located in southern resort destinations (SRI International, 2012). SRI International estimates that in 2011, golf travelers made approximately 115.9 million golf-related visits (where an overnight stay was involved), with golf-related travel expenditure amounting to an estimated US$20.6 billion in the same year. According to the National Golf Foundation (2013), golfers favor such destinations as Florida, North and South Carolina, and Arizona. Golfers who live in areas with harsh winter climates or a lack of facilities are more likely to travel to pursue their sport. Many harbor a dream to play a round at the ultimate mecca of golf, the Old Course at St. Andrews in Scotland.

The development of downhill skiing in the United States resulted in tourism activities similar to those that occurred with golf. Sun Valley, Idaho, the first all-inclusive ski resort in the United States, was designed to increase passenger volume on the new westward expansion of the railroad. Subsequently, ski resorts in Aspen and Vail, Colorado, Park City, Utah, and Lake Tahoe, California, among others, followed. Like the regions of the United States associated with golf, these towns became synonymous with skiing.

Like those in other segments of the tourism industry, operators of ski areas and resort managers realized at the start of the 1990s that to maintain profitability, they had to combat **seasonality**, or the variable pattern of visitation throughout the year at a destination. Most destinations have three seasons: a peak season, a shoulder season (which occurs just before and just after the peak), and an off-season. Ski resorts have a definite season (winter), and fall and spring skiing occurs on either side. Many ski areas have diversified operations by adding all-weather indoor and outdoor activities and facilities, operating chairlifts in the summer months to accommodate activities such as hiking and mountain biking, and actively targeting the convention market and nonskiing vacationers (Needham et al., 2011).

seasonality—The variable patterns of tourist visitation throughout the year at a destination. Most destinations have three seasons: a peak season, a shoulder season (which occurs just before and just after the peak), and an off-season.

With the Cliffs of Moher in the background, international travelers can participate in active sport tourism—while braving the rain and sea winds—by playing this links course in Doolin, a fishing village in Ireland.

For many family-owned resorts, becoming a year-round destination was not enough. Faced with increasing costs from aging lift equipment, rising liability insurance rates, and unpredictable snow seasons (a result of climate change) that led to investment in new technologies such as snowmaking equipment (Dawson & Scott, 2013), many independent resorts have merged with or been acquired by larger ski corporations.

To maintain profitability in the face of a declining number of skiers, the ski industry has actively targeted the destination skier, an active sport tourist who spends more than a day at the resort, buying accommodation, food, and transportation as well as lift tickets. Moreover, golf and skiing continue to forge a closer relationship. Ski resorts use golf to combat seasonality and have begun to diversify their holdings. Intrawest, for example, owns a beach and golf resort in Sandestin, Florida.

Event Sport Tourism

destination image—The impression that people (especially potential tourists) have of a certain location.

The second type of sport tourism pertains to sport events as tourist attractions and to the sport tourists who travel to watch them. To combat seasonality and create or enhance their **destination image**, towns and cities around the world are increasingly hosting sport events that draw spectators as well as active sport tourists (Walker et al., 2013). These can be hallmark events such as the Wimbledon Championships and the Super Bowl, mega events such as the Olympic Games and World Cup, regional events such as PGA golf tournaments and NCAA-sanctioned college sports, or amateur events such as road races and the Senior Games. The competition among communities to host these events is intense because their leaders focus on the economic impact from event patrons, sponsorship deals, and, for the major events, television rights (Ritchie, 1999).

synergy—The interaction between two components, such as tourism and sport.

As community leaders have recognized the **synergy** between sport and tourism (Fourie & Santana-Gallego, 2011), they have increasingly looked to develop a destination image by hosting sport events in order to generate tourism. In examining event sport tourism, it is useful to think about two levels: the major events that draw international attention, such as a hallmark event or mega event, and the small-scale sport event.

HALLMARK EVENTS

Ritchie (1984) defined hallmark events as

> major one-time or recurring events of limited duration, developed primarily to enhance the awareness, appeal and profitability of a tourism destination in the short or long term. Such events rely for their success on uniqueness, status, or timely significance to create interest and attract attention. (p. 2)

Hallmark events include carnivals and festivals such as Mardi Gras in New Orleans, important cultural or religious events such as a British royal wedding, and major sport events such as the Super Bowl or the Calgary Stampede. Ritchie (1984) further added the criteria of relative infrequency, uniqueness of the event, aura of tradition, excellence in participants, and international attention. Jago and Shaw (1998) suggested that in addition to hallmark events, mega events are another type of major international-level event. Mega events are those of extraordinary significance, scale, and reputation, such as the Olympic Games and the FIFA World Cup, that garner international-level participation from athletes, spectators, and the world's media.

Increasingly, the mega sporting events have become as much a media spectacle as they have a sporting competition. Cities around the world regard the Olympic Games and the FIFA World Cup as a chance to reimage themselves, boosting their tourism industry and attracting new businesses (Essex & Chalkley, 1998). When South Africa held the FIFA World Cup in 2010, the expressed intent was not only to achieve the domestic goals of social cohesion and economic impact, but also to establish an increased international prominence for the entire African continent (Walker et al., 2013). Likewise, the Australian Tourist Commission actively worked to **leverage** the tourism associated with the 2000 Olympic Games in the years following by inviting the international travel media to visit and showcase various aspects of Australia in their travel writing and television coverage. With the hosting of the 2012 London Olympic Games, Oxford Economics (2012) estimated that over a period of 12 years, from 2005 to 2017, the UK will experience a net increase in tourist visits of 10.8 million, with the extra tourism spending predicted to contribute £2 billion to the UK GDP.

leverage—Using strategies to optimize the benefits or outcomes associated with an event.

The concept of destination image drives many communities to invest significant resources in hosting one event. It is generally thought that the international media coverage associated with a mega event will increase awareness of the host city and lead to increased tourism and business investment in the years to follow (Ritchie & Smith, 1991). A host city, however, cannot always expect the media coverage to be positive. For example, in the months leading up to the 2004 Olympic Games in Athens, Greece, the media focused consistently on the construction delays of the venues. Beijing, the host city of the 2008 Olympic Games, hoped that the event would constitute China's coming-out party, announcing to the world that the country was an emerging superpower (Steinmetz, 2008). Although staging the Olympic Games went relatively well, China received a lot of negative press beforehand about the poor air quality in Beijing and the protests about the country's relations with Tibet, which were a constant part of the Olympic torch relay (Streets, Fu, Jang, Hae, & He, 2007). Nonetheless, studies of previous Olympic Games showed that hosting this hallmark event can raise awareness and the image of a country around the world (Kim & Morrison, 2005; Fourie & Santana-Gallego, 2011). For maximum benefit to occur, however, an organizing committee needs to implement strategies to encourage the media to showcase the sights of the city and country beyond the sport venues (Chalip, 2004; Chien, Ritchie, Shipway, & Henderson, 2012).

Olympic Legacy

By Brent W. Ritchie
University of Queensland, Australia

By Richard Shipway
Bournemouth University, United Kingdom

Despite the growing importance of a triple bottom line approach to mega sport event tourism, limited research has been carried out to understand resident perceptions of event impacts. In the context of the 2012 London Olympics and Paralympic Games, we conducted a study to investigate residents' perceptions of Olympic tourism development in Weymouth and Portland both before and after the Games. Weymouth and Portland, which hosted the sailing events for the 2012 Olympics, are located in Dorset in the southwest of England.

Audience members display their national pride at the 2012 London Olympics.

Unfortunately, as Roche (1994) observed, hallmark events are "short-term events with long-term consequences for cities that stage them" (p. 1). Often, these consequences are not positive ones. Such events present significant economic risks. Unfortunately, more often than not, the economic costs outweigh the economic or tourism benefits (Sun, Rodriguez, Wu, & Chuang, 2013; Tien, Lo, & Lin, 2011). For example, the 2008 Beijing Olympics was hailed as the most expensive Olympic Games held, costing more than US$40 billion (Leeds, Mirikitani, & Tang, 2009), while the 2004 Athens Games cost Greece more than €13 billion, accounting for around 6% of Greece's Gross National Product (GNP) (Prayag, Hosany, Nunkoo, & Alders, 2013).

Stories such as this are more common than not in the aftermath of mega events. As a result, since the mid-2000s, there has been a call by the IOC and others to encourage organizing committees to identify and plan for the legacies associated with hosting the Olympic Games (Agha, Fairley, & Gibson, 2012). Preuss (2007) defined legacy as "all planned and unplanned, positive and negative, intangible and tangible structures created for and by a sport event that remain for a longer time than the event itself" (p. 86). Subsequently, the 2010 Vancouver–Whistler Winter Olympics had a legacy

We found that residents' overall support for hosting the Games dropped from 89% in 2007 to 85% in 2010 and 78% in January 2013. In the 2013 study, questions were asked about perceived legacies resulting from hosting the Olympics. The most likely legacy was the sporting infrastructure and protection of the Dorset coastline (68% likelihood it would occur), followed by tourism and regional image benefits (59%), and increasing sport participation to improve physical activity (56%). However, the findings also illustrate a lack of certainty regarding potential legacies, with 38% of the respondents reporting they were unsure whether the Olympics would regenerate East London, while 33% were unsure whether the promised economic growth associated with hosting the Olympics would actually occur.

Although only 2.6% of respondents had worked as one of the official volunteers, or Games Makers as they were called during the Olympics, a total of 24% of respondents indicated that they would volunteer for future events held in the community. A relationship was found between those who had volunteered and their increased intention to volunteer at events in the future. A spirit of volunteering is often cited as a long-term legacy of hosting mega events such as the Olympic Games, and may be a more tangible legacy compared to the promises of regeneration and economic development.

International Learning Activity #1

Conduct an Internet search of the last four Olympic Games. What is the legacy that each of the Games left? What similarities or differences are present between the different Olympics, and why might these similarities or differences exist?

International Learning Activity #2

Volunteers are essential to the success of international sporting events. Think of an international sporting event with which you are familiar (e.g., Olympic Games, World Championships, World Cup) and discuss all of the ways in which the event would need volunteers to function successfully.

International Learning Activity #3

Go to www.rio2016.org and investigate strategies that the Rio Organizing Committee of the Summer Olympic Games and Paralympic Games has outlined for a sustainable mega event. Describe how Rio 2016 plans to build a sustainable Olympic Games. Do you think that the committee's plans for sustainability are achievable? Explain why or why not. How does the idea of legacy relate to the overall proposed sustainability of the Rio 2016 Summer Olympic Games?

committee responsible for recognizing and facilitating the long-term legacy of the Olympic Games. The London 2012 Olympic Games bid document mentioned the word *legacy* more than 150 times.

Oxford Street London dressed up for the 2012 Games.

Despite such thinking, host cities are often left with empty buildings and huge debts. Five months after the close of the 2008 Beijing Olympic Games, the iconic Bird's Nest (the Olympic Stadium) was "searching for a new purpose." It had yet to have any big events scheduled, and the government is worried about recouping the US$450 million required to build it. It has, however, become a tourist attraction, drawing thousands of visiting tourists per day.

Although communities continue to vie with one another to host these mega events, the realization is growing that hosting smaller-scale events might be more beneficial. Indeed, Ritchie (1999) suggested that hosting recurring events such as the Boston Marathon or the Calgary Stampede might be more valuable to a community and lucrative in the long run than one-time events such as the Olympic Games. The long-term effects of hosting mega events may lie in improved infrastructure and community pride rather than increased tourism (for more information on this topic, read the later section on social dimensions).

Small-Scale Event Sport Tourism

Although mega events such as the Olympic Games are regarded as the pinnacle for a community in terms of hosting a sport event, Higham (1999) suggested that small-scale sport events provide communities with more benefits and fewer burdens than the short-lived hallmark events. He defined small-scale sport events as "regular season sporting competitions (ice hockey, basketball, soccer, rugby leagues), international sporting fixtures, domestic competitions, masters or disabled sports, and the like" (p. 87). Small-scale sport events usually operate within the existing infrastructure of a community, require minimal investment of public money, are more manageable in terms of crowding and congestion, and may minimize the effects of seasonality for a destination (Gibson et al., 2012).

Many sport events around the United States fit the definition of a small-scale event, from professional and collegiate sports, to amateur sport events that represent the crossover between active and event sport tourism (discussed earlier) such as the Senior Games and Special Olympics. One form of small-scale sport tourism with much untapped potential is college sports. In terms of total attendance at sports events, college football and college basketball are second only to Major League Baseball (Humphreys, 2008; U.S. Census Bureau, 2012), illustrating the local importance of these events. A study by Lee, Harris, and Lyberger (2010) found that for Portage County (Ohio), the college football events of Kent State University contributed to more than US$1.6 million in event-associated sales, US$563,943 in personal income, and US$931,029 in value added, as well as the creation of 28.6 jobs. Other U.S. communities experience similar economic effects from hosting college sport events, and the contribution of these events often enable local stakeholders to boost their local economies. Thus, community tourism agencies such as **convention and visitors bureaus (CVB)** and **sports commissions** are often engaged in marketing and assisting amateur and professional sport organizations and events in their communities.

Communities around the United States and the world are recognizing that although hosting the Olympic Games may be out of the question, hosting small-scale sport events is a possibility. Even Walt Disney World in Florida recognized the potential associated with sport tourism by opening its Wide World of Sports in 1997, which caters to both active and event sport tourism.

Nostalgia Sport Tourism

The third type of sport tourism is nostalgia sport tourism. Redmond (1991) identified this type of sport tourism as traveling to visit sport halls of fame, taking sport-themed vacations on cruise ships or resorts, attending fantasy sport camps, and touring famous

convention and visitors bureau (CVB)—A community agency funded by the "bed tax," the local taxes paid for stays in commercial lodging facilities such as hotels. A CVB promotes tourism in a community and acts as a centralized source of information about events, accommodations, and other visitor-related information.

sports commission— Local or state agency responsible for attracting and organizing sport events to help communities capitalize on the potential benefits of sport tourism.

Professional Profile: Alex Alston

Title: sales and marketing director, SMG

Education: BS; MS (sport management), University of Florida

As an executive in the sport industry, Alex Alston is a good example of someone whose internship experiences as an undergraduate in sport management led him on a path to his current position. Alston was fortunate enough to attend the University of Florida at a time when sport-related tourism at the community events level was in its infancy and when the Gainesville Sports Commission (GSC or, as it was then, the Gainesville Sports Organizing Committee), led by Jack Hughes as executive director, was at the forefront of this type of small-event sport tourism. The GSC has always provided students at UF with hands-on experience in various aspects of event operations and, as such, it has started many students on the path to a career in sport tourism or working with various sports governing bodies. Alston's story is a good example of a path from undergraduate intern to executive director of a sports commission in a city considered a mid-to-large market. (After this interview was conducted, Alex moved back to Florida and is now working for SMG.)

What have been the key moves, steps, or developments in your career, and how did you arrive at your current position?

I secured an internship with the Gainesville Sports Commission during the final semester of my senior year at UF. After that, I was able to serve as an intern in three different capacities at the PGA Tour. On completion of that experience, a position opened with the Gainesville Sports Commission, and I was fortunate enough to be hired as the events manager. During my time in Gainesville, I was involved in numerous events including the FHSAA Football, Swimming and Diving, and Track and Field Finals, as well as events such as the USA Age Group Synchronized Swimming Championships, AAU Junior Olympic Track Championships, and numerous others. At this stage in my career, I was responsible for event operations, intern management, and recruiting potential events. After five years, I decided to go back to school to pursue my master's, and I pulled double duty as a student while keeping my position with the Gainesville Sports Commission. As I was graduating with my master's in sport management, I received an opportunity to go to Tulsa as the director of sales for the Tulsa Sports Commission. In this role, I was exposed to a greater number of potential event opportunities and was tasked with writing numerous event bids and building relationships with various events rights holders from across the country. My success in this role led to my promotion, after a little over a year, to executive director of the Tulsa Sports Commission.

What are your current responsibilities and objectives in your job?

I currently lead a five-person staff in the day-to-day operations of the organization, while still serving in a sales capacity. My role covers a broad range of responsibilities, ranging from board management, budget development and review, event sales, sponsorship development and sales, and staff evaluation. Our main objective is to create economic impact through sports events and meetings. We have an annual room night goal by which we are judged, and work closely with hotel partners to ensure proper reporting. Another aspect of our organization is fundraising. We host a number of fundraising events each year and also secure sponsors for particular events throughout the year.

What do you enjoy most about your current job?

Being able to hold a position in an industry built on relationships is the number one thing I enjoy about my work. The sports tourism industry is a small one, and the relationships that I am able to cultivate are good for business, and they have also led to lifelong friends and colleagues. You never know where you will end up or who you will work with in the future, so maintaining these relationships is critical.

What do you consider the biggest future challenge to be in your job or industry?

Competition. Our industry is extremely competitive now, but it will only get tougher as new cities develop an appetite for sports and realize the influence sport tourism can have on a community. As these new competitors surface, existing communities will continue to diversify their funding streams, creating an environment where events are essentially bought by the highest bidder. It is rapidly becoming an arms race, where the haves and the have-nots are being clearly defined. It will be up to the national governing bodies, conferences, NCAA, event rights holders, and so on to change the culture, but that is asking a lot when they are seeking the best deals for their organizations.

NE DAY

to the WSG
learn more
ut a typical day
he life for Alex Alston.
if he spends his
rking hours the way you
k he does.

ESPN Wide World of Sports Complex: The Ultimate Sport Tourism Destination

Since 1997 with the opening of its Disney's Wide World of Sports (the name was eventually changed to the ESPN Wide World of Sports Complex), Walt Disney World (WDW) in Orlando, Florida, has become an important venue for sport tourism. The area contains world-class facilities for hosting a range of sport events, from baseball and beach volleyball to basketball and gymnastics, and hosts about 350 professional and amateur events per year. The HP Field House, the indoor venue, has more than 70,000 square feet (21,336 m^2) of space for competitions and seating for 5,000 spectators. Similarly, the tennis complex has 10 clay courts and room for 1,000 spectators. Seating can be expanded to accommodate 7,500 people when hosting a professional event. The baseball stadium is the spring-training venue for the Atlanta Braves. But most of the sport events held at the ESPN Wide World of Sports Complex are youth and adult amateur competitions. These include the Special Olympics, high school field hockey championships, Amateur Athletic Union (AAU) wrestling competitions, the annual Walt Disney World Marathon, and the Walgreens Orlando International Dragon Boat Festival. The strategy behind the ESPN Wide World of Sports Complex is to use sport tourism to promote its core product, the theme parks. Athletes and spectators are actively encouraged to visit the parks during their stay. Theme park tickets are packaged with tournament fees and on-site hotel accommodations.

The complex uses volunteer sports enthusiasts to help run the larger events. On event days, guests can eat at the ESPN Wide World of Sports Grill and enjoy the PlayStation Pavilion. Moreover, on the WDW resort properties as a whole, many opportunities are available for guests to take part in sports, including golf, tennis, and jet boat racing. The Richard Petty Driving Experience helps guests realize the dream of being a NASCAR driver. The complex's auditorium hosts forums in which fans get a chance to listen to and interact with their favorite athletes. At the end of the day, guests can watch their favorite athletes on the TV screens of the ESPN Club on Disney's BoardWalk. In its diversity of sport tourism offerings, WDW provides opportunities for active, event, and nostalgia sport tourism in conjunction with visiting the four theme parks.

sport stadiums. The credit card company MasterCard once ran an advertising campaign that showcased the journey of two friends in a Volkswagen bus who visited the 30 MLB parks in the United States. This type of trip for a nostalgia sport tourist might be regarded as a dream vacation, a once-in-a-lifetime trip. Other nostalgia sport vacations might be more commonplace, involving such activities as visiting Cooperstown (home of the National Baseball Hall of Fame and Museum), the LPGA Hall of Fame, or the sport venues for the 2008 Beijing Olympic Games, as discussed earlier.

Most Olympic and major sport stadiums provide tours so that visitors can see behind the scenes, from the locker rooms to the press boxes and the VIP seating. These tours are generally guided by somebody who can provide in-depth information about the venue and its history. In the United Kingdom, soccer fans of a particular team can visit the football grounds, meet the players, and relive significant events in the history of the team. In the United States, an example of a company that specializes in sport vacations is Sports Travel and Tours. The company's baseball tour itineraries usually include four or more MLB games and a side trip to the Baseball Hall of Fame, thereby combining both event and nostalgia sport tourism.

Another trend over the past 15 years or so has been adult fantasy sport camps (Dwyer & Kim, 2011). These are a cross between a vacation and a training camp where participants pay for the privilege of spending a few days hanging out with their sports idols and receiving instruction from the pros while competing in a sport (Heydari, 2007). Golf, baseball, football, tennis, and NASCAR all have fantasy camps that range in cost, duration, and what is included. For example, for US$10,000, participants can take part in the weekend-long Coach K Academy, a basketball fantasy camp hosted by Olympic gold medalist and NCAA champion Duke University head coach Mike Krzyzewski, with former Duke players also serving as coaches (see www.basketballfantasycamps. com). The Gretzky Fantasy Camp is a weeklong event that features the chance to skate alongside Wayne Gretzky and other hockey greats. In 2013, the camp was held at the Bellagio in Las Vegas and cost participants US$11,999 for the experience (see www. gretzky.com/fantasycamp).

Nostalgia sport tourism is a relatively underdeveloped area of study, yet the growing popularity of this type of tourism suggests that scholars need to pay more attention to it. Researchers have argued that nostalgia may be associated not only with physical artifacts such as stadiums or sports equipment housed in halls of fame, but also with the social interactions of the group (Fairley 2003; Fairley, Kellett, & Green, 2007). While traveling by bus with a fan group, Fairley (2003) found that the fans reminisced about trips that they had previously taken together and enacted ritual activities as a way of reliving the nostalgia associated with those trips. Similarly, Kulczycki and Hyatt (2005) focused on the nostalgic feelings among Hartford Whalers hockey fans who traveled to watch NHL hockey games because their own team (the Whalers) had relocated to Raleigh, North Carolina.

Sustainability and Sport Tourism

Over the past couple of decades, the concept of sustainable development has become more commonplace. In general terms, sustainability takes the approach of balancing the needs of today with those of the future. Much of the focus has been placed on the environment and the conservation of natural resources. But the environment is only one prong of the three-pronged approach to sustainability, the other two being economics and social (cultural) well-being. The phrase "triple bottom line" is frequently used to describe the interrelationship among the three prongs of sustainability. In the tourism realm, the topic of sustainable development has been receiving a lot of attention in recent years (Mallen, Stevens, & Adams, 2011). If attention is not given to the long-term sustainability of a tourism destination, the effects of a large number of visitors can quickly destroy the attractiveness of a destination and its facilities (Collins, Munday, & Roberts, 2012; Mallen & Chard, 2012). In the realm of sport, less attention has been paid to sustainability. We argue that it is time to start thinking about the long-term sustainability of sport, particularly for those sports that rely on certain climate conditions such as skiing or golf, as well as for those that can have negative effects on the environment or local communities, both socially and economically. Thus, as sport tourism continues to grow in popularity, we need to be aware of the potential negative and positive effects of this sector on both the sport and the tourism industries, while at the same time working to improve the sustainable development of this particular niche. We will now look at each of the three prongs of sustainable development in turn.

Social Dimensions

Tourism studies have produced abundant evidence that tourism can have both positive and negative effects on a host community. Some of the positive social effects include improved political relations (Heere et al., 2012), improved cultural relationships (Schulenkorf & Edwards, 2012), and enhanced community pride, attachment, and excitement (Grieve & Sherry, 2012; Kim & Walker, 2012). This pride in community among the local residents results in what Burgan and Mules (1992) called the **psychic income**, which is often associated with hosting an event. Tourism has also been shown to open societies to new ideas and even bring about a liberalization of values in more

psychic income—The pride that people have in their community, generated by hosting a sport event.

Encouraging Youth Sport Tourism: Skate Park Facility Design

By Pamm Phillips, Australia
Deakin University, Melbourne

In Australia there are over 1,300 skate parks, and the sport of skateboarding has more participants than many organized sports. As such, skate parks have been identified as important facilities for cities to invest in for adventure sport tourism (Hinch & Higham, 2011). It is the young Generation Y and Z market that engage in skateboarding because of its individualistic nature, and buy associated products that meet their consumer needs (Kellett & Russell, 2009). The design of a skate park facility—the nature of the components that are installed, such as ramps, rails, and bowls, and how they are placed in relation to each other—makes the sport of skateboarding and its destinations attractive and unique. Many cities are realizing the power of using skate parks not only to cater for youths in their residential areas, but also to encourage youth sport tourism.

The Bondi Beach skate park attracts youth to Sydney, Australia's sunny shores.

rigid or closed cultures (Doğan, 1989). Tourism may also provide the funding and the impetus to preserve historic buildings, traditional practices (e.g., dances, crafts), and natural settings.

In recent years, there has been a growing focus on the social benefits of event sport tourism for communities. Many believe that the social benefits (e.g., sense of community, urban regeneration) are the true legacy of hosting a mega event. Positive outcomes, however, may not always result from sport events. In a study of the potential social costs associated with the hosting the Olympic Games, Minnaert (2012) found that mega events affect different segments of a host community unequally. In particular, socially excluded groups in the host community are rarely specifically targeted to be

The YMCA manages a number of skate parks in the state of Victoria, Australia. Their flagship facility, Riverslide Skate Park (Riverslide), is in the central business district (CBD) of Melbourne, and is managed on behalf of the local council (the City of Melbourne). Riverslide attracts youth from all over the state as it is easily accessible by public transport and is one of the largest supervised parks in Melbourne. Riverslide also provides a café, which has proven to be an excellent enticement for parents to accompany their children. Parents also spend additional money at the site and in retail stores in the CBD. The YMCA also offers holiday camps programming, which involve travel to other skate parks around Victoria that they manage. The camps become a win–win for the YMCA and other local councils in which the skate parks are located.

Skate parks, however, can offer destinations more than just tourism. The organizations that deliver skateboarding have been at the forefront of adopting technology to facilitate the delivery of and engagement in their sport. Sharing videos (taken with personal mobile phones), Internet streaming tricks skateboarders perform, and facilitating the use of social media to connect with other skateboarders have been key to the success of the sport. This is important for tourism, as what happens at any one skate park can be shared internationally in a matter of seconds. Any skate park that attracts youth and allows them to showcase their skills in unique ways through the installed components can gain international exposure for itself and the destination in which it resides.

Skate park construction companies in Australia have responded to the sophisticated needs of Generation Y and Z as consumers of skateboarding, as well as to the tourism needs of destinations (local councils), by designing and installing what they call youth precincts. Modern skate parks are being designed as destinations for youth that can bring skaters and their broader communities (including virtual communities) together in a sport and in a public space through integrating technology such as WiFi, visual screens, and speakers into the infrastructure of their installations.

International Learning Activity #1

Local councils grapple with strategic questions regarding youth sport tourism. For example, some questions that these councils may ask themselves include: How can we encourage youth sport tourism? How could a skate park be used to tap into motives for youth sport tourism? From the perspective of the host destination, what are advantages and disadvantages of a skate park as part of the destination portfolio? After studying this chapter, work together with your classmates to try to provide answers to these questions.

International Learning Activity #2

Conduct some research on the country of Australia and its culture. Additionally, study the culture of another country from a different part of the world. What is it about Australia's people, culture, and heritage that make skateboarding a popular youth sport tourism activity? Regarding the other country you study, what might be the most appropriate youth sport tourism options there and why? What similarities and differences exist between the two?

beneficiaries of the event. What's more, low-income residents often suffer the most because they are frequently displaced from their homes because of redevelopment plans (for more information on this topic, see the later section on ethics and the Vancouver 2010 Olympic Games).

Event sport tourism is not the only type of tourism to affect a host community. The crowding and congestion experienced by small ski towns or golf resort areas such as Myrtle Beach, South Carolina, also need attention. In most tourism regions, host communities experience a love–hate relationship with tourists. On the one hand, residents realize that their economic well-being often depends on tourists, yet the high prices, traffic congestion, and sometimes increased crime that accompany living in a tourist destination may lead to resistance and even hostility among community members (Doğan, 1989; Fredline, 2005). All these effects need to be carefully planned for in any proposed tourism development. But, as many of us argue, emphasis is too frequently placed on the potential economic benefits. The voices of the community are often overlooked and the social legacies are often ignored. The protests in Brazil over the costs associated with the 2014 FIFA World Cup and the upcoming 2016 Olympic Games are current examples as to how the local people may perceive the hosting of these mega events quite differently (Shaw, 2013). Arguably, the sustainability of most events may lie in the social dimensions, particularly enhanced community spirit, increased patriotism, and even an experienced event volunteer labor force that has the skills necessary to help with future events hosted by the community.

Economic Dimensions

When community leaders attempt to raise money to build a new stadium, secure a professional franchise, or host a sport event, they often point to the projected economic benefits arising out of these projects. But research has shown, particularly in relation to professional sport, that as many as 70% of spectators come from within the metropolitan area (Crompton, 1995; Sun et al., 2013) and therefore are not event sport tourists according to any definition of a tourist. Thus, although using sport as

Sport Volunteer Tourism: Traveling to Volunteer at Sporting Events

Because many sport events are not fixed to a particular location, volunteers must often travel some distance to the host venue. The travel requirement creates a sport tourism opportunity. An example of volunteer sport tourists are the members of the Sydney Olympic Volunteer (SOV) Social Club. The SOV Social Club was established as a web-based community in September 2000. The stated purpose of the club was to "keep the [Olympic] spirit alive" and to coordinate a concerted effort to volunteer at future Olympic Games and other sporting events. The website initially served as the primary communication medium for club members. A discussion section was posted on the website to facilitate dialogue among people interested in volunteering at the 2004 Athens Olympic Games. The discussion section included information about volunteering in Athens, a link to the official Athens 2004 website, and a suggestion that interested people should meet regularly to learn about Greek culture and to organize the trip to Athens collectively.

To prepare for volunteering in Athens, the SOV Club met every three months at a Greek restaurant in Sydney. At these meetings, they shared stories about their experiences at the 2000 Games, heard from guest speakers who were key to the Olympic subculture, exchanged information about logistical issues associated with travel to the Athens Olympic Games, and learned about Greek culture through language, food, and trivia. The main reasons people chose to travel to Athens to volunteer included nostalgia (i.e., wanting to relive volunteer experiences at the Sydney Olympic Games), camaraderie, being part of the Olympic subculture, and wanting to use the knowledge and skills that they had acquired while volunteering at the Sydney Olympic Games.

After arriving in Greece, group members used various means of accommodation, including staying with family or friends, participating in a Greek homestay program (i.e., living with a local family in Athens), or staying in a community facility that had been converted into a discount accommodation venue for the Olympic Games. Although some club members chose to stay only for the duration of the mega event, others extended their stay and explored other parts of Greece and Europe. After returning from Athens, the group changed its focus to the 2008 Olympic Games in Beijing, China, and subsequently met at a Chinese restaurant in the lead-up to the Beijing Olympic Games. After the closing of the 2008 Olympic Games, the focus shifted to the 2012 London Olympic Games.

a tourist attraction is a valuable strategy for economic and community development, we need to be sure when we read studies about the tourism-related impacts accruing from sport events that locals are not included in the people surveyed or the economic estimates generated.

We also need to be clear about how economic impact is measured. As Crompton (1995) explained, several common mistakes can occur when communities estimate economic impact, including using the wrong multiplier, measuring **time switchers** and **casuals**, and including people whose primary motivation was not to attend the event but who happened to be in the vicinity or switched the timing of their visit to coincide with the event. Another phenomenon that appears to be associated with hosting the mega event is the **displacement effect**: some potential visitors avoid a host city and region in the years leading up to, and during, the event, dissuaded by fear of congestion, construction-related hassles, and terrorism (Sun et al., 2013). Mules and Dwyer (2005) suggested that there is no accurate way to estimate how many visitors are displaced. But in conversations with various business owners, we have been told that regular tourism disappeared in Victoria, British Columbia, when the city hosted the 1994 Commonwealth Games. Similarly, in 2012 during the first week of the Olympic Games, hoteliers were slashing prices in an attempt to attract guests as the number of visitors to the city (both regular tourists and business travelers) had declined dramatically (Goss, 2012). This scenario is common in the months leading up to most mega events, and exemplifies the displacement effect noted earlier. Although the perceived risks associated with mega events appear to have heightened the displacement effect since the 2001 terrorist attacks (Neirotti & Hilliard, 2006), it is yet to be seen whether the terrorist bombings that specifically targeted participants and spectators at the 2013 Boston Marathon will lead to an increased displacement effect at other smaller hallmark events to the same degree.

Due to the numerous potential risks associated with hosting a mega event, security budgets for such events have been on the rise over the past several decades. For example, the UK invested at least five times the original estimated budget into security in the time period surrounding the 2012 Summer Olympic Games in London (Schroeder, Pennington-Gray, Kaplanidou, & Zhan, 2013). Despite the rising security budgets, the lure of the potential economic impacts associated with sport tourism will continue to grow as countries around the world rely more heavily on tourism to boost their gross national product. Members of the Cooperative Research Centre for Sustainable Tourism in Australia suggested, from their studies of the 2000 Olympic Games, that conducting a cost–benefit analysis may be more appropriate than emphasizing economic impact (Chalip & Green, 2001; Mules & Dwyer, 2005). Indeed, some of the preliminary lessons learned from hosting a hallmark event have been not to focus on the effects of an event but to use strategic leveraging to maximize the legacies and thus the sustainability of the event (Chalip, 2001).

Environmental Dimensions

As the popularity of sport vacations increases, we must consider the effects on the environment. Over the past 15 years, those in the tourism industry have begun to realize that the environment is the core of the tourism product. The growth in ecotourism and related products has been one outcome of this environmental concern. More recently, however, there has been a push toward extending sustainable development practices to all segments of the tourism industry. This new focus includes adopting a more comprehensive approach to sustainability that not only includes the social and economic dimensions (as discussed earlier) but also recognizes that forces such as global climate change may, in turn, affect the long-term viability of some tourism activities such as snow sports and scuba diving (Mallen & Chard, 2011).

time switchers—Visitors who had been planning to visit the destination and then switched their visit to coincide with the event; their spending cannot be attributed to the event.

casuals—People who happened to be visiting the destination and chose to attend the event instead of doing something else. Their attendance at the event was not their prime reason for visiting the destination.

displacement effect—The process whereby potential tourists are discouraged from visiting a destination because of perceptions of such hassles as crowding and construction or fear of terrorism.

Take, for instance, scuba diving. The growing popularity of the sport and recreational activity has resulted in increasing pressure on the environment: diver contact, specimen collecting, anchor damage, pollution from copper emissions in the antifouling paint, oil discharge, litter, untreated sewage, and toxic cleaning products all destroy the natural resource base (Ong & Musa, 2012). Moreover, from the perspective of global climate change, as temperatures increase, the health of the coral reefs is declining because of the increasing intensity and frequency of major storms, coral bleaching events, and other occurrences (Soutar & Lindén, 2000). Hence, the long-term viability of many diving locations around the world is being questioned.

Controversies surrounding skiing provide another example: long-term conservation efforts are often overlooked for the desire for optimal ski conditions in the short-term. In addition, due to climate-change impacts, regional ski areas are increasingly implementing adaption strategies that, ironically, often negatively affect the environment. Such strategies include building ski resorts at higher elevations to account for lower temperatures at altitude, investing in all-season resorts, delivering non-snow-based activities, and investing in snowmaking technologies (Dawson & Scott, 2013). In Southern Ontario, Canada, for example, heavy investment in snowmaking allows skiing to continue relatively unimpeded despite a warming world. However, snowmaking uses massive quantities of water, and pumping water for the process often either diverts or dries out mountain streams and lakes. One Alps-based study found that 2.8 million liters of water per kilometer of trail were required (Spector, Chard, Mallen, & Hyatt, 2012). From an ecological perspective, the alterations from the use of river water have cascading effects on species and ecosystems downstream. Pumping water from contaminated streams can introduce foreign acids and metals into the fragile alpine environments where the artificial snow is being laid. Artificial snow also melts at a slower rate than natural snow, thus potentially damaging grasses and flowers (Schmidt, 2006).

As Buckley, Pickering, and Warnken (2000) explained, ski resorts are among the most intensive forms of development in mountain regions, requiring tree clearing for ski runs and water for snowmaking and servicing the resorts. While the strategies implemented to extend the tourist seasons may reduce the economic effects of seasonality, they leave little time for grass and plant regeneration and relief from the noise and air pollution caused by the sheer number of people using the mountain roads to access the resorts.

Some of the same concerns have been raised in relation to the golf industry. Golf courses are land intensive, and the use of chemicals on the greens and water in desert areas have been of particular concern. One Philippines study found that the average golf course uses 24 million gallons of water per month—enough to irrigate 65 hectares of farmland (Woodside, 2009). Some golf courses have adopted strategies to protect the ecological balance of their courses with programs to protect wildlife, sponsored by partnerships between the United States Golf Association and Audubon International, among others (*Audubon International*, 2013). More needs to be done in this area, particularly in lesser-developed countries where national governments have identified golf tourism as a source of much-needed foreign currency, while ignoring the severe socioeconomic and environmental consequences that golf courses would have for their citizens (Palmer, 2004).

The IOC has charged host countries with implementing environmentally friendly practices in relation to the Olympic Games. The 1994 Winter Olympic Games in Lillehammer were called the first Green Games (Chernushenko, 1996). The Norwegian Parliament mandated Project Environment Friendly Olympics to protect the fragile ecology surrounding the small host city. Chernushenko argued that the Lillehammer Olympic Games provided a good example of event sport tourism and environmentalism that future events could copy; it produced not only a better event but also satisfied tourists and had a reputation as a clean and attractive destination.

Although the Sydney Olympic Games were also called the Green Games, Sparvero, Trendafilova, and Chalip (2005) contended that Sydney did not keep all its promises, citing the failure to detoxify Homebush Bay, where the main Olympics complex was located. The scholars questioned the traditional approach of using environmental guidelines mandated by sport governing bodies. They suggested that consensus-building approaches in which the local organizing committees and host communities are integrally involved in establishing environmental policies and practices for their events might be more successful. However, concern was raised in the media that the massive development involved in creating "a brand new ski resort from scratch" for the 2014 Sochi Winter Games displaced residents, and is likely to have long-term effects for the natural environment (Sanford, 2013).

Social Media and Sport Tourism

Social media has revolutionized the travel experience. More recently, this phenomenon has extended into sport tourism experiences. Specifically, the 2012 Summer Olympic Games were dubbed the first Social Media Games. While social media existed during the 2008 Summer Olympic Games, social media platforms experienced changes in functionality and dramatic increases in the number of users during the four years between the Beijing and London Games. During London 2012, the ways in which people consumed information about the Games was drastically altered. Information was disseminated by means of social media through various sources, ranging from official Olympic sources and the media to spectators. Social media allowed spectators to share experiences, pictures, and event updates with others. Those who were at home felt more connected to the Games than in the past because of unprecedented access to real-time information through social media, which sparked an unparalleled demand for live coverage through computers, mobile phones, and tablets. This led to a change in behavior and expectations. No longer did people have to wait for primetime television coverage. They were able to view the posts and pictures of spectators at the event, follow their favorite athletes and national teams, and view live videos and scores. Thus, a major part of London 2012's legacy is social media, which is a reflection of the current live and connected world in which we tend to turn to social media for current insider information.

Extraordinary access to information related to the Games, however, meant that people also had access to negative information. Not all information disseminated through social media was positive. For example, social media posts were made during several days of riots in London, which occurred approximately a year prior to the opening of the Games. Negative stories continued as the Games approached, with social media posts indicating that London did not have an adequate number of security personnel to ensure safety despite a record security budget. A large number of people could have been exposed to such negative news stories in social media through a variety of methods, including viewing posts by accounts followed, viewing a story shared by a friend, following a hashtag or keyword (e.g., #London2012), or viewing a picture or video, as well as through multiple platforms (e.g., Facebook and Twitter). Social media has also become an increasingly important information source in risky situations, including in the event of a crisis during travel, since people have perceived that social media provides information that cannot be found elsewhere at a rapid pace and promotes peer-to-peer communication during crises. Exposure to negative information through social media could occur at various stages of the travel process, and it has been found to influence travel-related decision making. In particular, international tourists who had read social media messages related to crises and disasters in London indicated a lower likelihood of traveling to London to attend the Games and higher perceptions of risk associated with London at the time of the Games. Given that people turned to social media for information related to the Olympics in record numbers, there may be an increased likelihood that they will be exposed to negative information about the host destination prior to and during future Games. This could be detrimental because exposure to negative information can affect the perceptions and behaviors of prospective and current sport tourists. While both positives and negatives are associated with social media, the social media landscape continues to evolve rapidly. It is expected that social media will continue to have an influence on future sport tourism events.

Written by Ashley Schroeder, University of Florida.

Critical Thinking in Sport Tourism

Certainly, there is evidence of a growing realization of the need for sustainable development in tourism of all kinds. The question becomes this: How do we balance the growing popularity of tourism in general and sport tourism in particular, along with the potential for greater economic profitability, with the need to protect the natural and sociocultural environments? A unified policy between sport and tourism agencies might be one way of balancing sustainability with profitability, in line with the three-pronged approach to sustainability.

Ethics in Sport Tourism

Winning a bid to host a mega event takes a lot of time, energy, and money. As noted earlier, mega events can bring many benefits to the host communities. For example, Vancouver raised its global profile considerably after hosting the 1986 World's Fair, Expo 86, and was looking for another event. When the Vancouver–Whistler sites in British Columbia were awarded the 2010 Winter Olympic and Paralympic Games, much celebration and excitement ensued.

But not everyone was pleased. Even before being awarded the Winter Olympic Games, there was controversy about how much it was going to cost to host the event and how that money could have been better spent on improving health care for residents of the province. Protests against seeking the Olympic bid were vocal, strong, and creative. A plebiscite was held for Vancouver and Whistler residents to determine whether they wanted the Olympic Games. When 64% said yes, they did want the Olympic Games, the bid went ahead and was ultimately successful. Government funding for the 2010 Winter Olympic Games came from federal, provincial, and municipal sources. A question to consider here is whether it is ethical to ask members of the host city about hosting the Olympic Games without asking residents of the entire province, who will share the debt load and the impacts of more visitors.

Canada may be a little hesitant about hosting mega sport events because in the past, cost overruns from infrastructure construction led to a debt load carried by locals for decades. With any large project seeking use of vast amounts of money, opinions will differ about appropriate ways of doing business. Mega sport events are no exception, and they probably have more than their fair share of ethical issues.

Written by Heather L. Bell, University of Florida.

Summary

You should now have a good overview of sport tourism in terms of both academic knowledge and some practices around the world. The chapter starts with an analysis of the sport and tourism connection, with a focus on understanding tourism and the tourism industry. Tourism, the world's largest industry, is composed of many segments, including transportation, accommodation, attractions, and the government and nongovernmental agencies responsible for planning, setting policy, and marketing. A tourist is defined in this chapter as a leisure traveler. Sport tourism is defined as travel to participate in sport (active sport tourism), to watch sport (event sport tourism), or to venerate (e.g., honor, revere) something or somebody associated with a sport (nostalgia sport tourism).

In reviewing the three types of sport tourism, the chapter discusses some possible explanations for the increasing popularity of active sport tourism over the past couple decades. Some of this popularity may be related to increased awareness of the benefits of an active lifestyle coupled with increased opportunities to take part in sport on vacation at resorts, on cruises, and at amateur sport events. Golf and skiing are the most popular types of active sport tourism. Golf is increasing in popularity as the population ages, whereas the alpine skiing industry has experienced some difficulties in sustaining its market share. All sectors of event sport tourism, on the other hand, are increasing in popularity. Cities around the world compete vigorously to host mega events such as the Olympic Games and the World Cup. This was evident in 2013 when Tokyo beat out Madrid and Istanbul to win the rights to host the 2020 Olympic and Paralympic Games. But communities around the United States and Canada are coming to realize that small-scale sport tourism events may be more manageable and beneficial than mega events. As a result, many communities now have sports commissions whose task is to attract sport events to their towns or cities. Sports commissions, coupled with convention and visitors bureaus, are helping many towns and cities throughout North America develop sport tourism. The third type of sport tourism discussed, nostalgia sport tourism, is the least well developed in terms of research and attention from tourism professionals. Nonetheless, in the United States and around the world, sport halls of fame, museums, and sport-themed events are becoming more popular. Even the cruise industry has developed a niche in the nostalgia sport tourism realm by offering cruises with various sport personalities.

Besides providing sections on critical thinking and ethical considerations, the chapter ends by addressing the issue of sustainable development as it relates to sport tourism. The three-pronged approach to sustainability includes social, economic, and environmental dimensions. All three dimensions are interrelated, and must be addressed to ensure not only the sustainability of sport tourism but also the overall sustainable development of communities. As communities around the world examine strategies for economic development, we need to urge governments and community leaders to think about the long-term effects of their decisions. One way of doing this is to pay attention to the triple bottom line of sustainable development. The economic impacts of sport and tourism always garner much attention. Closer cooperation between sport and tourism agencies at all levels may be one way of reaping both the economic benefits and the social benefits of sport tourism while decreasing the negative effects on the physical and social environment.

Review Questions

1. What are the major dimensions of sport tourism and the sport tourism industry?
2. If sport tourism is leisure-based travel, is a professional athlete a sport tourist? Why or why not?
3. How might climate change affect the growth and development of golf tourism and winter sport tourism in the future?
4. What strategies might you suggest to your community to leverage the tourism associated with college sports?
5. What are the arguments for and against a city's hosting of the Olympic Games?
6. Why has nostalgia sport tourism become popular in recent years?
7. How might we implement a sustainable development approach to future sport tourism ventures?
8. How do you think sport tourism will change over the next 10 years, given the increasing emphasis on sustainable development?
9. What sorts of career opportunities are available in sport tourism for sport management majors?

References

Adventure Travel Trade Association, The George Washington University, & Vital Wave Consulting. (2011, July). *Adventure tourism development index, 2010 report*. Retrieved from www.adventuretravel.biz/wp-content/uploads/2011/07/atdi_2010_report.pdf

Agha, N., Fairley, S., & Gibson, H. (2012). Considering legacy as a multi-dimensional construct: The legacy of the Olympic Games. *Sport Management Review, 15*, 125–139.

Audubon International. (2013). Audubon Cooperative Sanctuary Program for Golf Courses. Retrieved from www.auduboninternational.org/acspgolf

Buckley, R., Pickering, C., & Warnken, J. (2000). Environmental management for alpine tourism and resorts in Australia. In P. Godde, M. Price, & F. Zimmermann (Eds.), *Tourism and development in mountain regions* (pp. 27–45). Wallingford, UK: CAB International.

Burgan, B., & Mules, T. (1992). Economic impact of sporting events. *Annals of Tourism Research, 19*, 700–710.

Chalip, L. (2001, February). *Leveraging the Sydney Olympics to optimize tourism benefits*. Paper presented at the International Conference on Sports, Athens, Greece.

Chalip, L. (2004). Beyond economic impact: A general model for sport event leverage. In B. Ritchie & D. Adair (Eds.), *Sport tourism: Interrelationships, impacts and issues* (pp. 226–252). Clevedon, UK: Channel View.

Chalip, L., & Green, B.C. (2001, June). *Leveraging large sports events for tourism: Lessons learned from the Sydney Olympics*. Paper presented at the 32nd Annual Conference Proceedings: Travel and Tourism Research Association, 2001—a Tourism Odyssey. Fort Meyers, FL.

Chernushenko, D. (1996). Sports tourism goes sustainable: The Lillehammer experience. *Visions in Leisure and Business, 15*(1), 65–73.

Chien, P.M., Ritchie, B.W., Shipway, R., & Henderson, H. (2012). I am having a dilemma: Factors affecting resident support of event development in the community. *Journal of Travel Research, 51*, 451–463. Retrieved from http://jtr.sagepub.com/content/51/4/451

Coakley, J.J. (2009). *Sport in society: Issues and controversies* (10th ed.). Boston, MA: McGraw-Hill.

Coghlan, A., & Filo, K. (2013). Using constant comparison method and qualitative data to understand participants' experiences at the nexus of tourism, sport and charity events. *Tourism Management, 35*, 122–131.

Cohen, E. (1974). Who is a tourist? A conceptual clarification. *Sociological Review, 22*, 527–555.

Collins, A., Munday, M., & Roberts, A. (2012). Environmental consequences of tourism consumption at major events: An analysis of the UK stages of the 2007 Tour de France. *Journal of Travel Research, 51*, 577–590.

Crompton, J. (1995). Economic impact analysis of sports facilities and events: Eleven sources of misapplication. *Journal of Sport Management, 9*, 14–35.

Dawson, J., & Scott, D. (2013). Managing for climate change in the alpine ski sector. *Tourism Management, 35*, 244–254.

Doğan, H. (1989). Forms of adjustment: Socio-cultural impacts of tourism. *Annals of Tourism Research, 16*, 216–236.

Dwyer, B., & Kim, Y. (2011). For love of money: Developing and validating a motivational scale for fantasy football participation. *Journal of Sport Management, 25*, 70–83.

Essex, S., & Chalkley, B. (1998). Olympic Games: Catalyst of urban change. *Leisure Studies, 17*(3), 187–206.

Fairley, S. (2003). In search of relived social experience: Group-based nostalgia sport tourism. *Journal of Sport Management, 17*, 284–304.

Fairley, S., Kellett, P., & Green, B.C. (2007). Volunteering abroad: Motives for travel to volunteer at the Athens Olympic Games. *Journal of Sport Management, 21*, 41–57.

Fluker, M.R., & Turner, L.W. (2000). Needs, motivations, and expectations of a commercial whitewater rafting experience. *Journal of Travel Research, 38*, 380–389.

Fourie, J., & Santana-Gallego, M. (2011). The impact of mega-sport events on tourist arrivals. *Tourism Management, 32*, 1364–1370.

Fredline, E. (2005). Host and guest relations and sport tourism. *Sport in Society, 8*, 263–279.

Gibson, H. (1998a). Active sport tourism: Who participates? *Leisure Studies, 17*, 155–170.

Gibson, H. (1998b). Sport tourism: A critical analysis of research. *Sport Management Review, 1*, 45–79.

Gibson, H., Kaplanidou, K., & Kang, S. (2012). Small-scale event sport tourism: A case study in sustainable tourism. *Sport Management Review, 15*, 160–170.

Goeldner, C., & Ritchie, J.R.B. (2011). *Tourism: Practices, principles, philosophies*. New York, NY: Wiley.

Goss, A. (2012, August 5). You can still grab a holiday bargain at home or abroad. *Sunday Times*, Money section, p. 10.

Grieve, J., & Sherry, E. (2012). Community benefits of major sport facilities: The Darebin International Sports Centre. *Sport Management Review, 15*, 218–229.

Heere, B., Kim, C., Yoshida, M., Nakamura, H., Ogura, T., Chung, K.S., & Lim, S.Y. (2012). The impact of World Cup 2002 on the bilateral relationship between South Korea and Japan. *Journal of Sport Management, 26*, 127–142.

Heydari, F. (2007, November). Fantasy sport camps. *Travel and Leisure*. Retrieved from www.travelandleisure.com/articles/fantasy-sports-camps

Higham, J. (1999). Commentary—sport as an avenue of tourism development: An analysis of the positive and negative impacts of sport tourism. *Current Issues in Tourism, 2*, 82–90.

Hinch, T.D., & Higham, J.E.S. (2011). *Sport tourism development*. Bristol, UK: Channel View.

Humphreys, B. (2008, May). *The size and scope of the sports industry in the United States*. Paper presented at the 10th Annual IASE Conference, Gijón, Spain.

Jago, L., & Shaw, R. (1998). Special events: A conceptual and definitional framework. *Festival Management & Event Tourism, 5*, 21–32.

Kaplanidou, K., & Gibson, H. (2010). Predicting behavioral intentions of active event sport tourists: The case of a small scale recurring sports event. *Journal of Sport & Tourism, 15*, 163-179.

Kellett, P., & Russell, R. (2009). A comparison between mainstream and action sport industries in Australia: A case study of the skateboarding cluster. *Sport Management Review, 12*, 66–78.

Kim, S., & Morrison, A. (2005). Change of image of South Korea among foreign tourists after the 2002 FIFA World Cup. *Tourism Management, 26*, 233–247.

Kim, W., & Walker, M. (2012). Measuring the social impacts associated with Super Bowl XLIII: Preliminary development of a psychic income scale. *Sport Management Review, 15*, 91–108.

Kulczycki, C., & Hyatt, C. (2005). Expanding the conceptualization of nostalgia sport tourism: Lessons learned from fans left behind after sport franchise relocation. *Journal of Sport & Tourism, 10*, 273–293.

Lee, S., Harris, J., & Lyberger, M. (2010). The economic impact of college sporting events: A case study of Division I-A football games. *Event Management, 14*, 157–165.

Leeds, M., Mirikitani, J., & Tang, D. (2009). Rational exuberance? An event analysis of the 2008 Olympics announcement. *International Journal of Sport Finance, 4*(1), 5–15.

Lyons, K., & Wearing, S. (2008). All for a good cause? The blurred boundaries between volunteering and tourism. In K. Lyons & S. Wearing (Eds.), *Journeys of discovery in volunteer tourism* (pp. 147–154). Wallingford, UK: CAB International.

Mallen, C., & Chard, C. (2011). A framework for debating the future of environmental sustainability in the sport academy. *Sport Management Review, 14*, 424–433.

Mallen, C., & Chard, C. (2012). "What could be" in Canadian sport facility environmental sustainability. *Sport Management Review, 15*, 230–243.

Mallen, C., Stevens, J., & Adams, L. (2011). A content analysis of environmental sustainability research in a sport-related journal sample. *Journal of Sport Management, 25*, 240–256.

Minnaert, L. (2012). An Olympic legacy for all? The non-infrastructural outcomes of the Olympic Games for socially excluded groups (Atlanta 1996-Beijing 2008). *Tourism Management, 33*, 361-370.

Mintel Oxygen. (2006). *Sports and adventure travel—US—November 2006*. Retrieved from http://academic.mintel.com/display/168019/#

Mules, T., & Dwyer, L. (2005). Public sector support for sport tourism events: The role of cost-benefit analysis. *Sport in Society, 8*, 338–355.

National Golf Foundation. (2013). Frequently asked questions! Retrieved from www.ngf.org/pages/faq

National Senior Games Association. (2013). History of the NSGA. Retrieved from www.nsga.com/history.aspx

Needham, M., Rollins, R., Ceurvorst, R., Wood, C., Grimm, K., & Dearden, P. (2011). Motivations and normative evaluations of summer visitors at an alpine ski area. *Journal of Travel Research, 50*, 669–684.

Neirotti, L., & Hilliard, T. (2006). Impact of Olympic spectator safety perception and security concerns on travel decisions. *Tourism Review International, 10*, 269–284.

Ong, T., & Musa, G. (2012). Examining the influences of experience, personality and attitude on scuba divers' underwater behavior: A structural equation model. *Tourism Management, 33*, 1521–1534.

Oxford Economics. (2012, July). *The economic impact of the London 2012 Olympic & Paralympic Games*. Oxford, UK: Lloyds Banking Group.

Palmer, C. (2004). More than just a game: The consequences of golf tourism. In B. Ritchie & D. Adair (Eds.), *Sport tourism: Interrelationships, impacts and issues* (pp. 117–134). Clevedon, UK: Channel View.

Prayag, G., Hosany, S., Nunkoo, R., & Alders, T. (2013). London residents' support for the 2012 Olympic Games: The mediating effect of overall attitude. *Tourism Management, 36*, 629–640.

Preuss, H. (2007). FIFA World Cup 2006 and its legacy on tourism. In R. Conrady & M. Buck (Eds.), *Trends and issues in global tourism 2007* (pp. 83–102). Berlin, Germany: Springer.

Redmond, G. (1991). Changing styles of sports tourism: Industry/consumer interactions in Canada, the USA, and Europe. In M.T. Sinclair & M.J. Stabler (Eds.), *The tourism industry: An international analysis* (pp. 107–120). Wallingford, UK: CAB International.

Ritchie, J.R.B. (1984). Assessing the impact of hallmark events: Conceptual and research issues. *Journal of Travel Research, 23*, 2–11.

Ritchie, J.R.B. (1999). Lessons learned, lessons learning: Insights from the Calgary and Salt Lake Olympic Winter Games. *Visions in Leisure and Business, 18*, 4–13.

Ritchie, J.R.B., & Smith, B.H. (1991). The impact of a mega-event on host region awareness: A longitudinal study. *Journal of Travel Research, 30*, 3–10.

Roberts, K. (2006). *Leisure in contemporary society*. Wallingford, UK: CAB International.

Roche, M. (1994). Mega-events and urban policy. *Annals of Tourism Research, 21*, 1–19.

Sanford, D. (2013, February 6). Putin's Olympic steamroller in Sochi. Retrieved from www.bbc.co.uk/news/world-europe-21356953

Schmidt, C.W. (2006). Putting the earth in play. *Environmental Health Perspectives, 114*(5), A286–A295.

Schneider, P., & Vogt, C. (2012). Applying the 3M model of personality and motivation to adventure travelers. *Journal of Travel Research, 51*, 704–716.

Schroeder, A., Pennington-Gray, L., Kaplanidou, K., & Fangzi, Z. (2013). Destination risk perceptions among U.S. residents for London as the host city of the 2012 Summer Olympic Games. *Tourism Management, 38*, 107–119.

Schulenkorfk, N., & Edwards, D. (2012). Maximizing positive social impacts: Strategies for sustaining and leveraging the benefits of intercommunity sport events in divided societies. *Journal of Sport Management, 26*, 379–390.

Schumacher, D. (2012). *National Association of Sports Commission's report on the sports travel industry*. Retrieved from www.sportscommissions.org/Documents/NASC%20Report%20on%20Sports%20Travel%20Industry.pdf

Shaw, A. (2013, June 18). Brazil riots in pictures: Protesters rage against cost of World Cup and Olympics. *Mirror*. Retrieved from www.mirror.co.uk/news/world-news/brazil-riots-pictures-protesters-rage-1960888

Soutar, D., & Lindén, O. (2000). The health and future of coral reef systems. *Ocean & Coastal Management, 43*, 657–688.

Sparvero, E., Trendafilova, S., & Chalip, L. (2005, June). *An alternative approach to environmental dispute resolution in sport contexts*. Paper presented at the 20th Annual Conference of the North American Society for Sport Management, Regina, Saskatchewan, Canada.

Spector, S., Chard, C., Mallen, C., & Hyatt, C. (2012). Socially constructed environmental issues and sport: A content analysis of ski resort environmental communications. *Sport Management Review, 15*, 416–433.

SRI International. (2012). *The 2011 golf economy report*. St. Augustine, FL: World Golf Foundation.

Standeven, J., & De Knop, P. (1999). *Sport tourism*. Champaign, IL: Human Kinetics.

Steinmetz, T. (2008, July 6). Hosting Olympics can damage tourism. *ETN global travel industry news*. Retrieved from www.eturbonews.com/print/3530

Streets, D., Fu, J., Jang, C., Hae, J., & He, K. (2007). Air quality during the 2008 Beijing Olympic Games. *Atmospheric Environment, 41*, 480–492.

Sun, Y., Rodriguez, A., Wu, J., & Chuang, S. (2013). Why hotel rooms were not full during a hallmark sporting event: The 2009 World Games experience. *Tourism Management, 36*, 469–479.

Swarbrooke, J., Beard, C., Leckie, S., & Pomfret, G. (2003). *Adventure tourism: The new frontier*. Burlington, MA: Butterworth Heinemann.

Tien, C., Lo, H., & Lin, H. (2011). The economic benefits of mega events: A myth or a reality? A longitudinal study on the Olympic Games. *Journal of Sport Management, 25*, 11–23.

Tsaur, S.H., Lin, W.R., & Liu, J.S. (2013). Sources of challenge for adventure tourists: Scale development and validation. *Tourism Management, 38*, 85–93.

U.S. Census Bureau. (2012). Arts, recreation, and travel. *The 2012 statistical abstract of the United States: The national data book*. Retrieved from www.census.gov/compendia/statab/2012edition.html

Walker, M., Kaplanidou, K., Gibson, H., Thapa, B., Geldenhuys, S., & Coetzee, W. (2013). "Win in Africa, with Africa": Social responsibility, event image, and destination benefits. The case of the 2010 FIFA World Cup in South Africa. *Tourism Management, 34*, 80–90.

Woodside, A. (2009). Applying systems thinking to sustainable golf tourism. *Journal of Travel Research, 48*, 205–215.

World Tourism Organization. (1994). *Recommendations on tourism statistics*. Madrid, Spain: Author.

World Tourism Organization. (2013). *UNWTO tourism highlights, 2013 edition*. Retrieved from http://dtxtq4w60xqpw.cloudfront.net/sites/all/files/pdf/unwto_highlights13_en_lr.pdf

PART III

SELECTED SPORT MANAGEMENT FUNCTIONS

The five chapters in this section present valuable information about sport marketing and promotion; sport consumer behavior; communication, public relations, and community relations; finance and economics; and facility and event management. These functions are universal in sport in that they are performed at most sport-related sites, including those discussed in the previous section—community and youth sport, interscholastic athletics, intercollegiate athletics, professional sport, sport management and marketing agencies, and sport tourism.

In chapter 12, Ketra Armstrong defines sport marketing and explains the unique aspects of this key sport management function. Armstrong presents the elements of the marketing mix and shows how a marketing plan addresses those elements (i.e., purpose, product, projections, positioning, players, packaging, pricing, promotions, place, and promise). In addition to a sidebar on how social media affects sport consumers and the marketing of sport, she also covers the elements of a SWOT analysis, the various dimensions of sport products and events, product positioning and market niches, branding, market segmentation, pricing and promotion strategies, distribution channels, and the packaging and selling of sport products. The theme of socially responsible sport marketing runs throughout the chapter. The professional profile in this chapter is on Hunter Lochmann, the chief marketing officer and senior associate athletic director for the University of Michigan Athletics. In the international sidebar, Sanghak Lee examines the sport marketing strategy employed by the Lotte Giants, one of the best professional baseball teams in South Korea. Lee teaches at Korea Aerospace University in Seoul.

Andrea Eagleman, Cara Wright, and Christine Green address consumer behavior in chapter 13. In the first section, the authors examine the individual factors that influence active (i.e., sport participation) and passive (i.e., sport spectation) sport consumption. They explain in detail how consumers are influenced by certain motives and how perceptions and attitudes influence consumers' involvement and identification with a sport, team, athlete, or sport brand. In their second section, they discuss group influences on the sport consumer. Within this discussion are analyses of the influence of reference groups and socialization on consumer decision making. Eagleman, Wright, and Green conclude their chapter with an explanation of the decision-making process itself. They include a sidebar on the use of social media by event organizers and its influence on consumer behavior. The underlying theme of this chapter is that understanding how people make decisions about their consumption of the sport product will be valuable to sport managers as they compete with a multitude of other diversions for the time and money of consumers. Samantha Hicks, the director of ticket sales and service for the Indiana Fever and Pacers Sports & Entertainment, is the practitioner featured in this chapter. The international sidebar for this chapter contains an essay on consumer behavior associated with Japanese baseball. Yosuke Tsuji from the University of the Ryukyus in Nishihara (Japan) contributed this international vignette.

Clay Stoldt, Steve Dittmore, and Paul M. Pedersen address the broad segment of sport communication in chapter 14. After presenting basic information about communication in the sport industry, the authors explain the concepts (i.e., genres, context, process, elements, and effects) on which the theoretical framework of sport communication is established. The remainder of the chapter involves an in-depth examination of the strategic sport communication model (SSCM), which includes three major components: personal and organizational communication, mass media, and sport communication services and support. Stoldt, Dittmore, and Pedersen explain each of these components in detail, but they pay particular attention to the last component because it contains the areas of sport public relations, media relations, and community relations. Finally, in addition to providing a section on social media surveillance in the sport industry, the authors discuss careers in media relations and community relations by delineating the responsibilities involved and the skills needed for each. The sport industry practitioners featured in this chapter are Mike Kern, the associate commissioner of the Missouri Valley Conference, and Aprile Pritchet, who is now with Walker Marchant Group (Washington, D.C.) but at the time of the interview was the community relations director for Major League Soccer's D.C. United and the executive director of United for D.C. Reinhard Kunz (University of Bayreuth) and Florian Schnellinger (Quattro Media)—both based in Germany—contributed the international sidebar for this chapter. Kunz and Schnellinger describe the media rights scene in Germany and argue that to increase media value and viewership, extreme and niche sports should deliver nonexclusive, free-of-charge, and branded sport content through television, the Internet, and mobile platforms.

In chapter 15, Tim DeSchriver, Dan Mahony, and Marion Hambrick introduce basic information about finance and economics within the sport industry. After explaining the size and scope of the sport industry in economic terms, the authors describe the current financial situation of the professional and intercollegiate segments of the U.S. sport industry. They then present principles of the economics of sport. A discussion of microeconomics follows, addressing supply and demand and the economic impact of sport. Next, DeSchriver, Mahony, and Hambrick further explain the business structure of sport organizations and introduce basic tools of financial management, including financial statements and sources of revenues and expenses for sport organizations. In addition to providing a sidebar focused on sport finance and economics information provided through social media platforms, the authors conclude the chapter with advice for students who aspire to careers in financial management of sport organizations. Tim Whitten, the director of finance for the Kentucky Derby Festival, is the featured sport industry professional in this chapter. The chapter's international sidebar contains an essay on the financial aspects and development strategies associated with the 2014 Sochi Olympic Winter Games. Victor Timchenko, from the Herzen State Pedagogical University of Russia in Saint Petersburg, contributed the essay.

David Stotlar and Coyte Cooper address sport facility and event management in chapter 16. First, the authors note the current state of sport facility construction and the influence that the current economic climate has had on this segment of the sport industry. Stotlar and Cooper then differentiate among several types of facilities (e.g., single purpose, multipurpose, nontraditional) and explain the current trend toward the privatization of facilities. They examine facility and event management personnel and include a sidebar on using social media to assess elements of the stadium experience for sport consumers. A discussion of ways in which sport managers can minimize risks associated with facilities and events follows. The final sections of the chapter provide in-depth information on facility management personnel and their responsibilities as well as examples of event personnel assignments. Real-life scenarios illustrate the importance of proper planning for sporting events. John Brunner, the director of athletic event management at the University of North Carolina at Chapel Hill, is the profiled sport industry professional in this chapter. In the international sidebar, Babs Surujlal—who teaches sport management at North-West University in Gauteng, South Africa—examines the various aspects of staging the FIFA World Cup.

The five major functions of sport management covered in this section are sport marketing, sport consumer behavior, sport communication, sport finance and economics, and sport facility and event management. Because sport managers are often engaged in or at least affected by the various activities and issues examined in these five chapters, it is important to have an understanding of these selected functions and their application to the various segments of the sport industry.

For More Information

Professional and Scholarly Associations, Institutes, and Organizations

Academy of Marketing Science

The American Communication Association

American Marketing Association

American Sports Data, Inc.

American Sportscasters Association

Associated Press Sports Editors

Association for Education in Journalism and Mass Communication

Association for Women in Sports Media

Canadian Sporting Goods Association

College Sports Information Directors of America (CoSIDA)

Direct Marketing Association

European Arenas Association (EAA)

Female Athletic Media Relations Executives (FAME)

Football Writers Association of America

Golf Course Builders Association of America (GCBAA)

International Association for Communication and Sport

International Association for Sports and Leisure Facilities (IAKS)

International Association of Business Communicators

International Association of Venue Managers

International Facility Management Association

International Sports Press Association (AIPS)

Investigative Reporters and Editors

Licensing Industry Merchandisers' Association (LIMA)

National Association of Collegiate Marketing Administrators (NACMA)

National Collegiate Baseball Writers Association

National Communication Association (NCA)

National Recreation and Park Association

National Sports Forum

National Sports Journalism Center

North American Snowsports Journalists Association (NASJA)

The Poynter Institute

Public Relations Society of America

Society of Consumer Affairs Professionals

Society of Professional Journalists

Sport Marketing Association (SMA)

Stadium Managers Association (SMA)

United States Basketball Writers Association

United States Racquet Stringers Association (USRSA)

Professional and Scholarly Publications

Advertising Age

American Journalism Review

Athletic Business

The Business Journalist

Communication & Sport

CoSIDA Digest

Editor & Publisher

Electronic Journal of Communication

ESPN The Magazine

Facilities Manager Magazine

Facility Management Journal

International Journal of Sport Communication

International Journal of Sport Finance

International Journal of Sports Marketing & Sponsorship

Journal of Broadcasting & Electronic Media

Journal of Communication

Journal of Communication Management

Journal of Computer-Mediated Communication

Journal of Consumer Behavior

Journal of Consumer Research

Journal of International Communication

Journal of Marketing

Journal of Marketing Communications

Journal of Marketing Research

Journal of Public Relations Research

Journal of Quantitative Analysis in Sports

Journal of Sponsorship

Journal of Sports Economics

Journal of Sports Media

Journal of Venue & Event Management

Journalism & Mass Communication Quarterly

Mass Communication and Society

The Migala Report

Modern Sport Communication

Newspaper Research Journal

PRWeek

Psychology & Marketing

Public Relations Quarterly

Public Relations Strategist

Sport Marketing Quarterly

Sporting News

Sports Market Place Directory

Team Marketing Report

TV Sports Markets

HISTORICAL MOMENTS

- **1928**   Coca-Cola began marketing partnership with the Olympic Games
- **1934**   Lou Gehrig became first athlete to appear on a Wheaties box
- **1949**   Babe Didrikson Zaharias landed first major endorsement deal for a female athlete
- **1951**   Eddie Gaedel, at 3 feet, 7 inches (110 cm), pinch hit for St. Louis Browns
- **1960**   CBS paid US$50,000 for the rights to televise the Winter Olympic Games in Squaw Valley, California
- **1964**   Blue Ribbon Sports founded; renamed Nike in 1972
- **1973**   Battle of the Sexes: Billie Jean King defeated Bobby Riggs in tennis; attracted 30,492 attendees and millions of television viewers
- **1974**   Muhammad Ali defeated George Foreman in the Rumble in the Jungle
- **1979**   Mike Veeck put on Disco Demolition Derby Night during Chicago White Sox doubleheader
- **1989**   NBA initiated global marketing campaign
- **1992**   *Sport Marketing Quarterly* launched
- **1993**   "Got Milk?" ad campaign launched
- **1997**   MasterCard MLB "Priceless" campaign launched
- **1999**   FIFA Women's World Cup event attracted record setting attendance of 90,185 spectators
- **2004**   Social networking site Facebook launched
- **2008**   NBA China formed
- **2012**   Boost Mobile landmark sponsorship of WNBA
- **2013**   WNBA launched new logo and entered into long-term partnership with ESPN
- **2014**   January bowl games' title sponsors included Tostitos, Allstate, AT&T, Discover, BBVA, and GoDaddy
- **2014**   NASCAR overhauled its Chase for the Spring Cup title playoff by changing its postseason formula to include elimination rounds and a winter-takes-all season finale

12

SPORT MARKETING

Ketra L. Armstrong

LEARNING OBJECTIVES

> Obtain a working definition of sport marketing.
> Identify the unique aspects (i.e., challenges and opportunities) of marketing sport.
> Recognize the importance of embracing a structured (strategic and tactical) approach to marketing.
> Understand the process of developing a marketing plan and the elements (principles of the 10 Ps) contained therein.
> Discuss the influence of technology (notably the Internet, social media, and new media) on sport marketing success.
> Understand the role of research in effective marketing.
> Understand ethics and apply them to sport marketing.
> Engage in critical thinking to address challenges confronted by sport marketers.

Key Terms

branding	place
external factors	product life cycle
internal factors	promotions mix
marketing mix	sport marketing
marketing plans	sport sponsorship
marketing research	SWOT analysis
market segmentation	

GET A JOB

Continue on your journey in sport management by going to the web study guide (WSG) at www.HumanKinetics.com/ContemporarySportManagement. Check out the job opportunities and consider the skills and experiences that can help you succeed in sport management.

marketing is one of the oldest aspects of management (Barker, 2003). It is a complex function that is extremely important to the overall success of sport organizations. You probably have heard the term *sport marketing* in many contexts, and you might be wondering exactly what it means. Some corporate executives might describe sport marketing as selling sport goods and services to generate a profit. But sport marketing is more than selling. People who work in advertising and public relations might consider sport marketing as designing the content and delivery of commercials aired during the Sochi 2014 Winter Olympics, obtaining Super Bowl XLIX tickets for clients, or entertaining a corporate sponsor at the 2015 NCAA Women's Final Four in Tampa. But sport marketing is more than advertising and public relations. Those who provide services for professional athletes might view sport marketing as arranging for athletes to attend a charity event hosted by a children's hospital or arranging to have corporate executives play in a golf tournament with professional golfers. But sport marketing is more than community relations. Although sport marketing includes elements of selling, advertising, public relations, and community relations, it is by no means limited to these activities.

To better contextualize the complexity of what sport marketing entails, you may think of it as the collection of activities that transform the basic physical activity of football into the commercialization of the enterprise that is the NFL Super Bowl (i.e., attracting fans, securing adequate venues, obtaining media exposure, and securing corporate partners, ticket distribution outlets, and community outreach activities). Sport marketing also refers to the collection of activities that transformed the parking lot of the convention center in Long Beach, California, into the site of the 2004 U.S. Olympic Swimming Trials (i.e., attracting fans, creating a venue, obtaining media exposure, and securing corporate partners, city permits, ticket distribution outlets, and community outreach activities). Other similar transformations include the hosting of a nationally televised basketball game on an aircraft carrier and arranging for an NHL game to be held outdoors in a football or baseball stadium.

The role of marketing in transforming sport or physical activity into commercialized spectacles is important for a number of reasons. For instance, at the collegiate level, campus sport event spectacles enrich the student experience, and the network broadcasts of college and university sport teams offer national exposure and enhance student recruitment and alumni relations. At the professional level, professional sport teams and events add to the property values of real estate, contribute to local economies, and engender community pride in local and regional residents. However, as Fullerton and Merz (2008) asserted, "there is no consensus as to exactly what is meant by the term sports marketing" (p. 90). However, sport scholars have generally agreed that sport marketing refers to the composite activities and practices that seek to facilitate the experience and expedite the exchange between sport and its consumers. More specifically, Pitts and Stotlar (2007) defined sport marketing as "the process of designing and implementing activities for the production, pricing, promotion, and distribution of a sport product or sport business product to satisfy the needs or desires of consumers and to achieve the company's objectives" (p. 69).

This definition has been widely used by sport marketing scholars. However, to derive a more comprehensive definition of sport marketing, it is proposed here that the infusion of tenets of relationship marketing (e.g., O'Malley & Tynan, 2003), service marketing (e.g., Barker, 2003), and social marketing (MacFadyen, Stead, & Hastings, 2003) is warranted. As O'Malley and Tynan summarized, relationship marketing refers to commercial relationships between economic partners, service providers, and customers at various levels of the marketing channel and the broader business environment. Relationships are a crucial part of the sport consumption experience. For example, sport marketers must consider the interactions between their customers (i.e., spectators at their events) as well as the interactions between the organization and their customers (i.e., spectators and event staff, including ushers and ticket takers). Since sport offers a service to consumers, sport marketers must consider customer service encounters and customers' perceptions of service quality (as service marketing suggests). The premise of social marketing requires that sport marketers consider how marketing practices affect the consumer and the organization, and what is responsibly (and thus, ethically) in the best interest of society. Therefore, using Pitts and Stotlar's (2007) definition as a basis, the following is a slightly extended and thus more comprehensive definition of **sport marketing**: "the process of designing and implementing activities for the production, pricing, promotion and distribution of a sport product or sport business product to satisfy the needs or desires of consumers and to achieve the company's objectives" (p. 69) in a manner that creates socially responsible exchange relationships.

Now that you have a better understanding of what sport marketing is, let's turn our attention to why sport marketing is. Why is there a need for sport marketing? What is unique about sport as a property or entity to be marketed?

Students who are interested in marketing in general often ask why there is a specific need for sport marketing. They ponder why a general marketing course will not sufficiently provide them with the concepts that are relevant to sport. While there are some properties of sport that are similar to other general products, there are also some distinct characteristics that differentiate sport and thus require a unique application of basic marketing principles. A brief examination of sport's unique combination of characteristics proposed by Mullin, Hardy, and Sutton (2014) shows how sport differs from other products, goods, and services, and therefore why the approach to marketing sport is unique.

> Aspects of sport are intangible. For example, you cannot touch the dynamic competition that takes place between two football teams. This elusiveness of the sport experience is unlike other products or goods and makes sport a unique entity for marketers to describe and for marketing practices to encompass.

> Sport involves emotions. Some sport spectators become emotionally attached to their teams; they are referred to as fanatics or fans. Other consumers might buy licensed sport products with team logos and uniform replicas as a way of personally identifying with their teams. Consumers do not often display such heightened emotions or psychological attachment to other goods or products, such as vacuum cleaners.

> Sport is subjective and heterogeneous because the impressions, experiences, and interpretations about the sport experience may vary from person to person. Because sport marketers cannot easily predict the impressions, experiences, and interpretations that consumers will have about the sport consumption experience, it is often challenging to ensure that consumers will have satisfying sport experiences. Further complicating the process of satisfying sport consumers is their fleeting or fluttering demand for sport and the frequent change in their sport interests. This consumer heterogeneity is not as pronounced for other products.

> Sport is generally socially consumed and depends on social facilitation with others (such as friends and family). Such social references are not typical determinants of consumers' use and enjoyment of general products (e.g., appliances, household or industrial goods).

> Sport experiences and events are inconsistent and unpredictable for a variety of reasons. A few of the many factors that influence the sport experience include injuries to players, the emotional state of athletes, team momentum and fluctuating

sport marketing—"The process of designing and implementing activities for the production, pricing, promotion, and distribution of a sport product or sport business product to satisfy the needs or desires of consumers and to achieve the company's objectives" (Pitts & Stotlar, 2007, p. 69) in a socially responsible manner that creates a favorable exchange relationship.

performance, and the weather. These characteristics of sport are in stark contrast to the characteristics of other goods, where there is an expectation of consistency and predictability in the product.

› Sport is perishable because the sport experience is simultaneously produced and consumed. For example, as the athletes are competing (i.e., producing the action and experience), the spectators are watching the competition (i.e., consuming the action and experience). General products have a longer shelf life. Based on the perishability of sport competitions, sport marketers often offer tangible items (e.g., T-shirts, souvenirs) that serve as lasting reminders of the perishable sport experience.

As outlined here, the composite profile of sport (which represents a blending of goods and services) is quite unique! Balancing a company's business objectives with consumer wants and needs is a challenge in any industry; however, the distinguishing characteristics and symbolic appeal of sport (its product, its market, and its consumers) add several layers of complexity to this task for sport marketers. Unlike the job of marketers of general consumer and industrial products, the challenge for sport marketers is to market the experiences and manage the expectations of an emotionally laden, inconsistent, unscripted, unpredictable, and uncontrollable momentary social product, that will be desired and experienced differently from person to person and place to place. Ask yourself these questions: What other products have this composite profile? What other high-demand products do consumers have such an emotional affinity with? What other products would consumers purchase without warranty or guarantee of their performance? Most likely, your list is a very short one. Herein is the uniqueness of sport that makes its marketing both a challenging experience and a rewarding opportunity.

Because of the uniqueness of sport—intangible aspects, emotional involvement, subjectivity, socially consumed, unpredictable, perishable—sport marketers must market the experience and manage the expectations surrounding a sporting event.

Given the previous discussion, how do you think the unique characteristics associated with sport influence decisions about packaging, promoting, and delivering sport? How do marketers know who will be attracted to certain sport events based on its varied characteristics? How should the packaging, promoting, and delivering of sport events be customized to reflect its unique characteristics and to influence the consumers' perceptions, desires, and experiences? What changes will be needed in the packaging, promoting, and delivering of sport in the future? These are all questions that sport marketers frequently ask themselves. The answers to these questions lie in the art and the science of sport marketing. While some people seem to inherently have an innate creative gift for the artistry and aesthetics of sport marketing, others have a keen understanding of the science of doing so. The next part of this chapter focuses on the latter, primarily examining the science of effective sport marketing—developing a marketing plan.

Developing a Sport Marketing Plan

The complexity and uniqueness of sport require sport marketers to have a comprehensive approach or road map to guide their marketing activities. **Marketing plans** contain the science (i.e., methodological approach and theoretical foundation) for marketing. They serve as structured game plans for an organization's marketing activities. Having a well-developed marketing plan is essential to the marketing success of sport organizations. According to Shank (2008), marketing plans should contain marketing strategy (broad or big-picture ideas) as well as marketing tactics (specific details). For instance, a marketing strategy may be to increase consumers' interest in ice hockey; a marketing tactic may be a halftime promotion featuring a youth hockey competition. Marketing plans should also include relevant information about the various internal (organizational) and external (environmental) factors that may influence the success of marketing strategies and tactics.

At the core of the marketing plans are the elements of product, price, place, and promotion, which make up the **marketing mix**. These elements are well established in the marketing industry, and are universally known as the *four Ps*.

> Product—a tangible good (object), a service, or an intangible quality that satisfies consumers' wants or needs

> Price—the value of the product and the costs that the consumer must accept to obtain the product

> Place—the distribution channels that allow consumers to access or obtain the product

> Promotion—the integrated communication and public relations activities that communicate, inform, persuade, and motivate consumers to purchase the product

To maximize their success, sport marketers develop strategic and tactical plans to manipulate the four Ps in a variety of ways, depending on the mission of the organization, consumer perceptions and motivations, and fluctuations of the market (Pitts & Stotlar, 2007). These manipulations are critical to implementing a successful marketing plan. However, to devise a comprehensive plan for achieving marketing goals and objectives, sport marketers must consider factors beyond the four Ps. This chapter presents a 10-step process for developing a sport marketing plan that consists of 10 Ps—purpose, product, projecting the market, position, players, package, price, promotion, place, and promise. This process, shown in figure 12.1, illustrates that although the four Ps are central to the marketing plan, they must be integrated with other elements to achieve optimal sport marketing success. Following is a discussion of the 10 Ps of a marketing plan.

marketing plans—Comprehensive strategic and tactical frameworks for identifying and achieving a sport organization's marketing goals and objectives.

marketing mix—The elements of product, price, place, and promotion, which sport marketers alter, modify, or manipulate to achieve marketing goals and objectives.

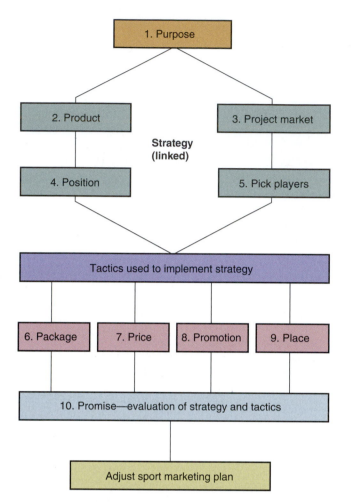

Figure 12.1 Steps in developing a sport marketing plan.

Adapted, by permission, from B.G. Pitts and D.K. Stotlar, 2002, Sport marketing theory. In *Fundamentals of sport marketing*, 2nd ed. (Morgantown, WV: Fitness Information Technology, Inc.), p.87. © Fitness Information Technology & West Virginia University.

Step 1: Purpose—Identify the Purpose of the Sport Marketing Plan

The first step in the marketing plan process involves clarifying the purpose of the sport marketing plan and linking the plan to the organization's mission and core values. Before packaging, promoting, and delivering can occur, sport marketers must establish a context to provide a direction for what they are trying to accomplish and how they expect to do so. As Covey (1989) noted, "an organizational mission statement is important because it creates in people's hearts and minds a frame of reference, a set of criteria or guidelines by which they will govern themselves" (p. 143). Every sport organization exists for a purpose. The organization defines this purpose in its mission statement. The mission statement of a sport organization must reflect the values and beliefs that are prevalent in the environments in which it operates. The mission statement answers two questions: Why does the organization exist, and what is the organization striving to achieve? Answering these questions establishes a context that enables sport marketers to select the best option and make appropriate and right (ethical) decisions that are consistent with the organization's mission and core values.

Besides allowing the mission statement to guide the marketing planning process, sport marketers must also have clearly defined and measurable goals and objectives. Goals are general summary statements of expected outcomes. Examples of sport marketing goals might be to increase attendance by 5% and to increase youth participation in community relations programs by 10%. Objectives are the specific activities that enable the sport marketer to obtain the expected outcomes. Examples of objectives linked to the earlier mentioned goals might be to increase preseason ticket sales by offering discount prices, adding game promotions giveaway items for youth, and offering youth sports clinics and camps. When the goals and objectives have been achieved and aligned with the mission of the sport organization, the marketing plan is deemed a success.

Step 2: Product—Analyze the Sport Product

The second step of the marketing plan process requires the sport marketer to analyze the dynamic and complex nature of the sport product. In additional to the unique aspects of sport previously discussed at the outset of this chapter, marketers must be mindful of three dimensions comprising the sport product: tangible goods, support services, and the game or event itself (Pitts, Fielding, & Miller, 1994). Tangible sport goods include items such as clothing and equipment. Support services include activities or programs ancillary to sport but necessary for its operation (e.g., game officials, athletics trainers, sport psychologists). The game or event itself is composed of two dimensions: the core product and product extensions (Mullin, Hardy, & Sutton, 2014).

Professional Profile: Hunter Lochmann

Title: chief marketing officer, senior associate athletic director, University of Michigan Athletics

Education: BS (education—sport management), University of Kansas; MS (sport management), University of Massachusetts at Amherst

NE DAY

to the WSG
learn more
ut a typical day
ne life for Hunter Loch-
nn. See if he spends
working hours the way
think he does.

Many of the concepts discussed in this chapter are illustrated in the marketing efforts of Hunter Lochmann at the University of Michigan (UM) department of athletics. Prior to his position at UM, Lochmann worked for the New York Knicks. To obtain the necessary background about the culture and traditions of UM, he read a book by the legendary UM football coach Bo Schembechler. Lochmann realized the need to respect what the Michigan brand represented, which meant refraining from promotional tactics such as having mascots and allowing advertising inside of Michigan Stadium for football games (Rothstein, 2012). While these practices are common for most collegiate sport teams, such practices would be inappropriate at Michigan because they are not congruent with the Michigan culture of sport marketing. As Rothstein notes, while Lochmann respected UM as the "staunch old guard in college sports, a program resistant to change, hesitant to new voices and lacking innovation" (para. 8), he responsibly and respectfully implemented some innovative and successful marketing practices. Among the noteworthy marketing changes were (a) his development of a marketing plan aimed at children and promoting student loyalty (market segmentation), (b) the decisions to have a UM night football game against Notre Dame and to revamp the ticketing department to identify different ways to sell tickets and expand the reach of UM athletics (place/product distribution), and (c) the decisions to restructure his staff to focus on the business of social media, to devise mobile apps for consumers, and to place a hashtag (#GOBLUE) on the Michigan Stadium field—an act that garnered the UM brand exposure to 31 countries and 48 states (a demonstrated embrace of technology and social media).

What have been the key moves, steps, or developments in your career, and how did you arrive at your current position?

To finish my undergrad degree, I needed to take part in an internship. I wanted to go back home (Massachusetts), and I had the opportunity for a year-long internship with the Harvard University athletic department on the athletic facility side. While there, folks recommended graduate school for my next step. I was lucky enough to get into a great sports management school in my backyard—UMass Amherst. To complete my master's degree, I had to do another internship, and a professor at UMass (Bill Sutton) recommended me to a small sports agency in Kansas City (where I had friends and contacts due to having gone to school at Kansas) called MAI Sports. MAI Sports had just landed an opportunity to help Sprint (based in KC) execute their new sponsorship of the NFL as the official telecommunications provider. Timing is everything. My summer internship turned into a four-year job as I helped Sprint execute their sponsorships (3 years with the NFL, 1 year with a NASCAR team). While at MAI Sports, Sutton was consulting for the National Basketball Association, and he knew of an open position that he thought I was a good match for. Sure enough, I jumped on the opportunity and moved to New York City to work in the newly formed team marketing and business operations department. During my four years there, I had the honor of working with all 30 NBA teams and their front offices—truly a great experience. When one of these teams—the New York Knicks—inquired about my interest in joining them as the director of marketing, I jumped at the chance. I joined them in 2004, and two years later, I was promoted to the VP of marketing, where I stayed for the next four years. During the summer of 2010, I was approached by a search firm with the newly created job of CMO for Michigan Athletics. When I read the job description and saw the brand, I knew it was my dream job. After a long interview process, I was offered the job and accepted it, starting in late 2010.

What are your current responsibilities and objectives in your job?

Within the Michigan athletic department, I contribute mainly to two of our strategic drivers—building the brand and growing in every way (revenue generation). Besides being the brand manager for our "Block M," I oversee the following departments and disciplines: ticketing, licensing, sponsorship (through our relationship with IMG), digital marketing, event presentation, marketing and promotions, and our website. All of these disciplines lead to the aforementioned goal of building our brand and creating revenue for our 31 teams and more than 900 student athletes.

(continued)

Professional Profile: Hunter Lochmann *(continued)*

What do you enjoy most about your current job?

I enjoy many things, including representing such a strong and well-respected brand, working for a leader and within a culture full of integrity, working with peers, coaches, and partners, knowing that my hard work is helping to create opportunities and experiences for student athletes, using our brand strength to innovate and to be a trendsetter, and creating "WOW" experiences for our fans.

What do you consider the biggest future challenge to be in your job or industry?

In my role, one of my biggest objectives is selling tickets. With the home viewing experience getting better by the year and our prices rising (like all sports), we have to make sure that nothing takes the place of attending a game in person. The bells and whistles, the sense of community, the memories, and so on. We are constantly attacking this problem through the event presentation as well as with technology (what is available at the game). Speaking of technology, we have to continue to be on the forefront of consumer and fan behavior and make sure we are engaged and leaders within these channels.

The core product of the event is the actual competition (e.g., the players and coaches on the competing teams, the sport activity itself, the facility in which the competition takes place). Brooks (1994) proposed the following tangible elements in the core sport product:

> Type of sport—football, basketball, gymnastics
> Participants—athletes (e.g., beginner, elite, professional), coaches (e.g., volunteer, part-time salaried, full-time professionals), and the environment (e.g., challenging golf courses, difficult or mountainous cross-country terrain)
> Team—University of Michigan, Miami Heat, Pittsburgh Steelers, Chicago Sky

Product extensions are the ancillary items, such as the mascot, music, halftime entertainment, concessions, bands, and cheerleaders associated with the overall sport experience. Because of the flair and excitement of product extensions that are created around the core product, sport events are often viewed as a form of entertainment (e.g., the NBA All-Star Game, the World Series, the NCAA Final Four). While the core product may be the primary attraction for some consumers, for others, it may be the product extensions. Therefore, marketers must understand and appreciate the elements of the core product of sport as well as the core product extensions before they can develop an appropriate and effective marketing plan.

It is also important that sport marketers recognize where a product is in its life cycle (Barker, 2003; Levitt, 1960; Shank, 2008). The life cycle seeks to depict the lifespan stages of a product, including the following: introduction (a product that is new to the market), growth (a product experiences an increase in sales, attendance, and support), maturity (a product that has sustained sales, attendance, and support), and decline (a product experiences a decrease in sales, attendance, and support). Each phase of the life cycle influences the marketing focus. For instance, in the introduction phase, the marketing focus is on increasing the consumers' awareness of the product; in the growth phase, the marketing focus is on differentiating the product from others in the market; in the maturity phase, the marketing focus is on sustaining the product sales and consumer support; and in the decline phase, the marketing focus is on extending the product (by repositioning it, identifying new consumers, or eliminating it all together).

Marketing plans must concurrently address the core product, product extensions, and the **product life cycle**.

product life cycle—The lifespan stages of a sport product include introduction, growth, maturity, and decline.

Step 3: Projection—Project the Market Climate

As alluded to previously, sport does not exist in isolation; market conditions have a profound influence on how it is perceived and on what consumers seek or demand from it. Therefore, the third step in the process of developing a sport marketing plan is a projection of the market climate. Projecting the climate requires a critical analysis of past market conditions and a keen understanding of present market conditions. Both phases of market assessment exert a direct or indirect influence on marketing effectiveness. Assessing the past market climate enables sport marketers to identify historical factors associated with successful or failed marketing efforts. Assessing the current market climate allows sport marketers to determine the timeliness and relevance of their existing marketing practices. This combined knowledge enhances sport marketers' ability to forecast the future market climate and to anticipate marketing changes needed (e.g., developing new and improved products, targeting emerging consumers, revising image).

As you may have concluded, projecting the marketing climate is a difficult task. It requires a continuous and thoughtful examination of internal and external factors and their subsequent effect on marketing efforts. For example, internal factors affecting the marketing climate of Major League Baseball (MLB) include players, owners, team management, and staff personnel. The media, corporate sponsors, advertisers, spectators, geographical location, sociocultural environment, the economy, and the federal government represent examples of external factors that affect the marketing climate of MLB.

Projecting the market climate requires an identification of positive (favorable) and negative (unfavorable) factors and conditions among a myriad of internal and external factors that may influence sport marketing. This type of assessment is often performed by conducting a SWOT analysis, which includes four elements: strengths, weaknesses, opportunities, and threats. They are defined as follows: (1) *Strengths* are internal factors that are advantageous to the sport organization's ability to achieve its marketing goals and objectives, (2) *weaknesses* are internal factors that are disadvantageous and may prevent a sport organization from achieving its marketing goals and objectives, (3) *opportunities* are external factors or conditions in the environment that may enhance a sport organization's ability to achieve its marketing goals and objectives, and (4) *threats* are the unfavorable factors or conditions in an environment that could interfere with a sport organization's ability to achieve its marketing goals and objectives. Marketing plans should maximize the strengths and opportunities and minimize the weaknesses and threats identified in the SWOT analysis. The sidebar on this page presents an example of a SWOT analysis applied to women's professional basketball.

Keep in mind that the key to marketing success is for a sport organization's strengths and opportunities to outweigh its weaknesses and threats. Applying the SWOT analysis to the Women's National Basketball Association (WNBA) and the American Basketball League (ABL) illustrates why the WNBA is still in existence and why the ABL suspended operations and eventually disbanded. Like the marketers of the WNBA, sport marketers should continuously examine market conditions and develop strategies that will enable them to maximize their products' or events' strengths and opportunities and eliminate or minimize their weaknesses and threats.

Step 4: Positioning—Position the Sport Product

According to Shank (2008), positioning refers to the process of establishing a sport entity in the minds of consumers in the target market. The objective of positioning is to differentiate the sport product from competing products by creating a distinctive image. Distinctive images are created in consumers' minds based on (1) the types of consumers who buy the product, (2) the design of the product as well as its benefits,

internal factors—Factors inside a sport organization that affect the sport marketing climate (e.g., players, owners, team management, staff personnel).

external factors—Factors outside of a sport organization that affect the sport marketing climate (e.g., media, corporate sponsors, advertisers, spectators, geography, culture, economy, federal regulations, regulations of sport governing bodies).

SWOT analysis—A management technique available to sport marketers to help them assess the strengths and weaknesses of an organization and the opportunities and threats that it faces.

SWOT Analysis of Women's Professional Basketball

A SWOT analysis for two professional women's sport leagues, the Women's National Basketball Association (WNBA) and the now defunct American Basketball League (ABL), provides another illustration of the manner in which internal and external factors can influence marketing success. The major strength of the WNBA was that it was a product of the NBA; a weakness of the ABL was its ownership by a small group of private investors. Consequently, the WNBA had the financial backing (from the NBA) to absorb deficits (a condition that was a strength), whereas the ABL had a limited budget, lacking the financial resources to absorb the financial losses incurred (a condition that was a weakness). The WNBA teams were located in large cities that were considered major U.S. markets (a condition representing an opportunity); the ABL teams were located primarily in midsize, medium-market cities (a condition representing a threat). The WNBA games were held in NBA arenas (a strength), whereas the ABL games were held in collegiate and other smaller venues within their respective cities (somewhat of a weakness). Another major strength of the WNBA was its national media distribution (i.e., NBC, ESPN, and Lifetime); a major weakness of the ABL was its regional media distribution (i.e., regional sports channels, Prime Network, and Black Entertainment Television). The ABL did not allow its players to participate in other professional women's basketball leagues (a weakness that limited players' appeal and exposure), whereas the WNBA allowed its players to participate in other leagues (a strength that maximized the players' appeal and exposure). The WNBA season of competition was held during the summer months, and did not compete with other girls' or women's basketball leagues (an opportunity), whereas the ABL season of competition was held during the winter months, competing with girls' high school basketball and women's college basketball games (a threat).

WEB

Go to the WSG and complete the web search activity, which invites you to analyze the importance of images on the website for the State Farm Bayou Classic.

(3) the price of the product, and (4) the place where the product is available or where the event occurs (e.g., arena, stadium, facility). Sport marketers often position products by means of verbal and nonverbal communications to consumers. Sport images can be communicated through logos, symbols, and messages through such avenues as TV and radio advertisements, public service announcements, jingles, press releases, and news articles.

Numerous examples of successful positioning in sport marketing exist. For example, the Paralympics does an excellent job in communicating positive images of elite athletes who are physically challenged by showing that they can compete in athletic events just like athletes who do not experience the same physical challenges. Another example is the New Orleans, Louisiana, State Farm Bayou Classic (the largest and most popular Black college sport event in America), which has been successfully positioned as a sociocultural and festive entertainment event that contains market features particularly salient to the Black community. Many Black consumers who are not football fans attend because the event has an image being exciting, racially affirming, and culturally supportive (Armstrong, 2002).

Several sport organizations have repositioned their images by revising associated symbols and images. For example, the WNBA recently changed its logo to depict a silhouette of a female basketball player who is stronger, more athletic, and more culturally diverse in appearance than the one in the previous logo. Relatedly, to respect the sacred values and customs of American Indians, a number of colleges and universities have replaced nicknames of their mascots and eradicated promotional routines conveying narratives and images that reflected aspects of American Indian traditions and practices. As a measure of respect for the many values of its diverse consumers, the NCAA announced that it would not allow universities that contained hostile, abusive, and offensive American Indian mascot nicknames to host postseason tournaments. Because of the special circumstances and unique relationships that exist between some

American Indian tribes and some NCAA universities, the approval of the use of Native American nicknames and mascots by American Indian tribes will be factored into the decision. Based on the increasing diversity of sport participants and consumers, the best way to position a sport product in the market is to use honest and nonoffensive verbal and nonverbal communication that creates a distinctive and socially responsible image.

The positioning of the sport product is established by the process called branding. **Branding** is the process of using a name, design, symbol, or any combination of them to help differentiate a sport product from the competition. According to Shank (2008), the branding process consists of several elements:

> Brand awareness—The consumers' recognition and recollection of the brand name

> Brand image—The consumers' perceptions and set of beliefs about a brand which, in turn, shape their attitudes

> Brand equity—The value that the brand contributes to a product in the marketplace

> Brand loyalty—The consistent purchase or repeat purchase of one brand over all others in a product category

Because branding seeks to distinguish the summary benefits of a product, it is a critical component of the sport marketing process. As the branding process indicates, the task for sport marketers is to convert product or brand awareness to loyalty. This requires favorably positioning the product to add value (brand equity) and to differentiate it by positively influencing consumers' affinity for it and enhancing their desire to consume it. Having consumers to believe in the brand value of a product makes the task of facilitating the marketing exchange with them easier for sport marketers. In other words, when products have good brand equity, they can virtually sell themselves. Product brands such as Nike athletic shoes and apparel, Louisville Slugger baseball bats, Titleist golf balls, and Penn tennis balls are just a few products that have achieved noteworthy customer loyalty based on their quality brand status.

branding—The process of using a name, design, symbol, or any combination of the three to help differentiate a sport product from the competition.

The key to market segmentation is being able to identify and group consumers based on elements such as their age, race, stage in life, interests, and so on.

Step 5: Players—Pick the Players and Analyze and Target Consumers

Levitt's (1960) seminal marketing myopia article in the *Harvard Business Review* revealed that the catalyst for organizations' unsuccessful marketing was due in part to their focus on their products. Levitt substantiated the need to shift from a product orientation to a customer orientation. Consumers are the lifeblood of sport marketing; a customer orientation is mandatory for sport marketing success. Consequently, marketing essentially begins and end with the customer. In this fifth step of the marketing plan process, the sport

marketer must identify (target or select) particular consumers who will allow for optimal sport marketing success. This process of selecting consumers can be envisioned as picking the players. This approach involves grouping consumers according to common characteristics (wants and needs) relative to the sport product or sporting event being promoted and delivered. Selecting the right consumers for sport marketing is a challenge because sport consumers are very heterogeneous (different). So, to appeal to the uniqueness of sport consumers, marketers must have information about them that will provide some insight into how they may be grouped.

The process of breaking large heterogeneous populations of sport consumers into smaller identifiable groups with similar wants and needs is referred to as **market segmentation**. Sport marketers use this process to identify target consumers. They often do so by grouping or segmenting consumers in four areas: demographics, psychographics, media preferences, and purchasing behavior. Demographic segmentation refers to clustering sport consumers based on their age, gender, income, race or ethnicity, education, and place of residence. The increasing economic power and growing sport interests among underrepresented racial and ethnic groups represent a huge opportunity for sport organizations. Sport marketers have also realized the importance of devising marketing strategies to appeal to female consumers. Until recently, women were not considered a viable target market segment for men's sports. But with increased buying of men's sport teams' merchandise by women, women's increased spectatorship of men's sports (e.g., the NFL, NBA, MLB, NHL), the growth of women's sports, the financial gains that women have made as consumers, and the general influence that women exert over family purchases and consumption decisions, women have become an important target market for sport marketers (Shank, 2008; Sutton & Wattlington, 1994). Moreover, the Title IX generation (women and girls born after 1972) is relatively young and affluent, two desirable attributes sought by sport marketers. Therefore, demographic segmentation has been a popular technique used by sport marketers. Psychographic segmentation refers to appealing to consumers' attitudes, interests, and lifestyles. Market segmentation based on media preference would cluster consumers based on their media and multimedia (e.g., TV, radio, Internet) preferences. Purchasing behavior as a means of market segmentation refers to grouping sport consumers according to the frequency of usage behavior (e.g., how often they attend basketball games, how frequently they purchase sport drinks).

Sport marketers often use combinations of these attributes in their market segmentation strategy. For instance, a sport equipment manufacturer using the combined demographic (sex and age), psychographic, and media preferences segmentation variables might identify the primary target audience as 12- to 16-year-old males who are interested in in-line skating and who watch MTV. The WNBA attracts combination markets: Their core consumers are family, women over the age of 35, and followers of college basketball, and the core television audience is mainly African American and male (Lombardo, 2011). Another group of consumers who are of interest to sport marketers and who represent the combined segmentation are Generation X (people born from 1964–1978) and Generation Y (people born from 1979–1990) consumers. Consumers from different generations exhibit unique behaviors that illustrate how demographics (age) and psychographics (attitudes and interests) interact to influence sport consumer behavior. Consumer characteristics such as race and ethnicity, age, and sex may also be integrated or combined to create specific target markets within the Generation X and Generation Y categories. Sport events such as the X Games and Dew Tour illustrate that the latest generations (e.g., X, Y) are target markets to be reckoned with. Sexual orientation offers another base by which to target sport consumers. It may represent a combined demographic and psychographic segmentation base. The WNBA is one

market segmentation— The process of identifying smaller and viable clusters of sport consumers who may exhibit similar wants, needs, and interests regarding sport.

sport organization that has recognized the significance of sexual orientation as a basis for market segmentation and has targeted lesbian consumers by tailoring marketing activities to reach them and welcome them to the WNBA experience. Other sport organizations have not expressly targeted lesbian, gay, bisexual, or transgender (LGBT) consumers to the same extent. It can be assumed that as masses of athletes from these groups become more open, visible, and successful in sports, marketing to attract these consumers will increase likewise.

As mentioned previously, sport marketing success requires that sport marketers target the right groups of consumers. Criteria for selecting the viable target markets include factors such as the size of the target group, the amount of resources available to the target group, and whether the target group is accessible to the organization. The determination of whether a target market is viable varies among sport organizations, based largely on the organization's marketing goals and objectives. For example, a target market of 100 students for a football event that attracts more than 100,000 consumers may not be of sufficient size to warrant specific marketing attention. On the other hand, a target market of 100 students for a fitness club with a membership of approximately 200 is an acceptable size, and it may have a significant effect on the overall marketing success of the fitness club.

After marketers have identified the target consumers for their product, they must engage in a number of strategies that will help them attract the targeted consumers to the sport organization or event. The remaining five steps of the development of a sport marketing plan describe tactics that help marketers attract their target audiences and facilitate a satisfying exchange relationship with them.

Step 6: Packaging—Package the Sport Product

The sixth step in the process is closely related to step 4 (positioning), and involves packaging tactical elements of the sport product. This step requires compiling or bundling the salient attributes of the product and presenting the product in the best possible manner to encourage selected target consumers to purchase it. Because consumers differ, sport marketers must package the product in different ways. Packaging tangible or industrial sport products involves explaining their benefits, such as the strength and longevity of metal bats, the comfort and safety of helmets, and the expanded sweet spot of oversize tennis rackets. Packaging the core product of the sport experience (the game or event itself), however, involves communicating the expectations of the product, and providing such information before the point of purchase (POP). For example, sport marketers might package the game or event as a family outing, offering family ticket plans and family entertainment. Marketers might also package sport as a good place to make business contacts, offering business ticket plans and a postevent business fair. A sport organization that wants to be seen as one that cares about the community might offer group discount ticket plans for social service and charitable community organizations, packaging the emotions that such events may elicit.

Another aspect of product packaging is the manner in which product extensions (discussed in step 2) are included in the overall sport experience. For instance, music, halftime promotions, and entertainment contribute to the overall packaging of a sport event. Some consumers may not be specifically attracted to the core product (e.g., the basketball game), but they may be attracted to the way in which the core product is packaged (e.g., music, fun, entertainment).

Another aspect of the sport product is the associated licensed merchandise. Many sport teams and events offer goods such as hats, T-shirts, and jackets, as well as non-apparel items such as watches, novelty items, memorabilia, and decorative items that consumers perceive as extensions and representations of the teams or events.

The Lotte Giants and Sport Marketing Strategy: "The Best Fans Make the Best Team"

By Sanghak Lee, South Korea
Korea Aerospace University, Seoul

"The New York Yankees of Korea." "The best value professional team in Korea." "The largest season attendance record in the KBO." These are phrases used to describe one of best professional baseball teams in South Korea, the Lotte Giants. However, there is another phrase that the Lotte Giants love even more: "The Giants have the most avid fans in the world." The team's enthusiastic fans have made the Lotte Giants the success story that they are. In a sense, having the best fans also creates the best sport marketing strategy.

The bright scoreboard of the Lotte Giants adds to the exciting atmosphere of the game.

The Korea Baseball Organization (KBO) is the most famous and financially successful professional sport in Korea. The KBO was founded in 1982 with six teams, and each team represents a city as well as a company. For example, the Lotte Group (the fifth largest conglomerate in Korea behind Samsung, Hyundai, and LG) established the Lotte Giants in Busan, the second largest city in Korea. The KBO has experienced expansion in terms of the number of teams and spectators, as well as in popularity and revenue, for the last 31 years. There are now nine teams in the league, and a tenth team is scheduled to join in 2015. The number of spectators in 2013 was estimated at more than 75 million. Because the KBO is the most competitive league in the most competitive sport in Korea, Korean baseball players have also become very competitive internationally. The Korean national baseball team (which is mostly stocked with players from the KBO) won the gold medal at the 2008 Beijing Olympics and advanced to the semifinal and final at the 2006 and 2009 World Baseball Classic (WBC), respectively. In addition, South Korean Hyun-Jin Ryu is the starting pitcher for the Los Angeles Dodgers and Shin-Soo Choo is the leadoff hitter for the Texas Rangers.

The Lotte Giants were one of the original six teams in the KBO when it was founded in 1982. They have won two KBO championships, one in 1984 and the other in 1992. More recently, they've made the postseason for the last five years (2008–2012). Their strong performance has brought with it a growing fan base. In 2009, the Lotte Giants recorded the largest season attendance in KBO history with 1,380,000 spectators, and they gathered more than a million fans in each of the last five years (2008–2012). Having the most fans has also made the Giants very profitable; one study estimated the value of the Giants at 128 billion Korean Won (about US$113 million), and the team contributed 231 billion Korean Won (about US$204 million) to the local (Busan) economy. In addition, the Lotte Giants are one of the favorite teams among corporate sponsors. Lotte Department Store and other Lotte Group–affiliated companies, as well as many other organizations, have become sponsors of the Giants. Each company typically spends between several million and a couple of billion Korean Won on these sponsorships.

One of the most important reasons behind the Giants' success, aside from their performance on the field, is the avid Lotte fans. One famous baseball commentator, Gu-Yeon Heo, once said, "You cannot evaluate the Lotte Giants' competiveness without considering Busan fans." Therefore, let's look at the avid Giants fans and the sport marketing activities related to those fans. First, everyone wears orange plastic bags on their heads, weaves bunches of torn newspapers, sings *Busan Seagull* (a 1980s famous K-pop song and now the Giants' official cheering song), and shouts "Chi-La!" (the phrase for *hit* in the dialect from the Busan region). This describes the typical Giants fan in the team's stadium in Busan. To satisfy and attract more enthusiastic Giants fans, the Lotte Giants and their sponsors have implemented a variety of programs. For instance, the Giants are trying to cultivate a new generation of young fans, so the team operates a playground for kids and even provides a mothers' room for baby fans and their parents. The Lotte Giants also operates its own Lotte Giants Museum to memorialize and honor the team's heritage, including the two championships and many franchise stars. The Giants also hold a Giants Cheering Song Contest. These programs keep avid fans involved with the Giants. Therefore, many say, "Once a Giants fan, always a Giants fan." These passionate Giants fans also allow sponsors to actively create fan-related marketing programs. For example, the main sponsor, the Lotte Department Store, organizes a Lotte Department Store Champions Day once a month, and the retailer supports 50% of every Lotte fan's ticket price on that day. Another sponsor, Busan Bank, provides a special savings account for Giants fans. The fans will receive an additional 0.1% to 0.3% savings rate based on the Giants' team performance. For example, if the Lotte Giants make the postseason, fans will receive an additional 0.1%, and they will get an additional 0.2% if the team takes the championship.

International Learning Activity #1

Using the Internet or other sources, search for Korean professional leagues. Which professional leagues exist in Korea? Which sports are famous in Korea?

International Learning Activity #2

Find and access the website for your favorite (or hometown) professional sports team. What sport marketing activities is the team currently engaged in? Are there any sport marketing actives related to fostering young sport fans? Which sport marketing activities look interesting to you? Why?

International Learning Activity #3

A sport sponsorship is one of the most common sport marketing activities and is an important revenue source for most professional teams. Using the Internet or other sources, find sport events, leagues, teams, or players that engage in large sponsorship contracts. Which sponsors spend the most money on sport sponsorship in your country?

sport sponsorship—The acquisition of rights to affiliate or associate with a sport product or sporting event in order to derive benefits from the affiliation or association (Mullin, Hardy, & Sutton, 2014).

promotions mix—The collection of integrated activities that seek to communicate, inform, and ultimately persuade consumers to participate in the sport consumption activity, experience, or event.

Packaging the sport product to secure financial support from corporations is an especially important aspect of the marketing plan called **sport sponsorship**. Sponsorship (which is also discussed in step 8 as an element of the **promotions mix**) involves an agreement between a sport organization or sport event and a business or corporate partner wherein the business pays a fee to the sport entity (organization or event) to acquire the rights to affiliate with it. This fee obtained from businesses to affiliate with sport provides the sport entity with financial support and needed products and services, and provides the business entity with benefits such as increased sales, change in attitudes, heightened awareness, and the establishment and maintenance of positive relationships with consumers. Sponsorships are successful when they create a partnership in which both entities prosper, fostering a win–win scenario.

The way that a product is packaged influences and is influenced by every other aspect of the 10-P process outlined in this chapter, such as who will be attracted to the product or event (be they individual consumers or corporate partners), how the product may be relevant to the current market climate, what the price of the product should be, how the product should be promoted, and how the product can be most effectively delivered. Therefore, sport marketers must understand how the elements that contribute to product packaging influence the success of the marketing plan.

Step 7: Pricing—Price the Sport Product

The seventh step in the marketing plan process is determining the value of the product by assigning it a price. Price is the most visible and flexible element because of discounts, rebates, and coupons. According to Pitts and Stotlar (2007), marketers should consider four factors when developing a pricing strategy:

1. Consumer—Analyze all aspects of the consumer, including demographics, psychographics, purchasing behaviors, and media preferences.
2. Competitor—Analyze the consumer's perception of the product value compared with all competing products and analyze the competitors' prices.
3. Company—Analyze the costs involved in producing the product (e.g., materials, equipment, salaries, rent) and set a minimum price to cover the costs.
4. Climate—Analyze external factors (e.g., laws pertaining to pricing, government regulations, the economic situation, the political situation).

Consumers obviously exchange money for sport products and services; however, they also invest and expend their time, emotions, and physical energy. For corporate consumers, trading is a common practice. For example, marketers of a tennis tournament might make trades with corporate sponsors, such as tickets for tennis balls, stadium signage for food and beverages for a hospitality tent, and scoreboard advertisement for the use of vehicles to transport players and officials.

Factors other than price help determine the value of a sport product. Each consumer has attitudes, preferences, beliefs, and a certain amount of expendable money. These factors, along with price, influence how people determine what sport products are worth. Because the meaning and value of sport is unique to each consumer, sport pricing strategy must appeal to as many different consumers as possible. For example, sport franchises set different prices for corporate season ticket holders, charitable organizations, group ticket purchasers, miniseason ticket purchasers, family ticket purchasers, and single-ticket purchasers. Prices are generally differentiated based on the consumer's interest, ability, and willingness to commit time and money to participate in the sport experience. Consumers who are highly identified or psychologically attached to a sport team may be less sensitive to the costs, and thus more willing to pay higher prices for tickets and merchandise.

Since price is a quantifiable statement of value, consumers tend to equate price with quality. Therefore, a new sport franchise should price tickets to be comparable with competing products (e.g., direct competitors such as other sport events, and indirect competition such as movies) rather than set a lower price. Consumers might equate a lower price with an inferior product.

Lead time is a concept that is very important to sport pricing. It refers to the time lag between the time a ticket is purchased and the time of the actual game or event. More day-of-the-game or walk-up sales occur at MLB games than at NBA games because many more games and seats are available at lower prices in baseball than in basketball (Mullin, Hardy, & Sutton, 2014). You may recall the discussion of market segmentation (in step 5) where marketers target certain groups of consumers. Prices are also segmented based on the consumer. For instance, collegiate sport marketers often segment their prices such that students pay one fee and the general public pays another. Prices are also segmented based on the experience they afford the consumer. For example, the price of courtside seats at an NBA game is much more expensive than the price of the seats located closer to the arena rafters.

As you may have surmised, sport pricing is complex, and it is an inexact science largely due to the difficulty of monetizing the uniqueness of sport. Price, however, is one aspect of the marketing plan that may be readily changed (i.e., increased or decreased slightly). For example, sport organizations often alter their prices to attract different consumers (e.g., offering special pricing for Girl Scouts attending a women's sport event). Sport organizations may also change prices according to the market environment (e.g., lowering prices during a recession or economic downturn) or the team's performance (e.g., increasing prices as a team's performance dramatically improves). In the final analysis, sport marketers must determine how consumers perceive the value of the product compared with all competing products and use that information to set an appropriate price that will not exceed consumers' price tolerance (i.e., the amount they are willing to pay for an event). Additionally, sport marketers should seek to offer consumers a satisfying experience with perceived benefits that surpass the personal and financial costs that consumers incur.

Step 8: Promotions—Promote the Sport Product

The eighth step in the market plan process is promotions. The core of promotions is effective communication. Promotions plays a key role in communicating, creating, and establishing the image of a product (discussed previously in step 4).

In their landmark work on public relations theory, Grunig and White (1992) suggested that effective communication practices consist of four key elements:

1. Open and honest communication with the public
2. Images and messages that are socially responsible
3. Cooperation with the public and response to their interests
4. Good faith relationships with the public

Please take a look at the following sidebar involving the story of an NBA team's name change from the Washington Bullets to the Washington Wizards. This is an historical yet classic application of the four steps in effective communication practices.

Promoting sport products involves implementing a mix of activities that will best (1) communicate the desired image of the product to the target audiences, (2) educate and inform the target audiences about the product and its benefits, and (3) persuade the target audiences to buy the product.

Elements that compose a promotion strategy are referred to as the promotional mix and include advertising, publicity, activities and inducements, public relations (including community relations and media relations), personal selling, and sponsorship.

Renaming the Washington Bullets

The name Bullets was associated for several decades with professional basketball, beginning in the 1960s as the Baltimore Bullets, who then became the Capital Bullets in the early 1970s and eventually the Washington Bullets in 1974. This was the name of the team before the arrival of the team's stars such as Gilbert Arenas (who in 2010 was suspended for the season for a locker room gun incident), Caron Butler, and even Michael Jordan, up through the mid-1990s. During the 1995–1996 season, however, Abe Pollin, owner of the Bullets, decided that the team nickname conveyed a negative image because bullets had nothing to do with basketball but everything to do with people being injured or killed by shooting incidents in Washington, D.C. and the surrounding communities. The actions by the team throughout the renaming process illustrate the four steps of effective communication practices (detailed in the text).

First, Pollin communicated openly and honestly with the public about the need to change the team's nickname (step 1). Second, Pollin involved the public in a promotional contest to determine a new team nickname, one that would convey a positive and socially responsible image of the team (step 2). Third, the contest was an example of how an organization should work cooperatively with the public and respond to the public's interest (step 3). Fourth, a corporate sponsor contributed prizes for some contestants, thus generating interest and publicity and establishing a good-faith relationship with the public (step 4). Moreover, an antiviolence campaign was launched in conjunction with the team nickname contest. This campaign communicated the message that the NBA franchise was a responsible corporate citizen that wanted to help the community solve an important social problem. The promotional contest resulted in a new name—the Washington Wizards.

> *Advertising*—One-way paid messages about the sport product. The messages can come through outlets such as newspapers, magazines, TV, radio, direct mail, scoreboards, arena signage, pocket schedules, game programs, posters, outdoor advertising, the Internet, and new media (smartphones, social media).

> *Publicity*—Nonpaid communication about a sport product in which the sponsor is usually not identified and the message reaches the public because it is newsworthy. Such publicity typically comes through news releases and TV and radio public service announcements.

> *Activities and inducements*—Endeavors to encourage consumers to purchase the sport product. These come in the form of giveaways, coupons, product samples, cash refunds, contests, raffles, and so on.

> *Public relations*—Activities and programs, especially those associated with community and media relations, that help the sport organization develop positive relationships with its publics and target consumers. For example, through their Be Fit campaign, the WNBA seeks to communicate the importance of being physically active. Moreover, through their Crucial Catch campaign, NFL players, coaches, and administrators are involved in a number of public relations activities that promote awareness of breast cancer and the need for women to take an active role in early detection.

> *Community relations*—Activities and programs, such as the NBA Cares initiative, designed to meet the interests and needs of the public and, by so doing, establish good-faith relationships with the respective communities. This area includes activities and programs such as youth sport clinics, athlete autograph-signing opportunities, and the collection of food items at sport arenas to help people in the community. With the growing need for sport organizations to be socially responsible, community relations activities that garner favorable relationships with the public are essential for marketing success.

› *Media relations*—Maintenance of networks and positive relationships with people in the media to obtain positive media exposure for a sport product. This goal can be accomplished by providing the media with press releases, having news conferences, hosting media-day events, and providing media guides. Positive media relations help to promote favorable relationships with publics.

› *Personal selling*—Direct face-to-face communication with individuals, groups, or organizations to sell tickets, luxury suites or boxes, or sponsorships. Personal selling is unique and highly effective because it allows salespeople to adapt messages based on feedback, communicate more information to the target audience, guarantee that the target audience will pay attention to the message being delivered, and develop a long-term relationship with the target audience.

› *Sponsorship*—A form of promotion that involves a partnership between sport organizations or events and corporate entities. Business partnerships are based on exchange theory. Corporations provide money, products, or services to sport organizations or events. In return, sport organizations or events provide rights and benefits of association such as use of the sport organization or event logo, name, or trademark; exclusive association with the event or facility; exclusive association within a product or service category; use of various designations or phrases in connection with the product, event, or facility, such as "official sponsor," "official supplier," "official product," or "presented by"; exclusive use of the product; and authorization to conduct particular promotional activities such as contests, advertising campaigns, or on-site product sales. Corporations make significant investments in sport for a number of reasons, such as to (1) establish or improve their image through association with high-visibility events, (2) promote their products, thereby increasing sales, (3) display goodwill, and (4) obtain access and exposure to the target audiences of events.

Just days after setting a new world record in the decathlon, eventual 2012 Olympic gold medalist Ashton Eaton accepts a $25,000 check for winning the Visa Championship Series at the 2012 U.S. Olympic Trials for track and field. Promotion strategy elements (e.g., publicity, sponsorship) are evident in this photo.

Step 9: Place—Distributing the Sport Product

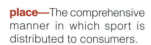

place—The comprehensive manner in which sport is distributed to consumers.

The ninth step in the marketing plan process is analyzing the place of the sport product. **Place** refers to consumers' abilities to access the sport event or experience. Place includes the location of the sport product (e.g., stadium, arena), the point of origin for distributing the product (e.g., ticket sales at the ice rink, sales by a toll-free telephone number), the geographic location of the target markets (e.g., global, national, regional, state, communities, cities), and other channels that are important to consider regarding how target consumers may access the product (e.g., time, day, season, or month in which a product is offered, media distribution outlets that consumers may use). Factors related to the physical location of a sport event can have a favorable or unfavorable effect on the marketing plan. To ensure a favorable effect, the sport facility must be easily accessible (e.g., highway systems, parking, walkways, ramps), have an attractive physical appearance (e.g., well maintained, painted), have a pleasant, convenient, and functional environment (e.g., quick and easy access to concessions, clean restrooms, smoke-free and odor-free environment), and have safe and pleasant surroundings (e.g., adequate public safety and security personnel, attractive neighborhood).

Since place pertains to the various channels by which the product is distributed to consumers, another term for place is distribution. Sport is unique in the way that it is distributed to consumers. The production and consumption of the product occur simultaneously for spectators attending sport events in stadiums or arenas. The sport product is also distributed to consumers, nationally and globally, through the electronic media of television (regular cable and pay-per-view), radio, Internet broadcasts, social networking endeavors, mobile technology, and a host of other forms of new media.

Ticket distribution is another critical aspect of sport distribution. The objective of a ticket distribution system is to make consumer purchases easy, quick, and convenient. Some approaches adopted by sport organizations include using outside companies such as Ticketmaster; ticket outlets at local banks, shopping malls, and grocery stores; mobile van units that transport ticket personnel and operations to various locations throughout the community; on-site stadium and arena ticket sales with expanded hours of operation; toll-free telephone numbers; and will-call pickup arrangements.

The overall objective of distributing the sport product is to facilitate consumers' ability to take part in the sport experience, or purchase the sport product, in a timely and convenient manner, thereby promoting marketing success.

Step 10: Promise—Evaluate the Promises of the Sport Marketing Plan

The last step in the marketing plan process is the evaluation of the plan. This step involves evaluating the extent to which the marketing plan met its promise to help achieve the sport organization's mission. This evaluation requires obtaining feedback about the marketing plan from internal and external sources. Some internal sources of feedback are ticket sales, merchandise sales, and an internal database of customer inquiries, complaints, and suggestions. Some external sources of feedback include consumers, corporate sponsors, advertisers, and media personnel. The sport marketer must analyze and evaluate the feedback. The evaluation should focus on determining the extent to which the plan helped the organization achieve its mission by acting in accordance with its core values and its marketing goals and objectives. For example, to evaluate the effectiveness of the marketing plans for some of the Black college sport events that specifically seek to empower the Black community sociologically and economically, marketers may evaluate the number of students who attended the event, examine the financial contributions that the event made to the respective HBCU (historically Black colleges and universities), and examine the economic contributions of the event to the local economies. To examine the effectiveness of ticket plans promotions, sport marketers can examine the attendance figures before and after such promotions.

In additional to an understanding and mastery of how to apply the 10-P principles previously discussed, several additional attributes will contribute to sport marketing success. Among the more notable ones are the embrace of (a) technology and social media, (b) marketing research, (c) critical thinking, and (d) ethics.

Market Research

Devising a comprehensive marketing plan to include the 10 Ps is no small feat! However, this process is dramatically easier when the sport marketer has good quality information to direct and inform marketing decisions. The type of information needed to develop a marketing plan includes but is not limited to information about (a) the product (its history, successes, and failures) and the respective organization, (b) targeted consumers (their attitudes, perspectives, purchase behaviors, demographic profile), (c) social, cultural, and economic trends of the environment, and (d) the direct and indirect competitors of the sport organization. Information used to develop marketing plans must be valid and reliable and should consider various sources. Sport marketers may obtain such information through both formal and informal means. For example, sport marketers may commission formal research investigations exploring consumer motivations for attending sport events or they may obtain consumer information informally by compiling the information fans provide when registering for a sport team raffle or by having conversations with spectators during sport events. Marketing information

ACTION

Go to the WSG and complete the Learning in Action activity, which tests how well you recall the 10 steps of creating a sport marketing plan.

Social Media and Sport Marketing

A pervasive influence on sport marketing success is technology (notably the Internet, social media platforms, tablets, and smartphones). The Internet has rapidly grown as a medium for consuming sport and has become one of the most important marketing tools for sport marketers (Hur, Ko, & Valacich, 2007). Sport teams' websites are an important component of their marketing mix (Seo & Green, 2008). This has prompted sport marketers to increase their understanding of online sport consumption motives and behaviors. As Blakely (2012) noted, social media is rapidly changing sport marketing. She reported that 35% of 18- to 35-year-olds regularly use social media to comment on, tweet/retweet, share, or link to online sport content; 45% of 18- to 35-year-olds follow sport teams or athletes on social media; and 53% of devoted sport fans are tablet and smartphone multitaskers.

Conway (2013) defined this segment of consumers as Generation HD. The HD stands for "heads down" and references the frequency with which this generation of consumers has their heads down and eyes focused on their smartphones and other multimedia devices. These consumers are also keeping their eyes down during various phases of the sport consumption and game experience (i.e., during actual competition to communicate with their social networks, to check sport scores of other teams and leagues, to see sponsored replays, while standing in line to purchase merchandise or concessions). Their mobile devices have been referred to as the second screen, even though it has become their first screen for consuming sports. Their behaviors have prompted some sport teams to create social media "Mission Control" centers to monitor messages, interact and engage with fans, and repost fan content.

The consumers' affinity for the second screen experience requires advanced and innovative technological skills of marketers seeking to reach these consumers and hold their attention. Generation HD also requires marketers to be more socially conscious. Conway (2013) portrayed this segment as a group of consumers who are raised with a "wider world view, social consciousness and values for sustainability, diversity and equality, which are important to them. A brand's engagement in topics such as the environment, social justice, or LGBT, for example is meaningful to Generation HD" (p. 25). Conway concluded that "marketers must listen, learn and understand how to connect and communicate to and with the Generation HD market segment. The long-term success of their sports property, product or brand may depend on it" (p. 25). Sport marketers must embrace the manner in which social media may influence each element of the marketing plan.

Table 12.1   **Marketing Research**

Modern or traditional approaches to marketing research	Postmodern approaches to marketing research
Quantitative methods (experiments, surveys)	Qualitative methods (ethnographies, focus groups, interviews)
Economical and psychological constructs	Sociological or anthropological constructs
Focus on buying	Focus on consuming
Emphasis on cognition	Emphasis on emotions
American	Multicultural

Adapted, by permission, from R.W. Belk, 1995, Studies in the new consumer behaviour. In *Acknowledging consumption*, edited by D. Miller (London: Routledge.), 58-96.

may also be obtained from Internal sources (e.g., sales records and attendance figures), or external sources (e.g., census data, information from the local chamber of commerce, or data from a league or conference office).

Belk (1995) offered a contrast in the modern and postmodern approaches used to obtain data for **marketing research**. The approaches can be seen in table 12.1. All of these approaches (be they rooted in the modern or postmodern domain) can offer valuable and insightful marketing information. Perhaps the best technique would be to include a combination of these methods when conducting marketing research. Regardless of the approach utilized, it is important to be mindful that the success of marketing plans is related to the quality of the information that informs it. Sport marketers must therefore embrace marketing research and must be very resourceful in developing a marketing plan. Additionally, sport marketers must develop databases, systems, and procedures for readily storing and retrieving marketing information.

marketing research— The systematic process of obtaining, analyzing, and interpreting data or information to evaluate and improve marketing practices.

Critical Thinking in Sport Marketing

Successful sport marketers engage in critical thinking as they consider the implications of their marketing practices. One area where critical thinking is required is in reference to the trend in sport marketing whereby nuances of the hip-hop culture are infused into the marketing plan. The term *hip-hop* is grounded in and reflects the burgeoning African American youth-oriented culture that originated in the Bronx, New York, during the 1970s (McLeod, 1999). Hip-hop symbolizes the voice of many urban Black youth and is reflected in the culture of their music, clothes, language, and overall way of life (Midol, 1998). The hip-hop genre has spawned a cultural revolution, and this trendsetting market has exerted a formidable influence on mainstream consumption patterns worldwide. Many companies and industries have made concerted efforts to capitalize on the popularity of hip-hop, and the sport industry is no exception. The overall appeal of the hip-hop culture has not been lost on sport marketers. Hip-hop artists frequently provide the pregame, postgame, and halftime entertainment of sport events. They are often featured in sport promotions and advertisements and used as sport product endorsers. The challenge of infusing cultural nuances of hip-hop into marketing practices is to be sensitive to its authenticity and to exercise the social responsibility needed to reach urban consumers and the markets of consumers that they influence (McLeod, 1999). Sport marketers must obtain and demonstrate a sincere responsiveness and respect for the cultural essence of hip-hop. The NBA has made concerted efforts to capitalize on the popularity and appeal of hip-hop to improve the league's overall market share. Some argue that the NBA's image and reputation is jeopardized because hip-hop often glamorizes violence, sexism, and consumerism, and it often depicts Black urban life in a negative manner.

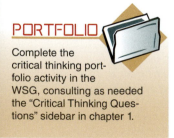

PORTFOLIO

Complete the critical thinking portfolio activity in the WSG, consulting as needed the "Critical Thinking Questions" sidebar in chapter 1.

Ethics in Sport Marketing

You may recall from the definition of sport marketing provided at the beginning of this chapter that the overarching purpose of marketing is to facilitate a socially responsible exchange relationship between a sport organization and its consumers. This means that sport marketing practices must be ethical and socially responsible. Although this seems like a reasonable thing for sport marketers to customarily do, it is not always an easy thing to do. Moreover, there may be some debate as to what is the right thing to do. Nonetheless, sport marketers are often pressured to increase their product sales to generate increased revenues for their organizations. This pressure poses a challenge. Because sport marketers are involved in persuading consumers to buy, they run the risk of exaggerating or misrepresenting their products and misleading their consumers in an effort to sell their products. Today, and in the future, sport marketers should recognize this risk and monitor their marketing strategies to ensure that they communicate honesty in images and integrity in messages about their products and to their consumers.

As discussed previously, the emergence of technology has had a dramatic effect on sport marketing practices and on consumers' wants and needs. Technology affects every phase of the marketing process (e.g., the product features, the channels of media and ticket distribution, sponsorship leverage). Technology bells and whistles have had a pervasive influence on the entertainment appeal of sport. In the future, sport marketers will have to decide how best to balance their use of technology to make the sport product and experience more entertaining for consumers without negatively affecting the true nature of sport. Overemphasizing the entertainment aspects that surround sport runs the risk of undermining sport or, worse, transforming it into what Hall (2002) called sportainment. According to Hall, sportainment is a marketplace reaction to consumers' increasing demand for greater human excellence and the desire to feel a sense of escape from ordinary life. Sportainment represents combining sport and entertainment in ways that will fulfill these consumer expectations. Although technology has allowed a number of improvements in the overall appeal of sport, sport marketers will need to guard against the temptation to overuse technology (e.g., the overuse of pop-ups and scrolls of statistical information can be distracting and detract from the game and can inadvertently increase the number of head-down moments) and therefore compromise the spontaneity and the dynamics of the sport experience. To sport purists, the uncontrolled filtration of technology into sport might jeopardize the integrity of sport and undermine its inherent value.

Increased consumer diversity is another factor that will influence sport marketing. The changing demographic and psychographic characteristics of sport consumers will increase the overall diversity that sport marketers must respond to as they seek to develop successful marketing plans. The trend toward increased diversity in the national and global markets will pose both a special challenge and a unique opportunity for sport marketers in the second decade of the 21st century. The increased diversity in the environments in which sport operates will require sport marketers to be equipped with not only the marketing fundamentals but also the skills to adapt them to multicultural sport consumers. Sport events play a critical role in the culture of most consumers, and many sport events have ethnocultural symbols, rituals, and emblems that may be more salient to some ethnic groups than others (Pons, Larouche, Nyeck, & Perreault, 2001).

Research (Kim & Cheong, 2011) has revealed that the match between the ethnicity of an athlete endorser and the audience moderates the effectiveness of sport advertisements. Nonetheless, there are still far too many incidents of ethnic and racial insensitivity in sport marketing, notably as conveyed in the promotional mix of advertising (Eagleman, 2011). Popular sport media have frequently employed offensive and demeaning narratives and images depicting Black, Hispanic, and Asian athletes. Consequently, racism pervades sport media. Additionally, while the racial and ethnic composition of sport participants and athletes is increasing, the racial and ethnic composition of their respective fan bases is not, as sport marketers have been reticent to really use race and ethnicity as a base for market segmentation. As the consumer base for sport continues to expand, sport marketers will have to develop appropriate and acceptable intercultural communications, packaging features, positioning strategies, and distribution channels to reach culturally diverse consumers in domestic and international environments (Armstrong, 2008). These associated strategies and tactics will enable sport marketers to communicate with people in these demographics and involve them in the sport consumption experience in an ethically and socially responsible manner.

As a matter of ethics, sport marketers should simply and consistently seek to (1) do the right thing (for the organization, consumers, and society), and (2) do things right (i.e., in a manner that is respectful, ethical, and socially responsible).

To help you think about the connection between ethics and sport marketing, consider the following hypothetical example. As the director of marketing for a minor league baseball team located in a city with a 15% Hispanic–Latino population base, you decide to plan three games during the season that focus on the Hispanic–Latino culture. Furthermore, you provide special pricing and promotions benefits to Hispanic–Latino fans who attend the games. Following the first Hispanic–Latino promotional game, the organization is confronted with negative media reaction to the event. Comments on radio and TV sports talk programs and in newspaper articles criticized the perceived special treatment offered to a particular ethnic group. The general manager schedules a meeting with you to discuss the situation and get your recommendations about whether to proceed with the next two Hispanic–Latino cultural game days.

PORTFOLIO

Complete the ethical issues portfolio activity in the WSG, consulting as needed the "Guidelines for Making Ethical Decisions" sidebar in chapter 1.

Summary

As this chapter elucidates, marketing is a complex and dynamic business process. Thus, the need is clear for a systematic and methodological approach to marketing, as seen in the 10-step process that can be used to develop a sport marketing plan. Although the core of the marketing process is the marketing mix, traditionally known as the four Ps, a more comprehensive approach to marketing includes factors such as organizational, environmental, and consumer-related considerations. It must be noted that marketing success is enhanced exponentially when each of the 10 steps outlined in this chapter are coordinated and integrated to complement each other. As a supplement to the 10 Ps, four additional factors contribute to long term-marketing success: (1) the recognition of the prominent role of technology and social media, (2) the need for marketers to embrace marketing research and to become connoisseurs of information, (3) marketing sport in ethically and socially responsible ways, and (4) critical thinking.

The challenge for sport marketers is to market the experiences and manage the expectations of an emotionally laden, inconsistent, unscripted, unpredictable, and uncontrollable momentary social product that will be desired and experienced differently from person to person and place to place. Sport marketers may embrace the task of marketing from a reactive or proactive perspective. As Covey (1989) noted, "Reactive people are driven by feelings, by circumstances, by conditions, and by their environment. Proactive people are driven by values—carefully thought about, selected, and internalized values" (p. 72). Effective sport marketers must exhibit characteristics of both orientations. Remember, marketing sport is both an art and a science. Having a passion for the art of marketing and a mastery of the science of marketing planning principles is a winning combination for creating a game plan for sport marketing success.

Review Questions

1. What is sport marketing, what is its role in the sport industry, and how do the unique characteristics of sport influence the sport marketing process?

2. Discuss the various elements and principles of developing a sport marketing plan. For instance, what is a mission statement and how does it influence the develop-

ment of sport marketing plans? What are the dimensions of a sport product? In what ways do the unique elements of sport influence sport marketing? What are the phases in the sport product life cycle, and what should the marketing focus be at each phase?

3. Identify the elements of a SWOT and discuss how they may inform marketing plans.

4. How do promotional activities help to position or establish an image of a sport product in the minds of consumers?

5. What are the methods used to segment a market in order to identify viable target audiences for a sport product?

6. What are some things to consider when pricing sport?

7. What elements comprise the promotions mix in sport marketing? Provide examples of each.

8. What factors should be considered when placing a sport product?

9. Regarding a sport marketing plan, what sources are used to obtain feedback about the plan's effectiveness? What role does research play in the development of the plan?

10. What challenges, critical thinking issues, technological influences, and ethical dilemmas must sport marketers be prepared to address? Name two of each.

References

Armstrong, K.L. (2002). An examination of the social psychology of Blacks' consumption of sport. *Journal of Sport Management, 16*, 267–288.

Armstrong, K.L. (2008). Consumers of color and the "culture" of sport attendance: Exploratory insights. *Sport Marketing Quarterly, 17*, 218–231.

Barker, J. (2003). *The marketing book* (5th ed.). Burlington, MA: Butterworth-Heinemann.

Belk, R.W. (1995). Studies in the new consumer behavior. In D. Miller (Ed.), *Acknowledging consumption* (pp. 58–96). London, UK: Routledge.

Blakely, J. (2012, December 6). How social media is changing sports marketing. *Postano*. Retrieved from www.postano.com/blog/how-social-media-is-changing-sports-marketing

Brooks, C.M. (1994). *Sports marketing: Competitive business strategies for sports*. Englewood Cliffs, NJ: Prentice Hall.

Conway, M. (2013, March 4). How sports marketers can hold attention of 'Generation HD'. *Street & Smith's SportsBusiness Journal*, p. 25.

Covey, S.R. (1989). *The seven habits of highly effective people*. New York, NY: Simon and Schuster.

Eagleman, A.M. (2011). Stereotypes of race and nationality: A qualitative analyses of sport magazine coverage of MLB players. *Journal of Sport Management, 25*, 156–168.

Fullerton, S., & Merz, G.R. (2008). The four domains of sports marketing: A conceptual framework. *Sport Marketing Quarterly, 17*, 90–108.

Grunig, J.E., & White, R. (1992). Communication, public relations and effective organizations. In J.E. Grunig (Ed.), *Excellence in public relations and communications management* (pp. 1–30). Hillsdale, NJ: Erlbaum.

Hall, M. (2002, August 19–25). Taking the sport out of sports. *Street & Smith's SportsBusiness Journal*, p. 23.

Hur, Y., Ko, Y.J., & Valacich, J. (2007). Motivation and concerns for online sport consumption. *Journal of Sport Management, 21*, 521–539.

Kim, K., & Cheong, Y. (2011). The effects of athlete-endorsed advertising: The moderating role of athlete-audience ethnicity match. *Journal of Sport Management, 25*, 143–155.

Levitt, T. (1960, July-August). Marketing myopia. *Harvard Business Review*, 45–60.

Lombardo, J. (2011, May 30). New president aims to widen WNBA's fan base. *Street & Smith's SportsBusiness Journal*, p. 10.

MacFadyen, L., Stead, M., & Hastings, G. (2003). Social marketing. In J. Barker (Ed.), *The marketing book* (5th ed., pp. 694–725). Burlington, MA: Butterworth-Heinemann.

McLeod, K. (1999). Authenticity within hip-hop and other cultures threatened with assimilation. *Journal of Communications, 49*(4), 134–150. Midol, N. (1998). Rap and dialectical relations. Culture, subculture, power, and counter-powered. In R. Genevieve (Ed.), *Sport and postmodern times* (pp. 333–343). Albany, NY: State University of New York Press.

Mullin, B.J., Hardy, S., & Sutton, W.A. (2014). *Sport marketing* (4th ed.). Champaign, IL: Human Kinetics.

O'Malley, L., & Tynan, C. (2003). Relationship marketing. In J. Barker (Ed.), *The marketing book* (5th ed., pp. 32–52). Burlington, MA: Butterworth-Heinemann.

Pitts, B.G., Fielding, L.W., & Miller, L.K. (1994). Industry segmentation theory and the sport industry: Developing a sport industry segmentation model. *Sport Marketing Quarterly, 3*(1), 15–24.

Pitts, B.G., & Stotlar, D.K. (2007). *Fundamentals of sport marketing* (3rd ed.). Morgantown, WV: Fitness Information Technology.

Pons, F., Larouche, M., Nyeck, S., & Perreault, S. (2001). Role of sport events as ethnocultural emblems: Impact of acculturation and ethnic identity on consumers' orientations toward sporting events. *Sport Marketing Quarterly, 10*, 231–240.

Rothstein, M. (2012, June 19). Wolverines push marketing envelope: Brandon hire Lochmann came from Knicks to help modernize Michigan. Retrieved from http://espn.go.com/colleges/michigan/football/story/_/id/8067187/michigan-wolverines-push-marketing-envelope

Seo, W.J., & Green, B.C (2008). Development of motivational scale for sport online consumption. *Journal of Sport Management, 22*, 82–109.

Shank, M.D. (2008). *Sports marketing: A strategic perspective* (4th ed.). Upper Saddle River, NJ: Prentice Hall.

Sutton, W.A., & Wattlington, R. (1994). Communicating with women in the 1990s: The role of sport marketing. *Sport Marketing Quarterly, 3*(2), 9–14.

HISTORICAL MOMENTS

- **1894**   *Daily Racing Form* made its debut
- **1908**   Pari-mutuel betting introduced at Kentucky Derby
- **1962**   Fantasy football began among beat writers for the AFL Oakland Raiders
- **1969**   Internet established
- **1976**   Basking in reflected glory (BIRGing) concept identified by Robert Cialdini and colleagues
- **1980**   Daniel Okrent started first Rotisserie Baseball League
- **1993**   Electronic Arts launched EA Sports brand
- **1994**   DirecTV founded
- **1998**   Sportvision debuted its 1st & Ten system, a yellow computer-generated line to aid TV viewers
- **1999**   TiVo made its debut
- **2000**   Major League Baseball Advanced Media founded
- **2003**   NFL Network launched
- **2005**   YouTube founded
- **2006**   Wii Sports game launched by Nintendo
- **2009**   US$40 million video board unveiled at the new US$1.15 billion Cowboys Stadium
- **2010**   Kinect device released to accompany Xbox 360 game console
- **2012**   Uniform changes unveiled by teams such as the Miami Marlins, Baltimore Orioles, and Toronto Blue Jays
- **2014**   Cristiano Ronaldo (24.6 million followers) and FC Barcelona (11.1 million) held top athlete and team spots in terms of number of Twitter followers

13

SPORT CONSUMER BEHAVIOR

Andrea N. Eagleman \ Cara Wright \ B. Christine Green

LEARNING OBJECTIVES

> Identify key motives for sport participation, spectation, and sport product purchases.
> Define consumer perception and its application for the sport industry.
> Describe the components of consumers' attitudes toward sport.
> Differentiate between consumer involvement and identification.
> Explain ways in which groups can influence the consumption behaviors of individuals.
> Discuss the process of consumer decision making in sport.
> Identify situational factors that can influence the decision-making process.
> Explain how new media offerings and social media opportunities contribute to sport consumers' behavior.
> Apply ethical reasoning and critical thinking skills to sport consumer behavior.

Key Terms

aspirational reference group
cognitive dissonance
diversion
eustress
extrinsic rewards
intrinsic rewards
market segment
need recognition
situational influence
target market

GET A JOB

Continue on your journey in sport management by going to the web study guide (WSG) at www.HumanKinetics.com/ContemporarySportManagement. Check out the job opportunities and consider the skills and experiences that can help you succeed in sport management.

Imagine that you have developed a new sporting event. Who will participate in your event? Who might watch it? The success of your new sporting event depends on your ability to attract customers. It is imperative that you learn as much as possible about your customers—what they want, what they need, what they think, what they feel, what they know, and what they value. Most important, you want to know *why* they make the choices that they do. Studying consumer behavior enables you to do just that.

Consumer behavior is made up of the processes involved in the search, selection, purchase, and use of products, services, and experiences that fulfill consumers' needs or desires. Consumer behavior helps you understand how personal and group factors influence consumer decisions and how people make purchase decisions. A detailed understanding of current and potential consumers enables an organization to develop marketing strategies that attract and retain customers, as well as products and services that meet their needs.

This chapter's purpose is to provide an overview of consumer behavior in sport. In the first section, you will learn about individual factors that influence sport consumption. This section describes the motives for two different types of sport consumption: active (i.e., sport participation) and passive (i.e., sport spectation). Additionally, it examines consumers' perceptions and attitudes toward sport, which influence their involvement with any particular sport and the ways in which they identify with a sport, team, athlete, or sport brand. The second section examines group influences on the sport consumer, including direct and indirect reference groups and the socialization process on consumer decision making. The final section of the chapter introduces the decision-making process itself.

Understanding the Individual as a Sport Consumer

Think for a minute about buying gifts for two of your close friends. Would you buy each one the same gift? Probably not. How, then, do you choose a gift suited to each of your friends? Most likely, you will consider what you know about them. You might consider things such as where they live, what they enjoy doing in their free time, and their personal values. The more information like this that you know about your friends, the easier it is to choose the perfect gift. The same is true for sport businesses. To sell more tickets, to sell more soccer cleats, or to entice more players and teams to join a league, sport organizations need to know their customers and potential customers well. The more a sport organization knows about these groups, the better it is able to design products and services to meet the needs of those customers, to design marketing messages that attract new customers and keep existing customers coming back, and to target these messages to those most likely to be receptive to them.

Although no two individuals are the same, people often have some characteristics in common. A standard practice in marketing is to try to group, or segment, people based on common characteristics. In marketing terms, groups that share a number of characteristics are called **market segments**. Marketers then choose to focus their efforts on one or more of the identified market segments. The selected market segments are referred to as **target markets**. Products and services are designed to meet the needs of the target market.

Marketers often segment sport consumers based on their motives, perceptions, and attitudes. Consumers build these attributes from experiences, which might depend on their interests and opinions. Sport consumers are often emotionally and psychologically involved with their sports. Many athletes and fans define themselves in terms of their sport identity. The following sections describe consumer needs and motivations, perceptions, attitudes, involvement, identification, and loyalty, and then explore the ways that each can be used to understand the sport consumer.

market segment—A portion of the population that is distinctive in terms of its needs, characteristics, or behavior.

target market—Market segment or segments identified as the focus of an organization's marketing efforts.

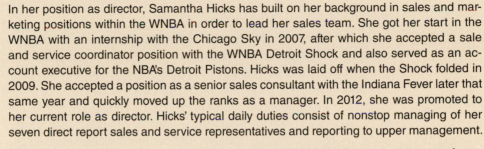

Professional Profile: Samantha Hicks

Title: director of ticket sales and service, Indiana Fever and Pacers Sports & Entertainment
Education: BS (business administration), Central Michigan University

In her position as director, Samantha Hicks has built on her background in sales and marketing positions within the WNBA in order to lead her sales team. She got her start in the WNBA with an internship with the Chicago Sky in 2007, after which she accepted a sale and service coordinator position with the WNBA Detroit Shock and also served as an account executive for the NBA's Detroit Pistons. Hicks was laid off when the Shock folded in 2009. She accepted a position as a senior sales consultant with the Indiana Fever later that same year and quickly moved up the ranks as a manager. In 2012, she was promoted to her current role as director. Hicks' typical daily duties consist of nonstop managing of her seven direct report sales and service representatives and reporting to upper management.

What have been the key moves, steps, or developments in your career, and how did you arrive at your current position?
After my internship with the Chicago Sky, I knew that I wanted to grow professionally within the WNBA, which is what motivated me to work with the organization. When I found myself without a position when the Detroit Shock folded, I had a few opportunities to work with other WNBA teams. I chose the Indiana Fever because I saw it as a place that I could advance my career with the experience I already had.

What are your current responsibilities and objectives in your job?
One of my main responsibilities is coaching the Fever Sales and Service team, which is responsible for generating revenue by selling ticket packages and group tickets, as well as renewing their season ticket base and customer service. Additionally, I oversee all ticket sales efforts and the renewal and retention plans for the Fever. I also monitor the growth of the sales consultants and provide guidance to maximize individual performance. Some of the major objectives in my job include implementing strategies to effectively grow our season ticket base, along with providing outstanding customer service.

What do you enjoy most about your current job?
Watching my sales reps accomplish goals. The highest enjoyment I will get is challenging sales reps and seeing them reach their highest potential in their current role and then advancing in their career.

What do you consider the biggest future challenge to be in your job or industry?
The biggest challenge will be hitting budget numbers following a championship season in the WNBA. Additionally, it will continue to be challenging to get a larger reach on WNBA fans in the state of Indiana.

Consumer Needs and Motivation

The fulfillment of needs is the essence of a marketing orientation (Shank, 2008). Everybody has needs. We are born with innate physiological needs—the need for food, water, air, clothing, and shelter. In order to live, these needs must be fulfilled. We also have acquired needs such as the need for esteem, affection, or power. These needs are not necessary for life, and they tend to vary from culture to culture and from person to person. They are better described as wants and desires. Motives can be thought of as the reasons that people behave the way they do. This driving force exists in response to an unfulfilled need. The key to the success of a sport organization (e.g., a minor league baseball team) is to identify and satisfy customers' unfulfilled needs better or faster than the competition (e.g., other minor league or professional teams, college teams, or other entertainment options such as concerts) does. Consequently, successful marketers define their target markets by the needs that they are trying to satisfy. Although individual needs and motives vary, researchers have identified some common participation and spectator motives. The following sections examine research involving sport participation motives followed by research related to sport spectator motives.

PARTICIPANT MOTIVATION

Green (1996) revealed that more than 100 motives for participating in sport have been identified. Fortunately, the reasons that people give to explain their participation can be grouped into three key motives: (1) achievement motivation, (2) social motivation, and (3) mastery motivation (Smith & Bar-Eli, 2007). The need to compete, to win, and to be the best are examples of achievement motivations. These needs nearly always require an element of social comparison. To attract participants motivated by achievement goals, sport marketers emphasize the competitive elements of their programs. Cyclists who are motivated by achievement, for example, would likely place importance on factors such as competitive age groups within a race and the opportunity to enter a race as a competitive team in which all members' race times or places contributed to an overall team placing. These athletes might also value **extrinsic rewards** such as medals, trophies, MVP awards, or competitive all-star events. These types of rewards provide an outward display of recognition for the athlete's achievement.

Marketing efforts directed toward participants seeking social opportunities through their sport participation should highlight social interactions among participants. Advertisers of both sport and nonsport products often use images of athletes enjoying themselves during and after competitions. Many clubs offer coeducational sport in an attempt to provide more extensive social interaction between female and male participants. For example, while some running clubs are focused on doing well in competition, many other running clubs clearly cater to social motivations. Unlike most sports, running does not require participants to train with others, and runners can compete

extrinsic rewards— Rewards given to a person by someone else.

A Swim Club in Crisis

A small suburban swim club was in trouble. Although the club enjoyed moderate success in the local summer swim league, substantial turnover of membership occurred from summer to summer. Each year, almost half the families from the previous season did not return. The club conducted a survey at the end of one of its seasons and discovered that families had many different reasons for joining the club. Some wanted their children to win ribbons, medals, and trophies (achievement motivation); some found that the club was a good way to get to know other people in the community (social motivation); and some wanted their children to improve their swimming skills (mastery motivation). The club had always assumed that its primary task was to help children become winning competitive swimmers. The club focused on achievement by helping its swimmers find a specialty event and train to win in that event. All members were required to compete at weekend swimming meets. Although the team had a picnic at the end of the season, the club did little else to foster social interaction among its members.

After the survey, the club changed its policies. Coaches implemented special coaching to help swimmers who wanted to develop swimming skills beyond their primary competitive events (mastery motivation). Members who did not want to compete were not required to enter weekend swimming meets. The club also introduced several social events for members, including pizza parties and midseason picnics (social motivation). Within two years, the club had grown from 62 families to over 300 families, and members typically stayed with the club for several years. By developing its programs to appeal to multiple motivations, the club increased its membership, improved its financial position, and became league champion.

without being part of a team. But that does not mean that people do not run for social reasons or that runners do not value social interactions. Two elements of club membership are important for socially motivated runners: (1) people can run with a group and thus do not have to run alone, and (2) socializing often continues after the run and thus is not limited to the training session itself.

The third key motivational category for participation in sport is mastery motivation. Skill development, learning, and personal challenge appeal to mastery-oriented participants. Programs that offer instruction, coaching, or mentoring often appeal to these participants. For people in this category, competition is for **intrinsic rewards** and is less about winning and more about challenging themselves. Training and instruction take place regularly in elite sport settings and in most sport programs for children and teens. But what about programs for adults? Although instruction is not the only way to appeal to mastery-motivated participants, it is certainly an underused element of adult sport programs. One example of an adult program that caters to mastery motivation is adult gymnastics, which is growing in popularity at gymnastics clubs in the United States. In these programs, adults of all ages and skill levels are coached and instructed on how to perform skills as basic as cartwheels and handstands or as advanced as back handsprings and back tucks. These programs allow adults to master gymnastics skills that they would likely never attempt otherwise, and to do so in a highly instructive and safe environment.

Now that we have identified three fundamental motives for sport participation: achievement, social, and mastery motives, think of the things that motivate you to participate in your favorite sport. It is likely that you have multiple motivations, as is the case for most sport participants. It is rare for people to take up a new sport strictly to socialize with others or just to beat the competition. Marketers of participatory sports must take into account the varying motives of current and potential participants and then communicate with these groups in a way that appeals to their achievement, social, and mastery motivations while highlighting benefits that appeal to each motivational segment.

intrinsic rewards— Rewards received by a person from the experience itself.

Spectators have many motives for watching sport, including escapism, drama, excitement, and diversion.

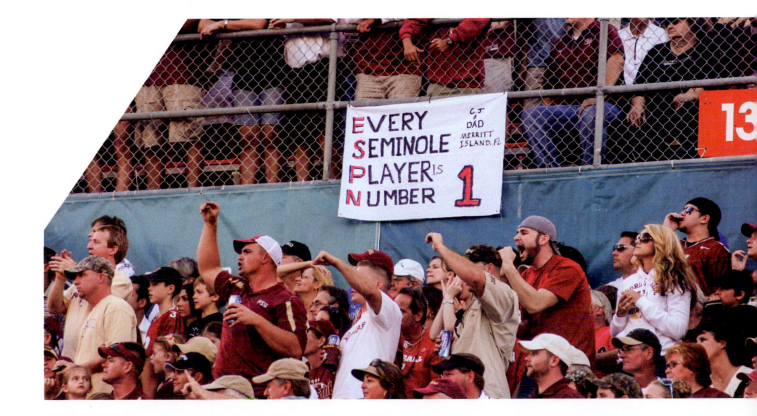

SPECTATOR MOTIVATION

The motivations that people identify for watching sport are quite different from their motivations for participating in sport. Like participation motives, spectator motives vary considerably. As we illustrate here, numerous motives have been found to capture the many reasons given for attending sporting events (Wakefield, 2014). For many, watching sport is a way to escape from everyday life, a **diversion** from stress or boredom.

> **diversion**—A distraction from a course or activity.

Others are driven by a desire for drama and excitement. When our favorite team wins an important game, most of us have felt the glow and satisfaction that accompany that victory. Basking in reflected glory (BIRGing), first labeled by Cialdini and colleagues (1976), is a key driver of attendance for fans seeking to enhance their self-esteem by associating themselves with a successful team or player (Trail, Kim, Kwon, Harrolle, Braunstein-Minkove, & Dick, 2012). Fans motivated by **eustress** seek excitement and stimulation. For example, fans motivated by eustress enjoy the uncertainty and anticipation felt when a basketball game is tied with just a few seconds left on the game clock. Economic gain is another powerful motive for a small but growing group of people. Although betting on sport is not a new phenomenon, it has become more commonplace since the advent of Internet gambling. Yet another spectator motive for many fans is the innate beauty of athletic performance. The aesthetic motive is most clearly associated with sports such as ice dancing and rhythmic gymnastics, but fans of all sports report being fascinated by the aesthetic elements of the sport. Soccer fans, for example, repeatedly mention the pure beauty of well-executed skills. Another spectator motivation is the desire to be part of something or to feel a sense of belonging. Similar to those who are motivated by the desire for affiliation, some people attend sporting events to spend time with their families. As you can see from these examples, there are several motives for attending sport events.

> **eustress**—Positive levels of arousal provided to sport spectators.

PARTICIPANT AND SPECTATOR MARKETS

Many people believe that the best place to find fans for a sport team is among players of that sport. Although some overlap is present between fans and participants of any particular sport, it varies from sport to sport and is much less common than one might think. For example, youth soccer leagues are ubiquitous in communities all across the country, and soccer is the second most played sport by working adults. Yet the average attendance for Major League Soccer (MLS) was around 18,000 fans per game in 2013 ("Major League Soccer," 2013). Given the number of soccer players in the United States, you might expect higher attendance figures for professional soccer matches. If you compare the key motives for participation with those for spectation, it is clear that different needs drive playing sport and watching sport.

Consumer Perceptions

While needs and motives are important for marketers to understand, they do not fully explain sport consumers' choices. The degree to which a consumer sees sport as meeting a particular need or motive depends on that person's experiences. Consumers must recognize the opportunity to watch or participate in a sport as a means to fulfill their needs. That recognition depends on experiences and the ways in which consumers perceive those experiences. This section considers the role of consumer perceptions.

Each of us perceives the world in our own way. Many Americans view the sport of cricket as confusing and uninteresting. The 20 million cricketers throughout the world would surely disagree with that perception, though. Similarly, some consumers consider boxing to be an exciting, physically challenging sport, whereas others may think of it as brutish and violent. Whose assessment is correct? Although perceptions often do not correspond to reality, people tend to act and react based on their perceptions rather than objective reality. Sport marketers attempt to alter consumers' views of specific products and services, which costs enormous sums of time and money. So what are the sources of our perceptions and how can sport marketers shape customers' perceptions of certain products?

Perception can be defined as a process by which a person selects, organizes, and interprets stimuli to create a meaningful picture of the world. Stimuli can include any input to any of the senses—physical inputs from the surrounding environment, such as sights, sounds, smells, tastes, and sensations, or cognitive inputs, such as expectations, motives, and learning as a result of experience.

Consider the following scenario. A group of friends attended a National Hot Rod Association (NHRA) drag race. Afterward, they discussed the race at a restaurant on their way home. James, a former competitive drag racer, dominated the conversation with talk about "reaction times," "spinning the tires," "nitro," and "dropping cylinders." He was especially impressed with Top Fuel racer Clay Millican's ability to deep stage and win on a hole shot in a head-to-head race against Tony Schumacher. No one else in the group recalled that taking place in the Millican vs. Schumacher race, including Dave, who is a college rowing coach. Dave was impressed with the precision of each driver's crew chief to tune the cars in a way that allowed them to reach speeds upwards of 300 miles (480 km) per hour. Betsy, an artist and writer with little interest in motorsports, talked incessantly about the design of the cars and the paint schemes on each one. It was almost as if the three friends had attended entirely different events. This story illustrates the idea of selective attention: choosing to pay attention to elements that are relevant to one's needs, attitudes, and experiences. These choices are often made subconsciously. People tend to be aware of stimuli that meet their needs and interests, and they filter out stimuli that are less personally relevant.

People rarely attend to each stimulus individually. Rather, they group stimuli together and perceive them as a unified whole. Sport teams have taken advantage of the grouping effect by associating their teams with particular images. For example, many teams choose their mascots to imply desired characteristics. As a result, American football teams tend to choose mascots such as Bears, Vikings, and Cowboys in the hope that fans will then associate their teams with strength, aggression, and toughness. Similarly, advertisements for a variety of products and services use sport imagery to associate their products with desired characteristics.

People then organize their selected stimuli into patterns and groupings. Perceptions ultimately depend on each person's interpretation of the stimuli—both are uniquely individual. Your experiences help form particular expectations that might provide alternatives that you would use to interpret the stimuli presented. The broader your experiences are, the more interpretations and alternatives you have to draw on.

Consumer Attitudes

The previous section explains and illustrates how experiences and attitudes can greatly influence our perceptions of various sports, teams, athletes, and other sport products and services. Marketing efforts are often directed at shaping people's perceptions of a particular product, service, or brand. Essentially, this marketing tactic attempts to form or change customers' attitudes about the product or service. But what exactly is an attitude, and how do we form our attitudes? In its simplest form, an attitude can be an expression of inner feelings that reflect like or dislike for something. Attitudes are based on a person's experiences (behavioral component), feelings (affective component), and beliefs (cognitive component) about an object (Shank, 2008). These three components work together to formulate an attitude (see figure 13.1).

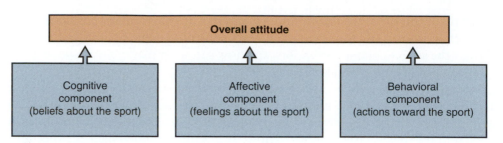

Figure 13.1 Model of attitude formation.

Consumer involvement can be characterized as a combination of people's interest in a sport product (e.g., team, athlete, sport) and the degree to which they consider the product an important part of their lives (Wakefield, 2014). Both sport spectators and sport participants often become highly involved with their favorite sports. Correspondingly, they think about, talk about, read about, and watch these sports frequently. Technological innovations in recent years have provided spectators and participants further opportunities to engage in conversation and consumption of their favorite sports through social media, online news sites and blogs, message boards, and smartphone or tablet apps. All of these innovations allow sport consumers to become more highly involved in their chosen sports. Sport consumers with higher levels of involvement tend to feel more deeply about their sports than do less involved participants and spectators. Sport marketers value involvement because high levels of involvement are associated with increased purchasing and consumer loyalty.

The more people become involved with a sport, a team, or some other sport product, the more it becomes a part of their identity. Consequently, involvement and identification are closely related. The process of identification occurs as people's role (as a participant or as a fan) becomes central to their personal sense of self—that is, their identity (Brown, Devlin, & Billings, 2013). Hence, the statements "I am a Blackhawks fan" and "I am a field hockey player" are expressions of identification with a team and with a sport, respectively. Highly identified consumers attend more games and invest more time and effort in being a fan, and are less sensitive to price (Wakefield, 2014). They tend to buy and display licensed products and to be more tolerant of performance slumps and losing seasons. Highly identified fans who display these attitudes and behaviors are desirable for sport marketers since a sport team's performance is beyond the marketers' control. These types of fans can be described as loyal rather than fair-weather fans.

Loyalty, involvement, and identification vary considerably from person to person. They are functions of individuals' motives for participating in or watching a sport, their previous experiences, and the perceptions and attitudes that they form about the sport, sport service, or product. These are largely internal, psychological processes. Sport consumers rarely make decisions or form attitudes or preferences based solely on their own experience, though. External groups exert tremendous influence on sport consumption decisions. This influence is sometimes subtle, as in the case of culture and ethnicity, and sometimes blatant, such as when your friends drag you to a local sporting event. We turn next to an examination of group influences on sport consumption decisions.

Group Influences on the Sport Consumer

This section examines external factors that influence sport buying behavior. Each of us is influenced by the people closest to us, by the groups with whom we choose to associate, and by the broader society in which we live. Take a moment to think about the intramural sports team options available at your college or university. The types of

ACTION

Go to the WSG and complete the Learning in Action activity, which has you identify how involved different fans are with a sport team.

sports offered are typically those sports valued by your national culture. Consequently, American college and university students might choose to play basketball, New Zealand students might choose to play rugby, and Malaysian students might choose to play badminton. This cultural influence can often be seen at a regional level also. For example, many colleges and universities in the East Coast region of the United States offer rowing as an intramural or varsity sport, while sports such as ice hockey are popular in Northern states. Along with national and regional influences, your membership in a group can greatly influence your choice whether or not to play intramural sports. Physical education majors would be expected to value sport participation highly, but music majors might not. If you choose to participate, your close friends might then influence your choice of sport.

Clearly, different people influence each of us, and we value the opinions of different groups. Thus, each of us has our own reference groups. These people and groups influence our values, norms, perceptions, attitudes, and behaviors by providing us with a valued point of comparison. Reference groups can be either direct or indirect. Direct reference groups require face-to-face interaction. Family and friends serve as reference groups throughout the lifespan. Think about your own sport participation. Who first encouraged you to play a sport? Parents or teachers usually introduce children to a sport. Later, peers play a more powerful role in participation choices. Similarly, you probably shared your first moments as a fan of your favorite team with friends or family members. Furthermore, friends and family usually reinforce your choices. For example, if you are a fan of golf, you might watch the Masters Golf Tournament with your family on television every April, you might attend a local tournament with friends, you might have a regular tee time at your local course, or your cousins might give you the popular golf movie *Caddyshack* for your birthday. Each of these actions subtly reinforces your attitudes and behaviors regarding golf.

Although friends and family can be powerful influences on a person's sport choices and purchases, they are not alone in their influence. Nearly everyone is part of a larger group of some kind. Some of these groups offer formal membership (e.g., sport teams, special interest clubs, service groups), but most do not (e.g., high school freshmen, college students majoring in journalism, residents of a particular neighborhood). The point is that each group shares something, and its values serve as a point of evaluation for a person's attitudes and behaviors.

Culture is perhaps the largest of the direct reference groups. Each of us is embedded in a national and ethnic culture. You could think of culture as the personality of society. It colors our values, expectations, attitudes, and opinions. It affects our view of the place of sport in society, the sports that we value, and the products and services that we seek. Its effects are subtle but powerful. Culture profoundly influences our view of what is normal, or at least of what is expected, and affects the sports we choose as well as the way we choose to become involved with sport. Even with the same sport (e.g., baseball), the culture is different depending on where the game is played. For instance, in this chapter's international sidebar, you can read more about consumer behavior affiliated with Japanese baseball.

Social class can sometimes place invisible boundaries on our choices by delineating appropriate and inappropriate behavior. We tend to associate certain sports with members of a particular social class. It often serves as a global referent—that is, it affects a person's choices and behaviors across a variety of settings—when choosing to participate (or not participate) in a particular sport. But not all reference groups have global influence.

Indirect reference groups do not require direct contact, but they can be highly influential. They might consist of people such as athletes, coaches, musicians, actors, or politicians; alternatively, they might be groups or subcultures. In either case, the influence

Japanese Baseball and Consumer Behavior

By Yosuke Tsuji, Japan
University of the Ryukyus, Nishihara

Baseball, or *yakyū*, has become the national pastime in Japan. Introduced in the late 19th century by several American professors, the sport caught the interest of many elite Japanese college students. The popularity of the sport surged with several Japanese victories over the Yokohama Athletic Club, which consisted mainly of Americans. These games attracted over 10,000 Japanese spectators, who brimmed with nationalistic pride with each victory. By the early twentieth century, the game had become so competitive that fights erupted in the stands, which led to the media denouncing the sport as countereducational. Despite these setbacks, baseball spread to schools, and eventually a professional league was formed in 1936.

Japanese baseball fans enjoy the unique atmosphere inside the stadium as they cheer for their favorite team.

Currently, over seven million people play baseball in Japan. In the early days of Japanese baseball, players approached the game from a martial arts perspective rather than as a form of entertainment. Sport in Japan was mainly practiced to train the body and the mind. Although this was unlikely to have been the intention of the American professors, it was easy for the students to link concepts such as courage, honor, team harmony,

aspirational reference group—A group to which an individual wishes to belong.

of the individual or group is not the result of direct, face-to-face contact. Instead, the influence derives from **aspirational reference groups**—groups in which a person is not currently a member but aspires to be one. Gatorade's legendary advertising campaign featuring Michael Jordan ("Be Like Mike") is perhaps the most unabashed use of an aspirational reference group to sell a product, but numerous, albeit subtler, examples of advertisements use athletes as aspirational referents. For example, companies such as Canon, Porsche, Tag Heuer, and Nike all use images of Russian tennis player Maria Sharapova in their ads to help sell their products to tennis fans and sports fans who admire Sharapova or who aspire to be like her.

Subcultures operate in much the same way as aspirational reference groups do. Let's assume for the moment that you want to be a surfer. Even before you learn to surf, chances are that you will be influenced by what you know about surfers and the surfing subculture. You might enjoy surfing movies such as *The Endless Summer, Dear Suburbia,* self-discipline, and sacrifice to the sport. To some extent, this mental approach has been passed on to current players.

For spectators, the *yakyū* experience is unique. First, there are a variety of food and beverage options. There are, of course, American foods, such as hot dogs and hamburgers, but there are also many Japanese foods, such as *yakitori* (chicken skewers) and *gyūdon* (beef bowls). Another unique aspect of Japanese stadiums is the way beer is sold—vendors carry beer kegs on their backs!

Seating options and prices are similar to American baseball stadiums. However, the manner in which the fans cheer on their favorite team or players differs. The cheers at baseball games are orchestrated by registered cheerleading groups, who lead the cheers, play music (trumpets and drums), and wave flags. Typical cheerleaders wear a *happi*, or jacket, in their team's colors and wave a flag when a player gets a hit or when the team scores. Cheerleaders can be found in the outfield bleacher seats, where other rowdy fans join them. A typical inning consists of cheerleaders playing music and leading songs and fans singing chants and songs. Usually there is one song for each everyday player (lyrics can be found on teams' homepages). While singing songs, fans also bang plastic megaphones to create a racket. Then, during the seventh inning stretch, fans sing the home team's song and collectively release balloons into the air. This unified cheering style gives the fans a sense of belonging and adds entertainment value to the game-day experience.

From the outside looking in, these unique experiences provide a glimpse into the role of Japanese culture in Japanese baseball and Japanese sport consumer behavior.

International Learning Activity #1

Visit the Major League Baseball website (www.MLB.com) as well as the International Baseball Federation website (www.Ibaf.org/en) to investigate the current efforts by MLB and IBAF to spread the sport in other countries. Additionally, from these websites, visit various countries' baseball league websites. What are some unique programs that these leagues organize?

International Learning Activity #2

Locate a sports bar in your community that caters to the international sports crowd. Attend a televised game there. Observe and compare the behaviors of the fans to those at American sports settings.

International Learning Activity #3

Conduct several quick interviews with fans at various sports games. What are their reasons for attendance? Do they come for social interaction? Or do they come for pure entertainment value? Compare their motives across different sports. What unique differences do you see?

or *Chasing Mavericks*. You might buy *Surfing* magazine, watch surfing events, talk to people who surf, and follow professional surfers or surfing organizations on social media sites. Your knowledge of the surfing subculture, however superficial, might influence the style and brand of clothing that you choose to wear, the music that you listen to, or even the way that you style your hair. Marketers are more than willing to sell you products that help you to look and feel as though you belong to the group.

As a marketer, you can take advantage of the ability of reference groups to change consumers' perceptions, attitudes, and purchase behaviors. But for the reference group to wield its influence, according to de Mooij (2004), it must be able to (1) make people aware of a product, (2) provide a chance for them to compare themselves with the group, (3) influence them to adopt attitudes and behaviors consistent with the group, and (4) support their decision to use the same product or service as the group does.

Your perceptions and experiences affect your choice of reference groups. Your choice of reference groups can affect your preferences for particular sports and the sport choices that you make. In other words, the reference groups that you choose are based, in part, on what you have learned, and the reference group might affect what you learn subsequently. This process is an effect of consumer socialization.

Consumer Socialization

We have seen that family, friends, teachers, and other reference groups can affect your decisions about participating in sport and about watching sport. Yet the effect of people who are significant in your life reaches even further. Through them you learn not merely *what* you prefer, but also *how* to consume what you prefer. Let's assume that you want to watch a baseball game. You have several choices. You could watch a game played by a local Little League team. You could watch a minor league game. You could watch an MLB game. If you choose an MLB game, you could attend the game or watch it on television. If you attend the game, you could sit in the bleachers, behind home plate, or behind a dugout. The choices that you make will be influenced, in part, by what you have learned about the ways to watch baseball. If when you were first learning to enjoy watching baseball, your family or friends typically preferred to watch on television, you will be more likely to choose to watch on television. On the other hand, if going to the ball game was something that your family or friends treated as a valuable choice, then you are likely to prefer going to the game instead of watching it on television.

As we grow and mature, we learn how to consume the sport that we prefer. Both direct and indirect reference groups influence the ways in which we consume sport. For example, Erin has season tickets to watch the Indiana University football team. When she was young, her parents took her to several university football games at the University of Illinois, which was near her hometown. Three things were always part of the college football experience for Erin. First, her parents always tailgated with friends before the games, where they would bring a charcoal grill and cook burgers and hot dogs. Second, they always took a football to the tailgate to toss around before the game started. Finally, they always sat next to the 50-yard line, which they considered to be the best seat in the stadium. Now that Erin is an adult, she has carried on these rituals. Unintentionally, she has also taught her young nephew, whom she takes with her to every game, that college football games require a person to grill food and toss a football at a tailgate party before the game, and that no seat in the stadium is acceptable unless it is along the 50-yard line. This is an example of socialization through modeling. Just as Erin learned from her parents as a child, her nephew now watched her behavior and has begun to copy it. Prompting and reinforcement can further assist in the socialization process. For example, Erin might prompt her nephew to bring his football or ask if he would like to make hamburgers or hot dogs before today's game. Similarly, he might reinforce her decision to sit along the 50-yard line by telling her that no other seats in the stadium are worth buying.

Socialization is a process that often goes unnoticed. Think of your own sport experiences. How did you develop your fan behaviors? Do you remember someone telling you when to clap or how to show your support for a great play, or teaching you the words to your favorite team's fight song? Chances are that your earlier experiences and reinforcement (or lack of reinforcement) by important reference groups shaped your current behavior.

Each of these processes—modeling, prompting, and reinforcing—also occur through indirect reference groups. Spectators seen on television broadcasts and in movies often influence our attitudes and consumption behaviors. In our current global era, people may not even need to attend live events to be aware of the appropriate behaviors or rituals of specific sports. As you learned in chapter 12, the mass media (e.g., sport programming on terrestrial, cable, and satellite television) and new media (e.g., streaming videos on sport websites) provide extended and comprehensive broadcasts of global sports and their environments. Advertisements, broadcasts, websites, and other types of indirect reference groups can prompt behaviors or reinforce our perceptions of appropriate ways to enjoy a game or a sport. Over time, we are socialized into a way of consuming sport that is shaped by our reference groups, both direct and indirect. Sport marketers are also interested in ways to socialize customers into particular consumption patterns.

Situational Influences on the Sport Consumer

The previous sections identify key internal factors and external group influences on sport consumers. In practice, isolating influences of either internal or external forces is difficult. Rarely does a single force influence sport consumption decisions. Rather, a person's relationship to a reference group or membership in a particular subculture forms and interprets internal attitudes, perceptions, and experiences. Further, different contexts and situations result in different decisions. A situation is a set of factors outside individual consumers and removed from the product that they buy or its advertisement. To develop marketing strategies that enhance the purchase of their products, marketers need to know how purchase situations influence consumers.

We can identify five categories of **situational influence**. First, physical surroundings include geographic location, decor, sound, smells, lighting, weather, and crowding. For example, weather would obviously influence the decision to swim laps at an outdoor pool. Retail organizations pay particular attention to the physical characteristics of their stores. For example, one Niketown store has a hardwood basketball court in its basketball shoe section and plays recordings of the unique sound of shoes squeaking during a basketball game. Second, social surroundings refer to the effects of the physical presence of others. For example, if you want to spend your Saturday on a long bike ride with friends, but the majority of your friends in the group prefer to go canoeing, you will probably comply with the group and find yourself sitting in a canoe on a lake. Third, task requirements speak to the context of the purchase (that is, the intent or requirement of the purchase). Consider the purchase of a pair of running shorts. If you are buying them for yourself, you might be more concerned with performance functions than with price. For example, you might want shorts that have a zippered pocket where you can store small items like your key or a packet of energy gel. You might also prefer shorts that have a pocket for your MP3 player if you listen to music while running. If you are buying the shorts as a gift, though, you might be more concerned with price and attractiveness than with performance. Fourth, time pressures, the time of day, and the season of the year are all examples of potential temporal influences on sport consumption. The Chicago Cubs serve as an example of this influence, since the majority of their games take place during the day when many people are at work. Therefore, if you work at a job that requires you to be in the office from 9 a.m. to 5 p.m., you likely won't attend as many Cubs games as you would if they played the majority of their home games in the evenings. Fifth, purchasing can be affected by antecedent states such as anxiety, excitement, or even hunger, and by momentary conditions such as cash on hand, fatigue, or illness. If you have ever attended a sporting event and wondered, on your return home, why you bought that gigantic foam finger, you have probably experienced the influence of excitement on the purchase decision process. Let's look more closely at the decision process.

situational influence—The influence arising from factors that are particular to a specific time and place and are independent of individual customers' characteristics.

Consumer Decision Making in Sport

You make hundreds of decisions each day, many of them related to sport. You decide whether to participate in sport, which sports you will try, whether you will watch sport, which sport you will watch, which team or player you will cheer for, whether you will buy season tickets, and whether you will wear your team jersey. The list of decisions seems endless. Some decisions are made more easily, while others require greater thought. In any case, the decision-making process has a common progression. It begins with the recognition of a need or problem that spurs you to gather information about potential solutions. You then evaluate alternatives, and the "best" alternative leads to purchase. The purchase experience is followed by a period of postpurchase evaluation that will influence your future purchase decisions (see figure 13.2). Notice that decision making does not happen in a void. Rather, each of the factors already discussed influences the process.

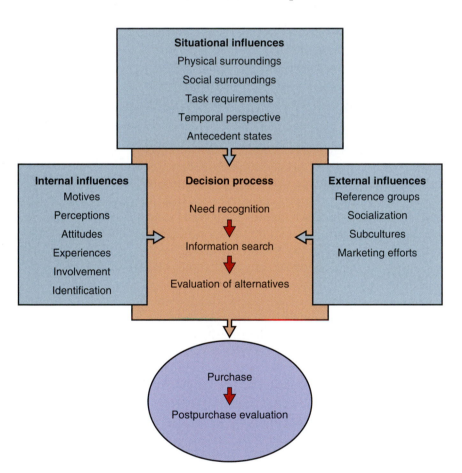

Figure 13.2 Model of the decision process.

Each of us arrives at a decision in a slightly different way. We begin with motives, perceptions, attitudes, and experiences that are uniquely our own. We are influenced by reference groups and subcultures that are important to us, and we have been socialized in different ways. In fact, we are rarely consistent in the way that we arrive at purchase decisions. We perceive each situation differently. Consumption decisions are not always rational, as can be seen with impulse purchases. As a result, we interpret and react to marketing efforts in varied ways. Despite these differences, the steps in the decision process are remarkably consistent from consumer to consumer.

Need recognition is the first step in the decision process. This stage is likely to occur when you confront a problem or recognize a difference between an actual state and a desired state. This stimulus can be as straightforward as

need recognition—Perception of a difference between a desired state and the actual situation; the first stage of the decision-making process.

the need to replace a pair of worn-out volleyball knee pads or as complex as a desire to be fit. In the first case, the need is obvious: The equipment is no longer effective, so you must replace it. In the second case, the need is less straightforward. The desired state is to be fit. In this case, the need emerges from the gap between your current and desired fitness levels.

After identifying the need, the consumer seeks information that helps resolve the problem or fulfill the need. Experience or brand loyalty might provide the consumer with enough information to determine alternatives. For example, Maya's satisfaction with her old road racing flats might be all the information that she needs to decide to buy the newer model of the same shoes. If she is loyal to a particular brand, she might limit her search by collecting information only about products produced by that company. She might ask the opinion of respected members of her reference group or be influenced by the acceptability of a brand or style within her running subculture. She might search out information on the Internet, in magazines, in catalogs, or at the local running store. In any case, she will collect enough information to determine her purchase options.

After Maya has determined her purchase options, she begins the evaluation process. When evaluating purchase options, consumers tend to use two types of information: (1) a list of the potential products, and (2) the features and characteristics that they will use to evaluate those products (de Mooij, 2004). Price or convenience might be two features important to Maya. People assess features and characteristics differently based on their values, attitudes, motives, and expectations. Notice that people's reference groups also influence their beliefs about which features and characteristics are important. Sport marketers need to understand which features are important to their target markets. Using the lightest materials possible for road racing shoes is useless if consumers evaluate these shoes based on their attractiveness and price rather than their weight. Consumers make their purchase decisions based on personal evaluations of particular products and their attributes.

You might think that the process ends with the purchase, but another step is yet to occur—the postpurchase evaluation (Shank, 2008). As consumers use a product, they evaluate it with respect to their expectations. Let's return to the example of Maya and the racing flats. Maya will have developed expectations about the performance of her new shoes. She might expect that they will look good, break in easily, and help her to run a few seconds faster in her next race. After wearing the shoes in her next race, she will evaluate their actual performance. If the shoes perform as well as or better than expected, Maya will be satisfied with her purchase. But if the shoes are uncomfortable or cause blisters to form on her feet, then she might be dissatisfied with her purchase. From a marketing standpoint, Maya's satisfaction is important for two reasons. One, her satisfaction will affect her future purchases of the product, and two, it will affect word-of-mouth communication about the product and the brand. She will tell others about her satisfaction or disappointment. With the increasing popularity of new and social media, this word-of-mouth communication about products and services is more important to sport organizations than it has ever been (Lim, Chung, & Pedersen, 2012). Comments posted on sites such as Facebook or Twitter have the ability to reach hundreds, if not thousands, of other consumers.

An important part of the postpurchase evaluation is consumers' attempts to reassure themselves that they made the right decision. Feelings of doubt about a decision are called **cognitive dissonance**. Consumers attempt to reduce postpurchase cognitive dissonance in several ways. They might rationalize their decision as being a wise choice (e.g., "This is definitely the best softball glove because it fits so well."). They might search for marketing materials that confirm their decision and avoid advertisements for competing products. They might try to persuade others to make the same purchase, or they could seek others who are satisfied with their purchase of the same product (e.g., talking with other players after practice). As previously mentioned, they might also take to social media websites to seek confirmation for their decision, or seek out positive online reviews of the product or service they purchased. Each of these strategies reinforces their satisfaction with the purchase. Reducing consumers' cognitive dissonance in the postpurchase period is a strategy that can increase repeat purchases.

cognitive dissonance—
Feelings of anxiety or doubt that can occur after an important decision has been made.

Sport Consumer Behavior Challenges and Issues

Analyzing and understanding sport consumer behavior is a complex endeavor. The challenges facing sport marketers are equally complex. Four issues are becoming increasingly important to understanding and marketing to sport consumers:

1. The meaning and emotion of sport consumption
2. The globalization of sport
3. Virtual consumption
4. Compulsive consumption

We know much about the ways that people think about sport purchases. Yet consumers consistently report emotional attachments to sport products, teams, events, and other sport services. To understand sport consumers, we need to know how they create these emotional attachments, what influences those attachments, and how the attachments vary as a function of culture or subcultural values. The globalization of sport is creating a related challenge for sport marketers. On one hand, consumers worldwide are being presented with the same sports, broadcasts, products, and advertisements. On the surface, sport is much the same across the globe. On the other hand, we know that culture influences the meaning and value inherent in sport consumption. In this respect, the world is made up of a multitude of consumer groups. We need to understand where similarities and differences exist and work to tailor our sport products and services for optimal sales.

The other two challenges to understanding and reaching sport consumers are emerging forms of sport consumption—virtual and compulsive. The Internet is a multifunctional space for sport consumption. Participants can purchase hard-to-find equipment; fans can buy tickets and licensed products for teams anywhere in the world. But actual purchases are only the tip of the iceberg. Fans can find a community of other fans online (e.g., by joining sport message boards, by posting thoughts on social media sites such as Facebook or Twitter). They can participate in online fantasy leagues. They can post photographs or short videos from sporting events on smartphone apps like Instagram. They can share their own thoughts and feelings about different sports or events on blogs and in the comment sections of news websites. Participants can receive or share information about their sport, team, players, and coaches instantly. The list is endless. Wireless technology has made it even easier for fans to stay involved with their teams. Scores and other statistics are routinely delivered to mobile phones. Digital photos and video can be sent by mobile phone. Recently, a college football coach complained that fans were able to see footage of a player getting hurt in practice before he could inform the player's parents. With sport content almost limitless, the challenge for sport organizations is to find ways to use new consumption technologies to reach their fans or participants more effectively.

As you can see from the football coach's complaint, sport consumption is not all positive. As sport consumption opportunities become ubiquitous, compulsive consumption is becoming more prevalent. Compulsive consumption refers to the repetitive consumption of sport such that it is addictive. Sports betting can be one of the most damaging forms of compulsive sport consumption, but there are others (e.g., sport video games). Fantasy leagues can become a compulsion as well; some participants spend astonishing amounts of time and money managing their teams. Compulsive consumption is not limited to fan behavior. Participants might spend well beyond their means traveling to pursue their sport participation. More likely, participants dedicate outrageous amounts of time to their sports and neglect other duties or important aspects of their lives. Compulsive consumption is a delicate issue for sport marketers, since effective marketing efforts taking advantage of in-depth knowledge of consumers' psychology

WEB

Go to the WSG and complete the web search activity, which challenges you to discover virtual sport consumption opportunities.

Social Media and Sport Consumer Behavior

The Magnificent Seven Race Series is a series of 35 annual races in south-central Indiana ranging in distance from 5K to the half marathon. After experiencing stagnant participation numbers in 2008 and 2009, series organizers began using social media on a more consistent basis to promote the series and increase its participation numbers at the races. The series began utilizing its Facebook and Twitter accounts as well as its website, which were updated sporadically in the past. They began engaging consumers on Facebook by asking trivia questions and rewarding participants with gift certificates to sponsors' stores, seeking input on topics such as places to run, and inviting participants to share their photographs from the races. Similarly, they held contests and posted reminders about races on Twitter. The increase in social media usage coincided with a 50% increase in series participation by 2011. Series organizers wondered how their usage of social media related to participants' correct identification of sponsors, and whether it influenced participants' intentions to purchase products or service from series sponsors. As noted in the study by Eagleman and Krohn (2012), participants were surveyed, and the organizers found out that those participants who spent more time on the series' Facebook page and website were able to correctly identify sponsors to a much greater degree than those who did not visit the sites. Additionally, those who frequently visited the website and Facebook page were found to be more likely to make purchases from sponsors. This information was important to the series organizers because it assisted them in retaining their current sponsors and in securing new sponsorships from other businesses.

can feed the addiction of compulsive consumers. Most sport consumption, however, is not destructive. Therefore, the challenge for sport marketers is to use knowledge of consumers to build effective marketing strategies without feeding consumers' addictions.

Today's sport marketers grapple with these challenges on a daily basis. Each challenge is representative of the broader society in which sport is embedded. All are interrelated. The emotion elicited by sport might be the high that compulsive consumers seek. Technologies such as the Internet and wireless services provide quick access to sport products and services from all corners of the world, at all times of day and night. Globalization of sport creates content that can be shared, often by technology, with people anywhere in the world. There is much to understand about sport consumers, and many ways to collect information. The challenges identified here also create opportunities for sport marketers to learn more about their consumers.

Critical Thinking in Sport Consumer Behavior

In 1999, the New Zealand government launched a physical activity campaign called Push Play to encourage more people to become active in order to combat increasing obesity and diabetes rates amongst the country's citizens. The Push Play campaign called on New Zealanders to engage in at least 30 minutes of physical activity on most days of the week. An example of one sport organization that responded to this call to action is the Manawatu Triathlon Club (MTC). It is a regional sport organization in New Zealand established in 1997 to create events that encourage people of all ages and abilities to participate in the sport of triathlon. In response to the Push Play campaign, MTC introduced a kids' triathlon series consisting of one triathlon a week for five weeks called "I Tri'd the Tri." Children as young as 4 and as old as 12 were eligible to participate, and the distance of the swim, bicycle, and run were modified for each age group to ensure that the distance of each race was age-appropriate. The entry fee was kept very low to encourage greater participation. Each race cost NZ$5 individually, or participants could preregister for all five events for a discounted rate of NZ$20. In the early years of the series, participation numbers ranged from approximately 75 to

PORTFOLIO

Complete the critical thinking portfolio activity in the WSG, consulting as needed the "Critical Thinking Questions" sidebar in chapter 1.

100 kids per event, but by the 2013 season, nearly 700 kids participated in each event. A wide range of skills and ability levels were present at each race. While some of the children who participated were extremely competitive, training several hours each week for the events, for other kids, the triathlon was the only physical activity they engaged in all week. The participants' times were not recorded and no awards were presented, though each child was given snacks such as yogurt, apples, and bottled water at the end of each triathlon. Despite these efforts and the dramatic growth in participation, obesity and diabetes continue to plague New Zealanders, and young people are no exception.

Ethics in Sport Consumer Behavior

You are a vice president (VP) of business operations for a professional soccer team. It is the beginning of the third quarter, and sales are up compared to the previous year. You need one last push to hit your budget. The sales team has been meeting to discuss the incentives that are most important to attract new season ticket holders for the upcoming season. Lisa, a sales and service representative, suggests a final season ticket sales promotion in which the organization highlights free parking at the facility as a new buyer incentive, even though parking is already an included season ticket holder benefit. The sales team is supportive of this new sale promotion except for Peggy, who has been a part of the sales team the longest and believes that the backlash from word of mouth will cause dissatisfaction with existing season ticket holders. Furthermore, Peggy believes it is manipulative to promote something that is already an included benefit. You leave the meeting not certain how you feel about the integrity of the sales promotion. As the VP of business operations, you must decide whether or not to execute the new sales promotion.

PORTFOLIO

Complete the ethical issues portfolio activity in the WSG, consulting as needed the "Guidelines for Making Ethical Decisions" sidebar in chapter 1.

Summary

The study of consumer behavior in sport helps you understand your customers. A better understanding of your customers can help you develop products and services that meet their needs and design marketing strategies to attract new customers while also retaining existing customers. This chapter explores the individual, group, and situational factors that influence sport consumption. Individual factors include motives, perceptions, attitudes, involvement, and identification. Reference groups, socialization processes, and subcultures are the primary group factors that affect decisions to attend sporting events, participate in sporting activities, and buy sport products and services.

It is rare for a single force to influence sport consumption decisions. More often, simultaneous group and individual influences work to exert influence at each stage of the decision process surrounding a purchase. The recognition of a need or problem is the first step in the process. After identifying a need, the consumer seeks information about potential products and services that can fulfill that need or solve the problem. The consumer then develops a set of possible purchase options and evaluates each before making the purchase.

The consumption process does not end with the purchase, since there are two ways for consumers to evaluate their purchase. They often evaluate their purchases in reference to prepurchase expectations. If performance meets or exceeds their expectations, then customers are satisfied. Customers tend to reassure themselves that they made the right purchase. This action is an attempt to reduce cognitive dissonance. Sport marketers can help customers feel good about their purchase by providing information after

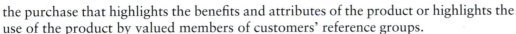
the purchase that highlights the benefits and attributes of the product or highlights the use of the product by valued members of customers' reference groups.

As a sport marketer, you have the job of enticing customers to buy your products, attend your games, compete in your events, and use your services. The consumer decision-making process identifies the steps leading to purchase. You can use your knowledge of the situational, group, and individual factors that can influence each step in the decision process to design products, services, and marketing campaigns that meet the needs of your customers. Furthermore, from the information that you learned in this chapter, you can rely on ethical guidelines and critical thinking skills to assist you in making marketing decisions and performing actions related to sport consumer behavior.

Review Questions

1. What are the key motives for sport participation? Explain them and provide an example of each.

2. What are the key motives for sport spectation? Explain them and provide an example of each.

3. You and a friend attend a football game at your university. Why might the two of you have different perceptions of the game?

4. What are the three components of an attitude? Describe each one.

5. What is the difference between consumer involvement and fan identification?

6. What are potential group influences on a person's decision to attend a sporting event? Give an example of the way that each would influence the decision.

7. How would you go about describing the decision process of parents who are choosing a youth sport program for their child?

8. What would you do to reduce postpurchase cognitive dissonance?

9. What benefits and challenges do new and social media present to sport marketers in terms of consumer behavior?

References

Brown, N.A., Devlin, M.B., & Billings, A.C. (2013). Fan identification gone extreme: Sports communication variables between fans and sport in the Ultimate Fighting Championship. *International Journal of Sport Communication, 6,* 19–32.

Cialdini, R.B., Borden, R.J., Thorne, A., Walker, M.R., Freeman, S., & Sloan, L.R. (1976). Basking in reflected glory: Three (football) field studies. *Journal of Personality and Social Psychology, 34,* 366–375.

de Mooij, M.K. (2004). *Consumer behavior and culture: Consequences for global marketing and advertising.* Thousand Oaks, CA: Sage.

Eagleman, A.N., & Krohn, B.D. (2012). Sponsorship awareness, attitudes, and purchase intentions of road race series participants. *Sport Marketing Quarterly, 21,* 138–146.

Green, B.C. (1996). A social learning approach to youth sport motivation: Initial scale development and validation. (Doctoral dissertation, University of Maryland, 1996). *Dissertation Abstracts International, 60,* 203.

Lim, C.H., Chung, J., & Pedersen, P.M. (2012). The influence of online consumer postings on purchase intentions: Investigating electronic word-of-mouth (eWOM) messages and sporting goods. *Sport Management International Journal, 8*(1), 55–75.

Major League Soccer stats: Team attendance—2013. (2013). ESPN FC: Major League Soccer. Retrieved from http://espnfc.com/stats/attendance/_/league/usa.1/major-league-soccer?cc=5901

Shank, M.D. (2008). *Sports marketing: A strategic perspective* (4th ed.). Upper Saddle River, NJ: Prentice Hall.

Smith, D., & Bar-Eli, M. (Eds.). (2007). *Essential readings in sport and exercise psychology.* Champaign, IL: Human Kinetics.

Trail, G.T., Kim, Y.K., Kwon, H.H., Harrolle, M.G., Braunstein-Minkove, J.R., & Dick, R. (2012). The effects of vicarious achievement on BIRGing and CORFing: Testing moderating and mediating effects of team identification. *Sport Management Review, 15*(3), 345–354.

Wakefield, K. (2014). *Team sports marketing.* Retrieved from http://teamsportmarketing.com/the-text

HISTORICAL MOMENTS

- **1883** *New York World* created first newspaper sports department
- **1895** *New York Journal* became first newspaper to publish an entire sports section
- **1939** First televised MLB broadcast on NBC—Cincinnati Reds v. Brooklyn Dodgers
- **1954** NCAA issued their first public relations (PR) manual for intercollegiate athletics
- **1954** First issue of *Sports Illustrated* published
- **1957** College Sports Information Directors of America (CoSIDA) founded
- **1961** ABC's *Wide World of Sports* made its debut
- **1963** Instant replay first used—Army v. Navy football game
- **1970** *Monday Night Football (MNF)* launched on ABC; *MNF* moved to ESPN in 2006
- **1979** Entertainment Sports Programming Network (ESPN) launched
- **1985** First all-sports radio station made its debut in Denver
- **1991** *The National* (daily sports newspaper) folded
- **1998** *Street & Smith's SportsBusiness Journal* launched
- **2006** *Journal of Sports Media* launched
- **2006** Microblogging service Twitter launched
- **2007** iPhone debuted, spurring the rise of numerous mobile sport applications
- **2008** *International Journal of Sport Communication (IJSC)* launched
- **2012** Manti Te'o hoax underscored complexity of social media communication in sport
- **2013** *Communication & Sport* launched
- **2014** *Modern Sport Communication* launched

14

COMMUNICATION IN THE SPORT INDUSTRY

G. Clayton Stoldt \ Stephen W. Dittmore \ Paul M. Pedersen

LEARNING OBJECTIVES

> Explain the definition and theoretical elements of sport communication.
> Identify the components of the strategic sport communication model (SSCM).
> Recognize the importance of interpersonal and organizational communication in sport.
> Demonstrate the components and workings of the sport media.
> Explain how communication technology affects the sport industry.
> Highlight the influence of social media in sport communication.
> Describe how media relations and community relations professionals serve their sport organizations.
> Identify ethical issues associated with aspects of and careers in sport communication.
> Explain how critical thinking skills relate to effective sport communication.

Key Terms

community relations

effects

electronic communication

new media

one-way model of public relations

print communication

social media

sport communication

sport public relations

strategic sport communication model (SSCM)

two-way model of public relations

GET A JOB

Continue on your journey in sport management by going to the web study guide (WSG) at www.HumanKinetics.com/ContemporarySportManagement. Check out the job opportunities and consider the skills and experiences that can help you succeed in sport management.

Sport communication is one of the most prominent and exciting aspects of sport management. Sport media personalities such as Sage Steele, Dan Patrick, Mike Tirico, and Erin Andrews are often as recognizable as the coaches and athletes whom they cover. Fans often look with envy at sport public relations professionals who are hard at work in some of the best seats in the house as they perform their duties from the press box or press row. Further, technological advancements are allowing sport consumers to interact with the organizations that they support and with one another in new and exciting ways. It is little wonder that so many sport management students are highly interested in communication.

In this chapter you will learn how sport communication is defined and understood using communication theory. You will also be introduced to a model that portrays the various facets of both the practical and academic aspects of the field (Pedersen, 2013b). You will see why effective interpersonal and organizational communication is critical to success in the field. You will learn about the various forms of sport media and how sport organizations deal with the media and other key publics in their community. You will see how technological advancements are changing the field, and you will be introduced to some of the key ethical issues confronting communication specialists in sport management.

social media—Web-based applications that enable people to share content such as information, opinions, and experiences.

sport communication—A process by which people in sport, in a sport setting or through a sport endeavor, share symbols as they create meaning through interaction.

Communication is such an integral part of our lives that it is easy to overlook just how complex and pervasive it really is. In sport settings, communication includes everything from a conversation between an event manager and a volunteer regarding the logistics of hospitality to the release of new information through social media to the presentation of a live event on television. Conceptualizing something so multidimensional is challenging, but Pedersen, Miloch, Laucella, and Fielding (2007) offered a helpful definition. They described sport communication as "a process by which people in sport, in a sport setting or through a sport endeavor, share symbols as they create meaning through interaction" (p. 196).

As you will see in the following section, a number of communication theories and concepts influenced the development of this brief definition. Each has important implications for students and practitioners.

Theoretical Framework of Sport Communication

Numerous communication models, from basic to sophisticated, have been developed to help explain how we communicate. An examination of the theory base as a whole reveals five key concepts: communication genres, context, process, elements, and effects.

Genres

Communication scholars have used a variety of approaches in studying their subject matter. Littlejohn and Foss (2008) described a number of categories that represent these approaches. They range in focus from the individual (e.g., how people learn, why they behave as they do) to the societal (e.g., how social systems function) to the interpretive (e.g., how meaning is discovered). Students who pursue in-depth study in sport communication will become familiar with these theories. Sport-focused publications such as *Communication and Sport* (Billings, Butterworth, & Turman, 2014) can introduce students to sport communication theories and concepts. The key point for now is that no single approach to studying communication can adequately address the subject. By recognizing the varied approaches to communication, students can position themselves for better understanding.

Context

Just as there are multiple approaches to studying communication, there are a number of contexts in which communication occurs. Common contexts for communication include interpersonal, group, organizational, and mass mediated. Interpersonal communication occurs between two people (e.g., ticket taker greets a fan). Group communication takes place among three or more people (e.g., focus group interview). Some communication scholars differentiate between small groups and large groups because the dynamics vary based on the number of people involved. Organizational communication occurs both internally (e.g., meetings, memos) and externally (e.g., news releases, website). Mass-mediated communication takes place when information is shared with large audiences through print, electronic, or new media channels. Each context is relevant in sport management, and prospective sport managers should build knowledge and develop competencies in regard to each.

At a sporting event, communication takes place in various contexts, such as interpersonal interactions between a fan and a guest services employee (as shown in this photo), a group meeting between a sales director and prospective clients in a luxury box, and media members receiving game notes from a media relations intern in the press box.

Process

As noted in the definition, sport communication is a process. This process involves multiple participants, dynamics, and influences at any given moment. For example, a public address announcer shares information about an upcoming event to people in a large, noisy crowd, many of whom are distracted by personal conversations that they are having. Some hear; others do not. Of those who hear, some will take note and plan to attend the event. They may even cheer. Others, meanwhile, will ignore the information.

This example conveys just some of the dynamics involved in the process of communication. The process becomes even more complex in mass communication settings. While the mass media commonly provides timely and accurate information, serious mistakes sometimes occur. Recent examples include the premature reporting of the death of football coach Joe Paterno and reports of related attacks elsewhere in Boston in the immediate aftermath of the Boston Marathon bombing. Serious consequences often result when we fail to communicate our message in situations in which accurate communication is important.

Elements

Communication is a process, and the value of communication models is that they help us understand that process. Most people do so by identifying the elements involved in the process.

The most basic components are portrayed in a model developed by Lasswell (1948):

> Sender

> Message

> Channel through which the message is delivered

> Receiver

ACTION

Go to the WSG and complete the Learning in Action activity, which helps you dissect the communication process between a coach and an athlete.

Using this model, the communication source could be a speaker at a community relations event, the author of a new company policy, or the writer of a news release. The message in each of these cases is the denotation and connotation of the spoken or written words and pictures that the sender produces. Although we can describe channels literally (e.g., broadcast or cable channels), communication scholars usually use the term to describe the delivery system or the way in which the message gets from the sender to the receiver (e.g., spoken word, gestures, over-the-air broadcast television, film). Thus, the channel through which a message is delivered could be face-to-face spoken words (with accompanying voice, expression, and gesture cues) or printed words (with accompanying graphics and layout). The receiver of the communication could be one person or several people who are listening to a speaker, reading a magazine, or visiting a website.

Shannon and Weaver (1949) created a communication model that added two additional elements—encoding and decoding—to this process. The encoding and decoding components of the communication process refer to the inescapable fact that every sender and receiver of communication assigns meaning to the communicated message. This meaning might or might not be readily apparent. Think about the times that you have heard or seen something that did not communicate the intended message. Key words might not have been familiar, or the speaker's language might have been communicating one message while her facial expressions communicated another.

Schramm (1954) expanded on earlier models by including the element of feedback. The resultant model portrayed communication as a two-way, rather than a one-way, process. Feedback helps the communicator understand whether the receiver got the correct message. It provides information for future communication. Phone calls concerning a change in the services offered by a recreation facility, fans erupting in cheers at a spirit rally, or the defeat of a municipal ballot initiative to help fund a team's new sports arena are all examples of feedback.

Another communication concept, noise, refers to elements that can impede successful communication. It can be literal, such as fans at a sporting event drowning out the public address announcer with their yelling. Noise can also be figurative; a poorly printed brochure would certainly hinder communication effectiveness and thus could be a form of noise. The goal in communicating is to minimize controllable noise and cut through uncontrollable noise so that as few impediments as possible are present in the communication process.

Schramm (1954) also argued that for communication to exist, the sender and the receiver must share something: a common language, vocabulary, or interest in or understanding of the subject being communicated. The more the sender and receiver share, the easier it is for them to communicate effectively. Schramm's point is a useful one to consider when you communicate. Ask yourself how much you and the receiver of your communication share. If you can increase the level of shared interest, you will increase the likelihood that your communication efforts will be successful.

Effects

One of the questions that has arisen as communication models have evolved over the years is just how much effect communication has on the parties involved in the interaction. More specifically, a number of theories have addressed the **effects** of the mass media on audiences. For instance, an early model of unlimited effects theorized that audiences are highly susceptible to the effects of messages conveyed through the mass media. Unable to resist the power of media messages, audience members are easily influenced, according to the unlimited effects theory. Research, however, did not support this theory, so a number of theories regarding the limited effects of the mass media have taken its place. These theories include the following:

> *Uses and gratification.* According to this theory, audience members self-select which mass media messages to embrace based on their psychological dispositions and needs. They reject messages that they do not find useful or personally gratifying.

> *Agenda setting.* As proposed by McCombs and Shaw (1972), the mass media are not powerful enough to tell people what to think about an issue. But the media do have the power to influence which issues people think about. In other words, the mass media influence the public agenda.

> *Innovation.* This theory recognizes that the mass media may influence audience members by providing information regarding new developments, products, or services. Accordingly, the media play a role in the process by which innovations are adopted.

> *Diffusion of information.* According to this theory, one of the ways that the mass media affect large numbers of people occurs when people who receive a message through the media then share that message with others.

> *Modeling and cultivation.* These two theories address the influence of the mass media on various audiences. Modeling theory proposes that children and young adults in particular may be inclined to alter their behavior based on media messages that they consume (e.g., following role models). Cultivation theory suggests that media messages influence opinions and attitudes based on the media consumption patterns of audiences. For example, audience members who frequently select violent programs may view the world as being more violent than people who do not as frequently select violent programs.

Each of these theories has implications for sport communication specialists. Combined, they provide the theoretical foundation on which the **strategic sport communication model (SSCM)** (Pedersen, Miloch, & Laucella, 2007) is built.

Strategic Sport Communication Model

The SSCM provides a framework for us to see how the dynamics of communication and the various settings for communication come together in sport. The model, depicted in figure 14.1, has four primary elements. One element is the sport communication process, which is displayed twice to emphasize that the process, elements, and effects described in the previous section pervade all the settings within the field. The other key elements are the personal and organizational communication in sport component, the sport mass media component, and the sport communication services and support components. Note that these key elements (i.e., components in the model) are related, and often overlap (Pedersen, 2013a; 2013b). The arrows pointing to and from component I denote that the types and forms of communication in the central component influence the forms of communication in components II and III, and vice versa.

Personal and Organizational Communication

Component I in the SSCM includes the various forms of personal communication and organizational communication in sport. Each is considered in the paragraphs to follow.

effects—Varied results of communication in regard to its effect on audience members and society in general.

strategic sport communication model (SSCM)—A model depicting the dynamics of communication and the various settings in which communication occurs in sport.

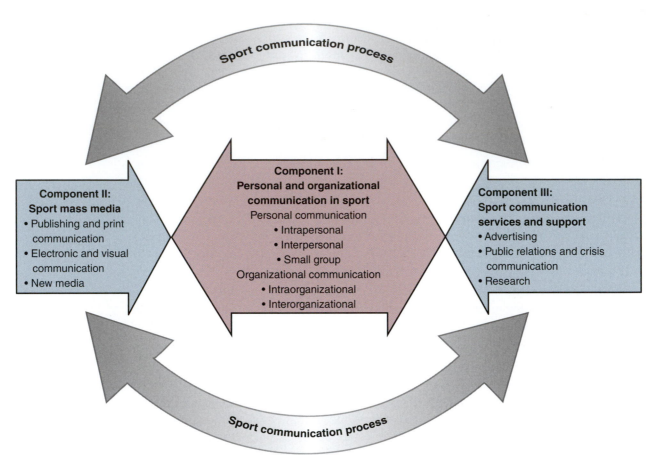

Figure 14.1 Strategic sport communication model.

Reprinted, by permission, from P.M. Pedersen, K.S., Miloch, and P.C. Laucella, 2007, *Strategic Sport Communication* (Champaign, IL: Human Kinetics), 85.

PERSONAL SPORT COMMUNICATION

Personal communication includes intrapersonal, interpersonal, and small-group communication. The prefix *intra* means "within," so intrapersonal communication is the internal communication that each of us experiences. The prefix *inter* means "between," so interpersonal communication is the exchange of messages between two people. Intrapersonal communication is individual in nature but so prevalent that it is arguably the most common type of communication. Intrapersonal communication is by definition private, but many people choose to share their thoughts in Internet forums such as blogs.

Interpersonal communication occurs in face-to-face interactions, may be verbal or nonverbal (e.g., facial cues), and may involve such actions as engaging in telephone conversations and exchanging information through notes, e-mail or social media correspondence, and text messages.

Small-group communication occurs in settings of three or more people. Although more people are involved, the means for small-group communication are identical to those for interpersonal communication. Small-group communication is also like interpersonal communication in that the communication has a shared purpose and the people involved influence one another in the process. It is more complex, of course, because more people are involved. The varying degrees to which people in the group engage in communication and the differing ways in which they respond can make group communication extremely complex.

The following example incorporates each of the three types of personal sport communication. The president of a professional baseball team desires to see her team enhance its relationship with its fan base. She engages in an internal dialogue (i.e., intrapersonal communication) regarding the various approaches that the team may take to address the issue. After she identifies a few ideas, she shares them with the team's director of public relations through an e-mail message (i.e., interpersonal communication). The director replies that he will forward the ideas to his staff members at their next meeting and will follow up with feedback after the meeting ends. The staff meeting (i.e., group communication) provides a forum for the discussion of the relative merits of the ideas. As a result, the best idea—a season-long fan appreciation campaign—is prioritized for development. The director of public relations then shares the idea with the president for final approval.

ORGANIZATIONAL SPORT COMMUNICATION

The three types of personal communication may occur in either an intraorganizational or an interorganizational setting. Again, because *intra* means "within," intraorganizational communication occurs within a particular sport organization setting. And because *inter* means "between," interorganizational communication occurs when members of a sport organization interact with those outside the organization.

The example in the previous section was of intraorganizational communication in its various forms. To carry that example to its next step, say that one of the fan appreciation initiatives that the organization develops is a caravan program in which members of the team, its coaches and manager, its broadcast team, and the team mascot make a series of appearances in the organization's surrounding area to promote the upcoming season. As the team representatives make speeches to the fans in attendance, conduct interviews with members of the media, and sign autographs afterward, they are engaging in interorganizational communication. That is, they are communicating with people outside their organization.

Communication Skills

The most basic personal and organizational communication skills that you need to develop are your writing and speaking abilities. To write effectively, you must be able to track down information, organize it, and record it in a way that interests and informs readers. Sentences must be grammatically correct, wording must be succinct, and ideas must flow from one point to another. Speaking effectively also entails organizing information. Strong speakers are able to boil down large amounts of information into key points that they carefully emphasize, and they are able to build on those points with additional information and humorous or insightful stories. They also connect with their audiences by using appropriate gestures and body language. Because sport communicators must routinely reach a variety of audiences, failure to develop effective communication techniques is usually a prelude to unproductive or even counterproductive efforts.

So how do you become an effective communicator? The same way you develop sports skills—training and practice. When you interview for an entry-level job in the field of sport communication, your prospective employer will expect you to have already developed strong communication skills and gained some related experience. You might get some of this experience through experiential learning activities in your classes, but that kind of practice probably will not be enough to distinguish you competitively. You will likely need to volunteer with a sport organization (e.g., media relations, community relations) or with a mass media outlet (e.g., campus newspaper, local radio station) to get the repetition necessary to hone your skills adequately. Significant volunteer experience will likely position you to gain a high-quality internship in which you can continue to build the skills necessary for a successful career in the field. Effective communication and interactions are just as vital once you secure a position in the sport industry. "Everything comes down relationships and reputation," noted Maxx Rapaport, a sport management graduate working in the league office of the NFL. "Realizing the importance of even the smallest interaction is vital. You never know who is going to be your next boss, or who will be on your team. Simply put, being respectful, polite, and positive will get you a lot further than you would think" (M. Rapaport, personal communication, September 20, 2013).

Component II of the SSCM includes publishing and print communication, electronic and visual communication, and new media. The three main categories are addressed in the following sections.

PRINT COMMUNICATION

print communication— Communication through printed publications, including sport sections in newspapers, sport magazines, and sport books.

The publishing and print communication setting includes sports sections in newspapers, sport magazines, and sport books. Accordingly, the people working in sport **print communication** positions include sports writers, sports columnists, and sports editors.

Although newspaper readership has been in decline, various readership trends reported by the Newspaper Association of America (2013) reveal interesting information. For instance, more than 169 million adults, or 69% of the adult population, read at least a portion of a newspaper every week. Sport coverage draws a significant number of those readers; 55% of newspaper readers report that they usually read that section (Newspaper Association of America, 2008). Sport magazines are also prevalent in the marketplace. These magazines range in scope from general interest periodicals such as *Sports Illustrated* and *ESPN the Magazine* to more specialized publications such as *Inside Triathlon* and *Golf Digest*. The print media are also prominent in other nations. For instance, the World Association of Newspapers and News Publishers (2011) reported that Iceland (96%), Japan (92%), Norway (82%), Sweden (82%), and Switzerland (82%) are the world's leaders in newspaper readership.

ELECTRONIC COMMUNICATION

electronic communication— Communication by electronic media, including sports broadcasting on television (e.g., broadcast, cable, satellite), sports radio, sport film (e.g., movies), and sport photography.

The electronic and visual communication setting encompasses sports broadcasting on television (e.g., broadcast, cable, satellite) and radio. **Electronic communication** includes sport film (e.g., movies) and photography.

Electronic media seem ubiquitous. Research indicates that 256 million Americans over the age of 12 watch television, 243 million listen to the radio, and 232 million use the Internet (Arbitron, 2013). Online radio reaches an estimated 120 million Americans per month, with users reporting they listen to online radio for almost 12 hours each week. On average, Americans spend nearly 8 hours and 15 minutes per day using radio, TV, and the Internet. People ages 12 to 34 are also more likely to watch TV shows on their computer rather than on TV (Arbitron, 2013). The U.S. Census Bureau (2013) reported that there were 14,400 radio stations and 1,800 TV stations in the country.

Broadcast media outlets are prevalent throughout much of the world. Table 14.1 displays the number of TV and radio stations broadcasting in a number of countries. Some TV and radio stations are noncommercial or educational, but most are commercial. TV stations may either be affiliated with a broadcast network (e.g., ABC, CBS, NBC, Fox, the CW) or operate as independent stations with limited or no network affiliation. Many major network affiliates have local news and thus sport programming. Many broadcast and TV networks have additional sport personnel to cover events on a regular or special basis (e.g., the NFL season, the Wimbledon Championships). Cable sports networks, ESPN and its sister channels in particular, require a large number of sport reporters and anchors to handle their all-sport format. Some programs that air on ESPN, however, are sold to the network as a package, complete with announcers and commentators under contract to the company that produces the programs, not the network airing them.

NEW MEDIA

new media— Communication through nontraditional media platforms, most of them Internet based and ranging from traditional websites to mobile applications to e-commerce systems.

New media include a variety of communication platforms, most of them Internet based. They range from traditional websites and social networking websites (e.g., Twitter, Facebook, Myspace) to sport web logs (i.e., blogs) and e-commerce systems. As of

Table 14.1   **Estimated Number of Television and Radio Stations**

Nation	Number of broadcast TV stations	Number of AM radio stations	Number of FM radio stations
Australia	104	262	345
Brazil	138	1,365	296
Canada	80	245	582
China	3,240	369	259
Russia	7,306	323	est. 1,500
United Kingdom	228	219	431

Data based on NationMaster.com: Television broadcast stations (most recent) by country (www.nationmaster.com/graph/med_tel_bro_sta-media-television-broadcast-stations) and Radio broadcast stations by country (www.nationmaster.com/graph/med_rad_bro_sta-media-radio-broadcast-stations).

2012, more than 2.4 billion people worldwide were using the Internet ("Internet usage," 2012). Many of these users go online to access sports information. Sport websites such as ESPN.com, CBSSports.com, FoxSports.com, Sports.Yahoo.com, NBCSports.com, SI.com, SportingNews.com, and NFL.com frequently draw heavy traffic. Growth in recent years has been significant. The percentage of the North American population using the Internet was over 78% in 2012, a number that has grown by 153% since 2000 ("Internet usage," 2012).

The emergence of new media has already had a profound effect on how many sport communication professionals practice their profession, and it seems certain that more changes are on the way. One advantage that many sport organizations have already realized through the Internet is the ability to disseminate messages to a mass audience quickly and inexpensively without having to go through the mass media. Only a few years ago, sport media relations professionals were completely reliant on the mass media to convey messages that originated with the sport organization through news releases. If the media did not use the releases, the information simply was not available to the public. Now, sport public relations practitioners can post that information on organizational websites where interested parties can access it at their convenience. Or the public relations professionals can use a distribution list to e-mail the information to interested parties who have previously provided their addresses to the organization. These options offer a level of message control previously unattainable in the field.

Additionally, the Internet provides a forum for a two-way flow of communication with the public. Social media, in particular, has become a particularly powerful platform for organizations and publics to interact. As members of the public share information, experiences and opinions through social media (e.g., Twitter, Instagram), organizations are able to assess the environment and, when appropriate, engage people in dialogue and shared experiences.

Of course, new technology also has a way of making things more complicated, and sport communication professionals are finding this to be true too. Sport journalists have to be able to work across various media (i.e., media convergence) and use a variety of new media platforms in their gathering and dissemination of sports news (Pedersen, 2014). Media relations specialists in particular are dealing with a couple of challenging issues. First, the specialists are receiving more requests from new media representatives for game credentials and interview access to players and coaches. Another issue that they

WEB

Go to the WSG and complete the web search activity, which invites you to explore the Real Madrid website.

Branded Entertainment in Extreme and Niche Sports: A Paradigm Shift in Media Marketing of Sports

By Reinhard Kunz, Germany
University of Bayreuth

By Florian Schnellinger, Germany
Quattro Media

Sky Sport News HD is the only sport news channel in Germany and one of the latest studios in Europe.

Sport and Audiovisual Mass Media in Germany

The German sport landscape is dominated by *Fußball* (i.e., football or soccer). Media rights to events such as the German Bundesliga and Cup (DFB Pokal), the UEFA EURO and Champions League in Europe as well as the FIFA World Cup are among the most valuable in the world. Besides soccer, only the FIA Formula 1 World Championship, certain winter sports events (primarily biathlon), and the Olympic Games are well represented on German television. TV is the leading mass medium in Germany, and popular sport content contributes to the audience reach, brand image, and advertising success of both free and paid subscription TV stations. Media coverage of extreme and niche sport events—being Olympic or not (e.g., rowing or base jumping)—is still low and is primarily provided by special-interest stations such as Eurosport or Sport 1. This situation is likely to change soon with the growing importance of Internet-based TV as well as a wide spread of new (mobile) media devices.

Revenue Sources for Sport Organizations

Long-term economic success is essential for every sport organization. A solid financial basis enables organizations to host their sport events again in the future. For many years, along with ticketing and sponsorships, media rights have become lucrative and codependent revenue streams for larger sport organizations. Spectators in the stadium or arena cocreate the value of the events, making these more attractive to media and sponsors that seek a large TV audience and high number of consumers. However, TV stations seem willing to pay high license fees only for exclusive premium sport content. Therefore, niche sports that generate small audiences are left out of the television broadcasting landscape in Germany. Niche sports often depend on patronage, sponsorships, and ticketing. They usually lack revenue from TV and have to accept disadvantageous media contracts. Thus, smaller sport organizations should be aware of a trade-off leading to a paradigm shift.

The Trade-Off Between Sponsorships and Media Rights

Sport organizations seek to increase their revenues by selling their media rights, ideally worldwide. In return, the broadcasting companies usually require exclusivity within their territory. This means that a maximum of one TV station per country owns the rights to report on a specific sporting event. Moreover, it is up to the broadcaster then to cover the sport event or not. In many countries, the events of smaller sport organizations are not broadcast at all since they are not considered to be relevant enough for their audiences. Additionally, other programming is often more likely to have a higher reach on the day of the event. Thus, sport organizations live with the uncertainty of their events not being covered. This happened to the World Rowing Cup in Germany, where Public Service Broadcasting (PSB) bought the rights, but the regattas were hardly covered. As a consequence, the media value of certain sport events is very limited for both the sport organization and the sponsors. If logos and advertising messages do not get communicated, the sponsors' cost per thousand consumers reached is high and the return on investment is low. Because sponsors could easily invest in different projects instead of with a sport organization, they have an enormous market power and can put pressure on the sport organizations.

The Paradigm Shift: Branded Sport Entertainment and Nonexclusive Media Coverage

In the future, German organizers of extreme and niche sport events should focus more pointedly on sponsors as their main revenue source. Producing branded entertainment and delivering nonexclusive content free of charge can increase their media value and total viewership. Branded entertainment in this context refers to embedding the sponsors' brands, products and services in sport events. The resulting content combines sport and brand messages without being intrusive. Instead of selling their media rights exclusively to one or a few media outlets, providing branded sport content to broadcasters for TV, Internet, and mobile gives extreme or niche sports much more flexibility and increases the chances that their events will be covered globally by the media. Thus, there still remains unused potential for sport organizations to maximize their audiences, revenues, and economic success.

International Learning Activity #1

From the media's perspective, discuss the most attractive sports in your country. Describe the relationships among sport organizations, sponsors, media companies, and viewers.

International Learning Activity #2

Discuss a communication strategy for an event of extreme or niche sports of your choice. Consider the branded entertainment concept and mass media such as TV, Internet, and mobile.

International Learning Activity #3

Go to the websites of FIFA and the X Games. Evaluate and compare the content, design, and usability of these sites. What changes would you recommend to each organization?

are facing is the growing amount of noncredible information (e.g., false rumors about a sport organization) and unauthorized credible information appearing on the Internet. These issues, and others, will call on sport public relations professionals to adjust their strategies as new technologies continue to develop.

Given the growing prevalence of technology in the field, one additional concern has begun to receive attention in recent years. Some sport communication professionals have become so reliant on technology that they may underuse the direct communication skills necessary to be effective (Battenfield & Kent, 2007). Although the ability to develop message content for online distribution is a powerful communication tool, informal interactions in the workplace and telephone conversations with members of important publics remain essential for effective sport communication.

Sport Communication Services and Support

Component III of the SSCM includes three elements—advertising, public relations and crisis communication, and research. A powerful form of interorganizational communication, advertising is primarily a marketing tool, and as such, it is addressed in chapter 12. Similarly, research is addressed in chapter 20. For now, we will simply emphasize that good research serves as the foundation of successful advertising and public relations efforts.

The remainder of this section focuses on public relations. **Sport public relations** has been defined as a "managerial communication-based function designed to identify a sport organization's key publics, evaluate its relationships with those publics, and foster desirable relationships between the sport organization and those key publics" (Stoldt, Dittmore, & Branvold, 2012, p. 2). Accordingly, public relations refers to organizational communication with various groups of people who are affected by the organization. Key publics often include the media, the community, employees, investors, donors, customers, and regulators. We now consider basic models of public relations practice and then address the two most common types of public relations practiced in sport—media relations and community relations.

sport public relations—A managerial communication-based function designed to identify a sport organization's key publics, evaluate its relationships with those publics, and foster desirable relationships between the sport organization and those key publics.

Models of Public Relations Practice

Some prominent public relations scholars have argued that public relations practitioners work under four basic models of communicating (Grunig & Hunt, 1984): two **one-way models** and two **two-way models**. The assumptions made about the communication process and the organization's purpose in communicating usually drives the decision about which model to use.

The first model is a one-way publicity and press agentry model. Organizations using this model do not seek input from their key publics, but they are extremely concerned about having messages disseminated to a wide audience. Sometimes, to get attention, they are willing to stray beyond the boundaries of what would be considered appropriate or ethical. If you have ever watched a news conference promoting an upcoming boxing match turn into a staged melee, you have seen this model in action at its worst. The boxers, and sometimes the promoters, are willing to risk their credibility, not to mention the well-being of anyone caught in the middle of the fracas, in exchange for the buzz that the prematch fight will generate among the public. This model has many ethical applications as well. Note that Grunig and Hunt (1984) suggested that the entertainment industry commonly employs the limited one-way model (one could argue that sport falls into that category much of the time). In such cases, feedback is limited to responses such as ticket sales.

The second one-way model is the public information model. Organizations that use this model are not as extreme in seeking public attention. Instead, they offer useful services to members of the mass media and the public by providing information in a credible manner. For example, they might assist members of the mass media in setting

one-way model of public relations—A communication model focusing exclusively on the flow of information from the sport organization to its publics.

two-way model of public relations—A communication model focusing on communication give and take between a sport organization and its key publics.

Professional Profile: Mike Kern

Title: associate commissioner, Missouri Valley Conference
Education: MA (communications management), Missouri State University

Most sport managers who enjoy successful careers are highly skilled and have established professional relationships that bring new opportunities their way. Mike Kern is an excellent example of a practitioner possessing both qualities. Kern serves as associate commissioner for the Missouri Valley Conference (MVC), a 10-team conference at the NCAA Division I level. The following is a snapshot of his development, education, duties, and insights as a sport communication leader.

What have been the key moves, steps, or developments in your career, and how did you arrive at your current position?

As you can imagine or expect, I got my start in this field through someone I knew. I was editor of my high school yearbook, and my advisor knew the sports information director at the University of Missouri (where I planned to pursue a degree in journalism). I was given a chance as a student assistant on that staff. After graduating from Mizzou, I pursued a graduate degree at Missouri State University (and also worked in the sports information office). Again, the opportunity was forged through a relationship that my boss at Mizzou had with the sports information director at Missouri State. That, in turn, developed into an opportunity for the position I currently hold (since 1991). If you aren't fortunate enough to have a pre-existing relationship, build one. Volunteer for as many events and opportunities as you can. Do a good job, and stay in touch with the managers who hired you on as a volunteer. Be persistent.

What are your current responsibilities and objectives in your job?

> Oversee all media relations for an 18-sport league
> Assist with men's basketball scheduling
> Assist with MVC's in-house television network
> Participate in strategic planning for the conference
> Help coordinate the MVC's marketing and promotions efforts in conjunction with MVC Sports Properties

What do you enjoy most about your current job?

We are a small staff, and we've had an opportunity to develop skills in a wide number of areas (television production, event management, championship administration, and traditional PR—writing, and so on). I think the fact that our field continues to change (websites were just beginning to launch when I first started, and we didn't have e-mail in 1991). The job is always moving and shaking, and I'm always presented with new challenges.

What do you consider the biggest future challenge to be in your job or industry?

Conference realignment and scheduling, and the continued pressure of keeping up with Division I conferences with seemingly unlimited revenue streams (our conference does not get the TV contract deals that you read about in the Big Ten, SEC, or ACC).

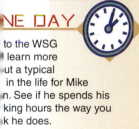

NE DAY

to the WSG
learn more
ut a typical
in the life for Mike
n. See if he spends his
king hours the way you
k he does.

up interviews, or they might provide a variety of other services such as dedicated work areas and game notes to members of the media who are covering a sport event. Many professional organizations and college athletics programs have media relations or sports information offices to perform these functions. By offering such services, they hope to receive greater amounts of favorable publicity.

Two-way communication models are based on the assumption that the most effective forms of communication require input from target publics. In other words, communication requires give and take. For example, if the owner of a sport team wants the community to vote in favor of a tax increase to help fund a new stadium, that owner would be smart to gather some information regarding public sentiment toward the team and public projects in general before attempting to craft public relations messages. In such an example, the owner is using the first two-way model, the asymmetrical approach. The goal is to use information about a public in a scientific way to communicate more effectively and induce that public to behave as desired. In the case of our example, the desired outcome would be for the community to vote in favor of the tax increase to fund the new stadium.

The second two-way model is the symmetrical approach. This method also employs planned information-gathering techniques to communicate more effectively, but it recognizes that the outcome of the communication process will likely mean that both the organization and the public will have to change their positions or behavior. In other words, the second two-way model is about negotiating mutually acceptable solutions. In her study of public relations practices in two English cricket clubs, Hopwood (2005) found that one of the clubs made considerable use of two-way symmetrical communication practices whereas the other was less proactive. The more proactive club was at the forefront of public relations practices among the clubs in its league.

Media Relations in Sport

The mass media devote considerable attention to sport. Because of that interest, most sport managers find that working with members of the mass media is an important part of their jobs. In many cases, sport organizations hire people specifically to manage media relations. These media relations professionals—or sports information professionals, as they are sometimes called—typically operate in a manner consistent with the public information model.

What Media Relations Specialists Do

Sport media relations professionals who work for a team, facility, or organization are responsible for creating, coordinating, and organizing information about that entity and disseminating it to the public indirectly through the mass media or through direct channels (e.g., organizational website). This chapter's profile of Mike Kern describes the background and work of one such professional. The following sections elaborate on a few of the more common duties assumed by media relations professionals.

WRITING NEWS RELEASES

The goal of a news release is to disseminate information to targeted publics in the most positive light possible. The media usually determine what is and what is not newsworthy. The job of a media relations professional is to get information into the hands of the media and persuade them to use it because it is newsworthy to some segment of the media's audience.

PLANNING NEWS CONFERENCES

The goal of a news conference, like a news release, is to disseminate noteworthy information from an organization to its targeted publics. News conferences allow face-to-face interaction with members of the media as an organizational spokesperson offers information or makes a statement. After the spokesperson finishes the statement, reporters usually have the opportunity to ask questions. Key considerations for media relations professionals concerning a news conference include who will speak on behalf of the organization and where the news conference will be held.

MANAGING GAME SERVICES

The primary purpose of a press box or area is to provide accredited working members of the media with a place to sit and record the actions of the event. The location of this space varies from sport to sport, but the media traditionally have an unobstructed view of the competition. Separate booths or spaces are generally provided for broadcast media

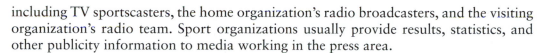

including TV sportscasters, the home organization's radio broadcasters, and the visiting organization's radio team. Sport organizations usually provide results, statistics, and other publicity information to media working in the press area.

CAREERS IN MEDIA RELATIONS

Competition for jobs in sport media relations is intense. Salaries are not always commensurate with similar communication positions in the corporate world because many people seem willing to work in sport almost for free. In addition, sport media relations professionals are frequently called on to work long hours. "First one to arrive, last one to leave" is a common reality in the profession. Work schedules of 60 to 80 hours per week are not uncommon during a particular season; for those working at the collegiate level, sport seasons usually run about 10 months.

Community Relations in Sport

Community relations activities tend to center on promoting charitable initiatives and developing opportunities for face-to-face contact with stakeholders. As such, they complement media relations. Sport organizations engage in **community relations** activities for many reasons, including demonstrating social responsibility, generating long-term goodwill in the community, and producing new revenue (Stoldt et al., 2012).

community relations— Often focuses on the promotion of charitable initiatives affiliated with the sport organization and the development of opportunities for face-to-face contact with sport organization stakeholders.

What Community Relations Professionals Do

Sport community relations professionals who work for a team, facility, or organization are responsible for creating, organizing, and executing charitable initiatives and other programs designed to involve the sport entity in community enhancement. The sidebar "Professional Profile: Aprile Pritchet" describes the work of one such practitioner. A common form of sport community relations activity is the donation of money to various charities. Some sport organizations, particularly those at the major professional level, execute a variety of fundraising events throughout the year and then donate the proceeds to charitable organizations. Other sport organizations may simply contribute autographed merchandise that the charity can then auction off in its own fundraising activities. A second form of community relations activities that sport organizations commonly employ involves initiatives to better the community through volunteering. For example, some organizations cultivate youth sport participation by constructing sport venues (e.g., ball fields) and sponsoring clinics. Others might establish partnerships with charitable organizations to advocate important messages (e.g., "stay in school") or generate an important service (e.g., building a home with Habitat for Humanity). These initiatives take place at multiple levels from the professional sport league to the member franchise to the individual player or coach. In addition, some sport organizations are looking to take their community relations efforts to a new level of effectiveness by creating strategic partnerships with corporate sponsors to serve their communities more effectively. A third form of common community relations activity does not directly benefit charitable organizations, but does enable the sport organization to build relationships with various constituents. Many community relations professionals coordinate public appearances by other members of their organizations. Still others organize promotional events such as the annual winter caravans that many MLB teams stage to rally support during the off-season. Some organizations, particularly those at the minor league level, find that the most popular personality at such appearances is the team mascot.

Careers in Community Relations

Community relations activity is common in a wide range of sport organizations from professional entertainment organizations to colleges and universities to for-profit fitness centers to sporting goods manufacturers. The larger the organization and the greater

Professional Profile: Aprile Pritchet

Title: operations director and senior account executive, Walker Marchant Group, Washington, D.C.

Education: MS (sport studies), University of Massachusetts at Amherst

Aprile Pritchet, who held the position of executive director of United for D.C. in addition to her duties as the community relations director for D.C. United, knows the value of experiential learning. She began her career with D.C. United of Major League Soccer (MLS) as an intern, as did many of her colleagues on D.C. United's staff. The results have been impressive. Pritchet is now considered an industry leader in community relations work, and she was the corecipient of the 2008 MLS Community Relations Executive of the Year award. After this interview was conducted, Pritchet joined the Walker Marchant Group, a public relations firm in Washington, D.C.

ONE DAY

Go to the WSG and learn more about a typical day in the life for Aprile Pritchet. See if she spends her working hours the way you think she does.

What have been the moves, steps, or developments in your career, and how did you arrive at your current position?

When I was in high school, I accepted an internship with the National Association of Collegiate Directors of Athletics (NACDA). Little did I know that internship would later lead to a full scholarship to the school of my choice, which ended up being the University of Massachusetts for a master's degree in sports management. After completing my degree, I was required to complete an internship. I knew I wanted to be in the Washington, D.C. area, so my two choices during the summer months were D.C. United and the Washington Mystics. Since I had previously worked with the Cleveland team, I figured I would try soccer. I interned for about four months; however, after my internship, there were no jobs available within the organization. I kept in contact with my former coworkers until something became available. I was hired as community relations coordinator, and I have spent the last nine years working my way up to head the department.

What are your current responsibilities and objectives in your job?

I am responsible for creating and implementing all of D.C. United's community outreach programs and initiatives, as well as overseeing programs and fundraising events directly related to United for D.C., the charitable arm of D.C. United. I also do the following:

> Oversee staff implementation and maintenance of each program

> Act as a liaison with local leaders relative to the team's community affairs

> Develop and coordinate appearance opportunities for players and coaches

> Develop off-the-field publicity strategies

> Take responsibility for the overall strategic and operational duties of the staff, as well as the expansion and execution of United for D.C.'s mission

> Maintain a strong board of directors by managing the governance, development, and strategic planning process

> Build partnerships in new markets, establish relationships with potential funders and political and community leaders to promote awareness of United for D.C., and raise support for its efforts

What do you enjoy most about your current job?

My job is extremely rewarding. Through our foundation, United for D.C., I have the opportunity to positively change the lives of kids by teaching them the importance of leading a healthy lifestyle and providing experiences they might not otherwise have the opportunity to be involved in.

What do consider the biggest future challenge to be in your job or industry?

Community relations and corporate social responsibility vary by industry, so there is no clean-cut answer. I think the challenge will continue to be whether organizations are good civic partners because it is the right thing to do or because it will help increase their profit. With sports, the community relations departments are typically not revenue generating, so it makes it difficult to spend money when there is little monetary gain. However, what the sports industry has that most organizations don't is the ability to be influential through its athletes, which could definitely translate monetarily.

its resources, the more likely it is that organization will have one or more employees assigned specifically to community relations.

On balance, fewer full-time positions are available in community relations than in media relations in sport. One primary reason is that hundreds of colleges and universities hire at least one full-time employee in sports information. Many community relations responsibilities are delegated to the student life skills division of the athletics department. Still, community relations is a viable career option in the sport industry.

Other Public Relations Positions

Many sport organizations employ public relations professionals in positions that extend beyond media relations or community relations. Some of the common positions are the following:

> *Corporate communications.* Tasks may include marketing communication such as media placement in support of a promotional effort, employee communications, community relations, investor relations, and customer relations. Corporate communications positions tend to be more common in sport organizations with relatively large public relations staffs.

> *Employee and volunteer relations.* These professionals build strong internal relationships by creating forums for communication and staging special events (e.g., volunteer appreciation day). Volunteer relations positions are more prevalent in settings such as state amateur sport festivals in which a large volunteer workforce is critical to successful execution of the event.

> *Digital media manager.* Work focuses on organizational websites and social media, so organizations can share information, interact with members of key publics, and accordingly build important relationships.

Social Media and Communication in the Sport Industry

With the ubiquity of social media, athletic departments have begun realizing the visibility student-athletes possess. Private companies have sprung up to assist athletic departments with social media monitoring of student-athletes. Varsity Monitor helps high school athletes sanitize their social media, delivers education for athletes, and provides monitoring "to ensure that athletes uphold their organization's standards and adhere to their code of conduct when using social media" (Institution, 2012, para. 1). Similarly, UDiligence utilizes apps to monitor student-athlete behavior and provides e-mail alerts "whenever a troublesome post occurs," so it can be addressed with the student-athlete before it becomes an issue (UDiligence, 2013). Fieldhouse Media only tracks publicly available information to respect student-athlete privacy (DeShazo, 2012).

The NCAA does not mandate social media monitoring; however, member institutions "feel pressure to monitor their student-athletes' online activity to demonstrate effective oversight that will stand up to scrutiny" if facing allegations of NCAA violations (Brutlag Hosick, 2013). When the Division I Committee on Infractions released their report in March 2012 on North Carolina's violations, the report showed "some of [the violations] were uncovered via social media" (Brutlag Hosick, 2013).

There are concerns with monitoring. Phillip Closius, a University of Baltimore constitutional law expert, noted "there are all kinds of unconstitutional statutes and governmental actions going on" in relation to monitoring (Gregory, 2012). Several state lawmakers agree. Delaware and California have passed laws banning colleges from requiring students to divulge personal social media information and banning third-party apps from accessing private student athlete information (Gregory, 2012). Other states have since followed their lead.

Student athletes should be aware of expectations in a new media world. Their lives are on display with the 24-hour news cycle. As representatives of the university and athletic department, they need education on positive branding opportunities through social media, in addition to the pitfalls that follow widely displayed negative behavior.

Depending on the setting, other public relations jobs in the sport industry may focus on donor relations, government relations, or relations with various governing bodies.

Critical Thinking in Sport Communication

Given the rapid ascension of nontraditional forms of communication such as message boards, blogs, and social media, sport communication professionals have found themselves needing to address ways to develop media policies for dealing with these emerging forms of media.

As potential future sport communication professionals, you will be put in a position to make decisions regarding how, when, and to whom to communicate. For instance, a common challenge facing sport communicators is determining whether and, if appropriate, how to respond to negative commentary on social media.

Additionally, the nature of how sports fans consume sport products such as games is changing. More options are available for television, mobile, and Internet video content. Future sport communication professionals who are creative in ways of distributing content, especially those who can monetize that delivery, will be in demand. So, the next time that you are watching a sporting event, either in person, on television, or on the Internet, think about what innovation might improve your experience. Perhaps it is providing additional services, such as highlights of other games in progress, to the mobile devices of those watching in a stadium. Or maybe it is pausing live television during a play to switch camera angles and watch a replay, much as the director of the broadcast could do.

Although we do not know how the sport mass media will change in the next several years, it is clear that the communication professional who has a firm understanding of how people communicate, whether through face-to-face interactions or computer applications, will be well positioned to contribute positively to organizational success.

PORTFOLIO

Complete the critical thinking portfolio activity in the WSG, consulting as needed the "Critical Thinking Questions" sidebar in chapter 1.

Ethics in Sport Communication

Sport communication professionals are frequently faced with ethical dilemmas. For example, those in sport mass media encounter ethical issues relating to their sources, coverage decisions, objectivity requirements, and so forth. Two examples in the areas of media relations and community relations in sport illustrate the myriad issues involving ethical and unethical actions in sport communication.

Ethical Issues in Media Relations

Media relations professionals frequently deal with a variety of ethics-related issues. Perhaps the most sensitive issues center on privacy. Media relations personnel have access to a great deal of information—much of it personal. If you work in the field, you need to be sensitive to this and release only information that will not compromise people's right to privacy. For example, it is unethical (not to mention illegal) for a college media relations professional to publicly release student-athletes' grade-point averages. An exception might be the authorized release of information about a student-athlete who earns academic all-star recognition. The College Sports Information Directors of America (CoSIDA) is a professional organization that has a prescribed code of ethics that guides members as they wrestle with privacy-related and other ethical issues. Please review this code (www.cosida.com/About/codeofethics.aspx) and identify the primary issues addressed. Refer to chapter 1 and read the section involving ethical guidelines. How could you use the CoSIDA code of ethics to help you in your application of ethical decision making? How could media relations professionals use the code as a framework by which to evaluate the propriety of one another's actions? For instance, Kant's categorical imperative states that an ethical action taken under a particular set of circumstances could be considered a universal rule of behavior. Kant's mandate is reflected in the CoSIDA code of ethics. For example, the code stipulates that sports information personnel avoid public criticism of their colleagues and support their coaches and student-athletes when they refrain from commenting on a question posed by the media. Both tenets align with Kant's principle.

Another ethics-related issue relevant to media relations has to do with social media and student-athletes. Some coaches ban their student-athletes from using social media, especially Twitter, so they do not have worry about inappropriate comments becoming public. But is such a ban an unethical violation of individual freedom? Athletes often make headlines with inappropriate tweets, but it is difficult to reconcile social media bans with the notion of building leaders, a commonly cited goal of athletics participation. Many institutions that do not ban athletes from using social media now monitor social media communications, a topic discussed at greater length in an earlier sidebar.

Ethical Issues in Community Relations

Community relations professionals also confront ethical issues. The notion of stewardship is particularly relevant when it comes to raising funds for charitable partners. A recent ESPN *Outside the Lines* investigation of 115 athlete charities found that 74% failed to meet commonly accepted standards for nonprofit organizations (Lavigne, 2013). In some instances, charitable foundations established by athletes failed to make any donations to the causes they purportedly supported, in spite of generating revenue through fundraising events. The ethical, not to mention legal dimensions, of being a good steward when soliciting support for charitable ventures is one that is relevant to both individual athletes and larger organizations, particularly in a field as high profile as sport.

PORTFOLIO

Complete the ethical issues portfolio activity in the WSG, consulting as needed the "Guidelines for Making Ethical Decisions" sidebar in chapter 1.

Summary

Communication is a core skill required of all sport managers, and it presents an exciting array of career options for prospective professionals. As noted earlier in the chapter, sport communication is defined as a process in which people share symbols in and through sport endeavors and settings and create meaning through their interactions. The strategic sport communication model (SSCM) depicts both the dynamic sport communication process and the various settings in which sport communication occurs. The components of the SSCM include personal and organizational communication, the sport mass media, and sport communication services and support.

Personal communication may occur on an intrapersonal, interpersonal, or small-group basis. It includes both intraorganizational communication (i.e., within the organization) and interorganizational communication (i.e., between organizational representatives and external constituents).

The many forms of sport media range from print to electronic to new media. The print media include sports sections in newspapers, sport magazines, and sport books. The electronic media encompass sport on television, on radio, and in the movies. New media include sport on the Internet and as communicated through other relatively recent technological innovations. The Internet is particularly powerful because it provides opportunities to reach constituents directly, instantaneously, and interactively. Social media are a particularly powerful form of engagement.

Sport communication services and support include both advertising and public relations. The latter topic received considerable attention in this chapter. Sport media relations professionals disseminate information to the public through the mass media or through organizational websites. They also manage additional media requests, service the media during games or events, and manage records and statistics. Sport community relations professionals generate goodwill for their organizations. They coordinate organizational participation in charitable endeavors, fundraisers that benefit various nonprofits, and public appearances by managers and players. By carefully executing these activities, they enhance their communities and the reputations of their organizations within their communities.

A variety of ethical issues are associated with sport communication. These range from protecting people's privacy to allowing for give and take in communication with key publics. Strong critical thinking skills are also important for sport communicators because they face a rapidly evolving communication environment. New technologies, accompanied by more frequent demand for bottom-line results from communication programs, mean that future professionals will be required to process significant amounts of information, apply appropriate value judgments, and define prudent actions.

Review Questions

1. Why is communication a critical concern to all sport managers, whether they are communication specialists or not?

2. What are the primary elements of the SSCM? What kinds of career opportunities pertain to the various elements?

3. What skills and experiences are most important to sport communication professionals?

4. What would you include in an inventory of the sport media that you commonly use?

5. How have social media changed the way people relate to sport? What are the ramifications of these changes for sport communicators?

6. Describe the work of sport media relations professionals. What sorts of tasks are included in their job descriptions?

7. How would you describe some of the tasks performed by sport community relations professionals?

8. What are some of the common ethical issues facing sport public relations professionals?

9. What are some of the nontraditional forms of communication now being used by sport managers?

References

Arbitron. (2013). *The infinite dial 2013: Navigating digital platforms.* Retrieved from www.arbitron.com

Battenfield, F., & Kent, A. (2007). The culture of communication among intercollegiate sport information professionals. *International Journal of Sport Management and Marketing, 2,* 236–251.

Billings, A.C., Butterworth, M.L., & Turman, P.D. (2014). *Communication and sport: Surveying the field* (2nd ed.). Thousand Oaks, CA: Sage.

Brutlag Hosick, M. (2013). Social networks pose monitoring challenge for NCAA schools. *NCAA.* Retrieved from www.ncaa.org/wps/wcm/connect/public/NCAA/Resources/Latest+News/2013/February/social+networks+pose+monitoring+challenge+for+ncaa+schools

DeShazo, K. (2012). Fieldhouse Media offers universities social media monitoring without violating the privacy of student athletes [press release]. Retrieved from www.prweb.com/releases/2012/3/prweb9261715.htm

Gregory, S. (2012). Jock police. *Time, 180*(7), 56–57.

Grunig, J.E., & Hunt, T. (1984). *Managing public relations.* New York, NY: Holt, Rinehart and Winston.

Hopwood, M.K. (2005). Public relations practice in English county cricket. *Corporate Communications: An International Journal, 10,* 201–212.

Institution. (2012). Varsity Monitor. Retrieved from www.varsitymonitor.com

Internet usage statistics. (2012). *Internet World Stats: Usage and Population Statistics.* Retrieved from www.internetworldstats.com/stats.htm

Lasswell, H.D. (1948). The structure and function of communication in society. In L. Bryson (Ed.), *The communication of ideas* (pp. 37–51). New York, NY: Harper.

Lavigne, P. (2013, March 31). Athlete charities often lack standards. Retrieved from http://espn.go.com/espn/otl/story/_/id/9109024/top-athletes-charities-often-measure-charity-experts-say-efficient-effective-use-money

Littlejohn, S.W., & Foss, K.A. (2008). *Theories of human communication* (9th ed.). Belmont, CA: Wadsworth.

McCombs, M.E., & Shaw, D.L. (1972). The agenda-setting function of mass media. *Public Opinion Quarterly, 32*(6), 176–187.

Newspaper Association of America. (2008). *Daily newspaper section readership report.* Retrieved from www.naa.org/~/media/NAACorp/Public%20Files/TrendsAndNumbers/Readership/Daily-Readership-Active.ashx

Newspaper Association of America. (2013, March 25). Across platforms, 7 in 10 adults access content from newspaper media each week. Retrieved from www.naa.org/en/Topics-and-Tools/SenseMakerReports/Multiplatform-Newspaper-Media-Access.aspx

Pedersen, P.M. (2013a). Reflections on communication and sport: On strategic communication and management. *Communication & Sport, 1*(1/2), 55–67.

Pedersen, P.M. (Ed.). (2013b). *Routledge handbook of sport communication.* London, UK: Routledge.

Pedersen, P.M. (2014). The changing role of sports media producers. In A.C. Billings & M. Hardin (Eds.), *Routledge handbook of sport and new media.* London, UK: Routledge, 101-109.

Pedersen, P.M., Miloch, K.S., & Laucella, P.C. (2007). *Strategic sport communication.* Champaign, IL: Human Kinetics.

Pedersen, P.M., Miloch, K.S., Laucella, P.C., & Fielding, L. (2007). The juxtaposition of sport and communication: Defining the field of sport communication. *International Journal of Sport Management and Marketing, 2,* 193–207.

Schramm, W. (1954). How communication works. In W. Schramm (Ed.), *The process and effects of mass communication* (pp. 3–26). Urbana. IL: University of Illinois Press.

Shannon, C.E., & Weaver, W. (1949). *The mathematical theory of communication.* Urbana, IL: University of Illinois Press.

Stoldt, G.C., Dittmore, S.W., & Branvold, S.E. (2012). *Sport public relations: Managing stakeholder communication* (2nd ed.). Champaign, IL: Human Kinetics.

UDiligence. (2013). UDiligence. Retrieved from www.udiligence.com

U.S. Census Bureau. (2013, June 19). *Guiding the airwaves.* Retrieved from www.census.gov/multimedia/www/radio/profile_america/profile-even-19.php

World Association of Newspapers and News Publishers. (2011, October 12). World press trends: Newspapers still reach more than Internet. Retrieved from www.wan-ifra.org/press-releases/2011/10/12/world-press-trends-newspapers-still-reach-more-than-internet

HISTORICAL MOMENTS

1966   Naming rights granted—Busch Memorial Stadium, St. Louis

1967   NFL Super Bowl 30-second ad cost US$42,500 on CBS and US$37,500 on NBC—the only time the game was broadcast on two networks; in 2013, the cost of some spots rose to more than US$4 million

1971   NFL New England Patriots Stadium became Schaefer Field in US$150,000 deal with Schaefer Brewing Company

1973   Buffalo Bills Stadium became Rich Stadium in US$1.5 million deal with Rich Foods

1985   The Olympic Partner (TOP) Programme created

1990s   Approximately 170 new pro sport teams and 13 new leagues formed during decade of U.S. economic expansion

1999   Enron Corporation agreed to pay Houston Astros US$100 million over 30 years to name the team's stadium Enron Field; after Enron declared bankruptcy, the Astros bought back the naming rights in 2002

2001   Alex Rodriguez signed 10-year, US$252 million contract with Texas Rangers

2002   YES Network, joint venture between MLB's New York Yankees and NBA's New Jersey Nets, established

2003   CBS signed TV contract for NCAA Men's Basketball Championship for over US$500 million per year

2004–05   NHL lockout resulted in cancellation of season when collective bargaining agreement (CBA) expired; NHL and NHL Players Association ratified a new CBA with a salary cap

2007   David Beckham signed US$250 million, five-year contract to play for MLS Los Angeles Galaxy

2009   Real Madrid paid Manchester United record US$131 million transfer fee for Cristiano Ronaldo

2010   Meadowlands Stadium built for US$1.6 billion, earning the distinction as the most expensive stadium built an surpassing the record set previously by the US$1.5 billion Yankee Stadium

2011   NBA experienced its fourth-ever lockout as owners and players debated issues surrounding revenue sharing and salary caps

2012   MLB salary average reached US$3.4 million, up from US$2.6 million in 2005 and US$1.07 million in 1995

2012   London hosted the Olympic Games for £8.9 billion, spending nearly £3.0 billion for operational expenses

2013   Destination Marketing Association International (DMAI) released sports module for its event-impact calculato

2014   Barclays Premier League's Wayne Rooney signed a contract extension with Manchester United paying him £85 million through 2019

15

FINANCE AND ECONOMICS IN THE SPORT INDUSTRY

Timothy D. DeSchriver ❭ **Daniel F. Mahony** ❭ **Marion E. Hambrick**

LEARNING OBJECTIVES

❭ Explain the basic principles of economics and relate the theories of economics to the sport industry.

❭ Discuss the concept of economic impact analysis and its relationship to sport events and facilities.

❭ Describe the business structures of sport organizations.

❭ Identify the basic principles and tools of financial management and apply them to the sport industry.

❭ Recognize the basic elements of balance sheets and income statements for sport organizations.

❭ Identify the various professional and career opportunities in the sport industry that are related to economics and financial management.

❭ Understand the influence of social media and the importance of ethics and critical thinking skills in the areas of sport finance and economics.

Key Terms

demand

economic interaction

law of demand

law of supply

market equilibrium

market shortage

market surplus

scarcity

sport economic impact studies

supply

GET A JOB

Continue on your journey in sport management by going to the web study guide (WSG) at www.HumanKinetics.com/ContemporarySportManagement. Check out the job opportunities and consider the skills and experiences that can help you succeed in sport management.

Sport is one of the most diverse industries in the business world. It is composed of subindustries such as professional sports, collegiate athletics, facility management, health and fitness, and sporting goods. This diversity increases the difficulty of measuring the overall economic size of the industry. For example, should the sale of fishing equipment be considered sport spending? Should the money that Sprint spends to be an official NASCAR sponsor be considered sport spending?

One unfortunate result of the lack of an exact definition of the sport industry is that few attempts have been made to measure the economic size of the industry. No empirical measurement of the overall size of the sport industry has been completed since the late 1990s. Meek (1997) estimated that the cumulative spending on sport-related goods and services in the United States was US$152 billion in 1995. Based on this estimate, Meek noted that sport was the 11th largest industry in the United States, larger than both the insurance and legal services industries. In 2009, *Street & Smith's SportsBusiness Journal* estimated the size of the sport industry at US$213 billion ("Advertise," 2009). Given the length of time that has passed since these estimates were made, it is likely that the current size of the sport industry may have increased two- to threefold. Although the U.S. Department of Commerce does not estimate the overall size of the sport industry, it does provide some financial information on the size of specific sectors within the sport industry (see table 15.1). For example, in 2009, approximately US$2.44 billion was spent at skiing facilities such as Aspen Mountain in Colorado and Shawnee Ski Area in Pennsylvania. The most recent numbers also revealed that the skiing industry employed more than 78,400 full-time workers (U.S. Census Bureau, 2012). Lastly, the Sports and Fitness Industry Association (SFIA, formerly called the SGMA) reported that Americans spent more than US$77 billion on the purchase of sporting goods and equipment in 2011 ("SGMA's Wholesale," 2012). Although the actual dollar amount that can be attributed to the sport industry might be debatable, all the estimates make it clear that sport contributes a great deal to the U.S. and global economies.

Although the sport industry has shown tremendous growth over the past decade, it is not immune to the fluctuations in the global economy that influence many other industries. The global recession that began in 2008 had major effects on the sport industry in areas such as layoffs and decisions to scale back on certain activities and endeavors. The economic troubles—in addition to some unethical and even illegal financial behavior—had a major effect on the sport industry. However, it appears that many segments

Table 15.1 **Economic Activity of Selected Sport Industry Sectors**

Sport industry subsector	2009 sales level (US$)	2008 full-time employees
Skiing facilities	$2.44 billion	78,400
Golf courses and country clubs	$20.33 billion	322,600
Fitness and recreational sports facilities	$21.91 billion	563,100
Professional sport teams and clubs	$20.64 billion	456,400
Racetracks (horse and dog)	$7.20 billion	50,700
Agents and managers for artists, athletes, and public figures	$4.93 billion	18,900

Adapted from US Census Bureau 2012.

of the sport industry have recovered from the global recession and are experiencing a growth in business activity.

Recognition of both the growth and possible contraction of the sport industry leads to a discussion of economic and financial concepts. This chapter presents basic principles of economics and financial management, addresses the relationship between these economic and financial principles and the sport industry, and discusses career opportunities related to the financial management of the sport industry.

Current Financial Situation of U.S. Professional Sport

One segment of the sport industry that has seen tremendous growth over the past decade is professional sport. For example, in 2012, the NFL had operating revenues of approximately US$9.5 billion, and the league's teams had an overall operating income of about US$1.3 billion ("NFL Team Valuations," 2012). Throughout the last decade, major professional men's sport leagues have seen their revenues increase more than 10% annually. Despite this growth in revenue, economic problems remain.

For example, MLB has seen a widening gap between the high- and low-revenue teams. In 2013, *Forbes* magazine estimated that the New York Yankees generated more than US$471 million, making the club the highest revenue team in MLB. In the same year, the Tampa Bay Rays ranked last in revenue with only US$167 million ("MLB Team Values," 2013). This imbalance is an economic concern because all MLB teams, regardless of revenue, compete for the same players. The current revenue disparity makes it difficult for teams that have older stadiums or are located in small markets, such as the Kansas City Royals and Pittsburgh Pirates, to acquire the best players and be competitive on the field. In the long run, this disparity may lead to a decrease in overall fan interest in MLB, particularly for fans of teams that are consistently poor.

To deal with this problem, most professional leagues attempt to equalize the differences in team revenues through revenue sharing. For example, all four of the traditional major men's leagues (i.e., NBA, MLB, NFL, and NHL) share revenue from national television rights fees and merchandise sales. Therefore, although an NFL team such as the New York Giants might be more popular than the Cincinnati Bengals, both receive the same amount of money from the NFL's US$5.18 billion annual television deals, the league's largest source of revenues. Revenue sharing equalizes team revenues and allows

Economic Cycles and the Sport Industry

All economies experience cyclical changes. For example, the world economy fell into a recession in early 2008. This recession brought higher unemployment rates and lower sales of consumer goods like automobiles and computers. Historically, most sport economists have believed that the sport industry has been recession proof, in other words, that sales of sport-related products have not fallen during past recessions. This steady demand is most likely due to the need for people, even in bad economic times, to engage in leisure and recreational activities. Also, sport has been considered a relatively inexpensive and affordable type of leisure. But this trend may be changing with the most recent recession. If the sport industry is no longer recession proof, the reasons most often cited are the increases in ticket prices and sport teams' increasing reliance on revenue from corporations in the form of sponsorship, advertising, and luxury suite sales. In retrospect, while some sectors of the sport industry were affected by the 2008 recession, it appears that they have recovered, and are prospering once again.

teams in smaller markets (e.g., the Green Bay Packers) to compete financially with the big-market teams. This equalization is important for professional sport leagues. As you learned in chapter 9, professional teams within a single league both compete and cooperate. Although their teams attempt to beat each other on the field, team managers must cooperate to ensure financial success for all. If some teams struggle financially, the entire league could decline.

As you might have already noticed, professional men's sport leagues rely heavily on the media. For example, teams in the NFL generate more money from their national and local media deals than they do from gate receipts. Table 15.2 shows the amount of money that some professional leagues and college events generate from media rights. Despite the fact that most major professional men's sport leagues have seen media and other revenue sources grow substantially over the past decade, this increase has not guaranteed overall profitability. Note that both revenues and costs determine the profits of a business. The following equation can be used to calculate the profit level for a sport organization:

$$\text{Profit} = \text{Total revenues} - \text{Total costs}$$

Table 15.2   Sports Television Rights Deals

Property	Networks	Annual average (US$)	Length
NFL	CBS, Fox, ESPN, NBC	$5.18 billion	2013–2022
NBA	ABC, ESPN, TNT	$930 million	2008–2016
MLB	Fox, TBS, ESPN	$1.55 billion	2014–2021
NHL	NBC	$187.5 million	2011–2021
NASCAR	TNT, Fox, ESPN, ABC	$560 million	2007–2014
NCAA Basketball Tournament	CBS	$770 million	2011–2024
Bowl Championship Series*	ESPN	$125 million	2011–2014

*The BCS deal with ESPN does not include the Rose Bowl.

Although MLB has seen tremendous growth in revenues over the past decade, owners still claim to be losing money. They base this claim on cost increases in areas such as team payroll, travel expenses, and coaching and staff salaries. Although many have questioned the accuracy of statements by league and team officials regarding the number of franchises experiencing revenue loss, some teams in major professional sport leagues are clearly not profitable because revenue growth has not kept up with the large increases in team operating costs. Specifically, team owners have been unable to control their spending on players. The average player salary in MLB was over US$3.44 million for the 2012 season. In comparison, the average player salary just 10 years earlier was US$2.38 million ("MLB Salaries," 2012). Twenty-one MLB players had contracts that paid at least US$20 million for the 2013 season, with some of the noteworthy salaries belonging to players such as Alex Rodriguez (US$29 million), Cliff Lee (US$25 million), Johan Santana, Vernon Wells, CC Sabathia, Prince Fielder, Mark Teixeira, and Miguel Cabrera ("Baseball Salaries," 2013).

Single-Entity Structure

As discussed throughout this book, the sport industry is unique in a variety of areas. One example is the use of the single-entity structure in professional sport. Although professional sport teams are all members in a particular league, and often share certain revenue sources (e.g., national television revenue) and expenses (e.g., league marketing), each team is generally operated as a separate entity. But some sport leagues (e.g., MLS) have gone with a single-entity structure. The advantage of using the single-entity structure is that the league members can work together more efficiently and make decisions that focus more on what is good for the league than what is good for an individual team. In addition, the league can set limits for player salaries in a way that would be illegal if the league were not using the single-entity structure. The long-term success of the single-entity structure is still unknown, but it has become popular for certain sport leagues.

As you learned in chapter 9, NHL team owners have also had difficulty controlling player salaries. As stated earlier, this problem has led to substantial losses for teams that have not been able to increase their revenues. The situation in the NHL became a crisis in the fall of 2012. In an attempt to change the economic system in the league, the owners agreed to lock out the players before the start of the 2012–2013 season. The club owners and the players' union (NHLPA) were unable to agree on a new economic system until January of 2013. More than two months of games were lost. After finally agreeing on a new collective bargaining agreement (CBA), a shortened 48-game schedule was played in 2013.

In contrast, the NFL and NBA owners have been able to negotiate agreements with players through the collective bargaining process, thus helping to control salaries. Recent exceptions to this were the 2011 NBA work stoppage, which lasted into December of that year, and the NFL lockout in the summer of 2011. No regular season games were lost due to the NFL lockout. For the NFL and NBA, the amount of money that owners spend on players' salaries is based on the level of revenues that they produce. Therefore, player salaries will increase only if teams are generating additional revenue. This arrangement reduces the likelihood that NBA and NFL owners will become as financially stressed as some MLB owners are. Team profitability is also more consistent in the NBA and NFL.

Current Financial Situation of U.S. College Athletics

Rising costs are also an important issue in collegiate athletics. Most collegiate athletics programs, even at the Division I level, do not produce enough revenue to cover their costs. A study of the finances in collegiate athletics for 2011 found that only 19% of Division I Football Bowl Subdivision (FBS) athletics departments produced revenues that exceeded costs; in many cases, this profit occurred only because the university provided institutional resources to the athletics department. Furthermore, the percentage of schools at which costs exceed revenues is even greater at the Football Championship Subdivision (FCS) and Division II and III levels (Fulks, 2012).

Many athletics departments face a difficult financial future as costs increase in areas such as team travel, equipment, coaches' salaries, and grants-in-aid. Some colleges and universities have also seen their costs increase as they increase opportunities for women. In response to the financial pressure from rising costs in all areas of collegiate athletics spending, some athletics departments have eliminated sport teams and reduced scholarships. For example, in 2012, the University of Maryland eliminated seven sports in a move to cut costs. These sports included men's and women's swimming, men's tennis, women's water polo, acrobatics and tumbling, men's indoor track, and men's cross country (Giannotto, 2012).

Rising costs have also placed additional emphasis on the need to increase revenues. Athletics administrators have turned to private donations, corporate sponsorship, television, and merchandising for additional revenue. At the Division I level, athletics administrators have used television rights fees and ticket sales to help their financial situation. Within the past decade, schools such as the University of Maryland and Ohio State University have expanded their football stadiums to increase ticket sales revenue and meet spectator demand. Penn State University generates more than US$5 million in ticket revenue from one home football game at the 107,000-seat Beaver Stadium. But not all institutions are able to find additional revenue sources so easily. Many athletics departments are increasingly relying on student fees and other forms of institutional support to avoid large budget deficits. Even Division I institutions are applying this remedy, and it has become increasingly common at lower-division levels in the NCAA and at NAIA schools where other revenue sources are limited.

The largest single source of revenue in collegiate athletics is the annual men's basketball championship. In 2011, CBS began paying the NCAA an average of US$770 million per year for the right to televise three weeks of men's basketball in March. The US$770 million will be about 90% to 95% of the overall revenues generated by the NCAA. Division I universities have been pleased with this deal because more than 75% of this money is distributed to them from the NCAA. The contract provided a sizable increase over the more than US$500 million per year received in the prior contract. This additional revenue has aided big-time college athletics departments as they attempt to pay for their growing expenses, but most programs will likely continue to experience annual deficits.

Another recent wave that hit collegiate athletics has been conference realignment. Many universities such as Syracuse, Pittsburgh, Utah, Colorado, and Nebraska, just to name a few, have shifted their conference affiliations. The primary reason for this movement is the belief that it will result in increased revenue for each of the teams.

Economics of Sport

The word *economics* intimidates many people. For some, it brings back memories of studying how intangible items such as widgets and utils are produced and sold. But this example is far from the whole story. Economics is one of the few academic disciplines that can be applied to almost any human action. Within the field of sport management, economics can help us understand issues such as the price paid by consumers for a pair of shorts in a sporting goods store, the escalating salaries of MLB players, and the decision made by an athlete to leave college early and play professionally.

Definition of Economics

scarcity—The basic economic problem facing all institutions, including sport. A sport product is considered scarce if people want more of the product than is freely available for consumption.

The economics of sport can be defined as the study of how people within the sport industry deal with scarcity. This statement leads to the obvious question, What is scarcity? Scarcity is present in the world today because resources are insufficient to meet the wants and needs of society. For example, a health club might want 200 machines available to its members. Unfortunately, because of the scarce resources available to club management, the club might be able to provide only 100 machines. Economics helps determine how the health club management will decide to distribute its scarce resources, not only to machines but also to staff salaries, rent, utilities, and office supplies.

Scarcity is an important issue in sport management because all managers encounter it. Managers have a maximum quantity of resources available for their use. Even the ultra rich Yankees have a limited amount of resources that they are willing to devote to players' salaries. The most successful managers are those who make the best use of limited resources. Although the fact that the Yankees have the most resources gives them a greater probability of winning the World Series, it does not guarantee a championship. Indeed, the team's World Series victory in 2009 was its first since 2000, and the Yankees did not even qualify for the postseason in 2008. Their management must make wise decisions about how to allocate resources to be successful.

The limited resources available to managers are used to produce goods and services that are then sold to consumers. Goods are tangible products (e.g., soccer cleats, tennis racquets, mountain bikes), and services are intangible products (e.g., marketing advice, business consulting, financial planning). Goods and services are exchanged through the **economic interaction** of individuals and organizations. For example, the purchase of a new tennis racquet at a store is an economic interaction. One product of value, a tennis racquet, is exchanged for another product of value, cash. Note that not all economic interactions involve cash. For example, a business might provide free equipment (e.g., computer, tables) or services (e.g., shuttle support, medical personnel) to an event organizer in exchange for advertising space on the event T-shirt.

economic interaction—The exchange of one product of value for another product of value.

Transactions such as those just described occur in markets, which can be defined as arrangements by which economic exchanges among people or business occur. A market could be an actual physical location such as a sporting goods store or a major league ballpark. It could also be an intangible idea such as a computerized stock exchange or the market for players in the WNBA. For teams such as the Washington Mystics and the Los Angeles Sparks, a market exists in which players are bought and sold but does not have an actual physical location. These markets are the core of economic activity. Without markets, the exchange of goods and services could not occur.

Economics has been traditionally separated into two areas of study: macroeconomics and microeconomics. For the sport manager, the principles of microeconomics have the most effect on the day-to-day operations of their organization. Therefore, the following section will examine that area of study within economics.

MICROECONOMICS AND THE SPORT INDUSTRY

Microeconomics is the study of the behavior of individual businesses and households (Keat, Young, & Erfle, 2014). It uses economic theories to explain specific industries such as sport and recreation, automobile manufacturing, and health care. Microeconomics studies variables such as price, revenues, costs, and profits for individual industries and organizations. For example, microeconomics helps to explain why you might walk into two sporting goods stores and see different prices for the same model of basketball shoe.

SUPPLY–DEMAND MODEL

Microeconomists often use models to explain the behavior of producers and consumers. These models are simplified descriptions of how markets operate. A market comprises two fundamental aspects: demand and supply. The supply–demand model is the most widely used and most powerful model in economics. As you will see, an accurate supply–demand model can provide information on the amount of a product or service that consumers are willing to buy at various prices, the amount that suppliers are willing to produce at various prices, and the final price that consumers will pay.

We will begin by discussing demand. **Demand** is the relationship between the price of a product and the amount of the product that consumers are willing to buy. The amount that consumers are willing to buy at various prices is referred to as the quantity

demand—The relationship between the price of a product and the amount of the product that consumers are willing to buy.

law of demand—Consumers will demand less of a product as its price increases and more of a product as its price falls.

demanded. In general, consumers will demand less of a product as its price increases, and they will demand more of a product as its price falls. This relationship is known as the **law of demand**. Demand can be shown through either a table or a graph. Let's use the example of a hypothetical market for WNBA-licensed jerseys. Table 15.3 shows the quantity of jerseys demanded by consumers at different price levels. Figure 15.1 illustrates the same relationship graphically. As you can see, the demand curve is downward sloping, as will always be the case because of the law of demand.

Table 15.3 **Demand Schedule for WNBA Licensed Jerseys**

Price	Quantity demanded
$160	400
$140	600
$120	800
$100	1,000
$80	1,200
$60	1,400
$40	1,600

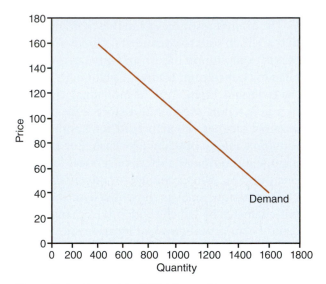

Figure 15.1 Demand for WNBA licensed jerseys.

supply—The relationship between the price of a product and the amount of the product that suppliers are willing to produce and sell.

law of supply—Suppliers will increase production as the price of the product increases and decrease production as the price falls.

market equilibrium—The price at which the quantity demanded equals the quantity supplied.

market surplus—A price at which the quantity supplied of a product is greater than the quantity demanded.

market shortage—A price at which the quantity demanded of a product is greater than the quantity supplied.

The other side of the supply–demand model is supply. **Supply** is the relationship between the price of a product and the amount of the product that suppliers are willing to produce and sell. The amount that suppliers are willing to produce and sell at various prices is known as the quantity supplied. Overall, suppliers will increase production as the price of the product increases and decrease production as the price falls. This relationship is referred to as the **law of supply**. Like demand, supply can be represented in both tabular and graphic forms. Let's continue with the WNBA jersey example. Table 15.4 shows the number of jerseys supplied by businesses in the market at various prices, and figure 15.2 presents the information in graphic form. Note that the supply curve will generally have this upward-sloping shape. Again, this relationship occurs because suppliers will increase production as the price that they can charge for their product increases.

The last phase of the supply–demand model is to determine **market equilibrium**. By analyzing tables 15.3 and 15.4, you can determine that at a price of $100, consumers are willing to buy 1,000 jerseys and suppliers are willing to produce and sell 1,000 jerseys. Thus, this point would be the market equilibrium. Graphically, the intersection of the supply and demand curves represents market equilibrium. As shown in figure 15.3, when the supply and demand curves intersect, the equilibrium price and quantity are $100 and 1,000 jerseys, respectively.

You might wonder what would happen if the price of jerseys was $120. Notice that at a price of $120, consumers are willing to buy 800 jerseys and suppliers are willing to sell 1,200 jerseys. Under these circumstances, the market is not in equilibrium. We would refer to this situation as a **market surplus** because producers are willing to sell more jerseys than consumers are willing to buy. Conversely, a **market shortage** occurs

Table 15.4   Supply Schedule for WNBA Licensed Jerseys

Price	Quantity demanded
$160	1,600
$140	1,400
$120	1,200
$100	1,000
$80	800
$60	600
$40	400

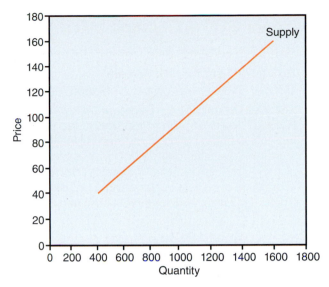

Figure 15.2   Supply for WNBA licensed jerseys.

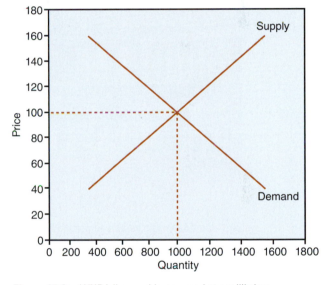

Figure 15.3   WNBA licensed jersey market equilibrium.

when consumers are willing to buy more jerseys than suppliers are willing to produce and sell. This condition would occur if the price was $80.

As you can see, the supply–demand model is a powerful tool in microeconomics. The model helps us determine the quantity of a product demanded and supplied at various prices and the equilibrium price and quantity. Additionally, it can show whether the market is in a state of surplus or shortage.

Economic Impact of Sport Events and Facilities

With the growth of the sport industry, major sport events seem to take place every week. Although these events bring enjoyment to a community, they can also bring a substantial amount of economic activity. Community leaders believe that events such as the Olympic Games, the Super Bowl, and the NCAA Final Four will stimulate their local economies because of increased spending by out-of-town visitors. This spending will, in turn, increase local tax revenues and produce jobs (Howard & Crompton, 2004). Although major events such as those mentioned might produce a significant amount of money for a local economy, smaller events such as road races, soccer tournaments, and festivals can also increase economic activity.

Sport economic impact studies are estimates of the change in the net economic activity in a community that occurs because of the spending attributed to a specific sport event or facility (Turco & Kelsey, 1992). These studies are helpful in measuring the increase in revenues, tax dollars, and jobs attributable to a sport event or facility. For example, New Orleans, Louisiana, hosted the 2013 NFL Super Bowl. A study conducted by the University of New Orleans estimated the overall economic impact of the Super Bowl to be US$480 million (*UNO Study*, 2013).

sport economic impact studies—Analyses of how expenditures on sport teams, events, or facilities economically affect a specific geographic region.

Sochi 2014 Olympic Winter Games and Regional Development Strategy

By Victor Timchenko, Russia
Herzen State Pedagogical University of Russia, Saint Petersburg

The XXII Olympic Winter Games were held from February 7 to 23, 2014, in Sochi, Krasnodar region, Russia. The official vision statement of the Sochi Olympic Organizing Committee (SOOC) declared: "The Games in Sochi are going to be highly innovative Olympic and Paralympic Winter Games, which will express the spirit of modern Russia and bring with them sustainable, positive change for the whole country." The main strategic aims of the committee included integrating efforts for organizing a unique and successful Games, giving a positive impression of Russia to competitors, guests, and global television audiences, and achieving a lasting legacy for Sochi, for Russia, and for the Olympic and Paralympic Movement.

With countdown clocks placed around the Krasnodar region of Russia, people were constantly reminded of the then upcoming 2014 Sochi Olympic Winter Games.

From 2005 to 2011, the effect of Olympic investments was most clearly manifested at the regional budget level, resulting in a stable annual 10% to 15% increase. The initial investment to the project was 327 billion roubles (approximately US$10.85 billion) for the total development, expansion, and hosting of the Olympic Games. A total of 192.4 billion roubles were funded from the federal budget and 7.1 billion roubles were funded from the Krasnodar regional and Sochi city budgets.

WEB

Go to the WSG and complete the first web search activity, which provides opportunity to research the results of an economic impact study conducted for a sport event or facility.

Researchers conduct economic impact studies by collecting information on the spending patterns of visitors to a sport event or facility. A researcher might distribute survey instruments to event spectators to determine how much they spent on things such as hotels, rental cars, food, game tickets, and merchandise. These data are then used to determine the overall new economic activity. Most often, researchers use computer software packages such as RIMS II (Regional Input-Output Modeling System) and IMPLAN to calculate the final economic impact.

Financing from non-budget sources (including private investment funds) was dedicated to the following aspects of the Sochi Winter Olympic Games:

> Tourist infrastructure—US$2.6 billion
> Olympic venues—US$500 million
> Transport infrastructure—US$270 million
> Power supply infrastructure—US$100 million
> Telecommunication infrastructure—US$580 million

The entire project was expected to cost close to US$48 billion, 65% of which was to come from investors and 35% of which was to come from the state. By the beginning of 2013, a total of US$38 billion had already been spent on the construction of Olympic venue structures and on regional infrastructure development.

In preparation for the Olympic Games, construction of new venues took place as well as a modernizing of the telecommunications, power, and transport infrastructures. A mobile network of new generation digital broadcasting infrastructure and a media center with an HDTV satellite channel were built before the start of the Winter Olympic Games. According to the SOOC's strategy, the capacity of the regional energy network was to increase two and a half times by 2014 in order to guarantee a stable power supply during and after the Games. The transportation infrastructure that was prepared to support the Olympics included Sochi Light Metro between the Olympic Park, airport and venues, a renovated railroad, 38 Siemens Mobility Desiro trains, a new terminal at the Sochi airport, backup airports in the neighboring cities, a new terminal at the Sochi seaport, and a new road network around the site.

As a result of the Sochi Olympics preparations, the Standard and Poor Agency's forecast for the Krasnodar region was changed in 2011 from stable to positive. In addition to this increasingly positive view of the region, there are many other noneconomic improvements for the region that could result from the Olympic project. Examples include employment opportunities, better job and earning prospects, improvements to the citizens' quality of life, an increase in cultural and educational activities, and long-standing improvements in health and well-being.

International Learning Activity #1

Using the Internet (www.olympic.org, www.gamesbids.com, www.aroundtherings.com), compare budget items of the 2014 Sochi Olympic Winter Games with previous Olympic Games. Explain the differences in strategic aims and expected financial results.

International Learning Activity #2

Try to forecast the long-term economic impact to the development of Krasnodar region of Russia. What are direct, indirect, and induced impacts? As statistics show, the economic benefits of hosting the Olympic Games increase significantly each year. What do you think are the main reasons for this growth?

International Learning Activity #3

Using the Internet (www.olympic.org, www.gamesbids.com, www.aroundtherings.com, www.sochi2014.com), examine marketing activity proposals for the 2014 Sochi Olympic Winter Games. Which ideas do you believe are the strongest, and what new ideas can you offer?

Experts disagree about the potential of sport events and facilities to generate economic activity. A study completed by the Maryland Department of Fiscal Services concluded that M&T Bank Stadium, home of the NFL's Baltimore Ravens, generates only about US$33 million per year in economic benefits for the state of Maryland. In addition, the stadium produced only 534 additional full-time jobs for the state. In comparison with other projects in the state, the new job creation was small. For example, Maryland's Sunny Day Fund for economic development cost taxpayers US$32.5 million and produced 5,200 full-time jobs (Zimmerman, 1997). Proponents of the public financing of sport facilities argue that the facilities and teams generate intrinsic benefits for a community that cannot be measured in monetary terms. Unlike the Ravens, the Sunny Day Fund cannot produce a Super Bowl–winning team.

As you can see, economic impact analysis is an important topic in the economics of sport. Economic impact studies have received a significant amount of media attention because civic leaders and team owners have used them to justify the use of public funding for new sport facilities. Any economic impact study is only as good as the methods used to generate its results. Educated readers should always ask two questions when seeing the results of an economic impact study:

1. Who conducted the research?
2. How was the research conducted?

Unfortunately, economic impact studies can be manipulated to generate a variety of results. A proponent of a new facility might greatly overestimate the economic impact, but a critic of the same facility might underestimate the economic impact. For example, a study done by PricewaterhouseCoopers (PwC) estimated the direct spending impact of the 2009 Super Bowl in Tampa to be about US$150 million ("Study," 2009). This finding is in stark contrast to a study completed by economist Philip Porter on the economic impact of the last Super Bowl hosted by Tampa in 2001. At that time, Porter estimated the impact of the Super Bowl to be around zero (Porter, 2001). Ironically, the two sides might be using the same statistical information; they are simply analyzing it in very different ways.

Overview of Financial Management

Generally, the functions of financial management fall into two broad areas—determining what to do with current financial resources (i.e., money) and determining how to procure additional financial resources. For example, in a given year, the NFL's Cleveland Browns might earn a profit of US$20 million. The question for the financial manager is what the Browns should do with that money. The franchise owners could decide to use the money to sign a high-priced free agent, renovate their practice facility, or increase the salaries of current employees. They could also decide to invest the money or distribute it among themselves.

Even after the organization decides how to use the money, the financial manager must choose the method for distributing the money. For example, if the Browns decide to spend the money on a free agent, they still must structure the player's contract. The financial manager would try to determine the difference in cost between giving the player a large signing bonus up front and structuring the deal in such a way that the player would receive most of the contract money in the future. Choosing what to spend the money on and how to spend it has significant long- and short-term implications for the team. For example, an MLB team that loads much of the contract onto later years might face financial difficulties when it is paying the player more while he is generating less fan interest. In addition, the team could have more difficulty trading the player because of the large amount of money that it still owes him. When the MLB's Texas Rangers decided to trade Alex Rodriguez and his large contract in 2004, only a few teams were interested. More recently, the Yankees are facing the same issue with Rodriguez. They signed him to a 10-year, US$275million contract in 2007, but in recent years, his production has declined and he has had problems with injuries. Even before his scandal relative to performance enhancing drugs, it would be difficult for the Yankees to find a team willing to take on the remainder of his contract. In order to help teams deal with unwanted long-term deals, the NBA developed the amnesty clause in the most recent collective bargaining agreement. While the team still has to pay for at least part of the player's contract when he is amnestied, they are able to get rid of the player, save some money, and avoid a hit to both the salary cap and the luxury tax. For example, when the Philadelphia 76ers used the amnesty clause on Elton Brand in 2012, they paid US$16.1million of his contract, while his next team, the Dallas Mavericks, paid US$2.1million. Also, none of his US$18.2million salary counted toward either the salary-cap limit or possible luxury tax computation for the 76ers.

Although the example of the Browns described earlier may generate an interesting discussion, few sport organizations have the luxury of deciding how to spend excess money. Because many sport organizations were struggling financially even before the recent financial crisis (Howard & Crompton, 2004), two of the key roles of the financial manager are determining how much money the organization will need to meet long-term obligations and how they will procure those funds. Although most involved with sport immediately think of selling tickets or merchandise as ways to increase available funds, a number of other means have potential. For example, good investments can produce significant income. Also, a few sport teams have sold stock in their organizations to raise funds, and many leagues have collected large fees from expansion teams.

Financial Statements

To allow both internal and external parties to monitor its financial situation, a sport organization develops financial statements on a regular basis. The limited scope of this chapter does not permit discussion of every detail included in financial statements and all the ways in which one might examine those statements to understand an organization's current financial situation. It does, however, give an overview of the major financial statements and the useful information that they provide.

BALANCE SHEET

Figure 15.4 is the balance sheet for a fictional professional football team, the Springfield Stars. In this example, the Stars are co-owned by Robert Goldstein and Connie Shumake. Connie owns 60% of the team, and Robert owns the remaining 40%. The balance sheet reflects the financial condition of the organization on a particular date. Although the balance sheet is generally reported at the end of a given financial period (e.g., the end of a year), a financial manager could generate a balance sheet any time such information is needed. The balance sheet includes three categories—assets, liabilities, and owners' equity. Assets are the financial resources of the company and include both current assets and long-term assets. Current assets are generally items that are cash or expected to be converted into cash within the next year, and will be used to meet current obligations. Long-term assets are items that are not expected to be turned into cash during the next year. Some examples include land, buildings, and equipment. All these items are initially recorded at the price paid for them, and some are reduced as their value declines (i.e., depreciation). Long-term assets also include the long-term investments, which might include government bonds that will not be converted to cash for a number of years.

Liabilities are obligations to pay money or provide goods or services to another entity. In other words, liabilities are money, goods, or services owed to others. Current liabilities are those that are due to be paid in the next year, and long-term liabilities are those that are due sometime after the current year. The owners' equity is Connie's and Robert's shares of the resources of the business. It includes both the money that they have personally put into the company (i.e., paid in capital) and their earnings from the Stars that they have decided to leave in the company (i.e., retained earnings). As you can see in figure 15.4, total assets are equal to liabilities plus owners' equity. This relationship is always true. Logically, all the resources (i.e., assets) either belong to the owner or owners (i.e., owners' equity) or are owed to another entity (i.e., liabilities).

Springfield Stars
Balance Sheet (in thousands)
March 31, 2014

Assets

Current assets

Cash and cash equivalents	$33,365,586
Marketable securities	58,132,669
Other short-term investments	95,558,465
Accounts receivable	3,213,175
Notes receivable	5,678,695
Prepaid expenses	2,616,407
Other current assets	5,900,586
Total Current Assets	**$204,465,583**

Long-Term Assets

Land	$52,495,823
Facilities	45,895,631
Equipment	1,689,954
Long-term investments	6,028,318
Total long-term assets	**$106,109,726**
Total assets	**$310,575,309**

Liabilities

Current liabilities

Accounts payable	$19,714,620
Deferred revenue	28,610,372
Ticket refunds payable	150,908
Long-term debt, current portion	14,365,096
Deferred compensation, current portion	16,209,896
Total current liabilities	**$79,050,892**

Long-term liabilities

Long-term debt, noncurrent	$75,000,000
Deferred compensation, noncurrent	48,850,057
Total long-term liabilities	**$123,850,057**
Total liabilities	**$202,900,949**

Owners' Equity

Paid-in-capital, Connie Shumake	$30,000,000
Paid-in-capital, Robert Goldstein	20,000,000
Retained earnings, Connie Shumake	34,604,616
Retained earnings, Robert Goldstein	23,069,744
Total owners' equity	**$107,674,360**
Total liabilities and owners' equity	**$310,575,309**

Figure 15.4 Springfield Stars balance sheet.

INCOME STATEMENT

In figure 15.5, you will see the income statement for the Springfield Stars. The income statement provides the financial results of the organization's operations over a specific period. As with the balance sheet, the income statement is often reported at the end of a year but can be generated at any point and for any period. For many people, the income statement is the most important financial statement because it presents the organization's bottom line (i.e., the net profit or net loss). Although developing a complete understanding of the organization's financial situation requires a thorough examination of all the financial statements, the bottom line gives the user a quick

---

Springfield Stars
Income statement
For the period ending March 31, 2014

Operating income

National television	$95,425,375
Road games	$13,919,710
Other NFL revenue	$15,075,968
Home games	$30,451,440
Private box income	$12,289,395
Marketing and sponsorships	$37,789,075
Local media	$7,721,250
Concessions and parking	$5,932,282
Miscellaneous	$3,393,293
Total operating income	$221,997,788

Operating expenses

Salaries	$115,868,020
Team expenses	$37,233,957
Marketing expenses	$4,854,095
Operations and maintenance	$13,838,354
General and administrative	$25,883,773
Total operating expenses	$197,678,199
Net operating income	$24,319,589

Other income (expenses)

Interest and dividend income	$6,231,027
Interest expense	($859,333)
Gain (loss) on sale of assets	$3,253,365
Net taxable income	$32,944,648
Income tax expense	$12,100,000
Net income	$20,844,648

Figure 15.5 Springfield Stars income statement.

assessment of the organization and its success in achieving the primary goal of profit-oriented companies—profitability.

The income statement includes two categories—revenues and expenses. Revenue is the inflow of value to the business. Note that revenue is the inflow of value, not the inflow of cash. Therefore, revenue is recorded when the good or service is delivered to a customer, not when the cash is received for that transaction. For example, when the NHL's New York Rangers sell a ticket to a December hockey game in July, the revenue from that sale is not recognized until the game is played in December. Likewise, if a customer receives a ticket for the December game for the promise that payment will be made in January, the revenue is recognized in December, not when the cash is received in January.

At the top of the income statement for the Stars is the organization's operating income. This figure represents the amount of revenue generated by the Stars from the team's main business. Note that some other revenue items (e.g., interest income) appear toward the bottom of the income statement. These items are separate from operating income because most financial analysts are more concerned with revenue from the company's main business, which is generally more useful for predicting future revenue.

The expenses are generally broken up into four categories—direct expenses (or cost of sales), operating expenses, other expenses, and income tax expense. Again, the income statement is more useful to analysts if the expenses are reported in this way. Direct expenses, or cost of sales, are expenses that can be directly matched to the main sources of revenue. For example, the cost of sales for a sporting goods company is the total cost to produce or manufacture all the items sold during the year. You will note that there are no direct expenses on the income statement for the Springfield Stars. Although it is relatively easy to tie the cost of a pair of shoes to the revenue produced from selling those shoes, it is not practical to directly tie the costs of a sport team to the revenue that is generated. Operating expenses are other normal business expenses, such as salaries, rent, and utilities that cannot be directly matched to specific revenue items. Other expenses are those that occur outside normal business operations for a given company. Items such as interest expense and unusual losses are often recorded here. For example, if the Stars lost $500,000 in a lawsuit, the company would report that loss under other expenses. Finally, income tax expense is the amount that the company pays to the Internal Revenue Service (IRS), the state, or the city related to the profits for the year. After subtracting all the expenses from all the revenue, the income statement provides the user with the net income (or loss) at the bottom of the statement; this number is, literally, the bottom line.

Sources of Revenues and Expenses for Sport Organizations

Organizations in the sport industry have various types of revenues and expenses, depending on the type of organization. In this section, we briefly discuss some of the business types in the sport industry and examine some sources of revenues and expenses in those businesses.

Types of Sport Organizations

As previously discussed, sport organizations can take many forms and have varied goals. Some organizations are geared toward encouraging sport participation. These include youth sport organizations, community recreation programs, and high school sports. Other organizations seek to make a profit by providing participation opportunities not offered by nonprofit organizations (or by providing better opportunities than those offered by nonprofits). These include sport organizations that rent their facilities to

WEB

Go to the WSG and complete the second web search activity, which challenges you to identify sources of expenses and revenues for three sport organizations.

participants (e.g., bowling alleys, health clubs), organizations that seek to train people (e.g., those that provide personal trainers, others who provide lessons in a particular sport), and organizations that provide the equipment necessary to participate in a certain sport (i.e., sporting goods companies).

Many companies focus more on sport spectators. These include both professional sports (e.g., WNBA, NASCAR, PGA Tour) and big-time college sports. Although these organizations receive a large portion of the money generated by sport spectators, other entities also benefit from sport spectating, including independent sport facilities that host sporting events, the sport media that bring sport events and information related to sport events to the consumer (e.g., television, radio, newspapers, magazines, the Internet), and companies that sell products licensed by these professional and college sport organizations. The diversity of the sport industry produces a variety of revenue and expense sources. The next two sections focus on types and aspects of revenues and expenses that are unique in the sport industry.

Sources of Revenues

Some of the sources of revenue unique to sport are items related to game attendance (e.g., concessions, personal seat licenses, luxury suite rentals, athletic department donations), media rights, sponsorships, and licensed merchandise. Although the ticket price is generally the major source of revenue related to attendance at events outside sport, this is not always true in sport. The total price of attendance is often much greater than the cost of the ticket. Consider the following:

> Most sport organizations charge fans an additional fee for parking during the event.

> Fans typically spend money on concessions at the stadium. Purchasing hot dogs, beer, and soda is considered by many fans to be an important part of the game experience. Some sport teams and facilities maintain complete control over the concessions at the stadium, but many prefer to hire a company with expertise in handling concessions. In the latter case, the contract outlines how these organizations share the profits from concessions.

> Some professional and college sport teams now charge fans for personal seat licenses (PSLs), which give them the right to buy a particular seat. For example, a fan may buy a 10-year PSL for $10,000. The fan must then pay for season tickets each year for the next 10 years. If the season ticket price is $1,000 per year, the fan will end up paying $20,000 [$10,000 + ($1,000 x 10)] over 10 years to watch games from that particular seat.

> A fan who wants a more exclusive setting for watching games might decide to rent a luxury suite or pay for a club seat. As with the PSL, the fan must still buy tickets for the game after paying the cost of renting the luxury suite. In the NBA, for example, the Brooklyn Nets' luxury suites at their new Barclays Center have an average annual lease price around US$260,000, with the 11 special suites in "The Vault" costing an average of US$550,000. These are still a bargain compared to some of the luxury suite prices, including the Yankees with suites more than US$800,000 and Madison Square Garden going for over US$1 million. Single-event luxury suite rentals can also be very high, including the Super Bowl, which have been leased for US$500,000. An average price for a club seat in the NFL would generally be above US$2,000, with some costing more than twice this amount.

College sport fans often donate money to an athletics department so that they can buy better seats or, in some cases, so that they can buy any seat. For example, a college

Fans are a vital revenue source for sport organization.

sport fan might have to donate $4,000 each year for the right to buy two $400 season tickets. In this case, the fan is actually paying $4,800 ($4,000 + $400 + $400) for the season tickets, or $2,400 per seat. Overall, donations to college athletics departments have increased from 5% of athletics department revenue to almost 21% of revenue at the Division I FBS level over the last four decades (Fulks, 2012).

Because of the increasing cost of attending games, many sport spectators watch or listen to games at home. This large audience for sport beyond those who attend games means that many sport teams make a large percentage of their revenue from media contracts. For example, the NFL recently signed new television agreements that increased the average annual television revenue from US$3.085 billion per year from 2006 to 2013 to US$4.95 billion during the period of 2014 to 2021. The largest single NFL agreement is the ESPN deal for *Monday Night Football* that averages US$1.9 billion per year. As noted earlier in the chapter, the NCAA's contract for the men's basketball tournament is highest on the list with a 14-year contract for US$10.8 billion, which was a nearly 37% increase over the prior record setting contract. Because the tournament takes place on only 10 days, the NCAA receives an average of more than US$77 million per day for the broadcast rights. The new college football playoff contract is expected to generate more than US$150 million per game in broadcasting rights. In many cases, television networks make little or no money directly from the broadcast of sporting events. The networks believe, however, that broadcasting games will be beneficial because they can use the broadcasts to promote other programming, and they believe that they will benefit from a positive association with sport.

Corporations also seek to take advantage of positive associations with sport events, leagues, teams, and players. Spending by corporate sponsors in North America is approximately US$20 billion, with nearly 70% of that going to sport sponsorships. Companies invest heavily in sport sponsorship because they believe that association with these sport organizations will create a positive image of their company and influence people to buy their products or services. The largest sums of money, such as the US$400 million paid by MetLife for the home of the NFL New York Giants and New York Jets, have generally been paid for naming rights of stadiums.

Likewise, corporations pay large amounts of money to athlete endorsers to promote their products and services. For example, Nike became the dominant force in the athletics footwear industry just as the career of its top endorser, Michael Jordan, was taking off. Nike, like other corporations, continues to sign large endorsement deals with athletes, including the deal with NBA MVP LeBron James.

Also looking to take advantage of the positive feelings that sport spectators have about teams and players are the sellers of licensed products. Once a rather small industry, sales of sport licensed products became big business during the 1980s. Although most people immediately think of players' jerseys and team hats, the licensed products industry includes a variety of items such as video games, blankets, framed pictures, and sport equipment. Although most of the money from these sales goes to the producers of the products, sport organizations receive a percentage of the sales revenue.

Sources of Expenses

Two critical sources of expenses for most sport organizations are the cost of sport facilities and the cost of salaries. Sport facilities can be extremely expensive. Most sport organizations try to persuade local communities to pay for stadiums, but many are finding that they have to pay at least part of the cost. This arrangement results in long-term payments, which can affect the financial stability of the organization for many years. Sport facilities are also costly to maintain, particularly large open-air facilities that might not be used for much of the year but must be maintained year round. In addition, sport facilities tend to become obsolete fairly quickly. If an organization has to make payments for 30 years, it could end up making payments on a facility that it is no longer using. In fact, some large sport facilities have been torn down before reaching their 30th birthdays. Combined, these factors require organizations that decide to build a new facility to proceed carefully and explore all options. For example, some sport organizations have been able to pay for some of the cost of a new facility by collecting PSL and rental fees for luxury suites before the opening of the stadium.

Salaries in both professional and college sport have increased dramatically during the last 40 years (Howard & Crompton, 2004). Players' and coaches' salaries often make up more than 50% of the expenses in professional sport, and big-time college coaches (e.g., John Calipari at the University of Kentucky, Rick Pitino at the University of Louisville) are often by far the highest-paid employees on campus. Alex Rodriguez's US$275 million deal with the Yankees is an astonishing contract, but there are other annual contracts above US$20 million. Average salaries in each of the four highest paid men's team sport leagues in the United States range from around US$2 million per year in the NFL to over US$5 million per year in the NBA. Some college coaches are also signing deals worth over US$5 million per year, and salaries around US$2 million are not unusual. Although many argue that the salaries are justified because of the revenue that players and coaches generate for an organization, some have questioned this assumption. Zimbalist (1999) suggested that even the best college coaches are worth much less than their annual salaries, and it is hard to explain how one player is capable of generating an additional US$25 million per year. Therefore, although profits are important to these organizations, some of these salaries are not related to the bottom line. Some organizations might pay more than they can afford because the owner or university official cares more about winning than about profits. The strong desire to win has probably led many sport organizations to make unwise financial decisions.

Careers in Financial Management for Sport Organizations

An increasing variety of jobs relate to financial management in sport. In the past, financial management jobs in sport were generally not complicated. Many organizations had business managers who were basically bookkeepers. They recorded receipts and distributions of money and made sure that organizational financial records were in order. Although these jobs still exist, many jobs today require far more sophisticated financial management skills. For example, negotiation of a player's contract requires both the team and the player to hire representatives who have a strong understanding of financial management. These contracts have both short- and long-term financial implications for the organization, as well as possible implications for league salary caps and luxury taxes. As the sport industry becomes more sophisticated at all levels, the need for people with sophisticated financial skills will become increasingly important.

A number of jobs are available for people who are interested in and have ability in the area of financial management. Because sophisticated financial management skills are needed for some activities, many professional teams and other large, for-profit sport organizations have people with such skills in positions of assistant general manager or vice president for financial operations. This arrangement is particularly common if the general manager or president does not possess the skills necessary to make complicated financial decisions. To help them make particularly complicated financial decisions, some sport organizations hire consulting firms. A number of companies provide such advice and have people who specialize in sport consulting.

Professional Profile: Tim Whitten

Title: director of finance, Kentucky Derby Festival, Inc.

Education: BS (business), Indiana University; certified public accountant (CPA); chartered global management accountant (CMGA)

As the director of finance at the Kentucky Derby Festival, Inc. (KDF), Tim Whitten provides financial support to the organization. KDF hosts nearly 70 events leading up to the annual Kentucky Derby. The organization's festivities include a full and half marathon, golf tournament, and one of the nation's largest fireworks displays. Together, the events combine to generate more than US$96 million in economic benefits in the local economy. The following question-and-answer session provides more information about his role as a finance professional in the sport industry.

What have been the key moves, steps, or developments in your career, and how did you arrive at your current position?
I started with KDF in 2005 after a series of finance and management positions with increasing levels of responsibility. I first worked in management with Winn-Dixie food stores, then became an auditor with the state of Indiana. After passing the CPA exam, I went into public accounting for five years, followed by a finance position with Humana Military Healthcare for five years. I later served as the chief financial officer for RSM Transportation/Elkins American Trucking, and then moved to my position with KDF.

What are your current responsibilities and objectives in your job?
My current responsibilities are complete oversight of all financial areas for KDF, including accounts payable, accounts receivable, general ledger, and audit preparation.

What do you enjoy most about your current job?
I enjoy working with the KDF staff and delivering the product we provide—our many Festival events—to the community.

What do you consider the biggest future challenge to be in your job or industry?
The biggest future challenge for KDF is the ever-increasing competition for sponsorship dollars, which we rely on to host our events. We also face competition from local sports facilities such as the KFC Yum! Center and Papa John's Cardinal Stadium as well as the potential addition of an NBA team.

ONE DAY

Go to the WSG and learn more about a typical day in the life for Tim Whitten. See if he spends his working hours the way you think he does.

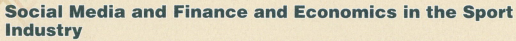

Social Media and Finance and Economics in the Sport Industry

The sport industry has witnessed a marked increase in social media usage. Twitter, Facebook, YouTube, Pinterest, and other social media platforms boast a sizeable presence of sports organizations and personnel. In fact, Twitter's expansive growth is largely attributed to the sport industry and celebrity athletes as early adopters of the platform (Fisher, 2009). Sport journalists and media outlets also use social media, particularly Twitter, to communicate with readers (Sanderson & Hambrick, 2012). Their tweets provide information about a variety of topics such as game scores, team updates, and other current events within the industry.

Sport consumers can also learn more about sport finance and economics issues through Twitter. Media outlets offering this information include *Street & Smith's SportsBusiness Journal* (@SBJSBD), *Forbes* (@SportsMoneyBlog), *USA Today* (@USATODAYsports), *Wall Street Journal* (@WSJSports), and CNBC (@CNBCSportsBiz). A number of prominent journalists also provide insights about sport finance and economics issues with writers such as ESPN's Darren Rovell (@darrenrovell) and Kristi Dosh (@SportsBizMiss), as well as Monte Burke (@monteburke), Kurt Badenhausen (@kbadenhausen), and Darren Heitner (@DarrenHeitner) from *Forbes*. News and other information provided through social media platforms can augment details and sources found in traditional media outlets. Accessing this information regularly can help readers stay apprised of current events and issues within the sport finance and economics realms.

As a student of sport management, you must understand that the skills needed for many of these jobs, particularly those that require highly sophisticated financial skills, require the student to take coursework beyond that needed for a typical undergraduate degree in sport management. One course in sport finance will not prepare you to handle a public stock offering.

ACTION

Go to the WSG and complete the first Learning in Action activity, which asks you to access and analyze the Twitter account of a well-known journalist.

Critical Thinking in Sport Finance and Economics

Critical thinking plays a key role in the financial management of a sport organization. Sport managers must continually develop new strategies to be financially efficient in the operation of their organizations. Ineffective strategies can have considerable short- and long-term effects for the overall financial success of the sport organization.

MLB's Miami Marlins represent one sport organization dealing with critical issues. In 2013, MLB attendance was down 3% from the previous year, but Marlin attendance was down 40% (Townsend, 2013). Industry analysts attributed the decline to an eroding relationship between fans and the organization, despite the opening of a new US$634 million stadium in 2012. The organization reported a US$47 million operating loss that same year, and has since taken significant financial measures. These actions include cutting payroll by US$55 million and lowering game-day operating costs. Yet industry analysts suggest that without an increase in fan support through attendance and other spending, the Marlins will face a tough road back to profitability (Egan, 2013). In a more favorable example, recreational sport participants are shifting away from traditional team sports to adventure sports. The latest offerings are obstacle races, particularly mud runs, which have grown in popularity over the last few years. The events allow participants to crawl through mud pits, jump over ditches, and scale walls. The number of participants increased from 41,000 in 2010 to more than 1.5 million in 2012. Entry fees range from US$60 to more than US$200 per event, and the largest event organizers generate millions, with industry leader Tough Mudder grossing US$70 million (Keneally, 2012).

Sport managers must critically analyze the markets in which they compete to ensure long-term financial success. Market changes such as shifting consumer tastes may have a significant influence on financial decisions related to expanding product offerings and production, hiring additional staff, and increasing marketing and promotional budgets. Failure to incorporate critical analysis into these financial decisions can have a negative effect on a sport organization.

Ethics in Sport Finance and Economics

Ethics can play a significant role in the financial management of a sport organization. Sport managers have a responsibility to act ethically and legally with respect to the organizations that they manage. Unfortunately, some people connected to the sport industry have violated this ethical responsibility. One all-too-common issue relates to performance-enhancing drugs (PED), and PED usage among professional athletes continues to trouble the sport industry. Examples in 2013 alone included the MLB's investigation of players Alex Rodriguez, Ryan Braun, and Melky Cabrera and their association with Anthony Bosch and the Biogenesis clinic (Thompson, Madden, O'Keeffe, & Red, 2013). The sport of cycling remains under intense scrutiny. In June of 2013, the U.S. government filed suit against Lance Armstrong in an attempt to reclaim US$40 million in sponsorship dollars and bonuses awarded to Armstrong and his team members during their Tour de France bids from 1998 to 2004 (Dye, 2013). Additionally, Vijay Singh allegedly used a prohibited deer antler spray, and the PGA Tour withheld nearly US$100,000 of his prize earnings in response to the allegations. Singh filed a lawsuit against the organization, citing unfair treatment during the investigation (Crouse, 2013).

As discussed throughout the chapter, the world of professional sports represents big business in terms of revenues generated by and salary and endorsement contracts awarded to star athletes. However, when detrimental issues such as PED use arise, should those same players be rewarded for their efforts? What financial ramifications should they incur in the face of such use? For instance, should Armstrong repay his salary and bonuses? What responsibilities and remedies do sport organizations have when handling these issues?

PORTFOLIO

Complete the critical thinking portfolio activity in the WSG, consulting as needed the "Critical Thinking Questions" sidebar in chapter 1.

PORTFOLIO

Complete the ethical issues portfolio activity in the WSG, consulting as needed the "Guidelines for Making Ethical Decisions" sidebar in chapter 1.

ACTION

Go to the WSG and complete the Learning in Action activity that tests how well you remember some of the key terms and their definitions used in this chapter.

Summary

This chapter introduces the basic concepts of economics and finance. Sport economics is the study of how people within the sport industry deal with scarcity. Ideas such as supply, demand, and price equilibrium are important for sport businesses such as professional teams, sporting goods manufacturers, and sport facility operators.

Financial management is the application of skills in the manipulation, use, and control of funds. Students need to have a thorough understanding of financial information available through financial statements. Balance sheets and income statements contain a plethora of data that are vital to the successful management of a sport organization. Lastly, students must have knowledge of the different types of revenues and costs that are present for sport organizations.

Review Questions

1. What does the term *economic impact* mean? Provide an example of how it can be used in sport.
2. How would you construct the supply and demand curves from this table to show the supply and demand for bicycles?

3. From the table, how would you determine the market equilibrium price and quantity for bicycles? What would happen if the price level were $250?

4. What are the different types of business structures in the sport industry? Give examples of each.

5. What is the main purpose of each of the financial statements?

6. What type of useful information does each financial statement provide?

7. What are the major sources of revenues and expenses in the sport industry? How are they different from or similar to revenues and expenses of nonsport organizations?

8. What types of positions are available in financial management in the sport industry?

Supply and Demand for Bicycles

Price	Quantity demanded	Quantity supplied
$500	30	180
$400	60	160
$300	90	140
$200	120	120
$100	150	80
$50	180	20

References

Advertise with us—the sports industry. (2009). *Street & Smith's SportsBusiness Journal*. Retrieved from www.sportsbusinessjournal.com/index.cfm?fuseaction=page.feature&featureId=1492

Baseball salaries for 2013. (2013). *Long Island Newsday*. Retrieved from http://data.newsday.com/long-island/data/baseball/mlb-salaries-2013

Crouse, K. (2013, May 8). Singh sues PGA over handling of doping case. *The New York Times*. Retrieved from www.nytimes.com/2013/05/09/sports/golf/vijay-singh-sues-pga-tour-over-doping-case.html?_r=0

Dye, J. (2013, April 23). Lance Armstrong sued by government over sponsor money. *Reuters*. Retrieved from www.reuters.com/article/2013/04/24/us-usa-armstrong-lawsuit-idUSBRE93N03M20130424

Egan, M. (2013, May 23). Miami Marlins' honeymoon cut short by acrimony. *FOX Business*. Retrieved from www.foxbusiness.com/industries/2013/05/23/miami-marlins-honeymoon-cut-short-by-acrimony

Fisher, E. (2009, June 1). Flight of fancy? *Street & Smith's SportsBusiness Journal*. Retrieved from www.sportsbusinessjournal.com/article/62656

Fulks, D.L. (2012). *2004–2011 Revenues and expenses of Divisions I intercollegiate athletic programs report*. Indianapolis, IN: National Collegiate Athletic Association.

Giannotto, M. (2012, July 2). Maryland cuts seven sports on 'sad day' in College Park. *The Washington Post*. Retrieved from http://articles.washingtonpost.com/2012-07-02/sports/35486395_1_athletic-programs-track-program-athletic-director-kevin-anderson

Howard, D.R., & Crompton, J.L. (2004). *Financing sport* (2nd ed.). Morgantown, WV: Fitness Information Technology.

Keat, P.G., Young, P.K., & Erfle, S. (2014). *Managerial economics: Economic tools for today's decision makers* (7th ed.). Upper Saddle River, NJ: Prentice Hall.

Keneally, S. (2012, October 22). Playing dirty. *Outside*. Retrieved from www.outsideonline.com/outdoor-adventure/multisport/Playing-Dirty-November-2012.html

Meek, A. (1997). An estimate of the size and supported economic activity of the sports industry in the United States. *Sport Marketing Quarterly*, 6(4), 15–21.

MLB salaries. (2012). *CBS Sports*. Retrieved from www.cbssports.com/mlb/salaries/avgsalaries

MLB team values: The business of baseball. (2013, March). *Forbes*. Retrieved from www.forbes.com/mlb-valuations/list

NFL team valuations. (2012, September 5). *Forbes*. Retrieved from www.forbes.com/nfl-valuations

Porter, P. (2001, January 15). Super Bowl impact figures a super stretch. *Street & Smith's SportsBusiness Journal*, p. 31.

Sanderson, J., & Hambrick, M.E. (2012). Covering the scandal in 140 characters: Exploring the role of Twitter in coverage of the Penn State saga. *International Journal of Sport Communication*, 5, 384–402.

SGMA's wholesale study reports $77+ billion in sales. (2012, May 23). *Sports & Fitness Industry Association (SFIA)*. Retrieved from www.sfia.org/press/464_SGMA's-Wholesale-Study-Reports-$77%2B-Billion-In-Sales

Study: Economy lessens Super Bowl economic impact. (2009, January 21). *Tampa Bay Business Journal*. Retrieved from www.bizjournals.com/tampabay/stories/2009/01/19/daily32.html

Thompson, T., Madden, B., O'Keeffe, M., & Red, C. (2013, June 4). *New York Daily News*. Retrieved from www.nydailynews.com/sports/baseball/a-rod-braun-face-100-game-suspensions-bosch-ready-talk-article-1.1363300

Townsend, M. (2013, June 2). Tom Verducci: Forty percent of MLB's attendance drop can be attributed to the Miami Marlins. *Yahoo! Sports*. Retrieved from http://sports.yahoo.com/blogs/mlb-big-league-stew/tom-verducci-40-percent-mlb-attendance-drop-attributed-081126007.html

Turco, D.M., & Kelsey, C.W. (1992). *Conducting economic impact studies of recreational and parks special events*. Arlington, VA: National Recreation and Park Association.

UNO study calculates $480M economic impact for Super Bowl XLVII. (2013, April 18). Retrieved from www.neworleanssaints.com/news-and-events/article-1/UNO-Study-Calculates-480M-Economic-Impact-for-Super-Bowl-XLVII/cbca86b4-b23c-42c2-8672-dfd075aba590

U.S. Census Bureau. (2012). *Statistical abstract of the United States: 2012*. Retrieved from www.census.gov/prod/2011pubs/12statab/arts.pdf

Zimbalist, A. (1999). *Unpaid professionals: Commercialism and conflict in big-time college sports*. Princeton, NJ: Princeton University Press.

Zimmerman, D. (1997). Subsidizing stadiums: Who benefits, who pays? In R.G. Noll & A. Zimbalist (Eds.), *Sports, jobs, and taxes* (pp. 119–145). Washington, D.C.: Brookings Institution Press.

HISTORICAL MOMENTS

- **1863** First covered skating rink in Canada opened in Halifax
- **1879** The first Madison Square Garden opened
- **1912** Fenway Park opened; Wrigley Field opened two years later
- **1912** First electronic timers introduced at Stockholm Olympic Games
- **1931** Maple Leaf Gardens opened in Toronto
- **1935** Cincinnati Reds played seven games under the lights
- **1959** First Daytona 500 held at Daytona International Speedway
- **1965** Astroturf developed; first used in the Houston Astrodome, which opened in 1965
- **1989** California earthquake caused 10-day interruption in A's v. Giants World Series
- **1999** Columbus Crew stadium opened—first soccer-specific stadium in the United States
- **2000** Pacific Bell Park (now AT&T Park) opened—first privately funded MLB stadium built since 1962
- **2005** Ski Dubai opened—world's largest indoor snow park
- **2006** Cardinals Stadium (now University of Phoenix Stadium) opened—first retractable grass playing surface in the United States
- **2008** Beijing National Stadium (Bird's Nest) opened—world's largest steel structure
- **2008** Washington Nationals opened first green stadium in the United States
- **2009** US$1 billion NFL Cowboys Stadium and US$1.5 billion MLB Yankee Stadium opened
- **2010** Stampede at Makhulong Stadium in South Africa injured 15 fans before World Cup
- **2011** Record crowd of 114,804 attended game at Michigan Stadium ("The Big House")
- **2013** Terrorist attack with two homemade bombs at Boston Marathon killed 3 and injured more than 260
- **2013** Protests mounted in Brazil in response to massive amounts of public money being spent on 2014 FIFA World Cup
- **2014** U.S. Pond Hockey Championships in Minneapolis, Minnesota, hosted nearly 2,000 skaters and 250 teams who competed on the 25 outside rinks on Lake Nokomis

SPORT FACILITY AND EVENT MANAGEMENT

David K. Stotlar \ **Coyte G. Cooper**

LEARNING OBJECTIVES

> Distinguish between the various types of venues that hold sport and entertainment events.

> Recognize the key steps that are necessary to manage a facility effectively.

> Identify the differences between public assembly facilities and those managed by private companies.

> Discuss the similarities and differences between event and facility management.

> Gain an understanding of the positions available in the field of event and facility management.

> Demonstrate an understanding of the procedures, principles, ethical practices, and current trends in planning and managing an event or facility.

> Recognize the importance of crowd management and identify critical elements for a proper crowd management plan.

> Use critical thinking skills to describe several major problems currently facing facility and event managers.

Key Terms

Americans with
  Disabilities Act
  (ADA)
boilerplate
booking
cost analysis
documentation

in-house
privatization
settlement
split
work order

GET A JOB

Continue on your journey in sport management by going to the web study guide (WSG) at www.HumanKinetics.com/ContemporarySportManagement. Check out the job opportunities and consider the skills and experiences that can help you succeed in sport management.

The number of sport and entertainment facilities constructed or renovated in the United States has increased dramatically during the past 10 to 15 years. For example, seven major facilities with a capacity over 10,000 were projected to open in 2014 in the United States. The estimated cost for these stadiums alone was nearly US$2 billion. This surge in construction is by no means specific to the United States. Brazil committed to spending more than US$3 billion in the construction and renovations of stadiums in preparation for the 2014 World Cup. Given the extensive price tag associated with construction, there has been backlash in the media and from community members not supportive of spending public money on these projects. In addition, reports have estimated that Russia spent about US$51 billion to deliver the 2014 Winter Olympics in Sochi, which is US$49 billion more than Salt Lake City spent to host the event in 2002 ("Sochi," 2014). While there were claims of corruption surrounding the financing of the event, Russian president Vladamir Putin maintained that the inflated prices were due to the honest mistakes of investors and that the actual figure that the government contributed was significantly lower (Myers, 2014; "Sochi," 2014). Regardless, the spending has received criticism given that it was spent amid a slow economy in Russia.

While select publicly constructed stadiums have been successful, some professional teams in the United States have experienced problems securing the necessary financing to complete their mega projects. One such example includes the proposed US$1.2 billion Chargers Stadium for the NFL's San Diego franchise. The Chargers had hoped to stay in San Diego County but have recently considered moving to Los Angeles because they have not been able to secure the funding for a new stadium in their current location (Schrotenboer, 2012). The mayor and others opposed to the project have stated financial concerns as a primary reason for not supporting the initiative.

Professional positions in these facilities provide students from a variety of majors, including sport management, with careers in planning, designing, and constructing facilities (Sawyer, 2013), as well as opportunities to work with facility operations, schedule events, oversee facility finances, equip facilities with TV and video connections, supervise maintenance and custodial services, conduct facility marketing and promotions, engage in event merchandising, and direct risk management services. The distinction between sport and entertainment has blurred to the point that sport and entertainment events are more similar than they are different. The competencies required to manage the facilities that host the events are comparable. Students who develop the right skill sets put themselves in a position to work in these areas of the sport industry.

Types of Facilities

Types of sport and entertainment facilities are as diverse as the events that they host (see table 16.1). Some facilities are single-purpose facilities that are used specifically

Table 16.1   Types of Sport Facilities

Type of facility	Examples
Single purpose	Softball complex, bowling alley, large stadium (e.g., Lambeau Field in Green Bay, WI)
Single purpose, specialized	Ice arena
Multipurpose	Large stadium (e.g., Staples Center in Los Angeles, CA), high school field house
Nontraditional	Skateboard park, convertible indoor–outdoor facility

for one sport or activity. An example is the New York Mets' Citi Field. Bowling alleys, golf courses, motorsport tracks, skate parks, swimming pools, and water parks are all other examples of single-purpose facilities. Other similar facilities are built for specialized events, but they might not be considered single-purpose facilities because they house other types of events. For example, some ice arenas are also used for instructional and recreational skating, figure-skating competitions, ice hockey, and curling, but not for rugby matches. This determination is often made based on who is controlling the facility.

Other facilities, called multipurpose facilities, host a variety of events, such as concerts, truck pulls, motocross races, home and garden shows, and recreational vehicle shows. In addition, these facilities might be home to intercollegiate and professional sport competitions. For example, Lucas Oil Stadium (home of the NFL's Indianapolis Colts), named by *Street & Smith's SportsBusiness Journal* as the Sports Facility of the Year in 2009, hosted the NCAA Men's Final Four in 2010, the NCAA Women's Final Four in 2011, the NFL Super Bowl in 2012, and the 2013 Chelsea FC and Internazionale contest in the Guinness International Champion Cup, and will host upcoming events such as the NCAA Division I Men's (2015) and Women's (2016) Final Four events. Originally, many types of events were held in large outdoor stadiums, going as far back as the chariot races in ancient Rome. In recent years, many stadiums and large arenas, some of them covered, have been built as sport organizations have attempted to improve their facilities to increase their chances of success. With the growing popularity of sports, stadium capacity increased a great deal in the last century and in the early decades of the 21st century. Two of the largest stadiums in the world are home to collegiate football teams in the United States. The University of Michigan's stadium ("The Big House") was built in 1927. The stadium's original capacity was 72,000, but it has since been increased to 109,901. Penn State University's Beaver Stadium has a slightly lower capacity at 106,572. In addition, four other collegiate football teams (Tennessee, Ohio State, Alabama, and Texas) have stadium capacities over 100,000. At the international level, stadiums have increased in size as well. The original seating capacity of San Siro in Milan, Italy, was 10,000 when it was built in 1926. Its capacity has since been expanded to 80,018. Rungrado May Day Stadium in Pyongyang, North Korea, built in 1989, is the largest stadium in the world and has a seating capacity of 150,000. The second largest stadium in the world is Salt Lake Stadium in Kolkata, India with a capacity of 120,000.

Not all sport and entertainment facilities are restricted to spaces that are roofed and walled. Golf courses, ski areas, and amusement parks are classified as sport and entertainment facilities. Another mistake would be to think that all facilities contain seating areas for large numbers of spectators. For example, a fitness center does not have seating areas, but instead has activity spaces, including cardiovascular equipment, free weights, fitness machines, jogging tracks, racquetball courts, and swimming pools. Finally, in some situations, the mission of a facility is broad, and the facility will incorporate many sports or activities. For example, a multipurpose high school gymnasium might be designed for interscholastic sport practices and competition, physical education classes, school plays, and graduation ceremonies. This same concept holds true for facilities such as gymnasiums on college campuses.

Regardless of the size or type of the facility or the kinds of events that it hosts, one factor remains consistent: To maintain a safe and enjoyable environment, proper management of the facility and events is crucial.

During the past 20 years, many sport and entertainment facilities have turned to private companies to handle their management tasks. **Privatization** is the term used to describe this move from public to private management. Either private owners or municipalities still own the facilities, but they outsource, which is the process of subcontracting services to an independent contractor, the management of their facilities to professionals who specialize in facility management (Steinbach, 2004).

privatization—Moving the management of facilities from the public sector to private companies or organizations.

The trend toward privatization began with U.S. professional team facilities and spread to intercollegiate facilities, the minor professional leagues, and sport and entertainment facilities in other countries. Some high schools and municipal recreation centers in the United States have also privatized. Often, the owners of private sport and entertainment venues and the managers of public facilities are not prepared to engage in the facility management business. In such cases, poor management can lead to less than optimal operational efficiency, and venue operations become a drain on financial resources. In public facilities, variables such as political red tape and even patronage (i.e., hiring people as payment for political favors) have caused financial difficulties. In most of these cases, gross operating expenses exceed gross revenues, causing the facilities to operate at a deficit. As you can imagine, this situation has led to reductions in services and the elimination of events, which in turn has led to privatization (Ammon, Southall, & Nagel, 2010). Another reason for privatization is that it allows sport organizations to outsource this area so they can spend their time on other areas to enhance operational efficiency as they see fit.

Facility Management

WEB

Go to the WSG and complete the web search activity, which asks you to identify and research the staff positions at various sport venues.

The number of managers in a given facility, as well as their specific titles and duties, varies depending on the size and purpose of the facility. Consequently, those interested in working in facility management need to read job descriptions carefully to determine the precise duties associated with particular titles. In the sections that follow, we describe several management positions and their accompanying responsibilities with the caveat that specific situations may differ. In general, however, three positions that exist in most facilities are the facility director, the operations manager, and the event coordinator.

The *facility director* (also called the facility manager or the chief executive officer) has overall responsibility for the entire facility. This person is mainly responsible for the creation and proper administration of the facility's standard operating procedures.

The *operations manager* reports directly to the facility director and is responsible for all personnel, procedures, and activities related to the facility. This manager has a variety of duties, such as defining the roles, responsibilities, and authority of facility staff; recruiting personnel to coordinate the various areas of the facility; coordinating personnel, policies and procedures, and activities within the facility; evaluating facility operations; and making recommendations to the facility director.

The *event coordinator*, who also reports to the facility director, is responsible for managing individual events held in the facility. These events can vary from concerts to ice shows and from political rallies to sport events. The event coordinator's responsibilities usually include transporting, assembling, erecting, and storing equipment; establishing a control system for venue and equipment logistics; recruiting, training, and supervising specific personnel; assisting in maintaining venues and equipment during the event; facilitating ticketing and ticket distribution at venue sites; and evaluating venue and equipment operations.

Event Management

Every event is a product, an outcome, and an occurrence. An event occurs in a specific year and month, on a specific date, and at a specific place. All preparation must be completed before the event begins. The total effort is much like the preparation of an actor who is waiting in the wings for the cue to go on stage. The pressure for perfection

Professional Profile: John Brunner

Title: director of athletic event management, University of North Carolina (UNC) at Chapel Hill Department of Athletics

Education: BA (sport management), Ithaca College; MS (sport administration), UNC

Named to his current position in 2006, John Brunner was previously employed in the UNC athletic ticket office, where he oversaw compliance, Olympic sports, and group sales. From 2001 to 2003 (before joining UNC), he was an employee at Harvard Athletics in the area of ticketing, marketing, and facility management. With his position at UNC, Brunner is responsible for managing the daily financial, operational, procedural, and human resource aspects of the UNC athletics operations office. In addition, he directs, coordinates, and supervises operations staffing at home football games and Olympic sports, and serves as the primary liaison with the National Collegiate Athletic Association (NCAA), the Atlantic Coast Conference (ACC), game officials, visiting teams, and television production staff.

What have been the key moves, steps, or developments in your career, and how did you arrive at your current position?

During my undergraduate education at Ithaca College, I came to the conclusion that I was committed to work in the sports industry. I tried to make sure I kept a positive attitude and made clear that no opportunity was too small. I proactively reached out to leaders I respected and kept in touch with them. I was able to get my first opportunity outside of my community with a professional soccer team—the Rochester Raging Rhinos of the A-League (2nd Division)—by utilizing a relationship I had with a friend of a friend, and I secured a meeting with the VP of communications. Following that meeting, I was given a part-time internship in media and community relations that turned into a full-time internship, which ultimately turned into a job offer. During my time with the Rhinos, they won the A-League Championship and a U.S. Open Cup Championship. My senior year of college, I decided to pursue an experience in intercollegiate athletics. After volunteering to assist in various event management roles, I successfully proposed an internship with the Cornell University athletic ticket office. During my internship, I continued to assist in events as well. After the director of events left for another position, I was asked to fill in as the interim director of events and was later offered the position on a full-time basis.

I ultimately decided to pursue a master's degree in sport administration at UNC. In graduate school, I made a deliberate effort to be exposed to as many people and experiences as possible. I did an internship in the director of athletics office. However, the UNC athletic ticket office was confronted with an unexpected challenge—hosting NIT games vs. Wyoming and Georgetown at the Dean E. Smith Center on very short turnaround, when they were shorthanded. I volunteered to help out, and I was ultimately offered a job shortly after. I took that job and focused on developing my core and fundamental competencies and on being responsive and treating people well. After several years, I was looking for a new challenge. Through my demonstrated competencies and commitment to maintaining good relationships with key leaders, I was afforded another opportunity in athletic event management at UNC. I was given new sport administrator responsibilities a year ago, and I was a part of UNC's first women's lacrosse NCAA championship in 2013. I now have an opportunity to work with our championship men's soccer program. I was given these opportunities because I expressed interest in having more responsibilities while showing over time that I could do well with my core responsibilities. I also took advantage of opportunities when they were open, even when the actual opportunity wasn't my passion.

What are your current responsibilities and objectives in your job?

I manage the daily financial, operational, procedural, and human resources aspects of the UNC athletic operations office. I also direct, coordinate, and supervise operations staffing at home football games and Olympic Sports and serve as primary liaison with NCAA, ACC, game officials, visiting teams, and TV production staff. Also, I serve as the sport administrator for women's lacrosse.

NE DAY

to the WSG
learn more
ut a typical day
he life for John Brun-
See if he spends his
king hours the way you
k he does.

(continued)

Professional Profile: John Brunner *(continued)*

What do you enjoy most about your current job?
I enjoy developing relationships with coworkers, student-athletes, fans, and university personnel, and helping our programs achieve their goals and provide excellent service and management. My job allows me to interact with people on a regular basis, and I enjoy getting the opportunity to build solid relationships with them. Given that my field is so relationship driven, this is an area where I have strived to improve regularly. I get the opportunity to be around people and sport on a daily basis and I love that!

What do you consider the biggest future challenge to be in your job or industry?
It's challenging to manage the results from the NCAA-related litigation and keep focus on student-athlete experience while navigating the financially related challenges. Higher expected revenues are needed to cover higher costs, prompting higher prices. These lead to higher fan and customer expectations and higher competition with other entertainment options, which all have fewer resources to achieve relevant goals.

ACTION

Go to the WSG and complete the first Learning in Action activity, which challenges you to design a unique experience for consumers who are attending a NCAA championship.

in event management is high. Many students in the United States think that obtaining a 90% (A) grade for academic work constitutes excellent performance. But if you are managing an event for 70,000 people and the satisfaction level is 90%, you will have 7,000 unhappy patrons.

Events come in many shapes and sizes, from a small corporate 5K run to the New York City Marathon, from an 18-hole community golf tournament fundraiser to the Masters, from a Little League Baseball game to the World Series. Event management includes the planning, coordinating, staging, and evaluating of an event. Most events have similar components, regardless of their scope.

Whether the event is a small golf tournament or the NFL Super Bowl, the planning of many components is crucial to its success. The components involved depend on the nature of the event, the time, the place, and the clientele. For example, a ticket to an event such as the Super Bowl is a prized possession, so serious attention is paid to ticketing in the NFL. Likewise, think of the preparation of the stadium maintenance crew for an NFL playoff game. Events like NCAA postseason championships present unique challenges because teams do not know where they will play until a few days before the competition.

Event Management Personnel

Because of the varied nature of events, no two events will have identical organizational structures. Many elements, however, are common across the industry of event management. Figure 16.1 shows a typical event management personnel structure for a moderately large (2,000–3,000 participants) sporting event. As you study the figure, you will notice that the executive director is at the top of the hierarchy, division managers are in the second tier, and the remaining positions are primarily coordinators. For the sake of brevity, we will discuss only three of the positions identified in figure 16.1: executive director; operations division manager; and the public relations, marketing, and hospitality division manager.

> *Executive director.* The executive director is responsible for the overall administration of the event. Some of the responsibilities include developing operational and strategic plans, preparing the financial statements and budgets for approval, anticipating problems, and implementing solutions. The director is responsible for hiring and recruiting division managers and coordinators, and defining their roles, responsibilities, and authority. The director also needs to provide administrative support for division

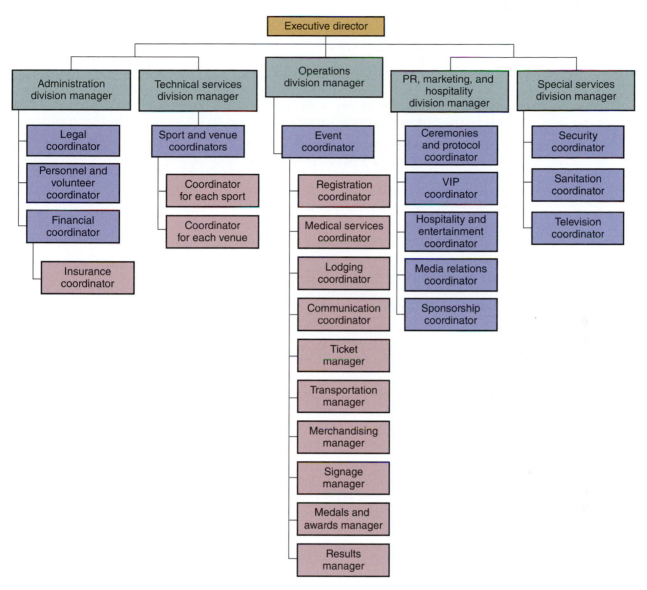

Figure 16.1   Event management structure.

managers and coordinators in the overall planning for each area. The executive director also must prepare an event manual with guiding principles, policies and procedures, and so on. The manual should clearly define the roles, responsibilities, and authority of each division manager and facilitate communication among the divisions. The director assumes responsibility for organizational duties not specifically assigned to division managers or coordinators; approves overall plans, strategies, and budgets; and monitors financial and human resources (e.g., budget, revenues, expenditures, staff, volunteers). Ultimately, the director is accountable for all aspects of the event.

› *Operations division manager.* The operations division manager is responsible for all personnel, procedures, and activities contained in the operations division. These items include registration, lodging, medical services, communications, merchandising and concessions, transportation, signage, medals and awards, and results. This person clearly defines the roles, responsibilities, and authority of each coordinator and manager while recruiting personnel to coordinate each operations area; helps coordinators and managers complete their assigned tasks; assists them in the overall planning for each area; coordinates personnel, policies and procedures, and activities within the operations division; and facilitates communication among all operations coordinators and managers and among other division personnel as needed. The operations division manager communicates with other division managers while supervising personnel and approving policies. Finally, the person in this position evaluates the operations division and makes recommendations to the executive director, to whom he or she reports directly.

> *Public relations, marketing, and hospitality division manager.* The public relations, marketing, and hospitality division manager works at the direction of the executive director in all matters pertaining to public relations (PR), marketing, and hospitality. This person is responsible for personnel, procedures, and activities contained in this division, including, but not limited to, ceremonies and protocol, sponsorship, VIP services, media and PR, and hospitality entertainment. He or she recruits personnel to coordinate each activity and helps staff complete assigned tasks and responsibilities. While coordinating personnel, policies, procedures, and activities within the division, this manager also assists other divisions with PR, marketing, and hospitality needs. This person develops, implements, and manages the overall event marketing plan and facilitates communications among personnel in other divisions as needed. He or she reports directly to the executive director. In addition, he or she evaluates the PR, marketing, and hospitality division and makes recommendations.

An effective organizational structure facilitates effective event planning. All events—from a local tennis tournament to the Wimbledon Championships at the All England Lawn Tennis Club—need effective event management plans. A management plan should include seven basic steps: scheduling, negotiating, coordinating, staging, settling with the promoter, cleaning up, and evaluating. The executive or facility director is ultimately responsible for developing this plan.

Preevent Tasks

The major tasks to be done before the event comprise scheduling the event, negotiating the details with the organization involved, and coordinating the management of every aspect of the event.

SCHEDULING THE EVENT

Scheduling an event entails a reservation process in which events are planned according to the philosophy of the facility. Because most facilities maintain a profit-oriented philosophy, a facility director tries to schedule the largest possible number of events without overburdening the facility or employees. Securing and contracting one specific event or attraction is known as **booking** an event.

Scheduling may involve difficult decisions about what events are acceptable to the owners and management of the facility. For example, a Harley-Davidson motorcycle rally or an Ultimate Fighting Championship (UFC) competition might be considered too controversial for some constituents, or might be distasteful to owners or managers. But these types of events might produce a large profit from significant ticket sales and the accompanying concession and merchandise revenues. The facility builds its reputation on how its directors handle such conflicts.

NEGOTIATING THE EVENT

After making the decision to schedule the event, the facility director (or his or her representative) negotiates the terms of the contract with a representative of the event, usually the promoter. Most facilities use a **boilerplate** contract that addresses the specific terms (e.g., cost of facility, division of revenue) agreed on by the facility and the promoter.

ACTION

Go to the WSG and complete the second Learning in Action activity, which requires you to identify the event management personnel mystery guest.

booking—Securing and contracting one specific sport or entertainment event.

boilerplate—Generic document that uses standard language and a fill-in-the-blank format to outline expectations between parties.

This type of document uses standard language and a fill-in-the-blank format (similar to most apartment leases) to describe the various clauses in the contract. Normally, a prearranged percentage known as a **split** is used to divide revenue from the sale of tickets, merchandise, and sometimes concessions. These financial negotiations are critical factors in establishing the cost of an event. If the amount is too high, additional negotiations ensue to determine which costs to adjust and which splits to modify. When a reasonable split is not found between two sides, it is possible that the facility director or the promoter will walk away from the negotiation.

split—A prearranged, negotiated percentage used to divide various sources of revenue between the promoter and the facility.

Stormy Weather

It was a dark and stormy Friday night in April, and the Big Band had just finished playing a rock concert at the World Arena in Colorado Springs, Colorado. The group was scheduled to perform on Saturday night at the Budweiser Events Center in Loveland, Colorado. The performers decided to sleep in and relax on Saturday instead of traveling to their Loveland hotel. The roadies left early to set the stage and lighting for the Saturday 7:00 p.m. show.

Spring weather in Colorado is notoriously unpredictable. On Saturday afternoon, a snowstorm blew in over the mountains. Frantically, the band members gathered their belongings and entourage, and the bus departed at 3:30 p.m. for the 125-mile (200 km) trip north. At 4:00 p.m. (three hours before the 7:00 p.m. show) the bus became mired in the snow in one of the mountainous areas along the route. It seemed that the trip would not be completed as planned.

The managers of the Budweiser Events Center got the call at 4:15 p.m.: "Our bus is stuck on Monument Hill, and I-25 is closed. We cannot arrive until 8:00 p.m. at the earliest."

What do you do?

Here is the play-by-play of what the Budweiser Events Center managers did.

1. They gathered the crisis management team at the arena and started their action plan. They were confident that the concert would begin only about an hour late based on highway reports from the Colorado State Police.

2. They secured ticket lists from the website database and divided the contact information into groups: e-mail and phone. Information technology (IT) people sent e-mail blasts to everyone with a known address and notified them of the problem.

3. All members of the crisis management team were responsible for calling roughly 50 people on the phone contact list. In addition, they created and printed flyers. As people came to the parking lot access gates, they received flyers so that they knew they could leave and come back later without getting out of their cars.

4. For patrons who had already arrived, notices were posted on the entry doors.

5. Patrons were allowed into the arena but were confined to the concourse until just before show time.

6. People who requested a refund were assigned a reference number, and all requests were granted.

7. In case too many people desired entry into the building, the team readied an adjacent venue (Expo Hall) for overflow from the concourse.

8. The scheduled intermission was cut in half so that the show would not extend too far into the night.

9. Staff members were instructed to deal with complaints right away and to be up front and honest; all messages on the team's phones were to be returned immediately.

10. At 7:20 p.m., the performers showed up and needed a few minutes to warm up.

11. At 8:10 p.m., it was show time at last.

It was a dark and stormy night.

COORDINATING THE EVENT

cost analysis—A systematic process used to provide an estimation of the revenues and expenses of an event.

After completing the preliminary negotiations with the promoter and calculating the **cost analysis**, the event coordinator sits down and studies all aspects of the event. This person is responsible for providing specific venue and equipment needs as requested by the promoter or appropriate representatives. An event coordinator needs to transport, assemble, erect, and store equipment while establishing procedures and guidelines for the rental, purchase, storage, and transportation of venue equipment. Securing a warehouse area for equipment storage and distribution as well as establishing a control system for venue and equipment logistics (e.g., inventory management, storage, transportation of equipment) are crucial steps in the process. After completing these tasks, the event coordinator works with the facility director to recruit and hire event personnel who will assist in maintaining the venues and equipment during the event. The event coordinator then trains and supervises these personnel.

work order—A detailed document that illustrates all requirements of the event.

The event coordinator designs a plan or **work order** for all employees to follow. The work order is the game plan for the event. It documents all requirements discussed with the promoter or other company representative. Anything not documented will be the responsibility of the event coordinator. The work order also defines the time required to do each assigned task.

Staging the Event

After much planning and anticipation, the day of the event arrives. During smaller events such as a local golf tournament, the event coordinator makes certain that items such as longest-drive and closest-to-the-pin markers are in place and that each group has received its caddy or electric cart. Finally, refreshments, award tables, and portable toilets should be properly located. For large events such as concerts and ice shows, an entire day is usually allowed for load-in and setup after the trucks carrying the equipment for the event arrive.

With larger events such as men's football games at stadiums such as Michigan Stadium, many planning elements often come into play. For example, when television crews are on campus for a primetime game, it is important that they have everything they need to carry out their broadcast. At a minimum level, this involves ensuring that crews have access to the stadium at least a day in advance of the game. Many similar elements need to be taken into consideration when planning a major event.

At the designated hour on the day of the event, the doors or gates are opened, the crowd flows inside, and the event begins. At this point, the event coordinator discovers whether he or she was effective in planning and coordinating the many facets of staging the event, including parking, seating, alcohol policies, and crowd control.

SEATING

Many facilities in the United States use reserved seats for events. This policy has not always been in place in sport stadiums around the world. Standing-room areas or terraces were permitted in many European stadiums until the late 1980s. In April 1989, thousands of football fans flocked to Hillsborough Stadium in Sheffield, England, to watch the FA (Football Association) Cup semifinal between Liverpool and Nottingham Forest. Too many fans were allowed into an already full terrace at one end of the stadium. In the resulting crush, 96 Liverpool fans were killed and many others were seriously injured. As a result, a government report (*The Taylor Report* by Lord Justice Taylor) required reserved seats and phased out the terraces from the Premier League levels of British soccer, although standing room is still allowed in the lower divisions (Warshaw, 2004).

With a reserved ticket, a spectator is assured of a specific seat, in a specific row, in a specific section at the event. With the use of trained ushers and an effective crowd control plan, few problems occur at events with this type of seating. Other types of seating are not as easy to manage. General admission (GA) seating is a first-come, first-served process that sometimes causes fans to line up outside for hours before the facility opens in the hope of gaining that prestigious front-row seat. Festival seating is a type of GA seating, but it is a misnomer because no actual seats exist. Festival seating allows spectators to crowd together standing shoulder to shoulder in open floor space. Although promoters can sell more tickets by using festival seating rather than reserved or general admission seating, it is a potentially deadly arrangement that continues to be a controversial topic in event management.

A variety of fatal incidents have occurred at entertainment events around the world, including the following:

> - May 1964, Lima, Peru—318 people were killed and 500 injured in riots at National Stadium after Argentina beat Peru in an Olympic qualifying match.
> - December 1979, Cincinnati, Ohio—11 were killed in a crush to get into a concert by The Who.
> - April 1989, Sheffield, England—96 people are crushed to death at an FA Cup semifinal between Liverpool and Nottingham Forest at Hillsborough Stadium.
> - January 1991, Salt Lake City, Utah—3 teenagers were killed when the crowd at an AC/DC concert rushed the stage.
> - May 1999, Minsk, Belarus—53 were killed when a crowd fleeing a severe rainstorm during a downtown rock concert and beer festival stampeded in an underground passage.
> - July 2000, Copenhagen, Denmark—8 were killed in crush of fans trying to get closer to Pearl Jam at an outdoor concert.
> - February 2003, Chicago, Illinois—21 died at a Chicago nightclub when guests stampeded to the exits after a security guard used pepper spray to break up a fight.
> - February 2003, West Warwick, Rhode Island—100 died after pyrotechnics ignited flammable foam lining the walls of the venue during a Great White concert.
> - July 2003, Moscow, Russia—17 people were killed when two explosions went off at a rock festival. Reports were that two suicide bombers set off the blasts in the crowd at the entrance to the festival when security guards prevented them from entering the gates.
> - April 2008, Quito, Ecuador—15 people died after pyrotechnics, lit by a band member, ignited a nightclub hosting a rock concert.
> - June 2010, Johannesburg, South Africa—Although not fatal, a stampede before a warm-up World Cup soccer match injured 15 fans.
> - February 2012, Port Said, Egypt—74 people were killed and 250 were injured when spectators at a football match broke onto the pitch and attacked players and rival fans.
> - July 2013, Nabire, Indonesia—18 people died and over three dozen more were injured in a brawl and the ensuing stadium stampede after a boxing match in the Kota Lama Sport Stadium.

CUSTOMER SERVICE

Tod Leiweke, former CEO of the NFL's Seattle Seahawks, emphasizes that for any sport or entertainment event to be a success, facility and event managers must concentrate on three fundamentals: brand, audience, and experience. The brand is the venue (the place), the audience comprises all those people driven by a passion for the product (the

Staging a Spectacular World-Class Mega Event: The FIFA World Cup in South Africa

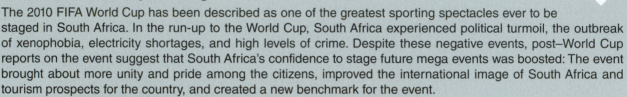

By Babs Surujlal, South Africa
North-West University, Gauteng

The 2010 FIFA World Cup has been described as one of the greatest sporting spectacles ever to be staged in South Africa. In the run-up to the World Cup, South Africa experienced political turmoil, the outbreak of xenophobia, electricity shortages, and high levels of crime. Despite these negative events, post–World Cup reports on the event suggest that South Africa's confidence to stage future mega events was boosted: The event brought about more unity and pride among the citizens, improved the international image of South Africa and tourism prospects for the country, and created a new benchmark for the event.

Despite some negative events prior to the 2010 World Cup in South Africa, the event was deemed a success due to the careful planning of event organizers.

event), and the experience is the relationship between the ticket buyer and the event itself (Deckard, 2005). Customer service, guest relations, and fan services are all terms used to describe the relationship that exists between the event (or facility) management and the people who attend the event.

The customers, or guests, are the fuel that the sport and entertainment industry relies on. Without patrons, there would be neither events nor facilities to house them. But the guests who attend sport and entertainment events are products of a society that has come to expect immediate results or instant gratification. Everyone knows that most businesses must have repeat customers to be profitable. In the same way, event managers depend on repeat customers to produce a profit. Thus, to guarantee repeat customers, event and facility managers must listen to their guests and respond

The success ars of debate, brainstorming, and planning. To stage the event, planners had to consider various factors to attract and satisfy spectators, fans, and tourists. Among the factors considered were marketing of the event, safety and security, quality of services, travel, cuisine, ease of obtaining tickets, side attractions, travel brochures, fan fests, volunteers, and affordability.

International perceptions regarding safety and security in South Africa prior to the World Cup were negative; therefore, aggressive marketing strategies to assure potential visitors of their safety were needed. In planning the event, organizers had to ensure that various modes of transport were available and accessible for travel between airports and hotels and hotels and stadiums, as well as for trips unrelated to the event. Ease of purchasing tickets also had to be considered, as this would have a direct bearing on attendance figures. Planners also had to consider the affordability of the event, not only for the locals but also for international visitors. Carefully planned information brochures clearly highlighting interesting places to visit on days between matches, possible related costs, and travelling time had to be available for tourists. These side attractions provided potentially positive opportunities to promote the country and encourage return visits. The quality of services in terms of cuisine and treatment of visitors was an important factor that also warranted consideration. Planners faced the dilemma of having to select approximately 18,000 volunteers from about 70,000 applications. This required careful screening of personnel who met the requirements of the job. Proper planning for fan fests within easy proximity to fans and spectators, giant high-quality screens, and sound and lighting to provide spectators with a near real-life experience of the event also had to be in place.

Although many people were pessimistic about South Africa's capabilities of staging this event, comments from those who were involved in many of the previous soccer World Cups indicate that the event was as good as the most successful World Cups ever. The number of visitors to the country far exceeded the anticipated number, the number of attendees to the event was the third highest ever recorded for the World Cup, and the TV viewership was the highest ever.

International Learning Activity #1

Using South Africa as an example, provide a detailed description of the factors you would consider when planning a mega event in the United States. What factors are similar between the two countries and which ones are different? Why is this the case?

International Learning Activity #2

Outline the steps you would take to ensure the safety of fans and spectators at an international sport mega event such as the World Cup. How might these steps differ based on the country in which the event was taking place?

International Learning Activity #3

Describe how you would go about attracting and retaining volunteers for an international mega event such as the World Cup. What duties are volunteers needed for at such events?

effectively to their concerns. These managers must adopt a customer-centered business philosophy because, as we all know, putting on an event without an audience is difficult. Although most facility and event professionals would assert that the customer is always right, "more important than serving one person is serving all the people" (Deckard, 2005, p. 2).

To enhance this process, sport organizations can use social media to gauge what consumers are saying about their product and their experience while at the stadium. In many instances, this can include topics such as congestion at the event, ease of product delivery, and other experiences while at the stadium. By taking a proactive approach to monitoring feedback, sport organizations can ensure that they develop loyal consumers who will maximize word-of-mouth initiatives.

Social Media and Sport Facility and Event Management

With the evolution of social media, sport managers have been provided the opportunity to enhance their efficiency in areas throughout organizations. This is true in facility and event management as well. With the two-way communication offered in social media outlets such as Twitter, managers have the ability to seek feedback from consumers who attend their events. In an article in *Street & Smith's SportsBusiness Journal*, one of the chapter contributors to this textbook (Sutton, 2012) explained that many top organizations outside of sports use social media as a strategy to get feedback to enhance their operations. For example, he noted that companies such as Orbitz and Southwest have used Twitter to find complaints about their product. As a result, they have taken a proactive approach to correcting issues with their operations to build customer loyalty.

As a consumer-based industry, sport organizations have the same ability to utilize social media to gauge their effectiveness in event- and facility-related areas. For example, when assessing the different elements of the stadium experience, sport organizations can hire a social media tracking service that gathers and provides evaluative feedback in areas that will improve the customer experience. In addition, Sutton further suggested that organizations can also hire a social media coordinator or intern to disseminate information about the stadium experience. Intercollegiate athletic departments have used this strategy with current employees when updating followers with changes to the event.

ALCOHOL POLICIES

A potential liability exists if intoxicated patrons create dangerous situations for themselves and others. Some people argue that revenue generated from beer sales is worth the risk, and some facilities would find it difficult to generate a profit without beer sales. Others have determined that the increased revenue produced by selling alcohol does not outweigh the liabilities. Even at college stadiums, administrators have found ways to serve alcohol in enclosed spaces such as suites because it is a desirable element for consumers. Although the controversy continues, alcohol probably will continue to be a part of many sporting events, and facility managers must continue to devise tactics to reduce the risks created by alcohol consumption.

Fan behavior at stadiums has become an increasing concern at all major sport venues. In 2008, the NFL released a fan code of conduct in response to numerous complaints from fans. Unruly fans who cause a disruption at the game can be ejected. Also, intoxicated fans can be asked to leave the game or can even be denied access into the stadium. In fact, for certain offenses, season ticket holders can lose their seats if they (or their guests) are ejected. On top of this, the NFL is now requiring fans who get ejected from a game to take a four-hour online course before they are permitted to come back to the facility again (Rovell, 2012).

CROWD MANAGEMENT

A facility or event manager needs a crowd management plan even when managing an event with a small number of spectators. Whether employed at a small high school basketball game, a local YMCA, or an NCAA Division I Softball Championship, the facility or event manager needs a crowd management plan because the manager must strive to provide a safe and enjoyable environment. The crowd control plan must be an integral element of a larger risk management plan. The components of such a plan are staff training, emergency planning, accessibility for spectators with disabilities, procedures for ejecting disruptive people, an efficient communication system, and effective signage.

> *Staff training.* The first component of an effective crowd control plan is training competent staff to carry it out. Management at some facilities choose to use their own staff to conduct crowd control duties. This approach is known as **in-house** security or crowd management. With in-house operations, the management must develop staff training protocol to ensure they are responding to the many critical areas discussed in this chapter. Given the in-depth nature of these tasks, management at other facilities outsource crowd management services to independent contractors.

in-house—Services provided by the facility staff.

> *Emergency planning.* An emergency plan is the second component of an effective crowd control plan. The intent of an emergency plan is to ensure that minor incidents do not become major incidents and that major incidents do not become fatal. Emergencies take many forms, such as medical problems (e.g., life-threatening issues, minor injuries), severe weather (e.g., lightning, tornadoes), natural disasters (e.g., earthquakes, floods), fires, bomb threats, power losses, and, in today's society, terrorist activities. Managers must not only design and implement an emergency plan but also practice it, because the courts will ask for documentation about when the plan was practiced. Because of the terrorist threat, managers at several venues use practice sessions to test the ability of their emergency services during a mock attack. In the hope of helping a wide range of sport organizations prepare for a disaster, the National Center of Spectator Sports Safety and Security has created a simulation software program called SportEvac that allows sport organizations to work through mock disaster situations. In addition to mimicking threat situations, the program allows facility managers to face a wide range of situations (e.g., full capacity stadium, emergency lights fail) to help prepare evacuation plans for stadiums ("SportEvac," 2012). In light of the 2013 terrorist bombing at the Boston Marathon, such training is essential.

> *Ensuring accessibility for spectators with disabilities.* The third component of an effective crowd control plan should address the procedures necessary to ensure facility accessibility for all citizens. Congress passed the **Americans with Disabilities Act (ADA)** in 1992. The ADA has had a major effect on the design of sport and entertainment venues. Sport and entertainment event managers must be familiar with the ADA because its various requirements pertain to facility features such as signage, restrooms, telephones, parking, and shower stalls. Furthermore, event managers must also develop plans for the evacuation of spectators with disabilities or special needs.

Americans with Disabilities Act (ADA)—Legislation that protects people with disabilities from discrimination. Specific to sport facilities, the law states that managers must provide "reasonable accommodations" for people with disabilities (Disability Resources, 2013).

> *Procedures for ejecting disruptive people.* The fourth component of an effective crowd control plan addresses the procedures necessary to eject disruptive, unruly, or intoxicated patrons. The ejection duties should remain the responsibility of trained crowd control staff and, in some jurisdictions, police officers, sheriff's department personnel, or state troopers. These individuals must understand the concepts of the reasonably prudent person and excessive force, and they should understand that they might be sued for negligence if they eject patrons incorrectly. Ushers should not undertake these duties if they are not trained in crowd control procedures. Removing disruptive or intoxicated fans will provide a safer environment for the remaining spectators and help protect the facility or event manager from potential litigation (Ammon & Unruh, 2013).

> *An efficient communication system.* An efficient communication network is the fifth component of an effective crowd control plan. Communication is critical in providing spectator safety, enjoyment, and security. The use of a centralized area for representatives from each group involved in the management of an event (i.e., law enforcement, maintenance, medical, and security) will facilitate communication and improve decision making.

> *Effective signage.* The creation and use of proper signage is the sixth and final component of crowd control. Informational and directional signs build a support network between fans and facility management staff. Spectators appreciate being treated fairly and, if previously informed, normally abide by facility directives pertaining to no-smoking sections, alcohol policies, and prohibited items. Directional signs have several important uses. As spectators approach the facility, road signs can indicate the correct exits and provide relevant parking information. Other signs serve to indicate the correct gate or portal and direct ticket-buying patrons to the box office. Signage will help facility patrons locate concession stands, first-aid rooms, telephones, and restrooms. Informational signs regarding prohibited items assist patrons in making decisions before entry (Ammon & Unruh, 2013).

Postevent Tasks

After the event has occurred, several additional items need to be completed before the event becomes history and the event coordinator can go home. The postevent procedures include activities such as event cleanup, **settlement**, and evaluation of the event.

settlement—Reconciling the expenses and revenues of an event and dividing the profits according to a contracted arrangement.

EVENT CLEANUP

After the event is over and the crowd has filed out, the equipment used in the event is gathered up and put away or stored in trucks, and cleanup of the facility commences. Another entire day is usually set aside for the load-out.

EVALUATING THE EVENT

documentation—Detailed records that describe the event.

Immediately after the event, the management team evaluates the process. Documentation of the entire process is critical, not only for protection against subsequent litigation but also for reference in planning future events.

Critical Thinking in Sport Facility and Event Management

Many aspects of ethical and moral conduct involve consideration and debate of possible actions and outcomes. One feature of critical thinking is the systematic evaluation of various arguments and positions. These discussions help managers weigh possible alternatives and their requisite outcomes. For example, consider the following event and facility management scenario about fans at a university basketball arena. At this university in the southern part of the United States, a fan at a basketball game stands and displays a poster with a Confederate flag. The flag, to some, represents the glory and pride of southern residents. To others, it represents a symbol of slavery and racism. It might be good to consider how you would go about handling a situation such as this to ensure that you maintain a safe environment at an event.

PORTFOLIO

Complete the critical thinking portfolio activity in the WSG, consulting as needed the "Critical Thinking Questions" sidebar in chapter 1.

Ethics in Sport Facility and Event Management

All employee-training programs should include a discussion of the role that professional ethics plays in facility and event management. Ethical behavior is not the sole province of employees. Most sport facilities have standards by which patrons are expected to comply. For example, the Seattle Seahawks have created a code of conduct that is committed to creating a safe, comfortable, and enjoyable experience for guests. To achieve this, their organization has created a list of behaviors that are not acceptable under any circumstances:

> Behavior that is unruly, disruptive, or illegal in nature
> Intoxication or other signs of alcohol or substance impairment that results in irresponsible behavior
> Foul or abusive language or obscene gestures
> Interference with the progress of the game (including throwing objects on the field)
> Failing to follow instructions of stadium personnel
> Verbal or physical harassment of opposing team fans, stadium guests, or staff members
> Smoking or tobacco use on CenturyLink Field Property

Fans who do not abide by them can be ejected from the stadium and have future ticket privileges revoked (Fan Code of Conduct, 2013).

PORTFOLIO

Complete the ethical issues portfolio activity in the WSG, consulting as needed the "Guidelines for Making Ethical Decisions" sidebar in chapter 1.

Summary

The FIFA World Cup, the Olympic Games, concerts, and high school track meets have two common denominators: They take place in some type of facility, and they are events. Given that they have these two traits, they must have people to manage them. However, as mentioned in the chapter, sport organizations can choose two options when carrying out an event. While some choose to keep things in-house, the management of many sport and entertainment events and facilities is being outsourced to private management companies. These private entities have been successful in raising the profit margins of many sport and public assembly facilities across the United States.

To ensure a successful event, facility directors must perform several important tasks. They need to know and understand how these tasks relate to the successful completion of every event. Scheduling and booking an event begin the overall process, and a cost analysis is critical in these initial operations. After the facility director has decided that the event will be held, the necessary contracts need to be signed, and the event coordinator must create and communicate a work order to the others on the event management team. Items such as seating arrangements, crowd management, alcohol policies, settlement, and event evaluation must be carried out for an event to be successful.

The number of facilities has grown significantly in recent years, and many of these facilities schedule sport and entertainment events with global implications. Worldwide terrorist attacks have changed the facility and event management industry dramatically. In addition, some areas of sport have downsized because of factors such as changes in the economy, corporate mergers, and business failures. Because of these trends, the future of facility and event management is not as clear as once imagined. Slower revenue growth has affected profit margins. This has had a domino effect on facility and event management that needs to be consistently monitored moving forward. In addition, sport organizations must also be aware of the ways that they can utilize technology to enhance the experience provided to customers who attend their events.

Review Questions

1. What is the nearest major single-purpose facility in your area? List the personnel who would be involved in the management at this type of facility.

2. What are some of the nearby multipurpose facilities in your area? How would the management of these facilities differ from the single-purpose facility you identified in question 1?

3. Currently, several companies privately manage more than 300 facilities nationally and internationally. What are some of the companies near you?

4. In reference to the previous question, why would a facility choose to contract with one of these companies? What are the potential benefits of contracting with these companies?

5. What is the purpose of a work order? Who compiles the work order?

6. Why do the management team members need to meet to evaluate the overall production after the event ends? Why should the team complete all the proper documentation at this meeting?

7. Why is employing trained people to reduce facility risks a less expensive alternative than reacting to potential disasters or litigation without such people? How can much of this litigation be avoided?

8. Why is it important for sport event and facility managers to develop proper ethical guidelines and critical thinking skills?

9. What role can technology play in the event management process to ensure that consumers are enjoying their experience at the facility?

References

Ammon, R., Jr., Southall, R., & Nagel, M.S. (2010). *Sport facility management: Organizing events and mitigating risks* (2nd ed.). Morgantown, WV: Fitness Information Technology.

Ammon, R., Jr., & Unruh, N. (2013). Crowd management. In D.J. Cotton & J. Wolohan (Eds.), *Law for recreation and sport managers* (6th ed., pp. 328–339). Dubuque, IA: Kendall/Hunt.

Deckard, L. (2005, January 19). Keynoter stresses customer service to ticketing professionals. *VenuesToday*, 4(3), 2–3.

Disability resources. (2013). *United States Department of Labor.* Retrieved from www.dol.gov/dol/topic/disability/ada.htm

Fan code of conduct. (2013). *Official site of the Seattle Seahawks.* Retrieved from www.seahawks.com/gameday/fan-code-of-conduct.html

Myers, S.L. (2014, January 27). Russians debate sticker price of Sochi Games. *The New York Times.* Retrieved from www.nytimes.com/2014/01/27/world/europe/russians-debate-sticker-price-of-sochi-games.html? r=0

Rovell, D. (2012, August 17). *NFL gets serious about fan conduct.* ESPN.com. Retrieved from http://espn.go.com/nfl/story/_/id/8278886/nfl-require-ejected-fans-take-online-fan-conduct-course

Sawyer, T.H. (Ed.). (2013). *Facility planning and design for health, physical activity, recreation, and sport* (13th ed.). Urbana, IL: Sagamore.

Schrotenboer, B. (2012, November 7). Will new mayor work with Chargers on new stadium? *USA TODAY.* Retrieved from www.usatoday.com/story/sports/nfl/2012/11/07/san-diego-chargers-mayor-stadium/1690099

SportEvac: Choreographing a stadium stampede. (2012). *Department of Homeland Security.* Retrieved from www.dhs.gov/sportevac-choreographing-stadium-stampede

Sochi costs $51 billion, $49 billion more than Salt Lake City Olympics. (2014, January 27). *New York Press.* Retrieved from http://nypost.com/2014/01/27/sochi-olympics-to-cost-51b-59b-more-than-salt-lake-city-games/

Steinbach, P. (2004, August). Special operations. *Athletic Business, 28*(8), 24–28.

Sutton, B. (2012, February 13). Sport organizations must deal with feedback more effectively. *Street & Smith's SportsBusiness Journal.* Retrieved from http://m.sportsbusinessdaily.com/Journal/Issues/2012/02/13/Opinion/Sutton-Impact.aspx

Warshaw, A. (2004, March). Making a stand. *Stadia*, 12–14.

PART IV

CURRENT CHALLENGES IN SPORT MANAGEMENT

A critical step in the process of becoming a responsible and effective manager of sport enterprises is recognizing the significance of sport as a major social and increasingly global institution. The first three chapters in this section provide the foundation for understanding the challenges presented by legal, social, and international aspects of sport. An appreciation of these facets of sport will increase the likelihood that you will make wise managerial decisions within the context of the broad social and global environment in which sporting activities occur. Chapter 20, the final chapter of the book, deals with research.

Anita Moorman, Chris Reynolds, and Samuel Olson address sport management's legal issues in chapter 17. The authors introduce basic concepts related to legislation affecting the management of sport in the United States. After presenting a brief introduction to the U.S. legal system, the authors discuss the influence of the U.S. Constitution on sport management and the effects of federal legislation, explicitly the Americans with Disabilities Act and Title IX of the Education Amendments Act. Then they examine state legal systems, including tort law, negligence, intentional torts, and contracts. For their social media sidebar, Moorman, Reynolds, and Olson include a discussion on the Federal Trade Commission's guidelines regarding endorsements promoted through social media. The authors conclude the chapter with a discussion of legal challenges that await prospective sport managers. The professional featured in this chapter is Jill Bodensteiner, the associate athletics director

for legal affairs and compliance at the University of Notre Dame. The topic of this chapter's international sidebar gives an introduction to sport law issues in China. Ma Hongjun, a sport law expert from the China University of Political Science and Law in Beijing, contributed this essay.

Chapter 18 focuses on the role of sport sociology in the management of sporting activities. Nicole LaVoi and Mary Jo Kane open with a discussion of the social significance of sport and then examine possible benefits of sport, such as its ability to socialize participants and unify people. Next, the authors present several examples of the darker side of sport, including sexism, homophobia and heterosexism, and racism. LaVoi and Kane, who include in their chapter a sidebar on the use of social media to market and promote sportswomen, conclude the chapter with a discussion of how sport can serve as a vehicle for social transformation and how you can apply your knowledge of sport sociology in the management of sport. Carley Knox, the director of business operations for the Minnesota Lynx (WNBA), is the sport industry practitioner profiled in this chapter. The international sidebar in this chapter is an essay on the media coverage in Canada provided to athletes with disabilities. Melinda Maika and Karen Danylchuk—from Western University in London, Ontario—contributed the essay.

In chapter 19, Ted Fay, Luisa Velez, and Lucie Thibault first define international sport. Next, the authors analyze the international growth of sport and provide examples to illustrate this phenomenon: changes to the Olympic Games, expanded opportunities for women, the redefinition of international sport, increased recruitment and marketing efforts at the international level, and increased participation in international sport by countries with emerging economies. They also discuss various current issues (e.g., corporate sponsorship, drug testing and arbitration, assistive devices, relocation of sporting goods manufacturing companies) in international sport. The authors' social media sidebar focuses on the increasing role that platforms such as YouTube, Facebook, Twitter, Google+, Foursquare, and Weibo have played in the publicity surrounding the Olympic Games and the Paralympic Games. After presenting the knowledge and skills necessary for a successful career in international sport, the authors conclude the chapter with a discussion of several trends that will affect international sport. The sport industry professional featured in this chapter is Kellie A. Cavalier, the event operations manager for USA Rugby. Lastly, the staging of hallmark sporting events in Brazil is the topic of this chapter's international sidebar. Ricardo João Sonoda-Nunes from the Federal University of Paraná (Brazil) contributed this essay.

Chapter 20 addresses research in sport management, a subject that sport managers should master in order to be more effective and efficient in their segment of the sport industry. The better sport managers become at interpreting and evaluating research, the less likely they will be to waste their time and their organization's resources on unsound suggestions. As a future sport manager, if you understand research, you will be able to make decisions grounded in the analysis of relevant data rather than depending on hunches or simply perpetuating tradition. The earlier you learn to evaluate research, the more meaningful those research article assignments will be later on. Moreover, as you develop greater skill in evaluating research, you will be more prepared to make the difficult decisions that surely will come your way as a sport manager. Therefore, chapter 20 provides an introduction to sport management research. Jess Dixon and Wendy Frisby begin their examination of this topic by explaining why asking good research questions and getting accurate answers are critical to the success of sport management ventures. The authors, after providing a sidebar on social media and sport management research,

discuss why sport managers should understand research and explain the academic and commercial aspects of sport management research. They then examine several key research concepts—ways of knowing, science and pseudoscience, basic and applied research, quantitative and qualitative data, research design, and validity and reliability of research instruments. The authors next detail the major issues influencing sport management research. They conclude the chapter by discussing the future of research conducted by sport managers, who will need research skills to operate successfully in a knowledge-based economy. The focus of the sport industry practitioner profile is Sydney Millar, the national program director for the Canadian Association for the Advancement of Women and Sport and Physical Activity. The international sidebar in this chapter examines researching the theory of authentic leadership in the sport industry. Shane Gibson and Lesley Ferkins—both from Unitec in Auckland, New Zealand—contributed this essay.

Before you take additional sport management courses and then enter the field, you are encouraged to become familiar with the topics (i.e., sport law, sport sociology, international sport, and sport management research) and issues presented in the four chapters of this final section of the textbook. For instance, think about its final chapter. As you progress through the curriculum at your college or university, some of your instructors will require you to write reports on research articles published in the sport management literature. Instructors assign these reports because they know that when you become a practicing professional, one of your obligations to your employer, your employees, the consumers of your products, and the public will involve being familiar with the research in your field. A problem with these assignments, however, is that students are seldom familiar with why people conduct research, how they conduct it, or how to evaluate the published product. Just as the preceding three chapters will provide you with a basic understanding of three current challenges (or opportunities) in sport management (i.e., law, sociology, and globalization), chapter 20 will give you a basic understanding of research concepts. This will assist you in your current educational pursuits and equip you for effective decision making as you commence your career as a sport manager.

For More Information

Professional and Scholarly Associations, Institutes, and Organizations

Academy of Legal Studies in Business

American Alliance for Health, Physical Education, Recreation and Dance (AAHPERD)

American Sociological Association (ASA)

Association Femmes Mixité Sports

Australia and New Zealand Sports Law Association

Australian WomenSport & Recreation Association (AWRA)

Black Entertainment and Sports Lawyers Association (BESLA)

Canadian Association for the Advancement of Women and Sport and Physical Activity (CAAWS)

Cerebral Palsy International Sports and Recreation Association

Court of Arbitration for Sport

European Paralympic Committee

European Women and Sport (EWS)

International Association of Physical Education and Sport for Girls and Women

International Association of Sports Law

International Committee of Sports for the Deaf/Deaflympics

International Cricket Council (ICC)

International Paralympic Committee (IPC)

International Working Group on Women and Sport

International World Games Association (IWGA)

LA84 Foundation

Maccabiah Games

National Center for Catastrophic Sport Injury Research

National Center on Health, Physical Activity and Disability (NCHPAD)

National Sports Law Institute

North American Society for the Sociology of Sport (NASSS)

Professional Football Researchers Association (PFRA)

SportAccord (International Sports Federations)

Sport and Recreation Law Association (SRLA)

Sport Business Research Network

The Sport, Health and Physical Activity Research and Policy Center (SHARP) for Women and Girls

Sport in Society

Sport Research Intelligence Sportive (SIRC)

Sports Lawyers Association

Statistics in Sports (section of the American Statistical Association)

STRI (formerly Sports Turf Research Institute)

Tucker Center for Research on Girls & Women in Sport

WomenSport International (WSI)

Women's Sports Foundation (WSF)

Women's Sports and Fitness Foundation (WSFF)

Youth Olympic Games

Professional and Scholarly Publications

American Business Law Journal

Catalyst eNewsletter

Culture, Sport, Society

DePaul Journal of Sports Law & Contemporary Problems

Entertainment and Sports Law Journal

Entertainment and Sports Lawyer

European Journal for Sport and Society

Florida Entertainment, Art & Sport Law Journal

Human Relations

International Gambling Studies

International Review for the Sociology of Sport

International Sports Law Journal

International Sports Studies

Journal of Business Research

Journal of ICHPER-SD (International Council for Health, Physical Education, Recreation, Sport & Dance)

Journal of the Legal Aspects of Sport

Journal of Quantitative Analysis in Sports

Journal of Sport & Social Issues

Journal of Sport Behavior

Journal of Sports Law & Contemporary Problems

Legal Issues in College Athletics

Marquette Sports Law Review

Paralympian: The Official Magazine of the Paralympic Movement

Quest

Research Quarterly for Exercise and Sport

Seton Hall Journal of Sports and Entertainment Law

Sex Roles: A Journal of Research

Soccer and Society

Sociology of Sport Journal

Sport, Education and Society

Sport in Society

The Sport Journal

The Sport Psychologist

Sports and Entertainment Litigation Reporter

Sports Law Forum at Fordham University School of Law

Sports Lawyer

The Sports Lawyers Journal

Sports, Parks and Recreation Law Reporter

Texas Review of Entertainment & Sports Law

University of Miami Entertainment and Sports Law Review

Villanova Sports & Entertainment Law Journal

Virginia Sports and Entertainment Law Journal

Willamette Sports Law Journal

Women in Sport and Physical Activity Journal

HISTORICAL MOMENTS

1922 *Federal Base Ball Club of Baltimore v. National League of Professional Base Ball Clubs* established MLB antitrust exemption

1938 *Pittsburgh Athletic Co. v. KQV* established baseball clubs' control of broadcast rights to a game

1961 Sports Broadcasting Act permitted sport leagues to pool their television rights package

1972 *Flood v. Kuhn*—Curt Flood (St. Louis Cardinals) challenged MLB's reserve clause

1987 Civil Rights Restoration Act overturned *Grove City v. Bell* (1984) ruling

1988 *NCAA v. Tarkanian*—U.S. Supreme Court held that the NCAA is not a state actor

1992 Professional and Amateur Sports Protection Act banned sports betting in all but a few states

1995 *Vernonia School District v. Acton*—U.S. Supreme Court upheld constitutionality of random drug testing of high school student athletes

1996 *Cohen v. Brown University*—class action Title IX lawsuit filed

1998 *Fraser v. Major League Soccer*—U.S. District Court ruling found that MLS' single-entity structure did not violate the Sherman Antitrust Act

2001 *PGA Tour v. Martin*—Supreme Court ruled that Casey Martin, a professional golfer with a disability, could use a golf cart in PGA Tour events

2004 *Clarett v. NFL*—Court ruled in favor of the NFL's age restriction rule

2007 *C.B.C. Distribution and Marketing, Inc. v. MLB Advanced Media*—Fantasy sports leagues won right to use MLB player statistics without license

2007 *TSSAA v. Brentwood Academy*—U.S. Supreme Court upheld TSSAA rules limiting high school sports recruiting

2008 *Borden v. East Brunswick*—Court upheld school district policy prohibiting coach's participation in student-led prayer

2008 Court of Arbitration for Sport ruled that South African sprinter Oscar Pistorius was eligible to compete with leg prosthesis in IAAF-sanctioned events

2010 Lawsuits filed by more than 4,000 former NFL players against league on basis of concussions and player safety were consolidated in federal court; in 2013, the NFL agreed to settle lawsuits for US$765 million

2013 NCAA Football 14 was the last NCAA-endorsed video game. Citing litigation costs as a key factor, NCAA decided to not renew contract with EA Sports

17

LEGAL CONSIDERATIONS IN SPORT MANAGEMENT

Anita M. Moorman ❭ R. Christopher Reynolds ❭ Samuel Olson

LEARNING OBJECTIVES

❭ Identify select legal issues affecting sport management stakeholders, operations, and organizations.

❭ Explain the American judicial system and its application to the sport industry.

❭ Identify situations involving the management or marketing of sport in which legal issues influence the decision-making process of those in leadership positions.

❭ Describe legal concepts in a sport context with matters involving Title IX legislation, tort law, and the Americans with Disabilities Act (ADA).

❭ Discuss the fundamental elements of contract law and apply them in a sport management context.

❭ Engage in critical thinking and problem solving regarding how the law can influence sport management decisions.

❭ Apply systematic guidelines to ethical dilemmas involving legal concepts in sport.

Key Terms

common law
constituencies
due process
precedent
proximate cause

restatements
stare decisis
statutes
tort

GET A JOB

Continue on your journey in sport management by going to the web study guide (WSG) at www.HumanKinetics. com/ContemporarySportManagement. Check out the job opportunities and consider the skills and experiences that can help you succeed in sport management.

constituencies—For purposes of this chapter, constituencies are any people influenced or effected by a particular decision.

As you learned in chapter 1, sport managers make numerous decisions each day. These decisions will be of various levels of importance and difficulty. All of them, however, require the sport manager to engage in a process of decision making. The manager's decisions are likely to affect numerous **constituencies**, including coworkers, supervisors, the media, spectators, and participants, just to name a few. All these groups are entitled to hold sport managers accountable for their decisions. Chapter 1 also introduced you to the value of critical thinking skills in responding to constituencies who challenge decisions that have been made and who may demand justification for chosen strategies. Now that you have acquired a fundamental understanding of the importance of critical thinking and have learned to ask the core critical questions, you can move on to a deeper understanding of how the law affects both your decision-making process and the results of your decisions.

This chapter will introduce you to situations requiring sport managers to examine how legal principles can influence decision making. We will introduce selected legal issues, discuss the situations in which these legal issues arise, and present questions for you to ponder. This chapter introduces the law and the legal system of the United States. You should keep in mind while reading this chapter, however, that as the sport industry continues to expand into the global marketplace, international law affects many sport organizations. Besides introducing the legal areas noted earlier, the chapter provides analyses of how the law intersects with sport on the amateur (e.g., interscholastic, intercollegiate) and professional levels.

Basics of Law

Black's Law Dictionary, a useful resource in legal research, defines the law as "the aggregate of legislation, judicial precedents and accepted legal principles" (Black, 2004). (See the sidebar on this page for the various sources of law.) The law is basically an accumulation of rules and regulations that govern our behavior. Failure to abide by the defined rules of law may result in either civil or criminal penalty. In the United States, the federal government and state governments are subject to a constitution. Both the United States Congress and state legislatures enact **statutes**, which create the need for government agencies to write or promulgate rules and regulations to implement the enacted laws. The courts are then required to interpret the statutes or rules and fill in any gaps left by legislatures.

statutes—Enactments made by a legislature and expressed in a formal document.

The American judicial system is divided into distinctly separate federal and state systems. The United States Constitution is the supreme law of the land. It governs conduct of the federal and state governments, as well as providing for the fundamental rights of private citizens. Each of the 50 states similarly has a state constitution that governs the conduct of the state government and protects citizens of that state. As noted previously, Congress and 50 state legislatures also enact laws (i.e., statutes) that address issues ranging from enforceability of contracts to product liability to the registration of trademarks. Each of the 50 states has its own court system, as does the federal government. These court systems, both federal and state, are hierarchical in structure. The highest court is usually a supreme or superior court. An intermediate appellate court is at a middle level, and a district or trial court is at the bottom. Most cases originate at the trial or district court level and work their way up through the court system. It can take years for a case to move through all levels of the court system.

precedent—A legal case establishing a principle or rule that a court may need to adopt when deciding subsequent cases with similar issues or facts. The term may also refer to the collective body of case law that a court should consider when interpreting the law.

stare decisis—Literally means "to stand by things decided." This principle expresses the notion that prior court decisions must be recognized as precedents, according to case law, and followed accordingly.

A fundamental premise of the law includes the concepts of **precedent** and **stare decisis**. The doctrine of stare decisis is the legal principle that compels courts to follow a previous decision or precedent when deciding a subsequent case in the same district or jurisdiction (Connors, 2009). A precedent is simply a decided case that furnishes a basis for determining later cases involving similar facts or issues (Black, 2004). These two concepts, precedent and stare decisis, work together to provide predictability and consistency to

Sources of Law

> Constitutions: United States Constitution and individual state constitutions
> Statutes: Federal laws enacted by Congress—United States Code (USC), state laws enacted by state legislatures
> Administrative law: Rules and regulations created by federal agencies—Code of Federal Regulations (CFR), rules and regulations created by state agencies
> Common law: Federal and state court decisions

judicial decisions. This predictability and consistency are important because those bound by the law are then able to make sound decisions and conduct themselves and their affairs in accordance with the law. For example, consider a situation in which a football player accidentally injures another player during a game and the injured player threatens to sue the first player. If players had to worry about being sued every time another player was injured, many sport competitions would probably never occur. But the majority rule as established by numerous judicial decisions provides that a player is liable to another player for an injury only if the player causing the injury acted recklessly (i.e., with conscious indifference to an extreme risk). The reckless standard is a much higher standard for determining liability than a traditional negligence standard (i.e., failing to act reasonably). Thus, the concepts of precedent and stare decisis would lead to the conclusion that a player is not liable to another player for accidental or negligent injuries. This precedent helps guide how sport participants conduct themselves and how sport organizations manage sport contests. Players, coaches, and event organizers in the sport industry can predict this judicial outcome because courts will rely on precedents when facing the same or a similar situation.

The law is dynamic and works to bring order to societal norms (Koller, 2006). As a result, legislatures adopt statutes reflecting, in part, the desires of those whom they represent. It should be no surprise that many of these adopted laws affect sport managers, sporting events, and sport organizations either directly or indirectly with the intent of better serving society as a whole. For example, many states have adopted the Uniform Athlete Agents Act (UAAA), which provides protection for student-athletes from unscrupulous sport agents and establishes uniform agent registration and disclosure requirements. Specifically, the UAAA identifies several provisions that must be included in an agency contract. For example, a couple of these provisions are language that requires notice to an educational institution after an agency contract has been entered into with one of its student-athletes and the right of the student-athlete to cancel an agency contract within 14 days after it is signed. Provisions of this kind in the contract between the student-athlete and agent can have the result of protecting institutions from harsh National Collegiate Athletic Association (NCAA) penalties and allowing student-athletes to terminate an agreement with an agent that effectively exploits them. Besides issues such as the illegal actions of agents, other societal influences and behaviors have spawned statutes governing concussion safety standards, steroid use, gambling, drug testing, and discrimination in athletics.

The next section of this chapter provides a basic overview of significant legal principles in the United States that have a direct or at least tangential effect on various decisions (e.g., managerial), activities (e.g., marketing), and personnel (e.g., athletics directors) in the sport industry.

WEB

Go to the WSG and complete the web search activity, which helps you identify and research laws that affect student, Olympic, and amateur athletes.

An Introduction to Chinese Sport Law

By Ma Hongjun, China
China University of Political Science and Law, Beijing

Professor Ma Hongjun, the author of this international sidebar, presents his research at an international conference on sports law.

In China, the term *sport law* means the summary of a series of legal norms, including administrative regulations, local codes, and regulations such as The Sports Law of the People's Republic of China and the National Health Regulations, as well as relevant clauses in constitutional law and common law. International and national sport organizations' constitutions, rules and contracts are also covered in sport law scholars' research. In China, the China Law Society Sports Law Seminar, which was founded in 2005, is the supreme academic institution in this field. Experts in sports circles, jurisprudential circles, and the legal profession have all joined. The Sports Law of the People's Republic of China was published on August 29, 1995. It included eight chapters covering general principles, social sports, school physical education, competitive

U.S. Constitution

The U.S. Constitution is the supreme law in the United States and is regarded as the document that provides the greatest source of individual rights to American citizens. The Constitution is made up of a preamble, seven articles, and 27 amendments. The first three articles of the Constitution establish and describe the functions of the legislative, executive, and judicial branches of government. The remaining articles address matters pertaining to states' powers and limits (Article IV), process for amending the Constitution (Article V), issues related to public officials taking an oath to support the constitution (Article VI), and the steps necessary to ratify the Constitution (Article VII).

Over the years, several amendments have been added to the Constitution. The first 10 amendments to the Constitution, commonly referred to as the Bill of Rights, were added in 1791. In short, the Bill of Rights preserves the basic and fundamental rights of the people. Subsequently, 17 amendments have been added over time. In total, there are 27 amendments to the U.S. Constitution.

Chemerinsky (2006) noted that the U.S. Constitution limits and empowers American government. The legal scholar adds that besides providing a framework for government, the Constitution protects individual rights by limiting governing authority. In the sport industry, such limitations by the U.S. Constitution have been evident. A number of sports, sports social organization, supporting conditions, and legal liability. Some issues were left out, such as a sport arbitration system, which does not currently exist in China.

In preparations for China to host the 2008 Beijing Olympic Games, the Olympic Symbol Conservation Regulation was passed on January 30, 2002. This was the first time special symbols were given legal protection in China. Next, antidoping regulation passed on December 31, 2003. This regulation contributed to the country's antidoping stance and provided a strengthened management system for dealing with doping incidents. The National Health Regulations passed on August 19, 2009, and it was an important supplement to The Sports Law of the People's Republic of China.

A practical example of sport law in China involves the Olympic Games. The IOC requires host countries to demonstrate that they will provide protection for Olympic intellectual property. In response, China enacted the Olympic Intellectual Property Protection Rules (OIPPR) in order to fully show the commitment of the Chinese government for this issue. The Chinese Olympic Committee sued the Golden Taste Food Company from Shantou for the company's illegal use of the Olympic rings logo on their packaging from 1996 to 1998. Beijing Higher People's Court, using the OIPPR, entered a judgment that Golden Taste immediately stop using the Olympic rings logo and ordered the company to apologize to the Chinese Olympic Committee on the China Sports Daily and Beijing TV station and other media outlets. The Golden Taste Company was also ordered to pay 5,000,000 yuan (approximately US$800,000) to the Chinese Olympic Committee for its illegal use of the Olympic logo.

International Learning Activity #1

A sport arbitration system has not yet been formed in China. Conduct an Internet search of the sport arbitration systems that exist in other countries, and then make recommendations for how China could build its own version.

International Learning Activity #2

Examine issues of illegal use of intellectual property in sports in your country. How were these issues handled? How do they compare to the case of the Golden Taste Food Company in China?

civil rights cases decided in the 1970s and 1980s raised issues of racial discrimination in public recreation areas. Sport management practitioners over the past few decades have witnessed landmark and other important decisions involving the intersection of constitutional, antitrust, and employment law with sport. Throughout this chapter, we will refer to some of these cases and issues that involve the sport industry and the U.S. Constitution.

A fundamental purpose of the U.S. Constitution is to protect the people from the government's unwarranted intrusion, discrimination, arbitrary and capricious treatment, and infringement of liberty and property rights without **due process**. The Constitution provides protections for its citizens whenever there is an infringement on a person's basic and fundamental rights. Moreover, an organization's public or nonpublic designation makes a tremendous difference in determining whether its policies and practices are subject to the Constitution.

Sport organizations governed by the U.S. Constitution include athletics programs in public schools, state university athletics departments; federal, state, and municipally owned park and recreation departments; and possibly a person or organization that leases state-owned property to host a sporting event. As a result, these public sport organizations must comply with a number of Constitutional requirements in the management of their business activities. Thus, if a state high school athletics association

due process—As it is embodied in the 5th and 14th Amendments to the United States Constitution, due process ensures that a law shall not be unreasonable, arbitrary, or capricious and that the means selected for enforcing a law shall have a reasonable and substantial relation to the objective sought by the government.

created a rule or regulation limiting or restricting eligibility to participate in high school athletics to male athletes only, this rule or regulation would have to pass Constitutional scrutiny, or "muster," to be enforceable. The 14th Amendment, which provides equal protection, would not permit the state high school association to make impermissible distinctions based on race, ethnic origin, or gender. For example, the 14th Amendment would require the state athletics association to demonstrate what important government interest was being served by a gender-based distinction and that there is a substantial likelihood that the government interest would be achieved by the regulation. Because it is unlikely that the state high school athletics association could articulate an important reason to exclude female students from high school athletics, this regulation would be an unconstitutional deprivation of their equal protection.

The U.S. Constitution was not intended to govern the operation of privately owned and operated sport organizations such as retail sporting goods stores (e.g., Dick's Sporting Goods), fitness clubs (e.g., YMCA), private golf courses (e.g., Augusta National Golf Club, whose membership is composed almost exclusively of men), or professional sports teams (e.g., the NBA's social media policy could be perceived as a restriction on how a player may choose to express himself through his online tweets or Facebook updates, but because the NBA is a private organization, no First Amendment [free speech and expression] challenges could be asserted against the league's policy).

Earlier, we discussed the U.S. Constitution and its various amendments. Take a closer look at the 14th Amendment, which was also examined earlier. This amendment provides citizens within a given state the same protections against unwarranted actions by state government. The provisions that regulate the acts of the federal government as embodied within the first 10 amendments were passed down to the operations of state governments. Thus, the first 10 amendments to the U.S. Constitution (i.e., the Bill of Rights) prohibit state-related unwarranted behaviors and intrusions on the people. For more on the application of the 14th Amendment, please read the critical thinking section near the end of this chapter. The critical thinking exercise will further illustrate how the protective intent of the U.S. Constitution can be applied to the sport industry.

The U.S. Constitution is an important source of individual rights and guarantees and is the highest legal authority in the United States. No statutes, laws, regulations, or policies may contradict its provisions. The next section introduces you to federal legislation and provides examples of federal laws that have application to sport.

Federal Legislation

The U.S. Constitution empowers Congress to enact legislation in a variety of subject areas (e.g., copyrights, patents, trade and commerce, taxation, securities regulation). Congressionally enacted legislation reflects societal interests regarding future conduct about a variety of issues including, for example, discrimination and business practices (e.g., sexual harassment, sports betting, and unfair trade practices). Statutory language may appear general in nature because of its emphasis on governing uncertain future conduct (i.e., situations demanding statutory application that have not yet arisen). In turn, judges, through their written judicial opinions, establish the application and interpretation of a statute. Oftentimes, the judiciary is guided by a detailed legislative history that may accompany a statute. On other occasions, the legislative history may be minimal or nonspecific, so instead the court may have more leeway in interpreting the language used by Congress. For example, Congress may have identified the purpose of a piece of legislation to eliminate discrimination against people with disabilities. In interpreting this legislation, the courts will take into account that the stated purpose is

Professional Profile: Jill Bodensteiner

Title: associate athletics director for legal affairs and compliance, University of Notre Dame

Education: BA (psychology and sociology), University of Notre Dame; JD, Washington University in St. Louis; MBA, University of Notre Dame

Jill Bodensteiner is relatively new to intercollegiate athletics administration, having spent the first 15 years of her career as a practicing lawyer. She has found a way to combine her legal interests and expertise with her passion for athletics. Bodensteiner has a particular interest in both Title IX and ethics in sport, and has lectured on both topics in a variety of settings. In addition to her work at the University of Notre Dame, Bodensteiner is very active in a variety of personal and professional service activities. She is particularly passionate about camps for children that she and friends operate in Kingston, Jamaica and Leogane, Haiti during the summer. The following is a snapshot into her role as a leader in the sport industry.

What have been the key moves, steps, or developments in your career, and how did you arrive at your current position?

My career path into intercollegiate athletics administration was unusual. I started my current position in July of 2009 as an internal transfer after spending 11 years as an attorney in the Office of the General Counsel at Notre Dame. Prior to coming to Notre Dame, I clerked for a federal district court judge in St. Louis and practiced employment law at two large law firms. I earned my BA from Notre Dame, my law degree from Washington University in St. Louis, and my MBA from Notre Dame (while working in the General Counsel's office).

Because my father is a lawyer and law professor, I knew from a young age that I wanted to practice law. Although I never envisioned transitioning into a career in athletics administration, I kept an open mind regarding new opportunities, and I am thrilled with where those opportunities have led me. I definitely plan to remain in college athletics.

What are your current responsibilities and objectives in your job?

In my current role, I wear three very different hats: (1) supervise a staff of five full-time employees and, with my staff, advise coaches, student-athletes, and the University community on NCAA compliance and governance issues; (2) serve as the liaison between Athletics and the General Counsel's office on legal matters involving athletics; and (3) provide sport administration oversight for Notre Dame's nationally prominent women's basketball program.

NE DAY

to the WSG learn more ut a typical day e life for Jill Boden- ner. See if she spends working hours the way think she does.

What do you enjoy most about your current job?

My favorite part of the position is the opportunity to make a positive influence on the lives of student-athletes, which comes in a variety of forms: e.g., mentoring a distressed student-athlete, drafting a successful waiver request of standard NCAA rules on behalf of a student-athlete, helping a student-athlete find a job after graduation, or helping a student-athlete become eligible for a Pell Grant and other permissible aid.

What do you consider the biggest future challenge to be in your job or industry?

There has arguably never been a more interesting time to be involved in intercollegiate athletics, and the issues are substantive and significant. These issues include conference realignment, new media and its future, legal threats to the concept of amateurism, NCAA reform, and the appearance of a crisis in ethics, just to name a few. The challenge for my colleagues and me is not to simply follow these issues and respond to change, but to help affect the outcomes to the best extent possible.

On occasion, I miss the intellectual challenge of practicing law, especially the exercise of working in a law library to research one issue for several hours, trying to identify supporting case precedent or develop a new theory that will help a client. However, the variety of issues in my current position, the camaraderie associated with being part of a team, and the people I work with make up for those occasional nostalgic moments.

broad. Therefore, the various provisions or remedies contained in the statute may also be interpreted broadly to maximize the reach of the statute and thereby better fulfill the purpose of the law. In addition to Court interpretations, many federal agencies are responsible for enforcing and implementing federal laws. For example, the Department of Education enforces Title IX prohibiting gender discrimination in educational programs and the Federal Trade Commission enforces laws prohibiting false or misleading advertising. These agencies' responsibilities can include adopting guidelines to aid organizations and persons subject to the law in question.

Many federal laws affect sport, some specifically and others only indirectly. For example, the Americans with Disabilities Act (ADA), which is discussed in the following section of this chapter, applies to a broad range of individuals and entities generally as well as sport organizations specifically. When Congress enacted this law, the elimination of discrimination was a broad and sweeping goal in employment, education, and public places throughout the United States. In addition to this general applicability, Title III of the ADA prohibits discrimination in places of public accommodation and contains specific provisions including sport venues such as stadiums and arenas. The legislation has had, and continues to have, a significant effect on the decision-making activities of those in various sport-related leadership and managerial positions. The Ted Stevens Olympic and Amateur Sports Act (2005), the Sports Agent Responsibility and Trust Act (2005), and the Unlawful Internet Gambling Enforcement Act (2006) all illustrate federal laws addressing specific activities or concerns within the sport industry. The following discussion elaborates on two federal laws and recent guidelines enacted by the Federal Trade Commission regarding the use of social media for product endorsements. These examples illustrate both the historical significance of our federal nondiscrimination laws as well as the challenges related to regulating new and emerging communication mediums such as social media.

Americans with Disabilities Act

The Americans with Disabilities Act (ADA), which was passed in 1990, prohibits discrimination against people with disabilities as well as people who are perceived to have a disability. Under the ADA, a person is defined as having a disability if he or she has (1) a physical or mental impairment that substantially limits one or more major life activities, (2) a record of a disability, or (3) a perception of possessing a disability. Title I of the ADA prohibits discrimination in employment. Employers cannot discriminate against a person with a disability who meets essential job qualifications with or without reasonable accommodation. Title III prohibits discrimination in places of public accommodation. In other words, people with disabilities must be provided reasonable accommodations that permit them access to places where the public congregates or participates for purposes of recreation or leisure (e.g., bowling centers, health and fitness centers, skating rinks, sport arenas, stadiums). An accommodation is not required if accommodating the disabled person poses a direct threat to other participants or if a requested accommodation creates an undue hardship by fundamentally changing the nature of the product offering (e.g., aerobic dance class), represents an excessive financial burden, or disrupts the environment itself.

Driven by the potential for additional revenue, many colleges and universities are expanding their stadiums, hoping to generate additional revenue for their athletics departments. Stadiums renovated to include suites and club seating attract financial support from alumni and donors. Although athletics facility enhancements throughout the country are being made in revenue-generating sports such as football and men's basketball, athletics directors must be certain that these facilities comply with ADA. Moreover, in sports that have grown in popularity in recent years, updates must be made to their facilities to accommodate the increasing number of spectators. The

University of Michigan recently encountered this situation during the US$226 million upgrade of its football stadium. The university characterized its renovation as a repair rather than a renovation, but was sued by a disabled veterans' group. Ultimately, the university settled with the disabled veterans' group and the Department of Justice by increasing the number of wheelchair-accessible seats.

Title IX of the Education Amendments Act

Congress enacted a law known as Title IX in 1972. Title IX precludes discrimination based on sex in any educational program or activity that receives federal financial assistance. With regard to sport, compliance with Title IX is generally evaluated in three areas. The first area looks at the school's distribution of financial aid among its women's and men's athletics teams. The second area evaluates other benefits, opportunities, and treatments within men's and women's sports programs. Areas evaluated include, but are not limited to, the following:

> Provision of equipment and supplies
> Scheduling of games and practice times
> Travel and per diem allowances
> Opportunity to receive coaching and academic tutoring
> Provision of locker rooms, practice facilities, and competitive facilities
> Provision of medical and training facilities and services
> Provision of housing and dining facilities and services
> Publicity and recruitment procedures
> Assignment and compensation of coaches
> Other support services provided (e.g., clerical or administrative)

The third area examines whether the interests and abilities of the underrepresented group have been accommodated.

The Department of Education has identified a three-prong test for examining the extent to which the interests and abilities of the underrepresented group have been accommodated. The three-prong test provides three ways to comply with Title IX. A university can demonstrate compliance under any of the three prongs. The first prong is both the most difficult to comply with and the most controversial. This prong compares the proportionality of the university's male and female students to the

Title IX ensures that women have an equal opportunity as men to participate in sports at institutions that receive federal money. There is still controversy, though, regarding how to ensure this equal opportunity exists.

proportionality of male and female student-athletes. For example, if the population of the student body at State University is 53% female, the percentage of female student-athletes should also be 53% under this first prong. Few college athletics programs meet this challenging standard. Opponents to the first prong have argued that it is an impermissible quota, but the courts have consistently rejected that argument because it is not the only way in which a university can demonstrate compliance.

The second prong allows a school to demonstrate compliance by showing that the school has a history and a continuing practice of program expansion responsive to the interests and abilities of the underrepresented sex. This is a dual requirement, because both a history and a continuing practice are required. The courts have said that the best evidence of expansion is expansion itself; thus, typically, proposals and plans may not satisfy this second prong. Also, a school cannot cite its elimination of men's programs under this prong. The courts have indicated that the action of eliminating opportunities for men is not the equivalent of expanding opportunities for women.

Lastly, the third prong allows a school to demonstrate compliance by proving that it is fully and effectively meeting the interests and abilities of its students with its current athletics programs. In other words, this prong conveys that although a disparity may exist between the percentage of males and females within the general student population versus the percentage of males and females among student-athletes, this inequity is due to legitimate, nondiscriminatory factors. Proving interest levels is not an exact science. Courts have identified several ways that a school may obtain information about interest levels in athletics participation: (1) student requests that a sport be added, (2) requests to elevate a club team to varsity status, (3) participation levels in club or intramural sports, (4) interviews with students, newly admitted students, coaches, administrators, or others regarding interest in a particular sport, (5) results of questionnaires of current and newly admitted students, (6) participation levels in interscholastic sports, (7) discussions with amateur athletics associations or community sports leagues, and (8) inclusion of participation and interest questions on university admissions forms. For more information on this aspect of Title IX, read *Pederson v. Louisiana State University* (2000).

As a result of the passing and enforcement of Title IX, women's athletics has witnessed tremendous growth and popularity. Moreover, recent landmark court rulings in this area have sent a message that discrimination against women in athletics is unacceptable and will be met with serious consequences. Fresno State University has paid out several million dollars as a result of lawsuits brought by its former women's basketball coach, volleyball coach, and associate athletics director (Steeg, 2008). Title IX is still highly relevant for sport managers working in high school and college athletics.

The next section of this chapter covers state legal systems and their application to the sport industry.

State Legal Systems

As mentioned in the previous paragraph, the legislature of each state is responsible for enacting laws to govern its citizens in matters where federal legislation is silent. Each state has a constitution that sets forth the rights of its citizens and the limitations of the state government. Furthermore, each state has a court system to interpret and apply the laws of that state. Two areas of law that are based solely on state law are torts and contracts. Although the concepts of precedent and *stare decisis* apply within the state court systems, a state court is not compelled to follow a precedent from another state. For example, suppose a suit is filed in New York state court against an MLB team in New York. The suit is based on a personal injury claim involving a spectator who is injured during a postgame fireworks display at the team's ballpark. Suppose further that the state supreme court in Minnesota has previously decided a spectator injury case

Social Media and Legal Considerations in Sport Management

As social media has grown in prominence and popularity, the industry has rushed to embrace its marketing potential (Hambrick & Mahoney, 2012). Most professional sports leagues, as well as the IOC, have created rules and policies regarding the use of social media by athletes (Hull, 2010; International Olympic Committee, 2014). In addition to these private contractual restrictions, the Federal Trade Commission (FTC) has enacted guidelines for the use of endorsements and testimonials in social media (Federal Trade Commission, 2009; McKelvey & Masteralexis, 2011). The FTC periodically publishes guides that are intended to help inform the public and businesses about how to comply with the law. The guides are a basis for voluntary compliance with the standards imposed by the law. Celebrity endorsers such as professional athletes are expressly addressed in the revised guides. Under the new guides, unlike the 1980 one, both endorsers and advertisers could be liable under the FTC act for statements they make in an endorsement on Twitter or Facebook. Potential liabilities include false or unsubstantiated claims made in an endorsement or failure to disclose material connections between the advertiser and endorsers. The revised guides also make it clear that athlete endorsers have a duty to disclose their relationships with advertisers when making endorsements outside the context of traditional ads, such as in social media. Professional athlete endorsers should disclose any material connections with the sponsors by using hashtags such as #spon or #ad. The guides are administrative interpretations of the law intended to help advertisers comply with the FTC act; they are not binding law themselves. In any law enforcement action challenging the allegedly deceptive use of testimonials or endorsements, the FTC would have the burden of proving that the challenged conduct violates the FTC act.

similar to the New York case. The decision in the state of Minnesota cannot serve as binding legal precedent for arguing a successful case in New York, but the New York court might find the reasoning of the Minnesota court persuasive and reach a similar conclusion. However, if that same issue came before the Minnesota courts again, the Minnesota courts would be bound to follow the prior precedent.

Regarding a state legal system, the state's constitution is the highest legal authority in the state. Moreover, its statutes must always be consistent with the federal Constitution. If they are not, the statutes will be deemed invalid by our courts. State laws also govern the citizens of a state in matters where federal legislation is silent.

The following section addresses issues involving tort law. Tort law cases can range from cases involving product liability (e.g., head injury because of a faulty helmet) to those associated with medical malpractice (e.g., misdiagnosis of a career-threatening injury).

Tort Law

A **tort** is a civil wrong or injury for which the law permits a recovery. Typically, a wrong or injury is either a negligent act or an intentional act by one person that causes an injury to another person or his or her property. Tort law focuses on whether a particular person (or persons) failed to perform appropriately based on her or his (or their) relationship with the injured plaintiff. The purpose of tort law is to remedy a wrong. Compensatory or punitive damages (or both) can provide a remedy for the wrong. Compensatory damages can reflect monetary damages for medical bills, lost days of work, payment for hired hands, lost earning potential, and pain and suffering. Punitive damages, in comparison, can impose additional monetary damages on defendants that serve to punish them for their wrongdoing and make an example of their conduct so that others do not engage in similar acts. Punitive damages often greatly exceed the actual costs of the injury and are generally available only for intentional torts.

tort—A civil wrong or injury for which the law permits a recovery. Typically, the wrong or injury is either a negligent act or an intentional act by one person that causes an injury to another person or his or her property.

As mentioned in the preceding paragraph, a person may have a cause of action in tort because of the negligent or intentional acts of another. Unintentional torts encompass claims based on negligence. Claims based on defamation, invasion of privacy, assault, and battery represent intentional torts. The next two sections will provide you with an understanding of the legal aspects of negligence and intentional torts and their application to sport.

NEGLIGENCE

proximate cause—A cause that directly produces an event and without which the event would not have occurred.

Negligence represents the failure to act as another reasonably prudent person would have acted in a like or similar circumstance. To prove negligence, a plaintiff must prove the following four elements: duty, breach of duty, **proximate cause**, and injury. The duty can be based on (1) relationship with the plaintiff (e.g., coach and student-athlete, teacher and student, manager of a sport facility and spectator), (2) voluntary assumption of a duty (e.g., a volunteer coach who agrees to assist student-athletes with their college application materials), or (3) duty imposed by a statute (e.g., a state law that requires lifeguards at all public swimming pools). Breach of duty, the second element, represents a failure to act as a reasonable, prudent person would have acted in the same or similar situation. Typically, liability is imminent when an injury is foreseeable by another reasonably prudent professional or the defendant's actions reflect a disregard for the relevant professional standards. Proximate cause relates to the linkage between the defendant's failure to adhere to the standard of care (breach of duty) and actual injury suffered (Spengler, Anderson, Connaughton, & Baker, 2009). This means that although the defendant may be negligent, the injury may have resulted from some other intervening act. Consider the following example: A swimming pool manager has a statutory duty to provide a lifeguard and fails to do so, and a child is injured when a table umbrella falls on top of him. The failure of the pool manager to provide a lifeguard did not *cause* the injury, since the injury would have occurred regardless of whether a lifeguard had been present or not. Additionally, being injured by a falling table umbrella was not the type of harm the legislature was trying to guard against when it enacted laws requiring lifeguards. Lastly, as noted earlier, an injury must actually occur. For example, a swimming pool operator could fail to provide a lifeguard, but if no one is injured from these acts, a claim for negligence would also fail. Defenses for negligence can include, but are not limited to, assumption of risk, comparative negligence, failure to meet one of the four elements of negligence, failure to meet procedural guidelines (e.g., statute of limitations), governmental immunity, volunteer immunity statutes, and recreational use immunity statutes.

INTENTIONAL TORTS AND OTHER STATE LAW RIGHTS

Tort claims may also result from intentional rather than negligent conduct. A number of intentional torts provide a plaintiff with a legitimate cause of action. Intentional torts include invasion of privacy, defamation, assault, and battery (see the sidebar "Types of Intentional Torts"). A state law right that is also highly relevant in the sport industry is the right of publicity. Publicity rights evolved from invasion of privacy rights, but are now recognized by many states by statute or common law as an independent right.

Right of publicity claims are similar to invasion of privacy claims but with a twist. Publicity rights protect the commercial value of a person's name or likeness from intrusion or misappropriation. For example, suppose that you are a sport marketing entrepreneur who is looking for an opportunity to capitalize on the success LeBron James has had with the Miami Heat. You decide to print up hundreds of T-shirts that have LeBron James' image printed on them. If you went through with your idea and then sold the T-shirts, you would be using James' image for profit and misappropriating his likeness without his permission in violation of Florida's state right of publicity laws.

Types of Intentional Torts

> Invasion of privacy: protects against unwarranted privacy intrusions and disclosures
> Defamation: protects against publication of false statements that are harmful to a person's reputation
> Assault: protects against threats that could result in physical harm
> Battery: protects against actual physical harm or offensive touching

The tort of defamation strives to protect a person's right to her or his reputation, pride, and integrity. For example, a coach who is terminated during an ongoing NCAA recruiting scandal investigation would find it difficult to find other employment if information were published implying that he or she had committed or contributed to the violations. Truth, however, is a defense to a defamation allegation. Thus, if the coach did in fact commit the violations, a defamation claim would be inappropriate. The proof required in defamation claims tends to be subjective. Hence, a successful defamation claim is difficult to prove and can require years to litigate.

Sport managers are better able to protect themselves and their employers, while also serving their fans, spectators, consumers, clients, and employees, when they understand the distinction between invasion of privacy and defamation, as well as the behaviors that can subject them and the sport entity to liability. Sport managers should know how to insulate themselves from legal claims. As you will see in the next section, a sound understanding of contract law is important for sport managers to create and enforce agreements that are beneficial to their organizations.

Contracts

The law of contracts is also known as the law of private agreements. Contract law enables private parties to enter into agreements and enforce those agreements legally. A contract represents an agreement between two or more parties to do, or not to do, a particular act. When a contracting party fails to abide by the terms of the agreement, the nonbreaching party has a legal cause of action. Contract law preserves and encourages the right of parties to make and enter into agreements as long as the parties abide by the legal tenants associated with contract law, including, for example, (1) legal subject matter, (2) defined offer, acceptance, and consideration, (3) terms within the realm of acceptable public policy, (4) parties in possession of capacity (i.e., appropriate age and without significant mental disability), (5) no economic duress or exercise of excessive bargaining power, and (6) clear and unequivocal contractual language. An offer, acceptance, and consideration represent the three basic tenets associated with contract law. Consideration refers to the bargained-for exchange (e.g., I'll pay you $75,000 in exchange for your employment as the marketing vice president for my sport management firm; I'll pay you $100 for your vintage rookie baseball card now worth $1,000). In the latter example, the agreed-upon consideration benefits the buyer of the baseball card much more than it does the seller. Common law and statutes that govern contractual agreements do not require that the agreed-upon consideration be equal (or even fair) to both parties as long as the agreement is made without fraud, duress, or deceit. In other words, one party may clearly benefit by the terms of the contract itself. Recourse for breach of contract actions can include court-imposed injunctions, restoring the parties (or a party) to a contract to their (or his or her) precontract condition, reforming the contract so that it better represents the intention of the parties or fairness, or total abandonment of the contract itself (i.e., rescission).

The 2012 Boston Marathon featured the hottest-ever temperature on the race course in the event's nearly 120 years of existence. Because of the protection provided through waivers, if marathon participants had sustained an injury because of their own negligence during the race, the organization would not be responsible for compensating them for that injury.

A variety of sport organizations routinely use exculpatory agreements as part of their daily operations. Waivers and releases both reflect exculpatory agreements, that is, agreements used to excuse an organization for its own acts of negligence. For example, health clubs typically require members to sign a waiver before they use the facility's programs and equipment. The signed waiver excuses an organization (e.g., a health club) from ordinary negligence liability even if an employee of the health club is responsible for negligence and a resultant injury.

Exculpatory agreements represent a conflict with the purpose of tort law. As mentioned earlier, tort law seeks to allow a person injured by another's negligence to recover damages as a matter of public policy; that is, the one causing the injury should be responsible to the injured person. On the other hand, contract law seeks to allow the enforcement of agreements entered into between private parties even though the agreed-upon terms may benefit one party more than another. Waivers jeopardize the legal rights of a few so that society may benefit. In sport and physical activity, the realm of possible injuries is extensive, ranging from mild muscle strains to sprains, heat exhaustion, heat stroke, broken bones, and even death. If people were allowed to sue for the minor injuries inherent in sport and physical activity, the expense associated with owning and managing a sport or recreational organization would be exorbitant and likely prohibitive. Insurance costs, litigation-related fees (e.g., discovery, attorney fees, expert witness testimony), and damaged public relations could result in the cessation of the sport and recreational industry. Judicial and legislative approval of the signed waiver, although it denies recovery to an injured plaintiff, benefits society through the continued solvency and sustained profitability of the sport and recreation industry.

If written correctly, waivers can provide legal protection to a sport entity for acts of ordinary negligence. As mentioned earlier, contract law is based on state common law and statutes. Some states permit complete enforcement of waiver agreements; others refuse to enforce waivers at all because they conflict with acceptable public policy. It is always important to review individual state statutes and common law cases regarding the enforceability of exculpatory contracts, as well as state and industry specifications required for a legally enforceable contract.

While contract and tort laws in all 50 states could theoretically vary from one state to another, many states strive to pattern their laws after one another, often creating common provisions adopted in each state. These common provisions are available in treatises known as restatements. **Restatements** are secondary legal research sources that seek to restate the legal rules that constitute the common law in a particular area. The American Law Institute (ALI), a prestigious legal organization composed of noted professors, judges, and lawyers, publishes the restatements. The ALI has completed restatements in 15 areas of law, including torts, contracts, property, conflict of laws, foreign relations law, and products liability.

restatements—Secondary legal research sources that seek to restate the legal rules that constitute the common law in a particular area such as contracts, torts, property, foreign relations, and product liability.

Summary of Fundamental Sport Law Components

The law in the United States is composed of a system of rules that are enforced through a variety of prescribed institutions. In the U.S. system of government, the process for interpreting and creating law on the federal level is clearly described in the Constitution. In this system, states are able to govern themselves in matters that do not have federal jurisdiction. The democratic form of government in the United States includes a system of checks and balances so that persons, regardless of their office or position, are held accountable for governing with integrity and respect for the rule of law. The power of the executive branch resides with the president of the United States, who acts as head of state and commander in chief. But as powerful as the president is in our form of government, the person who holds this office must work in concert with the judicial and legislative branches. For example, the president is empowered by the Constitution to sign legislation into law or veto bills enacted by Congress. But Congress (which resides in the legislative branch) may override a veto with two-thirds vote of both houses. Federal legislation such as the Education Act of 1972 (Title IX) and the ADA serves to protect citizens who have historically been discriminated against and denied the opportunity to participate in society with the rights and privileges that are extended to all citizens of the United States.

The Broncos elaborate no trespassing sign is designed to notify fans, photographers, and other people that trespassing is a criminal violation under Colorado state law.

Besides examining the legislative acts and constitutions at the state and federal level, the chapter also examines tort law and contract law. Because accidents and intentional misdeeds inevitably occur, tort law works to determine whether an injured party can receive compensation from someone who is legally responsible for the injury that has occurred. Furthermore, as covered earlier, contract law is instrumental in formalizing agreements between parties. Because we have examined the various fundamental components involved with sport law, we can now turn our attention to applying the legal aspects in sport management.

Earlier in this chapter, we discussed the U.S. Constitution. In reference to the critical thinking scenario presented later, let's look at the issue in the context of the language of the Constitution regarding religion. As you read the following paragraphs, consider the extent to which your new knowledge of critical thinking (from your reading of critical thinking in chapter 1) might influence how you would react to the later section "Critical Thinking in Sport Law."

common law—The body of law derived from the judgments and decrees of the courts rather than those laws created by legislatures.

Common law is the body of law derived from the judgments and decrees of the courts rather than those laws created by legislatures. In addressing the issue of school prayer, common law decisions have held that because young students have impressionable minds, what might begin as a tolerance for religious expression can later become coerced indoctrination. With this in mind, consider the following.

Future Challenges

The daily decisions of sport managers profoundly influence employee and customer recruitment and retention, as well as organizational solvency. Effective and efficient sport management entities require managers who are cognizant of how their actions influence others. Further, the law (e.g., constitutions, statutes, common law) is a dynamic environment that constantly changes and requires managers to adapt and respond. Failure to comply with the law can bring both individual and organizational liability. Liability risk increases when professionals fail to act as another reasonable professional would act in a like or similar circumstance (i.e., negligence).

Several issues will continue to challenge sport managers. For example, office conduct and related policy issues such as maintenance of personnel files, communication with the media, and inspection of employee e-mail communication can subject an organization to invasion of privacy or defamation litigation. Contract negotiation is becoming a vital skill for sport managers as the sport industry continues to expand. Compensation for an average NCAA Division I coach is often in the millions of dollars and flows from a variety of sources (e.g., salary, media shows, perks, endorsements, licensing opportunities, sport camps, personal appearances, performance bonuses), all of which must be provided for in a clear and enforceable contractual agreement. Sport managers in leadership positions today must thoroughly understand contract law and be prepared to make challenging decisions regarding the retention and hiring of coaches and administrators. Lastly, advances in technology continue to create legal issues that challenge sport managers. For instance, the increase in new media technology (e.g., Facebook, Twitter) has affected the sport industry with numerous legal challenges. The increasing influence of the Internet in the marketing and promotion of sport has led to a number of new legal challenges such as Internet domain disputes (e.g., recent suits filed over websites such as Vancouver2010.org, SteffiGraf.com, Chicago2016.com), ambush marketing, and defamatory blogging.

Critical Thinking in Sport Law

Earlier in the chapter, we discussed the U.S. Constitution. As you read in chapter 1, being able to apply critical thinking skills to the field of sport management is important to future sport managers. For example, an issue that requires sport managers to use critical thinking skills to evaluate a constitutional issue is the question of prayer at public school sporting events. This controversy, which is particularly prominent in the United States, presents an excellent opportunity for you to practice critically evaluating an issue of great concern to the public while also learning about how the law, specifically the U.S. Constitution, can be interpreted.

Assume that you were recently named to the position of athletics director at a public high school that had a long tradition of offering prayers over the public address system at

PORTFOLIO

Complete the critical thinking activity in the WSG, consulting as needed the "Critical Thinking Questions" sidebar in chapter 1.

athletic contests. Recently, following the Supreme Court decision in *Santa Fe Independent School District v. Doe* (2000), which held that such practices violated the establishment clause in the First Amendment, the practice of offering prayers over the public address system had been halted. But some students and parents have inquired about whether a moment of silence or reflection could be used to replace the prayer before athletic contests. You are not sure what to do.

Ethics in Sport Law

Sport law and ethics often intersect in a variety of ways, ranging from constitutional and contract law to intellectual property and agency law. The following are two illustrations of ethical dilemmas associated with the legal aspects of sport management. One example involves professional sports and the other has implications for intercollegiate athletics. After you read each dilemma, review the section in chapter 1 that deals with ethical guidelines and apply the appropriate guideline to each of the following problems.

The first ethical dilemma involves an NFL team's use of a trademark for its team name. The Washington Redskins, a longstanding NFL franchise, has faced legal challenges based on the argument that the name "Redskins" is a racially offensive term for Native Americans (Capriccioso, 2013). Federal law has long held that the granting of disparaging trademarks is strictly prohibited. Specifically, Section 2(a) of the Lanham (Trademark) Act precludes the registration of trademarks that may disparage or falsely suggest a connection with persons, living or dead, institutions, beliefs, or that bring them into contempt or disrepute.

The legal wrangling involving the Washington Redskins trademark in an attempt to get the team's nickname changed dates back more than two decades. In 1992, Suzan Shown Harjo sued the team regarding its trademarks, but the suit was eventually rejected based on the doctrine of laches (Swyers, 2013). Per the court, the Native Americans unreasonably delayed the pursuit of their rights under the Lanham Act. After several attempts to overturn the decision on appeal, Washington was permitted to keep the trademark. Seven years later, in 1999, it was determined by the Trademark Trial and Appeal Board that the Redskins trademark potentially may disparage Native Americans (Brady, 2013). Consequently, the federal trademark of the nickname held by Washington was cancelled. Subsequently, however, in *Harjo v. Pro-Football, Inc.* (2003), the Board's decision was overturned by the U.S. District Court for the District of Columbia on the following two bases: (1) the finding of the board lacked the support of strong evidence and (2) the case should not have been considered because of the doctrine of laches. Following unsuccessful subsequent appeals by the *Harjo* plaintiffs, the Washington Redskins were ultimately able to retain the trademark. *Blackhouse et al v. Pro Football, Inc.* represents an ongoing lawsuit that is challenging and attempting to cancel the Washington Redskins trademark.

The Washington Redskins trademark litigation presents an ethical dilemma because the franchise and the NFL enjoy substantial revenues from the Redskins name and trademark; however, the use and publication of the mark can be perceived as offensive to a class of citizens. Increasing public sentiment against the Redskins name coupled with a new group of plaintiffs and involvement from Congress in the spring of 2013 could result in a major change for the team and its trademark protection against third parties.

The second ethical dilemma describes the NCAA's use of a student-athlete's likeness or image. As the popularity of college sports video games (SVGs) increases and the graphic designs included in these games become more similar to the live competition, the debate over the likeness and the use of student-athletes in video games has reached unparalleled levels (Gullo, 2013). With the financial stake and commercial appeal of college athletics growing over the years due in part to record television contracts involving the NCAA and conference offices, the NCAA's claim that the primary interest of college athletics is to educate student-athletes has been scrutinized and debated (Elias, 2013).

Former UCLA basketball standout Ed O'Bannon is suing the NCAA, its licensing arm, and EA Sports in an effort to receive financial compensation based on the billions of dollars earned by the NCAA and it member institutions through memorabilia, video games, live broadcasts, and through other means. The lawsuit, which was originally filed in 2009, has expanded and the plaintiffs have included high-profile coplaintiffs like Oscar Robertson and Bill Russell (McCann, 2013). Initially, this lawsuit focused singularly on the use of former student-athletes' likenesses in products such as EA Sports' NCAA video games, for which the individuals are not compensated. However, in a motion for class certification filed in August of 2012, the plaintiffs have postulated that both current and former student-athletes should be included in the lawsuit and maintain that they should receive 50% of revenue produced by the NCAA and the conference television broadcast rights to college sporting events (Vinton, 2013). If successful, the NCAA and its member institutions could stand to lose billions of dollars in damages.

The O'Bannon case presents a legal and ethical dilemma because the NCAA and its member schools receive windfall financial profits from their various sponsorship agreements and television contracts while prohibiting student-athletes from receiving compensation based on this revenue in exchange for their participation in athletics. It is believed by some that student-athletes should receive financial compensation in exchange for their participation in college athletics, while others hold that providing compensation to student-athletes would jeopardize the amateur nature of college sports.

PORTFOLIO

Complete the ethical issues portfolio activity in the WSG, consulting as needed the "Guidelines for Making Ethical Decisions" sidebar in chapter 1.

Summary

This chapter discusses how to identify legal issues that affect sport management operations and introduces many basic legal concepts that affect sport managers. It also identifies and explains a number of ways in which legal issues influence the sport industry and emphasizes how important it is for sport managers to make effective decisions when confronting legal issues. To recognize and respond to legal issues successfully, effective sport managers must engage in critical thinking and prudent problem solving.

An effective sport manager must have a basic familiarity with the court system (e.g., constitutions, state law, federal law), legislative acts (e.g., Title IX, ADA), and myriad legal topics and issues (e.g., negligence, defamation). Moreover, because employment and sponsorship contracts are an integral part of professional sport and college athletics, sport managers and athletics administrators must be knowledgeable of and adept at working with the critical components of these agreements. Lastly, because of the increased litigiousness of our society, people are increasingly looking to the U.S. Constitution for protection in asserting fundamental rights in issues related to sport. This chapter introduces these and other legal issues that affect sport managers, sporting events, and sport organizations.

Review Questions

1. Why does society need laws that govern behavior?

2. What are the four elements of negligence that the plaintiff must successfully prove?

3. What guarantees included in the U.S. Constitution affect sport?

4. Can legal precedent of a sport issue in the state court of Ohio be used as the basis of a decision in the state court of Nevada? Please explain your answer.

5. Why is the concept of invasion of privacy based on intrusion, disclosure, and misappropriation? Provide an illustration of why a plaintiff may sue for invasion of privacy.

6. How have the ADA and Title IX legislative acts influenced the sport industry?

7. What are the benefits of contracts for sport organizations (e.g., athletics departments), nonsport entities that deal with sport (e.g., event sponsors), and sport personnel (e.g., coaches)?

8. What applications does tort law have to sport?

References

Americans with Disabilities Act of 1990, 42 USCA § 12101 et seq. (West, 1993).

Black, M.A. (2004). *Black's law dictionary* (8th ed.). St. Paul, MN: West.

Brady, Erik. (2013, May 11). New generation of American Indians challenge Redskins. *USA Today Sports*. Retrieved from www.usatoday.com/story/sports/nfl/redskins/2013/05/09/native-americans-washington-mascot-fight/2148877/

Capriccioso, R. (2013, March 21). A new generation takes on the Redskins; Asks team's lawyers to buy new dictionaries. *Indian Country Today Media Network.com*. Retrieved from http://indiancountrytodaymedianetwork.com/2013/03/21/new-generation-takes-redskins-asks-teams-lawyers-buy-new-dictionaries-148285

Chemerinsky, E. (2006). *Constitutional law: Principles and policies*. New York: Aspen.

Connors, J.W. (2009). Treating like subdecisions alike: The scope of stare decisis as applied to the judicial method. *Columbia Law Review, 108*(3), 681–715.

Elias, P. (2013, April 1). NCAA battles former players' lawsuit over revenues. *Associated Press*. Retrieved from www.utsandiego.com/news/2013/apr/01/ncaa-battles-former-players-lawsuit-over-revenues/

Federal Trade Commission. (2009, October 5). FTC publishes final guides governing endorsements and testimonials. Retrieved from www.ftc.gov/opa/2009/10/endortest.shtm

Gullo, K. (June 20, 2013) NCAA lawyer says student athletes can't sue for broadcast. *Bloomberg*. Retrieved from www.bloomberg.com/news/2013-06-20/ncaa-lawyer-says-student-athletes-can-t-sue-for-broadcast.html

Hambrick, M.E., & Mahoney, T.Q. (2012). "It's incredible—trust me": Exploring the role of celebrity athletes as marketers in online social networks. *International Journal of Sport Management and Marketing, 10*, 161–179.

Hull, M.R. (2010). Sports leagues new social media policies: Enforcement under copyright law and state law. *Columbia Journal of Law and the Arts, 34*, 457–490.

International Olympic Committee. (2014). Social media, blogging, and internet guidelines. Olympic.org. Retrieved from www.olympic.org/social-media-and-internet-guidelines

Koller, P. (2006). The concept of law and its conceptions. *Ratio Juris, 19*(2), 180–196.

McCann, M. (2013, June 19). O'Bannon expands NCAA lawsuit. *SI.com*. Retrieved from www.sportsillustrated.cnn.com/2012/writers/michael_mccann/09/01/obannon-ncaa-lawsuit/index.html

McKelvey, S., & Masteralexis, J. (2011). This Tweet sponsored by . . .: The application of the new FTC Guides to the social media world of professional athletes. *Virginia Sports and Entertainment Law Journal, 11*, 222–246.

Pederson v. Louisiana State University, 213 F.3d 858 (5th Cir. 2000).

Pro-Football, Inc. v. Harjo, 284 F. Supp. 2d 96 (D.D.C. 2003).

Santa Fe Independent School Dist. v. Doe, 530 U.S. 290 (2000).

Spengler, J.O., Anderson, P.M., Connaughton, D.P., & Baker, T.A. III. (2009). *Introduction to sport law*. Champaign, IL: Human Kinetics.

Sport Agent Responsibility and Trust Act, 15 USC § 7801–7807 (2005).

Steeg, J.L. (2008, May 13). Lawsuits, disputes reflect continuing tension over Title IX. *USA Today*. Retrieved from www.usatoday.com/sports/college/2008-05-12-titleix-cover_N.htm

Swyers, M. (2013, May 21). The Washington Redskins' trademark fight. *The Trademark Advocate*. Retrieved from www.inc.com/matthew-swyers/the-washington-redskins-trademark-fight.html

Ted Stevens Olympic and Amateur Sports Act, 36 USC § 220501 et seq. (2005).

Title IX of the Education Amendments of 1972, 20 USC § 1681–1688 (1990).

Unlawful Internet Gambling Enforcement Act, 31 USC § 5361–5367 (2006).

Vinton, P. (2013, May 6). Ed O'Bannon vs. the NCAA: Explaining the major decision coming. *SB Nation*. Retrieved from www.sbnation.com/college-football/2013/5/6/4291666/ed-obannon-ncaa-lawsuit-next-class-certification

HISTORICAL MOMENTS

- **1926**   Gertrude Ederle became first woman to swim the English Channel
- **1936**   Jesse Owens won four gold medals in athletics at Berlin Olympic Games
- **1943**   All-American Girls Professional Baseball League (AAGPBL) formed; disbanded in 1954
- **1957**   Althea Gibson became first African American woman to win Wimbledon singles title and appear on a *Sports Illustrated* cover
- **1968**   At Olympic Games in Mexico City, Tommie Smith and John Carlos raised black-gloved fists on medal stands
- **1972**   Title IX passed
- **1977**   Shirley Muldowney won National Hot Rod Association (NHRA) Top Fuel Championship
- **1989**   First *Racial & Gender Report Card* issued by the Center for the Study of Sport in Society
- **1997**   Dee Kantner and Violet Palmer became first female referees to officiate an NBA game
- **1999**   Women's World Cup match between the United States and China drew 90,000 spectators in Rose Bowl
- **2002**   Esera Tuaolo, former Green Bay Packers and Minnesota Vikings player, publicly announced that he is gay
- **2006**   WNBA celebrated 10th anniversary
- **2008**   NCAA prohibited member use of Native American mascots
- **2010**   Super Bowl became the most viewed television program of all time in the United States
- **2012**   For the first time, women competed in every sport on the program in the 2012 Olympic Games in London
- **2013**   Lance Armstrong confessed to a decade of blood doping and the use of banned performance-enhancing substances. Armstrong stripped of his 7 consecutive Tour de France titles from 1999–2006
- **2013**   Social media controversies included homophobic tweet (e.g., Tyler Seguin) and racist video rant (e.g., Riley Cooper)
- **2014**   More than 111 million viewers watched Super Bowl XLVIII, which had a blowout win by the Seattle Seahawks over the Denver Broncos

18

SOCIOLOGICAL ASPECTS OF SPORT

Nicole M. LaVoi \ Mary Jo Kane

LEARNING OBJECTIVES

› Define sport sociology and its importance for sport managers.
› Discuss the social and cultural significance of sport in our society.
› Identify positive and negative social effects of sport.
› Discuss significant research findings in sport sociology pertaining to sexism, racism, and homophobia.
› Discuss patterns of leadership in sport and media coverage patterns based on gender and race.
› Discuss race logic and stacking in sport.
› Discuss how homophobia affects athletes and sport practitioners.

Key Terms

empirical	role learning
gender roles	socialization
heterosexism	sport sociology
homophobia	stacking
race logic	Title IX

GET A JOB

Continue on your journey in sport management by going to the web study guide (WSG) at www.HumanKinetics.com/ContemporarySportManagement. Check out the job opportunities and consider the skills and experiences that can help you succeed in sport management.

An important step in becoming a successful sport manager is gaining in-depth awareness of sport as a social, political, and economic activity that permeates our society and influences both institutions and people in a variety of ways. To understand the complex dynamics of how and why people participate in sport and physical activity, you must have knowledge about both individual behavior (e.g., psychological aspects such as motivation to participate) and the social context in which that behavior occurs. For nearly 40 years, the scientific investigation of the relationships and social worlds that people create, maintain, change, and contest in and through sport has been at the heart of an academic discipline called **sport sociology.**

sport sociology—The scientific investigation of relationships, social interactions, and culture that are created, maintained, changed, and contested in and through sport.

The purpose of this chapter is to define sport sociology and highlight several domains of scholarly inquiry within this discipline. Particular attention is devoted to the areas where sport sociology and sport management intersect. Knowledge in this area can help you address social challenges, especially as those challenges relate to real-world concerns such as racism, sexism, and changing gender roles.

Given that sport is a significant part of many societies of the world, it is not surprising that scholars would be interested in studying its dimensions, scope, and influence. According to Coakley (2009), sport sociology is the "subdiscipline of sociology that studies sports as social phenomena" (p. 11). Sport sociologists rely on sociological theories and concepts to examine institutions and organizations (e.g., the International Olympic Committee [IOC]), microsystems (e.g., women's professional basketball teams), or subcultures (e.g., sport gamblers). As part of their analyses, sport sociologists do not typically focus on the behavior of specific people. Instead, they examine the social patterns, structures, and organizations of groups actively engaged in sport and physical activity.

Rather than examining the behavior of specific people, sport sociologists examine institutions, organizations, and subcultures. The sociological aspects, and prevalence, of legal and illegal gambling in sports are examined by some sport sociologists.

An underlying assumption of sport sociology is that sport is an important institution of the same magnitude as the family, the educational system, and our political structure. A fundamental goal of sport sociology is to describe the complex dynamics surrounding patterns of participation (e.g., the number of girls versus the number of boys involved in youth sports) and social concerns (e.g., an overemphasis on winning that may lead to the use of steroids) that make up this all-pervasive institution (Eitzen & Sage, 2009). Keep in mind that sport sociologists do far more than describe sport involvement by, for example, gathering data on how many people participate on an annual basis. They are ultimately concerned with understanding the social context in which this participation occurs, as well as the meaning of sport as an influential social, political, and economic institution.

Social Significance of Sport

Did you ever wonder why local television newscasts describe their content as news, weather, and sports? Why not news, weather, and technology? Why do they not highlight education? Or literature? Have you ever wondered why so many families spend discretionary resources and time at youth sport events? Or why advertising rates during the NFL Super Bowl are so astronomical? The entry cost for some 30-second ads for the 2013 Super Bowl ranged from US$3.8 million to US$4 million, or roughly US$130,000 per second (Stone, 2013)! Perhaps it is because sport influences almost every aspect of our lives. Undeniably, billions of corporate and personal dollars are spent annually on sport-related products and services. In fact, in 2011, US$77.3 billion was spent on sporting goods, apparel, footwear, fitness equipment, and licensed sport merchandise (Brettman, 2012), which demonstrates that the sport industry has an enormous economic impact on U.S. society.

Another way the significance of sport is highlighted is to see how individual acts and governance often come to symbolize broader social concerns. Some examples of this include racism (e.g., in 2008, the NCAA prohibited member use of Native American mascots), sexism (e.g., the public debate on whether women should be allowed membership at Augusta National Golf Club), criminal behavior (e.g., NFL quarterback Michael Vick's involvement in dog fighting), and drug use and abuse (e.g., the use of performance-enhancing drugs by cyclist Lance Armstrong). These examples clearly indicate that sport holds a prominent place in our society and that the consumption, valuation, and participation of sports have potential for both positive and negative outcomes and consequences. Sport can be a place where sexism, racism, homophobia, and violence occur and are perpetuated. Keep in mind, however, that sport also has incredible potential to serve as a vehicle for positive youth development and social change.

Benefits of Sport

Clearly, sport shapes and maintains many social values that are held in high regard, such as hard work and fair play, self-discipline, sacrifice, and commitment to oneself and others. Research documents that sport participation can lead to greater health and well-being, as well as social, emotional, moral, physical, and psychological development (LaVoi & Wiese-Bjornstal, 2007). In short, sport has the potential to contribute to the positive development and stability of both individuals and society as a whole (Coakley, 2009).

Sport as a Socializing Agent

The socialization process refers to the various ways in which a society's dominant values, attitudes, and beliefs are passed down from generation to generation. Socialization also pertains to the process of starting, continuing, changing, and discontinuing sports, as well as the effect of sport participation on the individual player (Coakley, 2009). Children learn from coaches, parents, teachers, peers, and siblings about what is normative, important, valued, and expected in a sport context—which helps them construct meaning of their experiences. In addition, what and who are portrayed in the sport media communicate values and attitudes to consumers and spectators about what is important.

socialization—The process by which people learn and develop through social interactions and come to know the environment around them.

Sport as a Unifier

Sport can bring people together by giving them a sense of personal identity, as well as feelings of group membership and social identification (Eitzen & Sage, 2009). For example, many U.S. citizens must have felt unified around the 2014 NFL Super Bowl, which was the most-viewed U.S. television program of all time, with 111.5 million viewers (Hibberd, 2014). Sport accomplishes feelings of unity in a number of additional ways, from the individual level (e.g., an athlete who feels that she is part of something bigger than herself because she is a University of Minnesota Golden Gopher), to the regional level (e.g., when citizens and professional sport teams like the Celtics, Bruins, and Red Sox banded together to raise money to help victims of the 2013 Boston Marathon bombing), to the national and international levels (e.g., the entire nation rooting for athletes in the Olympic Games). Few, if any, institutions can unite people the way that sport does, largely because the popularity of sport cuts across social categories like race and class.

Dark Side of Sport

Although sport can produce unity and beneficial outcomes for both individuals and society as a whole, involvement in sport does not bring only good things; it can also be exclusionary and divisive in terms of race, class, gender, age, ability, and sexual orientation—and their complex intersections. For example, not all families can afford the rising pay-to-play fees of professionalized youth sport. Seats inside professional sport stadiums funded by public tax dollars are so expensive that only a small minority of people can afford to attend a game in the very stadium that they helped fund! Participation rates are lowest and the number of barriers to sport participation and physical activity are greatest for underserved girls—girls for whom geography, class, race, gender, and ethnicity intersect (LaVoi & Thul, 2009). A change in cultural beliefs pertaining to impaired athletes is occurring. In early 2013, the U.S. Department of Education amended and released new guidelines for The Rehabilitation Act of 1973 that will help ensure equal access to school-based sports for disabled students. While this change is a move in the right direction, improvements in access and accommodation for impaired athletes have come slowly.

ACTION
Go to the WSG and complete the first Learning in Action activity, which challenges you to identify sociological issues at play in several scenarios.

As is apparent, sport participation can have a darker side. This dark side of participation includes such aspects as sexual and emotional abuse of athletes, burnout, dropping out, steroid use, chronic injuries, and eating disorders. Anxiety, yet another issue in sport participation, can result from a win-at-all-costs philosophy that characterizes the pressure-cooker world of big-time athletics. Furthermore, the same inclination increasingly characterizes youth sport. Besides the concerns just listed, research findings from sport sociology highlight four areas of sport that reflect and contribute to some of the most troubling aspects of the United States as we move into the second decade of the 21st century—sexism, homophobia and heterosexism, and racism.

Sexism in Sport

In the wake of the modern feminist movement that began in the early 1970s, a number of women's roles expanded into areas traditionally occupied by men; the world of sport was no exception. As you learned in chapters 7, 8, and 17, **Title IX** of the Education Amendments Act was passed in the United States in 1972. This landmark federal legislation prohibits sex discrimination in educational settings. Since its passage and implementation, enormous changes in the world of women's sports have taken place. For example, substantial gains have occurred in the number of sports offered, access to sport-related scholarships and facilities, and overall athletics budgets. However, while a record number of girls and women are participating in sports at all levels of competition, boys and men still outnumber their female counterparts and receive a disproportional amount of resources, and the number of women in positions of power in sport is declining. Sociologists argue these trends are due to maintenance of power hierarchies, organizational structure, policies, and societal beliefs that preserve sport as a space that is still primarily by, about, and for men (Cooky, Messner, & Hextrum, 2013).

Title IX—Federal legislation passed in 1972 that amended the 1964 Civil Rights Act and prohibited sex discrimination in educational settings.

FEMALE PATTERNS OF SPORT PARTICIPATION

With respect to sports offered on a nationwide basis, in 2012, the average number of teams (per college or university) that was available for women was 8.73—an all-time high. Compare that with 1972, when the average number was 2.5 sports per school (Acosta & Carpenter, 2012). The National Federation of State High School Associations (NFHS, 2012) reported that more than three million girls (3,207,533) are now involved in interscholastic sports nationwide, compared with only 298,000 before Title IX. In the 2011–2012 school year, 41.6% of high school athletes (NFHS, 2012) and 43% of NCAA athletes were female (National Collegiate Athletic Association, 2012)—compared with only 15% in the early 1970s. And more than just participation rates have skyrocketed in the wake of Title IX; the number of fans is exploding as well. Consider women's college basketball, one of the most popular women's sports around; 98.8% of member NCAA institutions have a women's basketball team. During the NCAA 2011–2012 season, 11.2 million women's basketball fans in all three divisions broke attendance records (Johnson, 2012), which have increased for 25 consecutive years. These statistics make it clear that because of Title IX, millions of girls and women are participating in and consuming a variety of sports at all levels in unprecedented numbers.

RESOURCES ALLOCATED TO FEMALE COLLEGIATE ATHLETES

Although women have made enormous progress in sport, assuming that they have attained equality would be a mistake. Consider the following examples. More than four decades after the passage of Title IX, women received 47% of athletic scholarships at the intercollegiate level, even though they represented 57% of all undergraduates nationwide (Civil Rights Data Collection, 2012). Although 47% is a vast improvement from the pre–Title IX era, female athletes received US$183 million less in scholarship money than did their male counterparts (Women's Sports Foundation, 2012; personal communication). Moreover, athletics budgets, salaries for coaches and athletics administrators, and access to facilities are nowhere near an equitable ratio. At the college level, women's programs in NCAA D-1A schools receive about half of the recruiting budget that men's programs receive (Equity in Athletics Data Analysis, 2011). These disparities not only put women's sports at a distinct disadvantage in building successful programs but also send a powerful message about which sports (and athletes) are considered the real or most important ones. These inequalities are particularly troubling given that most sports programs are housed within public institutions.

WOMEN IN POSITIONS OF LEADERSHIP IN SPORT

Ironically, with respect to leadership positions in women's sports in the United States, women have lost far more than they have gained since the passage of Title

WEB

Go to the WSG and complete the first web search activity, which helps you identify the outcomes of Title IX and determine what more could be done to support gender equity.

Four decades after the passage of Title IX, record numbers of girls and women are participating in sports. Some of the sport participation opportunities can lead to professional careers, such as playing on the LPGA Tour.

IX. In terms of national trends, before 1972, more than 90% of all head coaches in women's athletics were female; in 2012, that figure was just 42.9% (Acosta & Carpenter, 2012). And although the overall number of head coaching positions in women's sports has increased dramatically since the mid-1980s, males have benefited from this increase far more than their female counterparts have. For example, in college sports only 20% of head coaches are female, and women continue to represent only 2% to 3% of the coaches in men's sports (Acosta & Carpenter, 2012). At the professional level, the WNBA is the only sport league to have any female head coaches, but even then, in the 2012–2013 season, only 5 of the 12 head coaches were women. Data from outside the United States show similar patterns of underrepresentation of women in positions of power in sport (LaVoi & Dutove, 2012).

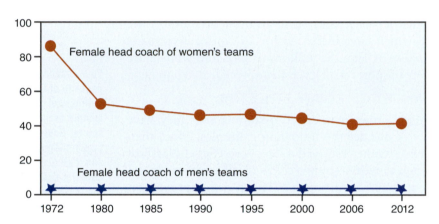

Figure 18.1 Percent of women head coaches in intercollegiate sport, as revealed in the analysis of longitudinal data (1972–2012) by Acosta and Carpenter (2012).

Data from R.V. Acosta and L.J. Carpenter, 2012, *Women in intercollegiate sport: A longitudinal, national study thirty five year update*. Available from www.acostacarpenter.org

The picture for women in key administrative positions in women's sports is even more disturbing. Research indicates that before Title IX, women occupied the vast majority (more than 90%) of all athletics director positions throughout women's intercollegiate sports. In 2012, however, they accounted for only 20.3% of those same administrative positions (Acosta & Carpenter, 2012). In professional sports, women in positions of power outside the WNBA are rare. Similarly, women make up 10% or less of the Associated Press sports editors, assistant sports editors, and columnists, and between 11% and 16% of sport reporters and copy editors or designers (Klos, 2013)—the people who decide what and how to write about sport.

These facts make it undeniably clear that in terms of employment opportunities, particularly in high-ranking leadership positions, men have fared far better under Title IX than women have, and women still face a labyrinth of barriers that impede entry and career advancement and have very few supports (LaVoi & Dutove, 2012). Even more troubling is that in spite of women's increasing experience and expertise, they remain only a token presence as leaders in men's sports and fight an uphill battle as leaders in women's sports. Some have suggested that this employment trend occurred (and persists) because men are better qualified, but **empirical** evidence does not support this belief. On the contrary, studies have indicated that women are often as qualified, or more qualified, than their male counterparts. Such hiring practices are rooted in outdated assumptions about gender and leadership. These findings suggest that sport is still a place that produces and reinforces male power (Fink, 2008), as well as perpetuates harmful gender stereotypes and traditional **gender roles** (Cunningham, 2008). The underrepresentation of women in positions of power exists even though research indicates that gender and marital and lifestyle status do not significantly affect a person's organizational commitment (Turner & Chelladurai, 2005).

empirical—Knowledge based on experimental method and observation versus theory or supposition.

gender roles—A set of perceived behavioral norms associated particularly with males or females in a given social group or system.

Why does it matter that fewer women occupy leadership positions? In the absence of visible female role models (role learning), women and girls may devalue their own abilities, accept negative stereotypes, fail to realize their potential, and limit their own sport career aspirations. Access and exposure to female role models in positions of leadership (i.e., power) is particularly important to girls, because they have fewer such role models in their lives than boys do, especially in sport contexts (LaVoi & Dutove, 2012). To create social change and challenge stereotypical beliefs pertaining to gender, power, and leadership, women must be seen in proportional or preferably equal numbers in all positions of power within the world of sport.

MEDIA COVERAGE OF FEMALE ATHLETES

A number of female athletes have become household names because of sport media coverage over the last several years—Abby Wambach, Gabby Douglas, Serena Williams, Danica Patrick, and Skylar Diggins immediately come to mind. In spite of such progress, the first wave of sport media scholars over the past three decades have convincingly demonstrated in two important ways how mainstream media treat sportswomen and sportsmen differently. First, although female athletes make up approximately 40% of all sport participants, they receive significantly less coverage than their male counterparts—on average receiving only 2% to 4% of the total sports coverage regardless of the medium, a figure that has declined. Numerous studies have documented this pattern in newspapers, in magazines such as *Sports Illustrated*, on television and sports talk radio, and through new media outlets (e.g., Cooky et al., 2013; Lisec & McDonald, 2012). This finding is true regardless of the period in relationship to Title IX, the age of the athletes, race, or the type of sport they are involved in.

A second way that the mainstream media treat female athletes differently involves type of coverage. Numerous investigations (e.g., Kane & Buysse, 2005; Kane, LaVoi, & Fink, 2013; Parker & Fink, 2008) have shown that the media portray male athletes in an array of images and stories that emphasize their athletic strength and mental toughness, but present women in ways that predominantly highlight their physical attractiveness and heterosexuality rather than their accomplishments as athletes. Similarly, sexualizing highly skilled sportswomen makes up much of the commentary of male sports reporters. Currently, a second wave of sport media scholars are using intersectionality (i.e., how gender, class, race, and sexual orientation intersect) and audience reception research frameworks to examine how diverse consumers (i.e., audiences) interpret media images of female athletes, and perceptions of whether sex sells women's sport (Kane et al., 2013; Fink, Kane, & LaVoi, in press). Emerging data from this growing body of research indicate that sexualized portrayals of female athletes are not an effective way to market and promote women's sport. As Kane (2011) emphatically stated in a piece she wrote for *The Nation*, "sex sells sex, not women's sport" (p. 28).

> **role learning**—A social process by which children learn various roles, such as neighbor, friend, student, sibling, daughter, or son, and the characteristics associated with them.

ACTION
Go to the WSG and complete the second Learning in Action activity, which encourages you to spend some time analyzing sports blogs and how they report on women in sport.

ACTION
Go to the WSG and complete the third Learning in Action activity, which asks you to follow and compare the tweets of popular male and female athletes.

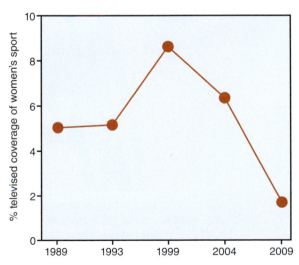

Figure 18.2   Gender in televised sport as detailed in a longitudinal study by Cooky, Messner, and Hextrum (2013).

C. Cooky, M.A. Messner, and R.H. Hextrum, *Communication and Sport*, Vol. 1(3): 203-230, copyright © 2013 authors. Adapted by permission of SAGE Publications.

Reframing Media Coverage of Paralympic Sport in Canada

By Melinda Maika, Canada
Western University, London, Ontario

By Karen Danylchuk, Canada
Western University, London, Ontario

In our modern society, media culture plays a critical role in socialization. Mediated sport can thereby be an important cultural platform upon which ideas about various aspects of social relations become naturalized. Accordingly, the stories that are told about Paralympic athletes have the potential to influence the public's understanding of the social construct of disability. Notwithstanding this potential, disability, particularly in sport, has routinely been excluded or poorly represented in the media. As the Paralympic movement gains momentum, there has been increased interest in examining the intersections among disability, sport, and the media.

Canada's Michelle Stilwell won gold and silver medals in the 2012 Paralympic Games in the 200-meter and 100-meter races, respectively. Here, Stilwell celebrates after winning the gold medal in the 200-meter race in the Olympic Stadium.

Homophobia and Heterosexism in Sport

Sport sociology scholars also examine one of the most oppressive aspects of sport—homophobia. Pat Griffin (1998), a leading scholar and advocate in this area and founder of Changing the Game: The Gay, Lesbian, and Straight Education Network Sports

The London 2012 Paralympic Games received unprecedented media attention in Canada and worldwide attention compared to previous iterations. However, the coverage of sport for persons with disabilities remains leagues behind that of mainstream, able-bodied sport. In 2012, Canada's official Games broadcaster—a partnership between Bell and Rogers dubbed Canada's Olympic Broadcast Media Consortium—offered limited Paralympic television coverage (hour-long daily highlights) along with 580 hours of online streaming. Comparatively, over 5,000 hours of multiplatform coverage were dedicated to the Olympics. In Canadian newsstand major dailies (print), the ratio of Olympic to Paralympic articles during the period two weeks prior through two weeks following each respective event was approximately 15:1.

In recent years, the Canadian Paralympic Committee (CPC) has taken steps to influence the amount and quality of media coverage that Canadian athletes receive during the Paralympic Games. A comprehensive pre- and post-Games media campaign was a mainstay in the CPC's London 2012 communications plan. In addition, a number of mission staff members were assigned to media-specific roles, and the CPC also implemented a media training program for the entire delegation of Canadian athletes prior to departure for the London 2012 Paralympic Games.

Traditionally, athletes with disabilities (AWD) have been portrayed in ways that focus attention on their impairments and depict disability sport as less legitimate than mainstream sport. The "supercrip" narrative, which is common in Paralympic coverage, frames AWDs as heroic because of their ability to overcome disability and perform feats normally considered not possible for people with disabilities. This frame communicates a somewhat contentious underlying story of rising above disability to achieve normalcy. The "cyborg" frame consists of stories that focus on the role of assistive devices and technology in Parasport performance. This narrative positions AWD as more than human and presents the possibility that technology has the potential to be used for the purposes of physical augmentation. Recent research in Canadian print media suggests a shift toward framing Paralympians largely as athletic, despite remnants of other frames. Athletic framing is more typical of mainstream sport coverage and consists of references to sport skill, performance, and training, generally carrying an element of competitiveness.

Interestingly, the most appropriate frame to legitimize Paralympic sport may not fall in line with the delivery of an enticing marketing campaign to the general public. Consequently, tension exists between these representations as managers, athletes, marketers, media, and researchers in Canada and around the world attempt to determine the best way to portray Paralympic athletes.

International Learning Activity #1

Investigate the coverage that Parasport has received in your country, specifically during recent major Games (e.g., Paralympics) and outside of major sporting events. What is the focus of the stories being told? How does this compare to Olympic coverage in your country?

International Learning Activity #2

Think about other groups that have been historically marginalized in sport (e.g., women, ethnic minorities, aboriginals). Has their status changed over time? How do you see the media playing a role in this process?

International Learning Activity #3

Collect information about opportunities for persons with disabilities to participate in sport in your area. What sport options exist for this population at the local, regional, and national levels? Is there a greater focus on leisure and recreation or on elite competition? Is this information readily available to the general public?

Project (GLSEN), defined **homophobia** as a universal fear or intolerance toward gay and bisexual people. Although significant progress has occurred in this area, stereotypes continue to link gender roles with highly competitive athletics, particularly in team contact sports such as basketball and football. Traditional definitions of masculinity

homophobia—An irrational fear, a contempt, or an antipathy toward homosexuals and homosexuality.

WEB

Go to the WSG and complete the second web search activity, which asks you to identify differences in pictures of two athletes, one male and one female, both in the same sport.

(and heterosexuality) were synonymous with "real" athletes. In contrast, traditional notions of femininity—sugar and spice and everything nice—were, by definition, the antithesis of athleticism. As a result, female athletes who challenge these stereotypes—in the 1980s and '90s, professional tennis player Martina Navratilova and, more recently, former Baylor University basketball All-American and now WNBA player Brittney Griner, both out lesbians—are often criticized as not being real women.

HOMOPHOBIA AND WOMEN'S SPORTS

Although homophobia is present in both women's and men's athletics, fears or concerns about being gay have long been associated with women's sports (Krane & Barber, 2005). Such fears range from historical assertions that women's participation will harm their reproductive capacity (and make them unable to fulfill what are presumed to be appropriate heterosexual roles such as wife and mother) to modern-day claims that athletic involvement (particularly those who engage in more masculine sports) will turn women into lesbians (Kauer & Krane, 2006).

Jennifer Harris, a student athlete at Penn State University (PSU), experienced firsthand how women who engage in sports such as basketball and softball are automatically assumed to be lesbian. Harris, a member of PSU's basketball team, filed a groundbreaking lawsuit against head women's basketball coach Rene Portland, PSU, and the PSU athletics director for discrimination based on race, gender, sexual orientation, and invasion of privacy after she was kicked off the basketball team in March 2005. The university's six-month internal investigation found that Portland created an offensive environment and an aura of hostility and intimidation because of Harris' perceived sexual orientation (Leiber, 2006). A settlement was reached out of court, and Portland resigned in March 2007. Harris' sexual orientation? Straight. Portland's discriminatory practices were documented in the film *Training Rules*. Kauer and Krane (2006) interviewed collegiate female athletes who, regardless of sexual orientation, experienced stereotypical labeling. One athlete in their study said, "It's if you're an athlete you must be a lesbian. . . . People will just flat out say, 'Oh a bunch of dykes'" (p. 46).

As this example indicates, those associated with women's sports, from athletes to coaches to athletics administrators, have often been stigmatized with the lesbian label.

Media Portrayals of Female Athletes

As stated in the chapter text, research has shown that the media portray female athletes in ways that predominantly highlight their physical attractiveness and heterosexuality rather than their accomplishments as highly skilled and dedicated athletes. Consistently, women are significantly more likely than men to be portrayed off the court, out of uniform, and in passive and sexualized poses. Take, for example, the historic *ESPN The Magazine* cover in the March 23, 2009, issue of the publication. The cover shot is of former University of Tennessee basketball standout and WNBA 2008 Rookie of the Year Candace Parker. The cover is historic because in the more than five years before Parker's cover, only 6 of the 168 (3.6%) of *ESPN The Magazine* covers featured female athletes. But how was she portrayed in the issue? A very pregnant Parker was pictured in a sleeveless white sundress alongside the cover headline "How Big Can Candace Parker Get?" The lead paragraph of the story inside started with "Candace Parker is beautiful. Breathtaking, really, with flawless skin, endless legs and a C cup she is proud of but never flaunts" (Glock, 2009, p. 28). Parker's *ESPN The Magazine* cover and cover story are classic examples of how the media continue to marginalize and sexualize female athletes and perpetuate heterosexism. To view a picture of Parker's cover shot, go to www.wnba.com/features/parker_espn_090312.html

Given this reality, those involved in women's sports feel a great deal of pressure to act or appear to be heterosexual: "The underlying fear is not that a female athlete or coach will appear too plain or out of style; the real fear is that she will look like a dyke or, even worse, is one" (Griffin, 1992, p. 254). To counteract such fears, female athletes have gone to great lengths to assure themselves, their parents and teammates, coaches, and corporate sponsors that sport can (and should) be consistent with traditional notions of femininity and heterosexuality.

Research has demonstrated how homophobic beliefs and heterosexist practices (**heterosexism**) affect the lives of female athletes on a daily basis. Coaches and athletics administrators often pressure sportswomen to embrace a feminine image by dressing in skirts when traveling to out-of-town games and by wearing makeup and jewelry (Krane, 2001; Theberge, 2000) or to hide or keep their sexual identity out of the media spotlight. Players suspected of being lesbian may be dismissed from their positions on a team—and lose their scholarships—or could be passed over in the selection of elite teams (Iannotta & Kane, 2002). We should not underestimate the harmful consequences of the homophobic beliefs and practices that surround women's sports. Although conditions for lesbian athletes (and those perceived to be lesbian) are far better than they used to be, it still remains the case that being labeled a lesbian is to be stigmatized as abnormal or deviant and to be threatened with the loss of employment, career, and family (Krane & Barber, 2005). Note that this labeling process affects all females in sport, homosexual and heterosexual alike.

Homophobia also puts female coaches at risk. Administrators, colleagues, and even their own athletes often monitor coaches' personal lives. For example, when a coaching position opens up, search committee members may place private, discrete phone calls to determine a female applicant's sexual orientation (Griffin, 1998). Female coaches are particularly vulnerable to being tagged (or targeted) with the lesbian label because it can affect a critical part of their job—recruiting. A dirty little secret in the world of women's sports involves a specific form of negative recruiting in which a coach suggests to a potential athlete (or her family members) that another coach or team has a lesbian reputation (Iannotta & Kane, 2002). An ESPN.com expose outlined that coaches in women's basketball suspected or labeled as lesbian fear negative recruiting by colleagues and losing their jobs for their inability to land top recruits due to this destructive and common practice (Cyphers & Fagan, 2011). High-profile Title IX jury verdicts, settlements, and cases at Penn State, California State University at Fresno, the University of California at Berkeley, and San Diego Mesa College raised awareness about systemic gender inequities and homophobia at major colleges and universities (National Center for Lesbian Rights, 2009). Given such an environment and the strong (and understandable) desire of many lesbians to keep their private lives private, the subject of homophobia in sport rarely surfaces, at least on any large, public scale.

HOMOPHOBIA AND MEN'S SPORTS

Up to this point, we have focused on how homophobia affects women's sports. But as all of us know, men's sports are particularly oppressive and intolerant when it comes to dealing with gay athletes. Scholars have suggested that this intolerance is due to the historical role of sport as a training and proving ground for men to establish their masculinity (Coakley, 2009). Because traditional definitions of masculinity are synonymous with athleticism, it is not surprising that being both a male athlete and gay is seen as a contradiction in terms (Anderson, 2005). Gay male athletes know this formula all too well. Former players such as Billy Bean in MLB, Esera Tuaolo in the NFL, and John Amaechi in the NBA are a few of the male athletes in major professional sports ever to come out, but they all waited until their careers were over to do so. Tuaolo stated that he knew that if his teammates discovered that he was gay, "that would be the end

heterosexism—An ideology and a behavior that promote privilege for dominant groups (e.g., heterosexuals are the norm and are therefore perceived to be better than homosexuals).

for me. I'd wind up cut or injured." He explained that he "was sure that if a GM didn't get rid of me for the sake of team chemistry, another player would intentionally hurt me, to keep up the image" (Tuaolo & Cyphers, 2002, para. 5).

Although professional female athletes, such as Rosie Jones in golf, Martina Navratilova and Amélie Mauresmo in tennis, Sheryl Swoopes and Brittney Griner in basketball, and Megan Rapinoe in soccer, have come out during their playing careers over the past decades, it wasn't until 2013 that NBA player Jason Collins became the first U.S. professional male athlete in a major sport to come out while still playing. Given the experiences of Tuaolo—who says that he spent hours lying awake, praying for his anxiety attacks and ongoing depression to end—who could blame Collins and others for remaining silent? The result of an openly gay high-profile male athlete is to be determined, but it certainly stimulates public dialogue—both homophobic and sympathetic. It is naive to suggest that a safe, tolerant, and open climate will soon be a reality for gay athletes, but public sentiment and laws are changing to protect and embrace them.

Recently, many groups and initiatives have blossomed to combat homophobia in sport, increase awareness, make sport a safer space for GLBT athletes, and increase visibility of gay athletes, such as the You Can Play Project, Hudson Taylor's Athlete Ally, and GLSEN. Historically, athletes did not come out because they rightly feared losing valuable endorsement opportunities (for example, Martina Navratilova). But as signs of the changing times, in June of 2013, Brittney Griner became the first openly gay athlete to be endorsed by Nike, and in February of 2014, University of Missouri defensive lineman Michael Sam became the first openly out NFL prospect. In addition, to reflect the increasing societal acceptance of the gay community, Nike signed Jason Collins to help them launch a new GLBT-themed line #BeTrue, in which proceeds go to the LGBT Sports Coalition, a nonprofit that works toward ending discrimination in all sports. It appears as if the institution of sport might finally be embracing principles of social justice. To achieve that end, we should remember that the "problem" of gays in sport is not the presence of gay and lesbian athletes; it is the presence of homophobia.

Racism in Sport

Since Jackie Robinson broke the modern color barrier in MLB in the 1940s, minorities have made important progress in all levels of sport. Even so, racism remains deeply entrenched throughout the sport world. Although sport sociologists have examined diverse ethnic minorities, the majority of research has pertained to African Americans and to the controversy related to the use of Native American mascots. Sport sociologists have identified four areas in which racial myths and prejudices about African Americans and other ethnic minorities in sport abound: assumptions about race and athletic ability, sport leadership, sport media coverage, and the role of sport in racially connected upward mobility.

RACE AND ATHLETIC ABILITY

race logic—An attributional pattern of athletic success in which Black athletes' successes are attributed to natural athletic abilities and genetic advantage and White athletes' achievements are attributed to discipline, intelligence, and hard work.

The popularly held belief that African American athletes owe their success to their natural athletic abilities suggests that they have some genetic advantage over Whites when it comes to achievement in sport (Buffington, 2005). A parallel belief is that White athletes achieve excellence because of their discipline, intelligence, and hard work. This attributional pattern is often referred to as **race logic.** Note, however, that when people of color dominate a particular sport, a strong need develops to explain this dominance, and a desire emerges to search for a "Black gene" or an "athletic gene" associated with race. Some scholars argue that the lack of visible professional success for African Americans outside sport, coupled with an overrepresentation in sport, has resulted in many scientific inquiries into the elusive athletic gene (St. Louis, 2003). Although the dialogue about the existence of the athletic gene has at times been contentious (see

Hoberman, 2007; Spracklen, 2008), conclusive scientific evidence regarding the athletic gene does not exist. But when Whites dominate sports such as golf and tennis (Tiger Woods and Venus and Serena Williams being notable exceptions), the need to explain patterns of success based on the racial compositions of the players seems to vanish. A sport sociologist illustrates this in his discussion about snow skiing. "When White skiers from Austria and Switzerland . . . win World Cup championships year after year, people don't say they succeed because their white skin is a sign of genetic advantages," explained Coakley (2009). On the other hand, however, he noted that "the success of Black athletes is seen as an invasion or a takeover—a 'problem' in need of an explanation focused on dark-skinned bodies" (p. 283). The implications for focusing on a genetic link to athletic success are far reaching. From a sociological standpoint, genetic-based reasoning ignores broader social and cultural explanations for ability differences such as differential access, quality of coaches, community resources, and socialization.

RACISM AND SPORT LEADERSHIP

The second area and one of the most widely studied forms of racial discrimination in sport is a phenomenon called **stacking,** whereby minority groups are steered away from (or into) certain player positions that are more (or less) central to key decision-making and leadership positions on the field (Eitzen & Sage, 2009). For example, in MLB, while Whites have dominated the position of catcher, pitcher, and infielder—baseball's primary "thinking positions"—African Americans have been overrepresented in the outfield, in positions that rely on speed (Lapchick, 2009). Similarly, NFL scouts rate African American quarterbacks higher on physical attributes (Bigler & Jeffries, 2008), and this pattern appears to continue with media narratives about Robert Griffin III and Cam Newton.

stacking—A disproportionate allocation of athletes to central (e.g., "thinking positions") and noncentral positions as a function of their race or ethnicity.

Although the number of African American quarterbacks starting on NFL teams has increased, the activities and attitudes surrounding stacking in sport have not been eliminated. If most African American athletes are, for example, steered away from critical decision-making positions such as catcher or quarterback during their playing careers, the practice reinforces the belief that African Americans do not have the leadership skills and judgment necessary to become coaches and managers. Stacking helps explain why, although progress has occurred, minorities remain underrepresented in proportion to the percentage of people of color in the population at nearly all levels of leadership positions in professional sports. To see the lack of racial diversity in positions of power in professional sports, look at the various reports on all leagues written for The Institute of Diversity and Ethics in Sport (www.tidesport.org). Racial equity is far from reality, but an example of progress is evidenced by the NFL's 2002 Rooney Rule, which mandates that each team include at least one person of color in the candidate pool for head-coaching positions in the NFL. It appears that this rule has positively affected hiring practices, but the long-term effect and sustainability of the Rooney Rule is yet to be determined. Up from two people of color as NFL head coaches in 2001, and after an all-time record number of eight in 2011, the number decreased in 2012 to six (Lapchick, Anjorin, & Nickerson, 2012).

As reported by Lapchick (2011), similar patterns of underrepresentation of minorities also occur in intercollegiate athletics. In fact, minority representation is even lower in intercollegiate athletics. In 2011, of the Division I athletics directors, 4.3% were African American men. Little, if any, progress has occurred when it comes to selecting African American women to occupy leadership positions in intercollegiate sports. In 2011, few athletics directors (0.3%) and head coaches (2.1%) across Division I were African American women. The encouraging news is that all of the men's major professional leagues, as well as the NCAA, have undertaken diversity initiatives to increase the numbers of minorities and women in leadership positions. Such initiatives complement the advocacy efforts of Black Coaches and Administrators (BCA) to increase minority participation and employment, particularly in intercollegiate athletics. For example, in nine years of publication of the BCA Report Card on the hiring practices of collegiate head football coaches, there was a 600% increase in the number of Football Bowl Series head coaches from 3 in 2003 to 18 in 2012 (Lapchick, Costa, Sherrod, & Anjorin, 2012).

SPORT MEDIA COVERAGE

A third area that reflects racial stereotypes of African Americans can be found in sport media coverage. For instance, scholars refer to one trend in media coverage as the hierarchy-of-naming pattern. This occurs when members of a less powerful group (minorities and women) are referred to by their first names only, whereas those in more powerful groups (White men) are referred to either by their last names or their full names. In a study by Duncan, Messner, and Cooky (2000), in 90% of the cases in which male athletes were referred to only by their first names, the athlete in question was a person of color. Examples from professional sports illustrate this point. All of us know who Kobe, LeBron, and K.G. are, but we do not think of Peyton Manning, Steve Nash, or Sidney Crosby as Peyton, Steve, and Sidney. Although certainly not intentional, this type of coverage can reflect and perpetuate a lack of respect toward minority athletes.

Sportscasters in basketball and football consistently describe African American athletes as naturally athletic in comparison to their White counterparts, who are described as intelligent or hard working (Bruce, 2004; Rada & Wulfemeyer, 2005). In the 2000 Summer Olympics, African American athletes were pictorially overrepresented in

How did the media's portrayal of 2012 Olympic gold medalist Gabby Douglas fit with typical media coverage of African American athletes?

newspapers when they were competing in strength sports, whereas White athletes were overrepresented in aesthetic sports such as swimming (Hardin, Dodd, Chance, & Walsdorf, 2004). These subtle forms of sport media coverage perpetuate racial stereotypes and race logic, suggesting that African American athletic success is primarily attributed to physicality or athletic ability.

SPORT AND UPWARD MOBILITY

The fourth area dominated by racial stereotypes and myths involves the notion that African Americans and sport are linked together as part of African Americans' biological and cultural destiny, especially in certain sports (Coakley, 2009). Sport is often perceived as one of the more progressive institutions in the United States because of the prevalence, visibility, and success of minority athletes. Although African Americans constitute 13.1% of the total population (United States Census Bureau, 2012), a majority of NBA (78%) and NFL (67%) athletes are African American (Lapchick, 2011). In short, the widely held belief is that sport—and in far too many cases, only sport—offers a path to upward mobility. Americans hold this view largely because African American athletes dominate the most visible and popular sports and because athletes such as Kobe Bryant (NBA) and Calvin Johnson (NFL) earn astronomical salaries and endorsement contracts. In addition, for many years, Americans have heard countless rags-to-riches stories about racial minorities making it in professional sports—from the Williams sisters to LeBron James. Probably for that reason, two-thirds of African American adolescent males believe that they can have a career in professional sports (Eitzen, 2006). How accurate are those beliefs? How often do African Americans succeed in the big-time world of sport?

Sport sociologists have addressed those questions by pointing out that although African Americans (particularly men) have been enormously successful in the most prominent professional and intercollegiate sports, the likelihood of having a professional sport career is "a dream for all but an infinitesimal number" (Eitzen, 2006, p. 178). Consider these statistics: Of all the professional sports available to men, African Americans have found the greatest success in basketball. Yet only a small percentage of high school seniors of any race continue to play football (5.7%) or basketball (3.0%) at NCAA institutions (Bracken, 2007). Additionally, Eitzen reported statistics from sociologist Wilbert M. Leonard, who calculated that for African American men, the odds of making an NBA team are 20,000 to 1 and the odds of playing for an NFL franchise are 10,000 to 1.

No one suggests that African Americans (and other racial minorities) should not strive for success in sport, despite the long odds against achieving and maintaining a professional career. But critics point out that achieving upward mobility is easier in other professions, such as medicine, law, education, science, and engineering. Equally important is the fact that people who follow such career paths have greater lifetime earnings than most professional athletes, who on average last 3 to 12 years in individual sports such as golf or tennis and 3 to 7 years in team sports such as basketball and football (Coakley, 2009). The late, great African American Arthur Ashe broke new ground in men's professional tennis. Although he used sport as a way to achieve success, Ashe understood the limitations—and warned against the dangers—of seeing sport as the only, or even the primary, path to social and economic mobility: "We have been on the same roads—sports and entertainment—too long. We need to pull over, fill up at the library and speed away to Congress, and the Supreme Court, the unions, and the business world" (Ashe, 1977, p. 2S). Unfortunately, more than 30 years after those prescient remarks, the need for African Americans to fill up professions beyond the sport world remains in play—although the 2008 and 2012 inaugurations of Barack Obama as President of the United States may turn the tide more quickly. Besides examining African American involvement in sport, scholars in the field of sport sociology have spent a lot of time researching the controversy surrounding Native American mascots in sport. This controversy is examined in the ethics section.

Professional Profile: Carley Knox

Title: director of business operations, Minnesota Lynx, WNBA

Education: MA (sport administration), Bowling Green State University; MA (women's studies), Bowling Green State University

Carley Knox is a nine-year front office veteran of the WNBA. As of 2013, she serves as the director of business operations for the Minnesota Lynx and is the primary liaison between the team and WNBA on league-wide business and marketing initiatives. Through all her educational, personal, and professional experiences a single passion has remained consistent—she is devoted to supporting and growing women's sports. Her commitment to achieving gender equity, social justice, and diversity in and through women's sport is unwavering. Through hard work and dedication, she has enjoyed franchise success on the court (four WNBA championships: 2006 and 2008 with the Detroit Shock and 2011 and 2013 with the Lynx), as well as in the boardroom as an agent of social change. The following is a snapshot into her role as a leader in the sport industry.

What have been the key moves, steps, or developments in your career, and how did you arrive at your current position?

On my way to a career with the WNBA, I earned degrees in both sports administration and women's studies at Ohio University in 2001 while playing on the soccer team. My professional trajectory began as an assistant college soccer coach, followed by an operations, marketing, and sales job for The Jamie Farr Owens Corning Classic LPGA tournament. In 2004, I earned a double master's degree at Bowling Green State University and completed a thesis titled "Behind Closed Locker Room Doors: How Homophobia Operates in Collegiate D-I Women's Athletics." Following graduate school, I took a position as the director of sales and marketing for the WNBA's Detroit Shock, and then moved to the Minnesota Lynx in 2010.

What are your current responsibilities and objectives in your job?

As the director of Lynx business operations, I oversee the day-to-day processes of business development, budget management, community relations, scheduling, and game-day operations. I manage interns and I also maintain my former job duties as development of corporate and tickets sales.

ONE DAY

Go to the WSG and learn more about a typical day in the life for Carley Knox. See if she spends her working hours the way you think she does.

What do you enjoy most about your current job?

One aspect of my job I enjoy is fighting the fight for women's athletics by bringing people together to celebrate powerful female role models. When consumers sample the WNBA and attend games, they often become fans because they see amazing athletes.

What do you consider the biggest future challenge to be in your job or industry?

As a woman in the male-dominated industry of professional sport, I face the daily challenge of overcoming stereotypes about gender and leadership. Through consistent and high performance, I believe I am opening minds to the fact that women can be competent sport leaders and can add value to a company. The biggest challenge I face is growing and sustaining the WNBA league.

Sport as a Vehicle for Social Transformation

Although sport certainly includes many problematic aspects, as highlighted in much of this chapter, it can also help us overcome injustice, prejudice, and oppression. Structured and reinforced with appropriate social values, the sport experience can instill people with a deep-seated commitment to make important and long-lasting contributions to society. Although we rarely think of sport in this manner, its enormous popularity, coupled with its ability to reach across social, political, and economic divides, make sport one of the few institutions that can serve as a catalyst for change. Perhaps the most celebrated example of sport as a vehicle for change occurred in 1947 when, as noted earlier, Robinson broke the modern color barrier in MLB and paved the way for countless athletes of color to participate across all levels of sport. We can only imagine what sport, and society, would be like if it were not for the contributions of athletes such as Muhammad Ali, Michael Jordan, Magic Johnson, Serena Williams, Candace Parker, Michelle Wie, and Tiger Woods.

Another area (and era) in which sport confronted society's ills and became a catalyst for significant change involved the turbulent 1960s. That period was marked by social unrest and assassinations of well-known leaders such as John F. Kennedy, Robert Kennedy, and Martin Luther King Jr. The decade was also a time of demonstrations in the streets and the killing of students on college campuses over U.S. involvement in Vietnam. Against this backdrop, the 1968 Summer Olympic Games took place in Mexico City. During the Games, two African American athletes, Tommie Smith and John Carlos, who had won the gold (Smith) and bronze (Carlos) medals in the 200-meter dash, used the awards ceremony to protest racial injustice. During the national anthem, Smith and Carlos lowered their heads and raised their black-gloved, closed fists in a gesture that was widely seen (and criticized) as an African American power salute. Although they were stripped of their medals and vilified back in the United States, their protest brought to light many of the injustices faced by African Americans and (in some quarters) revealed the hypocrisy of America as the "land of the free." Sport sociologists argue that the protest of Smith and Carlos was not only one of the most memorable moments in Olympic history but also a milestone in the civil rights movement.

In the early 1990s, sport—and a celebrated sports figure—challenged existing stereotypes and helped to transform society. Near the peak of his career, Magic Johnson stunned not only the NBA but all of America with the revelation of his HIV-positive status. Before his shocking announcement, many Americans were aware that thousands of people had died from AIDS and that millions more were infected with the deadly disease. Although by that time the public knew that celebrities such as Hollywood icon Rock Hudson had died of complications from AIDS, education, treatment, and research about the disease remained almost invisible to the public consciousness. But that all changed with Johnson's announcement. Almost immediately, his medical condition and subsequent retirement from professional basketball became the lead story, not just in the world of sport but throughout society. The event was a dramatic illustration of the power and widespread appeal of sport. It clearly demonstrated how sport, and sport heroes like Johnson, could enable us to see AIDS as an American and world tragedy and allow us to move beyond the stereotypic and inaccurate perception that AIDS was confined to gay men and that contracting HIV meant a death sentence.

Another example of sport as a vehicle for change is women's increasing and widespread participation in sport and physical activity. Before the early 1970s and the passage of Title IX, many segments of society, including many kinds of sporting activities, were considered off limits to most females. But many women and their male allies began to push for greater opportunities and a more level playing field for any female who wanted to become involved in sport. Such efforts have made an enormous difference in the lives of countless girls and women, their families, and their communities. For the first time in U.S. history, young girls, like countless young boys before them, grow up with a sense of entitlement to sport. They also experience the benefits of sport, from having a sense of identity, to being a part of something bigger than themselves, to facing (and overcoming) the physical, social, and intellectual challenges found in sport. Because of sport, girls and women feel a sense of pride and accomplishment, learn about their physical limitations and potentials, and create their own destinies, both in sport and in every part of society in which they participate. And because they do, we all benefit.

Finally, and perhaps most amazingly as outlined earlier in this chapter, some individuals in sport have taken some steps in challenging homophobic beliefs and practices. When 2013 WNBA 6'8" first-round draft pick Brittney Griner was asked about the effect of her public coming out, she stated, "If I can show that I'm out and I'm fine and everything's OK, then hopefully the younger generation will definitely feel the same way" ("Brittney Griner," 2013). By doing so, Griner and others have created some safe spaces for gay and lesbian athletes in the all-powerful institution of sport.

Implications for Sport Managers

Sport sociology has a number of implications for sport managers. We have already discussed how individuals face challenges, both on and off the court, and in so doing gain feelings of self-worth and empowerment. We have also examined broader social issues like the various (and harmful) ways in which mainstream media portray female athletes, how racism is perpetuated throughout the sport world, and how homophobic stereotypes put coaches and athletes at great risk personally and professionally. At the same time, however, we have seen how the Olympic Games, professional sports, and big-time college athletics can unify cities and nations and, as a result, challenge and transcend bigotry and oppression. What all these scenarios have in common are people. And knowing about people is critical to success in sport management because the sport manager must understand the social context of sport and the meaning attached to that context in order to get people involved with and stay committed to a certain activity.

One example that relates to the positive and negative aspects of sport illustrates this point. As we have seen, women's mass participation in sport and physical activity is a relatively recent phenomenon. As we have also seen, many who participated in the pre–Title IX era were stigmatized as not being real women. Yet we all know that people can gain tremendous benefits when they become involved in fitness or competitive sports programs. This is particularly true for females; adherence to sport and exercise

Case Study

The way in which University of Minnesota sport managers used research findings to guide decision making provides a good example of how sport sociology has direct implications for sport management. Anthony Brown is the assistant director of the university's Department of Recreational Sports; his boss, James Turman, is the director. They submitted a long-range proposal for recreational sport facilities to the university planning office. To inform their decisions regarding number of participants, design issues, and other factors related to on-campus sport facilities, they examined longitudinal survey data from the National Sporting Goods Association (NSGA).

Findings from this survey provide nationwide participation rates related to age, gender, geographic location, and popularity of activity. Brown and Turman concluded that exercise for fitness and physical appearance will remain popular among college students. They also used the research data to conclude that in team sports, interest in basketball will remain strong, soccer will continue to grow, and participation in extreme sports and outdoor pursuits such as snowboarding and skateboarding will increase. Brown and Turman's use of research findings had a direct effect on their facility and program master plan—more soccer fields, facilities for roller hockey and in-line skating, a skateboard park, a climbing wall, and another basketball gymnasium in the recreation center were included.

Social Media and Sociological Aspects of Sport

Some argue that digital, and particularly social, media is the most effective way to respectfully market and promote sportswomen. In social media, reliance on traditional sports editors and journalists—most of whom are White men (Lapchick, 2013)—to cover and promote female athletes and women's sport events in legitimate ways becomes immaterial. Social media has the potential to reduce reliance on gatekeepers, increase interest in and respect for women's sport, change the media landscape, resist sexist backlash, and shift the institutional and ideological control of sport away from men (Hardin, Zhong, & Corrigan, 2012) . . . but does it? One cannot assume those blogging or posting on digital sites respect female athletes. In fact, content on sport blogs is often ripe with unmediated backlash against female athletes (Lisec & McDonald, 2012). For social media to be used effectively, female athletes must also be explicitly taught how to employ such skills in order to best increase respect for and interest in themselves and their sport. Ineffective use of digital media may include oversharing, reproduction of stereotypes, and marginalization of their athleticism (e.g., post or share nude or seminude photos, focus on femininity over athleticism). These may help them personally gain visibility, promote their brand, and secure sponsorships but do little to advance women's sport. In fact, a recent study found that female athletes reproduced traditional gender roles and portrayed themselves in provocative and sexy ways in social media posts (Barnett, 2013). Some argue that social sport media sources have the potential to be a transformational, empowering, and positive space where sportswomen are valued, where women's sport is advanced, where masculine power can be contested, and where ideological and institutional control is shifted away from men. However, based on current data, this vision is currently unrealized (LaVoi & Calhoun, 2014).

can result in significantly lower rates of obesity and heart disease and can serve as an important counterweight to depression or a negative self-image (Women's Sports Foundation, 2005). Clearly, getting girls and women interested in regular (and serious) physical activity and providing safe opportunities for them to do so is the right thing to do. But given historical definitions of what it means to be an athlete and a female, many older women may need a more proactive approach by sport managers to help them get, and stay, involved. Sport managers who understand and respect the concerns of older women can provide creative and sensitive sports programs that reaffirm not only the benefits of participation, but also the notion that serious sport involvement can enhance, not undermine, participants' womanhood.

Critical Thinking in Sport Sociology

The following is a guest column ("Title IX Needs Change") by a male student that was published in a university newspaper:

> *Title IX is not good for collegiate sports. Universities are decreasing the athletic opportunities for men in order to make room for various women's sports. There has been a net loss of more than 17,000 opportunities for men in collegiate athletics. Title IX is merely a law of proportionality. Schools need to keep the same ratio of male athletes to male students as female athletes to female students. This is not fair to men's athletics. Universities need to be concerned about the economics of athletics by focusing mainly on those sports that are the most profitable. This should be common sense.*
>
> *The university should be putting money toward those sports that will return the greatest profits, not using funds for state-of-the-art women's athletic facilities. Earlier in the year the women's [sport withheld for privacy] team was promoting games for $1—$1 games . . . this is not a good*

investment. This sport does not attract fans. There are so few students that would go to a women's [sport] game for the purpose of being entertained. Most of those in attendance are family or friends that know the athletes. Now compare this to a men's [same sport] game. . . .

I just don't believe it is fair for men's programs to be cut in order to have more women's sports. . . . The female teams that benefit from Title IX do very little to benefit the university on an economic level. These teams are financial burdens to the university. Title IX was never expected to last 30 years. The number of women in college has increased, so the number of females athletes needs to increase according to Title IX. This does not take into account the fact that there is a greater proportion of men interested in sports than women. Title IX is now a threat to the history of men's athletic programs across the country.

PORTFOLIO

Complete the critical thinking portfolio activity in the WSG, consulting as needed the "Critical Thinking Questions" sidebar in chapter 1.

Ethics in Sport Sociology

The debate over the use of Native American sport mascots has been contested over the last 30 years. According to Davis-Delano (2007), Native American mascots were used by five professional sport teams (i.e., the Atlanta Braves, Chicago Blackhawks, Cleveland Indians, Kansas City Chiefs, and Washington Redskins), approximately 15 to 20 colleges and universities, and more than 2,900 high schools, middle schools, and elementary schools across the United States. Among other ethnic minority groups who experienced historic marginalization and discrimination, the use of related mascots is absent.

The position of scholars and activists pertaining to Native American mascots is based on three major points—imagery reflects and reinforces stereotypes, representations harm Native Americans, and Native Americans have no control over such images (Davis-Delano, 2007). For example, the Chief Wahoo (Cleveland Indians) mascot is representative of images at the center of the debate. Stereotypical depictions and inaccurate portrayals of Native Americans assume two forms: untamed savages (Washington Redskins) or noble savages (Chief Wahoo). This unfounded dichotomy of Native American culture ignores the role that the U.S. government played in the relocation and displacement of Native American tribes (King, 2004; Staurowsky, 2004).

PORTFOLIO

Complete the ethical issues portfolio activity in the WSG, consulting as needed the "Guidelines for Making Ethical Decisions" sidebar in chapter 1.

In contrast, individuals and institutions who defend the use of Native American mascots believe they are resisting political correctness. They claim that the images honor local tribes (Hofmann, 2005) or that the mascot has been supported by Native Americans (Cummings, 2008). Institutions have shown reluctance to comply or change their mascots to less offensive representations because they fear economic backlash from loyalist alumni donors (Williams, 2006) or fans. This controversy has inspired position statements from the U.S. Commission on Civil Rights and the American Sociological Association, as well as a 2005 NCAA policy change banning postseason hosting for schools with offensive mascots. But the vowed continuation by owner Daniel Snyder of the NFL Washington Redskins, coupled with the February 2014 letter to the NFL by two lawmakers calling for a name change or else they will hold hearings, illustrates that the debate is far from over.

Summary

Sport sociology involves the scientific study of the social context of sport. Although sport sociologists study the various ways in which people participate in sport, they are primarily interested in the meaning of sport and its influence on our social, political, and economic institutions. Sport management is directly linked in theory and practice to sport sociology because both areas are influenced by the cultural and societal aspects of sport and physical activity.

Sport has great prominence in society, shaping and perpetuating many important social and cultural values. The social benefits of sport include teaching children positive social roles and unifying diverse groups of people as they cheer for a particular team. Sport can also engender feelings of self-worth and a sense of empowerment. But sport has negative aspects as well—sexism, racism, and violence, both in and out of sport settings. Finally, sport may serve as a vehicle for social transformation. Sport figures can enhance awareness of and sensitivity to social problems such as AIDS, racial injustice, and homophobia.

Understanding and appreciating the field of sport sociology can provide an important foundation for understanding the field of sport management. To be effective, sport managers must be aware of the social aspects of sport. Considering that sport managers work with people in social settings, they must understand both individuals and their social environments because they are continuously interacting and affecting each other. Sport managers can play an essential role in developing safe, positive, and enriching sport environments. When they do so, people will participate more fully and effectively in all aspects of sport as athletes, employees, fans, clients, or consumers. As we have seen throughout this chapter, sport is a much-loved institution. The exciting challenge for sport managers is to harness that love in ways that emphasize not only sound management skills, but also a sense of social responsibility that enriches us all.

Review Questions

1. What is the definition of sport sociology, and how (and why) is it related to examining the social context of sport?

2. How and why do sports come to symbolize broader social concerns throughout society?

3. What do we mean when we say that sport is a socializing agent? How does participation in sport allow us to learn important societal roles?

4. What is Title IX, and how has it influenced participation patterns for girls and women on a nationwide basis?

5. Why has the number of women in key leadership positions in sport declined dramatically over the past three decades?

6. Do you think that stereotyping happens more often to African Americans or to Hispanics, or is the stereotyping just of a different type? Explain your answer.

7. How can homophobia negatively affect all women in sport, not just those who are gay?

8. What are some current examples of ways in which sport can serve as a catalyst for social change?

9. Why does sport sociology have significant implications for sport managers?

10. What are the two key patterns that sport media scholars have demonstrated over the last three decades pertaining to female athletes?

References

Acosta, R.V., & Carpenter, L.J. (2012). *Women in intercollegiate sport—a longitudinal, national study: Thirty-five year update 1977–2012.* Retrieved from www.acostacarpenter.org

Anderson, E. (2005). *In the game: Gay athletes and the cult of masculinity.* Albany, NY: State University of New York Press.

Ashe, A. (1977, February 6). Send your children to the libraries. *The New York Times*, p. 2S.

Barnett, B. (2013). *Girls gone web: Self-depictions of female athletes on personal websites.* Paper presented at the annual meeting of the International Association of Media and Communication Research, Dublin, Ireland.

Bigler, M., & Jeffries, J.L. (2008). "An amazing specimen": NFL draft experts' evaluation of Black quarterbacks. *Journal of African American Studies, 12*, 120–141.

Bracken, N. (2007). *Estimated probability of competing in athletics beyond the high school interscholastic level.* Retrieved from www.ncaa.org/wps/ncaa?key=/ncaa/ncaa/academics+and+athletes/education+and+research/probability+of+competing/methodology+-+prob+of+competing

Brettman, A. (2012, June 12). Wholesale spending on sporting goods up 4.2%, says Sporting Goods Manufacturers Association. *The Oregonian.* Retrieved from www.oregonlive.com/playbooks-profits/index.ssf/2012/06/wholesale_spending_on_sporting.html

Brittney Griner discusses being gay. (2013, April 21). ESPN.com. Retrieved from http://espn.go.com/wnba/story/_/id/9185633/brittney-griner-comes- says-just-are

Bruce, T. (2004). Marking the boundaries of the "normal" in televised sports: The play-by-play of race. *Media, Culture & Society, 26*, 861–879.

Buffington, D. (2005). Contesting race on Sundays: Making meaning out of the rise in the number of Black quarterbacks. *Sociology of Sport Journal, 22*, 19–37.

Civil Rights Data Collection (CRDC). (2012). Gender equity in education: A data snapshot. Retrieved from www.ecu.ac.uk/publications/files/equality-in-higher-education-statistical-report-2010.pdf/view

Coakley, J. (2009). *Sports in society: Issues and controversies* (10th ed.). New York, NY: McGraw-Hill Higher Education.

Cooky, C., Messner, M.A., & Hextrum, R.H. (2013). Women play sport, but not on TV: A longitudinal study of televised news media. *Communication & Sport, 1*, 203–230.

Cummings, A. (2008). Progress realized? The continuing American Indian mascot quandary. *Marquette Sports Law, 18*(2), 309–335.

Cunningham, G.B. (2008). Creating and sustaining gender diversity in sport organizations. *Sex Roles, 58*, 1–2.

Cyphers, L., & Fagan, K. (2011, January 11). Unhealthy climate: Some coaches' homophobia is polluting the recruiting trail. Retrieved from http://sports.espn.go.com/ncw/news/story?page=Mag15unhealthyclimate

Davis-Delano, L.R. (2007). Eliminating Native American mascots: Ingredients for success. *Journal of Sport and Social Issues, 31*, 340–373.

Duncan, M.C., Messner, M.A., & Cooky, C. (2000). *Gender in televised sports: 1989, 1993 and 1999.* Retrieved from www.aafla.org/9arr/ResearchReports/tv2000.pdf

Eitzen, D.S. (2006). *Fair and foul: Beyond the myths and paradoxes of sport* (3rd ed.). Lanham, MD: Rowman & Littlefield.

Eitzen, D.S., & Sage, G.H. (2009). *Sociology of North American sport* (8th ed.). Boulder, CO: Paradigm.

Equity in Athletics Data Analysis. (2011). Retrieved from http://ope.ed.gov/athletics/index.aspx

Fink, J.S. (2008). Sex and gender diversity in sport: Concluding comments. *Sex Roles, 58*, 146–147.

Fink, J., Kane, M.J., & LaVoi, N.M. (in press). The freedom to choose: Elite female athletes' preferred representations within endorsement opportunities. *Journal of Sport Management.*

Glock, A. (2009). The selling of Candace Parker. *ESPN The Magazine, 12*(6), 26–28, 30–32.

Griffin, P. (1992). Changing the game: Homophobia, sexism and lesbians in sport. *Quest, 44*, 251–265.

Griffin, P. (1998). *Strong women, deep closets.* Champaign, IL: Human Kinetics.

Hardin, M., Dodd, J., Chance, J., & Walsdorf, K. (2004). Sporting images in black and white: Race in newspaper coverage of the 2000 Olympic Games. *Howard Journal of Communications, 15*(4), 211–227.

Hardin, M., Zhong, B., & Corrigan, T.F. (2012). The funhouse mirror: The blogosphere's reflection. In T. Dumova & R. Fiordo (Eds.), *Blogging in the global society: Cultural, political and geographical aspects* (pp. 55–71). Hershey, PA: IGI Global.

Hibberd, J. (2014, February 3). Final Super bowl ratings: Most-watched TV event ever! *Entertainment Weekly.* Retrieved from http://insidetv.ew.com/2014/02/03/super-bowl-ratings-3/

Hoberman, J. (2007). African athletic aptitude and the social sciences. *Equine and Comparative Exercise Physiology, 1*(4), 281–284.

Hofmann, S. (2005). The elimination of indigenous mascots, logos, and nicknames. *American Indian Quarterly, 29*, 156–17.

Iannotta, J., & Kane, M.J. (2002). Sexual stories as resistance narratives in women's sports: Reconceptualizing identity performance. *Sociology of Sport Journal, 19*, 347–369.

Johnson, G. (2012). Attendance sets all-time high: Overall spectators pass 11 million for fifth consecutive year. Retrieved from www.ncaa.com/news/basketball-women/article/2012-06-06/attendance-sets-all-time-high

Kane, M.J. (2011, August). Sex sells sex, not women's sports. *The Nation Magazine, 293*(7), 28–29.

Kane, M.J., & Buysse, J.A. (2005). Intercollegiate media guides as contested terrain: A longitudinal analysis. *Sociology of Sport Journal, 22*, 214–238.

Kane, M.J., LaVoi, N.M., Fink, J.S. (2013). Exploring elite female athletes' interpretations of sport media images: A window into the construction of social identity and "selling sex" in women's sports. *Communication & Sport, 1*, 269–298.

Kauer, K., & Krane, V. (2006). "Scary dykes" and "feminine queens": Stereotypes and female collegiate athletes. *Women in Sport & Physical Activity Journal, 15*, 42–55.

King, C.R. (2004). This is not an Indian: Situating claims about Indianness in sporting worlds. *Journal of Sport and Social Issues, 28*, 3–10.

Klos, D.M. (2013). The status of women in the U.S. media 2013. *Women's Media Center*, p. 1–52.

Krane, V. (2001). We can be athletic and feminine, but do we want to? Challenging hegemonic femininity in women's sport. *Quest, 53*, 115–133.

Krane, V., & Barber, H. (2005). Identity tensions in lesbian intercollegiate coaches. *Research Quarterly for Exercise and Sport, 76*, 67–81.

Lapchick, R. (2009). *The racial and gender report card.* Retrieved from http://web.bus.ucf.edu/sportbusiness/?page=1445

Lapchick, R. (2011). *2011 race and gender report card.* Retrieved from www.tidesport.org/racialgenderreportcard.html

Lapchick, R. (2013, February 25). Diversity progress, diversity hiring in sports media still poor. *Street & Smith's SportsBusiness Journal.* Retrieved from www.sportsbusinessdaily.com/Journal/Issues/2013/02/25/Opinion/Richard-Lapchick.aspx

Lapchick, R., Anjorin, R., & Nickerson, B. (2012). Striving for sustained positive change: The BCA hiring report card for NCAA FBS and FCS head coaching positions (2011–2012). Retrieved from www.tidesport.org/Grad%20Rates/BCA/2012%20BCA%20Football%20Report%20Card.pdf

Lapchick, R., Costa, P., Sherrod, T., & Anjorin, R. (2012). The 2012 racial and gender report card: National Football League. Retrieved from www.tidesport.org/racialgenderreportcard.html

LaVoi, N.M., & Calhoun, A.S. (2014). Digital media and female athletes. In A.C. Billings & M. Hardin (Eds.), *Routledge handbook of sport and new media* (pp. 320–330). New York, NY: Routledge.

LaVoi, N.M., & Dutove, J. K. (2012). Barriers and supports for female coaches: An ecological model. *Sports Coaching Review*, *1*(1), 17–37.

LaVoi, N.M., & Thul, C.M. (2009, May). Sports-based youth development for underserved girls. San Francisco, CA: Team Up for Youth.

LaVoi, N.M., & Wiese-Bjornstal, D. (2007). Girls' physical activity participation: Recommendations for best practices, programs, policies and future research. In M.J. Kane & N.M. LaVoi (Eds.), *The Tucker Center research report, developing physically active girls: An evidence-based multidisciplinary approach* (pp. 1–5). Minneapolis, MN: The Tucker Center for Research on Girls & Women in Sport, University of Minnesota.

Leiber, J. (2006, May 11). *Harris stands tall in painful battle with Penn State coach*. Retrieved from www.usatoday.com/sports/college/womensbasketball/2006-0511-jennifer-harris_x.htm

Lisec, J., & McDonald, M. (2012). Gender inequality in the new millennium: An analysis of WNBA representations in sport blogs. *Journal of Sports Media*, *7*(2), 153–178.

National Center for Lesbian Rights. (2009). *Sulpizio and Bass v. San Diego Mesa College*. Retrieved from www.nclrights.org/site/PageServer?pagename=issue_caseDocket_sulpizio

National Collegiate Athletic Association. (2012). *2004–2010 NCAA gender equity report*. Retrieved from www.ncaa-publications.com/p-4267-research-ncaa-gender-equity-report-2004-2010.aspx

National Federation of State High School Athletic Associations. (2012). *2011–12 high school athletics participation survey*. Retrieved from www.nfhs.org/content.aspx?id=3282

Parker, H.M., & Fink, J.S. (2008). The effect of sport commentator framing on viewer attitudes. *Sex Roles*, *58*, 116–126.

Rada, J.A., & Wulfemeyer, K.T. (2005). Color coded: Racial descriptors in television coverage of intercollegiate sports. *Journal of Broadcasting & Electronic Media*, *49*(1), 65–86.

Spracklen, K. (2008). The holy blood and the holy grail: Myths of scientific racism and the pursuit of excellence in sport. *Leisure Studies*, *27*, 221–227.

Staurowsky, E.J. (2004). Privilege at play: On the legal and social fictions that sustain American Indian sport imagery. *Journal of Sport and Social Issues*, *28*, 11–29.

Stone, J. (2013, February 2). How much do Super Bowl commercials cost? Ad prices continue to rise, still a bargain. *International Business Times*. Retrieved from www.ibtimes.com/how-much-do-super-bowl-commercials-cost-ad-prices-continue-rise-still-bargain-1057574

St. Louis, B. (2003). Sport, genetics and the "natural athlete": The resurgence of racial science. *Body & Society*, *9*(2), 75.

Theberge, N. (2000). *Higher goals: Women's ice hockey and the politics of gender*. Albany, NY: State University of New York Press.

Tuaolo, E., & Cyphers, L. (2002, October 30). *Free and clear*. Retrieved from http://espn.go.com/magazine/vol5no23tuaolo.html

Turner, B.A., & Chelladurai, P. (2005). Organizational and occupational commitment, intention to leave, and perceived performance of intercollegiate coaches. *Journal of Sport Management*, *19*, 193–211.

United States Census Bureau. (2012). *State and county quick facts*. Retrieved from http://quickfacts.census.gov/qfd/states/00000.html

Williams, D. (2006). Patriarchy and the "Fighting": A gendered look at racial college sports nicknames. *Race and Ethnicity Education*, *9*, 325–340.

Women's Sports Foundation. (2005). *Her life depends on it: Sport, physical activity and the health and well-being of American girls*. Retrieved from www.womenssportsfoundation.org/binary-data/WSF_ARTICLE/pdf_file/990.pdf

HISTORICAL MOMENTS

1896	First modern Olympic Games held in Athens, Greece
1903	First Tour de France held
1904	FIFA established
1930	First British Empire Games (now Commonwealth Games) held in Hamilton, Ontario
1950	Inaugural Formula One World Championship held in Great Britain
1960	First Paralympic Summer Games held in Rome, Italy
1972	At Munich Olympics Games, Israeli athletes were taken hostage and killed
1975	First International Cricket Council (ICC) Cricket World Cup held
1976	First Paralympic Winter Games held in Örnsköldsvik, Sweden
1984	At Olympic Games in Los Angeles, Joan Benoit Samuelson won first Olympic women's marathon
1987	First Rugby Union World Cup held
1989	Hillsborough Stadium disaster claimed 96 lives during soccer match in England
1991	First Women's FIFA World Cup held
1995	Bosman case changed soccer transfer rules in European Union
2002	Japan and Korea cohosted FIFA World Cup
2006	Inaugural World Baseball Classic held
2007	United Nations' Convention on the Rights of Persons with Disabilities (Article 30.5) included sport as a human right
2009	United Nations awarded International Olympic Committee official observer status
2009	IOC awarded 2016 Olympic and Paralympic Games to Rio de Janeiro (first time to a South American city)
2010	Qatar awarded 2022 FIFA Men's World Cup (first time to an Islamic nation) in a controversial move by FIFA
2010	Canadian cross-country skier Brian McKeever became the first Paralympian named to an Olympic Winter Games team
2012	Muslim women from several countries in the Middle East and Asia (e.g., Saudi Arabia, Brunei, and Qatar) were allowed to participate in the Olympic Games by their respective countries for the first time
2012	Oscar Pistorius became first double amputee to compete in an Olympic Games athletics event
2012	IOC–IPC strategic partnership agreement granted games management, sponsorship, and broadcast rights to IOC and the Organizing Committee of the Olympic Games in hosting Paralympic Games through 2020
2013	The UEFA banned Turkish clubs, Fenerbahec and Besiktas, for three years from Champions League over match fixing
2014	Sochi, Russia, hosted the XXII Olympic Winter Games

A NORTH AMERICAN PERSPECTIVE ON INTERNATIONAL SPORT

Ted G. Fay \ **Luisa Velez** \ **Lucie Thibault**

LEARNING OBJECTIVES

> Explain factors one might consider when defining international sport.
> Identify five key changes that have resulted in the expansion of international sport.
> Discuss three factors that have redefined international sport during the first quarter of the 21st century.
> Explain how advances in recruitment of athletes and marketing of teams and events have affected international sport.
> Identify nations with emerging economies that are attractive hosts for international sport competitions.
> Critically analyze issues related to manufacturing sport products in countries that use sweatshop labor.
> Discuss the influence on sport governance of corporate sponsorship, new and social media, drug testing and doping, assistive sport devices and technologies, and the inclusion of Paralympic athletes in single-sport or multi-sport international competitions.
> Identify skills, experiences, and competencies that help aspiring international sport managers prepare for the job market.
> Discuss three factors that will affect the future of international sport.

Key Terms

mbush marketing

ALCO (Bay Area Laboratory Co-operative)

ood doping

RPD (Committee on the Rights of Persons with Disabilities)

J (European Union)

FIFA (Fédération internationale de football association)

GATT (General Agreement on Tariffs and Trade)

GGSP (gross global sport product)

International Olympic Committee (IOC)

International Paralympic Committee (IPC)

NAFTA (North American Free Trade Agreement)

position player

Title IX

Youth Olympic Games (YOG)

GET A JOB

Continue on your journey in sport management by going to the web study guide (WSG) at www.HumanKinetics.com/ContemporarySportManagement. Check out the job opportunities and consider the skills and experiences that can help you succeed in sport management.

FIFA—Fédération Internationale de Football Association (i.e., International Federation of Association Football).

Youth Olympic Games (YOG)—New, elite multi-sport event created by the International Olympic committee to provide competitive opportunities to youth aged 15 to 18 years old in 28 summer sports and 7 winter sports.

During the later part of the 20th century, a number of events, companies, teams, and personalities transcended the isolation and limitations of regional and national recognition to become international sport brands across a broad cross section of cultures, religions, and locations around the globe. International events in this category include America's Cup, the Solheim Cup, the Ryder Cup, the **FIFA** World Cup, the Tour de France, the Rugby World Cup, the **Youth Olympic Games (YOG)**, and the Olympic and Paralympic Games (Vancouver 2010, London 2012, Sochi 2014, Rio 2016, PyeongChang 2018, Tokyo 2020, and so on). Professional leagues that are also brands include, for example, the NBA for basketball, English Premier League in soccer, and IPL in cricket. Similarly, athletic apparel and shoe companies (e.g., Nike, adidas–Reebok, Puma) and sport teams (e.g., Manchester United and Real Madrid in soccer, New York Yankees in baseball) share a high degree of global brand recognition. Like movie stars and musicians, athletes such as Candace Parker, Sachin Tendulkar, Inbee Park, Kobe Bryant, LeBron James, Lewis Hamilton, Serena and Venus Williams, Cristiano Ronaldo, Lionel Messi, Alexander Ovechkin, Sidney Crosby, Marta Empinotti, Usain Bolt, Alan Fonteles Cardoso Oliveira, Michael Phelps, and Tony Parker have reached near-cult status. Against this contemporary backdrop, this chapter provides snapshots of people, organizations, and historical events that have shaped and will continue to shape the international sport industry in the first quarter of the 21st century, which we hope will give you a better understanding of the ever-changing and expanding dimensions of international sport. This chapter also emphasizes the special skills, experiences, and competencies that will help you, as a new sport management professional, gain access to a career in the management of international sport.

What Is International Sport?

We consider two factors in determining whether a sport is international: (1) the context in which an individual, organization, or event operates within the international sport enterprise and (2) the degree to which, or the regularity with which, action by an individual, organization, or event focuses primarily on the international stage.

With respect to the context in which an organization operates, it is clear that the Olympic Games and Paralympic Games, world championships such as FIFA's Men's and Women's World Cups, and major annual international events such as the Tour de France, the Ryder Cup, and the tennis Grand Slam events, are among the giants of international sport. The same is true for multinational sport product and service corporations such as Nike and adidas, sport marketing and representation agencies such as Octagon and International Management Group (IMG), and sport facility design and management firms such as Populous (formerly HOK Sport), Ellerbe Becket, AEG, and Global Spectrum.

Assessing the degree to which an organization is engaged in international sport can be more difficult, especially if it operates almost exclusively in one nation or is only occasionally involved with international athletes or clients. Examples of these types of organizations include United States, European, or Asian-based professional sport leagues. For example, from a North American perspective, the National Basketball Association (NBA), Women's National Basketball Association (WNBA), Major League Baseball (MLB), National Football League (NFL), National Hockey League (NHL), National Pro Fastpitch (NPF), Major League Soccer (MLS), and National Women's Soccer League (NWSL) have a wealth of talented players who originate from all continents of the world. These leagues broaden their regional or national bases through marketing, branding, and broadcasting events to international audiences. They also recruit and market international players in hopes of gaining new international fans, start developmental leagues in various countries, and allow their athletes to play for their home countries during the Olympic Games or world championships. The creation of

grand tours by some of the world's most famous soccer teams (e.g., Manchester United, Chelsea, Real Madrid, Arsenal, Liverpool, AC Milan, FC Barcelona, Juventus) to play high-profile exhibition matches, in the United States and China, for example, signals the recognition of the value of creating an international brand (Foer, 2004). Clearly, we can examine international sport in several ways. To avoid confusion, this chapter addresses only the organizations, events, and governance structures that are involved internationally on a regular basis or as one of their primary functions.

Similar to the NFL or NBA playing games overseas, the Guinness International Champions Cup is an opportunity for European teams to play exhibition contests in front of mainly U.S.-based audiences.

Expansion of International Sport

During the last two decades, sport enjoyed unprecedented international growth, mostly in the first-world economies of North America, Europe, and parts of Asia. This growth could be seen in (1) dramatic changes in the Olympic Games and Paralympic Games, (2) increased opportunities for women in sport, (3) the redefinition of international sport, (4) extension of international recruitment and marketing efforts, and (5) the introduction of countries from emerging economies such as Brazil, Russia, India, China, South Africa, and Turkey (BRICSAT) as potential hosts for major global sporting events.

Dramatic Changes in the Olympic Games

Between 1968 and 1984, several events occurred that produced lasting effects on the Olympic Games. Change began at the 1968 Mexico City Games with the compelling and symbolic Black Power salute on the medal podium by American sprinters Tommie Smith and John Carlos. The Summer Olympic Games of 1972, held in Munich, Germany, marked the birth of an international sport revolution. The West German government was eager to demonstrate its rebirth as a peaceful nation free of its dark past associ-

Sport Mega Events in Brazil: Initial Repercussions

By Ricardo João Sonoda-Nunes, Brasil
Federal University of Paraná, Paraná

The 2013 FIFA Confederations Cup was held in Brazil. It marked the beginning of the final preparations for the 2014 World Cup, which also took place in Brazil. The country has been planning future sport mega events since the Pan American Games were held in Rio de Janeiro in 2007. Along with the World Cup, the 2016 Summer Olympics Games are also set to take place in Brazil.

Brazilian children practiced soccer as the country prepared to host the 2014 FIFA World Cup.

Beyond this important moment in the history for Brazilian sport, however, the beginning of the Confederations Cup was marked by outside issues beyond the technical competitive activity of sport. A series of demonstrations swept the country, mobilizing hundreds of thousands of people in major Brazilian cities as the demonstrators demanded improvements in public transportation, education, and health. The protests, which took place during the start of the Cup competitions to draw international media attention, were also designed to display the citizens' opposition to the excessive spending that takes place in mega sporting events. The demonstrations, which lasted several days, were organized by social networks (e.g., Facebook), and reached audiences around the globe, as protests were also organized in the UK and Portugal.

WEB

Go to the WSG and complete the first web search activity, which asks you to investigate the legacy of the 2012 Summer Olympic Games held in London, England.

ated with the anti-Semitism of Hitler and the Nazis at the 1936 Olympic Games and the Holocaust of the late 1930s and early 1940s (Reeve, 2000). Even as the world watched the incredible performances of athletes such as triple gold and silver medalist Olga Korbut of the USSR in women's gymnastics and Jewish American Mark Spitz, who won seven gold medals in men's swimming, the prevailing idealistic sense that the Olympic Games were above international politics was about to be shattered forever.

In terms of sport, Brazil suffers from problems relating to planning and management. Amid the protests during the Confederations Cup, the Brazilian government continued to encourage sports training within the country including in schools, clubs, sports federations, and other institutions. In recent years the federal government has significantly increased investments to promote sport, especially at the high-performance level. This has been done in an attempt to strengthen the country's participation in the Rio Olympic Games in 2016.

Between 2013 and 2016, the federal government plans to invest R$2.5 billion (equivalent to US$1.15 billion) in sport, with R$1.5 billion (US$690 million) for the high-yield sports in which Brazil is more likely to have success, and R$1 billion (US$460 million) for the Brazil Plan Awards, which in turn will allocate R$690 million (US$317 million) in the form of athlete support (scholarships for athletes and coaching staff, equipment, sports equipment and training in Brazil and abroad) and R$310 million (US$142 million) in training centers (construction, renovation, and operation of 22 centers, one Olympic and one Paralympic). The aforementioned investments are only those made through the sports ministry (SM). The country's total investments are much higher when one considers the investments made by other ministries such as the education and culture ministry (ECM), which launched a training program for high school sports.

The SM is comprised of three departments: National Secretariat of Sport High Performance; National Secretariat of Sports, Education, Leisure and Social Inclusion; and the National Secretariat of Football and Defense of Rights Supporter. Of the five priority programs related to sports training in the SM, four are linked to the Secretary of High Performance and only one is linked to the Secretariat of Sports, Education, Leisure and Social Inclusion. Regarding the recent creation of a Secretariat specific for football (soccer), beyond the country's sociocultural bond with the sport, the World Cup also served as a factor.

These are just some of the initial effects in Brazil related to sport mega events. More changes are sure to come in the next few years with the country's hosting of the FIFA World Cup and the Olympic Games.

International Learning Activity #1

Along with the protests that took place surrounding the 2013 Confederations Cup, what other examples of social unrest surrounding major sporting events can you identify? Conduct a search to find similar events and discuss the repercussions of these events for the country in which they took place as well as the various sport stakeholders.

International Learning Activity #2

Choose a country other than the United States. Create a profile of your selected country by investigating its most popular sport activities, sport facilities, and famous athletes. Describe the prime sport exports and imports of this country, including the production of goods and services, the existence of prominent sport leagues and events, the development of players and coaches in particular sports, offices of international sport federations (IFs), and so on.

International Learning Activity #3

Research the country of Brazil and its successful bids to host the World Cup and the Olympic Games. What did sport managers in Brazil do to ensure that their country was granted hosting duties for these events? What can other World Cup or Olympic host country hopefuls learn from Brazil?

The perception that the Olympic Games were immune to the evils of the world changed dramatically on September 5, 1972, with the tragic murder of 11 Israeli Olympic athletes and coaches and a German police officer by Palestinian terrorists in the Munich Olympic Village. This 20-hour saga, watched by a worldwide audience of more than 900 million viewers, sent shock waves through the international sport establishment (Reeve, 2000). This horrific catastrophe permanently altered the safety and security procedures required for all subsequent Olympic Games and other major international sporting events.

The year 1972 also witnessed conflict between the competing principles of amateurism and professionalism in the Olympic Games. At both the Winter and Summer Games, some sporting goods manufacturers (e.g., adidas, Puma) were accused of under-the-table payments to alpine skiers such as Karl Schranz of Austria, track and field athletes such as Michel Jazy of France, and swimmers such as Mark Spitz of the United States. Such payments challenged the concept of amateurism that had been carefully promulgated and fiercely protected by American Avery Brundage, who reigned as **International Olympic Committee (IOC)** president from 1952 to 1972.

The controversy involving individual-sport athletes, however, paled in comparison to the debate over inequities in team sports (e.g., men's ice hockey, basketball), wherein the USSR was accused of fielding professional teams against the amateurs from Western countries. The fierce debate over the eligibility of professional athletes to participate in the Olympic Games reached a flashpoint in 1972 because of the controversial upset victory by the Soviet Union (51-50) over the favored U.S. team. This game marked the first loss by a U.S. men's basketball team in Olympic history. In response to this loss, some within the U.S. Olympic Committee and Western European national Olympic committees accused the Soviet players of being quasi-professionals who were paid by their government. Many observers believed that the idea of sending NBA all-stars instead of the best U.S. amateur collegians gained serious momentum as a result of this loss. A month after the 1972 Summer Olympic Games, the professionalism controversy deepened when a team of Canadian NHL all-stars challenged the reigning Olympic and world ice hockey champions ("amateurs") from the Soviet Union for the first time in history. The Canadian professionals barely emerged victorious in what ice hockey historians called "The Series of the Century" or "The Cold War on Ice."

A New Dawn in Women's Sports

The year also marked the passage of **Title IX** of the Education Reform Act of 1972, a law that set off a revolution in women's sports in the United States and, indirectly, around the world. Title IX challenged male privilege within the Olympic Movement and other international sport federations. As a result, by the time of the 2004 Athens Olympic Games, the level of women's participation in both the Summer and Winter Games, as measured by the number of athletes, number of sports, and number of events, had become nearly equal to that of men (King, 2005). In the 2012 London Olympic Games, a new record was set as 42% of the athletes were women, including Olympians from three Muslim-majority nations (Saudi Arabia, Brunei, and Qatar) that were allowing women to participate for the first time. In comparison, 26 nations did not send female athletes to the 1996 Atlanta Olympic Games. 2012 also marked the first time that the U.S. Olympic team was comprised of more women (269) than men (261). American women also won more total and gold medals (58 to 45, with 29 to 17 gold) than the U.S. men (Longman, 2012). This total exceeded the overall women's and men's medals won by all but four nations (Rapp, 2012).

A critical effect of Title IX has been the slow but steady growth in the number of women who are assuming leadership roles within international sport federations, including increased numbers of women being selected as members of the IOC. In 1995, then IOC president Juan Antonio Samaranch established a Women and Sport Working Group to advise the IOC executive board on policies regarding women's roles in international sport. This group, chaired by former U.S. Olympian and IOC vice president Anita DeFrantz, became a full-fledged IOC commission in March 2004.

International Olympic Committee (IOC)—A nonprofit, international, multisport federation responsible for the governance of the Olympic Movement and its premier event, the Summer and Winter Olympic Games. It is also responsible for the Youth Olympic Games. The IOC works closely with national Olympic committees, with international sport federations, and with the organizing committees of the Olympic Games.

Title IX—A U.S. law mandating equal opportunity for women and men in educational programs and activities that receive federal financial assistance.

Redefinition of International Sport

During the latter 20th century, many aspects of international sport changed profoundly. Primary among those changes were the advent of corporate sponsorship associated with the Olympic Games, a shift in the balance of power, and the emergence of soccer as a worldwide obsession.

THE OLYMPIC GAMES GO CORPORATE AND PROFESSIONAL

Faced with possible political and financial disaster, the IOC reluctantly altered its rules governing corporate involvement for the 1984 Summer Olympic Games in Los Angeles. For the first time in Olympic history, the IOC allowed the Los Angeles Olympic Organizing Committee (LAOOC), under the leadership of its entrepreneurial CEO, Peter Ueberroth, to charge significant fees for corporate sponsorship that included the use of the Olympic rings. The financial success of these Olympic Games touched off a sport marketing and event management revolution.

In 1985, yielding to increasing pressure to allow professional athletes to participate in the Olympic Games, the IOC eliminated all references to the term *amateur* and allowed each international sport federation (IF) to determine its own eligibility rules. This landmark decision opened the door for professional athletes to compete in both Summer Games and Winter Games and helped level the playing field between the state-supported athletes of the Soviet bloc and their Western counterparts.

NEW KIDS ON THE BLOCK: A SHIFT IN THE BALANCE OF POWER AND PLAYERS

Over the past several decades, the balance of power in international sport has shifted dramatically with each breakthrough victory by an individual, team, or nation. Beginning with Australia's win in the 1983 America's Cup, to the Tour de France successes of American cyclists Greg LeMond and Lance Armstrong (who admitted in 2013 to blood doping and the use of banned performance-enhancing substances), to China's Chen Lu becoming the first Asian to win a World Ladies Figure Skating Championship in 1995, the previously predictable world of international sport has been transformed. Although the United States claims to have the best baseball league in the world, Team USA did not make it to the semifinals in the 2006 and 2013 World Baseball Classics (WBC), and lost in the semifinals in the 2009 WBC. Although Japan took the crown in the 2006 and 2009 WBCs, the Caribbean island nations of Cuba, the Dominican Republic, and Puerto Rico emerged as serious baseball contenders in both years, with the Dominican Republic winning in 2013

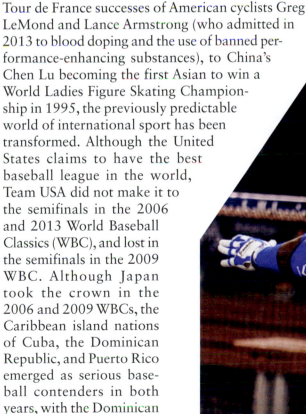

Team Dominican Republic is emerging as a power player in the global baseball arena.

over Caribbean neighbor Puerto Rico 3-0 (Torres, 2013). Europeans have taken turns dominating the professional women's and men's tennis tours, while European, African, Asian, and Australian golfers have consistently succeeded on the LPGA and PGA Tours. Clearly, single nations or regions no longer dominate specific sports.

SOCCER: THE WORLD'S SPORT OBSESSION

The period from 1992 through 2013 brought a dramatic shift in both men's and women's soccer. Teams from Africa, Asia, and the United States emerged to challenge the dominance of a few select European and South American teams. In 1994, the United States successfully hosted the FIFA Men's World Cup, played before record crowds of spectators (3.58 million) and television viewers (2.1 billion worldwide). Despite scandals and fan violence, soccer has continued to expand its presence globally. New professional leagues for men have formed in Japan, Korea, and China. An elite professional league in the United States was restarted with the MLS league in 1996, and the U.S. team surprised many by finishing second to Brazil in the FIFA Confederations Cup in 2009. Hosting the 2010 FIFA Men's World Cup was awarded to South Africa and returned to Brazil in 2014. Clearly, FIFA has successfully expanded from its traditional roots in Europe and South America to Asia, North America, Africa, and Russia, as highlighted by its highly controversial award to the Middle-Eastern emirate of Qatar for the Men's World Cup in 2022.

In 1991, the first FIFA Women's World Cup was held in China. It was followed by the 1995 Women's World Cup in Sweden and the 1999 Women's World Cup in the United States, where more than 90,000 fans watched in the Los Angeles Rose Bowl as a scoreless tie between China and the United States was settled by a shootout, won by the United States. This victory gave the U.S. team its second successive World Cup title. In the 2003 Women's World Cup, Germany defeated the favored Americans and thus joined the elite group of nations (i.e., United States, Norway, and China) that had ruled women's soccer in the 1990s.

The successful U.S. hosting of the Women's World Cup in 1999 and again in 2003 had a tremendous influence on the popularity of the game with girls and women throughout the world. Players such as Mia Hamm and Brandi Chastain (United States), Sun Wen (China), Sisleide do Amor Lima (known as Sissi) and Kátia Cilene Teixeira da Silva (known as Kátia) (Brazil), and Birgit Prinz (Germany) became well known. Endorsements, professional league contracts, and television deals became connected with the women's game for the first time. The ascent of the United States as a world power in women's soccer is often attributed to the role that Title IX played in supporting the development of sport for girls and women at the school, college, and elite club level. Following the 2003 demise of the Women's United Soccer Association (WUSA), efforts to create another league for women were undertaken by the Women's Soccer Initiative. As a result, the Women's Professional Soccer (WPS) league was established in 2007, and held its inaugural season in 2009, culminating in a championship by Sky Blue FC. Although the WPS was disbanded and ceased operations in 2012, a new women's professional league (the NWSL) began play in the spring of 2013. It will be interesting to see if a third shot at a women's professional soccer league in the United States will ultimately prove to be sustainable.

Recruitment and Marketing

Changes in the recruitment of international athletes and the expansion of teams and organizations marketing that began in the late 20th century with a more global focus have had a profound effect on the nature and conduct of international sport. Today, athletes and teams have numerous additional options, and consumers have enhanced access to performances, products, and services.

RECRUITMENT

The recruitment and development of top players from nontraditional locations has accelerated because most professional sport leagues scout the world for talent. This practice is common among the elite soccer leagues in Europe, where many of the top players on professional clubs are not from the home region, from the home nation, or even of European origin. It is common to find South American, North American, Asian, Australian, and African players starting in the first division of premier European soccer leagues. This trend is also seen among the top North American leagues. The NBA has players from Brazil, Argentina, Canada, Australia, Germany, Croatia, Congo, Nigeria, Senegal, Spain, Turkey, and China. Korean, Japanese, Caribbean, Latin American, Canadian, and Australian players are increasing in number in MLB. Players from Russia, Sweden, Finland, Czech Republic, Slovakia, and other European countries are prominent in the NHL, Canadians and Australians play on college teams in NCAA softball, and an array of international stars from Europe, Asia, Canada, Australia, and South America participate in the WNBA and NWSL.

With the appearance of NBA and European league professionals in world championship and Olympic tournaments and the recruitment of foreign players in Division I college basketball, players from Europe, Asia, Africa, and South America have gained a greater presence in the NBA. In the 2012–13 season, 84 athletes from 37 countries (other than the United States) played in the NBA. Many of the international athletes are stars in the league, including players such as Tim Duncan (U.S. Virgin Islands), Steve Nash (Canada), Luol Deng (Sudan), Manu Ginóbili (Argentina), Tony Parker (France), Pau Gasol (Spain), and Dirk Nowitzki (Germany).

In professional baseball, the 1990s produced an unexpected star in Hideo Nomo, a pitcher for the Los Angeles Dodgers of MLB's National League (NL). Nomo was the first Japanese player to play in the major leagues since 1963, when Masanori Murakami pitched briefly for the San Francisco Giants. In 1995, Nomo was named to the 1995 NL All-Star team and was the NL Rookie of the Year. In 2001, Ichiro Suzuki, another Japanese national, became an overnight phenomenon as the first Japanese **position player** in MLB when he won the American League's MVP award, batting title, and Rookie of the Year award in the same season. The success of Nomo and Ichiro set off a groundswell of signings of other Asian players by MLB teams (e.g., Kosuke Fukudome, Daisuke Matsuzaka, Hong-Chih Kuo). International athletes are now so common in professional sport leagues, it is taken for granted.

The increasing number of international athletes who compete in elite professional sport leagues based in North America, Europe, and Asia continues to broaden the definition of what constitutes international sport. The leagues use the influence and appeal of these players to market to new audiences at home while expanding their teams' brands through the sale of broadcast rights, team merchandise, and other product extensions overseas. An interesting result of increased access to international stars has been a corresponding drop in fan interest and attendance within regionally focused professional leagues. For example, the rise of Japanese players in MLB has resulted in an increased interest among Japanese fans in watching Japanese players play on television for MLB teams in the United States and a drop in attendance at Japanese professional baseball league games (Maguire & Nakayama, 2005).

In light of these developments, major professional leagues in soccer, basketball, baseball, and ice hockey have formed new working agreements. Leagues and franchises have sought to create a climate of cooperation and a more orderly international transfer of players. Both of these efforts have been affected by court rulings. In the early 1990s, a number of Canadian- and U.S.-based players migrated to the national teams of their ancestry, giving rise to issues over the eligibility of dual nationals to participate in the Olympic Winter Games. Issues involving transfer fees and freedom of movement of

position player—Any baseball player other than a pitcher.

Russian and other European players to the NHL also developed. The case that laid the foundation for future decisions occurred in 1995 when Jean-Marc Bosman, a Belgian soccer player, challenged the Belgian Football Association and the Union of European Football Associations (UEFA) over their system that allowed only a certain number of foreign-born players on each professional club. In this case, the European Court of Justice ruled that transfer fees for out-of-contract, foreign-born soccer players who were transferred between clubs from one EU nation to another were illegal and represented a restraint of trade.

SPORT MARKETING AS A GLOBAL PHENOMENON

The international expansion of sport has set off a flurry of activity in sport marketing. In 1989, the NBA launched a global marketing campaign to expand the brand awareness of its teams, players, and league-licensed merchandise. This campaign was perfectly positioned to capitalize on the gold medal performance of the 1992 U.S. Olympic men's basketball team led by the NBA's best. As much by design as by happenstance, Michael Jordan and Magic Johnson became even greater international sport icons. The NBA is now one of the most recognized sport brands in the world, and it is poised to consider expansion of team franchises into Europe in the coming years. Evidence of the success of the NBA's global recognition and its popularity among fans is the fact that in the 2008–09 season, the top-selling jersey in China was Kobe Bryant's while Yao Ming's jersey ranked 6th in sales (National Basketball Association, 2009).

Successful and popular professional sport teams such as the New York Yankees and Manchester United have experimented with forming unique business partnerships to broaden themselves as worldwide brands, particularly in China. Even the ownership of these teams is undergoing a radical international shift from national to international investment and ownership control. In 2005, American Malcolm Glazer began the invasion of American owners in English Premiership with his takeover of Manchester United. British soccer fans and sport media were outraged by this action, which was seen as anti-British, and could be compared with the purchase of the Yankees by a Russian business mogul.

The hosting of international competitions is increasingly done by countries looking to position themselves on the international sport scene. Iran is such a country. They hosted the Wrestling World Cup 2013 in Tehran.

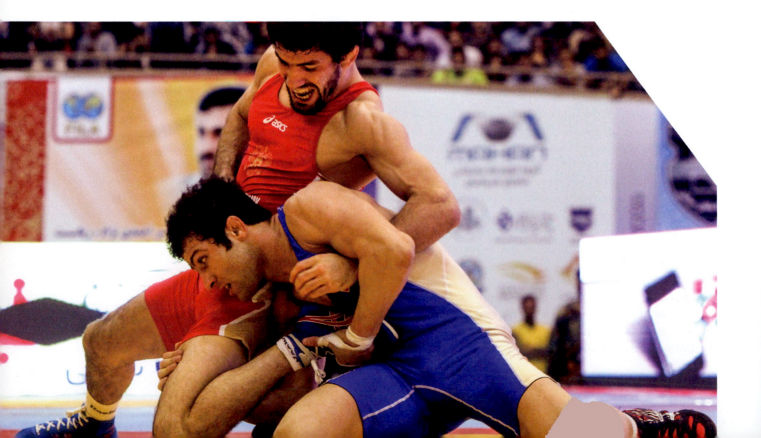

Emergence of China as a Sport Superpower

The most socially and politically significant sport-related event that occurred during the latter half of the 20th century was U.S. President Richard Nixon's decision to use sport as a diplomatic tool by sending a U.S. table tennis team to China in 1972. This historic event, which is often referred to as Ping-Pong diplomacy, marked the beginning of the normalization of diplomatic and economic relations between the United States and China.

Since that time, China has emerged as a new Olympic power, challenging the traditional powers led by the United States, Russia (formerly the Soviet Union), and other Western countries. China has invested heavily in a government-run and government-sponsored sport model that identifies children with talent in specific sports and then trains them intensively in residential training centers for elite and promising athletes.

Similar to its Soviet and East German predecessors, China, while not forgetting to support its burgeoning men's programs, has invested significant amounts of money and other resources into developing its women's programs in numerous sports. These efforts to develop elite Chinese athletes have produced numerous medals, as evidenced by China's finishing third overall in total medals behind the United States and Russia at both the 2000 and 2004 Olympic Games, dominating the gold medal count in the 2008 Beijing Olympic Games, and coming in second in total medals in 2012 behind the United States. China also topped the medal count at the 2004, 2008, and 2012 Summer Paralympic Games, sending shock waves through the traditional Paralympic powers.

This strategy of developing winning international teams in a variety of high-profile sports has created a strong sense of national pride. It has also assisted the government in garnering increased international respect. The potential growth in real **gross global sport product (GGSP)** for all segments of the international sport industry will come from new sport media (e.g., traditional, new media, social media) and marketing opportunities, the rise of new professional leagues, the exportation of elite athletic talent, the incredible growth of new facilities of all types, and expanded sport manufacturing and product development. With this boom in the establishment of a new sport infrastructure for China, other segments of the sport enterprise, such as finance and licensing, will continue to accelerate. We will also see the creation of joint ventures and alliances between established U.S. and European sport firms and their Chinese partners.

GGSP (Gross Global Sport Product)—Total economic output of the sport industry worldwide.

Emerging Economies

The end of the cold war and the dissolution of the Soviet Union and East Germany in 1989 helped spawn sport market economies in the new nation states of Central and Eastern Europe. A similar emergence of sport market economies has occurred in South America, Africa, the Persian Gulf States, and Asia. A vibrant global marketplace based on new sources and pathways in both the production and distribution of goods and services has stimulated a dynamic export–import exchange among many nations and regions. Sport is often seen as a universal product that bridges cultural differences, customs, and belief systems, and thus is a vital part of the growing international business exchange (Larmer, 2005).

In the 21st century, countries new to the international sport scene have positioned themselves as attractive for global commerce and, therefore, attractive as prospective hosts of international competitions. A shift has occurred from the so-called G20 group of industrialized nations to emerging markets in Asia (e.g., China, India) and the Middle East (e.g., the Gulf States of Abu Dhabi, Bahrain, Dubai, Qatar). Host countries have included South Africa with the 2010 Men's FIFA World Cup, Turkey with the 2010 FIBA World Basketball Championship (the country is also a finalist for consideration for hosting the 2020 Olympic Games), Brazil with the 2014 FIFA World Cup and the 2016 Olympic and Paralympic Games, Russia hosting the 2014 Olympic and Paralympic Winter Games and the 2018 FIFA World Cup, and Qatar hosting the 2022 FIFA World Cup.

Current Issues in International Sport

As a prospective sport management professional, you need to be aware of many issues in international sport. In this section, we examine several concerns associated with international sport governance. (See "Ethics in International Sport" later in this chapter for discussion of another issue, the relocation of sporting goods manufacturing companies.) A key step on your journey into international sport is developing an understanding of complicated international sport governance structures (see figure 19.1). Eligibility for each Olympic- and Paralympic-related sport is governed and controlled by international sport federations (IF) and their related national sport governing federations

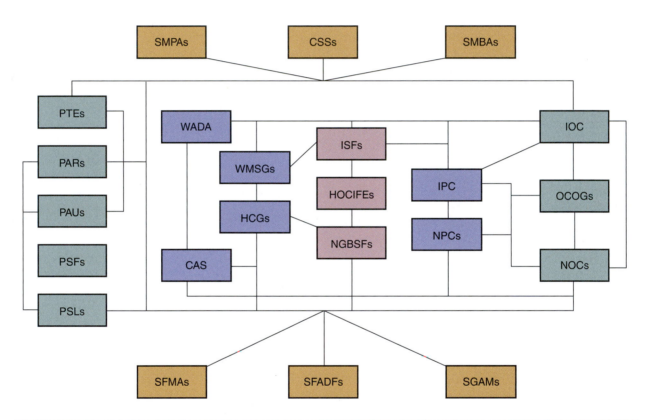

Figure 19.1 Universe of key international sport governance and industry interrelationships.
Created by Ted Fay 2006.

or bodies (NSF or NGB). Note that the IFs have relationships with the IOC and the **International Paralympic Committee (IPC)**, but they are not formally part of the IOC or the IPC. These federations, therefore, sometimes differ with the IOC and IPC with respect to rules, athlete eligibility, competitive opportunities, and funding, although the World Anti-Doping Agency (WADA) has tried to standardize drug testing sanctions for positive drug tests.

Before 1985, international sport focused on amateur sports that were included in the Olympic Games, Commonwealth Games, or hemispheric games (e.g., Asian Games, Pan-African Games, Pan-American Games). Over the past 30 years, a number of new entities have become involved in international sport governance. These changes reflect the evolution of international sport from a relatively small number of organizations that emphasized amateur sport to a highly complex set of interrelated organizations with billions of U.S. dollars at stake. The principal additions include (1) professional sport organizations, such as sport franchises, leagues, tours, and circuits; (2) professional athlete unions (PAUs), along with professional athlete representatives (PARs); (3) the Court of Arbitration for Sport (CAS), which adjudicates issues such as international athlete eligibility and breaches of fair play; (4) WADA, an independent testing, research, and education organization working to eliminate the use of banned performance-enhancing substances and techniques from international sport competition; and (5) sport organization and event sponsors that provide critical support and funding to athletes, organizations, and events.

Numerous problems confront the governance of international sport. The following sections focus on four primary issues: corporate sponsorship, drug testing and arbitration, the use of assistive devices, and concerns associated with the Paralympic Games.

Corporate Sponsorship

A classic example of the complexities of international sport governance involved the 1992 U.S. men's Olympic basketball team. Some members of the team were NBA players who had endorsement contracts with sponsors other than the official U.S. Olympic team sponsors. In 1992, Reebok was the official U.S. Olympic outerwear sponsor, providing warm-up jackets to Olympic athletes in all sports. As the gold medalist U.S. basketball team stood on the victory podium, some of them covered the Reebok name and logo on their warm-up jackets with American flags. Michael Jordan, a Nike-sponsored athlete, initiated this action because he did not want to be seen implicitly endorsing his company's competitor. This incident thrust the United States Olympic Committee (USOC), Nike, Reebok, USA Basketball, the NBA, the NBA Players Association, and Jordan into a high-stakes public relations battle. The USOC has since amended its code of conduct to include language that requires all U.S. Olympic athletes to wear the apparel provided by official U.S. Olympic sponsors.

In the years following the marketing success of the 1984 Olympic Games in Los Angeles, the IOC became an international sport marketing juggernaut. It has been fueled by billions of dollars in television rights fees from NBC and others, as well as millions from corporations in the TOP (The Olympic Partner) program. As shown in the sidebar "Rights and Opportunities for TOP Companies," TOP members have exclusive marketing rights to both the Summer and Winter Games. Because of the known effectiveness of an association with the Olympic Games, some non-TOP companies have engaged in **ambush marketing** by linking images of sports or athletes to the host city (e.g., "Good luck to our athletes in Vancouver"). Although these companies carefully refrain from the use of terms such as *Olympic* or *Olympic Games* in their ads, consumers psychologically infer a relationship between the product being advertised and the sporting event with which it is being linked. The IOC in partnership with the host

International Paralympic Committee (IPC)—A nonprofit, international, multisport federation responsible for the governance of the Paralympic Movement and its premier event, the Summer and Winter Paralympic Games. The IPC promotes sporting excellence for Paralympic athletes.

ambush marketing—A tactic whereby a company attempts to undermine the sponsorship activities of a rival that owns the legal rights to sponsor an event; intended to create the sense that the ambusher is officially associated with the event.

organizing committee for the Olympic Games, along with National Olympic Committees, have become forceful in limiting and counteracting ambush marketing campaigns by corporations and organizations intent on circumventing the costs of sponsorship. As noted earlier, to prevent future conflicts between official Olympic team sponsors and rival companies that have endorsement deals with Team USA players, the USOC has tightened its contracts and oversight.

Drug Testing and Arbitration

Another example of the complexities of international sport governance involves U.S. track and field athlete Butch Reynolds' challenge of the 1992 Olympic drug-testing procedures. Reynolds failed an out-of-competition drug test and was disqualified from participating in the 1992 Olympic Games. He subsequently filed suit against the International Association of Athletics Federations (IAAF), claiming that his urine specimens had been tampered with and that the analysis procedures had been flawed. The U.S. federal court's ruling in favor of Reynolds prompted several international sport federations to join the IOC in creating the Court of Arbitration for Sport (CAS), which mediates sport-related disputes that cross national boundaries (Hums & MacLean, 2008; Thoma & Chalip, 1996).

blood doping—The practice of illicitly boosting the number of red blood cells, which transport oxygen, to enhance athletic performance.

Bay Area Laboratory Co-operative (BALCO)—Founder Victor Conte and others have been implicated in providing designer performance-enhancing drugs and steroids to Major League Baseball players and several Olympic athletes.

Reynolds' dispute and other cases that followed led to the creation of WADA in 1999. As an independent agency, WADA has been willing to challenge sport federations and professional sport leagues by taking on the giants of sport such as Lance Armstrong and the International Cycling Union. Even so, issues related to **blood doping**, drugs, performance-enhancing supplements, steroids, and technologies that aid performance continue to challenge the foundation of international sport (Pound, 2004). Stemming from the government-sponsored cheating of the East Germans and other countries in the 1970s and 1980s and the free-market approach of companies such as U.S.–based **Bay Area Laboratory Co-operative (BALCO)**, the challenges facing sport governing bodies are staggering (Perez, 2008). One of the most staggering recent cases of the 21st century was the stunning confession of Lance Armstrong to a pattern of systematic blood

Rights and Opportunities for TOP Companies

Companies associated with The Olympic Partner (TOP) program receive exclusive marketing rights and opportunities within their designated product category. They may exercise these rights on a worldwide basis, and they may develop marketing programs with the various members of the Olympic Movement, The International Olympic Committee (IOC), the National Olympic Committees (NOCs), and the organizing committees (e.g., the London Organising Committee of the Olympic and Paralympic Games [LOCOG] for the 2012 Games). Besides exclusive worldwide marketing opportunities, partners receive the following benefits (Sponsorship, 2013, para. 7):

> Authorization to use all Olympic imagery as well as Olympic designations on products

> Opportunities for hospitality at the Olympic Games

> Direct advertising and promotional opportunities, including preferential access to Olympic broadcast advertising

> On-site concessions and franchise as well as product sale and showcase opportunities

> Protection from ambush marketing

> Acknowledgment of sponsors' support through a broad Olympic sponsorship recognition program

doping and use of performance-enhancing drugs over the course of his participation in the Tour de France, including from 1999 to 2006 when he won seven consecutive titles. Sadly, everyone else who joined him on the podium for those victories were also banned for various doping violations during this period as well (Jessop, 2013).

Assistive Devices

In the lead-up to the 2008 Olympic Games in Beijing, the world witnessed double-amputee Oscar Pistorius (a.k.a. the Blade Runner) in his efforts to qualify as a South African Olympic runner in the 400 meters. First banned by the IAAF for having an alleged competitive advantage for space-age prosthetics, Pistorius subsequently won his appeal in the CAS. Classification and eligibility of athletes with disabilities to compete in open competition in many sports using radical assistive technology is a new frontier in sport law and arbitration (Fay & Wolff, 2009; Wolbring, 2008). Although Pistorius was not able to compete in Beijing in 2008, he did subsequently qualify to compete in the individual 400-meter race and 4 x 400 meter relay at the 2012 Olympic Games in London.

Paralympic Governance Concerns

The Paralympic Games, which include elite athletes with physical or visual disabilities, are among the world's largest quadrennial sporting events. Both the Summer and Winter Paralympic Games occur two weeks after the Summer and Winter Olympic Games. Since 1988, they have been held at the same location and in the same facilities as the Olympic Games. An initial agreement in 2001 between the IOC and the IPC mandated that the city winning the bid to conduct the Olympic Games is obligated to organize the Paralympic Games as well (International Paralympic Committee, 2009). The host country is expected to modify its infrastructure where necessary to meet the accessibility needs of Paralympians. The IOC and IPC signed a new strategic partnership in 2012 that went beyond games management and infrastructure requirements to outline media and broadcast rights as well as corporate sponsorship regarding the Paralympic Games ("IOC and IPC," 2012).

Under the leadership of the IPC and its corresponding National Paralympic Committees (NPCs), the Paralympic Games have emerged as a viable international sport movement. Following the example regarding gender equity in U.S. sport, some people have begun to ask whether the national governing bodies of Olympic sports and the USOC should be required by law to integrate their structures, teams, management, and governance to include Paralympic athletes (Fay, Legg, & Wolff, 2005; Legg, Fay, Hums, & Wolff, 2009). In 1986, the U.S. Ski and Snowboard Association (USSA) became the

WEB

Go to the WSG and complete the second web search activity, which challenges you to investigate Lance Armstrong's confession to a decade of systematic doping and use of performance-enhancing substances and to consider the influence of national and international antidoping agencies.

Tool Kit for International Sport Managers

Essential equipment for a career in international sport includes an up-to-date world atlas, a current passport, appropriate visas, bilingual dictionaries, a pocket guide to currency exchange rates, several credit cards with reasonable credit lines, appropriate transportation tickets, a laptop computer with WiFi capability, a personal digital assistant (PDA), a cellular phone with international calling options, and items necessary to conduct business. You will be embarking on an adventure that will test your wits with respect to your personal habits, eating preferences, cultural understanding, business etiquette, patience, ability to develop a new network of friendships, and flexibility.

Sport Management Travel Tips

As a prospective sport manager preparing for a journey into international sport, what do you need to know? The first step in your journey is to develop an understanding of the primary trade treaties and agreements, such as the General Agreement on Tariffs and Trade (**GATT**), the North American Free Trade Agreement (**NAFTA**), and the rules and regulations that affect countries associated with the European Union (**EU**). This knowledge will provide a rudimentary foundation from which you can research other important trade regulations, currency exchanges, and legal issues concerning brand protection and intellectual property rights. You must also know how free or restricted the movement of goods, services, persons, and capital are from nation to nation. With an in-depth awareness of how well you, your employees, and your investments will be protected by a given legal system, you will know what recourse you have if problems occur. You also need to be highly attuned to security procedures, including visa requirements and other travel-related regulations.

GATT (General Agreement on Tariffs and Trade)—An agreement negotiated in 1947 among 23 countries, including the United States, to increase international trade by reducing tariffs and other trade barriers.

NAFTA (North American Free Trade Agreement)—A 1994 agreement reached by the United States, Canada, and Mexico that instituted a schedule for the phasing out of tariffs and eliminated a variety of fees and other hindrances to encourage free trade among the three countries.

EU—Known as the European Union, this is a unique economic and political partnership between 27 democratic European countries.

first national governing body of an Olympic sport to integrate Paralympic athletes into its operating structure. When the USSA assimilated the U.S. Disabled Ski Team (USDST), the USDST became, at least in theory, equal to the other U.S. ski teams (i.e., alpine and cross-country teams) of the USSA. This recognition allowed USDST athletes to compete in open USSA-sanctioned races, including the U.S. National Championships. In the future, governing bodies will likely continue to seek the best path to full and equitable inclusion of athletes with disabilities into international organizations and events (Fay, 1999).

Essentials for Aspiring International Sport Managers

Important segments of the international sport industry include arenas, event management, stadiums, sport products, ticketing, sport law, security, fitness centers, rehabilitation and sport medicine centers, sport marketing, accommodations, and travel. These segments are crucial to the conduct of international sport and are the areas in which the most growth will occur in the future, thereby providing the most opportunities for entry-level sport managers. To secure work in these venues, sport managers must master a wide knowledge and skill base.

International Sport Managers' Skill Set

Computer skills and the ability to navigate the Internet to conduct research and maintain daily business communication are basic skills for entry-level sport management positions. International sport has a personal relationship culture that requires strong oral and written communication skills as well as an understanding of electronic etiquette. A sales background or experience as an athlete is not a requirement, but both can be helpful in gaining a job and succeeding in it. As an international sport manager, you must be willing and able to travel, necessitating an adequate level of fitness and health.

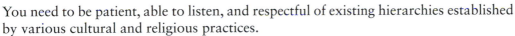

You need to be patient, able to listen, and respectful of existing hierarchies established by various cultural and religious practices.

Being able to communicate in the language of the country where you are working is extremely important. You might be told that your colleagues from other countries understand English better than they do or that you can obtain the services of an interpreter who, as it turns out, cannot or will not convey the nuances of key oral exchanges. Consequently, in international business and sport, even a rudimentary understanding of the language of the country in which you are doing business can gain you an invaluable advantage over the competition.

International Sport Managers' Worldview

If you aspire to a career in international sport management, you should consider (1) studying abroad, preferably in a country that speaks a language different from yours, for a minimum of one semester while still in school and (2) availing yourself of a wide range of publications, including industry and trade publications, Internet resources (e.g., websites, blogs, message boards), professional journals, newspapers, and magazines to keep you up to date on international political, business, and sport trends. This practice will give you knowledge of general business practices in a given culture, keep you current on what is happening in the global economy, and provide up-to-date information about world events.

A basic knowledge of how a sport operates internationally, how the specific rules of the game are applied, how the sport is structured, and where the locus of power resides with the sport (politically as well as on the field of play) can enhance your marketability. An understanding of trends in licensing, marketing, promotion, event management, and contracts is also helpful. Familiarity with international geography, such as shifting borders within geopolitical regions, will prevent a serious faux pas. Knowing as much as possible about a country's demography, geography, government, economy, and culture are extremely important to sport leaders working in the global context. Consider consulting *The World Factbook* developed by the Central Intelligence Agency (available online) to learn about the countries with which you are conducting business.

International Sport Management: It's Personal!

Success in the international sport and the business sphere is predicated on personal contact and friendship. Attending meetings of national sport federations, professional sport-related associations, and other conferences and symposia helps maintain and expand your network of professional contacts. Time availability, relevance to your professional interests, and financial resources are important factors to consider when choosing the associations or conferences and trade shows (e.g., China International Sporting Goods Show, Seoul International Sports and Leisure Industry Show) that you want to attend. Volunteering at a major international sports event, conference, or trade show is an effective way to gain access to the field and demonstrate your capabilities as a potential employee.

Forecasting the Future: International Sport 2014 and Beyond

In the beginning decades of the 21st century, the international sport industry has shifted and will continue to shift from being a niche in the sport marketplace to constituting the very foundation of the sport enterprise. In the following paragraphs, we discuss several trends that are destined to affect international sport.

Professional Profile: Kellie A. Cavalier

Title: event operations manager, USA Rugby

Education: BA (international studies), American University; MS (international sport management), State University of New York (SUNY) at Cortland; MS (international sport management), London Metropolitan Business School (LMBS)

Kellie Cavalier is a young professional working in event operations at USA Rugby, the national governing body for the sport located in Boulder, Colorado. For her undergraduate education, Cavalier graduated cum laude from American University in Washington, D.C. in 2007. She most recently completed a dual graduate degree program, graduating with honors from SUNY Cortland and from LMBS (a part of the London Metropolitan University) in 2013. Although happy in her current position, she would strongly consider moving onto a position in the future as a venue director of a large single-sport or multi-sport international event (e.g., Pan-American or Commonwealth Games, Olympic/Paralympic Games, America's Cup, Rugby 15s World Cup). Such a move would allow her to take on a progression of new and increasing professional challenges. She describes her career focus and goals as being "a sport manager with a background in international relations whose professional goal is to create sport events that resonate with both participants and spectators." By utilizing her significant experience in national team, VIP hospitality, and rugby event management, she hopes to produce events with impact and character.

What have been the key moves, steps, or developments in your career, and how did you arrive at your current position?

After finishing my undergraduate degree in 2007, I worked for three years for Events DC, first as a project coordinator and then as an assistant in the event operations, sport and entertainment division. During my time at Events DC, I liked the fact that my duties were varied, ranging from managing payroll systems for more than 150 employees, being responsible for coordinating venue, logistics, and volunteers at two college football bowl events, and assisting with logistics for four 2009 Presidential inaugural events, as well as developing and implementing a document management system for Events DC. Call me crazy, but during that time period, I also assumed a part-time position as manager for USA Rugby's women's sevens national team. My duties at USA Rugby ranged from managing the athlete player pool; running 5 to 10 domestic and international assemblies each calendar year, including tournaments in Dubai, Amsterdam, and Las Vegas; and collaborating with team, USOC, and national office staff to adhere to policies, standards, and best practices. I was also responsible for administering a US$5,000 to US$50,000 budget for each team camp or competition. By 2011, I had decided that I needed an advanced degree in business or management with an international focus. I was very lucky that I found a unique program in sport management that had a prominent international focus. While earning dual degrees from SUNY Cortland and London Metropolitan University, I still maintained my part-time position at USA Rugby, worked as a graduate assistant for internships at Cortland, and served as assistant program manager for London 2012 hospitality partner, Jet Set Sports, in helping manage their AT&T Olympic account. I strongly believe that maintaining relevant professional experiences and completing two advanced degrees helped me greatly in expanding my interests and skills and being hired at USA Rugby in my current full-time position.

What are your current responsibilities and objectives in your job?

In my current position as USA Rugby's event operations manager, I work in a three-person division. One of my prime job responsibilities was to plan and execute event operations for first-ever stand alone IRB Women's Sevens World Series event in Houston, Texas in 2013. I liaised with staff of participating teams to understand needs and provide services required at WSWS, and recruited, selected, trained, and oversaw team liaison officers; thus, I hoped to ensure high-quality team experiences. I also assisted incoming teams with selection of hotel, training venue, meals, and so on for international test matches. I was excited about being named tournament director for four-team Senior Women's 15s Nations Cup tournament in August 2013.

What do you enjoy most about your current job?

I love a workplace environment where I can be self-directed with a reasonable amount of autonomy and can work with great colleagues in a collaborative way. It helps immensely that I have an immediate supervisor who

ONE DAY

Go to the WSG and learn more about a typical day in the life for Kellie A. Cavalier. See if she spends her working hours the way you think she does.

values supporting professional development and growth where my (our) mistakes are an accepted part of the learning curve. I have become keenly aware that positive professional and work relationships are so critical to being successful in my job and that there are no guarantees that colleagues or supervisors will remain in place for any predictable length of time. There is a lot of movement from organization to organization in the sport governance and event management world. I also really enjoy my role at events as a troubleshooter, often more like a fire extinguisher.

What do you consider the biggest future challenge to be in your job or industry?
The biggest challenge in both my current job, as well as in the event management industry, is burnout and fatigue. Maintaining a healthy lifestyle is difficult, particularly when you are on the road more than 20% of the year. You are expected to put in 16- to 18-hour days during events that last 8 to 10 days, which can be really intense. During prime event season, there is little recovery time between events. Managing more routine, but important, tasks back at headquarters is also challenging.

The Shrinking Globe

As evidenced by the worldwide recession beginning in 2008, financial and credit markets are highly interdependent. In future years, countries around the world will be drawn closer as national and international sport federations compete more directly with professional leagues and franchises for global market shares of trademark licensing and merchandise. All domains of the international sport enterprise, both emerging niche sports and traditional professional sports, will profit from increased advertising revenues made possible through worldwide cable deregulation and integrated technologies that use the Internet, cell phones, and new media to deliver sport content to consumers through high-definition broadband providers. Advances in on-demand information technologies will allow the creation of strong fan affiliations and the development of new virtual fans in other nations and other continents. Cross-marketing and promotional agreements among partners on different continents and in different sports will change the way in which the sport industry organizes itself. Differences in cultures, national laws, and customs will compound the challenges of these developments (Smith & Westerbeek, 2004; Szymanski & Zimbalist, 2005).

International exchanges of athletes across a broad cross section of sports, ranging from youth to near elite levels, will become commonplace. Such exchanges will continue to include showcase tournaments and camps for the benefit of U.S. college coaches who use them to recruit athletes from Europe, Australia, and to a lesser extent Africa and South America. As the rate of export and import of international talent at all competitive levels escalates, international trade agreements will have a greater effect on the sport industry.

Social and Ethical Awareness

The United Nations (UN) proclaimed 2005 as the International Year of Sport and Physical Education. In so doing, it drew attention to its focus on a new human rights convention, which included access to sport and leisure activity for all people of the world as a basic human right. This and other trends indicate that the world will soon rediscover the importance and interrelationship of access to play and sport opportunities for all, regardless of socioeconomic status, gender, race, or ethnicity. In 2006, the United Nations passed and ratified a **Convention on the Rights of Persons with Disabilities (CRPD)** that included rights to sport, play, leisure, and culture for persons with disabilities (United Nations, n.d.).

CRPD—United Nations' Convention on the Rights of Persons with Disabilities. This convention recognizes the rights of people with disabilities. Countries that buy into this convention support, secure, and protect the rights for all people with disabilities.

The social consciences of elite athletes will become even more pronounced. Already, we see current and former athletes such as Dawn Staley, Drew Brees, Tamika Catchings, David Beckham, Mia Hamm, Roger Federer, Dikembe Mutombo, Julie Foudy, and Kristi Yamaguchi give back to society by establishing charities and foundations to support critical causes, from finding a cure for cancer to literacy to HIV and AIDS research. Another example of philanthropy is the generosity of Johan Olav Koss, multiple speed-skating gold medalist from Norway at the 1994 Lillehammer Olympic Winter Games. Koss used his accomplishments as an Olympic champion to call attention to a number of human rights needs by creating an organization originally called Olympic Aid, renamed Right to Play in 2003. This organization originally supported the survivors of ethnic cleansing in Bosnia in the 1990s, and has since evolved into Right to Play, an international organization focused on bringing sport and physical activity to children in developing countries in Africa, Asia, and South America.

Within the context of human rights, an expansion and application of the principles of equity will occur throughout all cultures. Such an effort will affect not only who gets to play sports but also who gets to control the sporting enterprise. The growth and expansion of professional team sport leagues for women, particularly in North America and Europe, will give rise to expanded marketing and management initiatives (Grundy & Shackelford, 2005; King, 2005). The Paralympic Games will achieve major event status through increased television, media, and spectator appeal, and will perhaps be fully integrated into the Olympic Games in the future. These trends will provide expanded job opportunities in the international sport marketplace for women, older people, and people with disabilities. Farsighted, socially responsible, consumer-oriented companies will stand to gain the most from these developments.

A new order of elite decision makers will assume command of a global sport industry based on pragmatic alliances among leagues, international federations, television networks, and corporate sponsors. Corporations will begin to seek brand identification with particular sports, leading to the formation of corporate and national team alliances (Smith & Westerbeek, 2004). Niche and action sports such as in-line skating, triathlon, snowboarding, and mountain biking will continue to emerge and grow. Sports such as roller hockey, beach volleyball, and endurance kayaking will redefine themselves and continue to expand. All these sports will flourish because of broad, cross-generational participation and their appeal as televised events that are distributed through a new array of broadband networks.

Critical Thinking in International Sport

Expanded leisure time for the elite and the growing middle classes in South America, China, India, other Asian countries, and parts of Africa will continue to fuel worldwide expansion of golf, tennis, and other recreational sports. Extended life expectancy will continue to affect the international sport and leisure travel industry, necessitating significant expansion of facilities. Serious concerns about the effect of recreational and sport facilities on the environment will accompany this expansion. Conflicts have already arisen regarding the construction of golf courses in sensitive mountain terrain and tropical rain forests. Concerns also exist about building large-scale leisure and sport resorts in the developing world and stadiums and arenas in environmentally or economically sensitive areas. In response, the IOC created a commission in 1995 and

ACTION

Go to the WSG and complete the Learning in Action activity, which investigates your opinion about the trends that are likely to occur in the international sport industry during the next 10 years.

Social Media and a North American Perspective on International Sport

We know that traditional media have been critical for the operations of large-scale sport events and sport organizations. They provide an important source of revenues for sport organizations and much-needed visibility to international audiences. This visibility also allows sports and sport events to become important commodities for corporations where they sponsor sports, sport events, and high-profile athletes as part of their core marketing strategies. Media is also important since it regularly reports on the results of amateur and professional sport competitions and, as such, keeps fans tuned in to their favorite sports and athletes. As evidence of the value of global media for sport, for the 2010 Olympic Winter Games and the 2012 Olympic Games, the broadcasting rights represented US$3.9 billion in revenue for the International Olympic Committee (IOC). Corporate support beyond these media rights for the IOC for the same time period is estimated to reach US$8 billion (IOC, 2012; Murray, 2012).

With the introduction of new media, the potential to reach even more spectators and to engage them actively in sport events has grown exponentially. Digital and social media coverage of the Olympic Games was officially introduced for Beijing 2008. It was, however, in London for the 2012 Olympic Games that digital and social media coverage exploded. In London 2012, for the first time, the IOC broadcasted live Olympic Games events on YouTube and developed partnerships with Facebook, Twitter, Google+, Foursquare, and Weibo, all in an effort to reach larger and younger audiences (IOC, 2011a). Thornton (2012, para. 21) explained that "the media is forging onto new screens well outside the living room." Social media is allowing organizers and athletes to directly connect with fans. In order to address issues that resulted from this increasing social media presence, the IOC had to develop social media, blogging, and Internet guidelines. These guidelines not only regulated the behaviors of athletes and accredited personnel during the 2012 London Olympic Games, but they also served to protect the IOC's sponsors and partners (IOC, 2011b). Some observers have coined London 2012 The Twitter Games, a fitting tribute given that "during the 17 days of the Olympics [London 2012], there were 82.6 million social media comments about the Games, its athletes, and its sporting events" (Dowling, 2012, para. 6).

Social media was also central to the coverage of the London 2012 Paralympic Games. The International Paralympic Committee (IPC) reported impressive social media figures; for example: 9 million views of videos uploaded on YouTube, 2 million visits of IPC's website during the Games, an increase of 130% of support for IPC's Facebook page, and a 50% increase in Twitter followers of @paralympic ("London 2012 Paralympics," 2012). As noted by an IPC official, "One of our objectives for London 2012 was to raise the profile of leading athletes. In terms of social media, we appear to have achieved this with many athletes enjoying significant growth in their Facebook and Twitter followings" ("London 2012 Paralympics," 2012, para. 11). The introduction of social media, however, has not been without some controversy. For example, after posting offensive and racist comments on Twitter during the Olympic Games, Greek triple jumper Voula Papachristou was expelled from the London 2012 Olympic Games (Magnay, 2012). As well, the IOC guidelines for social media, blogging, and Internet, also referred to as Rule 40, "encourages all social media and blogging activity at the Olympic Games provided that it is not for commercial and/or advertising purposes and that it does not create or imply unauthorised association of a third party with the IOC, the Olympic Games or the Olympic Movement" (IOC, 2011b, p. 1). Athletes, coaches, and officials cannot use social media to "report on competition or comment on the activities of other participants or accredited persons, or disclose any information which is confidential or private in relation to any other person or organisation" (IOC, 2011b, p. 1). These guidelines have been met with resistance from many athletes who feel they are being censored by the IOC (Whiteside, 2012).

Regardless of these controversies, it is evident from the London 2012 Olympic and Paralympic Games that social media is increasingly playing a central role in reaching and engaging even greater global audiences beyond the audiences reached by traditional media for large scale sport events.

PORTFOLIO

Complete the critical thinking portfolio activity in the WSG, consulting as needed the "Critical Thinking Questions" sidebar in chapter 1.

formed a policy position regarding concerns about the effect of the Olympic Games on local and regional environments (Sport and Environment Commission, n.d.).

In the next decade, more career opportunities will emerge in areas dealing with jurisdiction and dispute resolution related to international athletes' rights, blood doping, drug use and abuse, relocation of franchises from nation to nation, corporate social responsibility, and other policy matters. International and national sport federations, professional leagues, sport marketing agencies, media (e.g., cable, satellite, network television, and radio) and new media entities, arenas and facilities, fitness clubs, and sport product corporations will begin to give hiring preference to people with backgrounds oriented to the global marketplace.

Ethics in International Sport

In the past, many sporting goods manufacturing companies relocated most of their production of footwear, apparel, and equipment to Asia (e.g., China, Vietnam, Pakistan, Indonesia). Currently, however, such companies are seeking other locations that have low labor costs and minimal labor rights in places such as Latin America, Africa, and the former Soviet republics. These relocations create serious financial, legal, and ethical questions. For example, does the availability of a large, cheap labor force outweigh concerns over counterfeiting made possible by weak copyright laws, currency fluctuations and devaluations, and potentially restrictive export and import laws? What are the human rights and ethical considerations when large, multinational corporations profit from the toil of children and women in sweatshop conditions in Southeast Asian or Central American countries? Is it exploitive to move footwear, equipment, and sport apparel production from one emerging economy to another (e.g., from Korea to the Philippines to China, Indonesia, and Bangladesh) in search of the cheapest labor supply? What responsibility do companies have to the workers and countries that they leave behind?

PORTFOLIO

Complete the ethical issues portfolio activity in the WSG, consulting as needed the "Guidelines for Making Ethical Decisions" sidebar in chapter 1.

Ideally, ethical value systems and human rights principles are part of the decision-making process in the relocation of manufacturing centers. Companies should also consider the stability of political regimes and their diplomatic relations with the nations in which the corporate home offices are located. In the aftermath of the 2001 terrorist attacks in New York and terrorist bombings in Moscow (2003), Madrid (2004), London (2005), and Mumbai (2008), security issues have become paramount in decisions to locate new production facilities and sport events.

Summary

Organizations, events, and governance structures are deemed to be international if they are involved in the global context on a regular basis or as one of their primary functions. Over the past few decades, five key changes occurred that resulted in the expansion of international sport. These changes involved the Olympic Games; women's sporting opportunities; a redefinition of sport based on corporate sponsorship, a shift in the balance of power, and the world's obsession with soccer; advances in recruitment and marketing; and the emergence of new economies. As examples, China has recently become a sport superpower and Brazil became appealing as a host for international sporting events. Current issues include the relocation of manufacturing companies and governance concerns focused on corporate sponsorship, drug testing and arbitration, assistive devices, and concerns associated with the Paralympic Games. To be successful internationally, aspiring sport managers must have the appropriate tools, skills, world-view, and cultural understanding. The future of international sport will occur in a world that is becoming smaller because of technology, a global community that is aware of social and ethical concerns that can be addressed through sport, and a world citizenry that possesses a heightened commitment to environmental concerns related to reducing the carbon footprint. Career opportunities in international sport will expand for people who are oriented to the global marketplace and possess the ability to integrate new technologies, including the effective use of social media.

Review Questions

1. What is the definition of international sport? What factors are considered in determining whether a sport fits this definition?

2. Name three factors that served to redefine international sport. What was the effect of each?

3. What five key changes over the past few decades have contributed to the expansion of international sport? How have they done so?

4. How have advances in the recruitment of athletes in a given sport, along with a focus on more globalized marketing, affected international sport?

5. Name some of the emerging economies that are now or in process of becoming attractive hosts for international competitions. What makes them attractive?

6. How have corporate sponsorship, drug testing, assistive devices, and the inclusion of Paralympic athletes affected international sport governance, particularly in relation to the Olympic Games and other large multi-sport events?

7. What skills, experiences, and competencies would help aspiring international sport managers prepare for the job market?

8. Name three factors that will affect the future of international sport. Explain the effect of each.

References

Dowling, E. (2012, August 13). Final social TV data for the 2012 London Olympics. *Bluefin Labs*. Retrieved from https://bluefinlabs.com/blog/2012/08/13/final-social-tv-data-for-the-2012-london-olympics

Fay, T.G. (1999). Race, gender, and disability: A new paradigm towards full participation and equal opportunity in sport (Doctoral dissertation, University of Massachusetts Amherst). *Electronic doctoral dissertations for UMass Amherst*. Retrieved from http://scholarworks.umass.edu/dissertations/AAI9950151

Fay, T.G., Legg, D., & Wolff, E.A. (2005, June). *Inclusion of Paralympic events within the Olympic Games*. Paper presented at the annual meeting of the North American Society for Sport Management, Regina, Saskatchewan, Canada.

Fay, T.G., & Wolff, E.A. (2009). Disability in sport in the twenty-first century: Creating a new sport opportunity spectrum. *Boston University International Law Journal, 27*, 231–248.

Foer, F. (2004). *How soccer explains the world: An unlikely theory of globalization*. New York, NY: Harper Perennial.

Grundy, P., & Shackelford, S. (2005). *Shattering the glass: The remarkable history of women's basketball*. New York, NY: New Press.

Hums, M.A., & MacLean, J. (2008). *Governance and policy in sport organizations*. Scottsdale, AZ. Holcomb-Hathaway.

International Olympic Committee. (2011a). *IOC marketing: Media guide London 2012*. Retrieved from www.olympic.org/Documents/IOC_Marketing/London_2012/IOC_Marketing_Media_Guide_2012.pdf

International Olympic Committee. (2011b, August 31). *IOC social media, blogging and Internet guidelines for participants and other accredited persons at the London 2012 Olympic Games*. Retrieved from www.olympic.org/Documents/Games_London_2012/IOC_Social_Media_Blogging_and_Internet_Guidelines-London.pdf

International Olympic Committee. (2012). *Olympic marketing fact file 2012 edition*. Retrieved from www.olympic.org/Documents/IOC_Marketing/OLYMPIC-MARKETING-FACT-FILE-2012.pdf

International Paralympic Committee. (2009). *IPC-IOC Co-operation*. Retrieved from www.paralympic.org/release/Main_Sections_Menu/IPC/About_the_IPC/IPC_IOC_Cooperation/index.html

International Paralympic Committee. (2012, July). *IOC and IPC sign co-operation agreement until 2020*. Retrieved from www.paralympic.org/news/ioc-and-ipc-sign-co-operation-agreement-until-2020

International Paralympic Committee. (2012, September 19). *London 2012 Paralympics prove to be online success*. Retrieved from www.paralympic.org/news/london-2012-paralympics-prove-be-online-success

Jessop, A. (2013, January). Retrieved from www.huffingtonpost.com/alicia-jessop/lance-armstrong-doping-admission_b_2492552.html

King, B. (2005, April 25–May 1). What's up with women's sports? *Street & Smith's SportsBusiness Journal*, pp.18–23.

Larmer, B. (2005). *Operation Yao Ming: The Chinese sports empire, American big business, and the making of an NBA superstar*. New York, NY: Gotham.

Legg, D., Fay, T.G., Hums, M.A., & Wolff, E.A. (2009, Fall). Examining the inclusion of wheelchair exhibition events within the Olympic Games 1984-2004. *European Sport Management Quarterly, 9*, 243–258.

Longman, J. (2012, July 13). Before games, wins for women. *The New York Times*. Retrieved from www.nytimes.com/2012/07/14/sports/olympics/before-london-games-wins-for-women.html?_r=0

Magnay, J. (2012, July 25). London 2012 Olympics: Greece athlete Voula Papachristou expelled for racist comment on Twitter. *The Telegraph*. Retrieved from www.telegraph.co.uk/sport/olympics/athletics/9426669/London-2012-Olympics-Greece-athlete-Voula-Papachristou-expelled-for-racist-comment-on-Twitter.html

Maguire, J., & Nakayama, M. (2005). *Japan, sport & society: Tradition and change in a globalizing world*. London, UK: Routledge.

Murray, C. (2012, July). Olympic Games set to break $8bn revenues barrier in four-year cycle ending with London 2012. *Sportcal*, 26, 6–9. Retrieved from http://www.sportcal.com/magazine/issue26

National Basketball Association. (2009, October 8). Bryant's jersey remains top seller in China. Retrieved from www.nba.com/2009/news/10/08/bryant.jersey.china

Olympic.org: Official website of the Olympic movement. (2013). *Sponsorship*. Retrieved from www.olympic.org/sponsorship?tab=the-olympic-partner-top-programme

Perez, A.J. (2008, March 28). *Chemist describes work with BALCO*. Retrieved from www.usatoday.com/sports/2008-03-26-balco-chemist_N.htm

Pound, R.W. (2004). *Inside the Olympics*. Montreal, Quebec, Canada: Wiley & Sons.

Rapp, T. (2012, August). Olympic medal count 2012: US women stole the show in London. *Bleacher Report*. http://bleacher-report.com/articles/1294747-olympic-medal-count-2012-us-women-stole-the-show-in-london

Reeve, S. (2000). *One day in September*. New York, NY: Arcade.

Smith, A., & Westerbeek, H. (2004). *The sport business future*. London, UK: Palgrave Macmillan.

Sport and Environment Commission. (n.d.). *History and mission of the Commission*. Retrieved from www.olympic.org/content/The-IOC/Commissions/Sport-and-Environment

Szymanski, S., & Zimbalist, A. (2005). *National pastime: How Americans play baseball and the rest of the world plays soccer*. Washington, DC: Brookings Institution Press.

Thoma, J.E., & Chalip, L. (1996). *Sport governance in the global community*. Morgantown, WV: Fitness Information Technology.

Thornton, T. (2012). London 2012: The thrills (and agony) of the Social Olympics. *PBS*. Retrieved from www.pbs.org/mediashift/2012/07/london-2012-the-thrills-and-agony-of-the-social-olympics-208

Torres, C. (2013, March). World Baseball Classic 2013: Dominican Republic wins championship, defeats PR 3-0, *Bleacher Report*. Retrieved from http://bleacherreport.com/articles/1574353-world-baseball-classic-2013-dominican-republic-wins-championship-defeat-pr-3-0

United Nations. (n.d.). *Convention on the rights of persons with disabilities*. Retrieved from www.un.org/disabilities/default.asp?id=150

Whiteside, K. (2012, August 23). After London, athletes still pushing for Rule 40 change. *USA Today*. Retrieved from http://usatoday30.usatoday.com/sports/olympics/london/story/2012-08-23/olympics-rule-40-michael-phelpos-lashinda-demus/57225924/1

Wolbring, G. (2008, July). Is there an end to out-able? Is there an end to the rat race for abilities? *Media/Culture Journal*, 11(3). Retrieved from http://journal.media-culture.org.au/index.php/mcjournal/article/viewArticle/57

HISTORICAL MOMENTS

1966 *International Review for the Sociology of Sport* launched

1970 *Canadian Journal for the History of Physical Education and Sport* launched

1973 *Journal of Sport History* launched

1977 *Journal of Sport and Social Issues* launched

1984 *Sociology of Sport Journal* launched

1993 *Journal of Sport & Tourism* launched

1994 *European Journal for Sport Management* (now known as *European Sport Management Quarterly*) launched

1998 *Sport Management Review* launched

1999 *International Journal of Sports Marketing and Sponsorship* launched

2000 *International Journal of Sport Management* and *Journal of Sports Economics* launched

2005 *Journal of Quantitative Analysis in Sports* and *International Journal of Sport Management and Marketing* launched

2006 *International Journal of Sport Finance* launched

2007 *Sport Management Education Journal* launched

2008 *Journal of Issues in Intercollegiate Athletics* and *Journal of Intercollegiate Sport* launched

2009 *Journal of Venue and Event Management, International Journal of Sport Policy and Politics*, and *Journal of Applied Sport Management* launched

2011 *Sport, Business and Management: An International Journal* launched

2012 *Case Studies in Sport Management* launched

20

SPORT MANAGEMENT RESEARCH

Jess C. Dixon \ **Wendy Frisby**

LEARNING OBJECTIVES

> Explain the value and importance of asking and addressing research questions in sport management.

> Define research and understand why it is important to sport management students, practitioners, and researchers.

> Know what questions to ask when evaluating the quality of a research article.

> Identify the growing number of academic journals and other sources that contain relevant sport management research.

> Describe the critical contributions of the academic community and commercial research firms in answering questions that emerge in various sectors of the sport industry.

> Explain the differences between scientific and pseudoscientific approaches to sport management research.

> Differentiate among quantitative, qualitative, and mixed-methods approaches to research and data analysis.

Key Terms

action research
anonymity
confidentiality
empirical
pseudoscience

reliability
research design
science
theory
validity

GET A JOB

Start to wrap up your current journey in sport management by going to the web study guide (WSG) at www.HumanKinetics.com/ ContemporarySportManagement. Check out the job opportunities and consider the skills and experiences that can help you succeed in sport management.

Interest in research has paralleled the growth of the sport industry and sport management educational programs around the world. This interest has occurred because people in business and education understand that research can inform managerial decisions, uncover solutions to managerial problems, improve organizational effectiveness and efficiency, point out inequalities in sport leadership or participation, and help sport management continue to develop a relevant body of knowledge.

Regardless of the area that you are studying or your career aspirations, understanding research is critically important. Progressive sport organizations want to find out about the latest trends, evaluate whether their customers are satisfied, update their policies, attract new participants, provide data to sponsors and partners, and stay ahead of their competitors. Increasingly, these sport organizations are looking to sport management graduates for expertise in information searches, feasibility studies, evaluations, and marketing studies, to name a few.

Even if you do not expect research to be a major component of your future career, you need to be able to understand, evaluate, and use it when solving problems and making professional decisions. This chapter introduces key concepts and various types of research conducted in the sport management field. It also provides you with a foundation for becoming a responsible producer and consumer of research, so that you can become a more informed decision maker. To develop your skills further, you should seek out the growing list of references and courses in research methods.

Research Questions

Asking suitable research questions and getting the best possible answers are critical to every sport management sector in the current information age. Research questions are important because addressing them sets the stage for decision, action, profit, satisfaction, success, and other goals desired by sport managers. Questions in any industry, but particularly in sport, emerge because of changes in the economy, law, culture, technology, policy, politics, and other dimensions of the broader environment that affect the operations and bottom lines of organizations. Thus, sport organizations should not make decisions without having reliable data. The starting point for obtaining information is a focused and well-thought-out research question. Addressing such questions through research enables sport managers to know their environment, personnel, industry, market, customers, and current trends. Although some research questions emerge because of curiosity, most materialize as sport organizations design or revise strategies to cope with a problem or to influence change.

Why Sport Managers Need to Understand Research

Students who aspire to careers in the sport industry sometimes undervalue research because they assume that it is not practical and is done primarily in universities. While some students are intrigued by research and want to pursue it further in graduate school, others appear to gain satisfaction from the practical, hands-on elements of undergraduate preparation and are sometimes unimpressed with theory and research. It is often not until one has served in a management position that one comes to fully appreciate the importance of research in assisting with the managerial role. Now is the best time to begin developing an understanding of why research is critical to sport managers who want to stay on top of their field.

Only Research Can Keep You Current

If your family doctor graduated from a prestigious medical school in 2000, would you not expect him or her to be up to date with medical developments here in this second

Social Media and Sport Management Research

Many sport properties might be concerned about how consumers' television viewing behavior changes in light of new and emerging technologies. In 2012, Nielsen, the leading audience measurement firm in the United States, reported that 41% of tablet owners and 38% of smartphone owners were actively using their devices while watching television. And what are these viewers using their devices for? In most instances, tablet and smartphone users are interacting with others on Facebook, Twitter, LinkedIn, Pinterest, or other social networking sites (Nielsen, 2012). This type of behavior is only expected to increase in the coming years.

What are the implications of these changes in technology for sport managers? On the surface, these kinds of distractions would seem to pose a considerable threat to television producers and commercial advertisers who rely on viewers as the basis for their business models. However, when one digs beneath the surface, these same producers and advertisers see a wealth of opportunity through the use of second-screen apps to make viewers' experiences more personal and engaging. According to Crystalyn Stuart (2013), vice president of social marketing for IMRE Sports, "Gone are the days of experiencing the game as a static spectator. Instead, fans are gravitating toward social sites to enrich their viewing experience and cultivate a deeper connection with the games they watch" (para. 1). While it remains true that the majority of second-screen users are engaging in social media while watching television, Nielsen (2013) reports that 41% of all TV-related tweets are about sport-related programming. But sport fans aren't just chatting about the games they are watching on television. They are also using their second screens to shop online and look up information related to the programs and advertisements that they are consuming (Nielsen, 2013). By tapping into sports fans' appetites for supplementary content, story lines, and analysis, while simultaneously satisfying sponsors' desires for activation, brand recall, and product purchase opportunities, second-screen apps are bound to become a regular part of the television viewing experience for many years to come. Sport managers in the second decade of the 21st century need to understand the importance of asking relevant research questions and choosing the appropriate research methods to address them.

decade of the 21st century? The advances that have occurred since our doctors and countless other professionals received their initial certifications and credentials have come about largely because of research. Being able to read, understand, and apply scientific findings leads to progress. The world would be a far different place without the contributions of scientific studies.

The field of sport management is no different from other professional areas. By applying research findings from human resources, leadership, marketing, organizational development, and countless other areas, the practicing sport manager has a much better chance of identifying and implementing sensible solutions to everyday managerial problems.

Trial-and-Error Management Is Folly

Would any of us drive a car or take medicine that had not been thoroughly tested? Probably not. In similar fashion, we are well aware of the extensive research conducted on hockey sticks, baseball bats, tennis rackets, golf clubs, running shoes, and virtually every other piece of equipment related to the world of sport. We now consider it commonplace to conduct experimental studies to improve athletic performance by increments as small as one-tenth of a second.

But when it comes to the management of sport, the standards may not be as exacting. We can easily become enthralled by a new idea or by what is being done at another university or in a similar sport in another country. In real terms, the trial-and-error approach often seems to be standard practice in the everyday management of sport.

Hundreds of promotions are conducted, marketing plans are formulated, and strategic plans are developed—all without research. Even with a great deal of thought, many of these ventures are doomed to failure. Having sound intuition and a wealth of experience is useful, but a trial-and-error approach can be risky and expensive. Successful marketing strategies, comprehensive human resources policies, and many other aspects of the sport management domain are based on sound theories derived from research. Admittedly, we are all students of the trial-and-error process in that we make decisions without all the possible information. We may not always have the time or resources to explore all the options. But why do this intentionally? Why not gather as much data as possible about your research question and make decisions based on sound information?

What Is Sport Management Research?

Sport management research is a systematic way of examining hunches, assumptions, and questions about a wide range of sport management phenomena. In particular, sport management researchers are interested in questions related to marketing, finance, communication, human resources, policy, and a number of other topics highlighted throughout this textbook. Sport management researchers typically use a wide range of research designs in a variety of sport settings to conduct research on people in organizations (e.g., employees and volunteers); their clients or customers, suppliers, sponsors, or partners; the media; and sport products, events, and programs. Sport management research also sometimes considers the broader economic, legal, social, cultural, ecological, technological, and political environments that shape or are shaped by sport (Slack & Parent, 2006). The findings from these research investigations can inform managerial practice, build knowledge in a subject area, or both.

Sometimes research findings support our initial hunches and assumptions, while at other times, the findings contradict and challenge them. Such challenges encourage us to consider new and improved ways of managing sport. For example, we might assume that everyone in our community has equal access to the sporting opportunities available, but research might reveal considerable disparities in participation based on income, gender, ethnicity, age, sexual orientation, religion, (dis)ability, health status, and other factors. Paying close attention to this evidence will push us to consider new ways of marketing and delivering sport programs so that more people can enjoy the benefits of participation.

Regardless of whether the findings obtained from research confirm or challenge our hunches and assumptions, they will help us make better decisions. Thus, sport managers increasingly rely on research before investing financial, human, and other types of resources into new or ongoing projects. They want to avoid the costly errors that can occur when decisions are based on false or unfounded assumptions. Effective sport managers want assurances that their decisions will help them achieve desired goals based on evidence that has been carefully collected, analyzed, and interpreted.

Academic Research in Sport Management

Some authors, as noted in chapter 1, have suggested that sport management has been around since at least 11 BCE when Herod, King of Judea, staged elaborate athletic spectacles (Frank, 1984). The study and documentation of research in this area is a much more contemporary occurrence. A number of academic and professional associations formed since the mid-1980s have stimulated research and scholarly activity in sport management. The North American Society for Sport Management (NASSM), the European Association for Sport Management (EASM), and the Sport Management Association of Australia and New Zealand (SMAANZ) are examples of international associations that foster research as part of their mandates. These and several other continental

WEB

Go to the WSG and complete the web search activity, which asks you to evaluate the research ethics review board at your university.

associations came together in April of 2012 to form the World Association for Sport Management (WASM). Each association hosts a conference where members and invited guests share sport management research in the form of presentations, roundtable discussions, and keynote addresses. In addition, these academic associations publish research journals to help grow the body of knowledge in sport management.

Although these journals may differ slightly in overall quality, we can be somewhat confident in the findings published in them because they have been vetted through the peer-review process that serves as the hallmark for all academic publications.

Commercial Research in Sport Management

The Council of American Survey Research Organizations (CASRO, 2013) represents more than 325 research firms operating in the United States and abroad, each with the mission of conducting research on behalf of other organizations. An organization might need help in answering questions because in-house personnel may lack expertise in newly developing areas or because the organization is unable to hire full-time research staff. When sport organizations have research questions that they are unable to answer themselves, they often hire the services of a research firm.

Several research companies specialize in providing expert research services exclusively to sport organizations. Often, the most pressing research questions of teams, manufacturers, and retailers relate to consumers and marketing. Consequently, many commercial companies address marketing and promotional issues on behalf of sport organizations. Nike, NASCAR, and other large and small sport organizations have used the services of commercial research companies in their marketing and management planning. Table 20.1 lists some of the most visible sport research companies and their services.

Although a wealth of information can be derived by contracting with commercial research firms, the uniqueness of the issues facing today's professional sports leagues has driven many of them to take responsibility for their own research undertakings. In the past two decades, many professional leagues and some individual teams have established their own internal research departments dedicated to collecting, analyzing, and explaining research data. Given the premium that is placed on information and analytics in decision making throughout all sectors of the sport industry, executives of the future will need to be competent in conducting research.

Young subjects participate in an academic research study involving the effects of watching violent sports.

Key Concepts

Because approaches to sport management research vary, the choice of approach will depend on the purpose of the study and the nature of the question that one is attempt-

Table 20.1   **List of Consultants Specializing in Sport Management Research**

Consultant	Specialty
TSE Consulting	Provides customizable advice and services to public-sector sport clients in the area of events, performance, participation, and facilities
Luker on Trends	Produces the *ESPN Sports Poll,* which is quoted frequently by scholars, professional literature, and the popular press.
Joyce Julius & Associates, Inc.	Utilizes proprietary technology to measure, analyze, and evaluate corporate sponsorships through various forms of media and on-site sponsorship activations.
Performance Research	Evaluates sponsorship effectiveness for sports, music, theme parks, arts, and cause marketing fields. Specializes in on-site data collection and research.
Sports Business Research Network	Provides continuously updated market research and industry news on sports participation, equipment sales, broadcasting, sponsorships, and marketing.
Turnkey Sports	Specializes in providing custom market research, lead generation tools, and executive recruitment services to sport properties and sponsors.
Ipsos-Reid	Part of the Ipsos Group, a global leader in survey-based marketing, advertising, media, customer satisfaction, and public opinion research, Ipsos-Reid produces the *Canadian Sports Monitor*, which profiles Canadian sports fans.

ing to address. Familiarity with the following key research concepts will be useful in understanding sport management research: (1) ways of knowing, (2) science and pseudoscience, (3) basic and applied research, (4) quantitative and qualitative data, (5) research design, and (6) validity and reliability.

Ways of Knowing

According to Peirce's classic theory (as cited in Kerlinger & Lee, 2000), knowledge can be acquired in four ways: through tenacity, authority, intuition, and science. Each of these sources of knowledge has pros and cons associated with it.

1. *Tenacity.* With this form of knowledge, a person assumes that a fact is true because people have always believed it to be true, even though evidence may exist to the contrary. For example, many people subscribe to the theory that sport participation builds character, although much empirical evidence shows that no relationship exists between sport and moral development, good citizenship, and other valued traits (Sage & Eitzen, 2012). In fact, some evidence demonstrates that sport might bring out the worst character traits in athletes. Yet many people still hold firmly to the belief that sport builds character.

2. *Authority.* In this case, a person knows that something is right because someone with expertise has said that it is. For instance, when Sir Alex Ferguson, legendary manager (coach) of Manchester United Football Club, proclaimed that repetition is a key to success in the sport of soccer, people accepted his assertion based on his near 27 years at the helm of one of the most successful and profitable sport franchises in the world. In his autobiography, *Managing My Life,* Ferguson (2002) stressed: "in any physical activity, effective practice requires repeated execution of the skill

involved. . . [A]ny player working with me on the training ground will hear me preach the virtues of repetition—repeatedly" (p. 137). In honor of his contributions to the sport of soccer and his many coaching achievements—including 13 Premier League championships and two UEFA Champions League titles with the ManU Red Devils—Ferguson was knighted by Queen Elizabeth II in 1999. Needless to say, when it comes to the sport of soccer, it could be argued that no one is a greater authority on the topic than Ferguson. However, being an authority figure does not always guarantee that one will have accurate views. In this particular case, Ferguson's opinions on the virtues of repetition are supported by numerous studies that have found that expertise in any field requires no less than 10,000 hours of deliberate practice (Ericsson, Prietula, & Cokely, 2007).

3. *Intuition.* A person who believes that something is true because she or he thinks it is common sense or self-evident is relying on intuitive knowledge (Thomas, Nelson, & Silverman, 2011). An example might be that Canadians are naturally gifted in the sport of ice hockey because their women's and men's teams have won more international tournaments than the teams of any other country over the years. Because this conclusion appears to be self-evident to many around the world, it stands to reason that it must be so—at least according to the method of intuition. Research has an important role to play in debunking common-sense beliefs that are not always accurate. To be clear, Canadians are not inherently better ice hockey players than athletes from other countries. Rather, ice hockey is an important part of Canadian culture and is conducive to its wintery climate, so youngsters have more coaching, facilities, equipment, and encouragement to take up and excel at the sport (Wilson, 2006). This remains true despite the fact that there have been more Canadians participating in the sport of golf than ice hockey since 1998 (Canadian Heritage, 2013).

4. *Science.* With this method of knowing, one assumes that information is reliable and credible because empirical evidence in the form of quantitative or qualitative data has been collected to address a research question of interest. Most people accept scientific information because data were collected using a systematic protocol with as few outside factors as possible swaying the results. In most cases, the scientific method is the most reliable route to information that sport managers can use to answer their research questions.

empirical—Refers to data or the results of a study that can appear in many forms, including numbers, words, or pictures.

Science and Pseudoscience

When we hear the word science, we might associate it with experiments done in high school or with exercise physiology laboratories where subjects' heart rates are monitored to determine their fitness levels. This type of experiment-based laboratory science is known as natural science, and it has a long historical tradition in physical education and kinesiology programs in colleges and universities. Social science, another type of science, includes areas such as sport sociology, sport psychology, and sport management. In general, a social science approach to sport is concerned with individuals, groups, and organizations as they interact in a complex environment (Slack & Parent, 2006).

science—Information based on systematic research.

A growing body of research appears to have a scientific basis when, in fact, it does not. Theories promoting the latest managerial or marketing techniques that are not based on systematic research are known as pseudoscience. We can find numerous examples of pseudoscience in popular press books, in television infomercials, in newspaper or magazine articles, and on the Internet. Get-rich-quick schemes that provide unsubstantiated evidence to support the claims made are another example of pseudoscience. Although the latest scheme or trend might be endorsed by a purported expert or authority, explained in technical language, and supported by promises of dramatic outcomes, sport managers should be skeptical of pseudoscience masquerading as

pseudoscience—Information that appears to be based on systematic research when it is not.

science. Although several well-known management gurus have made personal fortunes by speaking about and selling popular how-to books on a variety of management topics, not all their theories and recommendations are supported by the systematic collection, analysis, and interpretation of data. To sort out what types of information are credible and to avoid basing decisions on information that is misleading or faulty, an understanding of sport management research is essential.

Basic and Applied Research

Social science research consists of two general types: basic and applied. Although the two types of research can be highly interrelated and may not always be easily distinguishable from one another, understanding some of the differences in their goals and approaches is helpful.

Basic research is usually done in universities or research institutes with the goal of advancing a body of knowledge in a subject area. It focuses on developing or testing theories or explanations for how the world operates in the way that it does. Direct practical outcomes from basic research are not always apparent, although research questions often arise from practical problems and the findings can provide a foundation for developing new managerial systems and approaches.

Simply put, a **theory** provides possible explanations for a phenomenon of interest to sport management researchers. Theory is integral to basic research in three main ways: (1) existing managerial theories can be used to explain sport management phenomena, (2) existing managerial theories can be built on or extended through the study of sport, and (3) alternative theories can be proposed if existing theories do not offer adequate explanations for sport phenomena. Applying, testing, advancing, and developing new theories can further develop the body of knowledge in sport management.

Most sport managers will be interested in applied research because it helps answer practical research questions, such as how to increase customer satisfaction or improve organizational performance. Although applied sport management studies often have a narrowly defined purpose and aim to produce practical results that are of immediate use, and they do not necessarily draw from theories, they should still use a systematic approach to research. That is, researchers must carefully define their research questions, consider how they will measure key concepts, select their study participants, and collect and analyze the data before they communicate the results. Some common types of applied research in sport management include marketing research, feasibility studies, economic impact studies, equity research, and program evaluations.

Quantitative and Qualitative Data

One way to determine whether a study uses a systematic approach is to examine the information source to ascertain whether the researchers collected empirical data. We usually associate data with numbers or statistics, but sport managers rely on many different types of data (Andrews, Mason, & Silk, 2005). Data in the form of numbers are known as quantitative data, whereas data in the form of words, pictures, or actions are known as qualitative data. The choice of data depends on the research question, and sometimes both types of empirical data are required to address it. When investigators collect both quantitative data and qualitative data in the same study, they are using a mixed-methods approach (Creswell, 2009). For example, an evaluation of a recreational sport program might entail counting the number of new and repeat participants, as well as conducting interviews with them to determine whether any program changes are desired.

Questionnaires, secondary data analyses, and content analyses are common techniques used in the sport management field to collect quantitative data for the purposes of establishing whether significant differences or relationships between variables of

theory—Provide possible explanations for a phenomenon of interest to sport management researchers.

ACTION

Go to the WSG and complete the Learning in Action activity, which challenges you to classify quantitative and qualitative research methods.

Professional Profile: Sydney Millar

Title: national program director, Canadian Association for the Advancement of Women and Sport and Physical Activity (CAAWS)

Education: BKin (kinesiology), McMaster University; MA (human kinetics—sport management), University of British Columbia

In her sport leadership position, Sydney Millar manages several national initiatives, including On the Move, the Women and Leadership Program, and Canadian Sport for Life. She has travelled across Canada delivering workshops and presentations about how to create positive programs and inclusive environments to engage more girls and young women in sport and physical activity. In terms of research methodologies used in her work, Millar stated that interviews and focus groups "with practitioners and decision makers inform most of CAAWS' work. Focus groups and surveys with girls and young women through our initiatives ensure community-based programs and CAAWS' services and publications reflect the realities of girls' and women's lives. We also conduct literature reviews and environmental scans of both popular sources and academic journals. Findings from all these methods are used to identify gaps in knowledge and practice and guide the development of new projects, publications, and partnerships." She added that over the years, she has been involved with several research projects including (1) Canadian Sport for Life (CS4L), (2) examining psycho-social factors affecting girls' and women's participation and leadership in sport and physical activity, and (3) evaluating participation barriers as well as supporting the development and delivery of community programs for newcomer girls and young women in several sites across the country. A project called Racialized Girls and Young Women involved researching "girls and young women from diverse ethnocultural communities about their sport and physical activity experiences." Another project called the Canadian Active After School Partnership (CAASP) entailed "examining the links between quality active after-school programs and positive mental health in children and youth." In terms of foreseeing where the future of sport research is going, Millar noted that it is her "hope that researchers will continue to focus on addressing the persisting gaps in the availability and utilization of quality opportunities and support for girls and women." She would also like to see "more practical, community-based research that examines how lessons from the community level and other nations can be used or adapted to influence change and enhance the system so everyone can benefit from participating in sport and physical activity." The following is a snapshot of Millar's career development, duties, and insights as a leader in the sport industry.

NE DAY

to the WSG
learn more
ut a typical day
he life for Sydney Millar.
e if she spends her
rking hours the way you
k she does.

What have been the key moves, steps, or developments in your career, and how did you arrive at your current position?

I connected with CAAWS in 1999 through a practicum placement in the second term of my master's degree and never looked back. My job evolved from a volunteer placement to part-time work, and then to a full-time contract while I was still living in Vancouver. In 2008, I moved to Ottawa, Ontario and accepted a full-time salaried position. Over my 13-plus years with CAAWS, my job has grown from a single project to developing and leading several complex national programs.

What are your current responsibilities and objectives in your job?

CAAWS is a national nonprofit organization dedicated to increasing opportunities for girls and women to participate and lead in sport and physical activity. As the national program director, I manage all aspects of several core initiatives, including developing funding proposals, managing program rollout, writing new educational resources, implementing performance management and evaluation systems, and supervising and mentoring staff and volunteers. I am also involved with the organization's strategic direction, partnership development and maintenance, and communication. My primary area of focus is On the Move, CAAWS' national initiative to increase opportunities for inactive girls and young women. In my years with CAAWS, I have led the expansion of On the Move to include targeted projects for Aboriginal communities, newcomer girls and young women, and girls and young women from diverse ethnocultural communities. I also lead projects related to CAAWS' involvement in the Canadian Sport for Life (CS4L) movement, and the Canadian Active After School Partnership

(continued)

(CAASP)—a collaboration of six national physical activity organizations that have come together to positively influence the health of Canada's children and youth. Finally, I manage CAAWS' Women and Leadership program, which provides a variety of professional development and networking opportunities for women working and volunteering in the sport and physical activity sector.

Managing several diverse programs requires advanced multitasking and time-management skills—no two days are the same, and there are always many competing priorities. Also required is a deep understanding of and familiarity with the Canadian sport and physical activity system, as well as with the current state of gender equity and the social and systemic barriers that limit the full engagement of all Canadians in the system. Partnership development and maintenance requires honed listening, facilitation, and collaboration skills, especially when working with others to influence social change. Finally, I need to be adept at reading and synthesizing great amounts of information from many different sources, as well as in carrying out research projects and evaluation initiatives on behalf of CAAWS and its many strategic partners.

Communication is a significant challenge facing our sector. It's difficult to share information, new resources, and opportunities across such a large and diverse country. Therefore, I rely on a number of sources to keep me in the loop:

> *Social media.* Sport and physical activity organizations have recently embraced Facebook and other social media. I scan these sources daily.

> *eNewsletters.* Most organizations have their own newsletters. I sign up for each one I find, not only those within the sport and physical activity sector, but also those associated with health, education, mental health, immigration, Aboriginal communities—anything related to current projects. These newsletters share popular and academic research and often present new opportunities for funding, partnerships, and collaboration.

> *Feminist sources.* To keep me up to date on trends and research relating to women in leadership, I consult Catalyst (a leading nonprofit organization with a mission to expand opportunities for women and business) and The Glass Hammer (a blog and online community created for women executives in the areas of finance, law, technology, and big business).

> *Management tips.* I find the Harvard Business Review's Management Tip of the Day useful for making my practice more intentional.

> *Sport Information Resource Centre (SIRC).* The information compiled by SIRC is great for keeping my finger on the pulse of the Canadian sports scene.

What do you enjoy most about your current job?

The ability to make a difference! Over the past 13 years, I have seen significant changes both at the individual level, in terms of the practitioners and decision makers we work with, and within the organizations that we collaborate with, but there is still a lot of work to do. I also get to travel a lot—delivering workshops, presenting at conferences, and meeting with community partners. During my time with CAAWS, I have been from coast to coast, to every Canadian province and territory except Nunavut. I also enjoy collaborating with diverse organizations, particularly with community organizations where I can see the impact of our programs. We work at the organizational level, not often directly with the girls and women whose lives we are trying to positively influence. Hearing from our partners about how our ideas and connections have affected their practice and programs, as well as the testimonials that they pass along from the girls within these various programs, is really energizing.

What do you consider the biggest future challenge to be in your job or industry?

With so many competing priorities and needs at the community level, and even amongst provincial or territorial and federal organizations and governments, gender equity sometimes slips down the priority list. However, continued efforts are needed to ensure girls and women are actively engaged as participants and leaders. This is especially true given that girls and women make up more than 50% of the Canadian population. We need to keep reminding practitioners, academics, and other types of decision makers that the unique needs, interests, and experiences of girls and women must be considered when making policy or developing new initiatives or strategies.

interest exist. In contrast, interviews, focus groups, field observations, and content analyses are common techniques for collecting qualitative data to shed light on actions and the meanings that people associate with various sport-related activities. Table 20.2 summarizes some of the major advantages and disadvantages of the common methods used to collect quantitative data. Table 20.3 summarizes some of the main advantages and disadvantages of the methods that sport management researchers commonly use to collect qualitative data.

Research Design

Li, Pitts, and Quarterman (2008) defined a research design as "the master plan that identifies the research methods and procedures for the development of the study, collection of the data, and analysis of the data" (p. 23). Common research designs in sport management research include experiments, surveys, ethnographies, case studies, and action research. Factors such as the purpose of the research, the research questions, the training and expertise of the researcher, available resources, and how the research will be utilized determine the choice of research design.

research design—A strategy or plan of action that links the research questions to the choice of research methods and the desired outcomes.

Table 20.2   Common Methods Used to Collect Quantitative Data

Method	Main advantage	Main disadvantage
Mailed surveys	Can be used on larger samples	Low response rate
Web-based or e-mail surveys	Quick response is possible	Only those with computers, tablets, or smartphones and a connection to the Internet can participate
Telephone surveys	Immediate response	Respondents may believe that their privacy is invaded
Intercept surveys	Immediate response	Ensuring a representative sample is difficult
Secondary data analysis	Avoids costs of primary research	Not all data required may be available
Content analysis	Budgets, marketing material, planning documents, and media broadcasts are usually available	Not all data required may be available in these documents

Table 20.3   Common Methods Used to Collect Qualitative Data

Method	Main advantage	Main disadvantage
Interviews	In-depth responses are possible	Time intensive
Focus groups	Less time intensive than interviews	Managing group dynamics can be difficult
Field observations	Can confirm or refute other types of data	Actions are often open to multiple interpretations

Researching Authentic Leadership and the Rugby World Cup

By Shane Gibson, New Zealand
Unitec, Auckland

By Lesley Ferkins, New Zealand
Unitec, Auckland

Consider the following quotations: "He can come across as quite abrupt, but he's just honest. He has fantastic integrity" (Bertrand, 2012). "I felt compelled to comment" (Martin, 2013). "He is a good listener, he's very fair … he has great mana" (McFadden, 2013). "It was a difficult one. It came quite early during my time as CEO. I made some mistakes" (Snedden, quoted in Romanos, 2011).

Martin Snedden led New Zealand's efforts to serve as a successful host of the 2011 Rugby World Cup.

Like exercise scientists, some sport management researchers use experimental designs to test the effect of a treatment condition or an intervention on an outcome. By exposing groups to different treatments or interventions, the researcher can examine whether the treatment or intervention is causing a change in an outcome of interest (Li et al., 2008). Because experimental designs cannot answer all questions of interest, sport management researchers also use other research designs.

Arguably the most common quantitative design, a survey provides a quantitative or numeric description of trends or attitudes of a population of interest. Researchers must carefully consider the questions that they will ask, the strategies that they will use to ensure that as many people as possible in their sample complete and return questionnaires, and the statistics that they will use to analyze the results. As more people gain access to computers, tablets, and smartphones, researchers are using online surveys more frequently than mail or telephone surveys (Li et al., 2008).

When you read the quotations, what comes to mind regarding the character of the person they are associated with? Are these the sorts of values that you would want your manager or leader to have? If we were to use a framework of thinking to research the possible leadership values evident within these quotations, it may be useful to apply authentic leadership theory.

Authentic leadership theory is a relatively new phenomenon within leadership research, and even more specifically within leadership in sport. Authentic leadership can be characterised by somebody who demonstrates honesty, integrity and a set of core values in everything that they do (Avolio, Gardner, Walumbwa, Luthans, & May, 2004). Authentic leadership requires more than just authentic attitudes and beliefs, as authentic leaders are also reported to possess the moral courage to act consistently with their beliefs when dealing with difficult moral issues, even if the end decision may be unpopular or unwelcome in some circles (George, Mayer, McLean, & Sims, 2007).

But how do we decide whether a person demonstrates these values or acts in this manner? Can we take for granted that the media representations of a person's ideals are a true reflection of the way that the person feels or acts? Looking at the quotations again, would your opinion of the person change depending on where you read or saw them—in a magazine article, in a newspaper, on a website, or in a live television interview?

Martin Snedden was the CEO of the Rugby World Cup 2011 in New Zealand. His role was to oversee the planning and delivery of this major event, focusing largely on stakeholder relationship building, looking out for issues that could cause problems, and concentrating on finding solutions. Previous to this, he was the CEO of New Zealand Cricket and a highly respected playing member of the New Zealand cricket team between 1980 and 1990. He currently holds a position of leadership (as CEO, Tourism Industry Association of New Zealand), but can we conclude that he is an authentic leader through the media representation of things that he has said and comments about him? Why or why not? How might the research process be used to further investigate such a curiosity? How would you go about researching this topic?

International Learning Activity #1

Using web-based information on the 2011 Rugby World Cup and media reports about Snedden's leadership, provide a rationale as to why this topic might be worthy of further investigation.

International Learning Activity #2

Drawing on authentic leadership literature and literature about the leadership of sport organizations, how might a research question be framed to address this topic?

International Learning Activity #3

Drawing on literature relating to sport management research, discuss what methods might be a good match for addressing the research question. Why?

Research questions are sometimes best answered by going out into the field and studying how sport is managed in a natural setting. Ethnography is one type of field research. The goal is often to understand the context or conditions that shape people's perspectives of their experiences as sport organizers, volunteers, consumers, or sponsors. Case studies are another popular research design in which the researcher explores a program, process, event, or organization in depth over time using a variety of data collection methods (Li et al., 2008).

As a consequence of being a practically oriented area of study, the sport management field is an ideal forum for what is commonly known as **action research**. Lewin (1946) is often given credit for coining the term, which refers to generating knowledge about a social system while at the same time attempting to change it. In sport management circles, this activity involves solving problems that come directly from those who currently are or would like to be involved in sport. Although action research is not

action research—Generating knowledge about a social system while at the same time attempting to change it.

commonly used in sport management, interest in this research design is growing because it is a way of bringing study participants, practitioners, and researchers together to tackle problems of mutual concern (Frisby, Reid, Millar, & Hoeber, 2005). The overall goal of action research is to produce knowledge about how everyday experiences of people can be improved to promote social change and social justice (Reason & Bradbury, 2007). For example, we know that those living below the poverty line are much less likely to participate in sport because of the high costs of programs, apparel, and equipment. By collaborating with those living in poverty on all phases of the research process, community sport managers can identify barriers to participation and develop action strategies for overcoming them.

Validity and Reliability

Before determining whether to collect quantitative data, qualitative data, or both types of data, sport management researchers must determine how they are going to measure the various managerial concepts under investigation. Because many concepts are abstract (i.e., we cannot touch them or observe them directly), coming up with perfect measures or indicators is rarely possible. For example, managerial concepts such as organizational effectiveness and customer satisfaction are abstract and multifaceted and are therefore difficult to define and capture. One way to measure abstract concepts is to create appropriate survey questions or other data collection techniques. Note, however, that our measures are never perfect indicators of the abstract concept under investigation.

validity—The degree to which measures capture the meaning of abstract concepts.

reliability—The consistency or dependability of measures of abstract concepts.

To determine how well our quantitative and qualitative data collection techniques measure abstract concepts of interest, validity and reliability are important considerations. Validity assesses how well our measures capture the meaning of abstract concepts, and reliability refers to the consistency or dependability of our measures. A sport manager can have more faith in research if the measures used capture the meaning of the abstract managerial concept and hold up over time and across different groups (Andrew, Pedersen, & McEvoy, 2011).

To illustrate, a manager of a fitness facility can assume that low prices, cleanliness, and qualified instructors contribute to customer satisfaction. If customers confirm that only these three factors contribute to their satisfaction, then the measures devised by the manager would have high validity because they fully capture the meaning of the concept. But, if customers reveal that other factors such as variety in program offerings and having the latest weight-training equipment also contribute to their satisfaction, then the survey or interview questions should incorporate those additional measures to improve validity.

Using this same example, the fitness facility manager should also consider whether the measures of customer satisfaction are reliable by testing whether they are consistent over time and across different groups when all other conditions remain constant. For example, if customers were asked to fill out a customer satisfaction survey twice in a year and the results of the two surveys were similar, then the measures could be assumed to be dependable over time.

Although quantitative and qualitative researchers often use different terminology and techniques to assess validity and reliability, both groups are interested in producing results that are credible, dependable, and believable. Some of the strategies that they use to achieve these goals are carefully defining abstract concepts, examining results over time and across subgroups, and using multiple sources of data.

Current Challenges in Sport Management Research

Several major issues will affect sport management research as we continue making our way through the second decade of 21st century. A few of the most urgent are addressed in the following sections.

Judging the Quality of Research

Sport managers who lack adequate training face considerable challenges when interpreting research. Because of the information explosion that has accompanied the emergence of a knowledge-based economy, sport managers are bombarded with research from a variety of sources including the media, the World Wide Web, trade publications, academic journals, consulting and governmental reports, workshops, and conference presentations, as well as research done for their own organizations. Because research varies considerably in quality, sport managers must be able to make accurate evaluations of the research methods used and the data analysis techniques employed to judge whether the conclusions drawn and the recommendations made are reliable and credible.

CONSIDER THE SOURCE

The source of the research is one element to consider. Many people are suspicious of research reported over the Internet, with good reason. Although some websites contain research information that has been carefully monitored or reviewed, many do not. Readers often have difficulty determining whether information on the World Wide Web is credible because the source may not report adequate details regarding the research design or the qualifications of the researcher.

QUESTIONS TO ASK TO JUDGE RESEARCH QUALITY

Sport managers should ask numerous questions when judging the quality of research. The following are some of the more critical questions that you should be asking:

> Are the purposes, research questions, or hypotheses of the research clearly stated?
> Is a strong rationale for conducting the study provided?
> Who conducted the research, and what are their credentials?
> Who sponsored the research, and how will they benefit from it?
> What is the source of the research, and is a rigorous review process in place for ensuring its quality?
> Are the key concepts or variables under investigation clearly defined?
> If applicable, was relevant literature or background information drawn from?
> Did the researcher consider ethical issues when conducting the research?
> Were the methods used to collect the data appropriate?
> What sampling techniques were used, and were they appropriate?
> Are the measures or indicators of key concepts valid and reliable?
> How were the data recorded and analyzed?
> What are the limitations of the study design?
> Were explanations for the findings provided, and are they justified?
> Are conclusions and recommendations provided, and are they supported by the findings?

If it is not clear who conducted the research or what their credentials are, if few details are provided about the sample or research methods, and if no mention is made of the validity and reliability of the measures or indicators used, you should be highly suspicious of the claims being made. A systematic approach to research may have been used, but until you can verify that, you should critically question whether the conclusions and recommendations are justified and be hesitant about relying on the information when making decisions.

The Gap Between Theory and Practice

As discussed previously, research in the field is increasing as the study of sport management spreads to all parts of the globe. Although the field is growing and research is proliferating rapidly, an area of concern has become apparent. Parks (1992) clearly outlined the problem when she noted the struggle between those doing the research and those who want to apply the knowledge. More than two decades later, the relationship between theory and practice in sport management remains a concern to many within the field. As Parks wrote, "Questions still remain how best to translate sport management theory into practice" (p. 221).

The key word is *translate*, and the meaning of that word leads to an important observation. Despite the proliferation of journals that have emerged in the field over the past two decades, the research that is published in them is geared toward the academic community and is written in such a way that other researchers can understand it, but many practitioners cannot because they do not have adequate training in research. In fact, the readership of academic journals (e.g., *Journal of Sport Management*, *Sport Management Review*, *Sport Marketing Quarterly*, *European Sport Management Quarterly*) is made up almost exclusively of professors and students in institutions of higher learning. Despite increased efforts by authors and journal editors to emphasize the practical implications of their research findings, many sport practitioners give little attention to those journals when making decisions.

At the opposite end of the spectrum are a great number of trade publications that cater to a membership that is actively engaged in providing sport to the masses. These publications include numerous articles written by sport professionals for the benefit of other professionals working in the field. Written in lay terms, these articles commonly highlight best practices for managing sport teams, programs, facilities, events, and the like. These articles also provide timely statistical information regarding industry trends. Although some of these articles report on research conducted by sport managers working in the field, rarely would any of these studies stand up to scientific scrutiny. Moreover, although some trade publications, like *Street & Smith's SportsBusiness Journal*, feature articles written by academics, they are not vetted through the same peer-review process as academic journals are, so readers should be cautious when basing decisions on the findings published in these outlets.

What should become clear from this analysis is that no publications occupy a common ground where both researchers and practitioners can contribute and reap the benefits from what is being written. Put on a continuum from theoretical to practical, the various publications show an obvious gap (see figure 20.1). The perceived gap between theory and practice can be narrowed as more sport management students learn about research. At the same time, academics cannot assume that the results of their well-conceived and eloquently written studies will reach or have an effect on the field. Consequently, some are actively striving to communicate their findings more broadly (e.g., in professional publications and conferences, in government reports, in

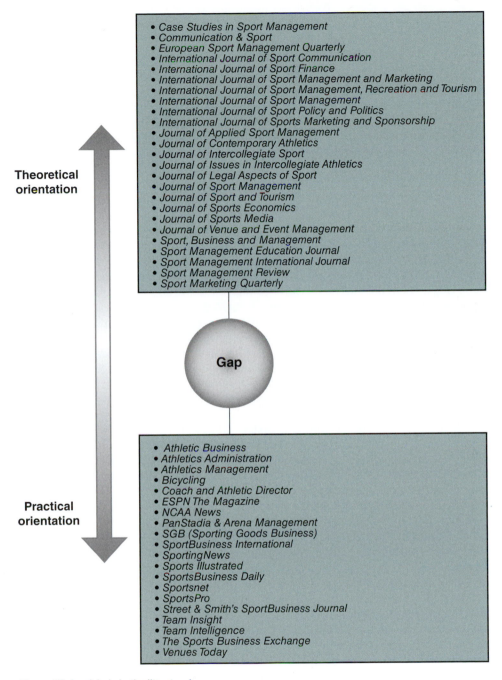

Theoretical orientation

- Case Studies in Sport Management
- Communication & Sport
- European Sport Management Quarterly
- International Journal of Sport Communication
- International Journal of Sport Finance
- International Journal of Sport Management and Marketing
- International Journal of Sport Management, Recreation and Tourism
- International Journal of Sport Management
- International Journal of Sport Policy and Politics
- International Journal of Sports Marketing and Sponsorship
- Journal of Applied Sport Management
- Journal of Contemporary Athletics
- Journal of Intercollegiate Sport
- Journal of Issues in Intercollegiate Athletics
- Journal of Legal Aspects of Sport
- Journal of Sport Management
- Journal of Sport and Tourism
- Journal of Sports Economics
- Journal of Sports Media
- Journal of Venue and Event Management
- Sport, Business and Management
- Sport Management Education Journal
- Sport Management International Journal
- Sport Management Review
- Sport Marketing Quarterly

Gap

Practical orientation

- Athletic Business
- Athletics Administration
- Athletics Management
- Bicycling
- Coach and Athletic Director
- ESPN The Magazine
- NCAA News
- PanStadia & Arena Management
- SGB (Sporting Goods Business)
- SportBusiness International
- SportingNews
- Sports Illustrated
- SportsBusiness Daily
- Sportsnet
- SportsPro
- Street & Smith's SportBusiness Journal
- Team Insight
- Team Intelligence
- The Sports Business Exchange
- Venues Today

Figure 20.1   A hole in the literature!

the media). Similarly, practitioners should not assume that research is too esoteric to be of practical use and should work with academics to identify problems of mutual concern that could be addressed through research to improve policies and managerial practices. Members of both groups must make a stronger effort to answer questions such as these: What does this research really mean? How can it be of use to me? How can we work together to promote progressive and innovative change?

Using Statistics Correctly

The following two sections of this sidebar deal with research and decision making in the sport industry. The first section examines MLB salaries to illustrate how sport managers need to be aware of the consequences associated with using mean scores as the basis for any decision. While statistics can provide precise information to help in the decision making process, they only provide part of the picture. Thus, sport managers should be careful in drawing conclusions from the numbers alone. The second section of this sidebar uses several sport management examples to illustrate the issues surrounding conducting surveys, selecting samples, drawing inferences, and arriving at sound conclusions.

Example 1: The Well-Chosen Average

According to a report filed by the Associated Press ("A-Rod," 2013), the average opening-day salary for MLB players was an estimated US$3.67 million in 2013. This figure represented a 6.1% increase from the previous season and marked the ninth consecutive year that average salaries increased for MLB players ("Yankees' payroll," 2013). The average (arithmetic mean) is a measure of central tendency that certainly provides some information. Yet we must be aware of how this average is used, as well as what it hides. For example, this US$3.67 million figure fails to inform us that the average player on the New York Yankees earned nearly twice this amount at US$7.15 million, making the Yankees MLB's leading spender for the 15th year in a row. Nor does this average indicate that the Houston Astros entered the 2013 regular season boasting an average salary of US$817,133, which is only 22.3% of the league average and 11.4% of the Yankees' average ("A-Rod," 2013). Although the same study reported these figures, the US$3.67 million league-wide average was likely the most quoted by the media and most used in salary negotiations during the off-season.

Intuitively, we also would want to question the effect that huge salaries, like those paid to the Yankees' Alex Rodriguez (US$29 million), Vernon Wells (US$24.6 million), CC Sabathia (US$24.3 million), and Mark Teixeira (US$23.1 million), have on this reported average. All four of these Yankee players will earn more on an individual basis than all of the players on the Houston Astros' opening-day roster combined ("A-Rod," 2013). No fewer than 103 players will earn in excess of US$10 million during the 2013 season, and more than 20 players will earn over US$20 million ("Yankees' payroll," 2013). Given the incredible disparity between the earnings of these players and the 44 players on opening-day rosters making the MLB minimum of US$490,000 in 2013 ("Yankees' payroll," 2013), the average may not be the best figure for understanding MLB salaries. Of all the measures of central tendency, the arithmetic mean is the one most affected by extreme measures (either high or low). Perhaps the median (the middle salary) or the mode (the salary most commonly earned) would be more appropriate measures to use when reporting player salaries. For sake of reference, the median salary of players on opening-day MLB rosters was US$1,262,500 in 2013, which illustrates how large salaries can skew the perception of player earnings in MLB ("Yankees payroll," 2013). Some other well-chosen averages to be wary of are (1) the average income of spectators at a professional sport event, (2) the average age of joggers, (3) the average amount spent on sport equipment in a year, and (4) the average length of employment for service employees at a stadium.

To summarize, we can fairly state that statistics can provide precise information that will assist in making sport management decisions. But we must be extremely careful in drawing conclusions from the numbers alone. They provide only part of the picture. For instance, in the example of MLB salaries, by employing the critical thinking questions posed in chapter 1 (e.g., what significant information is omitted?), sport managers can expose the consequences associated with using mean scores as the basis for decision making.

Example 2: Built-In Bias

Darrell Huff is the author of the book *How to Lie With Statistics*. "To be worth much," Huff wrote, "a report based on sampling must use a representative sample, which is one from which every source of bias has been removed" (1993, p. 18). Sometimes when doing research, we have a strong desire to produce a pleasing result. Surveys are used to gauge customer satisfaction, fan allegiance, and a host of other factors. Because we can rarely survey the entire population, we draw samples to represent a much larger number of people. If the sample is representative of the larger population, we can draw inferences and be more assured that our conclusions are sound. In some instances, however, the sample is not representative. Analyze the following hypothetical situations to see whether you can spot the problem:

> A MLS franchise (e.g., LA Galaxy) surveys spectators at a game to determine fan allegiance.

> The city council of Wichita, Kansas, hesitates on plans for a multipurpose recreational facility because of an outcry of opposition in the letters to the editor section of the local newspaper.

> The cost of playing youth lacrosse in a Canadian maritime province was increased to C$150 per season based on a survey that determined the average income of the players' parents.

> A survey of spectators at a local harness racing track revealed that 60% would be receptive to having nutritious offerings replace junk food.

On the surface, each of the scenarios is a legitimate way to use information to improve decision making in sport management. But we must be careful what we ask, whom we ask, how we ask, and most important, what we conclude. Take, for example, the previous hypothetical situations:

> The information derived from the LA Galaxy survey will be biased by the fact that the fan allegiance of spectators would be presumed to be quite high. A comparison between casual fans and regular fans would be more useful, but the best information might come from people who do not attend games at all.

> People who write letters to the editor are not necessarily representative of the population of a given city. The overwhelming majority may be in favor of a new recreational facility but do not find it necessary to have their thoughts appear in print. Also, a sampling process did not preselect the letter writers who volunteered to write. Thus, they create an imbalance of opinion that readers of the newspaper should consider.

> If the average income was self-reported, then the lacrosse officials should be careful in using the results because people tend to inflate their earnings when surveyed. And because we already know about the well-chosen average, we know that this income figure may not be representative of the parents of these young players.

> When surveyed, people almost always support habits and practices that are good for them. It is well established that survey subjects tend to report based on their attitudes rather than their actual behavior. People may say they would like to see food that is more nutritious at the concession stands, yet junk food may continue to be the biggest seller.

Refer to the critical thinking questions presented in chapter 1 to help you in your analysis of the preceding hypothetical situations. Can you think of other areas in statistics and research where you might be able to use critical thinking skills to elicit practical solutions to complex problems in the field of sport management?

Future of Sport Management Research

More sport managerial issues will arise as the field grows and the century progresses. Changing technologies, environments, workforces, spectators, venues, security measures, aging populations, and a plethora of other factors will influence sport and the ways in which it is managed. Sport scholars and practitioners foresee changes in media delivery, game management, and customer service to be at the forefront of concern. What issues and problems do you foresee? How will you solve them to the satisfaction of various stakeholders? What methods will you use to address your research questions?

In his best-selling novel *Moneyball*, Michael Lewis (2003) chronicled how the small-market Oakland Athletics relied on sophisticated statistical analyses to defy baseball logic by finishing near the top of the MLB standings and reaching the postseason despite having one of the smallest player payrolls in the league. In addition to serving as the impetus for a critically acclaimed motion picture, Lewis' book has also gained notoriety for spawning interest in the use of big data analytics for guiding decision making within a variety of organizational settings. "In business, as in sports, tracking the metrics that matter is fundamental to better performance" (Harris, 2012, para. 12). However, the simple availability of data is not sufficient to making better decisions. In order to be effective in the age of information, sport managers must be able to discern which data are meaningful and have a verifiable influence on organizational outcomes. Understanding how to read, interpret, and critically assess research data of all shapes and sizes is becoming an increasingly common job requirement within the sport industry. But the demand for these skills extends far beyond the front offices of professional sport teams.

An article published in the *Harvard Business Review* proclaimed that "data scientists" have the sexiest job of the 21st century (Davenport & Patil, 2012). Unfortunately, the demand for these positions is racing ahead of the supply of qualified talent to fill them. Outside of the sport industry, technology companies such as Yahoo!, Facebook, Google, Amazon, Microsoft, eBay, LinkedIn, and Twitter are at the forefront of this revolution. Just like with any good researcher, "the dominant trait among data scientists is an intense curiosity—a desire to go beneath the surface of a problem, find the questions at its heart, and distill them into a very clear set of hypotheses that can be tested" (Davenport & Patil, 2012, p. 73). Given the increasing value being placed on research skills in sport and other related industries, it is anticipated that research will eventually be included as a core content area in undergraduate curriculums for sport management degree programs around the world. Where such classes are not required, sport management students would be well served by seeking out courses in research methods, as well as in both quantitative and qualitative data analysis, to prepare themselves for a future career in the knowledge economy.

Critical Thinking in Sport Management Research

PORTFOLIO
Complete the critical thinking portfolio activity in the WSG, consulting as needed the "Critical Thinking Questions" sidebar in chapter 1.

You do not have to look far to realize that statistical information inundates our daily lives. Television commercials inform us that "four out of five dentists surveyed recommend Brand X toothpaste." News broadcasts mention that our chances of getting the flu this winter are 1 in 20 without a flu shot and 1 in 100 with the shot. Professional and amateur sport stars break records at what appears to be a record-breaking pace. Goals, home runs, coaching victories, and increased diversity in the workplace are all examples of what we count, put in some kind of chronology, and compare or contrast.

North America has clearly demonstrated a preoccupation with sport statistics. Although statistics can be useful, those aspiring to be sport managers should be aware of the indiscriminate and, in some cases, intentional misuse of statistical information. As mentioned earlier, in 1954, Darrell Huff wrote a book titled *How to Lie With Statistics*. The book was reprinted in 1982 and again in 1993, and has become a bestseller in a number of countries. In a lighthearted way, Huff described how the presentation of statistical data can often fool us and give us a sense of false confidence. In the earlier sidebar "Using Statistics Correctly," we adapted two of Huff's examples to illustrate how statistics influence sport managers and how they must be careful in using them. Used correctly, statistical information complements the research process. Used improperly, however, statistics can be misleading at best and incorrect at worst. As pointed out in this chapter, statistics are just one type of data, and much can be learned by talking directly to those involved in sport through interviews or focus groups to obtain information on how to improve it. The same care and critical thinking need to be applied to qualitative and mixed-methods research to avoid making faulty assumptions about future directions.

Ethics in Sport Management Research

A number of important ethical issues should be taken into account when conducting sport management research. Most colleges and universities have ethical guidelines that students and faculty members must follow when conducting research involving human subjects. These same ethical guidelines should be followed when sport management research is conducted outside of the university setting to ensure that it is conducted professionally. For example, people have a right to know what the research is about and how the data will be used before they agree to participate in a study, whether it is filling out a marketing survey or being interviewed on a topic of interest to sport managers. Participation in research should be voluntary, so even though researchers need to explain the importance of their studies and encourage people to take part in research, staff, volunteers, or customers should not feel as if they are being coerced into participating.

Research in sport organizations can often deal with sensitive topics, so **anonymity**, which means that names of study participants should not be included in the reporting of the results, is another ethical guideline that should be followed. Anonymity is closely tied to **confidentiality**, which means that researchers should not be specifying who said what, so study participants will feel free to speak honestly and openly about the topic without repercussions.

Violating ethical guidelines in sport management research can have serious consequences. For example, if an evaluation of the leadership of a sport organization is being conducted and researchers release the names and comments made by employees who have concerns, these employees may face negative sanctions from their supervisors and coworkers for expressing their views. To learn more about ethical guidelines in sport management research, students are encouraged to take research methods courses and read the research ethics guidelines at their college or university.

Summary

In our information-based economy, sport managers must raise and address research questions. Sport managers who ask relevant and focused research questions and obtain valid and reliable answers through sound research practices will enhance their planning and improve the likelihood of achieving success both on and off the playing field. The most successful sport managers in the second decade of the 21st century will be those who understand the importance of asking questions and using research to inform their decision making.

Sport management research is available from a variety of sources. The scholarly and professional literatures are both excellent sources of information, and they often lead readers to ask additional research questions of their own. In many cases, commercial research firms are contracted to aid sport organizations in identifying suitable research questions and obtaining appropriate answers. Regardless of the source, sport managers need a solid foundation in research to be able to assess what types of information are reliable and credible. Understanding key concepts such as ways of knowing, science and pseudoscience, basic and applied research, qualitative and quantitative data, research design, and reliability and validity can help sport managers judge the quality of research so that they can make more informed decisions. This understanding will also help bridge the gap between sport management theory and practice.

Engaging in the research process can be stimulating and rewarding for students. Besides incorporating research into their coursework, sport management students can attend conferences, join associations that promote sport management research (e.g., NASSM, EASM, SMAANZ), and refer to publications within the field. In addition,

PORTFOLIO

Complete the ethical issues portfolio activity in the WSG, consulting as needed the "Guidelines for Making Ethical Decisions" sidebar in chapter 1.

anonymity—Normally, the names of people who participate in research are not revealed in the reporting of the study.

confidentiality—What individual people say or report in research is not revealed in the reporting of the study.

students can also ask professors about how they might be able to get involved as volunteers or participants in their ongoing research studies, which often take place right on campus. This will lead some students to consider entering graduate sport programs for advanced study in sport management, which are growing around the world.

Review Questions

1. What value does a sport organization receive from research provided by the academic and professional literature?

2. Under what circumstances would a commercial research firm be able to make valuable contributions to a sport organization?

3. What are five key ways that pseudoscience differs from science? Why does the scientific approach provide sport managers with more trustworthy information on which to base decisions?

4. What are some of the differences between quantitative and qualitative data? Describe one common data collection technique for each and provide one main advantage and one main disadvantage of each data collection technique discussed.

5. What is a research design, and what are the key features of the most common research designs used in sport management research?

6. Why is it important to consider ethical issues when conducting sport management research?

7. What questions should be asked to judge the quality of sport management research?

8. Do you agree that the need for expertise in sport management research will continue to grow in the future? Justify your argument.

References

A-Rod will make more than Astros. (2013, March 29). *Associated Press*. Retrieved from http://espn.go.com/mlb/story/_/id/9109596/alex-rodriguez-make-more-houston-astros-combined-salary

Andrew, D.P.S., Pedersen, P.M., & McEvoy, C.D. (2011). *Research methods and design in sport management*. Champaign, IL: Human Kinetics.

Andrews, D.L., Mason, D.A., & Silk, M. (Eds.). (2005). *Qualitative methods in sport studies*. London, UK: Berg.

Avolio, B.J., Gardner, W.L., Walumbwa, F.O., Luthans, F., & May, D.R. (2004). Unlocking the mask: A look at the process by which authentic leaders impact follower attitudes and behaviours. *Leadership Quarterly, 15*, 801–823.

Bertrand, K. (2012, October 23). Martin Snedden: My biggest champion. *New Zealand Women's Weekly*. Retrieved from www.nzwomansweekly.co.nz

Canadian Heritage. (2013, February). *Sport participation 2010 Research Paper*. Retrieved from http://publications.gc.ca/collections/collection_2013/pc-ch/CH24-1-2012-eng.pdf

Council of American Survey Research Organizations. (2013). *About CASRO*. Retrieved from www.casro.org/?page=AboutCASRO

Creswell, J.W. (2009). *Research design: Qualitative, quantitative, and mixed methods approaches* (3rd ed.). Thousand Oaks, CA: Sage.

Davenport, T.H., & Patil, D.J. (2012, October). Data scientist: The sexiest job of the 21st century. *Harvard Business Review, 90*(10), 70–76.

Ericsson, K.A., Prietula, M.J., & Cokely, E.T. (2007, July-August). The making of an expert. *Harvard Business Review, 85*(7/8), 114–121.

Ferguson, A. (2002). *Managing my life: My autobiography*. London, UK: Hodder & Stoughton.

Frank, R. (1984). Olympic myths and realities. *Arete: The Journal of Sport Literature, 1*(2), 155–161.

Frisby, W., Reid, C., Millar, S., & Hoeber, L. (2005). Putting "participatory" into participatory forms of action research. *Journal of Sport Management, 19*, 367–386.

George, G.W., Mayer, D., McLean, A.M., & Sims, P. (2007). Discovering your authentic leadership. *Harvard Business Review, 85*(2), 129–138.

Harris, J.G. (2012, April 10). What business can learn from sports analytics. Retrieved from www.cnbc.com/id/46964446

Huff, D. (1993). *How to lie with statistics*. New York, NY: Norton.

Kerlinger, F.N., & Lee, H.B. (2000). *Foundations of behavioral research* (4th ed.). Orlando, FL: Harcourt.

Lewin, K. (1946). Action research and minority problems. *Journal of Social Issues, 2*, 34–36.

Lewis, M. (2003). *Moneyball: The art of winning an unfair game*. New York, NY: Norton.

Li, M., Pitts, B., & Quarterman, J. (2008). *Research methods in sport management*. Morgantown, WV: Fitness Information Technology.

Martin Snedden rips into Parker's campaign. (2013, April 7). *The Sunday News*. Retrieved from www.stuff.co.nz/sunday-news

McFadden, S. (2013, March 23). Martin Snedden: Mr. Fix-it. *The New Zealand Herald*. Retrieved from www.nzherald.co.nz

Nielsen. (2013, January 18). *State of the media: 2012 year in sports*. Retrieved from www.nielsen.com/us/en/reports/2013/state-of-the-media-2012-year-in-sports.html

Nielsen. (2012, December 4). *State of the media: The social media report 2012*. Retrieved from www.nielsen.com/us/en/reports/2012/state-of-the-media-the-social-media-report-2012.html

Parks, J.B. (1992). Scholarship: The other "bottom line" in sport management. *Journal of Sport Management, 6*, 220–229.

Reason, P., & Bradbury, H. (2007). *Handbook of action research*. Thousand Oaks, CA: Sage.

Romanos, J. (2011, January 27). The Wellingtonian Interview: Martin Snedden. *The Wellingtonian*. Retrieved from www.stuff.co.nz/dominion-post/news/local-papers/the-wellingtonian

Sage, G.H., & Eitzen, D.S. (2012). *Sociology of North American sport* (9th ed.). New York, NY: Oxford University Press.

Slack, T., & Parent, M. (2006). *Understanding sport organizations: The application of organization theory* (2nd ed.). Champaign, IL: Human Kinetics.

Stuart, C. (2013, January 28). How brands adapt marketing to the second-screen experience. *Street & Smith's SportsBusiness Journal*. Retrieved from www.sportsbusinessdaily.com/Journal/Issues/2013/01/28/Opinion/From-the-Field-of-Social-Markting.aspx

Taylor, J., & Frisby, W. (2010). Addressing inadequate leisure access policies through citizen engagement. In H. Mair, S.M. Arai, & D.G. Reid (Eds.), *Decentring work: Critical perspectives on leisure, social policy, and human development* (pp. 30–45). Calgary, Alberta, Canada: University of Calgary Press.

Thomas, J.R., Nelson, J.K., & Silverman, S.J. (2011). *Research methods in physical activity* (6th ed.). Champaign, IL: Human Kinetics.

Wilson, B. (2006). Selective memory in a global culture: Reconsidering links between youth, hockey, and Canadian identity. In D. Whitson & R. Gruneau (Eds.), *Artificial ice: Hockey, commerce, and Canadian culture* (pp. 53–70). Aurora, Ontario, Canada: Garamond.

Yankees' payroll hits $230 million. (2013, April 1). *Associated Press*. Retrieved from http://espn.go.com/mlb/story/_/id/9121461/new-york-yankees-set-opening-day-payroll-record-230-million

PHOTO CREDITS

Page 341 Courtesy of Paul M. Pedersen
Page 348 © Sky Deutschland/Fabian Helmich
Page 351 Courtesy of Dave Preston and
  Missouri Valley Conference
Page 354 Courtesy of D.C. United
Page 360 Brad Rempel/Icon SMI
Page 370 Courtesy of Victor Timchenko
Page 378 Courtesy of Paul M. Pedersen
Page 380 Courtesy of Tim Whitten
Page 384 Courtesy of Casey A. Gentis
Page 389 Courtesy of University of North
  Carolina Athletic Department
Page 396 Maurizio Borsari/AFLO SPORT/
  Icon SMI
Page 406 Javier Garcia/BPI/Icon SMI
Page 410 Courtesy of Zhang Yan
Page 413 Courtesy of University of Notre Dame
  Athletic Department
Page 415 Courtesy of Paul M. Pedersen
Page 420 Courtesy of Karl Eagleman

Page 421 Courtesy of Paul M. Pedersen
Page 426 Mark LoMoglio/Icon SMI
Page 428 Courtesy of Paul M. Pedersen
Page 431 Courtesy of Paul M. Pedersen
Page 434 Courtesy of Canadian Paralympic
  Committee
Page 440 Brian Peterson/Minneapolis Star
  Tribune/MCT/ZUMA PRESS
Page 442 Courtesy David Sherman/Carley Knox
Page 450 Courtesy of Paul M. Pedersen
Page 453 Courtesy of Paul M. Pedersen
Page 454 By Jeffix (photographer). Courtesy of
  NB Football Business / NBFB.
Page 457 Juan Salas/Icon SMI
Page 460 Zuma Press/Icon SMI
Page 468 Courtesy of Colleen Cavalier
Page 476 Shelly Castellano ICON SMI 740
Page 481 Courtesy of Paul M. Pedersen
Page 485 Courtesy of Mark Demeny
Page 488 Courtesy of Joanne Martin

INDEX

ABOUT THE EDITORS

Paul M. Pedersen, PhD, is a professor of sport management and the director of the sport management program in the School of Public Health at Indiana University–Bloomington (IU). He has worked as a sportswriter, sports management consultant, and sport business columnist. Pedersen's primary area of scholarly interest is the symbiotic relationship between sport and communication in addition to his research examining the activities and practices of various sport organization personnel.

A research fellow of the North American Society for Sport Management (NASSM), Pedersen has published seven books (including *Handbook of Sport Communication*, *Research Methods and Design in Sport Management*, and *Strategic Sport Communication*) and over 80 academic articles in outlets such as the *Journal of Sport Management*, *European Sport Management Quarterly*, *Sport Marketing Quarterly*, *International Journal of Sports Marketing and Sponsorship*, *Sociology of Sport Journal*, *International Review for the Sociology of Sport*, and *Journal of Sports Economics*. He has also been a part of more than 110 presentations at professional conferences or other gatherings, including invited addresses in China, Denmark, Hungary, Norway, and South Korea. He has been interviewed and quoted in publications as diverse as *The New York Times* and the *China Daily*.

Founder and editor in chief of the *International Journal of Sport Communication*, he serves on the editorial board of 10 journals, including founding editorial review board member of *Communication & Sport* and two other journals. A 2011 inductee into the Golden Eagle Hall of Fame (East High School in Pueblo, Colorado), Pedersen lives in Bloomington, Indiana, with his wife, Jennifer, and their four children, Hallie, Zack, Brock, and Carlie. His photo is courtesy of IU.

Lucie Thibault, PhD, is a professor in the department of sport management at Brock University in Ontario, Canada. She has taught at Brock since 2002. Thibault has also taught at the University of British Columbia and the University of Ottawa. In her quarter century of teaching, Thibault has instructed courses in organizational theory, organizational behavior, ethics in sport, globalization of sport, and policy and social issues in sport.

Thibault serves on the editorial board of the *International Journal of Sport Policy and Politics* as well as the *European Sport Management Quarterly*. She has held the roles of associate editor and editor of the *Journal of Sport Management*. She is a member of the North American Society for Sport Management (NASSM) and was named a research fellow of NASSM in 2001. In 2008, Thibault was awarded the Earle F. Zeigler Award from NASSM for her scholarly and leadership contributions to the field.

Her research interests lie in the formation, management, and evaluation of cross-sectoral partnerships in sport organizations. She also investigates the role of the Canadian government in sport excellence and sport participation and government involvement in developing sport policy. She has been an invited speaker featuring her research in many conferences around the world. Her research has appeared in numerous scholarly journals such as the *Journal of Sport Management*, *International Review for the Sociology of Sport*, *Journal of Sport and Social Issues*, *Human Relations*, *Leisure Studies*, *European Sport Management Quarterly*, *International Journal for Sport Policy and Politics*, and *Nonprofit and Voluntary Sector Quarterly*.

Thibault resides in the Niagara region of Ontario. Her photo is courtesy of Mike Armstrong, Brock University.

ABOUT THE CONTRIBUTORS

Robertha Abney, PhD, is an associate professor at Slippery Rock University (SRU) in the Department of Sport Management. She received her doctoral degree in athletics administration from the University of Iowa. Her areas of research include role models and mentoring women in sport (womentoring), and the status of minorities and women in leadership roles in sport. At SRU she teaches courses in sport management and ethics, sport communication, global sport management, and introduction to sport management. Dr. Abney has written several chapters in sport management textbooks. She was the associate athletic director and senior woman administrator at SRU for 17 years. She served on the following committees within the National Collegiate Athletic Association (NCAA): Division II Management Council, Management Council Subcommittee, Committee on Infractions, Administrative Review Subcommittee, Championship Task Force Committee, and Project Team to Review Issues Related to Diversity. Also, she served on the American Alliance for Health, Physical Education, Recreation and Dance (AAHPERD) Awards Committee. Dr. Abney is a past president of the National Association for Girls and Women in Sport (NAGWS) and is a member of the North American Society for Sport Management (NASSM). In addition to serving on the Commission on Sport Management Accreditation's (COSMA) Board of Commissioners, she was elected to serve as the organization's co-chair in 2013. Dr. Abney's photo appears courtesy of Herman A. Boler.

Ketra L. Armstrong, PhD, is the associate dean for graduate programs and faculty affairs and a professor of sport management in the School of Kinesiology at the University of Michigan (UM). Dr. Armstrong's scholarship converges on the topics of race, gender, and the social psychology of managing, marketing, and participating in sport. Her research has been featured in numerous journals (e.g., *Journal of Sport Management, Sport Marketing Quarterly, Journal of Sport and Social Issues, Journal of Sport Behavior, Innovative Marketing, Journal of Black Psychology, Journal of Black Studies*, and *Western Journal of Black Studies*). She received the 2001 Outstanding Probationary Faculty Research award from The Ohio State University; she received the 2002 Young Professional award from the American Association of Active Lifestyle and Fitness; she coauthored an article that received the 2004 Outstanding Research award by the Sport Marketing Association (SMA); she conducted national research for *Essence Magazine* on Black Women's Fitness; in 2008, she was inducted as a research fellow by the North American Society for Sport Management (NASSM); and in 2011, the article she coauthored, "Market Analyses of Race and Sport Consumption," was selected among the top 20 articles published in the past 20 years by *Sport Marketing Quarterly*. Dr. Armstrong teaches the Principles of Marketing, Race Relations and Cultural Images in Sport, and Gender and Sport courses at UM. In addition to Dr. Armstrong's scholarly pursuits, she has amassed a wealth of practical experience in the sport industry. She is a former NCAA Division I scholarship student athlete (basketball player), coach (women's basketball), and athletic administrator. Over the years, she has performed integral roles in advising/consulting, research, management, marketing, and media relations for numerous youth, community, collegiate, professional, and international sport events. She is a member of the UM Diversity Council, an internal advisory board member for the UM SHARP research center, the former vice president of the NCAA Scholarly Colloquium, the former president of the National Association for Girls and Women in Sport (NAGWS), a former board member of the National Women's Hall of Fame, and a former member of the prestigious Wade Trophy Selection Committee. Dr. Armstrong is also a freelance sport broadcaster, and she received the 2001 Newsmaker of the Year award from the Columbus, Ohio Association of Black Journalists. In 2010, she received the Honorary Guiding Woman in Sport award. Professor Armstrong's photo appears courtesy of Ketra L. Armstrong.

Kathy Babiak, PhD, is an associate professor in the Department of Sport Management at the University of Michigan (UM). She completed her doctoral degree at the University of British Columbia, where she explored the implementation, management, and evaluation of cross-sector partnerships in the Canadian sport system. From this doctoral work, a natural extension of her research became focusing on socially responsible issues in cross-sector partnerships. Her most recent research in the area has explored underlying motives that drive sports organizations to engage in socially responsible practices, as well as strategic aspects related to social involvement (such as community investment, philanthropy, and environmental sustainability) in commercial and nonprofit sports organizations. Her work appears in a variety of journals, including *Journal of Sport Management, Corporate Social Responsibility and Environmental Management, Journal of Business Ethics, Sport Management Review,* and *European Sport Management Quarterly.* Dr. Babiak's most recent edited book, *The Handbook of Corporate Responsibility in Sport: Principles and Practice,* was published in 2013. This book offers a comprehensive survey of theories and concepts of corporate social responsibility (CSR) as applied to sport, and considers the social, strategic, ethical, and environmental aspects of social responsibility

in the field of sport. She has taught a number of classes to undergraduate and graduate students related to organizations and business while at UM, including strategic management, human resource management, and organizational behavior. Babiak is a North American Society for Sport Management (NASSM) research fellow and is also the codirector of the Sport, Health and Activity Research and Policy (SHARP) Center for Women and Girls at the University of Michigan, a partnership with the Women's Sports Foundation. She lives in Ann Arbor, Michigan with her husband, Mark, daughters, Ruby and Vivian, and dog Pearl. Her photo appears courtesy of KGT Photography.

Jennifer E. Bruening, PhD, earned her BA in English from the University of Notre Dame (1992), her MA in English from Morehead State University (1994), and her PhD from The Ohio State University (2000). Bruening spent four years as a collegiate student athlete playing volleyball at the University of Notre Dame. She spent eight years as an athletics administrator and volleyball coach at Kenyon College in Ohio, including two years as athletics director. She has been a part of the sport management program at the University of Connecticut since January 2002. She is also a research fellow with Northeastern University's Center for the Study of Sport in Society. Dr. Bruening's research line has focused primarily on the barriers and supports for women and minorities in sport. Dr. Bruening is also the program founder and director for Husky Sport, which receives funding from the USDA SNAP-Ed program, AmeriCorps, and the City of Hartford. Husky Sport has both a program and a research component. The program provides mentors (UConn students) as planners of sessions at a recreation center, an elementary school, and a neighborhood Saturday program. These sessions emphasize exposure and access to sport and physical activity and advocate good nutrition and healthy lifestyles. Her research has focused specifically on the effect of involvement in such programs on both preadolescents and the college student mentors. For more information, see www.huskysport.uconn.edu. Her photo appears courtesy of Jennifer E. Bruening.

Coyte G. Cooper, PhD, is an assistant professor of sport administration at the University of North Carolina at Chapel Hill. While he has taught a variety of different sport management courses in the past, his area of specialization focuses on the business side of the sport industry. Dr. Cooper has developed a line of research that focuses on the identification of innovative marketing practices in NCAA athletic departments. In addition to teaching and conducting research initiatives, Dr. Cooper is involved with the National Wrestling Coaches Association (NWCA), helping promote its events on a local and national level. Some of his key duties in this role involve helping build interest in its highlight competitions while assisting with event management. Dr. Cooper is also active in outreach initiatives to help grow sport programs. In collaboration with the NWCA, he is currently active working with coaches to help them develop marketing strategies to enhance their programs. In addition, he developed Elite Level Sport Marketing (ELSM) (www.elitelevelsportmarketing.com), a resource for coaches interested in developing skill sets in marketing. Dr. Cooper received his doctorate in sport marketing and management from Indiana University-Bloomington. His photo appears courtesy of Abbey Doron of UNC Athletic Communications.

Corinne M. Daprano, PhD, is an associate professor in sport management in the Department of Health and Sport Science at the University of Dayton. She graduated from The Ohio State University, and she has more than 20 years of experience working in the sport and recreation industry. Her research interests include Paralympic sport, sport for development, and civic engagement in higher education and its application to sport management. At the University of Dayton, she teaches undergraduate courses in organizational behavior, principles of management, sport law, international sport business, and women in sport.

Dr. Daprano has published articles in *Sport Management Review, Recreational Sports Journal, Quest,* and *Future Focus.* She has coauthored a book chapter on the topic of service learning and has made numerous presentations at local, regional, national, and international conferences on volunteer management, Paralympic sport, and civic engagement. Dr. Daprano serves on the editorial review board of *Teaching, Research, and Media in Kinesiology.* She is a member of the North American Society for Sport Management (NASSM) and the Sport and Recreation Law Association (SRLA). Dr. Daprano's photo appears courtesy of the University of Dayton.

Timothy D. DeSchriver, EdD, is an associate professor of sport management in the Alfred Lerner College of Business and Economics at the University of Delaware. He earned his doctoral degree in physical education, with an emphasis in sport administration, from the University of Northern Colorado (UNC). He has worked as a field economist for the U.S. Department of Labor and has served as interim associate athletics director at UNC. He also spent four years as an assistant professor at Western Carolina University. He currently teaches classes on sport finance and sport marketing at both the undergraduate and graduate levels. Dr. DeSchriver's research interests are sport consumer demand, pro sport ownership incentives, and sport facility financing. He has published articles in the *Journal of Sport Management, Eastern Economic Journal, Sport Marketing Quarterly, International Sports Journal,* and *Street & Smith's SportsBusiness Journal.* He has been involved in research projects for the NCAA, the New York Red Bulls, the Major Indoor Soccer League, and the National Steeplechase Association. He was also coauthor of the textbook *Sport Finance* (first and second editions). Dr. DeSchriver is a member of the North American Society for Sport Management (NASSM) and the Sport Marketing Association (SMA). He has made numerous presentations at NASSM annual conferences as well as at international conferences. Before taking his position at the University of Delaware, Dr. DeSchriver was an assistant professor at the University of Massachusetts Amherst. Dr. DeSchriver's photo appears courtesy of the University of Massachusetts Amherst.

Stephen W. Dittmore, PhD, is an associate professor in the Department of Health, Human Performance and Recreation at the University of Arkansas, where he teaches undergraduate and graduate courses in the Recreation and Sport Management program. He earned his doctorate from the University of Louisville. He has taught a course in sport media and public relations at the AACSB-accredited sport management MBA program at the Instituto de Empresa in Madrid, Spain. Dittmore's research has appeared in the *Journal of Sport Management*, *International Journal of Sport Communication*, *Sport Marketing Quarterly*, and *Sport Management Review*. He coauthored *Sport Public Relations: Managing Stakeholder Communication,* now in its second edition. Dittmore has 10 years of practitioner experience in various sport public relations roles, and he served as a director of the Salt Lake City Organizing Committee for the 2002 Olympic Winter Games. His photo appears courtesy of the University of Arkansas.

Jess C. Dixon, PhD, is an assistant professor of sport management in the Department of Kinesiology at the University of Windsor. His primary research and scholarly interests are in the areas of strategic management in sport. His secondary interests include executive leadership and human resource management in sport, sport finance and economics, and sport management pedagogy. He currently teaches classes in sport management, strategic management in sport, human resource management, and sport finance. He has experience working within the golf and retail sporting goods industries, as well as with a boutique sport agency. He belongs to the North American Society for Sport Management (NASSM) and has made several presentations at its annual conference. His photo appears courtesy of the University of Windsor.

Marlene A. Dixon, PhD, is a professor at Troy University. Her research expertise is in the area of sport and life quality. In this area, she examines the ways that sport can be better designed and implemented to enhance the life quality of both sport providers and participants. Her most recent works include investigations of the characteristics of effective sport programs for girls and women, examinations of the work and family lives of intercollegiate coaches, and the role of sport in community building. Dr. Dixon completed her doctorate at The Ohio State University and served for eight years in the Sport Management Department at The University of Texas at Austin. She has more than 40 publications in a variety of journals, including the *Journal of Sport Management*, *Sport Management Review*, *Research Quarterly for Exercise and Sport*, *Sex Roles*, and *Quest*. She has been named a research fellow in the North American Society for Sport Management (NASSM). Her primary teaching areas are social and cultural aspects of sport, sport finance, and human resource management. She also enjoys mentoring graduate students and directing projects stemming from the Sport and Life Quality Laboratory. Before beginning her formal academic career, Dr. Dixon coached basketball and volleyball at the college level. She also competed as a varsity athlete in basketball and volleyball at Trinity University. She enjoys running, playing basketball, hiking, and fishing with her husband and three children. Professor Dixon's photo appears courtesy of Stacy Warner.

Andrea N. Eagleman, PhD, is a senior lecturer in the School of Sport and Exercise at Massey University in New Zealand, where she teaches undergraduate and graduate sport management courses. She earned her doctoral degree from Indiana University-Bloomington in 2008. She is a sport management researcher with a focus on communication and marketing, and her research examines portrayals of athletes of differing gender, race, and nationality in all forms of media, as well as the utilization of new media by sport organizations and athletes. She has published more than 30 peer-reviewed journal articles and book chapters in outlets such as the *Journal of Sport Management*, *Sport Management Review*, *Sport Marketing Quarterly*, *International Journal of Sport Communication*, and *International Journal of Sport Management*. Additionally, she has presented her research in countries such as New Zealand, the United States, Spain, and Germany. She was awarded the 2012 North American Society for Sport Management (NASSM) Janet B. Parks research grant, which allowed her to study the new media coverage of six countries during the 2012 Olympic Games. In addition to her research, Dr. Eagleman has held several leadership positions with professional sport management associations. She currently serves as the vice president of student affairs for the Sport Marketing Association (SMA) and is a member of the Publicity and Promotions Committee for NASSM. She also serves on the editorial boards of the *International Journal of Sport Communication*, *Journal of Applied Sport Management*, *Global Sport Business Association Journal*, and *Theories and Applications, International Edition*. Her industry experience includes three years as the public relations and marketing manager of Lehman Racing, a professional NHRA drag racing team, and a one-year position in the communications department at USA Gymnastics. Along with her scholarly pursuits, Dr. Eagleman remains active in the industry by partnering with sport organizations for research projects as well as by serving as a media relations volunteer at national and international sporting events. Dr. Eagleman's photo appears courtesy of Karl Eagleman.

Sheranne Fairley, PhD, is the head of event management in the School of Tourism at the University of Queensland, Australia. Her primary research interests are in the consumer behavior of sport and event fans, sport and event tourists, event volunteers, and umpires. Her secondary research streams focus on the internationalization and globalization of sport practice and education and event legacy. She has published in the *Journal of Sport Management*, *Sport Management Review*, *Sport in Society*, *Journal of Sport & Tourism*, and *Event Management*. She teaches classes in event marketing and international event management. Dr. Fairley's photo appears courtesy of the University of Queensland.

Ted G. Fay, PhD, is a professor and former chair of the Sport Management Department at the State University of New York (SUNY) at Cortland. Dr. Fay's doctorate is from the University of Massachusetts Amherst. In addition to being a senior fellow at the Institute for Human Centered Design (IHCD) for the Inclusive Sports Initiative, Dr. Fay is also a member of the Advisory Council for the Sport and Development Project at Brown University. Fay served as a senior research fellow at the Center for the Study of Sport in Society at Northeastern University and as a strategic consultant related to the Center's research and academic program initiatives from 1999 to 2010. Dr. Fay has focused much of his scholarly work in the areas of social and public policy, sport governance, leadership, sport for development, and strategic management. A particular focus in his research, advocacy, and activism has been placed on diversity and social justice issues involving a sport context, with an emphasis on individuals with disabilities. Dr. Fay was one of four keynote speakers at the 2011 NCAA Scholarly Colloquium, at which he delivered an address titled *Disability in Sport—It's Our Time: From the Sidelines to the Frontlines (Title IX – B)*. He currently consults with the NCAA regarding the inclusion of student athletes with a disability into intercollegiate athletics. Dr. Fay has presented more than 60 scholarly papers at a variety of international and national academic and professional conferences and has authored or coauthored more than 30 book chapters, academic articles, and monographs. A former Paralympic Games (1980–1991) and Olympic Games (1988) coach and an international cross-country ski official (1988–2010), Dr. Fay has an extensive background in international sport, including active involvement in the Olympic and Paralympic movements. He has had a varied career as an educator, advocate, and activist involving a number of human rights initiatives, environmental policy and protection campaigns, and community organizing efforts. Fay is recognized as an international expert on issues related to the integration and inclusion of athletes with a disability in mainstream sport. He was involved in drafting Article 30.5 of the United Nations Convention on the Human Rights for Persons with a Disability (2007), which addresses the universal right of persons with a disability to be fully included in all cultural, leisure, recreational, and sport activities. Fay was also involved in the development of new guidance issued by the U.S. Department of Education's Office of Civil Rights (OCR) in January 2013 regarding the inclusion of students with disabilities in scholastic and intercollegiate sports. He has been an active member of a number of professional associations, including the North American Society for the Sociology of Sport (NASSS), the North American Society for Sport Management (NASSM), the European Association for Sport Management (EASM), and the International Sport for Development and Peace Association (ISDPA). Professor Fay's photo appears courtesy of Eric Poggenpohl.

Lawrence W. Fielding, PhD, is a professor of sport management in the Department of Kinesiology in the School of Public Health at Indiana University-Bloomington. He received his doctorate from the University of Maryland in sport history in 1974. He has published more than 50 articles in sport history, sport management, and sport marketing. He has presented more than 75 papers at professional meetings. He has served on the editorial review boards for the *Journal of Sport History*, *Journal of Sport Management*, and the

Sport Marketing Quarterly. He is a research fellow in the North American Society for Sport Management (NASSM), and was selected for the North American Society for Sport History (NASSH) Staley Address, the highest recognition in sport history. Professor Fielding's photo appears courtesy of Indiana University-Bloomington.

Eric W. Forsyth, PhD, is a professor at Bemidji State University. He received his doctorate in sport administration from The University of New Mexico, with a minor in marketing management. Dr. Forsyth's two primary duties are teaching courses in sport management and supervising field experiences. He is a founding member of the interscholastic athletic administration graduate curriculum standards endorsed by the National Association for Sport and Physical Education (NASPE) and the National Interscholastic Athletic Administrators Association (NIAAA). With a passion for interscholastic athletics, he has published numerous articles in both juried and trade journals, presented at various conferences on the national and international level, and written several text chapters on issues related to high school athletics. Dr. Forsyth is the coeditor of the textbook, *NIAAA's Guide to Interscholastic Athletic Administration*. Dr. Forsyth has received the distinction as a certified athletic administrator through the NIAAA certification program. His most memorable role was serving as president of the Minnesota AAHPERD Association. When Dr. Forsyth is not in the classroom, you can bet he is in the woods during hunting season—he has even written stories about his bear hunting adventures, which have appeared in outdoor magazines and two hunting and fishing company profiles that were published in a sport brand textbook. Despite all his successes in his field, Dr. Forsyth considers himself truly accomplished when his wife considers him a good husband and his children consider him a good father. Professor Forsyth's photo appears courtesy of Eric Forsyth.

Wendy Frisby, PhD, is a professor in the School of Kinesiology at the University of British Columbia, Canada. The overall goal of her research program is to determine how those who have the least access to sport and recreation can become more involved as decision makers and participants to promote health, policy change, and other outcomes. She conducts feminist participatory action research (FPAR) with citizens and practitioners to analyze how the social and living conditions experienced by those living in poverty—which are often exacerbated by existing policies, programs, and structures in community sport and recreation—create barriers to participation. Dr. Frisby is a NASSM research fellow and a former editor of the *Journal of Sport Management*, and she was the recipient of the Earle F. Ziegler award in 2004. Professor Frisby's photo appears courtesy of John MacLeod, School of Kinesiology, University of British Columbia.

Heather Gibson, PhD, is a professor in the Department of Tourism, Recreation, and Sport Management at the University of Florida. She has an international reputation as a scholar in sport tourism and has written a number of foundational papers for work in this area. Her educational background encompasses both sport and tourism studies. She earned her doctoral degree in sport, leisure, and exercise science from the University of Connecticut. She has published both conceptual and empirical work on sport tourism, and she is the author of one of the most widely cited articles in sport tourism, "Sport Tourism: A Critical Analysis of Research," which was published in the *Sport Management Review* in 1998. Dr. Gibson, together with Dr. Laurence Chalip of the University of Illinois, was instrumental in initially bringing sport tourism to the attention of sport management professionals in the North American Society for Sport Management (NASSM). She is a member of the European Association for Sport Management (EASM), National Recreation and Park Association (NRPA), World Leisure, and the Leisure Studies Association (LSA). Professor Gibson's photo appears courtesy of Ray Carson, University of Florida.

James ("Jay") M. Gladden, PhD, is dean of the School of Physical Education and Tourism Management at Indiana University–Purdue University Indianapolis (IUPUI). Dr. Gladden's research expertise lies in the areas of sport brand management, sport sponsorship planning and evaluation, and college athletic fund-raising. Dr. Gladden has published numerous articles and book chapters on these topics in a wide variety of outlets, including the *Journal of Sport Management*, *Sport Marketing Quarterly*, *Sport Management Review*, and the *International Journal of Sports Marketing and Sponsorship*, and in trade publications such as *Athletic Management* and *Street & Smith's SportsBusiness Journal*. Dr. Gladden also brings more than 20 years of experience working with industry, first as a project director for DelWilber + Associates (from 1991–1994) and then later as a faculty member at the University of Massachusetts Amherst. Dr. Gladden has worked with a variety of organizations, including Compaq Computer Corporation, Iowa State University, the Los Angeles Dodgers, Major League Soccer, the National Collegiate Athletic Association, the Pittsburgh Pirates, Purdue University, and the United States Figure Skating Association. Professor Gladden's photo appears courtesy of IUPUI.

B. Christine Green, PhD, is an active researcher who studies consumer behavior of sport event volunteers, active sport participants, and fans in a variety of sport contexts. A professor in the Department of Recreation, Sport and Tourism at the University of Illinois and the founder of the Sport+Development Lab at the University of Texas at Austin, Dr. Green earned her doctoral degree in sport management from the University of Maryland. She has published more than 70 articles that span a variety of contexts, including sport participants, fans, event volunteers, and sport tourists. Her framework of sport development, published in the *Journal of Sport Management* in 2005, provided pivotal guidance to the sport management field concerning sport and talent development at both the local and international levels. She designed and implemented the volunteer management system for the British Olympic Association's pre-Games training camp and participated in the strategic planning efforts to redesign the Australian university sport system. Dr. Green was the head of the research team that studied the motivation and commitment of the 2000 Sydney Olympics volunteers. She has also supervised a number of student-run marketing projects that significantly increased student attendance at intercollegiate sporting events. She is a research fellow in the North American Society for Sport Management (NASSM). She has also been honored with the Academic Innovation Award from the RGK Center for Philanthropy and Community Service. Professor Green's photo appears courtesy of the University of Texas.

Marion E. Hambrick, PhD, is an assistant professor of sport administration at the University of Louisville. Dr. Hambrick has a BA in finance from Transylvania University, an MBA in finance from University of Kentucky, and a doctorate in educational leadership and organizational development with an emphasis in sport administration from University of Louisville. He has worked for General Electric Corp. in its finance and corporate audit departments. He currently teaches classes on sport finance at the undergraduate and graduate levels. Dr. Hambrick's research interests are social media usage in sports and innovations in the sporting goods industry. He has published articles in *International Journal of Sport Communication, Journal of Sports Media, Sport Marketing Quarterly, International Journal of Sport Management and Marketing,* and *Case Studies in Sport Management.* Dr. Hambrick is a member of the North American Society for Sport Management (NASSM) and the International Association for Communication and Sport (IACS). Dr. Hambrick's photo appears courtesy of Tom Fougerousse.

Mary Jo Kane, PhD, is the director of the Tucker Center for Research on Girls & Women in Sport in the School of Kinesiology at the University of Minnesota, where she also serves as a professor. She received her doctorate from the University of Illinois with an emphasis in sport sociology. Professor Kane is an internationally recognized scholar who has published extensively on issues related to sport and gender, particularly media representations of women's sports as well as the social, economic, and political effects of Title IX. Professor Kane is the recipient of the first endowed chair related to women in sport: The Dorothy McNeill Tucker Chair for Women in Sport & Exercise Science. She was elected by her peers to become a fellow in the National Academy of Kinesiology, the highest academic honor in her field. Professor Kane is a past recipient of the Scholar of the Year Award from the Women's Sports Foundation. In 2012, Professor Kane received a Distinguished Service Award from the Minnesota Coalition of Women in Athletic Leadership. This award is given to individuals who exemplify the highest levels of commitment and contributions to breaking barriers for girls and women in sports. In 2013, Professor Kane was named one of the 100 most influential sports educators by the Institute for International Sport. She is a member of the North American Society for the Sociology of Sport (NASSS) and serves on the editorial review boards of *Communication &*

Sport and the *Journal of Sport and Social Issues*. Professor Kane's photo appears courtesy of the University of Minnesota.

Shannon Kerwin, PhD, received her doctorate from Western University in Canada. She spent two years as an assistant professor at the University of Florida, where she taught graduate-level management and leadership in sport. During this time, she also sat on numerous graduate student committees. Dr. Kerwin is now an assistant professor at Brock University, where her research interest rests in management and leadership within sport organizations. Specifically, Dr. Kerwin has looked at the influence of value congruence on organizational outcomes, the role of conflict in the effectiveness of volunteer boards, and leadership within the context of sport teams and organizational culture. She has delivered presentations at national and international conferences and has published in academic journals, including but not limited to *Small Group Research*, *Journal of Sport Management*, and *Journal of Leisure Research*. Dr. Kerwin is an editorial board member of *Sport Management Review* and *Journal of Sport Management*, and remains an active member of the North American Society for Sport Management (NASSM). Dr. Kerwin's photo appears courtesy of Brock University.

Catherine Lahey, MBA, MSBM, works as director of consulting for Wasserman Media Group. In her current role, she is tasked with driving strategic ideation and execution for Nationwide Insurance, particularly around their motorsports platform. Prior to Wasserman, Lahey served as account director at International Speedway Corporation, where she developed and implemented strategic business solutions for a group of key corporate partners, including Ford, ServiceMaster, and Sprint. A graduate of the DeVos Sport Business Management program at the University of Central Florida, she worked as a graduate assistant at the National Consortium for Academics and Sports (NCAS) while earning an MBA and a master of sport business management. Before entering the DeVos program, Lahey attended Stetson University on the J. Ollie Edmunds Distinguished Scholarship, earning her undergraduate degrees in English and sport management with a minor in creative writing. In her years at Stetson, Lahey studied abroad at Oxford University's Magdalen College and coached high school and elite travel softball. She currently resides in Raleigh. Lahey's photo appears courtesy of Wasserman Media Group.

Nicole M. LaVoi, PhD, is the associate director of the Tucker Center for Research on Girls & Women in Sport (www.tuckercenter.org), cofounder of the Minnesota Youth Sport Research Consortium (www.MNYSRC.org), and instructor in the area of social and behavioral science in the School of Kinesiology at the University of Minnesota. Before returning to the University of Minnesota, where she earned both her MA and doctorate in kinesiology, LaVoi was a research associate in the Mendelson Center for Sport, Character & Culture at the University of Notre Dame and an assistant professor at Wellesley College, where she taught in the Department of Physical Education, Recreation and Athletics and served as the head women's tennis coach. LaVoi's multidisciplinary research has focused on the relational qualities of the coach–athlete relationship, the effect of background anger behaviors of adults (parents and coaches) on youth athletes, the emotional experiences of youth sport parents, the physical activity of underserved girls, the structural and personal barriers and supports experienced by female coaches, and media representations of girls and women in sport. She strives to answer critical questions that can make a difference in the lives of coaches and youth athletes—particularly females. To that end, LaVoi contributed to *The 2007 Tucker Center Research Report: Developing Physically Active Girls*, developed the Minnesota PLAYS (Parents Learning About Youth Sports), codeveloped the Parents And Coaches Together (PACT) program with colleagues at the University of Notre Dame, and helped produce and develop the Emmy-nominated *Concussion & Female Athletes: The Untold Story* in conjunction with Twin Cities Public Television. Dr. LaVoi has published book chapters, research reports, and a number of peer-reviewed articles. As a public scholar, she maintains a social media presence through Twitter (@DrSportPsych) and her personal blog *One Sport Voice* (www.nicolemlavoi.com). She also contributes to the *Women in Coaching* blog. Dr. LaVoi's photo appears courtesy of Jessica Fleming.

Ming Li, EdD, is dean of the College of Education and Human Development at Western Michigan University. He received his bachelor's degree in education from Guangzhou Institute of Physical Culture, his master's degree in education from Hangzhou University, and his doctor of education degree in sport administration from the University of Kansas. His research interests are in financial and economic aspects of sport and in management of sport business in a global context. Li served on the editorial board of the *Journal of Sport Management* and *Sport Marketing Quarterly*. He has published more than 29 articles in refereed journals, four books (*Economics of Sport, Research Methods in Sport Management, International Sport Management,* and *Badminton Everyone*). He has made numerous refereed presentations at state, national, and international conferences. Dr. Li is an honorary guest professor of a number of institutions in China, including Sun Yat-sen University, Central University of Finance and Economics, Beijing Sport University, Tianjin University of Sport, and Guangzhou Institute of Physical Education. Currently, he is president of the Alliance for Sport Business (ASB). He was an Olympic envoy for the Atlanta Committee for the 1996 Olympic Games and served as president of the North American Society for Sport Management (NASSM). Professor Li's photo appears courtesy of Ohio University.

Daniel F. Mahony, PhD, is a professor of sport administration and the dean of the College of Education, Health and Human Services at Kent State University. Dr. Mahony has a BS in accounting from Virginia Tech, an MS in sport management from West Virginia University, and a doctorate in sport management from The Ohio State University. He has worked for the accounting firm Peat Marwick Main & Co., the North Hunterdon High School Athletic Department, the West Virginia University Athletic Department, and the University of Cincinnati Athletic Department. Before becoming dean at Kent State University in 2008, he was a faculty member and administrator at the University of Louisville for 13 years. Dr. Mahony is an active researcher in the areas of sport consumer behavior and intercollegiate athletics and has published more than 50 articles in various journals including the *Journal of Sport Management, Sport Management Review, Sport Marketing Quarterly, International Journal of Sport Marketing and Sponsorship, International Journal of Sport Management,* and *Journal of Sport and Social Issues*. He is also coauthor of *Economics of Sport*. Dr. Mahony served as president of the North American Society for Sport Management (NASSM). He received the 2007 Earle F. Zeigler award from NASSM, and has been a NASSM research fellow since 2003. Professor Mahony's photo appears courtesy of Kent State University.

Tywan G. Martin, PhD, is an assistant professor of sport management in the Department of Kinesiology and Sport Sciences in the School of Education and Human Development at the University of Miami (Florida). He earned his doctorate from Indiana University-Bloomington (IU). While at IU, Martin received the prestigious Groups Student Support Services Fellowship and a School of Health, Physical Education and Recreation minority scholarship award. His primary research focus is on the influence, persuasion, and influence of media messages on consumer behavior across a variety of platforms (e.g., magazines, television, social media, mobile devices). Additionally, his research examines brand perception and how associated thoughts and ideas about sport brands are utilized to influence fan behavior. Martin has taught a number of undergraduate and graduate courses that are directly in line with his research interests. He has a wealth of experience as a former student affairs administrator, where he mentored numerous student athletes and general admission students. Martin has worked extensively in the sport industry, most notably as a basketball camp coordinator at the high school, collegiate, and professional levels. In his free time, he enjoys reading, writing, watching movies, working out, and attending live entertainment events. Dr. Martin's photo appears courtesy of Paul M. Pedersen.

Brian P. McCullough, PhD, is an assistant professor of sport management at Bowling Green State University. Before earning his doctoral degree from Texas A&M University, Dr. McCullough had industry experience working in college athletic fundraising and advancement as a development associate in the major gifts department of the 12th Man Foundation, the main fundraising arm for Texas A&M University's athletic department. His research interests include understanding the managerial and organizational processes to implement environmental sustainability initiatives within sport organizations. His work has been published in academic journals that include *Journal of Sport Management, International Journal of*

Sport Management and Marketing, and *Quest.* Dr. McCullough has taught undergraduate and graduate classes in several areas, including management, finance, research methods, history and philosophy. A former student athlete, he played Division III baseball at Ithaca College. He is a member of the North American Society for Sport Management (NASSM), the Sport Marketing Association (SMA), and the North American Society for the Sociology of Sport (NASSS). Dr. McCullough's photo appears courtesy of Bowling Green State University's Office of Communications and Public Relations.

Anita M. Moorman, JD, is a professor in sport administration at the University of Louisville (UofL), where she teaches sport law and legal aspects of sport. She joined the faculty at the University of Louisville in 1996. Professor Moorman is the interim cochair of the Department of Health and Sport Sciences, and was previously the program director for the Sport Administration Program at UofL. Professor Moorman has a law degree from Southern Methodist University. Before beginning her academic pursuits, she practiced law in Oklahoma City, Oklahoma, in the areas of commercial and corporate litigation for 10 years. Professor Moorman also holds an MS in sport management from the University of Oklahoma and a BS in political science from Oklahoma State University. She was the editor of a feature column in *Sport Marketing Quarterly* titled "Sport Marketing and the Law" for several years, and is coauthor of the text *Sport Law: A Managerial Approach,* which entered its 3rd edition in 2014. Professor Moorman's research interests include disability discrimination in sport, and legal and ethical issues related to sport marketing practices, brand protection, and intellectual property issues in sport. She has published more than 30 articles in academic journals, including the *Journal of Sport Management*, *Sport Management Review*, *Sport Marketing Quarterly*, *Journal of Legal Aspects of Sport*, *JOPERD*, *Leisure Science*, *International Sport Journal*, *Journal of Sport and Social Issues*, *Journal of the Academy of Marketing Science*, and *ACSM's Health and Fitness Journal*. She has given more than 60 presentations at national and international conferences. Professor Moorman's photo appears courtesy of the University of Louisville.

Samuel Olson, JD, earned his law degree from Michigan State University College of Law in 2010. Before taking his current position as an assistant compliance director at Eastern Michigan University, Olson completed his master's degree in sport administration at the University of Louisville. In addition to teaching an undergraduate course on the legal aspects of sport at the University of Louisville, Olson worked as an intern in athletics compliance at the University of Louisville and Bellarmine University. After earning his law degree, he worked as a law clerk and judicial advisory assistant to a chief probate judge in Genesee County, Michigan. He earned a BA from the University of Michigan. Olson's photo appears courtesy of the University of Louisville.

Brenda G. Pitts, EdD, is nationally and internationally known in sport management, particularly in sport marketing. Dr. Pitts is a professor of sport marketing and sport business management at Georgia State University. She was recently featured in the book *Women as Leaders in Sport: Impact and Influence* as one of the pioneers of the field of sport management in the United States. One of the first North American Society for Sport Management (NASSM) research fellows, Dr. Pitts has been the honored recipient of several scholarly awards in the field, such as the 2012 Diversity Award of NASSM, the prestigious Dr. Earle F. Zeigler award of NASSM, and the NASSM Dr. Garth

Paton Distinguished Service award. Her research work involves sport consumer behavior, fan and spectator analysis, sport sponsorship and brand awareness measurement, and economic impact and visitor spending. She is the author and coauthor of seven sport marketing textbooks published in several languages, coauthor of the textbook *Research Methods in Sport Management*, author and editor of three Sport Marketing Association's *Book of Papers*, and author of more than 200 publications and presentations. She has also been published in several scholarly journals, such as the *Sport Management Education Journal*, *Journal of Sport Management*, *Sport Marketing Quarterly*, *Journal of Vacation Marketing*, *International Journal of Sports Marketing and Sponsorship*, *Women in Sport and Physical Activity*, and the *International Journal of Sport Management*, and she has brought in more than $1 million in grants. Her research, consulting, and service work have taken her around the world as a speaker and lecturer in sport marketing. Dr. Pitts is a founding team member of the new World Association for Sport Management (2012). In 2013, she was an invited visiting scholar at the Johan Cruyff Institute of Sport Marketing and the Wagner Group Institute of Sport Marketing in the Netherlands. She has hosted numerous international students, and her international work has included such countries as Mongolia, Thailand, Sweden, South Africa, Hong Kong, Singapore, Malaysia, Spain, France, Australia, Germany, Hungary, Czech Republic, Mexico, England, the Netherlands, Japan, Canada, Portugal, Scotland, Cyprus, and China. As an athlete, she enjoys several sports. Along the way, she played in the first Women's Professional Basketball Association. She is a member of the A Club of the University of Alabama, where she played basketball and was one of the first five women to receive a scholarship. She was inducted into the Huntsville Sports Hall of Fame and the Women's Basketball Hall of Fame, and she is a nominee for the Alabama Sports Hall of Fame. In fact, Dr. Pitts' sports and research were interrelated from the beginning: Her 1984 dissertation was one of two studies used in the United States' decision to officially adopt the women's size basketball for competitive play. Recently, Dr. Pitts won a couple of golf tournaments, but she has made the wise decision to keep her day job. She enjoys spending time with her partner of more than 29 years and playing with their furry kids, Jazz the Corgi and Tucker the Terrier. Professor Pitts' photo appears courtesy of Brenda G. Pitts.

Jerome Quarterman, PhD, is an associate professor and the chair in the Department of Health, Physical Education, and Recreation at Benedict college in South Carolina. Prior to that, he was on the faculty at Howard University in Washington, D.C. and at Florida State University where he taught graduate students in research methods, organizational theory, and diversity in organizations of the sport industry. He was a tenured faculty member at Bowling Green State University of Ohio for 11 years. Prior to his position at Bowling Green, his teaching and administrative experiences were at historically black colleges and universities, including Southern, Alabama State, Kentucky State, Central State, Hampton, Florida A&M, and Lincoln universities. He is a member of the North American Society for Sport Management (NASSM), and was inducted as an NASSM Fellow in June 2010. He is also a member of the American Alliance for Health, Physical Education, Recreation and Dance (AAHPERD). Quarterman is an active researcher who has authored or coauthored 45 scholarly publications, including peer-reviewed journal articles, book chapters, and edited books. His research has appeared in the *International Journal of Sport Management, Sport Marketing Quarterly, Journal of Sport Management, Academic Athletic Journal, Journal of Teaching Physical Education, Applied Research in Coaching and Athletics Annual, The Physical Educator, International Journal of Sport Marketing and Sponsorship, Journal of Physical Education, Recreation and Dance,* and *College Student Journal.* He has also served on the editorial boards for the *International Journal of Sport Management, Athletic Academic Journal,* and *ICHPERSD Journal of Research.* He has served on and chaired numerous master and doctoral committees at Bowling Green, Florida State, and Howard universities. He teaches students in a variety of courses at the undergraduate, master's, and doctoral levels, including organizational theory, intercollegiate athletic administration, research methods in sport management, ethics and social issues in sport, human resources management, sport marketing, and diversity in sport organizations. Quarterman holds a doctoral degree from The Ohio State University, a master's degree from Kent State University, and a bachelor's degree from Savannah State University. He is the proud parent of Terrance and Michele. His photo appears courtesy of Dr. Quarterman.

Jezali Ratliff, MBA, MSBM, currently serves as senior director of consulting for Wasserman Media Group. Ratliff is responsible for driving strategic thought and implementation for key accounts, and is currently focused on PepsiCo's global sports marketing efforts. Prior to Wasserman, she worked at the Atlantic Coast Conference in the championships department and participated in the NIKE Adrenaline Internship program, working in the U.S. soccer sport marketing division. Ratliff is a graduate of Florida State University, where she earned a bachelor's degree in sport management with minors in Spanish and religion. While at FSU, she was a four-year starter and captain of the nationally ranked varsity women's soccer team. Ratliff earned her MBA and master of sports business management at the University of Central Florida's DeVos sport business management program, where she served as class copresident. In 2012, Ratliff was honored for her accomplishments by Forbes in its annual "30 Under 30," a list of the young disruptors, innovators, and entrepreneurs in the sports industry. Ratliff currently resides in Durham, North Carolina, with her husband, JD Lubenetski. Ratliff's photo appears courtesy of Wasserman Media Group, LLC.

R. Christopher Reynolds, PhD, JD, serves in the position of deputy director of athletics at Northwestern University and has held this role since 2012. Before arriving at Northwestern, Reynolds served in the position of senior associate athletics director at Indiana University-Bloomington and was utilized in a variety of key administrative roles over a nine-year period. He has more than 16 years of experience working in athletics administration at Division I institutions in the following areas:

human resource management, coaches' employment contracts, student-athlete welfare issues, legal issues, diversity matters, sponsorship contracts, NCAA compliance, event management, capital facility projects, equipment room operations, sport supervision, and recreational sports. Reynolds has taught graduate-level courses in sports marketing, sports law, NCAA compliance, and issues in intercollegiate athletics. He has served as chair of the NCAA committee on sportsmanship and ethical conduct, taught as an adjunct faculty member at Indiana University-Bloomington and Western Michigan University, and conducted leadership development workshops for Nike, Inc. and the NCAA. Reynolds was selected for an NCAA fellowship, a rigorous leadership development program sponsored by the NCAA national office for aspiring athletics directors and conference commissioners. Also, he completed professional development training at the Division 1-A Institute, which is a comprehensive program that exposes participants to prominent leaders in the business of athletics administration. Reynolds completed his PhD in sport management (2012), his law degree (1996), and his undergraduate degree (1993) from Indiana University-Bloomington. His photo appears courtesy of Northwestern University.

Sally Rea Ross, PhD, is an assistant professor of sport leadership at Grand Valley State University in Allendale, Michigan. Prior to earning her doctoral degree from the University of Illinois at Urbana-Champaign, Dr. Ross gained extensive practical experience in college athletics administration as an assistant athletics director, overseeing student-athlete support services at her alma mater. Before taking on that role, Dr. Ross was an academic counselor and life skills coordinator for student athletes and was also an academic advisor for the Department of Recreation, Sport and Tourism at the University of Illinois at Urbana-Champaign. Her research interests include girls' and women's experiences and opportunities in sport, media representations of athletes, and the social responsibility of sport entities. Her work has been published

in academic journals that include *Qualitative Research in Sport, Exercise and Health, Quest, Sex Roles, Sport Marketing Quarterly, International Journal of Sport Marketing and Sponsorship*, and *Sport Management Education Journal*. Dr. Ross has taught undergraduate and graduate courses in a variety of areas, including foundations of sport and leisure management, intercollegiate athletics administration, event and facility management, sport ethics, and popular culture. A former Big Ten All-Conference and Academic All-Conference student athlete, Dr. Ross was the recipient of the Distinguished Alumnus Award from the University of Illinois volleyball program. She is a member of the North American Society for Sport Management (NASSM), Sport Marketing Association (SMA), and North American Society for the Sociology of Sport (NASSS), and is a faculty affiliate with the Collegiate Sport Research Institute. Her photo appears courtesy of Grand Valley State University.

Ellen J. Staurowsky, EdD, is professor and graduate chair of the Department of Sport Management at Drexel University. She received her doctoral degree in sport management and psychosocial aspects of sport from Temple University. On more than 150 occasions, Dr. Staurowsky has presented to learned societies, professional associations, and conferences on gender equity and Title IX, pay equity and equal employment opportunity, the exploitation of athletes, the faculty role in reforming college sport, representation of women in sport media, and the misappropriation of American Indian imagery in sport. She has published numerous articles in scholarly and professional journals. In 1998, she coauthored the book *College Athletes for Hire: The Evolution and Legacy of the NCAA Amateur Myth*. Dr. Staurowsky is a member of the editorial board for the *Journal of Sport Management, Women in Sport and Physical Activity Journal*, and *Athletic Management*. She is past president of the North American Society for the Sociology of Sport (NASSS) and the Research Consortium. She is a founding member of the Drake Group, a group of faculty around the country interested in college sport reform. She is also on the executive board of the College Sport Research Institute. She is the former college field hockey and lacrosse coach at Oberlin College, and was the director of athletics at Daniel Webster College and William Smith College for nine years. Professor Staurowsky's photo appears courtesy of Ithaca College.

G. Clayton (Clay) Stoldt, EdD, is a professor and chair of the Department of Sport Management at Wichita State University. He teaches classes in sport public relations and sport marketing. Stoldt is the coauthor of *Sport Public Relations: Managing Stakeholder Communication (2nd edition).* His research activities have focused on sport public relations issues such as the roles of sport public relations professionals, the influence of social media, and the application of advanced public relations practices in the field. Stoldt serves on the editorial boards for the *International Journal of Sport Communication* and the *Journal of Applied Sport Management.* He received his doctorate from the University of Oklahoma in 1998. His master's degree was in sport management, and his bachelor's was in journalism and mass communication. Before coming to Wichita State University, Stoldt worked in the athletics department at Oklahoma City University, where he served as sports information director, radio play-by-play broadcaster, and development officer. He also served as an adjunct instructor at both Oklahoma City University and the University of Oklahoma. Dr. Stoldt's photo appears courtesy of Ryan Stoldt.

David K. Stotlar, EdD, is a professor of sport management in the areas of sport marketing and sport law at the University of Northern Colorado. He has had more than 90 articles published in professional journals and has written several

book chapters in sport marketing, fitness risk management, and sport law. He is the author of several textbooks, including *Developing Successful Sport Sponsorship Plans,* which is now in its 4th edition. He has made numerous presentations at international and national professional conferences and has conducted international seminars in sport management and marketing for various sport councils, federations, and institutes. Dr. Stotlar served as the media subcenter supervisor for the Soldier's Hollow venue at the 2002 Winter Olympic Games in Salt Lake City. He received the Dr. Earle F. Zeigler award from the North American Society for Sport Management (NASSM) in 1999, and was named a NASSM research fellow in 2001. Professor Stotlar's photo appears courtesy of Sylvia Stotlar.

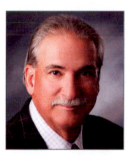

William A. Sutton, EdD, is a distinguished academician and a proven sport marketing practitioner. Sutton's body of work includes notable academic appointments and extensive industry experience. Dr. Sutton holds an appointment as founding director and professor at the sport and entertainment business management graduate program in the Management Department at the University of South Florida (USF). He is the founder and principal of Bill Sutton & Associates, a consulting firm specializing in strategic marketing and revenue enhancement. In addition to his role as cocreator and architect of the innovative and groundbreaking Sports Sales Combine, he teaches courses at USF in sport marketing and sales and promotional management in sport and serves as the internship coordinator for the program. His consulting clients include the NBA, WNBA, NHL, Orlando Magic, Phoenix Suns, MSG Sports, and the New York Mets. Prior to assuming his current positions, Sutton served as vice president of team marketing and business operations for the NBA. In this capacity, Dr. Sutton assisted NBA teams with marketing-related functions such as sales, promotional activities, market research, advertising, customer service, strategic planning, and staffing. Dr. Sutton has held previous academic appointments at Robert Morris University, The Ohio State University, the University of Massachusetts Amherst, and the University of Central Florida. Dr. Sutton—the coauthor of two textbooks (*Sport Marketing* and *Sport Promotion and Sales Management*) and coeditor of the *Handbook of Sport Marketing Research*—has authored more than 200 articles and has made more than 300 national and international presentations. He was a past president of North American Society for Sport Management (NASSM) and is a founding member and past president of the Sport Marketing Association (SMA) and the *Sport Marketing Quarterly*, where he has also served as coeditor. Dr. Sutton is a featured author *for Street and Smith's SportsBusiness Journal (SBJ)*, where his "Sutton Impact" column is a monthly feature. He is also a contributor for the basketball strategy and business magazines *Basketball Gigante* and *FIBA Assist*, published in Italy. Sutton is frequently called on by members of the media for his insight and commentary on the sports business industry, including *USA Today*, *The New York Times*, CNBC.com, *The Washington Times*, Fox Business, *The Orlando Sentinel*, *South Florida Sun-Sentinel*, *Advertising Age*, and *Brandweek*. In addition to working at the NBA, Dr. Sutton's professional experience also includes service as a special events coordinator for the city of Pittsburgh, a YMCA director, vice president of information services for an international sport-marketing firm, and commissioner of the Mid-Ohio Conference. A native of Pittsburgh, Dr. Sutton holds three degrees (BA, 1972; MS, 1980; and EdD, 1983) from Oklahoma State University,

where he was inducted into the College of Education Hall of Fame in 2003. Dr. Sutton is also an inaugural member of the Robert Morris University Sport Management Hall of Fame (2006), and received the lifetime achievement award from the Southern Sport Management Association (2012). Dr. Sutton serves on the board of directors for the Folds of Honor Foundation, and served on the Central Florida Sports Commission. Dr. Sutton and his wife, Sharon, reside in Tampa and Clearwater Beach, Florida. Professor Sutton's photo appears courtesy of William Sutton.

Luisa Velez, PhD, is an assistant professor of sport management at West Virginia University (WVU). She teaches the undergraduate internship course and coordinates the undergraduate internship program. She earned her doctoral degree in sport management from Texas Woman's University. Her research and scholarly interests include inequities in sport involving race, gender, and class. She has published in the journal of the *National Association for the Education of Young Children* and *Adapted Physical Activity Quarterly* and has made contributions to textbook chapters for Human Kinetics. She has had the opportunity to present her research internationally. Dr. Velez's photo appears courtesy of WVU, Cole Smith.

Warren A. Whisenant, PhD, is an associate professor of sport management and is associate chair in the Department of Exercise and Sport Sciences at the University of Miami (Florida). Whisenant, a North American Society for Sport Management (NASSM) research fellow, obtained his doctorate at Florida State University. He also holds an MA in kinesiology and an MBA in management from Sam Houston State University. His research, most of which has focused on gender and organizational issues within interscholastic athletics, has been published in such journals as the *Journal of Sport Management, International Journal of Sport Management, International Journal of Sport Management and Marketing, Sex Roles,* and *Sport, Education, and Society.* Dr. Whisenant's professional background includes more than 20 years of experience with three global organizations—Hewitt Associates, KFC-USA, and Frito Lay, Inc. His roles within those businesses were as an advanced project and process consultant, a director of restaurant operations (1 of 16 in North America), and region sales manager, respectively. In each of the positions noted, he was involved with coordinating promotional programs and sponsorships with various sport organizations. Dr. Whisenant's photo appears courtesy of the University of Miami.

Cara Wright, PhD, is an account executive with the 2012 WNBA Champion Indiana Fever for Pacers Sports and Entertainment, as well as an adjunct professor in the sport management undergraduate program at Indiana University-Bloomington and Purdue University of Indianapolis. Wright obtained her doctorate in human performance at Indiana University-Bloomington (IU). She is the first Black woman to pursue a doctorate in human performance (athletic administration) at IU. Wright also obtained her master's degree in athletic administration from IU, where she was a recipient of the Marjorie P. Philips award and the Doctoral Minority Fellowship award. She received her bachelor's degree in communications management from the University of Dayton, where she was the captain of the women's basketball team. Wright has experience in the sport industry as a student athlete, an athletic administrator, trainer, consultant, coach, and most recently as an instructor and fundamentals coach for the inaugural girls' NBA Basketball Without Borders Basketball Camp held in South Africa in 2011 and then repeated in 2012. She also has experience in athletic administration, compliance, marketing, ticket sales, fundraising, and event planning and execution. She has worked in intercollegiate athletic departments and for the National Foundation for Cancer Research in the area of sport fundraising. Dr. Wright's photo appears courtesy of Katie Terrell for Magnitude Agency.